THE
New Humanities
R E A D E R

RICHARD E. MILLER

KURT SPELLMEYER

Houghton Mifflin
Custom Publishing

Custom Publishing Editor: Dan Luciano
Custom Publishing Production Manager: Kathleen McCourt
Project Coordinator: Malti Sharma

Cover Design: Joel Gendron

Printed in the United States of America.

ISBN: 0-618-09533-0
3-98385

1 2 3 4 5 6 7 8 9 - CC - 02 01 00

 **Houghton Mifflin**
　　　　　　　　　Custom Publishing

222 Berkeley Street • Boston, MA 02116

Address all correspondence and order information to the above address.

CONTENTS

The New Humanities

READINGS FOR THE TWENTY-FIRST CENTURY

Richard E. Miller and Kurt Spellmeyer

This book probably differs from most you have encountered, at least those you've encountered in school. Initially, the readings collected here might appear to have nothing more in common than their concern with contemporary issues—the jobless future, the global economy, the degradation of the environment, the conflict between scientific expertise and spiritual conviction. Rather than arrange these readings under helpful rubrics like "Civilization and Nature" or "Society and the Individual," we have organized them alphabetically by author, with the result that an essay on the information society is followed by one that deals with women's labor in the new economy. Generally, the books taught in school tell students how to think but ours has a different purpose. We wanted to put in your hands a book that would permit you to make connections for yourself as you think, read, and write about the events that are likely to shape your future life. And as you make these connections, you will also cultivate the abilities most needed in a time of rapid change—to use information creatively and to communicate your discoveries.

Although the articles and essays in this book deal with subjects as diverse as the anthropology of art and the philosophy of science, the book is not really "about" art or science or any of the other subjects explored by the readings. Instead, this book is about the need for new ways of thinking, and it does not try to pretend that those ways of thinking are widely practiced today. Our world has seen more change in the last hundred years than it had seen in the previous thousand. From the media we get daily reports on subjects that our great-grand parents might have found incomprehensible: breakthroughs in cloning technology; mergers of U.S. firms with Japanese or German partners; a global treaty on biological weapons; a revision of trade agreements with China; a new account of the universe in the first seconds after the Big Bang; the rise of cancer rates in the mid-West; the melting of our polar ice-caps; new insurance policies for same-sex couples. Such events are truly without precedent.

Never before have people faced uncertainty in so many different areas. How, for instance, will the information technologies affect our personal lives?

Will the Internet contribute to the forces that have pulled apart our families, or will it strengthen our neighborhoods and communities? As corporations spread across continents, will our identity as Americans continue to be important, or will we need to see ourselves in other ways? And will the global economy create widespread unemployment and environmental decline or will it usher in an era of undreamed-of peace and prosperity? Will the encounters between different cultures, long separated by geography, lead to a new renaissance, or must such meetings always end in balkanization and terrorism? Will genetic technology lead to a brave new world of "designer babies" and made-to-order soldier-clones or will its breakthroughs be devoted to revolutionizing food production and eliminating congenital disease? Unlike most questions posed by textbooks, the right answers to these questions aren't waiting for any of us in the teacher's edition. Not even the best educated and the most experienced can foresee with certainty how the life of our times will turn out. If our problems today are much more sweeping than humankind has encountered before, they are also more complex. Globalization is not just an issue for economists, or political scientists, or historians, or anthropologists; it is an issue for all of them together. The degradation of the biosphere is not just an ecological matter, but a political, social, and cultural matter as well.

The uniqueness of our time requires us to devise new understandings of ourselves and the world. One purpose of this book is to provide a place for these understandings to emerge. It may seem strange, perhaps, that we would have such lofty goals in a course for undergraduates. Surely the experts are better equipped to respond to issues of the sort our world now confronts than beginning students in our colleges and universities. But this assumption may be unjustified. While the forms of expertise available today clearly have great value, most of the current academic disciplines and departments were created more than a century ago, and the divisions of knowledge they are based on reflect the needs of a very different society. It's worth remembering, for example, that in 1900, cars were a new technology, and airplanes and radios had yet to be invented. Scientists still debated the structure of the atom. The British Empire dominated three-quarters of the globe and "culture" meant the traditions of Western Europe's elite, never more than tenth of one percent of the population of that region. In a certain sense, the current generation of college students needs to reinvent the university itself, not by replacing one department or methodology with another, but by building broad connections across areas of knowledge which still remain in relative isolation.

Some readers of this book will be surprised at the absence of material from the traditional humanities: poems and plays; photos of paintings and statues; excerpts from great works of philosophy like Plato's *Republic* and Descartes' *Discourse on Method*. It seems to us that no one should leave Shakespeare or Plato or Toni Morrison unread. Anyone unfamiliar with Leonardo da Vinci, Frida Kahlo, Thelonious Monk, or Georgia O'keeffe has missed a priceless opportunity. Yet we also believe that the humanities today must reach farther then they have in centuries past. Without intending do so, modern humanists may have contributed to the decline of their own enterprise. One could even argue that the modern humanities have seen their principal task as the preservation of the past rather than the creation of the future. Humanists have often left real-world activities and concerns to other fields, while devoting themselves to passive contemplation, aesthetic pleasure, and partisan critique. Consequently, most people outside the university have come to think of the humanities as something closer to entertainment, wish-fulfillment, or a covert form of politics, while regarding the knowledge of the sciences as the only real truth. We reject this division.

We see humanities not as a particular area of knowledge but as the human dimension of *all* knowledge. Engineering, or course, does not belong to the humanities, but we enter the domain of the humanities when we begin to consider the impact of engineering on everyday life, as Henry Petroski does here in his chapter on the politics of bridge-building. When we define the humanities in this way, it becomes clear some of our society's foremost humanists work in field quite far removed from the traditional humanities. Steven Jay Gould, one of the writers in our collection, is a distinguished paleontologist who has played a leading role in American cultural life. Well-versed in Western arts and letters, he also brings to his writing the knowledge and insight of a highly accomplished scientist. Marcia Angell, a pathologist and editor-in-chief of the *New England Journal of Medicine,* has helped to protect our whole society by changing the way the legal system understands scientific evidence. In the brightest future we can imagine, this fusion of humanistic sensibility with scientific training will increasingly characterize the life of the mind. As we see it, the role of the New Humanities is to foster an ability to think across fields, training students in the arts of synthesizing knowledge by exposing them to the unprecedented breakthroughs in cosmology, cognitive science, ecology, behavioral psychology, and paleoanthropology that illuminate the thought of our time.

The New Humanities bring change in another way as well—they must be more than academic subjects left behind on the way to fulfilling degree requirements. The New Humanities must take the knowledge of the university beyond the university itself. In a certain sense, this means that students have to become their own best teachers: they need to find in their own lives—their own goals, values, dreams, and commitments—an organizing principle for a learning experience which is bound to seem disorganized. The great, unspoken secret of the university is that the curriculum has no center: specialization makes sure of that. Historians write primarily for historians; literary critics for other critics. As students shuttle back and forth between these specialized areas, the only coherence they can take away from their education is a coherence they have made for themselves. Under these conditions, what the New Humanities must teach is a different way of using knowledge, a way that fosters a sense of coherence across fields of study and institutional boundaries.

Specialized learning deals with the "how," but it leaves unanswered the "why." There has never been a course called "Life 101" and given the complexity of our world, such a course seems unlikely anytime soon. But something important will be missing from higher education if we leave the "why" questions altogether unexplored. Should we continue to pursue techno-utopia? Does modern science mean the end of religion? Is social inequality an acceptable price for economic growth? Any attempt to answer these questions will require specialized knowledge, yet knowledge alone is not enough. Because a cogent, well-informed case could be made on either side of almost every issue, the sources of our ultimate commitments must reach deeper. We might say that the "why" questions shape these commitments because they address our most basic and most personal relations to other people and to the world. In different ways, these questions always ask us how we choose to live. No expert can choose on our behalf, because no expert can live our lives for us or declare what our experience should mean to us.

The coherence missing from the curriculum is not a quality of knowledge, but of our own lives. In itself, no amount of learning can produce a sense of coherence. That sense arises, instead, from a creative and synthetic activity on our part as we interact with the world. Again and again, we need to make connections between separated areas of knowledge, and between knowledge and our personal experience. This coherence is never complete because something more always remains unconnected, but we might think of coherence, not as a goal reached once and for all but as an ideal worth pursuing continuously. Of course, cynicism and fragmentation are always options too, and they require no special effort. One can easily live as though nothing and no one matters; obviously, people do. But in that case, learning and living both become exercises in futility. The New Humanities mark an alternative path that we invite you to follow for yourself.

Knowledge in Depth and Knowledge of the World

As everyone understands, formal education has been carefully designed to keep everything separate from everything else. In economics classes, people typically read economics; in history classes, they typically read history. This approach serves the purpose of imparting information in small, efficiently managed packages. We can divide, say, biology from chemistry, and then we can divide biology into vertebrate and invertebrate, and chemistry into organic and inorganic. We start with the general and move to the particular: ideally, the student learns in depth, with greater and greater mastery over details that become more and more

refined. At the end of the semester, if everything goes well, a person can distinguish between an ecosystem and a niche, a polymer and a plastic, a neo-Kantian
and a neo-Hegelian. Students can contrast Hawthorne's treatment of the outsider
with Salinger's, or they can explain the debate about the weather slavery or
states' rights actually caused the Civil War.

Knowledge in depth is indispensable. But it can also create a sense of disconnection, the impression that education is an empty ritual without real-world
consequences beyond the assignment of a grade and the fulfillment of a requirement. Students learn to calculate sine and cosine without ever discovering how
these calculations might be used or why they were invented. Searching for symbols in a poem or a short story becomes a mental exercise like doing a crossword
puzzle. Instead of reflecting on why events have happened and how they get
remembered or recorded, students cultivate the ability to recapitulate strings of
dates and names. At its worst, learning in depth can produce a strange distortion:
the purpose of learning becomes learning itself, while activity in the real world
becomes incidental, even difficult to imagine. Post high-school students understand vaguely that they ought to know *Hamlet,* and should able to identify *The
Declaration of Independence* and explain how photosynthesis has influenced the
shape of leaves, but in response to an actual tragedy, a real-life legal crisis, or an
environmental disaster, they tend to feel unqualified to speak and unprepared
to act.

College-level learning can offer the chance to escape from this predicament
by giving students greater freedom to choose what they will study, and in many
cases the subjects they choose are closely related to their real-world objectives.
But even with this new-found freedom, the problem of disconnection returns in
other ways. After years of hard work, a person who has mastered electrical engineering can still leave college very poorly informed about the commercial environment in which most engineers must do their work. Students well-versed in
Renaissance drama, or the history of World War I, may find their lives after graduation much more difficult to interpret. For some students, this problem of disconnection may arise long before graduation. The person who sets out to
memorize facts in, say, an abnormal psychology textbook may find that these
facts grow increasingly stale. Easily memorized one day, they are quickly forgotten the next. The risk of knowledge in depth is that we lose our sense of the
larger world and we forget that a field like psychology, for all its sophistication
today, began with tentative and somewhat clumsy questions about the mind that
anyone might ask. Ironically, the more we treat an area of knowledge as reality
in itself, the less we may be able to understand and use what we supposedly have
learned.

There is another kind of knowledge which we begin to create when we ask
ourselves how our learning pertains to the larger world—the world outside the
classroom. This line of questioning is more complex than it might seem at first
because the larger world is never simply out there waiting for us. Initially, all

knowledge is a knowledge of parts and fragments, even knowledge of the private lives we know in most detail. Each of our private lives may seem complete in itself, just as a field like psychology can seem to explain everything once we are immersed in its methods and its facts. But this sense of completeness is an illusion produced by the limits of any perspective: beyond the reach of what we know here and now, nothing appears to matter. We begin to get a glimpse of the larger world, however, only when we move from one reality to another and we discover the insufficiency of our previous ways of thinking. Then it can become possible to think in a new and different way. it is this movement from the known to the unknown that is the essence of all learning; indeed, we believe that the most successful learners are those who have developed the highest tolerance for not-knowing—those who continue to question and explore issues beyond their own areas of specialization, and so can entertain alternatives others might find unimaginable.

Intensive Reading

The readings in this book are intended for writing. We believe the humanities should do more than covey information or give professors a chance to demonstrate their brilliance. After all, studies have consistently shown that people on average retain very little of what they are taught unless they put their knowledge to use. At its best, education should give beginners the chance to practice the same activities that more accomplished thinkers engage in: beyond receiving knowledge, beginners should participate in the making of knowledge. We conceive of these readings as opportunities for just such participation. All of our selections are challenging, some because they are long and complex, some because they draw on specialized disciplines, and some because they open up unusual perspectives. These are not readings that lend themselves to simple summaries and multiple-choice answers. Instead, they require discussion—they were written to elicit your own activity.

Most of our readings lack the obvious coherence of textbook prose; in fact, some of the readings seem to break the rules of "good" writing most students are taught. For example, if we try to make sense of Karen Armstrong by looking for a topic sentence at the beginning of every paragraph, we are likely to quit in frustration. Understanding an author like Armstrong is never achieved one sentence or one paragraph at a time. For many pages, we may feel that the writer is sweeping us along in a torrent of words and ideas, but gradually we begin to see where we have traveled and where we may be headed. Reading prose like this requires a high degree of patience and a generous tolerance for uncertainty, two capacities of value outside the classroom as well.

While each of these selections poses a challenge, we never intended them to be used in isolation from one another. In our view, the best assignments move from exploring the connections within one author's work to exploring the connections among multiple authors read in a sequence. Over six to eight weeks, a sequence might move from Peter Drucker to Benjamin Barber to Shirley Brice Heath, or from David Abram to Ellen Dissanayake to Karen Armstrong. Rather than read extensively—an author each week, let's say, or a cluster of authors all writing on the same topic—we intend for these selections to be read intensively, leaving time to think through the implications of the arguments in a way that has become all too rare in formal education and also in our society as a whole. At its best, extensive reading can provide the background knowledge that every discipline requires, but at its worst, it can discourage the sort of learning that is likely to be remembered and to prove useful later on. By contrast, intensive reading requires our own connective activity. Twenty years from now, we may or may not remember in detail the arguments made by Barber or Abram, but we will have learned something much more important by working closely with them: how to construct meaning from materials that may seem at first chaotic, overwhelming, or unrelated. What we will have learned is a special art of thinking.

Mimetic Thinking and Connective Thinking

Much formal education promotes mimetic thinking: the student learns to reproduce information already collected and organized by someone else. Mimetic thinking presupposes the adequacy of knowledge in its present state. But what happens when we discover that our knowledge leaves something out? Perhaps the lecture in English this afternoon contradicts a point made yesterday in Sociology class. Or perhaps an assigned author has described an aspect the social world in ways we find inaccurate or disconcerting. Once we encounter the limits or defects of knowledge on occasions like these, mimetic thinking cannot help; instead we are obliged to think connectively—to think across domains of knowledge rather than thinking from the inside. When a theorist of management like Peter Drucker looks at the emerging "knowledge society," he foresees an era of unprecedented personal freedom and upward mobility. One the other hand, Benjamin Barber, a political scientist and a contemporary of Drucker, describes an America that he regards as socially fragmented and politically paralyzed. Once we confront these two images of the same society, we are bound to ask ourselves about their relation to one another. Are the two in contradiction? Perhaps you will find Barber's view more persuasive—or perhaps you will prefer Drucker's. But no two essays are simply in contradiction. To a greater or lesser extent, they will also confirm and complicate one another. We might assume that democracy and the free market go together, as Drucker thinks; but the values of the free market may in some ways undermine democratic attitudes, as Barber fears. We might believe, as Barber does, that people ought to get more involved with their government, but perhaps, as Drucker argues, the apparatus of government is no longer in control of society. The point is not say "yes" to one writer or "no" to the other, but to explore the different ways their discussions might fit together. And instead of declaring, "Everyone has a right to his or her own opinion," we can evaluate the consequences that different opinions are likely to bring about.

Connective thinking is creative and independent in a way that mimetic thinking can never be. No matter how well we summarize Drucker and Barber, this is not the same as fitting their ideas together. To think connectively, we need to step back from what each of the writers has said in order to discover a common ground. Drucker's principal concern is the organization of work, Barber's the collapse of political life, and at first, when we consider these differences, no common ground may seem to be available. But often we can find a common ground on the level of broader implications which may never get discussed explicitly. A common ground between Barber and Drucker may emerge when we ask about the forms of political life that might be possible in a society where knowledge is power; or when we start to imagine the economic changes that might give Americans more time to be active in their communities.

To search for a common ground is to explore the "stakes" behind the readings: their consequences for life in the real world. Drucker praises the market economy; Barber, for his part, distrusts it. At stake in the two essays is the status of the market: is it a menacing presence or an engine of human freedom? At stake too is the nature of the "information age": will it worsen the divisions between rich and poor or will it prove to be an equalizing force? Mimetic learning requires students to recapitulate an author's own arguments, to dissect them or compare and contrast them to other arguments. But connective learning moves from an awareness of the stakes to an informed and original position.

Write-to-Tell, Writing-to-See

Mimetic learning tends to emphasize writing-to-tell—writing for the purpose of demonstrating mastery over an existing body of information. In American schools, the classic example of writing-to-tell is the venerable genre of the book report. Like mimetic learning, writing-to-tell has its appropriate place. But connective learning calls for writing of a different kind, which might be described as writing-to-see. In this case, the writer has to do something more than present the knowledge made by others. The writer needs to take that knowledge somewhere new. In the act of writing-to-tell, people give answers. But in writing-to-see, we start with a question raised by thinkers who have come before us, and we go on to explore what they have left unexplored: we engage in the kind of thinking that higher education at its best can foster—deliberative thinking. A good example is Ellen Dissanayake's "What is art?" Although Dissanayake draws extensively from previous thinkers on aesthetics, evolutionary biology, and ethology, she connects each thinker to the next in a way that gradually uncovers a new position of her own. While she could not have reached her final position without the help of her sources, her thinking goes beyond them.

For Dissanayake to become a source for our own writing, we need to start with a question that her work leaves unresolved. If art is, as she believes, a universal human behavior, then what are we to make of museums, galleries, and professional artists? Why is it that we call certain paintings "art" but not cartoons or popular movies? If we ourselves see cartoons and movies as trivial, we may find Dissanayake's ideas less than entirely persuasive. But her ideas may also force us to rethink our assumptions: where is it written, after all, that art has to be exclusive and difficult? As we set out to answer questions like these, we might also draw on David Abram's observations on the Balinese way of life. Or we might make fruitful connections to Drucker's thoughts on the increasingly specialized character of work. The position we eventually discover on the place of the aesthetic in contemporary culture could emerge from the synthesis of these three writers. We might decide that "entertainment" is actually art, or we might see the disappearance of art from everyday life as a development closely related to our growing distance from nature.

A position is not exactly an argument, in the ordinary sense of the word. In everyday speech, the term "argument" suggests an adversarial stance: we might argue for, or against, Drucker's positive assessment of corporate culture. "Making an argument" tends to mean deciding ahead of time what you think about an issue and then finding "support" to back up your points. We don't believe that much learning results from such a practice; instead, people simply ratify their existing beliefs. By inviting you to use the readings to formulate a position of your own, we are asking you to imagine yourself in a different way—not as a combatant but as a participant in an ongoing conversation. Even if we read a writer like Drucker with distaste, what matters most are the questions he raises and not the answers he gives. Precisely because the search for a position begins with some degree of uncertainty, it requires the willingness on our part to suspend judgment and to pursue ideas wherever they might lead. It's important to remember that this pursuit does not require complete assent or unswerving commitment. We can always explore ideas we eventually reject. The proper spirit for writing-to-see might be described as experimental.

An experiment requires a "dialogue" between projection and revision. First, we imagine or "project" an outcome based on our prior knowledge and experience. We make an educated guess about the conclusion we will probably draw from our reading of an author or authors. Perhaps we can start with the claim that Chris McCandless, the young man whose death Jon Karkauer retraces, was a spoiled, self-deceiving ingrate. Yet when we turn to Unni Wikan's discussion of Balinese culture, or to Alexander Stille's account of alternative attitudes toward the natural world, our opinion of Chris McCandless may grow less clear. As we write, our thinking may appear to lose its way and we may realize, after three or four pages, that we have contradicted ourselves. Instead of treating this change in our position as a failure or a lapse, we should appreciate its value as a discovery, which we could make only after a great deal of hard work. And rather than return to our original stance, we should revise what we have written in order to present our new position at the outset. But revision too involves experiment and discovery. The point of a new draft if never simply to change a position: the point is also to explain how and why the position has changed.

The Spirit of the New Humanities

Because we can learn from everything, no one should fear making mistakes. We should never forget that the greatest thinkers of every age have often been refuted later, while quite ordinary people have sometimes lived more wisely than they were given credit for. Not so long ago, the best educated Europeans believed that all celestial bodies beyond the moon hung immobilized in space. The learned taught that matter in every form could be reduced to the basic elements of earth, air, fire, and water. Medical experts sternly warned against the perils of regular bathing and eating whole grains. In the making of children, men were supposed to contribute the blueprint, while women provided the raw material. One could spend a whole lifetime enumerating the follies that have passed for knowledge. And when we pause to consider such a checkered history, we might decide that education is itself a folly.

But maybe not. Instead of expecting knowledge to be true once and for all, we might try to see it as pragmatic and provisional—always subject to revision given further evidence or new circumstances. In our society today, the sciences may offer the best example of this experimentalist attitude, but philosophers and artists of every generation have also refused the twin consolations of dogmatism and disillusionment. In the years ahead, our society will face challenges—environmental, social, cultural, economic, and political—that are sure to seem overwhelming. Given the high level of uncertainty that has become a constant feature of our lives, people may be drawn to ideologies which promise truths exempt from all revision and insulated from the challenges of diversity. If this book does nothing else, we hope that it will offer an alternative more compatible with the values espoused by the readings we have chosen: trust in the world, and trust in ourselves.

Reading 1

THE ECOLOGY OF MAGIC
A Personal Introduction to the Inquiry

David Abram

Late one evening I stepped out of my little hut in the rice paddies of eastern Bali and found myself falling through space. Over my head the black sky was rippling with stars, densely clustered in some regions, almost blocking out the darkness between them, and more loosely scattered in other areas, pulsing and beckoning to each other. Behind them all streamed the great river of light with its several tributaries. Yet the Milky Way churned beneath me as well, for my hut was set in the middle of a large patchwork of rice paddies, separated from each other by narrow two-foot-high dikes, and these paddies were all filled with water. The surface of these pools, by day, reflected perfectly the blue sky, a reflection broken only by the thin, bright green tips of new rice. But by night the stars themselves glimmered from the surface of the paddies, and the river of light whirled through the darkness underfoot as well as above; there seemed no ground in front of my feet, only the abyss of star-studded space falling away forever.

I was no longer simply beneath the night sky, but also *above* it—the immediate impression was of weightlessness. I might have been able to reorient myself, to regain some sense of ground and gravity, were it not for a fact that confounded my senses entirely: between the constellations below and the constellations above drifted countless fireflies, their lights flickering like the stars, some drifting up to join the clusters of stars overhead, others, like graceful meteors, slipping down from above to join the constellations underfoot, and all these paths of light upward and downward were mirrored, as well, in the still surface

Abram, David. "The Ecology of Magic." *The Spell of the Sensuous*. New York: First Vintage Books, 1997.

of the paddies. I felt myself at times falling through space, at other moments floating and drifting. I simply could not dispel the profound vertigo and giddiness; the paths of the fireflies, and their reflections in the water's surface, held me in a sustained trance. Even after I crawled back to my hut and shut the door on this whirling world, I felt that now the little room in which I lay was itself floating free of the earth.

Fireflies! It was in Indonesia, you see, that I was first introduced to the world of insects, and there that I first learned of the great influence that insects— such diminutive entities—could have upon the human senses. I had traveled to Indonesia on a research grant to study magic—more precisely, to study the relation between magic and medicine, first among the traditional sorcerers, or *dukuns,* of the Indonesian archipelago, and later among the *dzankris,* the traditional shamans of Nepal. One aspect of the grant was somewhat unique: I was to journey into rural Asia not outwardly as an anthropologist or academic researcher, but as a magician in my own right, in hopes of gaining a more direct access to the local sorcerers. I had been a professional sleight-of-hand magician for five years back in the United States, helping to put myself through college by performing in clubs and restaurants throughout New England. I had, as well, taken a year off from my studies in the psychology of perception to travel as a street magician through Europe and, toward the end of that journey, had spent some months in London, England, exploring the use of sleight-of-hand magic in psychotherapy, as a means of engendering communication with distressed individuals largely unapproachable by clinical healers.[1] The success of this work suggested to me that sleight-of-hand might lend itself well to the curative arts, and I became, for the first time, interested in the relation, largely forgotten in the West, between folk medicine and magic.

It was this interest that led to the aforementioned grant, and to my sojourn as a magician in rural Asia. There, my sleight-of-hand skills proved invaluable as a means of stirring the curiosity of the local shamans. For magicians—whether modern entertainers or indigenous, tribal sorcerers—have in common the fact that they work with the malleable texture of perception. When the local sorcerers gleaned that I had at least some rudimentary skill in altering the common field of perception, I was invited into their homes, asked to share secrets with them, and eventually encouraged, even urged, to participate in various rituals and ceremonies.

But the focus of my research gradually shifted from questions regarding the application of magical techniques in medicine and ritual curing toward a deeper pondering of the relation between traditional magic and the animate natural world. This broader concern seemed to hold the keys to the earlier questions. For none of the several island sorcerers that I came to know in Indonesia, nor any of the *dzankris* with whom I lived in Nepal, considered their work as ritual healers to be their major role or function within their communities. Most of them, to be sure, *were* the primary healers or "doctors" for the villages in their vicinity, and they were often spoken of as such by the inhabitants of those villages. But the villagers also sometimes spoke of them, in low voices and in very private conversations, as witches (or "lejaks" in Bali), as dark magicians who at night might well be practicing their healing spells backward (or while turning to the left instead of to the right) in order to afflict people with the very diseases that they would later work to cure by day. Such suspicions seemed fairly common in Indonesia, and often were harbored with regard to the most effective and powerful healers, those who were most renowned for their skill in driving out illness. For it was assumed that a magician, in order to expel malevolent influences, must have a strong understanding of those influences and demons—even, in some areas, a close rapport with such powers. I myself never consciously saw any of those magicians or shamans with whom I became acquainted engage in magic for harmful purposes, nor any convincing evidence that they had ever done so. (Few of the magicians that I came to know even accepted money in return for their services, although they did accept gifts in the way of food, blankets, and the like.) Yet I was struck by the fact that none of them ever did or said anything to counter such disturbing rumors and speculations, which circulated quietly through the regions where they lived. Slowly, I came to recognize that it was through the agency of such rumors, and the ambiguous fears that such rumors engendered in the village people, that the sorcerers were able to maintain a basic level of privacy. If the villagers did not entertain certain fears about the local sorcerer, then they would likely come to obtain his or her magical help for every little malady and disturbance; and since a more potent practitioner must provide services for several large villages, the sorcerer would be swamped from morning to night with requests for ritual aid. By allowing the inevitable suspicions and fears to circulate unhindered in the region (and sometimes even encouraging and contributing to such rumors), the sorcerer ensured that *only* those who were in real and profound need of his skills would dare to approach him for help.

This privacy, in turn, left the magician free to attend to what he acknowledged to be his primary craft and function. A clue to this function may be found in the circumstance that such magicians rarely dwell at the heart of their village; rather, their dwellings are commonly at the spatial periphery of the community or, more often, out beyond the edges of the village—amid the rice fields, or in a forest, or a wild cluster of boulders. I could easily attribute this to the just-mentioned need for privacy, yet for the magician in a traditional culture it seems to serve another purpose as well, providing a spatial expression of his or her symbolic position with regard to the community. For the magician's intelligence is not encompassed *within* the society; its place is at the edge of the community, mediating *between* the human community and the larger community of beings upon which the village depends for its nourishment and sustenance. This larger community includes, along with the humans, the multiple nonhuman entities that constitute the local landscape, from the diverse plants and the myriad animals—birds, mammals, fish, reptiles, insects—that inhabit or migrate through the region, to the particular winds and weather patterns that inform the local geography, as well as the various landforms—forests, rivers, caves, mountains—that lend their specific character to the surrounding earth.

The traditional or tribal shaman, I came to discern, acts as an intermediary between the human community and the larger ecological field, ensuring that there is an appropriate flow of nourishment, not just from the landscape to the human inhabitants, but from the human community back to the local earth. By his constant rituals, trances, ecstasies, and "journeys," he ensures that the relation between human society and the larger society of beings is balanced and reciprocal, and that the village never takes more from the living land than it returns to it—not just materially but with prayers, propitiations, and praise. The scale of a harvest or the size of a hunt are always negotiated between the tribal community and the natural world that it inhabits. To some extent every adult in the community is engaged in this process of listening and attuning to the other presences that surround and influence daily life. But the shaman or sorcerer is the exemplary voyager in the intermediate realm between the human and the more-than-human worlds, the primary strategist and negotiator in any dealings with the Others.

And it is only as a result of her continual engagement with the animate powers that dwell beyond the human community that the traditional magician is able to alleviate many individual illnesses that arise *within* that community. The sorcerer derives her ability to cure ailments from her more continuous practice of "healing" or balancing the community's relation to the surrounding land. Disease, in such cultures, is often conceptualized as a kind of systemic imbalance within the sick person, or more vividly as the intrusion of a demonic or malevolent presence into his body. There are, at times, malevolent influences within the village or tribe itself that disrupt the health and emotional well-being of susceptible individuals within the community. Yet such destructive influences within the human community are commonly traceable to a disequilibrium between that community and the larger field of forces in which it is embedded. Only those persons who, by their everyday practice, are involved in monitoring and maintaining the relations *between* the human village and the animate landscape are able to appropriately diagnose, treat, and ultimately relieve personal ailments and illnesses arising *within* the village. Any healer who was not simultaneously attending to the intertwined relation between the human community and the larger, more-than-human field, would likely dispel an illness from one person only to have the same problem arise (perhaps in a new guise) somewhere else in the community. Hence, the traditional magician or medicine person functions primarily as an intermediary between human and nonhuman worlds, and only secondarily as a healer.[2] Without a continually adjusted awareness of the relative balance or imbalance between the human group and its nonhuman environ, along with the skills necessary to modulate that primary relation, any "healer" is worthless—indeed, not a healer at all. The medicine person's primary allegiance, then, is not to the human community, but to the earthly web of relations in which that community is embedded—it is from this that his or her power to alleviate human illness derives—and this sets the local magician apart from other persons.

The primacy for the magician of nonhuman nature—the centrality of his relation to other species and to the earth—is not always evident to Western researchers. Countless anthropologists have managed to overlook the ecological dimension of the shaman's craft, while writing at great length of the shaman's rapport with "supernatural" entities. We can attribute much of this oversight to the modern, civilized assumption that the natural world is largely determinate and mechanical, and that that which is regarded as mysterious, powerful, and beyond human ken must therefore be of some other, nonphysical realm *above* nature, "supernatural."

The oversight becomes still more comprehensible when we realize that many of the earliest European interpreters of indigenous lifeways were Christian missionaries. For the Church had long assumed that only human beings have intelligent souls, and that the other animals, to say nothing of trees and rivers, were "created" for no other reason than to serve humankind. We can easily understand why European missionaries, steeped in the dogma of institutionalized Christianity, assumed a belief in supernatural, otherworldly powers among those tribal persons whom they saw awestruck and entranced by nonhuman (but nevertheless natural) forces. What is remarkable is the extent to which contemporary anthropology still preserves the ethnocentric bias of these early interpreters. We no longer describe the shamans' enigmatic spirit-helpers as the "superstitious claptrap of heathen primitives"—we have cleansed ourselves of at least *that* much ethnocentrism; yet we still refer to such enigmatic forces, respectfully now, as "supernaturals"—for we are unable to shed the sense, so endemic to scientific civilization, of nature as a rather prosaic and predictable realm, unsuited to such mysteries. Nevertheless, that which is regarded with the greatest awe and wonder by indigenous, oral cultures is, I suggest, none other than what we view as nature itself. The deeply mysterious powers and entities with whom the shaman enters into a rapport are ultimately the same forces—the same plants, animals, forests, and winds—that to literate, "civilized" Europeans are just so much scenery, the pleasant backdrop of our more pressing human concerns.

The most sophisticated definition of "magic" that now circulates through the American counterculture is "the ability or power to alter one's consciousness at will." No mention is made of any *reason* for altering one's consciousness. Yet in tribal cultures that which we call "magic" takes its meaning from the fact that humans, in an indigenous and oral context, experience their own consciousness as simply one form of awareness among many others. The traditional magician cultivates an ability to shift out of his or her common state of consciousness precisely in order to make contact with the other organic forms of sensitivity and awareness with which human existence is entwined. Only by temporarily shedding the accepted perceptual logic of his culture can the sorcerer hope to enter into relation with other species on their own terms; only by altering the common organization of his senses will he be able to enter into a rapport with the multiple nonhuman sensibilities that animate the local landscape. It is this, we might say, that defines a shaman: the ability to readily slip out of the perceptual boundaries that demarcate his or her particular culture—boundaries reinforced by social customs, taboos, and most importantly, the common speech or language—in order to make contact with, and learn from, the other powers in the land. His magic is precisely this heightened receptivity to the meaningful solicitations—songs, cries, gestures—of the larger, more-than-human field.

Magic, then, in its perhaps most primordial sense, is the experience of existing in a world made up of multiple intelligences, the intuition that every form one perceives—from the swallow swooping overhead to the fly on a blade of grass, and indeed the blade of grass itself—is an *experiencing* form, an entity with its own predilections and sensations, albeit sensations that are very different from our own.

To be sure, the shaman's ecological function, his or her role as intermediary between human society and the land, is not always obvious at first blush, even to a sensitive observer. We see the sorcerer being called upon to cure an ailing tribesman of his sleeplessness, or perhaps simply to locate some missing goods; we witness him entering into trance and sending his awareness into other dimensions in search of insight and aid. Yet we should not be so ready to interpret these dimensions as "supernatural," nor to view them as realms entirely "internal" to the personal psyche of the practitioner. For it is likely that the "inner world" of our Western psychological experience, like the supernatural heaven of Christian belief, originates in the loss of our ancestral reciprocity with the animate earth. When the animate powers that surround us are suddenly construed as having less significance than ourselves, when the generative earth is abruptly defined as a determinate object devoid of its own sensations and feelings, then the sense of a wild and multiplicitous otherness (in relation to which human existence has always oriented itself) must migrate, either into a supersensory heaven beyond the natural world, or else into the human skull itself—the only allowable refuge, in this world, for what is ineffable and unfathomable.

But in genuinely oral, indigenous cultures, the sensuous world itself remains the dwelling place of the gods, of the numinous powers that can either sustain or extinguish human life. It is not by sending his awareness out beyond the natural world that the shaman makes contact with the purveyors of life and health, nor by journeying into his personal psyche; rather, it is by propelling his awareness laterally, outward into the depths of a landscape at once both sensuous and psychological, the living dream that we share with the soaring hawk, the spider, and the stone silently sprouting lichens on its coarse surface.

The magician's intimate relationship with nonhuman nature becomes most evident when we attend to the easily overlooked background of his or her practice—not just to the more visible tasks of curing and ritual aid to which she is called by individual clients, or to the larger ceremonies at which she presides and dances, but to the content of the prayers by which she prepares for such ceremonies, and to the countless ritual gestures that she enacts when alone, the daily propitiations and praise that flow from her toward the land and *its* many voices.

All this attention to nonhuman nature was, as I have mentioned, very far from my intended focus when I embarked on my research into the uses of magic and medicine in Indonesia, and it was only gradually that I became aware of this more subtle dimension of the native magician's craft. The first shift in my preconceptions came rather quietly, when I was staying for some days in the home of a young "balian," or magic practitioner, in the interior of Bali. I had been provided with a simple bed in a separate, one-room building in the balian's family compound (most compound homes, in Bali, are comprised of several separate small buildings, for sleeping and for cooking, set on a single enclosed plot of land), and early each morning the balian's wife came to bring me a small but delicious bowl of fruit, which I ate by myself, sitting on the ground outside, leaning against the wall of my hut and watching the sun slowly climb through the rustling palm leaves. I noticed, when she delivered the fruit, that my hostess was also balancing a tray containing many little green plates: actually, they were little boat-shaped platters, each woven simply and neatly from a freshly cut section of palm frond. The platters were two or three inches long, and within each was a little mound of white rice. After handing me my breakfast, the woman and the tray disappeared from view behind the other buildings, and when she came by some minutes later to pick up my empty bowl, the tray in her hands was empty as well.

The second time that I saw the array of tiny rice platters, I asked my hostess what they were for. Patiently, she explained to me that they were offerings for the household spirits. When I inquired about the Balinese term that she used for "spirit," she repeated the same explanation, now in Indonesian, that these were gifts for the spirits of the family compound, and I saw that I had understood her correctly. She handed me a bowl of sliced papaya and mango, and disappeared around the corner. I pondered for a minute, then set down the bowl, stepped to the side of my hut, and peered through the trees. At first unable to see her, I soon caught sight of her crouched low beside the corner of one of the other buildings, carefully setting what I presumed was one of the offerings on the ground at that spot. Then she stood up with the tray, walked to the other visible corner of the same building, and there slowly and carefully set another offering on the ground. I returned to my bowl of fruit and finished my breakfast. That afternoon, when the rest of the household was busy, I walked back behind the building where I had seen her set down the two offerings. There were the little green platters, resting neatly at the two rear corners of the building. But the mounds of rice that had been within them were gone.

The next morning I finished the sliced fruit, waited for my hostess to come by for the empty bowl, then quietly headed back behind the buildings. Two fresh palm-leaf offerings sat at the same spots where the others had been the day before. These were filled with rice. Yet as I gazed at one of these offerings, I abruptly realized, with a start, that one of the rice kernels was actually moving.

Only when I knelt down to look more closely did I notice a line of tiny black ants winding through the dirt to the offering. Peering still closer, I saw that two ants had already climbed onto the offering and were struggling with the uppermost kernel of rice; as I watched, one of them dragged the kernel down and off the leaf, then set off with it back along the line of ants advancing on the offering. The second ant took another kernel and climbed down with it, dragging and pushing, and fell over the edge of the leaf, then a third climbed onto the offering. The line of ants seemed to emerge from a thick clump of grass around a nearby palm tree. I walked over to the other offering and discovered another line of ants dragging away the white kernels. This line emerged from the top of a little mound of dirt, about fifteen feet away from the buildings. There was an offering on the ground by a corner of my building as well, and a nearly identical line of ants. I walked into my room chuckling to myself: the balian and his wife had gone to so much trouble to placate the household spirits with gifts, only to have their offerings stolen by little six-legged thieves. What a waste! But then a strange thought dawned on me: what if the ants were the very "household spirits" to whom the offerings were being made?

I soon began to discern the logic of this. The family compound, like most on this tropical island, had been constructed in the vicinity of several ant colonies. Since a great deal of cooking took place in the compound (which housed, along with the balian and his wife and children, various members of their extended family), and also much preparation of elaborate offerings of foodstuffs for various rituals and festivals in the surrounding villages, the grounds and the buildings at the compound were vulnerable to infestations by the sizable ant population. Such invasions could range from rare nuisances to a periodic or even constant siege. It became apparent that the daily palm-frond offerings served to preclude such an attack by the natural forces that surrounded (and underlay) the family's land. The daily gifts of rice kept the ant colonies occupied—and, presumably, satisfied. Placed in regular, repeated locations at the corners of various structures around the compound, the offerings seemed to establish certain boundaries between the human and ant communities; by honoring this boundary with gifts, the humans apparently hoped to persuade the insects to respect the boundary and not enter the buildings.

Yet I remained puzzled by my hostess's assertion that these were gifts "for the spirits." To be sure, there has always been some confusion between our Western notion of "spirit" (which so often is defined in contrast to matter or "flesh"), and the mysterious presences to which tribal and indigenous cultures pay so much respect. I have already alluded to the gross misunderstandings arising from the circumstance that many of the earliest Western students of these other customs were Christian missionaries all too ready to see occult ghosts and immaterial phantoms where the tribespeople were simply offering their respect to the local winds. While the notion of "spirit" has come to have, for us in the West, a primarily anthropomorphic or human association, my encounter with the ants was the first of many experiences suggesting to me that the "spirits" of an indigenous culture are primarily those modes of intelligence or awareness that do *not* possess a human form.

As humans, we are well acquainted with the needs and capacities of the human body—we *live* our own bodies and so know, from within, the possibilities of our form. We cannot know, with the same familiarity and intimacy, the lived experience of a grass snake or a snapping turtle; we cannot readily experience the precise sensations of a hummingbird sipping nectar from a flower or a rubber tree soaking up sunlight. And yet we do know how it feels to sip from a fresh pool of water or to bask and stretch in the sun. Our experience may indeed be a variant of these other modes of sensitivity; nevertheless, we cannot, as humans, precisely experience the living sensations of another form. We do not know, with full clarity, their desires or motivations; we cannot know, or can never be sure that we know, what they know. That the deer does experience sensations, that it carries knowledge of how to orient in the land, of where to find food and how to protect its young, that it knows well how to survive in the forest without the tools upon which we depend, is readily evident to our human senses. That the mango tree has the ability to create fruit, or the yarrow plant the power to reduce a child's fever, is also evident. To humankind, these Others are purveyors of secrets, carriers of intelligence that we ourselves often need: it is these Others who can inform us of unseasonable changes in the weather, or warn us of imminent eruptions and earthquakes, who show us, when foraging, where we may find the ripest berries or the best route to follow back home. By watching them build their nests and shelters, we glean clues regarding how to strengthen our own dwellings, and their deaths teach us of our own. We receive from them countless gifts of food, fuel, shelter, and clothing. Yet still they remain Other to us, inhabiting their own cultures and displaying their own rituals, never wholly fathomable.

Moreover, it is not only those entities acknowledged by Western civilization as "alive," not only the other animals and the plants that speak, as spirits, to the senses of an oral culture, but also the meandering river from which those animals drink, and the torrential monsoon rains, and the stone that fits neatly into the palm of the hand. The mountain, too, has its thoughts. The forest birds whirring and chattering as the sun slips below the horizon are vocal organs of the rain forest itself.[3]

Bali, of course, is hardly an aboriginal culture; the complexity of its temple architecture, the intricacy of its irrigation systems, the resplendence of its colorful festivals and crafts all bespeak the influence of various civilizations, most notably the Hindu complex of India. In Bali, nevertheless, these influences are thoroughly intertwined with the indigenous animism of the Indonesian archipelago; the Hindu gods and goddesses have been appropriated, as it were, by the more volcanic, eruptive spirits of the local terrain.

Yet the underlying animistic cultures of Indonesia, like those of many islands in the Pacific, are steeped as well in beliefs often referred to by ethnologists as "ancestor worship," and some may argue that the ritual reverence paid to one's long-dead human ancestors (and the assumption of their influence in present life), easily invalidates my assertion that the various "powers" or "spirits" that move through the discourse of indigenous, oral peoples are ultimately tied to nonhuman (but nonetheless sentient) forces in the enveloping landscape.

This objection rests upon certain assumptions implicit in Christian civilization, such as the assumption that the "spirits" of dead persons necessarily retain their human form, and that they reside in a domain outside of the physical world to which our senses give us access. However, most indigenous tribal peoples have no such ready recourse to an immaterial realm outside earthly nature. Our strictly human heavens and hells have only recently been abstracted from the sensuous world that surrounds us, from this more-than-human realm that abounds in its own winged intelligences and cloven-hoofed powers. For almost all oral cultures, the enveloping and sensuous earth remains the dwelling place of both the living *and* the dead. The "body"—whether human or otherwise—is not yet a mechanical object in such cultures, but is a magical entity, the mind's own sensuous aspect, and at death the body's decomposition into soil, worms, and dust can only signify the gradual reintegration of one's ancestors and elders into the living landscape, from which all, too, are born.

Each indigenous culture elaborates this recognition of metamorphosis in its own fashion, taking its clues from the particular terrain in which it is situated. Often the invisible atmosphere that animates the visible world—the subtle presence that circulates both within us and between all things—retains within itself the spirit or breath of the dead person until the time when that breath will enter and animate another visible body—a bird, or a deer, or a field of wild grain. Some cultures may burn, or "cremate," the body in order to more completely return the person, as smoke, to the swirling air, while that which departs as flame is offered to the sun and stars, and that which lingers as ash is fed to the dense earth. Still other cultures may dismember the body, leaving certain parts in precise locations where they will likely be found by condors, or where they will be consumed by mountain lions or by wolves, thus hastening the re-incarnation of that person into a particular animal realm within the landscape. Such examples illustrate simply that death, in tribal cultures, initiates a metamorphosis wherein the person's presence does not "vanish" from the sensible world (where would it go?) but rather remains as an animating force within the vastness of the landscape, whether subtly, in the wind, or more visibly, in animal form, or even as the eruptive, ever to be appeased, wrath of the volcano. "Ancestor worship," in its myriad forms, then, is ultimately another mode of attentiveness to nonhuman nature; it signifies not so much an awe or reverence of human powers, but rather a reverence for those forms that awareness takes when it is *not* in human form, when the familiar human embodiment dies and decays to become part of the encompassing cosmos.

This cycling of the human back into the larger world ensures that the other forms of experience that we encounter—whether ants, or willow trees, or clouds—are never absolutely alien to ourselves. Despite the obvious differences in shape, and ability, and style of being, they remain at least distantly familiar, even familial. It is, paradoxically, this perceived kinship or consanguinity that renders the difference, or otherness, so eerily potent.[4]

Several months after my arrival in Bali, I left the village in which I was staying to visit one of the pre-Hindu sites on the island. I arrived on my bicycle early in the afternoon, after the bus carrying tourists from the coast had departed. A flight of steps took me down into a lush, emerald valley, lined by cliffs on either side, awash with the speech of the river and the sighing of the wind through high, unharvested grasses. On a small bridge crossing the river I met an old woman carrying a wide basket on her head and holding the hand of a little, shy child; the woman grinned at me with the red, toothless smile of a beetle nut chewer. On the far side of the river I stood in front of a great moss-covered complex of passageways, rooms, and courtyards carved by hand out of the black volcanic rock.

I noticed, at a bend in the canyon downstream, a further series of caves carved into the cliffs. These appeared more isolated and remote, unattended by any footpath I could discern. I set out through the grasses to explore them. This proved much more difficult than I anticipated, but after getting lost in the tall grasses, and fording the river three times, I at least found myself beneath the caves. A short scramble up the rock wall brought me to the mouth of one of them, and I entered on my hands and knees. It was a wide but low opening, perhaps only four feet high, and the interior receded only about five or six feet into the cliff. The floor and walls were covered with mosses, painting the cave with green patterns and softening the harshness of the rock; the place, despite its small size—or perhaps because of it—had an air of great friendliness. I climbed to two other caves, each about the same size, but then felt drawn back to the first one, to sit cross-legged on the cushioning moss and gaze out across the emerald canyon. It was quiet inside, a kind of intimate sanctuary hewn into the stone. I began to explore the rich resonance of the enclosure, first just humming, then intoning a simple chant taught to me by a balian some days before. I was delighted by the overtones that the cave added to my voice, and sat there singing for a long while. I did not notice the change in the wind outside, or the cloud shadows darkening the valley, until the rains broke—suddenly and with great force. The first storm of the monsoon!

I had experienced only slight rains on the island before then, and was startled by the torrential downpour now sending stones tumbling along the cliffs, building puddles and then ponds in the green landscape below, swelling the river. There was no question of returning home—I would be unable to make my way back through the flood to the valley's entrance. And so, thankful for the shelter, I recrossed my legs to wait out the storm. Before long the rivulets falling along the cliff above gathered themselves into streams, and two small waterfalls cascaded across the cave's mouth. Soon I was looking into a solid curtain of water, thin in some places, where the canyon's image flickered unsteadily, and thickly rushing in others. My senses were all but overcome by the wild beauty of the cascade and by the roar of sound, my body trembling inwardly at the weird sense of being sealed into my hiding place.

And then, in the midst of all this tumult, I noticed a small, delicate activity. Just in front of me, and only an inch or two to my side of the torrent, a spider was climbing a thin thread stretched across the mouth of the cave. As I watched, it anchored another thread to the top of the opening, then slipped back along the first thread and joined the two at a point about midway between the roof and the floor. I lost sight of the spider then, and for a while it seemed that it had vanished, thread and all, until my focus rediscovered it. Two more threads now radiated from the center to the floor, and then another; soon the spider began to swing between these as on a circular trellis, trailing an ever-lengthening thread which it affixed to each radiating rung as it moved from one to the next, spiraling outward. The spider seemed wholly undaunted by the tumult of waters spilling past it, although every now and then it broke off its spiral dance and climbed to the roof or the floor to tug on the radii there, assuring the tautness of the threads, then crawled back to where it left off. Whenever I lost the correct focus, I waited to catch sight of the spinning arachnid, and then let its dancing form gradually draw the lineaments of the web back into visibility, tying my focus into each new knot of silk as it moved, weaving my gaze into the ever-deepening pattern.

And then, abruptly, my vision snagged on a strange incongruity: another thread slanted across the web, neither radiating nor spiraling from the central juncture, violating the symmetry. As I followed it with my eyes, pondering its purpose in the overall pattern, I began to realize that it was on a different plane from the rest of the web, for the web slipped out of focus whenever this new line became clearer. I soon saw that it led to its own center, about twelve inches to the right of the first, another nexus of forces from which several threads stretched to the floor and the ceiling. And then I saw that there was a *different* spider spinning this web, testing its tautness by dancing around it like the first, now setting the silken cross weaves around the nodal point and winding outward. The two spiders spun independently of each other, but to my eyes they wove a single intersecting pattern. This widening of my gaze soon disclosed yet another spider spiraling in the cave's mouth, and suddenly I realized that there were *many* overlapping webs coming into being, radiating out at different rhythms from myriad centers poised—some higher, some lower, some minutely closer to my eyes and some farther—between the stone above and the stone below.

I sat stunned and mesmerized before this ever-complexifying expanse of living patterns upon patterns, my gaze drawn like a breath into one converging group of lines, then breathed out into open space, then drawn down into another convergence. The curtain of water had become utterly silent—I tried at one point to hear it, but could not. My senses were entranced.

I had the distinct impression that I was watching the universe being born, galaxy upon galaxy. . . .

Night filled the cave with darkness. The rain had not stopped. Yet, strangely, I felt neither cold nor hungry—only remarkably peaceful and at home. Stretching out upon the moist, mossy floor near the back of the cave, I slept.

When I awoke, the sun was staring into the canyon, the grasses below rippling with bright blues and greens. I could see no trace of the webs, nor their weavers. Thinking that they were invisible to my eyes without the curtain of water behind them, I felt carefully with my hands around and through the mouth of the cave. But the webs were gone. I climbed down to the river and washed, then hiked across and out of the canyon to where my cycle was drying in the sun, and headed back to my own valley.

I have never, since that time, been able to encounter a spider without feeling a great strangeness and awe. To be sure, insects and spiders are not the only powers, or even central presences, in the Indonesian universe. But they were *my* introduction to the spirits, to the magic afoot in the land. It was from them that I first learned of the intelligence that lurks in nonhuman nature, the ability that an alien form of sentience has to echo one's own, to instill a reverberation in oneself that temporarily shatters habitual ways of seeing and feeling, leaving one open to a world all alive, awake, and aware. It was from such small beings that my senses first learned of the countless worlds within worlds that spin in the depths of this world that we commonly inhabit, and from them that I learned that my body could, with practice, enter sensorially into these dimensions. The precise and minuscule craft of the spiders had so honed and focused my awareness that the very webwork of the universe, of which my own flesh was a part, seemed to be being spun by their arcane art. I have already spoken of the ants, and of the fireflies, whose sensory likeness to the lights in the night sky had taught me the fickleness of gravity. The long and cyclical trance that we call malaria was also brought to me by insects, in this case mosquitoes, and I lived for three weeks in a feverish state of shivers, sweat, and visions.

I had rarely before paid much attention to the natural world. But my exposure to traditional magicians and seers was shifting my senses; I became increasingly susceptible to the solicitations of nonhuman things. In the course of struggling to decipher the magicians' odd gestures or to fathom their constant spoken references to powers unseen and unheard, I began to *see* and to *hear* in a manner I never had before. When a magician spoke of a power or "presence" lingering in the corner of his house, I learned to notice the ray of sunlight that was then pouring through a chink in the roof, illuminating a column of drifting dust, and to realize that that column of light was indeed a power, influencing the air currents by its warmth, and indeed influencing the whole mood of the room; although I had not consciously seen it before, it had already been structuring my experience. My ears began to attend, in a new way, to the songs of birds—no longer just a melodic background to human speech, but meaningful speech in its own right, responding to and commenting on events in the surrounding earth. I became a student of subtle differences: the way a breeze may flutter a single leaf on a whole tree, leaving the other leaves silent and unmoved (had not that leaf, then, been brushed by a magic?); or the way the intensity of the sun's heat expresses itself in the precise rhythm of the crickets. Walking along the dirt paths, I learned to slow my pace in order to *feel* the difference between one nearby hill and the next, or to taste the presence of a particular field at a certain time of day when, as I had been told by a local *dukun,* the place had a special power and proffered unique gifts. It was a power communicated to my senses by the way the shadows of the trees fell at that hour, and by smells that only then lingered in the tops of the grasses without being wafted away by the wind, and other elements I could only isolate after many days of stopping and listening.

And gradually, then, other animals began to intercept me in my wanderings, as if some quality in my posture or the rhythm of my breathing had disarmed their wariness; I would find myself face-to-face with monkeys, and with large lizards that did not slither away when I spoke, but leaned forward in apparent curiosity. In rural Java, I often noticed monkeys accompanying me in the branches overhead, and ravens walked toward me on the road, croaking. While at Pangandaran, a nature preserve on a peninsula jutting out from the south coast of Java ("a place of many spirits," I was told by nearby fishermen), I stepped out from a clutch of trees and found myself looking into the face of one of the rare and beautiful bison that exist only on that island. Our eyes locked. When it snorted, I snorted back; when it shifted its shoulders, I shifted my stance; when I tossed my head, it tossed *its* head in reply. I found myself caught in a nonverbal conversation with this Other, a gestural duet with which my conscious awareness had very little to do. It was as if my body in its actions was suddenly being motivated by a wisdom older than my thinking mind, as though it was held and moved by a logos, deeper than words, spoken by the Other's body, the trees, and the stony ground on which we stood.

Anthropology's inability to discern the shaman's allegiance to nonhuman nature has led to a curious circumstance in the "developed world" today, where many persons in search of spiritual understanding are enrolling in workshops concerned with "shamanic" methods of personal discovery and revelation. Psychotherapists and some physicians have begun to specialize in "shamanic healing techniques." "Shamanism" has thus come to connote an alternative form of therapy; the emphasis, among these new practitioners of popular shamanism, is on personal insight and curing. These are noble aims, to be sure, yet they are secondary to, and derivative from, the primary role of the indigenous shaman, a role that cannot be fulfilled without long and sustained exposure to wild nature, to its patterns and vicissitudes. Mimicking the indigenous shaman's curative methods without his intimate knowledge of the wider natural community cannot, if I am correct, do anything more than trade certain symptoms for others, or shift the locus of dis-ease from place to place within the human community. For the source of stress lies in the relation *between* the human community and the natural landscape.

    Western industrial society, of course, with its massive scale and hugely centralized economy, can hardly be seen in relation to any particular landscape or ecosystem; the more-than-human ecology with which it is directly engaged is the biosphere itself. Sadly, our culture's relation to the earthly biosphere can in no way be considered a reciprocal or balanced one: with thousands of acres of nonregenerating forest disappearing every hour, and hundreds of our fellow species becoming extinct each month as a result of our civilization's excesses, we can hardly be surprised by the amount of epidemic illness in our culture, from increasingly severe immune dysfunctions and cancers, to widespread psychological distress, depression, and ever more frequent suicides, to the accelerating number of household killings and mass murders committed for no apparent reason by otherwise coherent individuals.

    From an animistic perspective, the clearest source of all this distress, both physical and psychological, lies in the aforementioned violence needlessly perpetrated by our civilization on the ecology of the planet; only by alleviating the latter will be able to heal the former. While this may sound at first like a simple statement of faith, it makes eminent and obvious sense as soon as we acknowledge our thorough dependence upon the countless other organisms with whom we have evolved. Caught up in a mass of abstractions, our attention hypnotized by a host of human-made technologies that only reflect us back to ourselves, it is all too easy for us to forget our carnal inherence in a more-than-human matrix of sensations and sensibilities. Our bodies have formed themselves in delicate reciprocity with the manifold textures, sounds, and shapes of an animate earth—our eyes have evolved in subtle interaction with *other* eyes, as our ears are attuned by their very structure to the howling of wolves and the honking of geese. To shut ourselves off from these other voices, to continue by our lifestyles to condemn these other sensibilities to the oblivion of extinction, is to rob our own senses of their integrity, and to rob our minds of their coherence. We are human only in contact, and conviviality, with what is not human.

Although the Indonesian islands are home to an astonishing diversity of birds, it was only when I went to study among the Sherpa people of the high Himalayas that I was truly initiated into the avian world. The Himalayas are young mountains, their peaks not yet rounded by the endless action of wind and ice, and so the primary dimension of the visible landscape is overwhelmingly vertical. Even in the high ridges one seldom attains a view of a distant horizon; instead one's vision is deflected upward by the steep face of the next mountain. The whole land has surged skyward in a manner still evident in the lines and furrows of the mountain walls, and this ancient dynamism readily communicates itself to the sensing body.

In such a world those who dwell and soar in the sky are the primary powers. They alone move easily in such a zone, swooping downward to become a speck near the valley floor, or spiraling into the heights on invisible currents. The wingeds, alone, carry the immediate knowledge of what is unfolding on the far side of the next ridge, and hence it is only by watching them that one can be kept apprised of climatic changes in the offing, as well as of subtle shifts in the flow and density of air currents in one's own valley. Several of the shamans that I met in Nepal had birds as their close familiars. Ravens are constant commentators on village affairs. The smaller, flocking birds perform aerobatics in unison over the village rooftops, twisting and swerving in a perfect sympathy of motion, the whole flock appearing like a magic banner that floats and flaps on air currents over the village, then descends in a heap, only to be carried aloft by the wind a moment later, rippling and swelling.

For some time I visited a Sherpa *dzankri* whose rock home was built into one of the steep mountainsides of the Khumbu region in Nepal. On one of our walks along the narrow cliff trails that wind around the mountain, the *dzankri* pointed out to me a certain boulder, jutting out from the cliff, on which he had "danced" before attempting some especially difficult cures. I recognized the boulder several days later when hiking back down toward the *dzankri's* home from the upper yak pastures, and I climbed onto the rock, not to dance but to ponder the pale white and red lichens that gave life to its surface, and to rest. Across the dry valley, two lammergeier condors floated between gleaming, snow-covered peaks. It was a ringing blue Himalayan day, clear as a bell. After a few moments I took a silver coin out of my pocket and aimlessly began a simple sleight-of-hand exercise, rolling the coin over the knuckles of my right hand. I had taken to practicing this somewhat monotonous exercise in response to the endless flicking of prayer-beads by the older Sherpas, a practice usually accompanied by a repetitively chanted prayer: *"Om Mani Padme Hum"* (O the Jewel in the Lotus). But there was no prayer accompanying my revolving coin, aside from my quiet breathing and the dazzling sunlight. I noticed that one of the two condors in the distance had swerved away from its partner and was now floating over the valley, wings outstretched. As I watched it grow larger, I realized, with some delight, that it was heading in my general direction; I stopped rolling the coin and stared. Yet just then the lammergeier halted in its flight, motionless for a moment against the peaks, then swerved around and headed back toward its partner in the distance. Disappointed, I took up the coin and began rolling it along my knuckles once again, its silver surface catching the sunlight as it turned, reflecting the rays back into the sky. Instantly, the condor swung out from its path and began soaring back in a wide arc. Once again, I watched its shape grow larger. As the great size of the bird became apparent, I felt my skin begin to crawl and come alive, like a swarm of bees all in motion, and a humming grew loud in my ears. The coin continued rolling along my fingers. The creature loomed larger, and larger still, until suddenly, it was there—an immense silhouette hovering just above my head, huge wing feathers rustling ever so slightly as they mastered the breeze. My fingers were frozen, unable to move; the coin dropped out of my hand. And then I felt myself stripped naked by an alien gaze infinitely more lucid and precise than my own. I do not know for how long I was transfixed, only that I felt the air streaming past naked knees and heard the wind whispering in my feathers long after the Visitor had departed.

I returned to a North America whose only indigenous species of condor was on the brink of extinction, mostly as a result of lead poisoning from bullets in the carrion it consumes. But I did not think about this. I was excited by the new sensibilities that had stirred in me—my newfound awareness of a more-than-human world, of the great potency of the land, and particularly of the keen intelligence of other animals, large and small, whose lives and cultures interpenetrate our own. I startled neighbors by chattering with squirrels, who swiftly climbed down the trunks of their trees and across lawns to banter with me, or by gazing for hours on end at a heron fishing in a nearby estuary, or at gulls opening clams by dropping them from a height onto the rocks along the beach.

Yet, very gradually, I began to lose my sense of the animals' own awareness. The gulls' technique for breaking open the clams began to appear as a largely automatic behavior, and I could not easily feel the attention that they must bring to each new shell. Perhaps each shell was entirely the same as the last, and *no* spontaneous attention was really necessary. . . .

I found myself now observing the heron from outside its world, noting with interest its careful high-stepping walk and the sudden dart of its beak into the water, but no longer feeling its tensed yet poised alertness with my own muscles. And, strangely, the suburban squirrels no longer responded to my chittering calls. Although I wished to, I could no longer focus my awareness on engaging in their world as I had so easily done a few weeks earlier, for my attention was quickly deflected by internal, verbal deliberations of one sort or another—by a conversation I now seemed to carry on entirely within myself. The squirrels had no part in this conversation.

It became increasingly apparent, from books and articles and discussions with various people, that other animals were not as awake and aware as I had assumed, that they lacked any real language and hence the possibility of thought, and that even their seemingly spontaneous responses to the world around them were largely "programmed" behaviors, "coded" in the genetic material now being mapped by biologists. Indeed, the more I spoke *about* other animals, the less possible it became to speak *to* them. I gradually came to discern that there was no common ground between the unlimited human intellect and the limited sentience of other animals, no medium through which we and they might communicate with and reciprocate one another.

As the expressive and sentient landscape slowly faded behind my more exclusively human concerns, threatening to become little more than an illusion or fantasy, I began to feel—particularly in my chest and abdomen—as though I were being cut off from vital sources of nourishment. I was indeed reacclimating to my own culture, becoming more attuned to its styles of discourse and interaction, yet my bodily senses seemed to be losing their acuteness, becoming less awake to subtle changes and patterns. The thrumming of crickets, and even the songs of the local blackbirds, readily faded from my awareness after a few moments, and it was only by an effort of will that I could bring them back into the perceptual field. The flight of sparrows and of dragonflies no longer sustained my focus very long, if indeed they gained my attention at all. My skin quit registering the various changes in the breeze, and smells seemed to have faded from the world almost entirely, my nose waking up only once or twice a day, perhaps while cooking, or when taking out the garbage.

In Nepal, the air had been filled with smells—whether in the towns, where burning incense combined with the aromas of roasting meats and honeyed pastries and fruits for trade in the open market, and the stench of organic refuse rotting in the ravines, and sometimes of corpses being cremated by the river; or in the high mountains, where the wind carried the whiffs of countless wildflowers, and of the newly turned earth outside the villages where the fragrant dung of yaks was drying in round patties on the outer walls of the houses, to be used, when dry, as fuel for the household fires, and where smoke from those many home fires always mingled in the outside air. And sounds as well: the chants of aspiring monks and adepts blended with the ringing of prayer bells on near and distant slopes, accompanied by the raucous croaks of ravens, and the sigh of the wind pouring over the passes, and the flapping of prayer flags, and the distant hush of the river cascading through the far-below gorge.

There the air was a thick and richly textured presence, filled with invisible but nonetheless tactile, olfactory, and audible influences. In the United States, however, the air seemed thin and void of substance or influence. It was not, here, a sensuous medium—the felt matrix of our breath and the breath of the other animals and plants and soils—but was merely an absence, and indeed was constantly referred to in everyday discourse as mere empty space. Hence, in America I found myself lingering near wood fires and even garbage dumps—much to the dismay of my friends—for only such an intensity of smells served to remind my body of its immersion in an enveloping medium, and with this experience of being immersed in a world of influences came a host of body memories from my year among the shamans and village people of rural Asia.

I began to find other ways, as well, of tapping the very different sensations and perceptions that I had grown accustomed to in the "undeveloped world," by living for extended periods on native Indian reservations in the southwestern desert and along the northwestern coast, or by hiking off for weeks at a time into the North American wilderness. Intermittently, I began to wonder if my culture's assumptions regarding the lack of awareness in other animals and in the land itself was less a product of careful and judicious reasoning than of a strange inability to clearly perceive other animals—a real inability to clearly see, or focus upon, anything outside the realm of human technology, or to hear as meaningful anything other than human speech. The sad results of our interactions with the rest of nature were being reported in every newspaper—from the depletion of topsoil due to industrial farming techniques to the fouling of groundwater by industrial wastes, from the rapid destruction of ancient forests to, worst of all, the ever-accelerating extinction of our fellow species—and these remarkable and disturbing occurrences, all readily traceable to the ongoing activity of "civilized" humankind, did indeed suggest the possibility that there was a perceptual problem in my culture, that modern, "civilized" humanity simply did not perceive surrounding nature in a clear manner, if we have even been perceiving it at all.

The experiences that shifted the focus of my research in rural Indonesia and Nepal had shown me that nonhuman nature can be perceived and experienced with far more intensity and nuance than is generally acknowledged in the West. What was it that made possible the heightened sensitivity to extrahuman reality, the profound attentiveness to other species and to the Earth that is evidenced in so many of these cultures, and that had so altered my awareness that my senses now felt stifled and starved by the patterns of my own culture? Or, reversing the question, what had made possible the absence of this attentiveness in the modern West? For Western culture, too, has its indigenous origins. If the relative attunement to environing nature exhibited by native cultures is linked to a more primordial, participatory mode of perception, how had Western civilization come to be so exempt from this sensory reciprocity? How, that is, have we become so deaf and so blind to the vital existence of other species, and to the animate landscapes they inhabit, that we now so casually bring about their destruction?

To be sure, our obliviousness to nonhuman nature is today held in place by ways of speaking that simply deny intelligence to other species and to nature in general, as well as by the very structures of our civilized existence—by the incessant drone of motors that shut out the voices of birds and of the winds; by electric lights that eclipse not only the stars but the night itself; by air "conditioners" that hide the seasons; by offices, automobiles, and shopping malls that finally obviate any need to step outside the purely human world at all. We consciously encounter nonhuman nature only as it has been circumscribed by our civilization and its technologies: through our domesticated pets, on the television, or at the zoo (or, at best, in carefully managed "nature preserves"). The plants and animals we consume are neither gathered nor hunted—they are bred and harvested in huge, mechanized farms. "Nature," it would seem, has become simply a stock of "resources" for human civilization, and so we can hardly be surprised that our civilized eyes and ears are somewhat oblivious to the existence of perspectives that are not human at all, or that a person either entering into or returning to the West from a nonindustrial culture would feel startled and confused by the felt absence of nonhuman powers.

Still, the current commodification of "nature" by civilization tells us little or nothing of the perceptual shift that made possible this reduction of the animal (and the earth) to an object, little of the process whereby our senses first relinquished the power of the Other, the vision that for so long had motivated our most sacred rituals, our dances, and our prayers.

But can we even hope to catch a glimpse of this process, which has given rise to so many of the habits and linguistic prejudices that now structure our very thinking? Certainly not if we gaze toward that origin from within the midst of the very civilization it engendered. But perhaps we may make our stand along the *edge* of that civilization, like a magician, or like a person who, having lived among another tribe, can no longer wholly return to his own. He lingers half within and half outside of his community, open as well, then, to the shifting voices and flapping forms that crawl and hover beyond the mirrored walls of the city. And even there, moving along those walls, he may hope to find the precise clues to the mystery of how those walls were erected, and how a simple boundary became a barrier, only if the moment is timely—only, that is, if the margin he frequents is a temporal as well as a spatial edge, and the temporal structure that it bounds is about to dissolve, or metamorphose, into something else.

Notes

1. This work was done at the Philadelphia Association, a therapeutic community directed by Dr. R. D. Laing and his associates.

2. A simple illustration of this may be found among many of the indigenous peoples of North America, for whom the English term "medicine" commonly translates a word meaning "power"—specifically, the sacred power received by a human person from a particular animal or other nonhuman entity. Thus, a particular *medicine person* may be renowned for her "badger medicine" or "bear medicine," for his "eagle medicine," "elk medicine," or even "thunder medicine." It is from their direct engagement with these nonhuman powers that medicine persons derive their own abilities, including their ability to cure human ailments.

3. To the Western mind such views are likely to sound like reckless "projections" of human consciousness into inanimate and dumb materials, suitable for poetry perhaps, but having nothing, in fact, to do with those actual birds or that forest. Such is our common view. This text will examine the possibility that it is civilization that has been confused, and not indigenous peoples. It will suggest, and provide evidence, that one perceives a world at all only by projecting oneself into that world, that one makes contact with things and others only by actively participating in them, lending one's sensory imagination to things in order to discover how they alter and transform that imagination, how they reflect us back changed, how they are different from us. It will suggest that perception is *always* participatory, and hence that modern humanity's denial of awareness in nonhuman nature is borne not by any conceptual or scientific rigor, but rather by an inability, or a refusal, to fully perceive other organisms.

4. The similarity between such animistic worldviews and the emerging perspective of contemporary ecology is not trivial. Atmospheric geochemist James Lovelock, elucidating the well-known Gaia hypothesis—a theory stressing the major role played by organic life in the ceaseless modulation of the earth's atmospheric and climatic conditions—insists that the geological environment is itself constituted by organic life, and by the products or organic metabolism. In his words, we inhabit "a world that is the breath and bones of our ancestors." See, for instance, "Gaia: the World as Living Organism," in the *New Scientist,* December 18, 1986, as well as *Scientists on Gaia,* ed. Stephen Schneider and Penelope Boston (Cambridge" M.I.T. Press, 1991).

Reading 2

HONOR AND SHAME

Lila Abu-Lughod

Say to the believing men that they should lower their gaze and guard their modesty; that will make for greater purity for them. And God is well acquainted with all that they do.

And say to the believing women that they should lower their gaze and guard their modesty; that they should not display their beauty and ornaments except what (ordinarily) appear thereof; that they should draw their veils over their bosoms and not display their beauty except to their husbands, their fathers, their husbands' fathers, their sons, their husband's sons, their brothers or their brothers' sons, or their sisters' sons, or their women, or the slaves their right hands possess, or male attendants free of sexual desires, or small children who have no carnal knowledge of women.

Qur'an 24:30–31

In a letter dated July 30, 1989, Kamla, another daughter of Gateefa and Sagr, wrote to tell me her good news.

In the Name of God the All-Merciful and Compassionate. It gives me pleasure to send this letter to my dear sister, Dr. Lila, hoping from God on high, the All-Powerful, that it reaches you carrying love and greetings to you and your family while you are all in the best of health and in perfect happiness.

By name she mentioned my brother and sisters (none of whom she has met) and asked me to convey her greetings and those of her family to them and to my parents, as well as to the one American friend of mine they had met ten years ago—in short, to everyone they knew about in my life in America. I had confided

Abu-Lughod, Lila. "Honor and Shame." *Writing Women's Worlds: Bedouin Stories.* Berkeley, Los Angeles, Oxford: U of California P, 1993. 205–242.

during my last visit that I would be getting married soon. She asked if I had; if so, she wrote, she sent a thousand congratulations and hoped, God willing, that he was a good man who would understand me. She hoped also that their new in-law was a noble man, the best in all of America, and that they would meet him soon. After wishing me many children (six boys and six girls) and more greetings, she squeezed her piece of news onto the bottom of the page.

Your sister Kamla has become engaged to Engineer Ibrahim Saleem, Aisha's brother.

I could hardly believe it. We had teased Kamla about him ever since his name had been floated four years before as a prospect. This was the match she scarcely dared hope her father would arrange. Not that she had ever met the young man. What mattered was that he was educated, came from a family that believed in educating girls, and lived in a town. She would be able to escape the kind of life her family lived, a life that annoyed her—the only one in her family, male or female, to have made it through high school—more and more.

Because she complained so much, I had asked her in the summer after she graduated to write me an essay on how young Bedouin women's lives were changing and what of the past she hoped the Awlad 'Ali would retain and what she wished they would abandon. She had proudly told me that her teacher had sent off for publication an essay on Awlad 'Ali weddings she had written in school. You can trace, in the stilted words of her essay and the candid comments (in parentheses) she made as she read it aloud to me, the outlines of the new world she hoped to gain by marrying the likes of Engineer Ibrahim Saleem.

The Education of Girls

*An Essay on the Young Bedouin Woman of Egypt
and the Changes in Her Life over 40 Years*

If we are to speak of the Bedouin girl in Egypt we find that her life differs from one era to another. The circumstances of the home and family relations change from one age to another. If we go back to discuss the way she was around forty years ago, we find that the Bedouin girl was living a life in which she was of no value. When she came of age, or maturity (as the Egyptians say—I mean the years when she is ready for marriage), *she had to do housework at her family's home—for example, cooking, washing clothes, and preparing firewood.* (Her only value was in the housework she did—the sweeping and washing—and if she didn't do it they'd laugh at her and gossip about her laziness. She was forced to do it, even if she weren't capable. No matter what her health was like. I'm talking about those who were my age, from around the age of twelve on.)

Also, she used to spin and weave, even though it is very difficult, painful, and strenuous. (When she was around fifteen, her mother or any woman in the household, an aunt for instance, would teach her. It's supposed to be the mother, though. Her goal was to teach her daughter to spin and to make something, anything. The important thing was for her to weave something, if only a border for the tent.) *She had to learn this skill.* (This is what is important for the Bedouins, housework, weaving, and such things. Forty years ago this was what a girl had to put up with.)

Kamla had been resenting housework. Now that she had finished school she rarely left the house. With two sisters, she was responsible for the cooking and cleaning one day out of three. On another of those days she was in charge of baking bread with them. She was on call much of the rest of the time, seeing to it that her little brothers and sisters were bathed, dressed, and staying out of mischief. Piles of laundry collected in the back room to be done when there was time.

Where before she had worn clean clothes for school, studied with her brothers in a quiet room of her own, and been given few household duties, now she had no privileges. Her clothes were as caked with dough and soot as her sisters'. Kamla's only escape was listening to the radio. She carried my transistor with her wherever in the house or courtyard she was working. She kept an eye on the time so as not to miss the radio soap operas. When she was free, she stared into space as she listened to Egyptian music, talk shows, and the news. So attached was she to the radio that I called it her sweetheart. Her mother, irritable from fatigue herself, scolded her and threatened to lock up the radio. When Gateefa complained, "My daughters are becoming lazy sluts," Kamla, like her sisters, simply ignored her.

Kamla had scored high enough on her final exams to secure a place in the agricultural college for which her high school had prepared her. She had no special interest in agriculture and had gone to this secondary school only because the regular high school was on the far side of town. Her uncles had given her a choice: quit school or go to the nearby agriculture school. School was still much on her mind. Her essay continued:

Education for the Bedouin girl used not to exist. It was impossible for her to study. (Forty years ago she lived a life, as I said earlier, that had no value at all.) *She was governed by the customs and traditions that the Bedouin families followed. These customs and traditions forbade a girl to leave the house under any circumstances. So going to school* (this is an example) *would be the greatest shame. She couldn't say that she wished to study, no matter what. Even if, as they say, she was the daughter of a tribal leader.* (So for example, a girl's father would be a tribal leader and she'd want to study, but her relatives would say no you can't. She'd say, but I'm the daughter of the head of a lineage. I must learn. They'd forbid her.)

This hypothetical example was, of course, from her own experience. She had been allowed to continue her schooling against the wishes of her uncles. They wanted to pull her out when she was no longer little. Because she was so determined, she and her parents had put up with the uncles' general suspicion and occasional accusations. She was a fierce child who had early on decided she wanted to go to school. She was not allowed to enroll in the public school, though, because, as is often the case, her father had never registered her birth. Yet still she went each day, as a visitor, borrowing her brothers' books. After three years of this her teacher finally required her to register officially. Haj Sagr went and had her papers drawn up. From then on she came in at the top of her class, while her brothers and male cousins flunked out. I had recorded in my notes from 1979 her bashful reaction when her brother told their father she had been appointed school monitor. Sagr had been hugging his youngest son, then in his first year of school, proudly predicting that his son would come out above the rest.

The primary school had been within sight of the camp, and its students were mostly relatives and neighbors. The secondary school, though, was about three kilometers away. Kamla's class had only four Bedouin girls; the rest of the girls were Egyptians from town. To get to this school she had to walk along the road past houses of people who did not know her. She said she walked with her head down, looking neither right nor left, but she still had to endure catcalls from men driving by.

Her relatives' suspicions were harder to cope with. One aunt had come twice to Gateefa to accuse Kamla of taking her son's schoolbook to give to a boy from a neighboring tribe. Kamla's mother had defended her. True, she had given the boy a schoolbook, but it was in exchange for a book that he had given her the pervious year. And the book was one that her father had bought her, not one she had taken from her cousin. Fortunately, when they questioned the aunt's son, he backed Gateefa.

Kamla and her mother were angrier when Kamla's uncle told Haj Sagr that he had seen his niece Kamla walking home with a boy. Gateefa felt she'd been hit in the stomach with a rock. She argued, to me, "If it were true, why didn't he stop for her and put her in the car? Why didn't he get out and beat her right there, if he really saw her? If he's so afraid for her, why doesn't he ever offer to drive her to school?"

Kamla told the story as she knew it. She believed the problem began during her second year of high school. Her uncle had not wanted her to continue, but Sagr had defended his daughter's right to stay in school. Furious, her uncle did everything he could to prevent her from studying. If, for example, guests came to the house, he would knock on her door to ask her to make the tea. She'd try to escape, sneaking off to study outdoors under the trees. Two days before her final exams (when, as we all know, she added, nerves are on edge), she was walking home from school. Across the road a boy she had known since she was small was going the same direction. Because she always walked with her head down, she noticed her uncle drive by only after he had passed. He went straight to her father and told him, "Your daughter was walking hand in hand with a boy." Her father had questioned him carefully, then called in Kamla's mother. Gateefa in turn had come to her ("And you know how upset she gets!" she said to me) to ask her about it. Kamla refused to say "yes, no, or maybe" unless her uncle came and accused her to her face.

Her father, she said lovingly, believed in her. He asked her why she didn't walk home from school with her cousin, and she explained that she was not about to go out of her way just to walk with him. If he wished to walk with her along her route before cutting off to his house, he was welcome to. Kamla's uncle had also told her father that this cousin had informed him that the boy waited for Kamla at the school gates to walk home with her every day. Fortunately for Kamla, her cousin happened to pass by the house that afternoon. Sagr called him over to question him—right in front of her uncle. The boy swore that he had never said such a thing. That ended it.

Arranged Marriage

The next paragraph of Kamla's essay took up the matter of marriage. Commenting on it, Kamla said, "This was a topic the Bedouin girl would hear nothing about and wasn't supposed to have anything to do with."

> *She had no right to an opinion in any matter, however much the matter might concern her personally. She had no say even in the choice of a husband. She had absolutely no say in this matter.* (And to this day, no matter how educated she's become, very seldom does she have any opinion. The Bedouin girl has no say.) *In this matter what she had to do was carry out her family's orders even if she didn't want to. It was not right for her to refuse.* (Even if she didn't want him, she had to agree to it against her will. Even if he was older than she was, for example, or very different from her, she had to agree to what the family wanted. For example, if they said I had to marry someone and I didn't want him—I hated him—but if my kinsmen had agreed to the match and told me I had to marry him, what I would have to do, despite my wishes, was marry him.)

I was surprised that Kamla depicted women as powerless in decisions about marriage. She had heard the same stories I had—stories, like her grandmother Migdim's, of resistance to marriages arranged for them by their kinsmen. She knew plenty of young women like one who, in love with someone else, had married Kamla's cousin but then had gone home to her father's household at the slightest provocation, eventually forcing her husband to divorce her. The specter of forced marriage, especially to paternal cousins, may have loomed large for Kamla because she, like her sister Sabra, was waiting. As her mother joked with a friend, "Kamla's got her diploma. Now we're going to give her the other diploma!"

Her religious training at school had given Kamla moral ammunition against arranged marriage. The Prophet, she would explain, says that it is wrong to marry someone you have never seen. Moreover, the girl must give her consent: the bride's relatives are supposed to ask her opinion. Kamla is not sure her opinion will be sought. Already she has made it known throughout the women's community that she does not want to marry her cousin Salih, the young man closest to her in age who has been lined up with her, at least according to the calculations of his father and uncles about marriages between their children.

Kamla is fond of Salih, but he is "like a brother." She and her sisters boldly ask him to get them things they want from town; they reach into his pockets to grab the latest cassettes he has brought for himself. Kamla sometimes teases him, threatening to make him wash the dishes and sweep the floor if he marries her. Kamla even jokes with his mother. I had seen the woman grab Kamla and warn her to be good or else she'd exercise her prospective rights as a mother-in-law and make her quit school. Kamla broke free easily, laughing as she shouted defiantly, "Not until I come to live with you!"

Women in the camp mutter that Salih is not right for Kamla. Even her grandmother half supports her. Although Migdim tries to persuade her granddaughters of the virtues of marrying cousins, she is angry with her sons for wanting "what nothing good will come of"—this set of matches within the family between children who have grown up together and say they feel like siblings. She fumed, "Her father wants Kamla for Salih, and Kamla says she won't marry him. And Salih says he won't marry Kamla. She's older than he is!"

Her unmarried granddaughters enjoy provoking Migdim by maligning cousin marriage. They say they want out: they want to marry men who live far away so they can have new lives.

"They're good for nothing!" insisted one of Kamla's cousins once about her male cousins.

Migdim scolded her, "You slut! What is this outrage? You gypsy!"

She and her sister laughed wildly, "Damn them, our cousins! What do you see in them?"

A cousin agreed, "They're all ugly. Not a handsome one among them. No, we'll marry outsiders, Grandma, ugly or handsome."

Kamla shook her head. "I'm marrying an Egyptian! Someone educated."

Her grandmother retorted, "Your father won't agree to it!"

Kamla hugged her grandmother. "We're just talking with you to see what you'll say. Is there anything in our hands, Grandma? Or in my father's? Only God knows what will happen."

Generations

In the past, according to Kamla, a girl had no say in the matter of marriage because, as her essay continued,

> *They thought that girls shouldn't be concerned with anything but clothing and food and drink. In her kinsmen's eyes a girl had no value.* (Even now it's true. You might think conditions had changed and advanced a bit, but it's still true.) *They did not know that a girl had something she valued more than food and such things—and that was feelings.* (Feelings were forbidden to the girl.) *But she had feelings and sensitivity and affections just like any other person on this earth.* (This is true. There is no person God has created without feelings or sensitivity.) *Her kinsmen had feelings and sensitivities and affections.* (Take my father, for example. My father loved in the days of his youth; but then he thinks a girl doesn't have any such feelings.) *But they did not care if the girl had feelings. Her feelings and desires were not important.*

Kamla laughed conspiratorially as she read the next section.

> *So, for example, if she loved a person, she could not show this love, however precious and strong her love was. She would be very afraid that her relatives would hear about it, because they considered it a big scandal for a girl to love, even though they had. They say that only men have the right—a young woman does not have the right to know or speak with any man except her brothers and their relatives. All of this has governed the Bedouin girl for as long as she has lived on this earth.* (This is true. For example, if a boy meets a girl and talks with her, they say it doesn't matter—"He's a man." But you, the girl, if you do this? They don't say anything to him. If my father heard that my brother was in love with someone and talked with her, he wouldn't say anything. But if it was me? That would be dealt with very differently.)

This talk of love and vocabulary of feelings was new. Ever since I had known Kamla, from the age of twelve or so, she had been a tough little girl, the kind who would say to her uncle's new wife, "I don't even know what this 'love' is. I hear about it in songs and hear about this one giving her necklace and that one her ring, but I don't know what they are feeling." She used to amuse her great-aunts when they hugged her and teased her about which of her young cousins she would grow up to marry by proudly shouting, "I'm never going to marry."

Just a year before she wrote this essay she had demanded of her mother, "Does a woman have to marry? Does she have to have someone to tell her what to do, to boss her around?"

"Yes, a woman has to marry," Gateefa had answered. "If she doesn't, people will say, 'The poor thing!'"

But things had changed. Kamla now quoted from a book she had read at school: it was natural as one entered adolescence to begin thinking about members of the opposite sex. She admitted that such things had never even crossed her mind before. But then it had happened. It was at her cousin Selima's wedding that she had first revealed to me the new experiences she had begun to have at school. During a quiet period of the day before the wedding we had gone for a stroll on the hillside. Scattered on the ridge were groups of women in twos and threes, sisters who rarely saw each other, aunts and their nieces, old friends, also talking privately.

Looking into the distance—and, as it turned out, toward a certain house—Kamla had asked me, "What do you think, Lila? Is it wrong for two people to think about each other all the time?" I was puzzled. She told me about a young man at school—a well-behaved and good person, she added quickly—who had taken notice of her. He had asked her friends whether they could persuade her to agree to talk to him. She had refused at first. Finally she agreed to a brief meeting, with friends present. He wanted to know if she would be willing to marry him if he got his father to request her from Haj Sagr. She wondered if there was any hope that her father would accept. Knowing the family, I said I doubted it.

Usually she was more realistic. When I would ask whom she wanted to marry she would give various answers. She was adamant about her cousins: "If they think I'm going to take any of these, my cousins, or anyone from the camp, they're wrong." Then she would deny that she cared whether or not it was the boy she knew from school. The brother of their family friend Aisha would be just fine. As long as the man was educated. Backtracking she would say, "It's not even important that he's well educated. But he must be knowledgeable." The boys in her camp didn't know anything; they would not know how to get on in the world. Dependent on their fathers to feed, dress, and marry them off, they were incapable of taking care of themselves. "They're men in name only," she scoffed.

She blamed her elder kinsmen, especially her father, for her cousins' failures. Despite the double standard in matters of the heart, she acknowledged that her cousins and her brothers were having almost as hard a time dealing with their old-fashioned elders as she was. One time when I returned from a short trip to Cairo, Kamla greeted me with the news that her grandmother was distraught because her cousin Salih, the woman's favorite grandson, had run away from home after his father had hit him. No one knew where he had gone.

I would hear the story several times from Migdim, once as she told it to a visiting niece who began by asking, "Who hit Salih?"

"His father hit him."

"And why?"

"He went to a wedding at So-and so's and they say he drank liquor."

"Liquor? What kind of liquor?"

Migdim didn't know much about it. "The stuff you drink that makes them drunk. They said he drank. Each of the men came and asked him. They'd told his father on him."

"Beer, must have been beer." Migdim's niece knew things. Her husband, now dead, was rumored to have been a womanizer and an alcoholic.

Migdim did not want her story interrupted. "His father came here and hit him."

"Beer. Liquor?—why a bottle costs twenty-five pounds! There is beer and white water. The beer costs two pounds fifty a bottle."

Migdim went on. "I said, 'Son, listen, sometimes he hits his sisters just to get half a pound from them. Another time he'll need a pound. By God, he doesn't have a piaster.' I said, 'Son, your boy didn't drink. He doesn't have any money.' Salih told him, 'Father, I didn't buy any. Dad, I didn't taste it. Dad, I didn't drink.' Every time he said something, his father would give him a slap. And in the end he looked for something big to hit him with, but we grabbed it away."

Her niece was shocked.

"The women stopped him. The boy cried and cried—and I was crying too— until his eyes were red. And he said, 'Swear to God, I'll go to Libya. I'm leaving.' I thought maybe he'd go stay with his maternal uncle. That would have been fine. In the end, though, they said he headed east."

Migdim went on about her own feelings. The night Salih left, she says, her head never touched the pillow. She and his sisters sat up crying all night. "It was hard on me. He really was so generous, he was generous. I swear to God, that time he got a job with his uncle out west and had some money, he'd give me five pounds, his sister five pounds, his aunt five pounds, and his nephews one pound each. So generous. And in the morning, he never left without coming to say, 'Good morning, Grandmother. How are you, Grandma?' And he'd kiss me from this side and that. He was always there around me."

Although they thought Salih was wrong to run away, the other women in the community were angrier with his father. One of them had tried to calm the man, saying, "It's something that's already happened. If the boy went astray it has passed, and if it didn't really happen, then people lied. He's your son." The man had refused to be calmed.

Migdim was upset that her son was now threatening to pursue the boy. She says she cursed him, "You've gone crazy, my son, and you've made him go crazy. If you got him angry, may God bring you no success! May God not grant you success!"

Her niece commiserated.

Migdim continued, "I told him, 'If you hit him, may God not favor you! You should just talk to him. How can you say you're going to make him go out to herd the camels, living for three or four months on unleavened bread? You drove him crazy! Why didn't you scold him gently and say, 'Son, this is wrong, this is shameful?'"

Migdim's niece gave an alternative. The man should have said to his son, "Okay, it was the first time. Now say it will be the last time." She added, "After all, someone invited him, rottenest of invitations. The boys figured it would pass, but they caught it."

Had Salih really bought the liquor? Who was with him? The women of the family disagreed. Migdim cursed the family that held the wedding. "May God ruin their houses, those who had a wedding and brought—I don't know what dog it was who brought a box and sold bottles from it—who was it?" Others knew that beer was often sold at these kinds of weddings, where professional performers entertained. They suspected that the drinking had gone on. All the women agreed that the boys were just kids who didn't know better; his father should have reprimanded the boy, "My son, this is wrong. This is the Devil's work."

Kamla, too, criticized her father and her uncles, but not just for the way they had reacted to this rumor of alcohol. She thought they were mistaken to be so strict with the boys. They wanted the boys to be straight, but all they would get from applying this pressure was stubbornness. The pressure, she warned, would produce the opposite of what they wanted. She gave examples. The men wouldn't let the boys play soccer. "What's wrong with soccer? It's exercise." They wouldn't let them have a television, go to cafés, or visit the local cafeteria where videos are shown. Needless to say, they wouldn't permit them to grow their hair long. The men wouldn't even let the boys get jobs, making them stay on the land and tend the new fig trees. Noting that her brothers and cousins had no money, Kamla added, "They treat them like girls. If only they would give them a bit of freedom."

The freedom she wants for them, and perhaps for herself, is the subject of a popular song, an early recording by 'Awadh al-Maalky, that includes a comical tale of woe. The singer is moved, he begins, by the suffering that customs of the past have caused a young man. Hundreds of others have come to him to complain. Assuming the voice of the aggrieved young man, the poet describes what happened in the three marriages his kin arranged for him: when he reached out on the wedding night to touch his first bride, he discovered she was completely bald; the second bride, though beautiful with long thick braids, could not speak; the third tried to strangle him in his sleep—she was insane. The young man declares he won't marry again unless he is allowed to choose his own bride. Resuming his own voice the singer comments on the young man's predicament with some advice to the elders:

> My warnings are to the old man
> who imprisons the freedom of the young,
> who has forgotten a thing called love,
> affection, desire, burning flames,
> forgotten the strength of lovers' fire,
> the fire of lovers who long for one another.

What's exquisite is that they're afraid,
they say, any minute my prying guard will turn up:
my father's about to catch us.

The Dangers of Schooling

Kamla thinks her elders are wrong to fear an abuse of freedom. Her essay described what happened when her generation began to go to school.

Life began to change for the Bedouins, a change of conditions and location. Those Bedouins who began living in town started sending their sons and also their daughters to school to learn right from wrong, prayer, and writing. (That was my father's single goal in educating us. He wanted us to know this. They don't put us in school to learn—who cared if I got educated? My own reason for being there was to learn right from wrong and the Qur'an. That's all.) *After that they would pull them out of school.* (Even if a girl was clever and came out first in her class, once she had learned right from wrong and had come to understand, they would say to her, "Come on, that's enough.") *Some might let her stay through secondary school.* (Like me. After I finished secondary school, that was it.) *The Bedouin girl could even gain such a mastery of learning and knowledge* (it would be great if every girl could go to high school) *that she could enter university.* (In Alexandria you'll find Bedouin girls who've gone to university.)

Kamla was grateful to have been allowed to continue so long in school. She had dreamt, when still in primary school, of going to college to study politics and economics. At the time, she says with amazement, she didn't understand the problem of being a girl. She had hope. Now they tease her younger sister for similar ambitions. Her father had proudly congratulated the younger girl for a good report card and said it was a pity her brothers had given her such a hard time when she announced that she wanted to be a doctor. Kamla was scornful. "They'll make her quit long before she becomes a doctor."

The problem with being a girl, as Kamla explained in her essay, was what other people would say and think about her family if they let her go to school.

What happened was that people began competing over the schooling of girls. (For example, my father sees Aisha's father, who has educated all his daughters; so my father looks at him and says, "Why should he educate his daughters and not me? I have to educate my daughters." One looked at the next until all of them started educating their daughters. . . . But around here, they see that others' daughters aren't in school. No one here has daughters in university. In Marsa Matruh they all sent their girls to school, each imitating the other. My father looks over at Aisha's father and his daughters. If one of them did anything wrong—may God protect us!—*anything* wrong, my father and all of them would decide not to follow. But when I look, I see that the Bedouin girl does not give up her Bedouin values. The girls went to school and nothing bad happened.) *They put them in school, and the girls repaid their precious trust. The Bedouin girl made them see clearly that their daughter was as good as any girl from the biggest city—in intelligence and level of learning. She would get the highest grades in all fields of learning.* (This is true. If, for example, you compare someone from Marsa Matruh and someone from Cairo who've both graduated from the same school, you'll find them equally good. You'll even find that the Bedouin girl is better because she is also modest, pious, and respectful of her traditions and customs—better than the Egyptian girl who may have graduated from medical school but does not dress properly. Everything in her lifestyle is not right. Even if she gets educated, the Bedouin girl is better. You know, the Bedouins used to think that girls were a scandal. They used to think that if a Bedouin girl left the house she would have to do something wrong. They were sure of it. They'd say she can't go out—she's an idiot, she can't think. Like a beast of burden, she wouldn't know right from wrong. But when she got educated she showed them that what they had thought was wrong.)

Kamla still struggled against community opinion. Her relatives opposed sending her to college. An aunt put it bluntly: "What? Let her study in Alexandria? She's a kid. What does she know? Someone might take advantage of her. If it were here in our territory, it would be fine. But it's in Alexandria. She's gotten enough schooling."

Her father was more honest about their concerns. He had defied his brothers (with Aisha and perhaps even me in mind) to let her complete high school. The summer she graduated a school friend of Kamla's came to visit. She was dressed differently from the girls in our camp, having adopted the modern Islamic modest dress that included a severe headcovering. Haj Sagr knew her family; she spoke freely to Kamla's father, while his own daughter sat silent. The young woman told him how they wished they could go on to college. At first he tried to dismiss the idea by asking what use agricultural college (the only kind they were qualified to enter) would be for a girl. Then he got to the heart of the problem: "What would people say? 'His daughter's in college. I wonder if she's really studying or just going out a lot.'" Even if she were truly doing nothing wrong, he said, people would talk. The young woman argued with him, but he ended, as Kamla had predicted, by saying, "Listen, if your father agrees to it, tell him I'll agree too."

He inquired about her family situation, and she told him her father was refusing to marry any of his daughters to cousins. His excuse was that blindness ran in the family. Kamla was encouraged, momentarily, when her father agreed that a girl who is educated should be married to an educated man so there could be mutual understanding. But then Haj Sagr suddenly reversed his argument. He told Kamla's friend that he had been willing to send his daughters to school because he wanted them to know how to organize their lives, their home, and their children. An educated mother could help her children with their schoolwork.

Therefore, he said, he would prefer to keep these girls in the family: even if their husbands were not educated, the next generation of the family would benefit. If you give women to outsiders, he noted, the benefits go to the other tribe.

His model was Aisha, the woman whose father had been an old friend, whose husband was Sagr's business partner, and whose brother he was eventually to accept as a son-in-law. Aisha was the only college-educated Bedouin woman they knew. Whenever she and her children accompanied her husband on a visit, Kamla assumed special charge. Although all the women were warm, it was Kamla who saw to it that Aisha got water for ablutions, a prayer mat when she wanted, and who kept the conversation going.

Aisha was tall, slender, and elegant. She wore nicely styled full-length, long-sleeved dresses. Instead of the usual black headcloth, she wore the fashionable modern headcovering that now marks Muslim modesty and piety. Unlike the Egyptian women who sometimes visited, she did not turn up her nose at the food that was offered her, and she was relaxed with the women of the household. She'd just laugh when old Migdim teased her about her husband. "After He created your husband's tribe, God created the donkey." Insults were expected between people from Aisha's tribe and that of her husband.

Aisha was and was not part of their world. A distant relative, she had people and interests in common with Migdi, Gateefa, and the others, but she was defensive about her family. Although they lived in the city, she was quick to tell stories that showed her brothers to be proper Bedouins. Describing her own wedding, she recalled how her husband—whose family were real desert Bedouins—came to her house the evening before the ceremony. He had brought along a Western-style suit, intending to have his photograph taken with her. Her brothers, she reported, had said, "If you're coming to have dinner with us, that's fine, you are very welcome. But if you're coming for anything else, don't bother."

Later she would try to cover for her sister, who made an unconventional marriage. We had met this young woman once, a student of pharmacology at Alexandria University who came to visit dressed in a long woolen suit, her hair covered with a turban and scarf, an alternative "Islamic" style. We heard later that her brothers had agreed to a marriage offer from an Egyptian doctor living in Marsa Matruh. Aisha insisted that even though the groom was Egyptian, her brothers had required a Bedouin engagement ceremony, where sheep are brought and eaten, first, before the Egyptian-style engagement party the groom's family wanted. She also claimed that they held a traditional henna party on the eve of the wedding—before the Egyptian-style wedding in a club. She denied that anyone except one brother had attended the wedding itself, but I didn't believe her: I knew she knew how scandalous it would be to admit that the bride's relatives had attended such a wedding.

Aisha switched easily between the Bedouin and Egyptian dialects. When she and her husband entertained Bedouins in their home, she served the men the customary lamb and rice but otherwise remained in a separate room from them.

When they were with Egyptian friends, she served different foods and they all ate together. They even got different videos to entertain their guests. For Bedouins they always rented the same film about the Libyans' struggle against the Italian colonists. Their guests, Aisha explained, loved the early scenes showing a traditional Libyan Bedouin wedding and the scenes of men fighting on horseback. Egyptian films, she said, contained risqué scenes, so these were never shown to Bedouin guests. Aisha also owned two photo albums: one she showed to their more traditional Bedouin friends and family; the other one she kept hidden because it contained photographs, taken with a self-timer, of herself holding hands with her husband. Yet Aisha worried about trying to raise her two small children in an apartment on the outskirts of Alexandria. She did not want them to play with the neighbors. She feared they were learning bad language, and she apologized for their having picked up the Egyptian dialect. Her five-year-old daughter had just begun school and had started to deny that she was an Arab. "She says she's Egyptian," her mother reported. "You know," Aisha said earnestly to Kamla, "Egyptians aren't like us."

Egyptians

Could Bedouin identity be maintained after schooling? Kamla's essay took up this question.

> *The Bedouin girl preserves the traditions and customs she was raised by.* (People stay with what they have grown up with because they came of age with it. Me, for example, I grew up knowing this was shameful and that was not right, there are customs, there's respect and modesty. Even when I'm old and my hair is grey, I'll have to follow these.) *She has sense and preserves her family's reputation.* (Of course, she'd be afraid that if she did something wrong they'd pull her out of school.) *The Bedouin girl tries to overcome the special obstacles she must confront.* (For example, she doesn't let her customs and traditions, or people's talk— saying this is wrong and that is shameful—make her fall behind other girls. The Bedouin girl follows her customs but in a way that doesn't tie her up or block the path before her.) *She attempts to live a life enlightened by learning, happiness, and contributions to her country and family.* (She gives to her country. The Bedouin girl feels for her country and understands the meaning of Egypt as much as any girl from Cairo. The girl living in the Western Desert has feelings for Egypt that may be even stronger than the Egyptian girl's. The educated Bedouin girl knows the meaning of her country. . . . Boy, if my father heard this!)

Kamla's comment about her father gives a clue as to the obstacles she faces as she moves between home and her state school run by Egyptian teachers. While Haj Sagr bemoans the Awlad 'Ali's lack of foresight in failing to request an independent state from the British and chafes against every government restriction on his activities, Kamla patriotically defends Egypt and speaks proudly of President Mubarak. Once, when her father confronted her for being a few hours late from a school trip, she argued back. He then scolded her for raising her voice and waving her hands as she spoke. "This is the work of Egyptians!" he yelled. Anger fighting fear, she answered, "I *am* an Egyptian. And they are the best people, and this is the best country!"

Kamla listened closely to the detailed reports of city life that Safiyya, her father's second wife, gave each time she returned from visits to her brothers' homes. These were brothers whose sons were becoming lawyers. Kamla was also riveted to broadcasts of Egyptian radio melodramas, with plots like that of "Bride by Computer," about a young man whose life is nearly ruined by computer matchmaking. Kamla can envision this world better than her sisters can, although she was as puzzled as they were about what a computer might be, and just as disapproving of the female characters in this conservative morale tale.

The plot of this serial, as the girls explained, followed the usual formula: A man loves someone but cannot marry her; in the end, though, he succeeds in getting her. The main character was a young Egyptian who worked in a company. When his mother objected to him marrying a co-worker whom he loved, a friend suggested he "talk to the computer to find a bride." The results, predictably, were disastrous. The first bride was a doctor. "She worked day and night," Kamla recalled. "Even the night of the wedding she was busy."

"You know what she was doing?" Kamla's neighbor intervened. "She was doing experiments with mosquitoes and rats."

"So he divorced her," Kamla went on. "He got engaged to another girl but didn't marry her. After he got engaged to her, she wanted him to go swimming with her and to dance with her, to act like foreigners."

The neighbor was excited. "The day he wanted to marry her she told him she wanted him to come over. He went there and found it wild. There was loud music."

Sabra explained. "She was at a nightclub. When he got there she said, 'Play that music,' and people started dancing. She asked him if he knew how to dance. He said no. She said, 'Look, see that man who's moving wildly on the floor?' The girl moved wildly as well, asking them to play a foreign tape."

The young women laughed as they described her. "She said to him, 'Get up, get up.' But he wouldn't go with her. He wouldn't dance with her."

When they paused I asked, "What was the problem with the third bride?"

The girls were confused. Sabra ventured, " I don't know, she had put . . . she had made a workshop in the house. They had a guest room, and she put her workshop in that room."

"No, she turned the bedroom into a factory."

"And she started fighting with her in-laws. She experimented on the old woman. She gave her something to try that made her almost die. When the man came home from work he asked his wife, 'Where is my mother?' She told him, 'I took her to the hospital.' He asked, 'Why, what's the matter?' He couldn't bear that any harm would come to his mother. When he went to see her she talked to him. She said, 'She was doing an experiment and I'm the one who drank the medicine.'"

They giggled as Kamla repeated, "The old woman almost died. He said, 'No, if she wants to kill my mother, I don't want her.'"

"He loved his mother," Sabra noted.

"And the fourth one, he brought her and then couldn't get any peace. She gave him a headache. She'd bring the onions and potatoes to peel. The man would be resting on the bed and she'd climb up next to him at night to peel potatoes. She'd say, 'Put down that newspaper and let's talk, me and you.'"

The girls found it hilarious to think of the woman peeling potatoes in bed. One of them explained, "She was a real peasant."

Kamla argued, "It's just lies. A peasant woman wouldn't do that."

Her neighbor was emphatic. "She was a peasant from Upper Egypt. They are like that."

Kamla will only go so far in her defense of Egyptians. She often criticized their neighbors, a poor family who had lived among Egyptians and had picked up different ways. As evidence of their immorality she disclosed that the men and women ate together. Another nearby household fared little better. They knew no modesty, she said: the son listened to cassettes in front of his father, and the young daughter-in-law neither covered her hair with a black headcloth nor avoided her father-in-law.

In her essay, and even more clearly in her commentary, Kamla underlined this distinction between Bedouin morality and Egyptian immorality. Still writing about the young Bedouin woman who had become educated, she said:

> *She doesn't forget her origins or her customs and traditions. She raises her children as well as the people of the city do.* (Now we're talking about what the Bedouin woman does after she gets educated. Does she forget her duties as a mother? The difference between the Bedouins and the Egyptians is that when the Egyptian woman has a baby, she gives it to her mother to raise for her, and she takes it to day care. She doesn't do her duty to the child nor give it the required care. For example, she nurses only up to the fortieth day or at most for two months. And then she leaves it with her mother, her sister, or day care and goes out to work. But the Bedouin woman gives the child its due, even if she's educated and has an advanced degree. Not her mother, not anyone else—she herself does the work.
>
> And she raises her child according to her customs. Let's say she's a Bedouin who marries an Egyptian or an educated Bedouin. She doesn't raise her child by the customs or traditions of the Egyptians. She raises her child with the customs and traditions of the Bedouin, except that she is slightly more informed. I mean, she tells her daughter, "This is shameful" and "That is right." Take an

educated Bedouin girl like me, for example. If I were to marry an educated man and live the city life, I wouldn't let my daughter follow the ways of the Egyptians where a girl wears short dresses or goes out to clubs. No, of course that is wrong. We must be modest. It is wrong for us Bedouins, and we must respect our traditions. This is necessary. You wouldn't find an educated Bedouin woman allowing her daughter to do things that she could not do when she was with her family. Or maybe even if her parents permitted it, the girl herself would not do it. "No," she'd know, "that's wrong." Bedouin women are the ones who really know how to raise their daughters. They are better than Egyptians because the Egyptian woman won't hit her daughter. Very rarely do you find an Egyptian who can hit her daughter. But the Bedouin woman, if her daughter does something wrong, she must hit her. Even if she's not that young. She must hit her to teach her right and wrong. You don't learn right from wrong if you're not beaten. The Egyptians don't do it and their girls—well, you know . . .)

Poets have long reflected on the differences between Bedouins and their peasant neighbors. Only fragments are remembered, however, like the lines of a love story about a wealthy peasant and a beautiful Bedouin girl named Khawd. Drought had driven her family into his fields in search of pasture for their herds. He allowed them to stay and graze their animals when he saw Khawd. One day, though, his beloved announced that her family had decided to return to the desert; she asked him to migrate with them. In despair the young man answered:

O Khawd, I have no camels that I might travel your distances
I have nothing but buffalo and cows, who will find no pastures near you

Kamla's aunt Dhahab had once recited a short poem on a similar theme—it was her comment when I declined her polite suggestion that I marry her son so that I could come live with her. The song came, she said, from a story about a bull who fell in love with a camel and tried to follow her into the desert. She warned him that he would exhaust himself if he tried, since he had to eat and drink every day and she drank only every five days. He said that for her sake he'd drink only every other day, but she knew he couldn't keep up with her. She told him:

You'll kill yourself bellowing
O bull, if you try to follow . . .

Some women were tolerant of moral differences between themselves and Egyptians. I talked once about television with two poor women who had recently moved to the area from near the Libyan border. They said they found television entertaining to watch when they had no work to do. Their favorite shows, of course, were the Egyptian serialized dramas.

I was curious. "But the Egyptians on these programs are not like you, are they?"

One of them laughed. "The Egyptians are citified, not like the Bedouins, the poor things."

They explained that it didn't matter because they would never watch television with people they should respect and be modest in front of. Girls would never watch if their fathers were there; women would leave the room if their husbands had visitors.

"So you don't you feel embarrassed by what you see on television?"

"No, if you're by yourself it doesn't matter," replied the older of the two.

"What if you see people in love?"

The younger of the two women laughed. "They're free to do that. We don't worry about them. The Egyptians have no modesty. They have no religion. They just do everything. It's their way."

The older one agreed. "Yes, let them do what they want. We just laugh at them."

Kamla and Sabra had a younger sister who loved television. She thought her father was wrong not to let them have a TV set. Although she conceded that foreign films were immoral, she argued that Egyptian films were different. Haj Sagr had taken away the television set when he heard that the girls were watching films in which people hugged and kissed each other. "He didn't want us watching. He said it was shameful." But these films and stories, she persisted, always showed the correct path in the end, even though they had people doing such things in early scenes. Egyptian films show how the girl who went off with a man later realized that he had tricked and used her. The importance of proper moral behavior always became clear ultimately.

Kamla's sister wondered anyway what her father could be thinking when he worried about his daughters' exposure to these things. Realistically she asked, "Where do we ever go? Nowhere but this house or the rest of the camp, where it's all family. Where does he think these things could happen?"

Kamla's father did fear the influence of Egyptians on the Bedouin community. In his opinion, the most serious problem the Bedouins faced was that of intermarriage between Bedouins and Egyptians. In the past, he maintained, no Arab, even the simplest shepherd, would give his daughter in marriage to "a peasant," as they used to call all Egyptians, even if the man were a company president. Things were more difficult now. Whereas before the area had been almost completely Bedouin, now, in regions like theirs that were close to large towns, Egyptians made up fifty percent of the population.

The trouble with the Egyptian presence, he went on, was that the Egyptian girls looked so pretty. They always dressed up, combed out their hair, and wore short dresses. A group of Bedouin elders had met recently to discuss what to do about these women who "walk around naked." Their concern was that the young men would find them attractive and want to marry them. And their fathers, wanting to make them happy, might agree. If the young men married Egyptian girls, there would no longer be any difference between Bedouin and Egyptian in the next generation. Sagr had warned the elders of this danger at the meeting. He admitted, though, that the process would be hard to stop now that the boys see these girls in school. Although he was afraid that Bedouin girls might pick up attitudes and habits from Egyptians—like having boyfriends, which the Egyptian girls don't think twice about—his real fear was intermarriage. That would bring about the end of tribal bonds.

Europeans

Sagr sensed the gradual shift in the boundaries of the moral community. Egyptians and Awlad 'Ali are being brought together by roads, newspapers, radio, television, schools, agricultural cooperatives, the army, and Parliament. With foreigners—Europeans—however, the divide remains absolute. Even Kamla, who sometimes pleaded with me, exasperated with her rambunctious little brothers and sisters, to take her away with me ("Put me in your suitcase and get me out of here!") and who proudly told me about several young Bedouin women with M.A.'s in veterinary medicine who had been sent, tattoos and all, to London for further training—even she did not approve of the Godless Europeans. Unlike Egyptian Christians, she argued, Europeans do not recognize God. "Every Muslim, even the most ignorant and uneducated, knows that there is a God and that He created all things." Worse, Europeans do not pray. When I contradicted her to say that many prayed in church, she challenged me. "What? What kind of person prays with his shoes on? May God protect us!"

The Westerner's lack of faith in god provides powerful imagery for inhumanity. Kamla's uncle's wife once lamented her lost brother with a poem that exploited this view:

> The European, with all his lack of faith,
> wept when I told him of my condition . . .

To show the magnitude of their compassion for girls, women sang a wedding rhyme that also mentioned Europeans:

> God protect every girl
> even the Christian woman's daughter

Kamla has not seen the new tourists who visit the Western Desert, but she has heard about them. In 1986 a favorite commercial cassette was the song called "The Japanese Woman" by the young Bedouin star Si'daawy al-Git'aany. The singer, identifying himself by tribe, says he lost his heart to a foreigner. (Although he calls her Japanese, the details of his song suggest a melding of many nationalities.)

Spanning many verses, the tale begins with his first sight of the woman. She had come to Egypt to relax, he sings, and in the gardens of a summer resort hotel in Marsa Matruh she was swinging on a swing. Her father, sitting on a chair ("like a boss") was grotesque and frightening: a European Christian with a long beard eating platefuls of pork and drinking quantities of beer. "We are Bedouins who like the desert," the singer goes on, "and they are Europeans. Fate brought us together." In her company he forgot his cares, and although they were accustomed to different ways, she made him lose interest in Bedouin women, who only cared about tying up goats and waiting for the sheep to come home in the evening.

She wore a cross and made him sit on chairs. Oh, he knew their ways were different, but he went astray, unable to stop himself from falling in love with a Christian. As she sat under an umbrella they talked. He had been to school and knew her language. She asked him to come home with her, but he first wanted to show her his home and the desert snail shells. Then she telephoned the governor and got permission for him to travel with her. So there he found himself, walking behind her, carrying her suitcases to board an airplane. Like a bird it took off, and he was scared. Everything is by God's will—that a man from the desert should end up with a Japanese woman.

Contrasting her country with his, he finds that the sea is to the south instead of the north. Her country is famous for its buses and trucks, he sings, whereas our women know only how to spin and to churn butter in goatskin bags. The moral contrasts are harsher. There, women's hair is uncovered and men wear straw baskets on their heads instead of skull caps. Women go wherever they wish and everyone says hello to them.

Accompanying his lover to a nightclub, he found people dancing like birds as someone howled while playing the piano. People got drunk and started fighting and throwing things around. His story would make a good soap opera, he sings. Things were different once they got to her country and she lost interest in him. The song ends with a refrain about the treachery of women, an ending that always got a rise out of Kamla and her sisters. "He got what he deserved," they insisted. "Who told him to go chasing after the foreigner, carrying her suitcases?"

Piety

Kamla reflected, in her essay, on what aspects of Bedouin life she would like to see preserved. Her father would have been proud of the list of positive features she drew up.

We all know that everything in life has its good qualities and its bad. (Weren't you asking what was good about the Bedouins and what wasn't?) *The virtues of the Bedouins are:*

1.   *Their piety and their total adherence to the traditions of the Prophet, despite their lack of education.* (This is the think I hope will continue until Judgment Day. This is the best thing—that they are religious. Even though ninety percent of them aren't educated, they are pious. Long clothing, respect, and modesty. The woman is as pious as the man. No woman can talk with a man she doesn't know or have him visit her at home. And she doesn't show her face or talk with any older man. This is what I hope Bedouin women and girls will never abandon.)

2.   *Their total respectfulness. The old respect the young, and the young respect the old, whether they are strangers or kin.*

3.   *Their generosity.* (It's true. You won't find anything on this earth like the generosity of the Bedouins. Even someone they don't know—they must invite him to the house and bring him food. Maybe no one else has this quality. I hope the Bedouins will hold on to this.)

4.   *Hospitality and respect for the guest.*

5.   *The ties of kinship that link various parts of the family and the cooperation of relatives in all situations.* (The other thing I want them to hold onto is this mutual assistance—they help each other in all circumstances. For example, even someone from a family that is related distantly to another must help a person from that family. Even among the women. When a Bedouin woman sets up a loom, for instance, her neighbors come to help her. Others always come to help. I wish the whole world—never mind just families—the whole world would help each other and that Muslims would cooperate the way our religion tells us to. Ninety-nine percent of Bedouin women haven't been educated. But they are pious. They're ignorant and illiterate, but they dress the right way, they fear God, and they pray. Sometimes they don't even know how to pray properly, but they pray anyhow. They are totally respectable, and they follow the traditions of the Prophet. They say the Prophet used to do this, the Prophet used to do that. They learn it from their husbands or their educated sons.)

Interestingly, Kamla had little to say about any of the traditional virtues except the first, piety. Although she was vehement in asserting their importance, perhaps she could not afford to think through their implications. She was proud of her father's generosity and hospitality, for instance, but it was also a source of tension, since the burden of feeding his many guests fell on the overworked women of the household. And if she were to think about how the extensive bonds between kin are to be maintained, she would have to admit the virtues of marriages to paternal cousins, the kind of marriage she wanted desperately to avoid.

Piety was a different matter. Like many, Kamla was becoming defensive in the face of new pressure from those sympathetic to Islamic activists in Egypt. She was correct to point out how tied up with their faith her kin were. They reckoned the months by the Islamic lunar calendar, the years by the annual religious feasts, age by the number of years a person has fasted the month of Ramadan, and the hours of the day by the five times for prayer. All the older women and many of the younger ones prayed regularly. Doing without the accouterments of city people, women simply prayed where they were, facing southeast and laying a small kerchief on the ground before them. The men like Kamla's father tended to know more. They would have learned as children to recite the Qur'an, and they continued to learn from the lectures at the mosque every Friday.

Their reactions to the sanctimonious Egyptians—and now to some Bedouins from the cities, who were becoming, as they put it, "followers of the model," meaning the life of the Prophet—have been mixed. The older women are not cowed. They argue, as Kamla did, that they have always worn modest clothing and covered their hair with a headcloth. They resent being told that some of the ways they have demonstrated their devoutness are wrong.

Kamla is more unsure. Sometimes she defends these Muslim Sisters and Brothers and sometimes she goes along with the old Bedouin women as they make fun of them. One evening, having recited some poetry and told some traditional tales for my benefit, Kamla's aunt Dhahab turned to her niece and asked, "Hey Kamla, have you given Lila any songs?"

Kamla was coy. "I'm not a song person. I'm just a simple person minding my own business. I'm with God. I'm pious and know my Lord."

Her sister hooted, perhaps thinking of Kamla's love of the radio and scandalous movie magazines. But Kamla went on, only half joking, "Auntie, I've become pious. I don't have anything to do with songs."

Her aunt mocked her. "What's this? You've become pious?" Everyone laughed as the old aunt continued, "God's blessings! God's blessings! So, you're joining the 'Beard Family'?"

There was a commotion, with everyone talking at once about the topic that was so often in the air these days: the Islamists. Kamla spoke on their behalf. "They say, 'We are religious people, . . . following God's path, the path to heaven.'"

Her aunt was hardly convinced. "I swear to God, they've never seen heaven. God is the only judge. God is present."

Sabra thought they should be more respectful. But she admitted, "May God protect them, they do some things that aren't necessary. Do you know what our aunt who lives out west says? She says they say that the sugar dolls are wrong, even the food we make to celebrate the Prophet's birthday. Rotten life! The special food for the birthday that the whole world celebrates—they say it is forbidden!"

Her aunt concurred. "Have you ever heard of such a thing!"

Some women were even more irreverent. Once when an old friend from the nearby town was visiting, the evening conversation turned to the topic of these new religious types. She complained that they had forbidden celebrations of saints' birthdays, including the candy and meat eaten at them. They had said it was wrong to call any holyman "Saint So-and-so." She said, "They have forbidden everything. Why, the next thing you know they'll forbid the clothes we wear and make us go around naked."

She then described to the group gathered around her how these people dressed. She told them about the wife of a Muslim Brother called Mr. Muhammad who had moved to her town. The woman was offering lessons on religion every Tuesday afternoon for any woman who wished to learn. She wore a veil that covered her head and her face, "except for her eyes"; she wore gloves, a dress down to the ground, and shoes. As the old woman put it, "She looks like a ghost."

Kamla showed off her knowledge of religion. "It is wrong for a woman to veil her face. What is required is that your head be covered; it is fine to expose your hands, your feet, and your face."

The old woman then commented on the men. "They all run around with those beards. Why, Doctor Ahmed's sticks out like this! It looks like pubic hair."

Kamla had to raise her voice to be heard over the wild laughter. "But Auntie, the beard is a tradition of the Prophet."

Kamla's cousin Salih had tried briefly to grow a beard, but the teasing had been merciless. No matter how many times Kamla told them it was the tradition of the Prophet, Gateefa and his other aunts accused him of looking like a Coptic priest. He finally shaved it off.

Kamla had confided to me that she would have liked to replace her kerchief with the new Islamic headcovering but she was afraid her family would object. A photograph of her with her school friends revealed that she was the only one among them not wearing the new modest dress. Yet Kamla criticized some of her classmates who wore this type of clothing but added flowers and multicolored headbands to their veils. She said their religion teacher had given them a real talking to and had confiscated their flowers and headbands saying, "If you want to take on the veil, do it seriously." Kamla said she would adopt this kind of headcovering "if God opens the way for me and I get to marry someone educated."

A New Order

The final part of Kamla's essay was to have been about what she hoped would change in her community. All she had written, though, was this:

As for the bad things, I will talk about them.

She read this final sentence and looked at me. "What are the wrongs I wish the Bedouins would finish with? I've already discussed these. First, their ideas about girls. They are totally meaningless and wrong. I wish they would give her the opportunity to get educated. They see her as a worthless being. You know this, Lila. . . . This is what I hope the Bedouins will leave behind. They should see that a girl is a person, a noble person created just as God created men. She has feelings, sensitivities, and desires.

"Another thing I wish is that they wouldn't let their customs and traditions rule them to such an extent that they believe that the customs of the city people are wrong and theirs right. Whenever they see that a person is educated, they say he's wrong, we're right. I wish they would respect the educated. I wish they would preserve their customs and traditions but be a bit more advanced. A girl who goes to school doesn't forget her customs and traditions, no matter how educated she becomes. Even if she goes to Europe or America, the Bedouin girl will preserve her customs and traditions. They should give her more freedom.

"Another thing I wish is that they would get more organized. I wish they would put a little order in their lives. Among Bedouins, order is completely lacking. In every area of their lives—in terms of food, in having too many children, in the way they raise the children—there's no order. And in the house—anything goes!"

I was curious about what Kamla meant by "order." She gave examples from close to home. "Say you've got two brothers living in one house. If they organized their lives, they'd put each one in his own house. And the business of marrying more than one wife—I wish they'd change their views on this. It is the biggest sin. The Prophet—it is not forbidden, but the Prophet said only if you can treat them fairly. But a man can't, it can't be done. Even if he has money, he can't. As a person, in his thoughts and his actions, he can't be fair. He'll like one more than another.

"The generation that's coming now, after my father's and mother's, they wouldn't think of it or do it. Why? So they won't have a house with thirty or forty people living in it. A household with two women in it will have thirty or forty people in it. Their lives will be lousy. They won't have good food, good clothes, or good childrearing. They won't be clean. A woman alone in her own house can handle her children. When there are two women, one will say, 'Why should I hit my children when that one doesn't hit hers?' They watch each other. When one does something, the other is looking. If one cleans and washes and the other doesn't, she says, 'Why should I do this when she doesn't?' If she is alone, a woman won't be able to say that. Who's going to do it for her? She'll do it herself and she'll know what's what. When she's alone she doesn't have to depend on anyone. And even her daughter will turn out well, like her mother. The other way they're always getting into fights over any little thing. Even without my saying this, you know it, Lila. This is what I wish would change.

"Bedouins think that as long as they have a house and can eat, drink, and be clothed, that's enough. That's life. And they marry and have kids and marry again. But a man should live a more ordered and relaxed life. Should a man come home at the end of his day tired from working and find it filthy and the kids and women fighting? He comes wanting to relax, and finds this? This is what makes someone say, 'No, there should be order.'"

For years I had heard Kamla's call for order. Living in a household of twenty or more, half of whom are under ten years old, can be chaotic. Fed up, Kamla would sometimes say, "This isn't a house, it's a breeding station!" She and Sabra often teased their mother, calling her Shalabiyya, the name of a character they had seen in a family planning advertisement on television. Shalabiyya was a woman with too many children: in her lap, on her shoulders, on her head. When she tried to draw water or milk the cow, they climbed all over her and trailed behind her. Gateefa would apologize, "We can't change the way we are."

When Kamla was young, she would come home from school announcing that she was going to marry an Egyptian doctor and have only one child. Other times she'd say she was going to have only two children, both daughters. She was going to live alone in a house with her husband, just them, no relatives. Bedouin men, she would say, make women work hard and don't pay attention to them. Even if the woman is ill, the man won't lift a finger to help, not even to pick up a crying baby. Egyptian men help their wives, respect them, and treat them well. When Kamla's younger sister, echoing their father, accused Egyptians of being stingy and not offering food to their guests, Kamla defended them to support her favorite theme. She argued that they just did things in an organized manner; they had special meal times, unlike the Bedouins who brought out food whenever anyone stopped by.

Perhaps because tensions between her father's wives had recently intensified, Kamla was impassioned in her final commentary. "Even without becoming educated, the Bedouins could organize their lives. It is enough to marry just one. Or if a man wants to marry more than one, he should put each wife in her own house. They won't fight then. But if the two are together, you'll always find this one saying, 'That one did and said' and that one saying, 'This one said this and did that.' Even if they are friends, the people outside the household won't let them be. Someone will come and say, 'That one said this' and 'This one said that.' Women are famous for this kind of talk.

"Yes, Bedouin women are famous for their talk. The Prophet said, 'Women—if not for their tongues, women would go to heaven.' They asked him, 'Why should a woman go to heaven?' He said, 'Because she gives milk.' Praise be to God, milk flows from her. And beyond that, she works harder than a man. She's weaker—that's right, she's weak compared to the man, whom nothing bothers—but she has to work more. She has children and cares for them. They asked the Prophet, 'So what is it that keeps her from entering heaven?' He said, 'It is because of her tongue.' In a second she'll turn things around. She'll gossip about everyone. Women talk about people more than men do."

Kamla is critical of the older women in her community. She confessed, too, that she belonged to two worlds. With her sisters and cousins she talked about the things they knew, not letting on that she was different. But there were so many things she could talk to her school friends about that she could not talk about with the girls in her family—things like politics. Sometimes she seemed to accept her double life with equanimity. When I saw her spinning with her aunt one day, I asked, "Hey Kamla, so you know how to spin too?" She had laughed. "Yes, I can go either way. If it turns out I'm to be citified, I'll do that. And if it turns out I'll be a Bedouin, I'll know how."

When I suggested that she might be lonely if she moved into a house of her own, she was adamant: "No, I won't miss them at all." Yet this is someone who is fiercely proud of her father for being an important man who is also generous and pious. Despite occasional confrontations, she spends, like her sisters, nearly every evening sitting close to her mother and talking. Even her brood of little siblings only sometimes drives her really crazy. The youngest she can rarely resist grabbing to hug. Delighted by this two-year-old's every new accomplishment, she whispers new words in her ear and kisses her when she repeats them.

Most of the time, though, she says she wants to get out. I worry about Kamla's blithe confidence that life in the city will be so much better. I disagree with her assessment of Bedouin women's lives. I argue with Kamla that she deliberately ignores the richness of their relationships and the way they have always struggled back (and were expected to). Her own life is evidence. There was not a single woman in the camp who had not admired her for being a willful little girl. Even her father had been amused by her opinions and determination. As she had grown up, her strength of purpose had enabled her to withstand the social pressure against her going to school. The independence she displayed reminded me of her grandmother Migdim, with her stories of resistance to marriage and her struggles to have her way with her sons. It even reminded me of her mother, Gateefa, who had earned the respect of her husband.

Yet when her letter arrived I was happy for her—happy that it was her fate not to have to marry her cousin after all and glad that her father had been willing to take her wishes into consideration. Armed with romantic visions inspired by Egyptian radio melodramas, cloying love songs, and her tattered collection of hokey postcards showing blonde brides and grooms looking deeply into each other's eyes, she will go off to live with her Egyptianized, educated husband in a small and ordered household. She will never work outside the home. She will rarely even leave her apartment. She expects to clean house, cook meals, and serve her husband. If God brings children, she'll take care of them and raise them well.

Because she has none of his sister Aisha's feminine refinement, I was worried. What would her husband think when he first saw this sturdy young woman with her wide feet and callused hands? Because she is the daughter of a wealthy tribal leader, the fabric of her dresses would be expensive and she would bring many with her; but they would have been tailored by local seamstresses, whose renditions of city clothes are always awkward. And would she know how to dress for the wedding night, this girl who had to fight her mother's horrified

accusations of immodesty when she wore a home-made bra? Would Engineer
Ibrahim Saleem find charming her outspoken ways?

I wrote back to wish her all happiness and to apologize for not being able to
attend the wedding. An older sister would sing at the henna party on the eve of
the wedding, so I looked through my collection of Bedouin wedding songs to
see if any seemed right. I ended my letter with three that I hoped would mean
something to her. The first let her know how much I thought of her family:

> Her father has a good name
> and those who have come to marry will find happiness . . .

The second reminded her that I knew how much she wanted this:

> Her morning is blessed
> she got what she desired and was honored . . .

And the third expressed my best wishes for this young woman, vulnerable and
beautiful as are all young brides heading off into the unknown:

> Neighbors, come say farewell
> a gazelle from our land is about to journey . . .

Reading 3

SCIENCE IN THE COURTROOM: OPINIONS WITHOUT EVIDENCE

Marcia Angell

> Dow's conduct in exposing thousands of women to a painful and debili-
> tating disease, and the evidence that Dow gained financially from its con-
> duct, may properly be considered in imposing an award of punitive
> damages.
>
> *—Judge Procter Hug, August 26, 1994*

[. . .] Maria Stern and her lawyer, Nancy
Hersh (with fellow attorney Dan Bolton's help), were the first to go for the legal
brass ring by alleging that implants cause connective tissue disease. Stern's disease was never clearly defined in the media, although some press reports
referred to it as "arthritis." Until this case, product liability suits against breast
implant manufacturers, of which there was a small trickle, had been limited to
settlements of no more than $15,000 to $20,000 for local complications.[1] With
the 1984 Stern case, all that changed. It was inevitable that after Stern there
would be more such cases. After all, many women had connective tissue disease
(about 1 in 100) and many had breast implants (also about 1 in 100). Thus, one
could expect—on the basis of chance alone—that about 10,000 of the roughly
100 million adult women in the United States would have both.

Once it got out that a link between the two conditions had been accepted in
court, women who had both implants and connective tissue disease would be bound
to consider whether they, too, should sue. Even those who only thought they might
have connective-tissue-like disease also began to take notice. For any who lagged
behind, there was plenty of encouragement from many plaintiffs' attorneys.

Angell, Marcia. "Science in the Courtroom: Opinions Without Evidence." *Science on Trial: The
Clash of Medical Evidence and the Law in the Breast Implant Case.* New York: WWNorton & Co.,
1997. 111–132.

The issue in the Stern case, as would be true of any product liability suit, was whether the manufacturer of the implants (Dow Corning, in this case) had sold her a defective product that caused her harm. To make the case required that Stern demonstrate two conditions: first, that she was harmed, and second, that the harm was most likely caused by the implants. In addition to demonstrating these conditions, which would satisfy the standard known as "strict liability," there was the question of negligence. Was the manufacturer guilty of knowingly or heedlessly selling a dangerous product? To show negligence required that a third condition be demonstrated—that the manufacturer knew or should have known that the implants were harmful. Theoretically, the first two of these conditions must be met for any product liability suit to be successful. That is theory. In practice, as we shall see, a product liability suit can be spectacularly successful without any of the conditions being fulfilled.

Conditions two and three depend on the satisfaction of the one before it. The manufacturer cannot be held negligent if the implants didn't cause the harm, and the implants cannot be blamed if there is no harm. In most of the breast implant cases that have been brought to trial (but not necessarily in the far more numerous cases settled out of court), the plaintiff has been clearly ill. (In the Stern case, because the records were sealed as a part of an out-of-court settlement after the verdict, it is difficult to be certain about the nature of her medical problems.) The major job of the plaintiff's attorney, therefore, has not been to show that the plaintiff is ill, but to show that the illness was caused by the implants. To do so requires convincing the jury by a "preponderance of the evidence." This is a more relaxed standard than the requirement in a criminal case that the verdict be "beyond a reasonable doubt." But aside from its relative liberality, the phrase "preponderance of the evidence" tells us less than it might seem. It suggests confusingly that there are two kinds of medical evidence—evidence for and evidence against a causal relationship. In practice, this is highly unlikely: either there is evidence for a relationship or there isn't. In the absence of such evidence, the default position must be that there is no link. The burden of proof is on those who assert the relationship.

Sometimes the phrase "preponderance of the evidence" is translated to mean that the jury finds the disease more likely than not to be caused by the breast implants. Or sometimes the same concept is expressed by saying that the breast implants contributed more than 50 percent to the causation of the disease—that is, but for the implants, the disease would not have developed.[2] While neither of these alternative formulations is entirely satisfying, they are an improvement over the vague term "preponderance of the evidence." Furthermore, they can be translated into epidemiologic terms. If connective tissue disease in a typical woman with implants is more likely than not to be caused by implants, it follows that in a large population of women, the majority of cases of connective tissue disease would be due to breast implants. In other words, this cause would have to outweigh all other contributing causes put together. To outweigh all other causes means that women with implants would have to be at least twice as likely to develop the disease as women without implants. ([. . .] There is no evidence that they do.)

Notice that what is at issue here is not how certain we are of the effect of implants, but how big the effect is. The degree of certainty is an entirely different matter. I mention the distinction, because some legal scholars confuse the concepts of the size of the effect (as, for example, when it is said that implants contribute more than 50 percent to the disease) with the degree of confidence we can have that it is true. For a scientific finding to be accepted, it is customary to require a 95 percent probability that it is not due to chance alone (I am here giving a shorthand version of a much more complicated statistical concept). Comparing the size of an effect with the probability that a given finding isn't due to chance is comparing apples and oranges. It would be possible to find a huge effect with a low degree of certainty, or a tiny effect with a high degree of certainty. The distinction between the size of an effect and the probability that a particular finding is not due to chance is important in debates about science in the courtroom. It is sometimes said that the reason plaintiffs in court may be awarded damages without good scientific evidence is that the legal standard is more liberal than the scientific standard. According to this argument, all the plaintiff has to do is show preponderance of the evidence, whereas science requires 95 percent confidence about a finding. Not only does this argument confuse size with certainty, but is also confuses the whole with the part. The degree of certainty scientists require refers to the results of a given study, not to a limitless body of evidence. The fundamental issue in both science and the courtroom should be the same—that is, the quality of the evidence. Can we rely on it?

So far, I have been speaking mainly about populations. But courtroom trials are not about populations, they are about individuals. The question is whether breast implants caused disease in *this* woman. Is there any basis for such a judgment? I do not believe there is. Given the absence of any scientific information on individual differences in women's responses to breast implants, we can only look at the individual as an *average* woman with implants. We have no basis, at least in the current state of knowledge, for making a judgment about a particular woman. We therefore *must* appeal to epidemiologic data—that is, to studies of populations. We have to assume that whatever is true on average is true on average is true of the particular woman. As it happens, we think this way intuitively. When we wonder whether someone we know developed lung cancer because he smokes, we automatically consider what we know about the risks of smoking in a population. We can't be sure that cigarette smoking caused disease in this particular man, because there is no test to answer that question in his case, but we think it probably did because we know a lot about the risks of smoking in populations. Without considering what we know about populations, we have no basis for our opinion. Despite our intuitive realization that particular cases must be considered in the light of what we know about the general situation, that is not what juries are instructed to do. They are asked to judge the particular case on the basis of the evidence presented in court, and no matter how unsatisfactory that evidence is, they must reach a verdict. They cannot say, as scientists can, that they will not form an opinion until they get more or better evidence.

Science in the courtroom is paradoxical in that it always yields a firm conclusion, yet never does. Each plaintiff who claims that breast implants caused her connective tissue disease requires a verdict, and a verdict is always reached. But even though the issue is settled for the last plaintiff, it is not settled for the next one. The question must be revisited over and over, for every woman who comes to court claiming a connection. Even so, it is not argued completely from scratch. An earlier verdict for a plaintiff provides a powerful presumption in the next case (for technical reasons, a verdict for a defendant does not). Nevertheless, verdicts can differ, no matter how similar the women's cases. In contrast, scientists almost never claim to have settled a "case." Their findings are conditional. More work is nearly always required. But for any one scientific question, the weight of the accumulated evidence tends to converge toward an answer. Eventually the probability of the answer will be great enough to warrant general acceptance of the conclusion.

In product liability cases, expert testimony by scientists is usually central. The question of causation is, after all, a scientific one. But scientific questions are handled very differently in the courtroom than they are outside the courtroom. The difference turns on the relationship between evidence and opinion. In both science and law, of course, "expert" opinion is important. But what that means in the two professions is as far apart as day and night. [. . .] Scientists, no matter how expert, must provide the evidence on which their opinions are based. When they complete a research study, it is necessary to present their evidence before their conclusions will be accepted. Even when they are commenting on the general state of their field, it is customary for them to cite explicitly the basis of their opinions. For example, medical researchers sometimes publish summaries of what is already known about a subject. Called "review articles," these summaries are analogous to expert testimony in court, in that they are evaluations of the state of knowledge. But even review articles must refer to the published research being evaluated (unpublished work usually counts for very little in science). In addition, it is expected that authors of review articles will be as even-handed as possible—that is, reasonably comprehensive and unbiased in the selection of the work they discuss. Indeed, an important question for peer reviewers is whether a review article is objective and balanced.

Expert testimony in the courtroom is very different. In contrast to scientific procedures, an expert witness in court is *expected* to give an educated guess, not to produce evidence.[3] Whether expert testimony is admitted in court turns largely on the witness's "credibility"—which means his or her credentials. Does the expert have the appropriate training and experience? Even these rather mini-malist standards are often loosely applied. In the courtroom, one scientist can seem much like another. Some distinctly second-rate scientists testify in trial after trial and consult in case after case, sometimes even earning their living that way. In essence they become well-practiced, professional witnesses, whose major talent is convincing juries, not evaluating evidence. In fact, they may cite no evidence at all, or allude to evidence only vaguely, without giving its source. Sometimes, they refer to their own, unpublished work as evidence, but no one has the opportunity to evaluate its validity or even to know whether it exists. Many reputable scientists refuse to be expert witnesses in court, probably in part because they find the adversarial process an unsatisfactory way to arrive at sci-entific conclusions and therefore feel uncomfortable participating in it. Often experts are chosen whose field is not relevant to the scientific question that needs answering. In many of the breast implant cases, for example, plaintiffs' attor-neys have relied on pathologists or toxicologists to speculate about how breast implants might cause connective tissue disease, rather than calling on epidemi-ologists who would get to the question of whether they actually do. In the Stern case, for example, her key witnesses consisted of a pathologist, a toxicologist, and an immunologist.[4] Even more troubling, expert witnesses are selected by the contesting lawyers, paid by them, and their testimony is rehearsed in ad-vance—circumstances unlikely to ensure competence, let alone objectivity. In fact, the whole point is precisely to find a "qualified" witness who will be scien-tifically committed to your side. The irony here is that a lawyer may employ a scientist to offer eccentric views in a court proceeding that is supposed to hold manufacturers to generally accepted, mainstream standards.

After contributing so decisively to the handsome verdict in the Stern case, Dan Bolton was on a roll. He left Hersh and Hersh and went on to become a partner in another firm and a magnet for breast implant suits. The decision in Bolton's next big case—the case of Mariann Hopkins—was appealed all the way to the Supreme Court, which refused to review it. In its own way, this case was even more influential than the Stern case, because it was instrumental in the FDA ban.

Mariann Hopkins, of Sebastopol, California, a secretary at Sonoma State University in nearby Rehnert Park and the wife of a San Francisco firefighter, was in her early thirties when she underwent a double mastectomy in 1976 because of fibrocystic disease of the breast.[5] This is a very common condition that produces tender nodules in the breasts, particularly just before menstrual periods. Whether it is a precursor of breast cancer or not has been debated for decades. The consensus is that it usually isn't, although some forms of it may increase the risk. In any case, Hopkins evidently did not want to take the chance. After her mastectomy she had her breasts reconstructed with silicone-gel-filled implants, manufactured by Dow Corning. Within a few months, one of them ruptured, and to maintain symmetry she had them both replaced.

Three years later, in 1979, she was told she had an autoimmune disorder called mixed connective tissue disease. This is a devastating disease, with clinical features of systemic lupus, rheumatoid arthritis, polymyositis, and scleroderma, all rolled into one. Typically, the disease produces very high levels of antibodies against constituents of the patient's own cells. Mixed connective tissue disease is incurable, and Hopkins had to be treated indefinitely with corticosteroids, which can produce a variety of serious side effects. In 1986, seven years after the diagnosis. Hopkins gave up her job because of her disabling disease. The same year she again had her breast implants replaced because one had ruptured.

In 1987, Hopkins's mother told her that she had heard there was a link between ruptured breast implants and autoimmune disorders. Hopkins queried her doctors, who told her they knew of no such connection. She later said the rheumatologist who was treating her mixed connective tissue disease, Dr. Stephen Gospe, was "very patronizing. He said people always need something to blame and I might as well accept my illness." The next year, however, Hopkins happened to turn on the evening news as she came into her house from the grocery store and saw a clip of Bolton, along with Sybil Goldrich, talking about the effects of silicone leakage on the immune system. (Goldrich [. . .] is co-founder of the advocacy group Command Trust Network; Bolton was at the time testifying before the November 1988 FDA advisory panel.) To Hopkins, seeing Bolton on television was little short of a miracle. As she said later, "If I'd turned it on one minute later, I would have missed it." But she didn't miss it, and she straightaway phoned Bolton in San Francisco. Hopkins said of that conversation, "I learned there were other women besides myself who'd had problems with implants. I said 'Why haven't I heard of this?' He said, 'Because there have been suits filed against Dow Corning and they have settled out of court, and then all the documents are kept under lock and key.'" The next month, she and Bolton filed suit against Dow Corning in federal court in San Francisco.[6]

At the trial three years later, in 1991, Bolton called three expert witnesses to testify as to the cause of Hopkins's disease—Marc Lappé, Nir Kossovsky, and Frank Vasey. Because these three have been so important in breast implant litigation, it is worth examining their credentials in some detail. Lappé, who [. . .] has a Ph.D. in experimental pathology, testified in the Stern case, as well as the Hopkins case, according to an article in *American Lawyer.*[7] In both cases, his testimony primarily concerned his interpretation of the Dow Corning laboratory studies. In his view Dow Corning's animal studies indicated that breast implants may have contributed to Stern's and Hopkins's illnesses. A 1995 computer search of Lappé's own publications, as compiled by the National Library of Medicine, is revealing. [. . .] He published his theory about the way in which implants might cause autoimmune disease in an article in the journal *Medical Hypotheses,* confidently titled, "Silicone-Reactive Disorder: A New Autoimmune Disease Caused by Immunostimulation and Superantigens." As a hypothesis, it contributed no new evidence. In its 1994 review of the scientific evidence in the breast implant controversy, the British Department of Health said Lappé's paper "has nothing to add to the issue of a causal relationship between silicones, immunological responsiveness and disease."[8] Of Lappé's 50-some scientific papers in the National Library of Medicine's database, only one other dealt with the subject of breast implants. (His other papers have dealt mainly with the ethics of genetic screening.) He also published a 1991 book, *Chemical Deception: The Toxic Threat to Health and the Environment.*[9]

Kossovsky is an M.D. certified in anatomic pathology, the study of diseased tissues.[10] An assistant professor at the UCLA Medical Center, he has been a very popular and effective plaintiffs' witness in breast implant cases. At the time of the Hopkins trial, Kossovsky was in his early thirties and looked younger. Pleasantly voluble, with an engaging, eager manner, Kossovsky gives the impression of wanting nothing more than to explain the immune system to the jury. He believes that silicone changes body tissues in such a way that the body no longer recognizes them as native. In its effort to reject what it interprets as "foreign" invaders, the body mounts an autoimmune reaction that leads to connective tissue disease. Despite Kossovsky's long-standing attachment to this theory, there is still no good evidence for it.

Bolton's third witness on causation was Frank Vasey, the chief of the Division of Rheumatology at the University of South Florida College of Medicine.[11] Rheumatology is the medical specialty concerned with connective tissue disease. Vasey, a physician, has reported a group of patients with breast implants who had connective tissue disease or symptoms suggestive of it, most of whom felt better after the implants were removed.[12] In medical practice, it is not unusual for a specialist who attracts patients with a certain type of problem to gain erroneous impressions about its frequency or its association with other conditions. Without controls and appropriate population sampling techniques, it is easy to draw conclusions that will not stand up to later, more careful epidemiologic analysis. Even a large clinical experience, while possibly suggestive, cannot substitute for a cohort or case-control study in getting at whether implants cause disease. The history of medicine is replete with examples of mistaken "clinical impressions" based on uncontrolled and often undocumented personal experience. One of the major advances in modern medicine is the realization that to be reliable, personal experience must be supported by rigorous research.

None of Bolton's witnesses was an epidemiologist. Yet this is the only kind of specialist who could authoritatively speak to the issue of a possible link between breast implants and connective tissue disease.

Perhaps the most startling testimony on the other side was that of Hopkins's own rheumatologist, Stephen Gospe. Gospe had definitively diagnosed Hopkins's mixed connective tissue disease in 1979, but he believed her symptoms began even before she received her first set of implants in 1976. Indeed, because of suggestive symptoms, her internist, Dr. Louis Pelfini, had in 1975 ordered a test for autoimmune disease, which at the time was inconclusive. Because her symptoms persisted, Pelfini sent her to Gospe in 1979. Gospe's testimony that her symptoms had begun before her first implants were placed in 1976 might have been expected to undermine the plaintiff's case. But evidently it didn't trouble the jurors. On December 13, 1991, the jury awarded Hopkins $7.34 million. Dow Corning was found guilty of fraud and malice in marketing the implants.[13] The evidence included the Dow Corning memo instructing salespeople to wash off demonstration implants so that plastic surgeons would not notice the oiliness of the envelope. The Hopkins case reached its climax just as David Kessler [commissioner of the FDA appointed by President Bush in 1990] was deciding whether to permit implants to stay on the market. This timing, nearly everyone agrees, greatly influenced the FDA's ultimate decision.

Dow Corning (which went out of the implant business a few months after the Hopkins decision)[14] appealed to the U.S. Court of Appeals for the Ninth Circuit. Signaling the significance of the case, two renowned lawyers joined the fray in the appeal. Harvard Law School professor Laurence Tribe headed the Hopkins-Bolton team. Shirley Hufstedler, Jimmy Carter's former secretary of education and a former judge of the Ninth Circuit, joined Frank Woodside III for Dow Corning's defense. The defense's appeal was based on two arguments. The first concerned the statute of limitations, a technical argument of interest to lawyers but probably no one else. The second argument was whether the testimony had established that it was more probable than not that there was a causal connection between Hopkins's breast implants and her mixed connective tissue disease—the second necessary condition for a product liability judgment. The first condition had clearly been met: no one doubted that Hopkins was sick. But the other two conditions were in contention, and the satisfaction of the third (that Dow Corning had been negligent or wanton) was contingent on proving the second (that the implants most likely caused the mixed connective tissue disease). The appellate court was asked to consider whether the lower court had adequate evidence for this finding. And in particular, was it correct in relying on the expert testimony Bolton had assembled?

Dow's Woodside (a physician as well as a lawyer) had argued in lower court that Lappé, Kossovsky, and Vasey were not qualified to testify as experts on causation, but the trial judge had disagreed. The appeal was largely based on the same argument, and again it was dismissed. Although the appeals court noted that scientific testimony must be "not only relevant, but reliable," it ruled that the testimony of Kossovsky, Lappé, and Vasey had met this standard. Kossovsky and Vasey, according to the court, had based their opinions in part on "preliminary results" of epidemiological studies they were conducting. Four years later, in a search of the medical literature, I was unable to find that either of them has published a rigorous epidemiologic study that could shed light on the question of causation. Lappé was said to be "a recognized expert on the immunological effects of silicone in the human body," although a search of the National Library of Medicine's comprehensive database shows that he has published very little on the subject.

Judge Procter Hug, writing for the Court of Appeals, not only accepted the testimony of the three witnesses, but his opinion indicated that he was utterly convinced about the substance of the matter—not just about the procedural questions.[15] He was certain, even if most scientists were not, that breast implants cause mixed connective tissue disease. Referring to the many thousands of women who have Dow Corning implants, the judge said, "Each of these women was at risk of encountering the same fate from which Hopkins suffered." As for Dow Corning, he said, "Dow's conduct in exposing thousands of women to a painful and debilitating disease, and the evidence that Dow gained financially from its conduct, may properly be considered in imposing an award of punitive damages." The harshness of Judge Hug's conclusion reflected the emphasis in the case on the Dow Corning documents. Dow Corning petitioned the U.S. Supreme Court for review. The petition was refused, thus letting stand the appellate court's decision.[16] Bolton's experts had done their job well.

With the astonishing explosion of scientific knowledge over the last century, and particularly in the last 50 years, expert testimony has become increasingly important in the courts. In particular, there are few product liability suits in which expert testimony is not central. In the *Hopkins* case, for example, the testimony of Lappé, Kossovsky, and Vasey was pivotal. But even as expert testimony became commonplace in the courtroom, legal scholars and judges began to fret about its role. Who was an expert? How should expert testimony be received and what weight should it have? As far back as 1858, the U.S. Supreme Court foresaw the problems in store. It observed then that "experience has shown that opposite opinions of persons professing to be experts may be obtained to any amount," and it went on to complain that cross-examination of all these experts was virtually useless, "wasting the time and wearying the patience of both court and jury, and perplexing, instead of elucidating, the questions involved."[17]

In 1897, possibly because it had heard enough, the Supreme Court decided to cut things short by limiting cross-examination of experts. In considering an insanity defense for a man accused of murder, an expert witness had been asked in lower court, "What does medical science teach as to that?" Incredibly, the witness was told by the trial judge that he didn't have to answer that question. On appeal, the Supreme Court agreed, saying that once an expert gives his opinion, the court should take it or leave it. It would be "opening the door to too wide an inquiry to interrogate him as to what other scientific men [sic] have said upon such matters, or in respect to the general teachings of science thereon, or to permit books of science to be offered in evidence." The message, then, was not to delve into something as arcane as scientific evidence. Whatever a qualified witness said was okay.

This decision pretty much settled the issue until a federal trials court in 1923 reached the polar opposite conclusion in *Frye v. United States*. In *Frye*, the issue in contention was whether a "lie detector test" (which in those days was simply a blood pressure reading) would be admitted as evidence. The court refused to admit it, on the grounds that there was not yet a scientific consensus about the validity of this new method. Far from agreeing with the Supreme Court that experts needn't take into account the work of other scientists, the *Frye* court said that testimony *must* speak to the work of others—that is, it was admissible only if it incorporated principles and methods generally accepted by the relevant scientific community. The Court of Appeals agreed. Thus was born the "general acceptance" standard for expert testimony, a subject of intense legal debate for the next 70 years. This standard had the effect of excluding a good deal of what has become known as "junk science"—patently absurd testimony by zealots, incompetents, or opportunists. But the *Frye* standard was by no means accepted in all courts. Its opponents claimed, somewhat improbably, that it would tend to exclude novel, farsighted testimony by modern-day Galileos.[18] There is no record of this happening once, let alone often. Furthermore, even if a modern-day Galileo did not make it into court at first, that fact would not stop him from prevailing in the scientific community. Courts do not determine scientific acceptance, as implied by the argument that we need to keep our courts open to the hidden Galileos in our midst.

What the don't-ask-don't-tell approach of the 1897 Supreme Court had in common with the *Frye* decision was that both avoided coming to grips with the substantive issue of how to define good scientific evidence that would qualify for admissibility in court. *Frye* evaded the issue by setting up a proxy, and a very good proxy it was: Good science was determined by other scientists through their usual methods—peer review and publication, criticism, replication—and, most important, by its reliability in predicting future results. (These were not the words of *Frye*, but they are its effect.) In 1975 new Federal Rules of Evidence were signed into law by President Ford. These detailed rules for admitting evidence into federal courts contain criteria for scientific testimony that include validity but omit the requirement for general acceptance in the scientific community. Whether the new, more liberal Rules superseded *Frye* or not was not clear. Some courts went with *Frye*, others with the Rules, and others simply followed their own instincts. The courts thus continued their chaotic approach to the problem, even while product liability suits were burgeoning and scientists themselves were having a difficult time keeping up with the rapid advances in their own fields.

In 1993 the U.S. Supreme Court finally grasped the nettle and attempted to deal substantively with the problem of expert testimony in the courts. The case that occasioned the Supreme Court's attention, *Daubert v. Merrell Dow Pharmaceuticals*, was in many respects similar to the breast implant cases.[19] The case was brought against Merrell Dow Pharmaceuticals in 1984 by the parents of two boys who had been born with only rudimentary arms, a well-known congenital mishap (these sorts of defects occur in about 1 in 1,000 births). The parents alleged that the defect had been caused by Merrell Dow's Bendectin, an antihistamine-like drug that the two mothers had taken during pregnancy to combat morning sickness. Bendectin was an extraordinarily popular drug, prescribed for pregnant women almost as routinely as vitamins. Some 17 million women took it (as did I) between 1958 and 1983. It is not surprising, then, that even if there were no connection, babies with upper-limb defects would sometimes be born to mothers who had taken Bendectin, just as connective tissue disease would sometimes develop in women who had breast implants even if there were no causal connection between the implants and the disease.

Merrell Dow's Frank Woodside (who would later be Dow Corning's attorney in the Hopkins case) had argued at first that the case should not be tried at all. He pointed out that there had been many epidemiologic studies published in the scientific literature, involving some 130,000 women, none of which had been able to show a connection between Bendectin and birth defects. The plaintiffs, however, produced eight expert witnesses who testified to Bendectin's ability to cause birth defects, although they could point to no epidemiologic evidence. One witness testified that she had reanalyzed the published studies that Woodside cited and had come to the opposite conclusion, although she had not published her work. The trial court, citing *Frye,* agreed that the plaintiffs had produced no admissible evidence. The appeals court agreed. The Supreme Court was then asked to speak to the narrow issue of whether Frye was the appropriate standard or whether it had been superseded by the 1975 Rules of Evidence. Merrell Dow favored *Frye,* since it had worked well for them, but the plaintiffs wanted the less stringent Federal Rules of Evidence to prevail.

The Supreme Court dispensed quickly with the narrow question. Yes, the Federal Rules did supersede *Frye,* and the case was passed back to the appeals court to hear again under those rules. The Supreme Court made no attempt to decide whether Bendectin caused birth defects, only what the standards for the admissibility of expert evidence should be. But the Court also devoted considerable attention to elucidating the meaning of those standards and how they were to be applied, thus finally dealing with the issue of what constitutes good science. A large number of interested individuals and organizations, including the *New England Journal of Medicine* [Angell is the executive editor of the NEJM], were aware of the enormous impact the *Daubert* decision might have. The Court was therefore flooded with amici briefs on both sides. These revealed interesting schisms within the scientific community. Many favored the *Frye* standard (as did we), because they felt it would reduce the amount of junk science finding its way to the courts. We argued that testimony should be based on research that had been duly published in peer-reviewed journals. But equally reputable scientists came down on the other side, because they felt the "general acceptance" criterion was too restrictive and elitist. And many lawyers also opposed the *Frye* standard because they believed it would preempt the responsibility of juries to decide the facts.

In the end both sides in the *Daubert* case claimed victory—or defeat, depending on whether one is inclined to see the glass as half full or half empty. The Supreme Court said that while the Federal Rules applied, this did not mean that all expert testimony would be admissible. Far from it. Federal judges are now required to undertake "a preliminary assessment of whether the reasoning or methodology underlying the testimony is scientifically valid and of whether that reasoning or methodology properly can be applied to the fact in issue." Thus, judges are to be the gatekeepers who decide whether to admit expert testimony. This was not what either side thought they wanted. The *Frye* proponents wanted the scientific community to be gatekeepers. The other side didn't want any gatekeepers; let the juries decide on the basis of the cross-examination. But in *Daubert,* the Supreme Court said that judges must decide, and they must do so by learning how to think like scientists. Expert testimony must be both "reliable" and "relevant," and judges should decide in advance whether it was. Writing for the majority, Justice Harry Blackmun emphasized the importance of relevance by pointing out that testimony about the effect of the phases of the moon on irrational behavior might be quite valid as to the astronomical data, but totally irrelevant in drawing any inference about behavior. What is relevant in one context may not be in another. This requirement that expert testimony be apposite to the matter at hand was at issue in the appeal of the *Hopkins* decision.

Many concerned about the increasingly contentious relations between law and science welcomed the *Daubert* decision. Bert Black, a lawyer and then-chair of the American Bar Association's Standing Committee on Scientific Evidence, and Francisco Ayala, a scientist and then-president of the American Association for the Advancement of Science, together with a colleague, Carol Saffran-Brinks, wrote a celebratory analysis in the *Texas Law Review.*[20] Despite the fact that both Black and Ayala had participated in an amicus brief on behalf of Merrell Dow—technically the losing side—they saw the actual written judgment as a cause for hope that the days of junk science in the courtroom were numbered. In particular, they approved of the sophisticated analysis of what good science is. The Supreme Court embraced the notion of Karl Popper, the philosopher of science, that good science requires formulating a question that can be answered. In other words, any hypothesis must be capable of being tested. It is useless to come up with a theory, no matter how plausible, that cannot be proved or disproved. Black and his colleagues, in a section on the "pathological science" that stems from ignoring the necessity for testing and corroboration, describe it as "characterized by a fixation on effects that are difficult to detect, a readiness to disregard prevailing ideas and theories, and an unwillingness to conduct meaningful experimental testing." This description is relevant in the breast implant controversy. The common contention that breast implants cause diseases that cannot be objectively described is a theory that cannot be tested. Doctors who believe in it simply assert that such diseases exist and that they know them when they see them.

For those who might have thought the Supreme Court's *Daubert* decision heralded a new, more rational era in the courts, let alone mere consistency, subsequent events are instructive. The Supreme Court decided the *Daubert* case in 1993, sending it back to the Ninth Circuit Appeals Court for reconsideration. By coincidence, this was the same court that considered the appeal in the Hopkins case in 1994. The *Daubert* decision was handed down after the Hopkins verdict but before the appeal. A major issue in the petition to the U.S. Supreme Court was the failure of the Ninth Circuit Appeals Court to adhere to the *Daubert* criteria. As we have seen, the appellate court found the expert testimony in Hopkins admissible even though its decision was handed down after the *Daubert* decision. Just a year later, however, the same court found that the testimony that Bendectin caused birth defects was *not* admissible.[21] I believe that in *neither* case had the testimony clearly met the Supreme Court's requirement for reliability and relevance. Even more difficult to comprehend is the fact that the Supreme Court itself, after its insightful analysis of good science in *Daubert* in 1993, let stand the Hopkins decision in 1995. (If you are having trouble following all this, it is not your fault, or even mine.) The inconsistency of the decisions surely underscores the continuing confusion about what kind of scientific evidence should be admitted in court. The *Daubert* decision doesn't seem to have helped much, at least not yet.

As I have noted, scientific testimony in the courtroom is often at most only marginally related to scientific evidence. To be sure, there are superficial matters of form that may suggest a resemblance between science in and out of the courtroom. Expert witnesses may wear white coats, be called "doctor," purport to do research, and talk scientific jargon. But too often they are merely adding a veneer to a foregone, self-interested conclusion. Sometimes they spin theories that they say are supported by their expertise or experience. Or they may refer vaguely to research. Very often, however, the "research" is their own and it is unpublished and unavailable. The point is that they are not required to produce their evidence, and they usually do not. The result is a growing gap between scientific reality and what passes for it in the courtroom. The *Daubert* decision was a brave step toward remedying the situation, but it was not enough.

Notes

1. See A. Frankel, "From Pioneers to Profits," American Lawyer, June 1992:82.
2. For a fuller analysis, see B. Black, "Matching Evidence about Clustered Health Events with Tort Law Requirements," American Journal of Epidemiology, 132 (1990):579–86.
3. For more information on the role of expert testimony in the courtroom, see L. Loevinger, "Science as Evidence," Jurimetrics Journal, winter 1995:153–90. Also B. Black, "Evolving Legal Standards for the Admissibility of Scientific Evidence," Science, 239, no. 4847 (1988):1508–12.
4. See A. Frankel, "From Pioneers to Profits," American Lawyer, June 1992:82.
5. Biographical details about Mariann Hopkins, and the case chronology, primarily come from two sources: the decision of the United States Court of Appeals for the 9th Circuit, August 26, 1994 (Mariann Hopkins v. Dow Corning Corp. 33F.3d 1116 1994), and the Petition for a Writ of Certiorari to the U.S. Supreme Court (Dow Corning v. Mariann Hopkins, No. 94-861, 1994). See also J. M. Adams, "Victim of Silicone Breast Implants Wants Value Placed on Women's Lives," Chicago Tribune, February 9, 1992, p. 21.
6. Hopkin quotes are taken from J. M. Adams, "Victim of Silicone Breast Implants Wants Value Placed on Women's Lives," Chicago Tribune, February 9, 1992, p. 21, and A. Frankel, "From Pioneers to Profits," American Lawyer, June 1992:82.
7. See A. Frankel, "From Pioneers to Profits," American Lawyer, June 1992:82.
8. See D. M. Gott and J. J. B. Tinkler, "Evaluation of Evidence for an Association between the Implantation of Silicones and Connective Tissue Disease: Data Published from the End of 1991 to July 1994" (London: Medical Devices Directorate, December 1994).
9. See. M. Lappé, Chemical Deception: The Toxic Threat to Health and the Environment (San Francisco: Sierra Club, 1991).
10. Kossovsky's credentials are documented in the Official ABMS Directory of Board Certified Medical Specialists, 27th ed. (Philadelphia: Reed Reference Publishing, 1995).
11. Vasey's credentials are documented in the *Official ABMS Directory of Board Certified Medical Specialists,* 27th ed. (Philadelphia: Reed Reference Publishing, 1995).
12. For Vasey's position, see his book, F. B. Vasey and J. Feldstein, The Silicone Breast Implant Controversy: What Women Need to Know (Freedom, Calif.: Crossing Press, 1993).
13. The verdict was widely publicized. See, for example, W. Carlsen, "Jury Awards $7.3 Million in Implant Case," San Francisco Chronicle, December 14, 1991, p. A13, and J. M. Adams, "Victim of Silicone Breast Implants Wants Value Placed on Women's Lives," Chicago Tribune, February 9, 1992, p. 21. See also the decision of the United States Court of Appeals for the 9th Circuit, August 26, 1994 (Mariann Hopkins v. Dow Corning Corp. 33F.3d 1116 1994).
14. Dow Corning announced it was pulling out of the breast implant market in March 1992. See E. Neuffer, "Maker Quits Implant Market," Boston Globe, March 20, 1992, p. 1.
15. See the decision of the United States Court of Appeals for the 9th Circuit, August 26, 1994 (Mariann Hopkins v. Dow Corning Corp. 33F.3d 1116 1994).
16. The U.S. Supreme Court's refusal to review the Hopkins case received widespread attention. See, for example, R. Carelli, "Justices Uphold Breast Implant Award," Boston Globe, January 10, 1995, p. 6.

17. For an account of the history of science in the courtroom, including *Frye* and the Federal Rules of Evidence, see L. Loevinger, "Science as Evidence," *Jurimetrics Journal,* winter 1995:153–90.

18. For more on the debate, see S. Begley, "The Meaning of Junk," *Newsweek,* March 22, 1993, and D. Freedman, "Who's to Judge? New Guidelines for Scientific Evidence," *Discover,* 15, no. 1 (1994):78.

19. Details of the *Daubert* case come primarily from the Supreme Court's decision (*Daubert v. Merrell Dow Pharmaceuticals,* No. 92-102, June 28, 1993, 113 S Ct 2768 1993) and "Brief of the New England Journal of Medicine, Journal of the American Medical Association, and Annals of Internal Medicine of Amicus Curiae in Support of Respondent" (*Daubert v. Merrell Dow Pharmaceuticals,* No. 92-102), Kaye, Scholer, Fierman, Hays & Handler (New York), January 19, 1993.

20. See B. Black, F. J. Ayala, and C. Saffran-Brinks, "Science and the Law in the Wake of *Daubert:* A New Search for Scientific Knowledge," *Texas Law Review,* 72, no. 4 (1994):715–802.

21. The 9th Circuit's decision in the Bendectin appeal was written by Judge Alex Kozinski. See *Daubert v. Merrell Dow Pharmaceuticals,* No. 90-55397, January 4, 1995. The decision received widespread attention in the popular and scientific press. See, for example, "Birth Defect Lawsuit that Set Science Standard Is Dismissed," *New York Times,* January 8, 1995, p. 19, and M. Baringa, "Bendectin Case Dismissed," *Science,* 267 (January 13, 1995):167.

Reading 4

DOES GOD HAVE A FUTURE?

Karen Armstrong

As we approach the end of the second millennium, it seems likely that the world we know is passing away. For decades we have lived with the knowledge that we have created weapons that could wipe out human life on the planet. The Cold War may have ended, but the new world order seems no less frightening than the old. We are facing the possibility of eco-logical disaster. The AIDS virus threatens to bring a plague of unmanageable proportions. Within two or three generations, the population will become too great for the planet to support. Thousands are dying of famine and drought. Gen-erations before our own have felt that the end of the world is nigh, yet it does seem that we are facing a future that is unimaginable. How will the idea of God survive in the years to come? For 4000 years it has constantly adapted to meet the demands of the present, but in our own century, more and more people have found that it no longer works for them, and when religious ideas cease to be effective they fade away. Maybe God really is an idea of the past. The American scholar Peter Berger notes that we often have a double standard when we com-pare the past with our own time. Where the past is analyzed and made relative, the present is rendered immune to this process and our current position becomes an absolute: thus "the New Testament writers are seen as afflicted with a false consciousness rooted in *their* time, but the analyst takes the consciousness of *his* time as an unmixed intellectual blessing."[1] Secularists of the nineteenth and early twentieth centuries saw atheism as the irreversible condition of humanity in the scientific age.

There is much to support this view. In Europe, the churches are empty-ing; atheism is no longer the painfully acquired ideology of a few intellectual

Armstrong, Karen. "Does God Have a Future?" *A History of God: The 4000-Year Quest of Judaism, Christianity and Islam.* New York: Knopf, 1993. 377–399.

pioneers but a prevailing mood. In the past it was always produced by a particular idea of God, but now it seems to have lost its inbuilt relationship to theism and become an automatic response to the experience of living in a secularized society. Like the crowd of amused people surrounding Nietzsche's madman, many are unmoved by the prospect of life without God. Others find his absence a positive relief. Those of us who have had a difficult time with religion in the past find it liberating to be rid of the God who terrorized our childhood. It is wonderful not to have to cower before a vengeful deity, who threatens us with eternal damnation if we do not abide by his rules. We have a new intellectual freedom and can boldly follow up our own ideas without pussyfooting around difficult articles of faith, feeling all the while a sinking loss of integrity. We imagine that the hideous deity we have experienced is the authentic God of Jews, Christians and Muslims and do not always realize that it is merely an unfortunate aberration.

There is also desolation. Jean-Paul Sartre (1905–80) spoke of the God-shaped hole in the human consciousness, where God had always been. Nevertheless, he insisted that even if God existed, it was still necessary to reject him, since the idea of God negates our freedom. Traditional religion tells us that we must conform to God's idea of humanity to become fully human. Instead, we must see human beings as liberty incarnate. Sartre's atheism was not a consoling creed, but other existentialists saw the absence of God as a positive liberation. Maurice Merleau-Ponty (1908–61) argued that instead of increasing our sense of wonder, God actually negates it. Because God represents absolute perfection, there is nothing left for us to do or achieve. Albert Camus (1913–60) preached a heroic atheism. People should reject God defiantly in order to pour out all their loving solicitude upon mankind. As always, the atheists have a point. God had indeed been used in the past to stunt creativity; if he is made a blanket answer to every possible problem and contingency, he can indeed stifle our sense of wonder or achievement. A passionate and committed atheism can be more religious than a weary or inadequate theism.

During the 1950s, Logical Positivists such as A. J. Ayer (1910–91) asked whether it made sense to believe in God. The natural sciences provided the only reliable source of knowledge because it could be tested empirically. Ayer was not asking whether or not God existed but whether the idea of God had any meaning. He argued that a statement is meaningless if we cannot see how it can be verified or shown to be false. To say "There is intelligent life on Mars" is not meaningless since we can see how we could verify this once we had the necessary technology. Similarly a simple believer in traditional Old Man in the Sky is not making a meaningless statement when he says: "I believe in God," since after death we should be able to find out whether or not this is true. It is the more sophisticated believer who has problems, when he says: "God does not exist in any sense that we can understand" or "God is not good in the human sense of the word." These statements are too vague; it is impossible to see how they can be tested; therefore, they are meaningless. As Ayer said: "Theism is so confused and the sentences in which 'God' appears so incoherent and incapable of verifiability or falsifiability that to speak of belief or unbelief, faith or unfaith, is logically impossible."[2] Atheism is as unintelligible and meaningless as theism. There is nothing in the concept of "God" to deny or be skeptical about.

Like Freud, the Positivists believed that religious belief represented an immaturity which science would overcome. Since the 1950s, linguistic philosophers have criticized Logical Positivism, pointing out that what Ayer called the Verification Principle could not itself be verified. Today we are less likely to be as optimistic about science, which can only explain the world of physical nature. Wilfred Cantwell Smith pointed out that the Logical Positivists set themselves up as scientists during a period when, for the first time in history, science saw the natural world in explicit disjunction from humanity.[3] The kind of statements to which Ayer referred work very well for the objective facts of science but are not suitable for less clear-cut human experiences. Like poetry or music, religion is not amenable to this kind of discourse and verification. More recently linguistic philosophers such as Antony Flew have argued that it is more rational to find a natural explanation than a religious one. The old "proofs" do not work: the argument from design falls down because we would need to get outside the system to see whether natural phenomena are motivated by their own laws or by Something outside. The argument that we are "contingent" or "defective" beings proves nothing, since there could always be an explanation that is ultimate but not supernatural. Flew is less of an optimist than Feuerbach, Marx or the Existentialists. There is no agonizing, no heroic defiance but simply a matter-of-fact commitment to reason and science as the only way forward.

[. . .] However, [. . .] not all religious people have looked to "God" to provide them with an explanation for the universe. Many have seen the proofs as a red herring. Science has been felt to be threatening only by those Western Christians who got into the habit of reading the scriptures literally and interpreting doctrines as though they were matters of objective fact. Scientists and philosophers who find no room for God in their systems are usually referring to the idea of God as First Cause, a notion eventually abandoned by Jews, Muslims and Greek Orthodox Christians during the Middle Ages. The more subjective "God" that they were looking for could not be proved as though it were an objective fact that was the same for everybody. It could not be located within a physical system of the universe, any more than the Buddhist nirvana.

More dramatic than the linguistic philosophers were the radical theologians of the 1960s who enthusiastically followed Nietzsche and proclaimed the death of God. In *The Gospel of Christian Atheism* (1966), Thomas J. Altizer claimed that the "good news" of God's death had freed us from slavery to a tyrannical transcendent deity: "Only by accepting and even willing the death of God in our experience can we be liberated from a transcendent beyond, an alien beyond which has been emptied and darkened by God's self-alienation in Christ."[4]

Altizer spoke in mystical terms of the dark night of the soul and the pain of abandonment. The death of God represented the silence that was necessary before God could become meaningful again. All our old conceptions of divinity had to die before theology could be reborn. We were waiting for a language and a style in which God could once more become a possibility. Altizer's theology was a passionate dialectic which attacked the dark God-less world in the hope that it would give up its secret. Paul Van Buren was more precise and logical. In *The Secular Meaning of the Gospel* (1963), he claimed that it was no longer possible to speak of God acting in the world. Science and technology had made the old mythology invalid. Simple faith in the Old Man in the Sky was clearly impossible, but so was the more sophisticated belief of the theologians. We must do without God and hold on to Jesus of Nazareth. The Gospel was "the good news of a free man who has set other men free." Jesus of Nazareth was the liberator, "the man who defines what it means to be a man."[5]

In *Radical Theology and the Death of God* (1966), William Hamilton noted that this kind of theology had its roots in the United States, which had always had a utopian bent and had no great theological tradition of its own. The imagery of the death of God represented the anomie and barbarism of the technical age, which made it impossible to believe in the biblical God in the old way. Hamilton himself saw this theological mood as a way of being Protestant in the twentieth century. Luther had left his cloister and gone out into the world. In the same way, he and the other Christian radicals were avowedly secular men. They had walked away from the sacred place where God used to be to find the man Jesus in their neighbor out in the world of technology, power, sex, money and the city. Modern secular man did not need God. There was no God-shaped hole within Hamilton: he would find his own solution in the world.

There is something rather poignant about this buoyant sixties optimism. Certainly, the radicals were right that the old ways of speaking about God had become impossible for many people, but in the 1990s it is sadly difficult to feel that liberation and a new dawn are at hand. Even at the time, the Death of God theologians were criticized, since their perspective was that of the affluent, middle-class, white American. Black theologians such as James H. Cone asked how white people felt they had the right to affirm freedom through the death of God when they had actually enslaved people in God's name. The Jewish theologian Richard Rubenstein found it impossible to understand how they could feel so positive about Godless humanity so soon after the Nazi Holocaust. He himself was convinced that the deity conceived as a God of History had died forever in Auschwitz. Yet Rubenstein did not feel that Jews could jettison religion. After the near-extinction of European Jewry, they must not cut themselves off from their past. The nice, moral God of liberal Judaism was no good, however. It was too antiseptic; it ignored the tragedy of life and assumed that the world would improve. Rubenstein himself preferred the God of the Jewish mystics. He was moved by Isaac Luria's doctrine of *tsimtsum,* God's voluntary act of self-estrangement which brought the created world into being. All mystics had seen God as a Nothingness from which we came and to which we will return. Rubenstein agreed with Sartre that life is empty; he saw the God of the mystics as an imaginative way of entering this human experience of nothingness.[6]

Other Jewish theologians have also found comfort in Lurianic Kabbalah. Hans Jonas believes that after Auschwitz we can no longer believe in the omnipotence of God. When God created the world, he voluntarily limited himself and shared the weakness of human beings. He could do no more now, and human beings must restore wholeness to the Godhead and the world by prayer and Torah. The British theologian Louis Jacobs, however, dislikes this idea, finding the image of *tsimtsum* coarse and anthropomorphic: it encourages us to ask *how* God created the world in too literal a manner. God does not limit himself, holding his breath, as it were, before exhaling. An impotent God is useless and cannot be the meaning of human existence. It is better to return to the classic explanation that God is greater than human beings and his thought and ways are not ours. God may be incomprehensible, but people have the option of trusting this ineffable God and affirming *a* meaning, even in the midst of meaninglessness. The Roman Catholic theologian Hans Kung agrees with Jacobs, preferring a more reasonable explanation for tragedy than the fanciful myth of *tsimtsum.* He notes that human beings cannot have faith in a weak God but in the living God who made people strong enough to pray in Auschwitz.

Some people still find it possible to find meaning in the idea of God. The Swiss theologian Karl Barth (1886–1968) set his face against the Liberal Protestantism of Schleiermacher, with its emphasis on religious experience. But he was also a leading opponent of natural theology. It was, he thought, a radical error to seek to explain God in rational terms not simply because of the limitations of the human mind but also because humanity has been corrupted by the Fall. Any natural idea we form about God is bound to be flawed, therefore, and to worship such a God was idolatry. The only valid source of God-knowledge was the Bible. This seems to have the worst of all worlds: experience is out; natural reason is out; the human mind is corrupt and untrustworthy; and there is no possibility of learning from other faiths, since the Bible is the only valid revelation. It seems unhealthy to combine such radical skepticism in the powers of the intellect with such an uncritical acceptance of the truths of scripture.

Paul Tillich (1868–1965) was convinced that the personal God of traditional Western theism must go, but he also believed that religion was necessary for humankind. A deep-rooted anxiety is part of the human condition: this is not neurotic, because it is ineradicable and no therapy can take it away. We constantly fear loss and the terror of extinction, as we watch our bodies gradually but inexorably decay. Tillich agreed with Nietzsche that the personal God was a harmful idea and deserved to die:

> The concept of a "Personal God" interfering with natural events, or being "an independent cause of natural events," makes God a natural object beside others, an object among others, a being among beings, maybe the highest, but nevertheless *a* being. This indeed is not only the destruction of the physical system but even more the destruction of any meaningful idea of God.[7]

A God who kept tinkering with the universe was absurd; a God who interfered with human freedom and creativity was a tyrant. If God is seen as a self in a world of his own, an ego that relates to a thou, a cause separate from its effect, "he" becomes *a* being, not Being itself. An omnipotent, all-knowing tyrant is not so different from earthly dictators who made everything and everybody mere cogs in the machine which they controlled. An atheism that rejects such a God is amply justified.

Instead we should seek to find a "God" above this personal God. There is nothing new about this. Ever since biblical times, theists had been aware of the paradoxical nature of the God to which they prayed, aware that the personalized God was balanced by the essentially transpersonal divinity. Each prayer was a contradiction, since it attempted to speak to somebody to whom speech was impossible; it asked favors of somebody who had either bestowed them or not before he was asked; it said "thou" to a God who, as Being itself, was nearer to the "I" than our own ego. Tillich preferred the definition of God as the Ground of being. Participation in such a God above "God" does not alienate us from the world but immerses us in reality. It returns us to ourselves. Human beings have to use symbols when they talk about Being-itself: to speak literally or realistically about it is inaccurate and untrue. For centuries the symbols "God," "providence" and "immortality" have enabled people to bear the terror of life and the horror of death, but when these symbols lose their power there is fear and doubt. People who experience this dread and anxiety should seek the God above the discredited "God" of a theism which has lost its symbolic force.

When Tillich was speaking to laypeople, he preferred to replace the rather technical term "Ground of being" with "ultimate concern." He emphasized that the human experience of faith in this "God above God" was not a peculiar state distinguishable from others in our emotional or intellectual experience. You could not say: "I am now having a special 'religious' experience," since the God which is Being precedes and is fundamental to all our emotions of courage, hope and despair. It was not a distinct state with a name of its own but pervaded each one of our normal human experiences. A century earlier Feuerbach had made a similar claim when he had said that God was inseparable from normal human psychology. Now this atheism had been transformed into a new theism.

Liberal theologians were trying to discover whether it was possible to believe and to belong to the modern intellectual world. In forming their new conception of God, they turned to other disciplines: science, psychology, sociology and other religions. Again, there was nothing new in this attempt. Origen and Clement of Alexandria had been Liberal Christians in this sense in the third century when they had introduced Platonism into the Semitic religion of Yahweh. Now the Jesuit Pierre Teilhard de Chardin (1881–1955) combined his belief in God with modern science. He was a paleontologist with a special interest in prehistoric life and drew upon his understanding of evolution to write a new theology. He saw the whole evolutionary struggle as a divine force which propelled the universe from matter to spirit to personality and, finally, beyond personality to God. God was immanent and incarnate in the world, which had become a sacrament of his presence. De Chardin suggested that instead of concentrating on Jesus the man, Christians should cultivate the cosmic portrait of Christ in Paul's epistles to the Colossians and Ephesians: Christ in this view was the "omega point" of the universe, the climax of the evolutionary process when God becomes all in all. Scripture tells us that God is love, and science shows that the natural world progresses towards ever-greater complexity *and* to greater unity in this variety. This unity-in-differentiation was another way of regarding the love that animates the whole of creation. De Chardin has been criticized for identifying God so thoroughly with the world that all sense of his transcendence was lost, but his this-worldly theology was a welcome change from the *contemptus mundi* which had so often characterized Catholic spirituality.

In the United States during the 1960s, Daniel Day Williams (b. 1910) evolved what is known as Process theology, which also stressed God's unity with the world. He had been greatly influenced by the British philosopher A. N. Whitehead (1861–1947), who had seen God as inextricably bound up with the world process. Whitehead had been able to make no sense of God as an-other Being, self-contained and impassible, but had formulated a twentieth-century version of the prophetic idea of God's pathos:

> I affirm that God does suffer as he participates in the ongoing life of the society of being. His sharing in the world's suffering is the supreme instance of knowing, accepting, and transforming in love the suffering which arises in the world. I am affirming the divine sensitivity. Without it, I can make no sense of the being God.[8]

He described God as "the great companion, the fellow-sufferer, who understands." Williams liked Whitehead's definition; he liked to speak of God as the "behavior" of the world or an "event."[9] It was wrong to set the supernatural order over against the natural world of our experience. There was only one order of being. This was not reductionist, however. In our concept of the natural we should include *all* the aspirations, capacities and potential that had once seemed miraculous. It would also include our "religious experiences," as Buddhists had always affirmed. When asked whether he thought God was separate from nature, Williams would reply that he was not sure. He hated the old Greek idea of *apatheia,* which he found almost blasphemous: it presented God as remote, uncaring and selfish. He denied that he was advocating pantheism. His theology was simply trying to correct an imbalance, which had resulted in an alienating God which was impossible to accept after Auschwitz and Hiroshima.

Others were less optimistic about the achievements of the modern world and wanted to retain the transcendence of God as a challenge to men and women. The Jesuit Karl Rahner has developed a more transcendental theology, which sees God as the supreme mystery and Jesus as the decisive manifestation of what humanity can become. Bernard Lonergan also emphasized the importance of transcendence and of thought as opposed to experience. The unaided intellect cannot reach the vision it seeks: it is continually coming up against barriers to understanding that demand that we change our attitudes. In all cultures, human beings have been driven by the same imperatives: to be intelligent, responsible, reasonable, loving and, if necessary, to change. The very nature of humanity, therefore, demands that we transcend ourselves and our current perceptions, and this principle indicates the presence of what has been called the divine in the very nature of serious human inquiry. Yet the Swiss theologian Hans Urs von Balthasar believes that instead of seeking God in logic and abstractions, we should look to art: Catholic revelation has been essentially Incarnational. In brilliant studies of Dante and Bonaventure, Balthasar shows that Catholics have "seen" God in human form. Their emphasis on beauty in the gestures of ritual, drama and in the great Catholic artists indicates that God is to be found by the senses and not simply by the more cerebral and abstracted parts of the human person.

Muslims and Jews have also attempted to look back to the past to find ideas of God that will suit the present. Abu al-Kalam Azad (d. 1959), a notable Pakistani theologian, turned to the Koran to find a way of seeing God that was not so transcendent that he became a nullity and not so personal that he became an idol. He pointed to the symbolic nature of the Koranic discourse, noting the balance between metaphorical, figurative and anthropomorphic descriptions, on the one hand, and the constant reminders that God is incomparable on the other. Others have looked back to the Sufis for insight into God's relationship with the world. The Swiss Sufi Frithjof Schuon revived the doctrine of the Oneness of Being (*Wahdat al-Wujud*) later attributed to Ibn al-Arabi, which asserted that since God is the *only* reality, nothing exists but him, and the world itself is properly divine. He qualifies this with the reminder that this is an esoteric truth and can only be understood in the context of the mystical disciplines of Sufism.

Others have made God more accessible to the people and relevant to the political challenge of the time. In the years leading up to the Iranian revolution, the young lay philosopher Dr. Ali Shariati drew enormous crowds from among the educated middle classes. He was largely responsible for recruiting them against the Shah, even though the mullahs disapproved of a good deal of his religious message. During demonstrations, the crowds used to carry his portrait alongside those of the Ayatollah Khomeini, even though it is not clear how he would have fared in Khomeini's Iran. Shariati was convinced that Westernization had alienated Muslims from their cultural roots and that to heal this disorder they must reinterpret the old symbols of their faith. Muhammad had done the same when he had given the ancient pagan rites of the *hajj* a monotheistic relevance. In his own book *Hajj,* Shariati took his readers through the pilgrimage to Mecca, gradually articulating a dynamic conception of God which each pilgrim had to create imaginatively for him- or herself. Thus, on reaching the Kabah, pilgrims would realize how suitable it was that the shrine is empty: "This is not your final destination; the Kabah is a sign so that the way is not lost; it only shows you the direction."[10] The Kabah witnessed to the importance of transcending all human expressions of the divine, which must not become ends in themselves. Why is the Kabah a simple cube, without decoration or ornament? Because it represents "the secret of God in the universe: God is shapeless, colorless, without simularity, whatever form or condition mankind selects, sees or imagines, it is not God."[11] The *hajj* itself was the antithesis of the alienation experienced by so many Iranians in the postcolonial period. It represents the existential course of each human being who turns his or her life around and directs it toward the ineffable God. Shariat's activist faith was dangerous: the Shah's secret police tortured and deported him and may even have been responsible for his death in London in 1977.

Martin Buber (1878–1965) had an equally dynamic vision of Judaism as a spiritual process and a striving for elemental unity. Religion consisted entirely of an encounter with a personal God, which nearly always took place in our meetings with other human beings. There were two spheres: one the realm of space and time where we relate to other beings as subject and object, as I-It. In the second realm, we relate to others as they truly are, seeing them as ends in themselves. This is the I-Thou realm, which reveals the presence of God. Life was an endless dialogue with God, which does not endanger our freedom or creativity, since God never tells us *what* he is asking of us. We experience him simply as a presence and an imperative and have to work out the meaning for ourselves. This meant a break with much Jewish tradition, and Buber's exegesis of traditional texts is sometimes strained. As a Kantian, Buber had no time for Torah, which he found alienating: God was not a lawgiver! The I-Thou encounter meant freedom and spontaneity, not the weight of a past tradition. Yet the *mitzvot* are central to much Jewish spirituality, and this may explain why Buber has been more popular which Christians than with Jews.

Buber realized that the term "God" had been soiled and degraded, but he refused to relinquish it. "Where would I find a word to equal it, to describe the same reality?" It bears too great and a complex a meaning, has too many sacred associations. Those who do reject the word "God" must be respected, since so many appalling things have been done in its name.

It is easy to understand why there are some who propose a period of silence about "the last things" so that the misused words may be redeemed. But this is not the way to redeem them. We cannot clean up the term "God" and we cannot make it whole; but, stained and mauled as it is, we can raise it from the ground and set it above an hour of great sorrow.[12]

Unlike the other rationalists, Buber was not opposed to myth: he found Lurianic myth of the divine sparks trapped in the world to be of crucial symbolic significance. The separation of the sparks from the Godhead represent the human experience of alienation. When we relate to others, we will restore the primal unity and reduce the alienation in the world.

Where Buber looked back to the Bible and Hasidism, Abraham Joshua Heschel (1907–72) returned to the spirit of the Rabbis and the Talmud. Unlike Buber, he believed that the *mitzvot* would help Jews to counter the dehumanizing aspects of modernity. They were actions that fulfilled God's need rather than our own. Modern life was characterized by depersonalization and exploitation: even God was reduced to a thing to be manipulated and make to serve our purposes. Consequently religion became dull and insipid; we needed a "depth theology" to delve below the structures and recover the original awe, mystery and wonder. It was no use trying to prove God's existence logically. Faith in God sprang from an immediate apprehension that had nothing to do with concepts and rationality. The Bible must be read metaphorically like poetry if it is to yield that sense of the sacred. The *mitzvot* should also be seen as symbolic gestures that train us to live in God's presence. Each *mitzvah* is a place of encounter in the tiny details of mundane life and, like a work of art, the world of the *mitzvot* has its own logic and rhythm. Above all, we should be aware that God needs human beings. He is not the remote God of the philosophers but the God of pathos described by the prophets.

Atheistic philosophers have also been attracted by the idea of God during the second half of the twentieth century. In *Being and Time* (1927) Martin Heidegger (1899–1976) saw Being in rather the same way as Tillich, though he would have denied that it was "God" in the Christian sense: it was distinct from particular beings and quite separate from the normal categories of thought. Some Christians have been inspired by Heidegger's work, even though its moral value is called into question by his association with the Nazi regime. In *What Is Metaphysics?*, his inaugural lecture at Freiburg, Heidegger developed a number of ideas that had already surfaced in the work of Plotinus, Denys and Erigena. Since Being is "Wholly Other," it is in fact Nothing—no thing, neither an object nor a particular being. Yet it is what makes all other existence possible. The ancients had believed that nothing came from nothing, but Heidegger reversed this maxim: *ex nihilo omne qua ens fit*. He ended his lecture by posing a question asked by Leibniz: "Why are there beings at all, rather than just nothing?" It is a question that evokes the shock of surprise and wonder that has been a constant in the human response to the world: why should anything exist at all? In his *Intro-duction to Metaphysics* (1953), Heidegger began by asking the same question. Theology believed that it had the answer and traced everything back to Some-thing Else, to God. But this God was just another being rather than something that was wholly other. Heidegger had a somewhat reductive idea of the God of religion—though one shared by many religious people—but he often spoke in mystical terms about Being. He speaks of it as a great paradox; describes the thinking process as a waiting or listening to Being and seems to experience a return and withdrawal of Being, rather as mystics feel the absence of God. There is nothing that human beings can do to think Being into existence. Since the Greeks, people in the Western world have tended to forget Being and have con-centrated on being*s* instead, a process that has resulted in its modern technologi-cal success. In the article written toward the end of his life titled "Only a God Can Save Us," Heidegger suggested that the experience of God's absence in our time could liberate us from preoccupation with being*s*. But there was nothing we could do to bring Being back into the present. We could only hope for a new advent in the future.

The Marxist philosopher Ernst Bloch (1885–1977) saw the idea of God as natural to humanity. The whole of human life was directed toward the future: we experience our lives as incomplete and unfinished. Unlike animals, we are never satisfied but always want more. It is this which has forced us to think and develop, since at each point of our lives we must transcend ourselves and go on to the next stage: the baby must become a toddler, the toddler must overcome its disabilities and become a child, and so forth. All our dreams and aspirations look ahead to what is to come. Even philosophy begins with wonder, which is the experience of the not-knowing, the not-yet. Socialism also looks forward to utopia, but, despite the Marxist rejection of faith, where there is hope there is also religion. Like Feuerbach, Bloch saw God as the human ideal that has not yet come to be, but instead of seeing this as alienating he found it essential to the human condition.

Max Horkheimer (1895–1973), the German social theorist of the Frankfurt school, also saw "God" as an important ideal in a way that was reminiscent of the prophets. Whether he existed or not or whether we "believe in him" is super-fluous. Without the idea of God there is no absolute meaning, truth or morality: ethics becomes simply a question of taste, a mood or a whim. Unless politics and morality somehow include the idea of "God," they will remain pragmatic and shrewd rather than wise. If there is no absolute, there is no reason that we should not hate or that war is worse than peace. Religion is essentially an inner feeling that there *is* a God. One of our earliest dreams is a longing for justice (how frequently we hear children complain: "It's not fair!"). Religion records the aspirations and accusations of innumerable human beings in the face of suf-fering and wrong. It makes us aware of our finite nature; we all hope that the injustice of the world will not be the last word.

The fact that people who have no conventional religious beliefs should keep returning to central themes that we have discovered in the history of God indicates that the idea is not as alien as many of us assume. Yet during the second half of the twentieth century, there has been a move away from the idea of a personal God who behaves like a larger version away from the idea of a personal God who behaves like a larger version of us. There is nothing new about this. As we have seen, the Jewish scriptures, which Christians call their "Old" Testament, show a similar process; the Koran saw al-Lah in less personal terms than the Judeo-Christian tradition from the very beginning. Doctrines such as the Trinity and the mythology and symbolism of the mystical systems all strove to suggest that God was beyond personality. Yet this does not seem to have been made clear to many of the faithful. When John Robinson, Bishop of Woolwich, published *Honest to God* in 1963, stating that he could no longer subscribe to the old personal God "out there," there was uproar in Britain. A similar furor has greeted various remarks by David Jenkins, Bishop of Durham, even though these ideas are commonplace in academic circles. Don Cupitt, Dean of Emmanuel College, Cambridge, has also been dubbed "the atheist priest": he finds the traditional realistic God of theism unacceptable and proposes a form of Christian Buddhism, which puts religious experience before theology. Like Robinson, Cupitt has arrived intellectually at an insight that mystics in all three faiths have reached by a more intuitive route. Yet the idea that God does not really exist and that there is Nothing out there is far from new.

There is a growing intolerance of inadequate images of the Absolute. This is a healthy iconoclasm, since the idea of God has been used in the past to disastrous effect. One of the most characteristic new developments since the 1970s has been the rise of a type of religiosity that we usually call "fundamentalism" in most of the major world religions, including the three religions of God. A highly political spirituality, it is literal and intolerant in its vision. In the United States, which has always been prone to extremist and apocalyptic enthusiasm, Christian fundamentalism has attached itself to the New Right. Fundamentalists campaign for the abolition of legal abortion and for a hard line on moral and social decency. Jerry Falwell's Moral Majority achieved astonishing political power during the Reagan years. Other evangelists such as Maurice Cerullo, taking Jesus' remarks literally, believe that miracles are an essential hallmark of true faith. God will give the believer anything that he asks for in prayer. In Britain, fundamentalists such as Colin Urquhart have made the same claim. Christian fundamentalists seem to have little regard for the loving compassion of Christ. They are swift to condemn the people they see as the "enemies of God." Most would consider Jews and Muslims destined for hellfire, and Urquhart has argued that all oriental religions are inspired by the devil.

There have been similar developments in the Muslim world, which have been much publicized in the West. Muslim fundamentalists have toppled governments and either assassinated or threatened the enemies of Islam with the death penalty. Similarly, Jewish fundamentalists have settled in the Occupied Territories of the West Bank and the Gaza Strip with the avowed intention of driving out the Arab inhabitants, using force if necessary. Thus they believe that they are paving a way for the advent of the Messiah, which is at hand. In all its forms, fundamentalism is a fiercely reductive faith. Thus Rabbi Meir Kahane, the most extreme member of Israel's Far Right until his assassination in New York in 1990:

> There are not several messages in Judaism. There is only one. And this message is to do what God wants. Sometimes God wants us to go to war, sometimes he wants us to live in peace. . . . But there is only one message: God wanted us to come to this country to create a Jewish state.[13]

This wipes out centuries of Jewish development, returning to the Deuteronomist perspective of the Book of Joshua. It is not surprising that people who hear this kind of profanity, which makes "God" deny other people's human rights, think that the sooner we relinquish him the better.

Yet as we saw in the last chapter, this type of religiosity is actually a retreat from God. To make such human, historical phenomena as Christian "Family Values," "Islam" or "the Holy Land" the focus of religious devotion is a new form of idolatry. This type of belligerent righteousness has been a constant temptation to monotheists throughout the long history of God. It must be rejected as inauthentic. The God of Jews, Christians and Muslims got off to an unfortunate start, since the tribal deity Yahweh was murderously partial to his own people. Latter-day crusaders who return to this primitive ethos are elevating the values of the tribe to an unacceptably high status and substituting man-made ideals for the transcendent reality which should challenge our prejudices. They are also denying a crucial monotheistic theme. Ever since the prophets of Israel reformed the old pagan cult of Yahweh, the God of monotheists has promoted the ideal of compassion.

[. . .] Compassion was a characteristic of most of the ideologies that were created during the Axial Age. The compassionate ideal even impelled Buddhists to make a major change in their religious orientation when they introduced devotion *(bhakti)* to the Buddha and *bodhisattvas*. The prophets insisted that cult and worship were useless unless society as a whole adopted a more just and compassionate ethos. These insights were developed by Jesus, Paul and the Rabbis, who all shared the same Jewish ideals and suggested major changes in Judaism in order to implement them. The Koran made the creation of a compassionate and just society the essence of the reformed religion of al-Lah. Compassion is a particularly difficult virtue. It demands that we go beyond the limitations of our egotism, insecurity and inherited prejudice. Not surprisingly, there have been times when all three of the God-religions have failed to achieve these high standards. During the eighteenth century, deists rejected traditional

Western Christianity largely because it had become so conspicuously cruel and intolerant. The same will hold good today. All too often, conventional believers, who are not fundamentalists, share their aggressive righteousness. They use "God" to prop up their own loves and hates, which they attribute to God himself. But Jews, Christians and Muslims who punctiliously attend divine services yet denigrate people who belong to different ethnic and ideological camps deny one of the basic truths of their religion. It is equally inappropriate for people who call themselves Jews, Christians and Muslims to condone an inequitable social system. The God of historical monotheism demands mercy not sacrifice, compassion rather than decorous liturgy.

There has often been a distinction between people who practice a cultic form of religion and those who have cultivated a sense of the God of compassion. The prophets fulminated against their contemporaries who thought that temple worship was sufficient. Jesus and St. Paul both made it clear that external observance was useless if it was not accompanied by charity: it was little better than sounding brass or a tinkling cymbal. Muhammad came into conflict with those Arabs who wanted to worship the pagan goddesses alongside al-Lah in the ancient rites, without implementing the compassionate ethos that God demanded as a condition of all true religion. There had been a similar divide in the pagan world of Rome: the old cultic religion celebrated the status quo, while the philosophers preached a message that they believed would change the world. It may be that the compassionate religion of the One God has only been observed by a minority; most have found it difficult to face the extremity of the God-experience with its uncompromising ethical demands. Ever since Moses brought the tablets of the Law from Mount Sinai, the majority have preferred the worship of a Golden Calf, a traditional, unthreatening image of a deity they have constructed for themselves, with its consoling, time-honored rituals. Aaron, the high priest, presided over the manufacture of the golden effigy. The religious establishment itself is often deaf to the inspiration of prophets and mystics who bring news of a much more demanding God.

God can also be used as an unworthy panacea, as an alternative to mundane life and as the object of indulgent fantasy. The idea of God has frequently been used as the opium of the people. This is a particular danger when he is conceived as an-other Being—just like us, only bigger and better—in his own heaven, which is itself conceived as a paradise of earthly delights. Yet originally, "God" was used to help people to concentrate on this world and to face up to unpleasant reality. Even the pagan cult of Yahweh, for all its manifest faults, stressed his involvement in current events in profane time, as opposed to the sacred time of rite and myth. The prophets of Israel forced their people to confront their own social culpability and impending political catastrophe in the name of the God who revealed himself in these historical occurrences. The Christian doctrine of Incarnation stressed the divine immanence in the world of flesh and blood. Concern for the here and now was especially marked in Islam: nobody could have been more of a realist than Muhammad, who was a political as well as a spiritual genius. As we have seen, later generations of Muslims have shared his concern to incarnate the divine will in human history by establishing a just and decent society. From the very beginning, God was experienced as an imperative to action. From the moment when—as either El or Yahweh—God called Abraham away from his family in Haran, the cult entailed concrete action in this world and often a painful abandonment of the old sanctities.

This dislocation also involved great strain. The Holy God, who was wholly other, was experienced as a profound shock by the prophets. He demanded a similar holiness and separation on the part of his people. When he spoke to Moses on Sinai, the Israelites were not allowed to approach the foot of the mountain. An entirely new gulf suddenly yawned between humanity and the divine, rupturing the holistic vision of paganism. There was, therefore, a potential for alienation from the world, which reflected a dawning consciousness of the inalienable autonomy of the individual. It is no accident that monotheism finally took root during the exile to Babylon, when the Israelites also developed the ideal of personal responsibility, which has been crucial in both Judaism and Islam.[14] [. . .] The Rabbis used the idea of an immanent God to help Jews to cultivate a sense of the sacred rights of the human personality. Yet alienation has continued to be a danger in all three faiths: in the West the experience of God was continually accompanied by guilt and by a pessimistic anthropology. In Judaism and Islam there is no doubt that the observance of Torah and Shariah has sometimes been seen as a heteronymous compliance with an external law, even though we have seen that nothing could have been further from the intention of the men who compiled these legal codes.

Those atheists who preached emancipation from a God who demands such servile obedience were protesting against an inadequate but unfortunately familiar image of God. Again, this was based on a conception of the divine that was too personalistic. It interpreted the scriptural image of God's judgment too literally and assumed that God was a sort of Big Brother in the sky. This image of the divine Tyrant imposing an alien law on his unwilling human servants has to go. Terrorizing the populace into civic obedience with threats is no longer acceptable or even practicable, as the downfall of communist regimes demonstrated so dramatically in the autumn of 1989. The anthropomorphic idea of God as Lawgiver and Ruler is not adequate to the temper of post-modernity. Yet the atheists who complained that the idea of God was unnatural were not entirely correct. [. . .] Jews, Christians and Muslims have developed remarkably similar ideas of God, which also resemble other conceptions of the Absolute. When people try to find an ultimate meaning and value in human life, their minds seem to go in a certain direction. They have not been coerced to do this; it is something that seems natural to humanity.

Yet if feelings are not to degenerate into indulgent, aggressive or unhealthy emotionalism, they need to be informed by the critical intelligence. The experience of God must keep abreast of other current enthusiams, including those of the mind. The experiment of Falsafah was an attempt to relate faith in God with the new cult of rationalism among Muslims, Jews and, later, Western Christians. Eventually Muslims and Jews retreated from philosophy. Rationalism, they decided, had its uses, especially in such empirical studies as science, medicine and mathematics, but it was not entirely appropriate in the discussion of a God who lay beyond concepts. The Greeks had already sensed this and developed an early distrust of their native metaphysics. One of the drawbacks of the philosophic method of discussing God was that it could make it sound as though the Supreme Deity were simply an-other Being, the highest of all the things that exist, instead of a reality of an entirely different order. Yet the venture of Falsafah was important, since it showed an appreciation of the necessity of relating God to other experiences—if only to define the extent to which this was possible. To push God into intellectual isolation in a holy ghetto of his own is unhealthy and unnatural. It can encourage people to think that it is not necessary to apply normal standards of decency and rationality to behavior supposedly inspired by "God."

From the first, Falsafah had been associated with science. It was their initial enthusiasm for medicine, astronomy and mathematics which had led the first Muslim Faylasufs to discuss al-Lah in metaphysical terms. Science had effected a major change in their outlook, and they found that they could not think of God in the same way as their fellow Muslims. The philosophic conception of God was markedly different from the Koranic vision, but Faylasufs did recover some insights that were in danger of being lost in the *ummah* at that time. Thus the Koran had an extremely positive attitude to other religious traditions: Muhammad had not believed that he was founding a new, exclusive religion and considered that all rightly guided faith came from the One God. By the ninth century, however, the *ulema* were beginning to lose sight of this and were promoting the cult of Islam as the one true religion. The Faylasufs reverted to the older universalist approach, even though they reached it by a different route. We have a similar opportunity today. In our scientific age, we cannot think about God in the same way as our forebears, but the challenge of science could help us to appreciate some old truths.

[. . .] Albert Einstein had an appreciation of mystical religion. Despite his famous remarks about God not playing dice, he did not believe that his theory of relativity should affect the conception of God. During a visit to England in 1921, Einstein was asked by the Archbishop of Canterbury what were its implications for theology. He replied: "None. Relativity is a purely scientific matter and has nothing to do with religion."[15] When Christians are dismayed by such scientists as Stephen Hawking, who can find no room for God in his cosmology, they are perhaps still thinking of God in anthropomorphic terms as a Being who created the world in the same way as we would. Yet creation was not originally conceived in such a literal manner. Interest in Yahweh as Creator did not enter

Judaism until the exile to Babylon. It was a conception that was alien to the Greek world: creation *ex nihilo* was not an official doctrine of Christianity until the Council of Nicaea in 341. Creation is a central teaching of the Koran, but, like all its utterances about God, this is said to be a "parable" or a "sign" *(aya)* of an ineffable truth. Jewish and Muslim rationalists found it a difficult and problematic doctrine, and many rejected it. Sufis and Kabbalists all preferred the Greek metaphor of emanation. In any case, cosmology was not a scientific description of the origins of the world but was originally a symbolic expression of a spiritual and psychological truth. There is consequently little agitation about the new science in the Muslim world: [. . .] the events of recent history have been more of a threat than has science to the traditional conception of God. In the West, however, a more literal understanding of scripture has long prevailed. When some Western Christians feel their faith in God undermined by the new science, they are probably imagining God as Newton's great Mechanick, a personalistic notion of God which should, perhaps, be rejected on religious as well as on scientific grounds. The challenge of science might shock the churches into a fresh appreciation of the symbolic nature of scriptural narrative.

The idea of a personal God seems increasingly unacceptable at the present time for all kinds of reasons: moral, intellectual, scientific and spiritual. Feminists are also repelled by a personal deity who, because of "his" gender, has been male since his tribal, pagan days. Yet to talk about "she"—other than in a dialectical way—can be just as limiting, since it confines the illimitable God to a purely human category. The old metaphysical notion of God as the Supreme Being, which has long been popular in the West, is also felt to be unsatisfactory. The God of the philosophers is the product of a now outdated rationalism, so the traditional "proofs" of his existence no longer work. The widespread acceptance of the God of the philosophers by the deists of the Enlightenment can be seen as the first step to the current atheism. Like the old Sky God, this deity is so remote from humanity and the mundane world that he easily becomes *Deus Otiosus* and fades from our consciousness.

The God of the mystics might seem to present a possible alternative. The mystics have long insisted that God is not an-Other Being; they have claimed that he does not really exist and that it is better to call him Nothing. This God is in tune with the atheistic mood of our secular society, with its distrust of inadequate images of the Absolute. Instead of seeing God as an objective fact, which can be demonstrated by means of scientific proof, mystics have claimed that he is a subjective experience, mysteriously experienced in the ground of being. This God is to be approached through the imagination and can be seen as a kind of art form, akin to the other great artistic symbols that have expressed the ineffable mystery, beauty and value of life. Mystics have used music, dancing, poetry, fiction, stories, painting, sculpture and architecture to express this Reality that goes beyond concepts. Like all art, however, mysticism requires intelligence, discipline and self-criticism as a safeguard against indulgent emotionalism and projection. The God of the mystics could even satisfy the feminists, since both Sufis and Kabbalists have long tried to introduce a female element into the divine.

There are drawbacks, however. Mysticism has been regarded with some suspicion by many Jews and Muslims since the Shabbetai Zevi fiasco and the decline of latter-day Sufism. In the West, mysticism has never been a mainstream religious enthusiasm. The Protestant and Catholic Reformers either outlawed or marginalized it, and the scientific Age of Reason did not encourage this mode of perception. Since the 1960s, there has been a fresh interest in mysticism, expressed in the enthusiasm for Yoga, meditation and Buddhism, but it is not an approach that easily consorts with our objective, empirical mentality. The God of the mystics is not easy to apprehend. It requires long training with an expert and a considerable investment of time. The mystic has to work hard to acquire this sense of the reality known as God (which many have refused to name). Mystics often insist that human beings must deliberately create this sense of God for themselves, with the same degree of care and attention that others devote to artistic creation. It is not something that is likely to appeal to people in a society which has become used to speedy gratification, fast food and instant communication. The God of the mystics does not arrive readymade and prepackaged. He cannot be experienced as quickly as the instant ecstasy created by a revivalist preacher, who quickly has a whole congregation clapping its hands and speaking in tongues.

It is possible to acquire some of the mystical attitudes. Even if we are incapable of the higher states of consciousness achieved by a mystic, we can learn that God does not exist in any simplistic sense, for example, or that the very word "God" is only a symbol of a reality that ineffably transcends it. The mystical agnosticism could help us to acquire a restraint that stops us rushing into these complex matters with dogmatic assurance. But if these notions are not felt upon the pulse and personally appropriated, they are likely to seem meaningless abstractions. Secondhand mysticism could prove to be unsatisfactory as reading the explanation of a poem by a literary critic instead of the original. [. . .] Mysticism was often seen as an esoteric discipline, not because the mystics wanted to exclude the vulgar herd but because these truths could only be perceived by the intuitive part of the mind after special training. They mean something different when they are approached by this particular route, which is not accessible to the logical, rationalist faculty.

Ever since the prophets of Israel started to ascribe their own feelings and experiences to God, monotheists have in some sense created a God for themselves. God has rarely been seen as a self-evident fact that can be encountered like any other objective existent. Today many people seem to have lost the will to make this imaginative effort. This need not be a catastrophe. When religious ideas have lost their validity, they have usually faded away painlessly: if the human idea of God no longer works for us in the empirical age, it will be discarded. Yet in the past people have always created new symbols to act as a focus for spirituality. Human beings have always created a faith for themselves, to cultivate their sense of the wonder and ineffable significance of life. The aimlessness, alienation, anomie and violence that characterize so much of modern life seem to indicate that now that they are not deliberately creating a faith in "God" or anything else—it matters little what—many people are falling into despair.

In the United States, [. . .] ninety-nine percent of the population claim to believe in God, yet the prevalence of fundamentalism, apocalypticism and "instant" charismatic forms of religiosity in America is not reassuring. The escalating crime rate, drug addiction and the revival of the death penalty are not signs of a spiritually healthy society. In Europe there is a growing blankness where God once existed in the human consciousness. One of the first people to express this dry desolation—quite different from the heroic atheism of Nietzsche—was Thomas Hardy. In "The Darkling Thrush," written on December 30, 1900, at the turn of the twentieth century, he expressed the death of spirit that was no longer able to create a faith in life's meaning:

> I leant upon a coppice gate
>   When Frost was spectre-grey
> And Winter's dregs made desolate
>   The weakening eye of day.
> The tangled bine-stems scored the sky
>   Like strings of broken lyres,
> And all mankind that haunted nigh
>   Had sought their household fires.
>
> The land's sharp features seemed to be
>   The Century's corpse outleant,
> His crypt the cloudy canopy,
>   The wind his death-lament.
> The ancient pulse of germ and birth
>   Was shrunken hard and dry,
> And every spirit upon earth
>   Seemed fervourless as I.
>
> At once a voice arose among
>   The bleak twigs overhead
> In a full-hearted evensong
>   Of joy illimited;
> An aged thrush, frail, gaunt, and small,
>   In blast-beruffled plume,
> Had chosen thus to fling his soul
>   Upon the growing gloom.

So little cause for carolings
　　Of such ecstatic sound
Was written on terrestrial things
　　Afar or nigh around,
That I could think there trembled through
　　His happy good-night air
Some blessed Hope, whereof he knew
　　And I was unaware.

Human beings cannot endure emptiness and desolation; they will fill the vacuum by creating a new focus of meaning. The idols of fundamentalism are not good substitutes for God; if we are to create a vibrant new faith for the twenty-first century, we should, perhaps, ponder the history of God for some lessons and warnings.

Notes

1. Peter Berger, *A Rumour of Angels* (London, 1970), p. 58.
2. A. J. Ayer, *Language, Truth and Logic* (Harmondsworth, 1974), p. 152.
3. Wilfred Cantwell Smith, *Belief and History* (Charlottesville, 1985), p. 10.
4. Thomas J. J. Altizer, *The Gospel of Christian Atheism* (London, 1966), p. 136.
5. Paul Van Buren, *The Secular Meaning of the Gospel* (London, 1963), p. 138.
6. Richard L. Rubenstein, *After Auschwitz, Radical Theology and Contemporary Judaism* (Indianapolis, 1966), passim.
7. Paul Tillich, *Theology and Culture* (New York and Oxford, 1964), p. 129.
8. Alfred North Whitehead, "Suffering and Being," in *Adventures of Ideas* (Harmondsworth, 1942), pp. 191–92.
9. *Process and Reality* (Cambridge, 1929), p. 497.
10. Ali Shariati, *Hajj,* trans. Laleh Bakhtiar (Teheran, 1988), p. 46.
11. Ibid., p 48.
12. Martin Buber, "Gottesfinsternis, Betrachtungen zur Beziehung zwischen Religion und Philosophie," quoted in Hans Kung, *Does God Exist? An Answer for Today,* trans. Edward Quinn, (London, 1978), p. 508.
13. Quoted in Raphael Mergui and Philippa Simmonot, *Israel's Ayatollahs; Meir Kahane and the Far Right in Israel* (London, 1987), p. 43.
14. Personal responsibility is also important in Christianity, of course, but Judaism and Islam have stressed it by their lack of a mediating priesthood, a perspective that was recovered by the Protestant Reformers.
15. Philipp Frank, *Einstein: His Life and Times* (New York, 1947), pp. 189–90.

Reading 5

MAKING CIVIL SOCIETY REAL
Practical Strategies

Benjamin R. Barber

There are three obstacles to civil society as the mediating domain between the government and the private sector: government itself, when it is arrogant and overweening; market dogmas, when they presume that private individuals and groups can secure public goods; and the yearning for community, when it subordinates liberty and equality to solidarity.

As to the first, the tendency of all institutions to ossify and become distanced from their constituents (the so-called iron law of oligarchy) turns government representatives into enemies of their citizens and, eventually, makes even democratically elected governments rigid and hierarchical, with the representatives regarding themselves as the sole civic actors on the political scene, governing on behalf of citizens instead of facilitating citizen self-government. When that happens, the democratic citizenry in whose name the governments govern is actually disempowered, at once both dependent and alienated.

As to the second, the myth of the invisible hand encourages market enthusiasts to believe that privatization is a synonym for democratization and empowerment, and for civic liberty to flourish, one need only get government out of the way. But the results are quite otherwise: an eclipse of the public, a one-dimensional culture of privatism and greed, and an addictive materialism that turns autonomous citizens into dependent consumers.

As for the third, the communitarian thirst for the restoration of lost values and value communities encourages people to impose on others their own cultural values through either government or quasi-censorious institutions of civil

---

Barber, Benjamin R. "Making Civil Society Real: Practical Strategies." *A Place For Us: How to Make Society Civil and Democracy Strong.* New York: Hill and Wang.

society. In the resulting solidaristic community, insiders favor identity over equality as the most precious of all social values and everyone else is left feeling like outsiders.

Ironically, although government itself has recently been seen as part of the problem, it has an opportunity here to be part of the solution. For a disciplined, self-limiting government can behave modestly. Such modesty is characteristic of President Clinton's new Democrats (prompted by the Democratic Leadership Council's Progressive Policy Institute), Tony Blair's "New" Labor Party, and Lionel Jospin's new socialists. Yet these new progressives do trust government to help ameliorate the crushing effects of monopoly corporations and counter their imposition of commercial uniformity and cultural homogenization. Through its courts and legal system government can also assure that liberty is protected against corrosive side effects of the all-too-human longing for solidarity.

The true enemy of civil society is, in fact, neither government nor corporations per se, but bureaucracy, dogmatism, unresponsiveness, totalism, bloat, unaccountability, absolutism, and inertia wherever they are found. While laissez-faire obsessives are loath to admit it, these defects are unfortunately found as much in private commerce as in the government, among firms and fraternities no less than in welfare bureaucracies. Had President Clinton announced not the "end of big government" but the "end of Leviathan, the end of big bureaucratic bloat," he would have declared war more symmetrically on the ills that afflict us. That he did not and that he has shown so little appetite to address the private sector attests to its intimidating power (as well as its campaign finance leverage).

Where government is at fault, laws must help it move to self-limitation and reform; and where the private sector is the problem, government must be the public's ally in curbing commercial and market abuses, and in forbidding the moral encroachments that conformist communities make when they try to impose their own values and way of life on all of us. Ultimately, democratic government is but an extension of the common power of citizens, and citizens must use that common power while working to reform its susceptibility to abuse. Power corrupts, and private power, neither accountable nor, often, even visible, may be much more corrupting (and far less tractable) than the power of democratic government. We can always "throw the buggers out!" when politicians get too big for their britches or forget to whom they are accountable. But there is no recall power against managers of the marketplace when they are not accountable to the sovereign public. That is a lesson worth remembering in an age when government is so disdained and markets so widely celebrated, when the prevailing orthodoxy is so insistently laissez-faire. It is a shameful reminder of the hypocrisy of those who benefit from privatism when they pretend that government has no role in defending those whom privatism cripples.

Democracy is not a synonym for the marketplace, and the notion that by privatizing government we can establish civil society and civic goods is a dishonorable myth. The freedom to buy a Coke or a Big Mac or a video of the Lion King eating a Big Mac is not the freedom to determine how you will live and under what kind of regime. Coke and McDonald's and MTV thrive in undemocratic Singapore and China as well as they do in chaotic, semi-democratic Russia and in the genuinely democratic Czech Republic. Historically, it is not capitalism that produced democracy but democracy that produced capitalism. Capitalism needs democracy but does not know how to create or sustain it, and frequently it produces circumstances that can undermine it.

The myth of the market is our most insidious myth, not just because so many believe it, but because the market's invisible bonds slip on so easily and feel so very much like freedom. Is shopping really a synonym for choice, even when, in a hyper-consumer society, consumption is more addiction than voluntary activity? I have written elsewhere and at length on the disastrous confusion between the moderate, mostly well-founded claim that flexibly regulated markets are the most efficient instruments of economic productivity and wealth accumulation, and the zany, overblown claim that unregulated markets are the sole means by which we can produce and distribute everything we care about—from durable goods to spiritual values, from capital development to social justice, from profitability to sustainable environments, from private wealth to the essential commonweal. This second claim has moved some people to insist that goods as diverse and obviously public as education, culture, penology, full employment, social welfare, and ecological survival should be handed over to the profit sector for arbitration and disposal, but the argument of this book [*A Place for Us*] shows how inadequate and dangerous this misapprehension is.

Markets are simply not designed to do the things democratic polities or free civil societies do. Markets give us private, not public, modes of discourse: we pay as consumers in currencies of consumption to producers of material goods, but we cannot use this currency when we deal with one another as citizens or neighbors about the social consequences of our private market choices. Markets advance individualistic, not social, goals and they encourage us to speak the language of "I want," not the language of "we need." Markets preclude "we" thinking and "we" action of any kind at all, trusting in the power of aggregated individual choices (the "invisible hand") somehow to secure the common good. In the name of diversity and private choice, markets foster a kind of consumer totalism, turning multidimensional citizens into one-dimensional, solitary shoppers. Consumers speak the divisive rhetoric of "me." Citizens invent the common language of "we."

Markets are also contractual rather than communitarian, which means they flatter our solitary egos but leave unsatisfied our yearning for community; they offer durable goods and fleeting dreams but not a common identity or a collective membership. Virulently negative expressions of communitarian solidarity are in fact often reactions to the market's desocializing features. The thinner the market's social nexus, the thicker and more bloody the response to it—and so what I have called McWorld engenders the Jihad that resists it.

Beyond our markets, then, we need the virtues of democracy and the social relations of civil society; and our markets and our ideal of civil society need democracy to survive. Markets are as likely to undermine as to sustain full employment, environmental safety, public health, social safety nets, education, cultural diversity, and real competition. These common goods are the result of common thinking, cooperation, and sharing of the kind democratic civil society makes possible. The task today, in theory no less than in practice, is to reilluminate public space for a civil society in eclipse. Making space for citizens and giving them a civil voice in their affairs must be the goal of all our practical strategies.

A government pledged to give practical support to citizenship and civil society can effectively and legitimately act through legislative initiatives and reform as a positive facilitator of civil society, as a partner of citizens in removing governmental obstacles to civil-society practices, and as an ally of civil society in challenging the totalizing, private commercial sector as well as overly zealous communitarian groups whose fraternal ministrations shrink the purview of citizenship.

There is no legislative domain that cannot be reframed and improved by thinking how it might promote civil society. After all, government programs, regulatory policy (or its absence), and political ideology expressed in laws helped to create our present world. The corporation, that dominating leviathan of the private sector, was itself a creature of government and in American law exists as an "artificial person" only through its status under the law. Happily, both Democrats and Republicans have shown some interest in "legislating civil society"—the Clinton Administration in its ongoing fascination with civil society and public-private partnerships, and the Republicans in the legislative agenda offered by Bill Bennett and Senator Dan Coats for government intervention to sustain civic practices.[1] Government agencies like the United States Information Agency, private philanthropies like George Soros's Open Society Institute, and the Institute for Civil Society and Civicus (the international NGO umbrella organization) all try to strengthen civil society in transitional societies and in the international arena. Some programs are obviously more easily enacted than others. I would propose six possible areas where innovative and liberating laws could nourish civil society without incurring unreasonable new operating costs. In many cases, the new tactics would build on legislative strategies that are already in place (e.g., campaign finance reform, free TV time for candidates, using new telecommunication technologies for the public weal); in others, they could embody new initiatives. The consequences not just of an absence of government intervention but of maladroit and destructive government policy need to be addressed afresh.

In every case, the specific initiatives I suggest here aim to reorient and reconceptualize our policy goals so as to downplay government as an end in itself or as the direct solution to social problems, and to emphasize it as a facilitating instrument of citizens who want to get their own public work done. Far from disappearing, government is strengthened—but by turning it back into what it should always be in a democracy: the agent and instrument of highest resort for the highest and most general objectives of civil society and free citizens; the entity that expresses the "we" of our commonalty; civil society in its legislative mode. The aim is to remove rather than reinforce barriers between the people as a citizenry and their government as their sovereign voice.

Here are six pertinent arenas for legislative action in support of civil society:

1. Enlarging and reinforcing public spaces: specifically, retrofitting commercial malls as multi-use and thus genuinely public spaces.
2. Fostering civic uses of new telecommunications and information technologies, preventing commercialization from destroying their civic potentials: specifically, a civic Internet; public-access cable television; a check on mass-media advertising for (and the commercial exploitation of) children.
3. Domesticating and democratizing production in the global economy: protecting the labor market, challenging disemployment practices; making corporations responsible members of civil society without surrendering the government's regulatory authority.
4. Domesticating and democratizing consumption in the global economy: protecting just wage policies, workplace safety, and the environment; the labeling and/or boycotting of goods produced without regard for safety, environment, or child-labor laws.
5. National and community service, service learning programs, and citizen-nurturing voluntarism.
6. Cultivating the arts and humanities as an indispensable foundation for a free, pluralistic society; treating artists as citizens and citizens as artists in government-supported arts education and service programs.

Public Spaces

In our mostly privatized, suburbanized world, there are not enough physical places where citizenship can be easily exercised and civil society's free activities can be pursued. Citizens need physical spaces where they can interact and work to solve public problems. "The trouble with socialism," Oscar Wilde once quipped, "is that it takes up too many free evenings." Civil society and its activities encroach on Wednesday afternoons and Saturday mornings, too. And they require space and place. There can be no civic activity without a palpable civic geography. Ducks, to be ducks, need their pond, and the public needs its town square.

Traditionally, town squares, village greens, general stores, city parks, community halls—even barbershops, post offices, watercoolers, and saloons—have been places for informal civic interaction: neighborly conversation, political argument, the search for shared ground. But when more than half of us now live in suburban developments that are anything but neighborhoods and that have no obvious public spaces—neither civic centers nor even sidewalks—or in inner cities where public space is often unsavory or unsafe, we have fewer and fewer of these formal and informal meeting places. In the suburbs, people go almost everywhere by car, and often bank and eat without leaving those cars. Suburbanization follows the automobile and the kinds of mobility that attend economic development: and there is good reason to think, in the absence of alternatives, that all the world may one day be New Jersey.

In New Jersey, the commonly available public spaces are commercial malls, designed to encourage and facilitate purchasing, indeed, to make material consumption a habit. Stores cater not to traditional needs (try to find a hardware store or dry cleaners or pharmacy in a mall!) but to the manufactured needs of the post-modern economy. Boutiques and novelty chains (The Nature Store, The Sharper Image, the Disney Store, Brookstone's) proliferate. Even food is proffered like fuel in "food court" pit stops that maximize caloric intake and minimize the time spent fueling up for more shopping.

Meanwhile, more traditional urban milieus have been mauled and malled by architects who think of Las Vegas (or Disneyland) as an opportunity to do a Times Square theme park, and of Times Square as an opportunity to bring Las Vegas to New York. In Washington, D.C., Union Station and the old Post Office are examples of traditional public spaces that have been recast as commercial spaces. (Ironically, the National Endowments for the Arts and the Humanities are sequestered upstairs in the commercialized old Post Office.) Might not both buildings have been refurbished to include civic and social space as well as shops? Public space means more than the accidental open areas left behind in cavernous buildings after commercialization has run its course. Even airports are coming to resemble malls with airplanes.

If our world is to be malled, is it possible to transform malls into usable civic spaces? Is an architecture geared to commerce malleable enough to permit alterations to fulfill civic needs? How might malls be designed and developers encouraged to make space for neighborhood health clinics, speakers' corners, child-care centers? for political and community meeting spaces, community theaters and art galleries, charitable organizations? for information and media groups and other civic associations? What kind of incentives might governments offer to make this happen? Could zoning regulations be used to make developers take a more civic approach? Might "curb cut" permits (which let developers have rights-of-way from public highways) do the same thing? Why not a "model" civic-mall competition sponsored by the National Endowment for the Humanities? A contest for architects to design model civic space?

Celebration, the Disney Corporation's "new-town" in central Florida, suggests a new architecture of public space, but it looks more like a mall-plus-homesites than the traditional town its architecture tries to ape. It is a kind of perfect counterparadigm to what I am talking about. It has taken the principles of comic-book spectatorship—sanitized vacations, safety-conscious adventure, vicarious history, homogenized variety, and simulated ethnicity—from their entertainment venue and applied them to a living environment that simulates a "public" from which it is in fact insulated in the manner of the gated community. It is but a short hop from Celebration to Orlando, a real city, but Celebration is as far away from the dark side of the public square—unemployment, welfare poverty, race bias, grand larceny, rape, and murder—as it can get. It is about "a signature golf course, tennis courts, acres of parks, ponds, and open spaces" as well as "homes with front porches and a vibrant downtown where you'll see friends and neighbors," as its publicity brochure puts it. It promises all the accouterments of the public square, the "building of a community," but Disney has prefabricated it along with instant "Celebration traditions" (a "fun-filled interactive orientation session"—a novel "tradition," to be sure!). Disney's traditions are no more traditional than its public squares are public. They are not born of blood, sweat, and tears—hard times and common experience forged over generations—but are "imagineered" by the same people who make the movies and create the rides and design the theme parks. In Celebration, lifelong community and permanent traditions are for sale today—public living without risk, diversity without tension, community without pain, tradition without history.

The true architecture of authentic public space is about diversity, and creating diversity is no easy architectural feat. Disney's style in Celebration has an archetainement feel to it—a Disneyclectic hodgepodge on the surface, with a comforting homogeneity lurking underneath. Like the Hollywood whose defining spirit and alter ego it has always been, Disney is necessarily parasitic: it creates nothing, living instead off other people's cultural capital. It homogenizes diversity just as it domesticates foreignness, contemporizes history, and privatizes public space. It gives you just enough history and culture and ethnicity and diversity to make sure you never have to deal with the real thing: the real public. Mexico without poverty or assassinations, Kashmir without altitude sickness or tribal war, Europe without foreign languages, France without snobbish waiters and people who think they're better than us, Germany without Dachau—community without hierarchy or clannishness, tradition without prejudice or inflexibility, friends without commitment or loyalty, public space for private use only, a town without pity or passion. Corporations like Disney imagine we have come to fear the very idea of real public space (space inhabited by the real, multicolored, multicultural public), and that makes the challenge of re-creating it particularly daunting.

Still, retrofitting commercial space as multi-use public space is a significant first step in giving our civil society a real geography. There are a few impressive examples: Mashappe Commons on Cape Cod or Ronald Sher's Crossroads in Seattle. But there are legal obstacles (many state courts have ruled that closed malls are wholly private), and there are political challenges: the danger of middle-class flight to private enclaves, for example, leaving "public" space to the poor, the unemployed, and the marginalized who are without the resources or tax base to create a usable commons of their own. Yet, without a commons, how are the poor, upon whom we heap new responsibilities in the era after big government, supposed to realize in practice the great ideals of civil society? Can reconstituted malls cut off from public transportation fulfill public purposes? These are the challenges.

The New Public Telecommunications Technologies

As the world enters a new telecommunications and information age whose venue is cyberspace and whose viaduct is the information superhighway, those of us who care about civil society must have effective strategies to guarantee widespread public access and broad civic usage. As the new technologies evolve, we must find ways to counter wholesale commercialization of what Congress defined as "public airwaves" and the new Internet conduits. Deregulation has focused on insulating productive market forces from government intervention. President Clinton's policy paper released in the summer of 1997 on "A Framework for Global Electronic Commerce" made clear that, despite Vice President Gore's outspoken endorsement of the educational value of the new telecommunications technology, the Administration intends to expend more energy fostering the private and commercial uses of the Net than on its public and civic uses.* With the private sector focused on profit and the government looking the other way, how can we insulate civic and educational forces from the market in telecommunications?

There is a risk that those developing information technology will focus either on national security (the Internet was born of Information Technology Warfare "ITW" research) or on profitable commerce. Yet the rewarding civic domain, though profitless, promises enormous potential benefits for democracy, civic culture, and education. The challenge of a civic technology is particularly important when government regulation and tax policy, the conventional tools of the public good, are in such disrepute. Yet they remain indispensable if the technology's civic is to be realized. The World Bank offers and innovative model: it

---

*"A Framework for Global Electronic Commerce" offers government support for common international technical standards, open access, privacy, and wholesale commercialization, and suggests that the new technologies are to be viewed, above all, as a vital component of world trade policy.

is examining the ways in which technology can assist economic and civic development. Satellite surveillance, for example, can aid agriculture by monitoring ecological change; cellular technology can allow areas still unwired for telephone to leapfrog over existing technologies and to join the twenty-first century without even going through the twentieth. Since roughly half the globe is currently without phone service, this would be a striking development.[2]

It has been five years—an eon, these days—since Speaker Gingrich talked casually about providing laptops for Americans below the poverty line. But to use computers, one must be user-literate, and literacy is founded on lifelong education and an economy that supports it, conditions that Gingrich did not address. Perhaps he was merely posturing. More recently, President Clinton has endorsed an initiative (it is called Netdays) in which volunteers help to hardwire inner-city schools with donated equipment. Demonstration projects like this are useful, but they are not the same thing as a national policy, for if the Net becomes wholly commercial, hard-wiring the schools is tantamount to commercializing them. To avert this, an ongoing governmental effort is needed. The government need not and should not run programs that are platforms for Net use or control the Net directly, but it can and should ensure that commercial markets remain competitive, and that ample space is left for local and regional public use, and it can and should fund pilots so that we can inspect and try out various experimental civic uses. For example, a civic chat-room facilitated by the League of Women Voters or a publicly oriented electoral and political information site such as Project Vote-Smart or Minnesota E-Democracy (nonprofit sites that try to make nonpartisan information available to journalists and the public during elections).

The World Wide Web was, in its conception and compared to traditional broadcast media, a remarkably promising means for point-to-point lateral communication among citizens and for genuine interactivity (users not merely passively receiving information, but participating in retrieving and creating it). But those who are busy commercializing it are already moving away from the "pull" programs that made the Net's early days interactive and participant-driven, and moving forward (backward!) to "push" programs, which look more like traditional advertising programming and pacify "clients" by using interactive information to anticipate ("guess") their interests and needs in order to sell them goods. Push technology wants to shape and guide your choices by inferring one want from another: if you logged on to the Boston Marathon's home page, you must like jogging, and if you like jogging, then you will probably want the latest Walkman. But if you spend your afternoons accessing films, you must be a couch potato, so here's a bargain on snack food, or, if it's film noir that's your passion, here's imitation art-deco jewelry.

There is nothing wrong with trying to make a profit by selling people what you guess they want, but when the Net becomes primarily or exclusively commercial, our capacity to choose is reduced to market appetites, and our potential for participation and interaction is reduced to rudimentary clientelism. In other words, without public intervention, the "new" Net technology becomes very much like the older technologies: passive, commercial, and monopolistic. First radio, then television, then cable were initially advanced as great new democratizing civic technologies in the public interest. Each in its turn grew into the commercial, privatized medium we know today, in which the public interest in civic culture, public education, and civil and political debate is marginalized and in which commercial selling and entertainment are front and center.

Government regulation, for which there is in any case little appetite, has not kept up with technological innovation. The Bill of Rights was written for a print world; the Federal Communications Act of 1934 was conceived for radio. The American government has yet to catch up to the implications of broadcast television, let alone of satellite and cable or fiber optics and computer chips. The public need for and civic use of these technologies have never been systematically contemplated. The government cannot and need not control them directly, but it has a fundamental responsibility to assure the American public and its civil-society institutions free and equal access and usage. Cyberspace is no less public than broadcast airwaves, and the information highway is a public, not private thoroughfare; it ought not to be commercialized and then sold back to its true owners, the American public.

We already face the irony that the "public airwaves" are leased by the government on behalf of the people to private commercial interests, which then sell them back to the American people for outrageous prices—corrupting the electoral process and making office-holding a privilege of the rich (or those willing to devote themselves to endless fund-raising). And we now face the added insult to our sovereignty of a government policy that simply donates the new digitalized broadcast spectra (roughly six new broadcast outlets for every television station now broadcasting) to current licensees, in what even Republican Presidential candidate Robert Dole labeled in 1996 the "giveaway of the century."

Paul Taylor, a former *Washington Post* journalist, has a project to persuade both broadcasters and politicians voluntarily to make prime-time television slots available for serious political expression and debate during election campaigns. It is one useful starting place, an excellent example of voluntary civil-society strategy in this domain. It has been endorsed by President Clinton but is being resisted by the networks, which do not wish to pay the costs. Why not make compliance with the Taylor proposal a condition for commercial use of the new digitalized broadcast spectra? Or invite rivals to propose other civic uses of the new spectra, and ask current license-holders to match them or give up their licenses? Realists will of course point out that the extraordinarily powerful current license-holders, not just as a lobby but as corporations controlling public information and influencing public opinion, will not stand for such government tactics. But their power is, precisely, another reason we need the countervailing power of democratic government. The object is not to have government monopolize the airwaves or own the information highway; it is guarantee that no one else be allowed to do so. That is presumably why the U.S. Justice Department has finally challenged the Microsoft Corporation's habit of compelling hardware manufacturers to carry only Microsoft's Web browser if they want to carry Microsoft's Windows.

Another useful strategy would have government use education and humanities funding to offset the baleful encroachment of corporate advertisers and promoters on America's higher-education telecommunications research programs and public-school media classrooms. The market makes its inroads through incentives—let us call them bribes—to institutions that cannot afford computers or television sets or software. Inner-city public schools in nearly every state— schools that need innovative hardware and software—are currently being forced to bid for new equipment and satellite broadcasts by selling their pupils as forced audiences for commercials. This is the mind-corroding tactic used by the K-III Corporation's Channel One, originally Chris Whittle's blunt instrument for exploiting the need of poor schools for equipment they cannot afford; they now have their three minutes of Channel One's hard advertising and nine minutes of soft news in more than 12,000 classrooms in nearly every state in the Union. Surely, if broadcasters "deserve" free access to the new digitalized bands which they are getting from the government, our children deserve free and equal access to the new technologies out of which digital broadcasting grows. Public schools and public libraries must be the primary, not the tertiary, beneficiaries of the information revolution, and the only body that can make that happen is the federal government. Netdays are fine, but it will take more than volunteers or even hardwired schools to create a civic internet.

One powerful way to utilize the new technologies on behalf of civil society is to establish a "national civic forum," in which civil speech and reasonable political argument among geographically and economically dispersed communities becomes possible. Such a forum could pull together via satellite uplinks dozens of groups, each a meeting of several hundred citizens gathered in their own neighborhood, so that they might converse and deliberate with one another on two-way television hookups, as well as with some primary national forum to which they are all linked. Think of an ABC Nightline Town Meeting hooked up to a dozen sites where other meetings have been convened, with people talking within their own groups but also to other assemblies all across the nations, and to a national television audience. This big electronic town meeting linking up smaller regional meetings might well ameliorate the damage done by demagogic talk-radio shows and a commercially dominated electoral process. Such a deliberative form of satellite interactivity invites vigorous public participation but, by its very nature, it would demand tolerance, mutual respect, and independent rational argument. It would originate in local communities, but still offer a genuine national conversation. A civic forum such as this, funded by the federal government but administered independently (say, again, by an experienced non-profit group such as the League of Women Voters), would take some of the organizational and financial responsibility for our electoral debates off the television media and give them an incentive to sponsor free time for candidates. Eventually it could support international dialogues linking NGOs and foundations in several nations in a single conversation.

A national civic forum has many attractive features for civil society. It facilitates horizontal conversation among citizens rather than the more usual vertical conversation typical of communication between citizens and elites. It offers ongoing deliberation rather than a single event (such as a debate between Presidential election candidates) and utilizes both traditional (television) and new (satellite and interactive) media. This kind of direct interaction among citizens is already the preferred mode of communication for many civil-society organizations such as American Health Decisions (a national health-education organization with multiple state sites), the Industrial Areas Foundation (founded decades ago by the progressive Saul Alinsky, a community-organization movement that teaches ordinary women and men from every walk of life to educate and empower themselves politically), the National Issues forums of the Kettering Foundation (which has organized hundreds of citizen groups around the country to reach consensual positions on fundamental policy issues), the Study Circles Movement (based on the Swedish practice of bringing together small groups of neighbors to discuss anything from fly-fishing to abortion policy, and supported in an active civic form today by the Topsfield Foundation), policy juries (that convene small groups of citizens who consider and deliver recommendations on tough policy questions), and so-called deliberative video town meetings (a project of Professor James Fishkin of the University of Texas, who, taking the idea of Theodore Becker and others, has pioneered prime-time televised gatherings of citizens who over several days discuss issues with experts and politicians and modify their opinions and prejudices as a result). These and other practical, ongoing experiments among citizens, who—without thinking of themselves as constituting a government or public authority—come together to express their common aspirations as well as their conflicting interests, suggest that a national civic forum is not just pie in the sky but would offer real nourishment for hungry citizens. The advantage it has over many local experiments already under way is that it extends the compass of interest and the membership of the participants by utilizing computer and Internet technology and thereby overcomes some of their special-interest parochialism.

The Committees of Correspondence created during the Revolutionary War by citizens who felt unrepresented were a remarkable example of civil-society politics. Men gathered together informally in these committees, which, being neither governmental nor private, were the first independent civic entities in a nation experimenting with autonomy, and in time they produced trained citizens who had had a common experience of institution-building. A little more than a century later, populists and progressives sent speakers and facilitators to "ride the circuit," bringing together communities of dispersed rural people in gatherings where the visitor was educator, political mobilizer, and conversation facilitator. Throughout the nineteenth century, New England town meetings and rural groups like the Grange gave America's new citizens forums that brought communities together around larger regional issues, tying them to people elsewhere with shared aspirations yet different experiences (urban workers and rural tenant farmers, for example). But by the twentieth century, America's pell-mell growth had rendered these forms of association less feasible—until now, with the advent of the new technologies. We have yet to reckon with the consequences of low-frequency broadcasts, public-access cable channels, videoconference up-and down-links, and private-sector satellite transmission, let alone with the possibilities of digitalized broadcasting, fiber optics, and a worldwide communications net. Panglossians exult, but technology has usually mirrored rather than transformed the society that creates it. Europe's emerging civic society in the Renaissance used gunpowder to enhance burgeoning democratization, but its discoverers in China used it to secure the hold of tyranny. The new telecommunications technologies certainly change the boundaries of our lives, but whether this will help or hurt democracy and civil society is not yet clear.

"Local" loses much of its limiting force with technologies in which global *is* local, for example; but whether this merely internationalizes commerce and consumerism or opens doors to international civic cooperation depends on factors other than the technology. An American civic forum (or French or Swiss or European or sub-Saharan African forum) is technically feasible, but its success will depend on political and cultural rather than technological factors. A national civic forum would push the technology in a democratic direction. As happens with New England's Representative Town Meetings in communities too large to convene the entire citizenry (where delegates are chosen to meet on behalf of the entire town population), civic-forum meetings might develop cross-sectional national representation with a sampling of "institutional" citizens from foundations, schools, voluntary associations, civic groups, and social movements. These delegates (and the local assemblies hooked up by satellite) might even be chosen by lot, as happened in many ancient Greek city-states. Sortition (the lottery) assumes civic competence on the part of every player in civil society, and in doing so helps to forge that competence. It assumes that any group of players drawn from civil society's constituents is as likely as any other group to be able to work for common goods and civic interests.

Some may object that a civic forum is redundant in a democratically governed nation where legislatures and representative assemblies already give civil society ear and voice. Surely democratic government itself offers citizens opportunities for public voice and social organization. In a well-ordered polity, it might actually do this; according to democratic theory, it is certainly supposed to. But America's political house is in a state of disorder, and so are many other nations' houses. Citizens are deeply suspicious of the professional political classes, cynical about government and, hence, about democracy itself. Here again the Committees of Correspondence seem apt models, for they were fostered by British subjects with quasi-colonial representative institutions of their own which, however, they did not feel belonged to them. They were meant to be a novel means of interaction—political but at the same time (because the colonial "government" was the enemy) extra-governmental. The aim in a modern democracy is not, of course, to create an alternative or parallel government or even an alternative legislative forum, but to help citizens and their many voluntary civic institutions speak in a common voice both to the private sector and to the government. Rather than displacing government or market institutions, a national civic forum facilitated by the new technologies could reinvigorate them and prepare the way for the relegitimation of strong democratic government, allowing citizens to rediscover their civic competence.

The fact that the United States is so vast and decentralized, geographically and ethnographically if not economically, means that a civic forum is both more necessary and more difficult to create than it might be for a smaller nation (although Europe as an emerging transnational entity faces the same challenges). Necessary, because when economic and political power are concentrated and monopoly is the rule, democratic power must also be concentrated effectively to offer monopoly a countervailing force; harder because participation is easiest locally and hardest nationally. Participation is parochial, power cosmopolitan: how does one unite the two? Can technology facilitate perhaps a forum of civic interaction that will bridge space and unite a nation's, even a whole continent's, hyper-diversified fragments?

It was the vast scale and heterogeneity of modern mass societies that created the imperative for representative government in the first place; and it was representative government that, following the iron law of oligarchy, in time distanced citizens from their delegates and compromised its own legitimacy. The solution to the problem of mass society became, in time, the problem. Revitalizing a strong democratic civil society can circumvent the abuses of representation while at the same time refurbishing its legitimacy. A credible public voice gives citizens an alternative mode of expression and weans them from dependency on public-opinion polls and the media, permitting the better angels of their nature (usually muzzled in a privatized, cynical society) to speak freely, and re-legitimizing democratic institutions that depend on their participation. Technology, properly used, can help give expression to this credible public voice.

Production in the Global Economy

Like everything else in a privatizing society dominated by commerce, technology's possibilities are circumscribed by its ownership. Ironically, at the very moment in the history of the West when the transformation of a traditional durable-goods industrial society into a post-industrial information society has given a handful of vertically integrated media, entertainment, and information conglomerates global influence over our thoughts, tastes, feelings, and ideas— hence our lives—we have voluntarily abjured our democratic sovereign power to control them. Unlike the nineteenth-century trusts in oil, steel, and railroads to which they are often compared, the new telecommunications monoliths— Disney/ABC, Time-Warner/CNN, the News Corporation/Fox, Bertelsman, Viacom/ Paramount, and Microsoft—monopolize not natural resources and durable goods, muscles of an industrial society's growing body, but pictures, information, and ideas, the sinews of post-industrial society's soul. Can these private corporations be made publicly responsible for the outcome they produce?

By law, corporations are of course themselves creatures and beneficiaries of the states they now assail: the limited-liability corporation and the trade policies under which it operates are all products of government: the "private" corporation is, in fact, public, and at best a forgetful child of its true parents, at worst an ingrate and parricide. As Hobbes made clear enough in his great book on sovereign power, *Leviathan*, in the state of nature there is neither "mine" nor "thine," neither private property nor contractual association, only the war of all against all, and the life of man nasty, brutish, and short.

To attack what one derogates as the "social collectivism" of democratic institutions is a very convenient tactic for corporations celebrating a private-market collectivism all their own. Their kind of privatizing "individualism," which defines so much of our ideological politics today, disempowers American citizens just when they most need their commonalty to contain the corporate entities trying to control their lives. We are thankfully rid of the political totalitarianism of communist statism, but we seem largely oblivious to the subtler forms of economic totalism for which "free" markets are responsible.

Among the fundamental principles that California Governor Pete Wilson enunciated during his unsuccessful 1996 Presidential campaign was one averring that "individuals should be responsible and accountable for their actions" and that "we should value family as the foundation of our society." Responsibility has become the leading principle of the new minimal-government politics shared by Tories and Labor, Republicans and Democrats—a politics that asks high-school community-service volunteers, welfare mothers, and disemployed workers to shoulder the burdens of the economy and the community, and to stop expecting government to remedy every social ill. It is time to make the same demand of corporations and businesses. Responsibility and power go hand in hand: nothing has greater power today than a multinational corporation; no group has been left with less responsibility. Citizens and politicians worry about ethics, character, and family values in a modern, secular world. The firms whose products, marketing strategies, and commercialism are often deeply anti-family (in consequence if not intent) have a responsibility. Jobs are being exported, communities decimated, health, safety, and environmental standards protected by American or German or French law regularly circumvented in foreign markets. The firms which downsize, sell off, or close down subsidiaries they have taken over, or which flee abroad to profit from the absence of public regulation in other nations have a responsibility. As the boundaries separating information and entertainment are deliberately blurred, films and music deliberately infused with violence and misogyny, colleges and classrooms deliberately commercialized, the companies that have done these things and are the financial beneficiaries have a responsibility.

Business people sometimes try to claim that they are subservient to consumers and merely give people what they want. They protest that the market is the perfect instrument of liberty since it empowers individual consumers to determine what is produced and how it is priced simply by the power of their choices. So it is the consumers who are responsible! But this claim is little more than a useful fiction. The ancient capitalist economy, in which products were manufactured and sold to meet the demands of consumers who made their independently forged needs known through the marketplace, has long since disappeared. In its place is a post-industrial economy in which needs themselves are manufactured to meet the supply of producers who make their products "necessary" through promotion, "spin," packaging, advertising, and "scientific" marketing. The market today has reversed the polarities of demand and supply, so that producers strive to create a market for products that are not necessarily related to essential human needs at all. The corporations that do this have a serious responsibility for the kinds of need they create, the kinds of life-style they encourage, and the kinds of innovation they press.

There was a time in America's history when greater civic demands were placed on business. Throughout the nineteenth century, it was assumed that free enterprise was a key agent of citizenship-building and moral character. At its outset, Jefferson had lauded the democracy of yeoman farmers and free artisans; at its end, moralists still lauded the democracy of shopkeepers and entrepreneurial small businessmen. No wonder observers worried that the great trusts and cartels of the Gilded Age, and later the catalogue and chain stores like Sears and Montgomery Ward, were not only existential obstacles to fair trade but a clear and present danger to civic life as well—"contrary to the whole genius of the American people and American Government, which is local self-control of affairs," wrote Montaville Flowers in his *America Chained*.[3] Flowers worried that the new conglomerates would reduce workers from the "status of independence to that of hirelings under humiliating regulations, thus . . . lowering the spirit of communities and the nation."

The political philosopher Michael Sandel has convincingly demonstrated that, throughout the 1920s and 1930s, only part of the reaction to trusts and chains was really about monopoly. He cites Justice Louis Brandeis's dissent in *Liggett Company v. Lee* (1933), which overthrew Florida's tax on chain stores:

Florida's "purpose may have been a broader and deeper one [than revenues]. They may have believed that the chain store, by furthering the concentration of wealth and of power and by promoting absentee ownership, is thwarting American ideals; that it is making impossible equality of opportunity; that it is converting independent tradesmen into clerks; and that it is sapping the resources, the vigor and the hope of the smaller cities and towns."[4]

In the same spirit, the clergyman Henry A. Stimson insisted that business was "a school of character second only to church."[5] What these moralists understood was that in a society in which business influences so many aspects of private and public life it bears a shared responsibility for the ethical and civic atmosphere. Following their logic, it seems apparent that Wal-Mart is no less a threat to turn the United States into that nation of "hirelings and clerks" alluded to by Brandeis and Sandel than was Sears, Roebuck. By the same token, Disney's entertainment and information services present an even greater risk of corruption by materialism, greediness, and passivity than the Standard Oil or Ford Motor Company. What Sandel calls "the political economy of citizenship" that "from Jefferson to the Knights of Labor" had "sought to form the moral and civic character" of the nation through the cultivation of "producers—as farmers, or artisans, or small businessmen and entrepreneurs"—is in danger of vanishing and, with it, the notion that corporations have a civic responsibility.

Justice Brandeis was prescient. He thought the new production-consumption mentality, severed from civic concerns, would breed a new kind of noncitizen: "Thoughtless or weak, he yields to the temptation of trifling immediate gain, and, selling his birthright for a mess of pottage, becomes himself an instrument of monopoly."[6] Trifling immediate gain and a mess of "pottage" have now become our era's high moral ambitions.

The new moralists who applaud the containment of government like to make vigorous civic demands on pregnant children and unemployed immigrants; they might more appropriately make them on Time-Warner and Microsoft. We rightly ask whether schools adequately provide for the moral education of children. We also have the right to ask whether Disneyland and MTV and the mall do the same.

What was true for shopkeepers and entrepreneurs surely holds for the multinationals. If in Brandeis's time absentee ownership and financier control presented a "grave danger to democracy,"[7] do not fax-paper merger-and-acquisition deals and international currency markets still more gravely endanger democracy today? Neither Brandeis nor his later advocates like Hubert Humphrey were anti-capitalist or anti-business. Rather, their point was and is to give business a good dose of genuine competition and consumers a fair playing field.[8]

The current crop of progressives are critical of business, but often cast their criticism in the language of capitalist efficiency. As Sandel is quick to notice, contemporary consumer affair critics like Ralph Nader and Mark Green appeal not to virtue but to consumer interests and "efficient" production and distribution. This inverts the progressive agenda, and ironically, turns the villains with whom the century started into the heroes with whom it is preparing to conclude:

> For progressives of old, the chains had been the villains, cut-throat competitors whose discounts would destroy the small, independent druggists and grocers and small businessmen on whom democracy depended. For modern progressives, the discounters have become the heroes, whose low prices enabled consumers to avoid paying the Bloomingdale's price.[9]

Civic responsibility, being a partnership between government, civil society, and the private market, necessarily depends on the active collaboration of political leaders, citizens, and business people. Executives have for too long suffered a kind of corporate schizophrenia in which they hived off and buried their civic identities—the small voices within that screamed "I cannot do that to my spouse, my children, my neighbors, my world!" even as their corporate hands signed orders doing exactly "that" to everyone, including their loved ones. Unless they want to live divided lives, they must accommodate their business to their human side.

It is not really so hard. The logic of the social contract enacts a set of mutual obligations among the parties who establish and benefit from democratic government. As citizens, whether of France, Germany, Russia or Untied States, we have already convenanted to establish a free democratic government, although we seem to have forgotten its origin in our sovereign contract. But the wall between public and private sectors has insulated corporations and their personnel from civic responsibility and allowed this corporate schizophrenia to insulate their women and men, whether employers or employees, from their obligations as citizens. As Donella Meadows has observed, "every day decent people clear-cut forests, fish the oceans bare, spray toxins, bribe politicians, overcharge the government, take risks with the health of their workers or neighbors or customers, cheapen their products, pay people less than a living wage for a day's work, and fire their friends."[10] It is not, she adds, that businessmen "sit around plotting how to poison rivers or subvert democracy . . . (or) conspire to pollute"; it is just that as executives they seem unable to act as citizens. Quite the contrary: the very citizens who otherwise might see government as an ally have as corporate managers encouraged and participated in dismantling the strong state society and the democratic regulatory institutions that enforced civic standards on them. This gives them self-imposed responsibilities they might have avoided in a strong state society (and, in a well-ordered society, *should* have avoided). In an ideal world I would prefer to have democratic government enforce public standards and leave corporations to the business of productivity and profit-taking; in the world we actually live in, the predicate for reestablishing a robust civil society is a new civic compact that specifically obligates corporations. Here is a template:

A Corporate Civic Compact for Private Sector Citizens

Preamble. Recognizing that democratic government is an instrument of a free society and that its elected officers and representatives are but accountable trustees of those who elect them; and

that the primary responsibility for the civic health both of government and society thus belongs to the citizens and associations that constitute civil society and the private sector; and

that the productive economy requires a free-market private sector to flourish, while civil association requires a free civil-society sector to flourish; and

that civil society occupies a space between the governmental and private sectors that can be destroyed by bloat and aggressive expansion from either side; therefore,

We the free citizens of civil society and the corporate managers, producers, shareholders, and workers of the private sector, integrating our economic and civic identities and acknowledging our primary responsibility for democracy, do therefore freely obligate ourselves to the following principles:

1. We will respect the independence and noncommercial character of civil society and actively work to prevent the privatization or commercialization of its spaces—whether those spaces are educational (no advertising in or commercial exploitation of the classroom), religious (no commercialization of religious holidays), public broadcast (no charge for civic and political use of public airwaves), or environmental (protection of parks, waterways, and outer space* from advertising and commercialization).

2. We will support the civic diversification of public space and support the redevelopment of what have become exclusively commercial spaces such as malls and theme parks back into true public spaces, creating a balanced social environment in which production and consumption are complemented by the cultural, religious, educational, philanthropic, and political-social activities of civil society.

3. We will work to guarantee full public and equal access by every part of civil society to the media, traditional and innovative, broadcast and cable, passive and interactive, on which information, culture, democratic discussion, and productive capacity depend; and we will support information equality and combat a gap between the information-rich and the information-poor that destroys the conditions of political and civic equality on which democracy depends.

---

*The technology is available to put electronic billboards on satellites or Mickey Mouse ears on the moon.

4. We will pay special attention to diversity and independence in the information and entertainment sectors where creativity, spontaneity, and innovation, which are indispensable to a free society, are cultivated and where the heterogeneity of information and debate that is the chief object of the Bill of Rights is secured.

5. We will treat employment not only as a function of economic efficiency and the profitability of production but as a fundamental social commitment, for work, whether commercial or civic, private or public, is the measure of human dignity and civic status, and social stability and labor morale depend on private, commercial, or civic work for all.

6. We will treat fair compensation and reasonable pension plans as rights that are indispensable to workers' dignity and status as citizens as well as their efficiency as producers and their power as consumers.

7. We will make a safe workplace and a safe environment the necessary conditions of doing business in a responsible manner that honors our owners, managers, and producers in their capacity as members of civil society.

8. We will encourage worker participation and worker shareholding through employee stock-ownership plans, codetermination, worker participation in management, and other forms of active worker engagement.

9. We will establish standards for safety, health, working hours, pension plans, and child-labor regulations that will be universally applicable, whether our facilities are located within or outside our company's headquarter nation; and we will pressure host foreign governments to accept and enforce these standards on all producers as a condition of our doing business in the host country.

10. We will establish standards for compensation that, while they may vary from country to country, offer a reasonable living wage by the measures of the host country; and we will pressure host governments to accept and enforce such standards on all producers as a condition of our doing business in the host country.

11. We will establish standards for compensation that link the salaries of all personnel to productivity, proportionally relate increases in executive salaries to those in workers' wages, and maintain a differential ratio of lowest and highest salaries, whether stockboy or CEO, of no more than twenty to one (that's $20,000 for the clerk, $400,000 for the executive).

12. We will nourish diversity and competition and oppose monopolies, trusts, and cartels, not only because they restrict fair trade and capitalist innovation, but because they diminish the independence, liberty, and dignity of those who work for and manage them in ways destructive to civic virtue and democratic civic culture.

13. We will not take over or merge with other firms unless we intend to maintain their work forces; we will not use the sell-off or close-down of

subsidiary companies to finance the takeover of parent companies; we will not engage in mergers and acquisitions whose only product is paper profits for buyers or sellers and the lawyers, accountants, and brokers who service them.

14. We will treat the placement of our facilities and plant in particular venues as a primary social and civic commitment and will not operate or uproot them without considering the social consequences for our employees and their communities, and without adequate compensation.

15. We will treat children and their education as special priorities of a free society, and will protect them from exploitation, from advertising that might distort their capacity for critical inquiry, and from products injurious to their health or polluting to their minds.

16. We will commit the resources necessary to execute the above obligations and treat them as a necessary cost of doing business in a democratic society, where executives and workers are citizens first and economic beings afterward.

17. We will spread the cost of this commitment of resources equally among all those who are social beneficiaries of social expenditures, including executives (modestly reduced salaries), shareholders (modestly reduced profits), and customers (modestly higher prices).

18. We will encourage personnel at all levels to overcome the civic schizophrenia that forces us to regard ourselves as citizens in our social role but as corporate producers and managers in our economic role, and instead acknowledge that our civic identity is primary and must play a primary role in our economic decision-making.

I believe a commitment to this corporate civic compact will benefit the private sector no less than civil society. Rapacious capitalism that brutalizes workers and rides roughshod over the common goods of civil society in the long run only befouls its own nest. A free market undisciplined by civic concerns destroys citizens in the short term but also destroys consumers in the long term. Henry Ford understood well enough that a living wage and a fully employed public were conditions on which the selling of his cars depended. If his workers couldn't buy his cars, to whom would he sell them? If "the end of work," as Jeremy Rifkin has warned in his book of the same title, is an unavoidable economic consequence of post-industrial capitalism, then capitalism will have to look to something other than pure economics for a guarantee of employment. Family values and civic virtue are products of socialization, which means that the behemoths ever more responsible for socialization will have to consider the moral and civic effects of their mind-bending software and their durable products, and look to the social consequences of their economic and fiscal policies. If they wish to indulge their self-serving propensity to discipline and curtail government in the name of free markets, free-market multinationals will have to discipline themselves from within—or spin off into a self-destructive anarchy of cartelism, gargantuanism, privatism, and disemployment that will in effect knock the pegs out from under them as efficient economic organizations. They have conspired in delegitimizing those who once did their civic work for them, and in any case now operate in an international arena where there are no countervailing governmental institutions, so they now have to shoulder the burden themselves. Capitalism needs democracy and civility, which means it needs to democratize its practices and civilize its executives. Where once we looked appropriately to the sovereign polity to bring justice and comity to an otherwise anarchic economic realm, we must now also look to the newly sovereign corporations. Either they must give us back our government and, while pursuing profits, accommodate governmental encroachments and regulation in the name of the public weal, or they themselves will have to become more civic-minded and democratic, no matter what the cost to their profits. Anything less means the end of democracy.

Consumption in the Global Economy

We can demand from corporations greater civic responsibility, but we do not have to await a new corporate spirit in order to counter the current irresponsibility. We can do plenty of things on the consumer side to nurture greater corporate virtue, using a civil-society strategy to form "civic consumers cooperatives" aimed at changing corporate behavior.

Once upon a time, the goods Americans purchased were unknown entities, safe or unsafe, clean or polluted—there was no way for us to know. In time, the safety of goods was assured by government-imposed standards. But the ideology that made regulation of this kind politically viable is no longer popular and the globalization of markets, which has permitted corporations to flee the control of sovereign national governments and set up production facilities in countries where reasonable standards may not exist, has created problems for consumers and for American workers—whose high wages in part reflect the high standards of American-produced goods.

A civil-society approach to solving this problem would enhance corporate responsibility by using the demand side, the consumer side, to modify corporate behavior. This strategy borrows from traditional voluntarist tactics of the kind used in, say, the "union label" approach, or the *Good Housekeeping* "Seal of Approval," or the Underwriters' Laboratory (U.L.) label for safely wired electrical products, or the Consumers' Union's testing and branding of goods for safety, quality, and plausible pricing. The same approach has been used more recently in the international domain by the Rugmark program, originating in Germany (a large importer of rugs), which identifies rugs that are made without child labor, and the Dolphin Safe Tuna program, which induces tuna fishermen to avoid the netting practices that kill dolphins. After a great deal of adverse publicity (Kathy Lee Gifford with her Wal-Mart line and Michael Jordan with his Air Jordan shoes for Nike were both assailed for representing companies that violated American standards), the clothing industry is also moving in this direction with its Apparel Industry Partnership. These positive strategies are an affirmative version of another, better known but less effective one—the boycott. Boycotts, however, have a punitive aspect and can be offset by counterboycotts: a company like Disney can as easily be boycotted by gays for honoring Baptist anti-gay sentiments as by Baptists for pro-gay employment benefit practices. Trade boycotts also risk being declared illegal internationally where free trade agreements reign. (The World Trade Organization had declared consumer boycotts incompatible with membership!)

The idea of a civic consumer coalition is intended not to punish "bad" producers but to reward "good" ones. To work, programs like Rugmark and the Apparel Industry Partnership need strong public support. The premise is that consumers, while primarily concerned with variety, quality, ease of purchase, and (above all) price of goods, also care enough about civic and social values to include them as part of their calculation about which goods (or which brand of goods) to buy. A significant proportion of consumers prefer to buy goods and brands that are produced without child labor, unfair employment practices, or indecent wages (as measured in-country), and without endangering workplace safety or the environment—especially when the goods are made in countries where American or European standards do not prevail by corporations that went to those countries precisely to increase profits and lower costs. We might say that civilized (civil) consumers want good-quality products at a good price which are also *child-labor safe, fair-wage safe, workplace safe, and environmentally safe.*

Firms that produce such goods and can verify that they do so with trustworthy (external) inspection and certification*—a "Safe" label, say, certifying the four safe categories—would have a clear marketplace advantage, even if their prices were marginally higher. Indeed, the added volume of sales might enable them to keep prices down. This demand-side market approach, it should be emphasized once again, does not punish corporations that disregard the civic-consumer rules, but it does benefit the civic-minded corporations that do play by the rules.

Once upon a time, a label announcing "Made in America" or "union made" gave products a trade advantage. Today, a CCC (Civic Consumers Coalition) SAFE label would enable consumers to offer producers powerful economic incentives voluntarily to meet "American" safety standards in these four domains,

---

*The Belgrade Manual of Rules of the International Law Association stipulates all human-rights inspections must be made by independent experts, not by those being inspected.

no matter where their facilities are located. Such a label, incorporating Rugmark and the "No Sweat" benchmarks, would provide a universal standard recognized around the world. The burden would be shifted from negative control via regulation of production to positive control via consumer oversight. At the same time, firms that stayed at home and met the already high government and state standards that prevail in the United States and Europe would find their higher-priced goods and higher production costs competitive after all, since the foreign-made goods would eventually bear some of the same costs. Companies would have less incentive to leave home in the first place, and those that did would no longer be rewarded for recklessness and irresponsibility.

A civic consumer cooperative would also help consumers to formulate their economic decisions as civic decisions, with the social consequences now calculated as part of a product's cost. How much would civic consumers pay for the label? The market itself would answer the question, though surveys suggest declining consumer cooperation when prices rise more than five or ten percent. Traditionally, the civic purpose of public decision-making and the commercial function of private decision-making were separated, and properly so, with government carrying the main burden. As early as 1930, Congress passed a law prohibiting the import of goods manufactured with the participation of forced or indentured labor (convict labor, for example), and a bill is currently pending that would extend that prohibition to goods made with child labor, a bill which if passed would represent "an incredible breakthrough" in curbing the abuse of children around the world, as one journalist has put it."[11] Whether or not this bill becomes law (and there are inevitable questions about its compatibility with the World Trade Organization's insistence that governments remain laissez-faire with respect to such issues), in this era of political skepticism and animus against regulations, the responsibilities once shouldered by government must be taken on by producers and consumers. And since producers are not likely to do their part without prompting from consumers, consumers must learn to think like citizens, bringing their private choices into line with their public responsibilities. A Civic Consumers Coalition with the means to influence producers becomes a new and powerful tool of the public good, another way to take civil society seriously.

As I have noted, consumer pressure, celebrity embarrassment, and pressure from the political side have already offered an immediate test of the idea of a civic consumers cooperative in one specific sector: the apparel industry. The Workplace Code of Conduct agreed to in the spring of 1997 by a Presidential task force (jawboned into being by President Clinton under the inviting title Apparel Industry Partnership and including not only Liz Claiborne and Nike but other major manufacturers such as Reebok and Nicole Miller) prohibits signatories to the code from using forced labor and young children, and requires companies and their contractors to pay the minimum wage as stipulated by local law, and to abide by other safe workplace standards.[12] The signatories' "No Sweat" logos on their labels will alert consumers to the salutary conditions under which their products were manufactured. In this case, we are actually on the verge of doing something effective to control a supposedly uncontrollable international market.

Civic Education and Community Service

The fostering of national and community service programs has been one of the Clinton Administration's great bipartisan success stories, yet it has come under fire from the congressional Republicans and seems forever at risk. Still, the Administration has been firm in treating service as a crucial attribute of citizenship and an activity of civil society rather than as a "government program," and this could go a long way to securing its future in America. After all, what is more civic than community service? But because the Clinton program was seen in some quarters as either an attempt to mandate voluntarism (it was not) or a device to find a new basis for a school-loan program (which it was only secondarily), it became a target of partisan wrangling. Congress tends to focus on "outcomes" and effectiveness (how many meals dispersed to homeless people? how many hours spent tutoring? how many senior shut-ins assisted?), and while this may be politically useful, it diverts attention from the primary goal: to teach social responsibility and citizenship to those doing the service. Underlining the learning dimension, and gaining a better sense of how these service programs promote civic education, can lower the "outcome" expectations and earn more credit for the good public work the programs actually do—to and for volunteers and the communities they serve—and not just in the near term.

An important first step has been taken by the Partnering Initiative on Education and Civil Society, a ten-year program launched by the Department of Education, the National Association of Education, and important public and private education groups.[13] By putting civic education on a par with other basic school skills, this initiative repositions education as critical for citizenship. A number of states, most notably Maryland, under the leadership of Lieutenant Governor Kathleen Kennedy Townsend (who was an advocate of school-based service long before her election), have introduced mandatory high-school community-service programs that are closely linked to classroom learning.[14] Putting service in the context of civil society and treating it as a concomitant of education makes it the first step toward lifelong citizenship, not just a temporary job that buys the government some social benefits in return for a wage measured in scholarship dollars.

Civil society depends on members serving what Alexis de Toqueville aptly called the arduous apprenticeship of liberty. We must learn to discuss public schooling, pedagogical standards, and federal money for education in terms of this crucial civic dimension. One of the most important original justifications for public and common schools was democracy's need for its young people to be educated, cognitively and behaviorally, as competent citizens. We do more nowadays to educate immigrants as citizens than we do to teach our own native-born Americans.

The federal government, through the Department of Education, can model civic curricula and service learning programs without spending large sums of money. The Department of Education might, indeed, strengthen its own case by focusing on this civic dimension, where its function as a national standard-setter is paramount. "Standards" might be more relevant if they included civic competence along with literacy and numeracy. By the same token, the volunteer effort on behalf of America's children, launched by General Colin Powell at the Presidents' Summit on America's Future in 1997, might better sustain civic and private momentum if it were more closely tied to the education of volunteers as well as to the education of those whom volunteers, through their service, educate in turn.

The partnership of government and civil society in fostering community service makes particular sense today, given the widespread popularity of education-based service programs in America's high schools and colleges. Community service was once an isolated Saturday afternoon extracurricular activity, but now it is recognized as a crucial component of a responsible academic curriculum that accepts schools as parts of their communities and that treats students as prospective citizens whose education must include civic competence. In recent years, to take just one example, the Ford Foundation has worked closely with the United Negro College Fund to nurture the development of education-based service learning programs in a dozen or more historically black institutions. Modest philanthropic dollars and robust outside guidance have allowed the colleges to build good programs without becoming dependent on external resources. A modest government program on this model, supporting a partnership with community organizations, colleges, and the non-profit sector, could accomplish a great deal without breeding dependency or overburdening taxpayers.

The European Commission has done its own experimentation with a European volunteer service program, presumably in the hope that service on this scale might help foster a more genuine sense of European citizenship.

Art and Humanities in a Civil Society

The relationship of art and the humanities to a free democratic society, to its diversity and pluralism, its manifold liberties, its openness and flexibility is complex and often problematical. The arts can flourish in democracy, but it is also true that they have often developed with remarkable vibrancy in autocratic societies as well as in cultures of dissent or rebellion. Still, democracy needs the arts and the humanities, since they constitute the cultural infrastructure of civil society. Yet the democratic impulse has sometimes been at odds with art and been threatened by avant-garde or anti-majoritarian or aristocratic cultures.

So democracy perhaps needs the arts more than the arts need democracy—although the symbiosis between the two is obvious and vital in a functioning free society. For a free society affirms its liberty and democratic vitality in civil society, and the arts and humanities invest that civil society with its creativity, its diversity and liberating spontaneity. What complicates the relationship is the market, which offers space to art and culture that insulates them from governmental direction and censorship. Yet because market space is also commercial space, commerce and exchange can imperil the autonomy of the arts.

Art and culture are, to be sure, resilient. Without subsidy, even without democracy, and under the conformist pressures of political autocracy or majoritarian mass opinion, the arts have survived. They are rooted in indelible human genius and an irrepressible need for authentic self-expression and communication, which surface under—indeed, sometimes are catalyzed by—the most repressive imaginable conditions, including the Gulag and the extermination camp. They are as difficult to root out and destroy as the human spirit itself. We were never so free, said Jean Paul Sartre, as during the Nazi Occupation.

But this durability of art is not an adequate reason to avoid asking the hard questions about arts policy in a democracy. After all, democracy and the arts share common roots in their common relationship to a robust civil society. As John Dewey noted, democracy is as much a way of life as a form of government, and its success depends on the existence of a vigorous civil society.

The arts are civil society's driving engine, the key to its creativity, its diversity, its imagination, and hence its spontaneity and liberty. As democracy depends on civil society for its liberal spirit, so civil society depends on the arts; thus democracy needs the arts' commitment to free creativity, liberal diversity, and unfettered imagination. A government that supports the arts is not engaging in philanthropic activity but assuring the conditions of its own flourishing. This is perhaps the most important single argument in favor of a democratic government caring about and nurturing the arts: not because the arts need it, but because democracy needs the arts. Europe has learned this lesson.

Under normal circumstances, the arts can survive without democratic support—indeed, without a democratic constitution—however much a democratic way of life needs their creativity and critical imagination, however much it is enhanced by a robust civic infrastructure nourished by art. Our circumstances today in the United States are not entirely normal, however. Under the adverse conditions of pervasive mass commerce, and given our growing ambivalence about diversity and pluralism, the arts may both be at risk and be necessary in unprecedented ways. Consequently, there are new arguments to make in favor of a modest government commitment to arts education, and for incentives and

subsidies for creation and performance in the overweening commercial environment, and our ever more diversified and (some fear) fragmented society.

Art today has more to fear from the uncoerced, largely invisible constraints
of commercialization than it does from pushy or censorious governments.
Although artists certainly have the "right" to isolate themselves from society
and pursue their muses free of interference, they may discover that by taking on
responsibilities for arts education and civic engagement they contribute to a climate from which they benefit. Artists as artists are responsible only to their art,
but artists are also citizens, and as citizens they have a particular responsibility:
in contributing to and nourishing an arts-supportive civil society, they serve both
democracy and themselves, both their fellow citizens and their art.

Advocates of laissez-faire privatizing, suspicious of government meddling
in the arts, may believe that they are supporting a merely private (and liberal)
domain. But when civil society is collapsed into the commercial market sector,
as has happened today, privatization means commercialization, and the arts are
subjected to the harsh interventionist dynamics of commerce. Neither high art
nor rebellious art nor even ordinary amateur art (community theater, for example) can thrive under such conditions. The market pushes toward a uniformity
of taste, a leveling of standards, and radical commodification. Yet "art products"
satisfy almost no one. Magazines trump books, newspapers trump magazines,
tabloids trump newspapers, television trumps tabloids, MTV trumps television—until not even popular culture in its full diversity can survive, let alone
anything else.

When the market for arts, "free" in theory, is in practice often monopolistic
in ownership and conformist in taste, not just high art and rebellious art but popular culture, too, needs the incentives and balancing support of government and
arts-council subsidy. "Public" television in America has offered a place on the
broadcast spectra where "other" tastes—some "high," some "popular," but in
any case not likely to flourish in a pure market environment—can educate, cultivate, and entertain audiences. Why should so modest a presence, for so modest a
cost, be seen as a harbinger of government-sponsored taste or a usurpation of an
otherwise quite nearly sovereign set of commercial market mechanisms and
commercially uniform values?

Ours is not only a democratic market society but also a pluralistic society
that has recently become so diversified and differentiated that historians have
begun to worry about the disintegration of our cultural fabric. (Arthur
Schlesinger, Jr., made this point in his *The Disuniting of Democracy*, for example.) In this regard, we must remember that the arts can simultaneously
express the particular identities of communities and groups (including those that
feel excluded from the dominant community) *and* capture universalities that
bring distinctive local communities together in a national whole. The Southern
novel did not fragment America: it helped to define an American perspective.
The Hudson River School of painters represented an emerging American taste in

the nineteenth century, just as New England transcendentalism helped to create and American philosophical perspective. Jewish culture in New York helps to tie the city together even as it gives special expression to a particular identity. In music and theater, American blacks have stamped our national culture with many of its best-known American themes. Jazz, tap, blues, and the broader popular music culture of which they are a part at once define America and define one special contribution of African-Americans to it. This power to give voice to, hence to empower and recognize, marginalized and minority cultures, and at the same moment to constitute them as an inclusive common culture from which none is excluded, is unique to the arts.

Imagination is the link to civil society that art and democracy share. When imagination flourishes in the arts, democracy benefits. When it flourishes in a democracy, the arts and the civil society the arts help to ground also benefit. Imagination is the key to diversity, to civic compassion, and to commonalty. It is the faculty by which we stretch ourselves to include others, expand the compass of our interests, and overcome the limits of our parochial selves. Only then do we become fit subjects to live in democratic communities. The democratic citizen needs critical imagination to ward off tyranny and defend liberty. The artist needs critical imagination to ward off convention and defend creation. Even where the arts defy convention, outrage taste, and flaunt democratic mores, democracy needs them. It is only a mature democracy that fully appreciates these links. Ironically, youthful democracies, which most need the arts to grow and mature, are least likely to have governments that support art. It has been a mark of America's maturity as a free society that it has become less fearful of the positive European model, and had sustained the arts without becoming either proprietary or censorious.

To be sure, art will not perish in the absence of active support and understanding from a democratic people and their government. Nor will democracy wilt and die in the absence of a robust arts policy and a vibrant arts community. But democracy will do better, and the arts will do better, when democratic citizens and their governments support them. Democracy has most to gain by cultivating and supporting artists and the arts. Though they remain stubborn, independent, cranky, rebellious, sometimes ungrateful, and always subversive, our artists cultivate and manifest the liberty that lies at the very core of democracy's liberal soul.

These six examples of practical approaches to reestablishing civil society (or, where it survives, reinvigorating it) argue for social realism, for a strong democratic vision of civil society in which citizens occupy an independent space between government and the private sector. They demonstrate that civil society is far from being an esoteric normative ideal or a remote subject of nostalgic memory or, worse yet, some social-science construct invented by scholars to let them play self-righteous scold to wayward citizens. On the contrary, it has vital political and civic importance in defining legislative and corporate strategies that can make society both more civil and more democratic. The theory of civil society has a potential practice that is realistic and pragmatic—and hence transpartisan but also progressive.

Yet the six areas portrayed here as ripe for legislative action and government/civil society partnerships do not address two troubling questions raised by the weakness of modern civil society: the growing incivility of our political discourse; and, in an ever more automated workplace, the continued hiving off of wage-earning work from every other kind of public work and activity (including leisure activity), which has left labor markets roiling and created such frustrating anomalies as a welfare strategy intent on evicting mothers from their deeply consequential "jobs" raising children and maintaining a home life alleged to be indispensable to family values and civic virtue, in the name of securing them inconsequential "real jobs" in a commercial sector whose long-term problem is an absence of meaningful employment. These two sets of challenges cannot be addressed by developing simple government/civil society partnerships. They pose basic dilemmas regarding the meaning of civility and the future of work in societies trying to mobilize their dormant civic realms and energize their citizen resources in what is a promising but daunting age of advances in telecommunications technology, downsizing of labor forces, and globalization of markets.

Notes

1. See Senator Dan Coats, "Can Congress Revive Civil Society?" *Policy Review,* Jan./Feb 1996.
2. See "Harnessing Technology for Development" (The World Bank, 1997).
3. Montaville Flowers, *America Chained* (1931).
4. Sandel, *Democracy's Discontent,* p. 229. It was not a stretch, Michael Sandel shows, to get from such concerns to anxiety about how catalogues from Sears, Roebuck and Montgomery Ward could destroy the independence of farmers. When Justice Hugo Black was still a senator, he condemned the "wild craze for efficiency in production, sales, and distribution [that] has swept over the land, increasing the number of the unemployed, building up a caste system, dangerous to any government. Chain groceries, chain dry-goods stores, chain clothing stores, here today and merged tomorrow, grow in size and power . . . The local man and merchant is passed and his community loses his contribution to local affairs as an independent thinker and executive." (Cited Boorstin, *The Americans,* pp. 111–12).
5. "The Small Business as a School of Manhood," in *Atlantic Monthly,* vol. 93, 1904.
6. Citation from Sandel, p. 74.
7. Brandeis, *Business: A Profession* (reprint, 1996), pp. 252–53.
8. Humphrey asked in 1952: "Do we want an America where the economic market place is filled with a few Frankensteins and giants? Or do we want an America where there are thousands upon thousands of small entrepreneurs, independent businessmen, and landlords who can stand on their own feet and talk back to their Government or to anyone else?" Senate Debate, 82nd Congress, 2nd session, July 1–2, 1952.
9. Sandel, pp. 94–95.
10. "The Global Citizen," *The Berkshire Eagle,* Aug. 14, 1995.
11. Steven Greenhouse, "Measure to Ban Import Items," *The New York Times,* Oct. 1, 1997.
12. The White House collaborated in this initiative in the spirit of its voluntary Model Business Principles, issued by the Department of Commerce in 1996, and aimed at "Provision of a safe and healthful workplace, fair employment practices, and responsible environmental protection." (Department of State Publication 10486, Washington, D.C., June 1997). This administrative jawboning is welcome but does not by itself constitute a sufficient consumer-side strategy. In his 1998 State of the Union Address, Clinton proposed a program to ban child labor globally.
13. See Peter Applebome, "Plan Adds Civil Education to the Basics of Schooling," *The New York Times,* Monday, April 24, B8.
14. For details, see Richard M. Battistoni, *Experiencing Citizenship: Concepts and Models for Service Learning in Political Science* (1997), and my *An Aristrocracy of Everyone* (1994)

Reading 6

SELECTIONS FROM:

HUNGRY GHOSTS: MAO'S SECRET FAMINE

Jasper Becker

False Science, False Promises

'Practical success in agriculture is the ultimate criterion of truth.'

Stalin

'Seeing all men behaving like drunkards, how can I alone remain sober?'

Tang dynasty poem

To launch the Great Leap Forward, Mao whipped up a fever of expectation all over China that amounted to mass hysteria. Mao the infallible, the 'great leader', the 'brilliant Marxist,' the outstanding thinker and genius, promised that he would create a heaven on earth. Even in the 1940s, the Party had encouraged a personality cult around Mao but now this reached new and grotesque heights: Mao was an infallible semi-divine being. The nation's poets, writers, journalists and scientists, and the entire Communist Party, joined him in proclaiming that Utopia was at hand. Out of China, the land of famine, he would make China, the land of abundance. The Chinese would have so much food they would not know what to do with it, and people would lead a life of leisure, working only a few hours a day. Under his gifted leadership, China would enter the final stage of Communism, ahead of every other

Becker, Jasper. "False Science, False Promises: and "How Many Died?" *Hungry Ghosts*. New York: The Free Press, 1996. 58–83 and 266–274 + notes.

country on earth. If the Soviets said they would reach Communism in ten or twenty years, Mao said the Chinese could get there in a year or two. In fact, he promised that within a year food production would double or treble. Even Liu Shaoqi entered into the spirit of things by coining the slogan 'Hard work for a few years, happiness for a thousand.'[1]

The Great Leap Forward was preceded by a new campaign to raise Mao's personality cult to a level rivaling that of Stalin. From the end of 1957, his portraits, large and small, began appearing everywhere. Mao was compared to the sun and people declared that the era of Mao was already like heaven on earth. The *China Youth Daily* wrote that 'the dearest people in the world are our parents, yet they cannot be compared with Chairman Mao'. In songs, too, Mao was eulogized:

> Chairman Mao is infinitely kind,
> Ten thousand songs are not enough to praise him.
> With trees as pens, the sky as paper
> And an ocean of ink,
> Much would be left unwritten.[2]

Officials toured the country in 1958 describing what happiness and bliss were at hand. Tan Chen Lin, the Minister of Agriculture, painted a fantasy of peasants jumping in one leap from mud huts to skyscrapers, travelling not on donkeys but in aeroplanes.

> After all, what does Communism mean? . . . First, taking good food and not merely eating one's fill. At each meal one enjoys a meat diet, eating chicken, pork, fish or eggs . . . delicacies like monkey brains, swallows' nests, white fungi are served to each according to his needs . . .
>
> Second, clothing. Everything required is available. Clothing of various designs and styles, not a mass of black garments or a mass of blue outfits. After working hours, people will wear silk, satin and woollen suits . . . Foxes will multiply. When all people's communes raise foxes, there will be overcoats lined with fox furs . . .
>
> Third, housing. Housing is brought up to the standard of modern cities. What should be modernised? People's communes. Central heating is provided in the north and air-conditioning in the south. All will live in high buildings. Needless to say, there are electric lights, telephones, piped water, receiving sets and TV . . .
>
> Fourth, communications. Except for those who take part in races, all travellers and commuters will use transport. Air services are opened in all directions and every *xian* [county] has an airport . . . The time is not remote when each will have an aeroplane.
>
> Fifth, higher education for everyone and education is popularised. Communism means this: food, clothing, housing, transportation, cultural entertainment, science institutes, and physical culture. The sum total of these means Communism.[3]

This fantasy of American life was repeated even to peasants in faraway Tibet where people had never even seen an aeroplane or heard of a skyscraper: 'Everyone would live in one big family . . . We would have no worries about food, clothing and housing as everyone would wear the same clothes, eat the same food and live in the same houses . . . practically everything would be done by machines. In fact a time would come when our meals would be brought by machines right up to our mouths.'[4]

Such fairy-tales of overnight prosperity had been spread as early as 1956. One interviewee, a former journalist from Shaanxi, recalled going to a meeting of propaganda chiefs in 1956 and hearing Mao say that after three years of hard work, China would enjoy such prosperity that no one would need to work hard, or grow much, yet all would live in great luxury.

Writers, too, were busy painting pictures of this happiness. A character in Qin Chaoyang's *Village Sketches* described what would happen:

> Socialism means that our mountain district will be clothed with trees, that our peach blossom and pear blossom will cover the hillsides. Lumber mills will spring up in our district, and a railway too, and our trees will be sprayed by insecticide from aeroplanes, and we will have a big reservoir . . .
>
> Can we cover more and more of the mountains in the whole district with green trees, and make the streams clearer each year? Can we make the soil more fertile and make the faces of the people in every village glow with health? Can we make this mountain district of ours advance steadily on the path to socialism? If you ask me, I tell you it can be done! We have the heart, and we have the hands! It can be done!

Another novel, *Great Changes in a Mountain Village* by Zhou Libo, describes how the secretary of a village youth league envisages a future with all modern conveniences:

> It'll be soon, we won't have to wait for ten or even five years. Then we'll use some of the co-operative's accumulated funds to buy a lorry and when you women go to the theatre in the town, you can ride a lorry. With electric light, telephones, lorries and tractors we shall live more comfortably than they do in the city, because we have the beautiful landscape and the fresh air. There'll be flowers all the year round and wild fruit, more than we can eat: chinquapins [dwarf chestnuts] and chestnuts all over the hills.[5]

Naturally enough, peasants all over China began to ask when they would get to Communism and were told soon, very soon. Such fantastic optimism was based on Mao's fundamental ignorance of modern science. Although he had barely ventured outside China and had never studied Western science, Mao believed that science could make his dreams come true. While in the remote hills of Yanan, Mao and his colleagues carefully studied Moscow's propaganda works eulogizing the great achievements of such Soviet scientists as Pavlov, Lysenko and others, and became convinced that they were genuine.

Marxism claims, above all, to be a 'scientific' philosophy, one which applies the principles of science to politics and society. In like manner, Mao believed, modern science could transform the lives of those millions of ignorant peasants sunk in the mire of centuries of feudal superstition. There was no time to wait for them to become convinced, they would have to be forcibly dragged into the twentieth century. Everything connected with traditional beliefs was smashed in the Great Leap Forward (although many observers tend to assume that this happened later, in the Cultural Revolution) but, ironically, what Mao put in place of these beliefs was a pseudo-science, a fantasy that could not be validated by science, or stand up to rational examination, any more than could the peasant superstitions which the Party ridiculed.

Kang Sheng, Mao's loyal henchman, exemplified this casual approach to facts: 'We should be like Marx, entitled to talk nonsense,' he told everyone, and he toured the country lecturing about the need to add imagination to science. 'What is science?' he asked teachers in Zhengzhou, Henan province, in 1958. 'Science is simply acting daringly. There is nothing mysterious about it.' In Hefei, Anhui province, he continued on the same theme: 'There is nothing special about making nuclear reactors, cyclotrons or rockets. You shouldn't be frightened by these things: as long as you act daringly you will be able to succeed very quickly . . . You need to have spirit to feel superior to everyone, as if there was no one beside you . . . You shouldn't care about any First Machine Building Ministry, Second Machine Building Ministry, or Qinghua University, but just act recklessly and it will be all right.'[6]

In Shanghai that year he told cadres that 'if by national day next year, Shanghai's schools are able to launch a third-grade rocket to an altitude of 300 kilometres, they should get three marks . . . A third-grade rocket with a satellite should get five marks. This is very easy. At New Year, the [ordinary] Shanghainese fire rockets, so surely the schools can launch [real] rockets!'[7]

Trained scientists such as Professor Qian Xusen, the American nuclear physicist who returned to serve Mao and help build China's nuclear bomb, gave credibility to this optimism. He wrote articles and gave lectures to agricultural experts stating that it was quite realistic to increase crop yields ten or a hundred times. Qian said that one small plot of land could yield over a dozen tonnes of grain if just a small percentage of the energy from sunlight were properly utilized.[8]

Such carelessness with the truth shocked even visiting Soviet scientists like Mikhail Klochko. He discovered first-year chemistry students at a teacher training school rewriting their organic chemistry textbooks as they went along. For example, the students had decided they would only learn about copper, because they lived in Yunnan province which is rich in copper ore, so there was no need to bother with the other metals and elements.[9] This approach to science mirrored that in Soviet Russia when Stalin launched his first five-year plan. Then, the message of countless books and articles was the same: the impossible could only be achieved by ignoring the advice of timid experts, the 'bourgeois specialists' who lived in ivory towers, pedantically inching their way forward. True scientists were peasants filled with intuitive knowledge and led by Party members driven by revolutionary fervour—that was how miracles were achieved. The Soviet novel *Izbrannoe (The Select)* by I. Babel, for example, contains a discussion in which a noted oil expert is reprimanded by a young Party member who says: 'We do not doubt the knowledge or goodwill of the professor . . . but we reject the fetishism of figures which hold us in thrall . . . We reject the multiplication table as the basis for policy.'

In the Great Leap Forward, much the same happened in China, only in real life. The *People's Daily* reported how students in one faculty of science and mathematics showed their disdain for basic theory by putting decimal points in the wrong place while others deliberately made mistakes when calculating square roots.[10] Still worse, the message was put out that science was so simple, even a child could excel at it. A propaganda book, *They Are Creating Miracles*, described how children at a primary school 'developed ten more new crops on its experimental plot', a feat presented as hard fact: 'It's a story out of a science-fiction book! But, no, my young friends, it is not! This is a true story. There are no fairy-tale magicians, no white-bearded wizards of never-never land. The heroes of our story are a group of Young Pioneers studying in an ordinary village primary school.'[11]

All over China in 1958, the Party created thousands of new colleges, universities and research institutes, while real scientists were imprisoned or sent to do manual labour. In their place, thousands of untrained peasants carried out 'scientific research'. Many kinds of miracles were announced but the Great Leap Forward was above all about creating huge increases in grain and steel production. These were the 'two generals' that Mao said would modernize China.

Just as Stalin saw a huge increase in steel production as the cornerstone of his crash industrialization programme, Mao envisaged a doubling or trebling of steel output within a year. The entire country, from peasants in remote villages on the Tibetan plateau to top Party officials in Zhongnanhai in Beijing, set up smelters in 1958 and 1959 to create 'steel' in backyard furnaces. Everyone had to meet a quota by handing over their metal possessions. People handed in bicycles, railings, iron bedsteads, door knobs, their pots and pans and cooking grates. And to fire the furnaces, huge numbers of trees were cut down. In the countryside people worked day and night fuelling these furnaces. While they did so, they could eat as much as they wanted out of the communes' collective food stores. The lumps of useless metal that emerged were supposed to be used in the mechanization of agriculture. Had China really produced a lot more steel then it could have been used to make the necessary tractors, ploughs, threshing machines, trucks, diesel engines and pumps. Instead the peasants relied on *tu fa*—literally 'earth methods'—to mechanize their work by inventing hundreds of Heath Robinson-type contraptions of pulleys, ropes and cogs, all made out of wood, not steel. Propaganda photographs showed wooden conveyor belts, wooden threshing machines, wooden automatic compost-appliers—a sort of wheelbarrow with a box on top—wooden rail tracks, wooden railcars, wooden rice-planting machines, wooden wheat harvesters, wooden jute harvesters and, in Shandong, a whole truck made of wood. They were all a great credit to the considerable ingenuity of the Chinese peasant but, in the end, perfectly worthless. Not one has survived in use. Yet, for all the waste and folly of the backyard furnace campaign, it was never more than a minor contributory factor to the starvation that was to result from the Great Leap Forward.

Rather, it was the half-baked ideas on growing more grain, Mao's second 'general', which he insisted the nation should follow, that led to a substantial decline in grain yields. Many Chinese believe his ideas were rooted in traditional Chinese peasant lore, but though this may explain their appeal to a peasant's son like Mao, in fact he merely adopted them from the Soviet Union. To understand what happened in China, therefore, one must first step back in time to the Stalin years and examine the theories of such pseudo-scientists as Lysenko, Michurin and Williams.

For twenty-five years Trofim Denisovitch Lysenko ruled over Soviet agricultural scientists as a dictator. Those who opposed him were shot or perished in labour camps, and his victims were not rehabilitated until 1986 when Mikhail Gorbachev came to power.[12] Until then, Lysenko's portrait hung in all scientific institutions. At the height of his personality cult, art stores sold busts and bas-reliefs of him, and cities erected statues in his honour. When he gave a lecture, he was preceded by a brass band and people sang songs in his honour:

> Merrily play one, accordion,
> With my girlfriend let me sing
> Of the eternal glory of Academician Lysenko.

Lysenko dismissed the developing science of genetics as an 'expression of the senile decay and degradation of bourgeois culture'. Instead, he advocated a mumbo-jumbo of his own which muddled up Darwin's theories on evolution and the competition in nature between different species and among members of the same species. His school rejected the 'fascist' theories that plants and animals have inherited characteristics which selective breeding can develop. Lysenkoists believed that, on the contrary, environmental factors determine the characteristics of plants and animals. Just as Communists thought that people could be changed by altering their surroundings, so Lysenko held that plants acquire new characteristics when their environment is changed and that these changes are transmitted to the next generation. As one observer pointed out, this was tantamount to saying that lambs would be born without tails just because you cut off their mother's tail. Yet Lysenko asserted that he could make orange trees flourish in Siberia, or change them into apple trees, not by selective breeding but by following Stalin's unintelligible teachings on evolution. As the

Lysenkoist journal *Agrobiologiya* put it: 'Stalin's teachings about gradual, concealed, unnoticeable quantitative changes leading to rapid, radical qualitative changes permitted Soviet biologists to discover in plants the realisation of such qualitative transitions that one species could be transformed into another.'

Lysenko was a semi-literate peasant from Azerbaijan whom *Pravda* praised in 1927 as a 'barefoot scientist' after he claimed to have found a way of growing peas in winter. These peas, he said, would green the mountains of the Caucasus in winter and solve the problem of winter forage. His next, and equally bogus, achievement went under the name of 'vernalization' (from the Latin, *vernalis,* for spring). Most Russian wheat is sown in winter but the seeds are sometimes damaged by severe weather. The yield from spring wheat is higher so when Lysenko claimed he could turn winter wheat seeds into spring seeds, he was promising to raise yields in many parts of the Soviet Union. His method was simple: change the environment of the seeds by soaking them in very cold water and they themselves would change.

The second verse of the Lysenko song, quoted above, also commemorates another Soviet hero, Michurin:

> He walks the Michurin path
> With firm tread.
> He protects us from being duped
> By Mendelist-Morganists.

If the Austrian monk Gregor Mendel and the American scientist Thomas Morgan are the fathers of genetics, then I.V. Michurin, an impoverished nobleman turned tree-grafter, is the true founder of Lysenkoism. He first rose to fame in the early 1920s when a Soviet leader praised his hybrid creations, including a part melon, part squash vegetable, on show at the First All Russian Agricultural Exhibition. Michurin claimed to have created hundreds of hybrid fruit trees, and because he had received only primary education, he qualified as a genuine peasant hero. The whole nation had to follow his methods, although he insisted that 'intuition' was as vital an element in matching his success as his theories. Michurin dismissed real scientists as 'the caste priests of jabberology', especially those who espoused the theories of Mendel.

Although Michurin was later conclusively shown to be a fraud, he was hailed during Stalin's first five-year plan as an example of what could be done with the correct attitude to science. The daring, untrammelled spirit of his thinking was evoked in this call to arms published in the magazine *October*: 'Knock out sleepiness with punches, with demands, with insistence, with daring. With daring to master and transform the earth, nature, fruit. Is it not daring to drive the grape into the tundra? Drive! Drive! Drive! Into the furrows, into the gardens, into the orchards, into the machines of jelly factories . . . Faster, faster, faster, comrade agronomists!'

Another hero of the Lysenko school was the son of an American engineer, Vasily Williams, who became a professor at the Moscow Agricultural Academy. Williams thought that capitalism and American-style commercial farming based on the application of chemical fertilizers were taking the world to the brink of catastrophe. This was in the early 1930s when American farmers in Oklahoma saw their fields turn to dust. Williams believed that the answer was to rotate fields as medieval peasants had done, growing grain only every third year. The rest of the time the fields would be left fallow, allowing nitrogen to accumulate in the roots of clover and other grasses which would enrich the soil. He was opposed by other experts, among them Pryanishnikov, who stressed the importance of mineral fertilizers and shallow ploughing, but Williams dubbed them 'wreckers of socialist agriculture'. Khrushchev later explained: 'The debate was essentially decided on the basis of capital investments. Pryanishnikov's theory of mineral fertilizers would have required enormous capital investments in order to build fertilizer plants and new machinery. We were short of capital at that time and so Williams' theory was more attractive. That is how Williams' grasslands theory came to reign supreme.'[13]

Khrushchev was one of those who supported Williams, but he admits in his memoirs that 'the fact of the matter is that Williams' system didn't work. Even after it had been consistently implemented throughout the Ukrane, there was no improvement in our agricultural production.'

Stalin also turned to the ideas of Terenty Maltsev, a pupil of Williams, who recommended ploughing furrows four or five feet deep as a way of improving the soil texture and obtaining higher yields. New ploughs to do this were designed and manufactured and Stalin gave Maltsev the Lenin prize for science.

All these ideas helped transform a rich farming nation into one beset by permanent food shortages. On the collectives, farmers could use neither chemical fertilizers nor the hybrid corn that America was using to boost yields by 30 per cent. Furthermore, their fields were left fallow most of the time, and when the crops were sown, the 'vernalized' wheat did not sprout; nor did Lysenko's frost-resistant wheat and rye seeds, nor the potatoes grown in summer and the sugar beet planted in the hot plains of Central Asia. They all rotted. One year, Lysenko even managed to persuade the government to send an army of peasants into the fields with tweezers to remove the anthers from the spikes of each wheat plant because he believed that his hybrids must be pollinated by hand. Under banners proclaiming 'Greater harvests with less dung', Soviet farmers also had to create artificial manure by mixing humus with organic mineral fertilizers in a rotating barrel. This method removed the phosphate and nitrogen, and when the muck was spread on the fields, it was useless. Ignoring Lysenko's repeated failures, the Soviet press continued to trumpet his endless successes: cows which produced only cream, cabbages turned into swedes, barley transformed into oats, and lemon trees which blossomed in Siberia.

Lysenko's greatest triumphs came after the Second World War when he dreamt up the 'Great Stalin Plan for the Transformation of Nature'. To create a new and warmer climate in the vast lands of Siberia, Lysenko proposed planting millions of trees. The peasants had to plant the seeds and saplings close together because, according to Lysenko's 'law of the life of species', individuals of the same species do not compete but help each other survive. Naturally all the seedlings died but not before the composer Shostakovich had written his choral symphony, *The Song of the Trees*, and Bertolt Brecht had penned this poem:

> So let us with ever newer arts
> Change this earth's form and operation.
> Gladly measure thousand-year-old wisdom
> By new wisdom one year old.
> Dreams! Golden if!
> Let the lovely flood of grain rise higher!

In China, Mao became greatly taken with the theories of Williams, Lysenko and Michurin. He read Williams' book on soil while still in Yanan and later frequently quoted both him and Lysenko. Mao, too, wanted the Chinese to plant seeds close together because, as he told colleagues, 'with company they grow easily, when they grow together they will be comfortable.'[14] Lysenko's theories meshed perfectly with Mao's obsession with class struggle. He readily believed that plants from the same 'class' would never compete against each other for light or food. While the Chinese Communists were still in Yanan, the chief Chinese Lysenkoist, Luo Tianyu, propagated the Soviet teachings: and in the 1942 rectification movement, a purge of Party members, Luo enthusiastically persecuted those who believed in genetics.[15]

After the Communist victory in 1949, Luo was put in charge of the new Beijing Agricultural University and Soviet-style science now reigned supreme. In the 1950s, all Soviet methods, textbooks and ideas had to be followed, while Western-trained scientists were either arrested or forced publicly to disown their 'fascist eugenics' theories. All research in genetics came to a stop. Lysenko's Soviet disciples toured China giving lectures, and Chinese peasants studied his theories at Michurin societies. China had her own Michurin, a peasant called Shi Yiqian who became a professor at the Henan Agricultural College after he grew grapes on a persimmon tree, and apples on a pear tree. In schools, children also set up a Michurin corner in their classrooms to study how to create such hybrids. Some reportedly managed not only to graft one vegetable on to another but also to cross-breed animals such as rabbits and pigs.

Soviet ideas also dominated other fields, notably that of medicine. Perhaps the most absurd notion introduced to the Chinese was the work of Olga Lepeshenskaya, who supposedly proved that living cells could be created from non-living organic material.[16] None of this could be challenged, as a former doctor in Beijing explained:

We were told the Soviets had discovered and invented everything, even the aeroplane. We had to change textbooks and rename things in Lysenko's honour. So the Harving Cushing Syndrome—a disease of the adrenalin gland—became Lysenko's Syndrome to show it had been discovered by him. Since genetics did not exist, we were forbidden to talk about inherited diseases such as sickle cell anaemia, even to students. This meant that all through Mao's lifetime there was no policy to stop people in the same family marrying each other and passing down their genes. A lot of idiots were born as a result.[17]

Adherence to Lysenkoism meant that when a potato virus struck large areas of China in the 1950s, nothing could be done because, as in the Soviet Union, the changes had to be attributed to environmental factors. Chinese scientists who had invested years of research into the blight were ignored, and their work was not published until 1979. Some believe that potato output in the Mao era was half what it might have been had the cause of the problem been correctly identified.

Lysenkoism reached its apogee in the Great Leap Forward when in 1958 Mao personally drew up an eight-point Lysenkoist blueprint for all Chinese agriculture. Every farmer in every commune in the country had to follow it. The eight elements of this 'constitution', as it was called, were:

1. The popularization of new breeds and seeds
2. Close planting
3. Deep ploughing
4. Increased fertilization
5. The innovation of farm tools
6. Improved field management
7. Pest control
8. Increased irrigation

The Popularization of New Breeds and Seeds

All over the country in 1958 people began to announce remarkable achievements like those of China's Michurin, Shi Yiqian. In Guangzhou, children and teachers crossed a pumpkin with a papaya, and runner beans with soybeans. In Henan, they produced sunflowers crossed with artichokes. In Beijing, scientists crossed tomatoes with aubergines, corn with rice, and sorghum with rice. One of the most glorious claims was a cross between a cotton plant and a tomato—the result red cotton![18]

In addition to these vegetable freaks, the New China (Xinhua) News Agency also trumpeted claims that peasants were growing super-big plants—pumpkins weighing not 13 lbs, but 132 lbs, wheat with extra-large ears, and rice of exceptional weight. The country's top national agricultural worker, Yang

Guangbo, set the pace by growing paddy rice with 150 grains per ear instead of 100. Others, too, were held up for emulation, amongst them Jiang Shaofang of the Yuli Botanical Normal School in Guangxi province whose achievements were described in *China Youth News*:

> The grains of sorghum are as big as those of corn, one full spike weighing as much as one pound, and one stalk may have several ears of corn giving a yield much greater than normal corn . . . Jiang Shaofang now plans by crossbreeding and grafting sorghum and corn and sugar cane to produce a plant that will be all three—sorghum, corn and sugar cane. He is also preparing next year to plant a high-yield field of wet rice that will produce 600–1,000 lbs per 0.04 acre.* The methods he plans to use will be a) to breed a very high yield of wet rice and b) to apply highly advanced agricultural techniques.

Specimens of these miraculous plants appeared at exhibitions or on giant pictures paraded through every city. The Chinese also claimed to produce extraordinary animals. The Ministry of Agriculture boasted in 1960 how peasants at the Golden Dragon Commune near Chongqing had been the first in the world to cross a Yorkshire sow with a Holstein Friesian cow using artificial insemination. The Xinhua News Agency described how after a year the litter was still thriving: some of these curious creatures were white but others were patched like the Holstein and 'in general they had shorter snouts and sturdier legs than ordinary pigs.'[19]

These fantasies were not without consequences in the real world. One interviewee, condemned as a 'rightist', was sent to a farm near Shanghai where he ran the pig pen. Cadres ordered him to start the pigs breeding prematurely. Normally, pigs do not breed before they are a year old and weigh at least 160 lbs. Instructions came down from above first to start breeding when the pigs weighed 66 lbs and later to start when the piglets were just four months old and weighed only 33 lbs. There was also a scheme to cross Chinese pigs, which produce small litters of two or three piglets, with much bigger Russian sows which have up to fourteen piglets in a litter. The result was indeed larger litters but all the piglets died because the sow could not produce enough milk to feed them. The interviewee said he tried but failed to save the piglets by bottlefeeding them. Attempts in Inner Mongolia and Tibet to crossbreed local sheep and goats with Ukrainian breeds were no more successful because the offspring, ill-adapted to the harsher climate, died in the first winter.

Close Planting

Mao's faith in high-density planting led nearly every commune in China to start an experimental field growing grain in this way. These experimental fields were begun in 1958 and in many places were retained until 1980. In some provinces,

*The Chinese measure of land is the *mu*, equivalent to 0.17 acres.

like Guangdong, close planting was initially obligatory in all fields. A density of 1.5 million seedlings per 2.5 acres is usually the norm in the south, but in 1958 peasants were ordered to plant 6–7.5 million seedlings and the next year 12–15 million per 2.5 acres. The same close planting was done throughout China with wheat, cotton, sorghum, millet and every other important crop: the results were identical—the seedlings died. Yet the press published photographs apparently showing wheat growing so densely that children could sit on top of it. A retired Xinhua photographer later told the author that the pictures were faked by putting a bench underneath the children.

Fortunately, in most places the peasants knew that close planting was dangerous nonsense and avoided carrying it out on a large scale, otherwise there would have been no food at all in China. Party officials knew this too. One interviewee recalled that before Mao visited the Xinli experimental field in the suburbs of Tianjin in 1958, the cadres brought rice plants from other fields and pushed them close together by hand. 'They were so close together, you really could walk across them,' the interviewee remembered. When Mao left, the cadres immediately removed and replanted the shoots. Mao's doctor, Li Zhisui, recalls how the same thing happened in Hubei: 'Party Secretary Wang Renzhong ordered the peasants to remove rice plants from away fields and transplant them along Mao's route to give the impression of a wildly abundant crop . . . All of China was a stage, all the people performers in an extravaganza for Mao.'

Deep Ploughing

Mao took the idea of deep ploughing to even greater extremes than had Stalin, in the belief that if it was good to plough deep, it was better to plough deeper still. In some places furrows dug by hand were ten feet deep although generally they were around three to four feet. The exhausting, backbreaking work was often done by crack teams of peasants who sweated around the clock. In 1958 Liaoning province's Governor, Huang Oudong, ordered 5 million people with tens of thousands of animals to toil non-stop for forty-five days to deep-plough 3 million hectares of land. Where the top soil was too shallow, he instructed the peasants to transport soil from fields elsewhere. All this was intended to treble yields in Liaoning.[20] In Heilongjiang in the far north, where for part of the year the soil is frozen solid, peasants blasted open furrows with dynamite. In labour camps on the high plateaux and mountains of Qinghai, the inmates tried to soften the iron-hard soil by digging little holes and filling them with straw and grass which were set on fire. In the rice fields of the south, peasant women waded through the deep paddies up to their waists and many caught infections as a result. In Anhui, where the soil is thin, the deep ploughing destroyed the fertility of the fields for many years to come. In some regions, fields were excavated to a depth of thirteen feet.[21] Indeed, in Guizhou province the trenches were so deep that peasants had to tie ropes around their waists to prevent themselves from drowning. Later, the same province claimed to have the biggest yield in the entire country, an absurd 130,000 *jin*, or 65 tonnes per 0.17 acres.[22]

Of course, there was never any real proof that any of this was effective, but agricultural halls displayed exhibits showing how much taller wheat plants grew the deeper they were planted. In February 1959, agronomists in Anguo county reportedly dug up wheat plants to prove that deep ploughing worked: 'Land ploughed 5 inches had roots only 13 inches long after two months' growth. Land ploughed 5 feet had roots 5 feet long and wheat plants growing in land ploughed 8 feet deep had roots 7 feet 8 inches long.'[23] The deep ploughing was not practised everywhere all of the time, but in some places peasants kept it up for three years or more.

Increased Fertilization

Lysenkoist agrobiology ruled out the use of chemical fertilizers so the Chinese government halted investment in chemical plants and, instead, instructed peasants to use a new method to replace lost nutrients. The Russians claimed that earth when mixed with manure would acquire the qualities of manure and recommended a ratio of 10 per cent manure to 90 per cent earth. So all over China millions of peasants started mixing all sorts of earth and rubbish with real manure and laboriously hauled this to their fields and spread it. To ease the transport of massive amounts of this 'fertilizer', peasants build carts running on wooden rails to carry it to the fields.

The most extraordinary rubbish was thrown on to the fields as fertilizer. People in Guangzhou took their household rubbish to the outskirts of the city where it was buried for several weeks before being put on the fields. Near Shanghai peasants dumped so much broken glass that they could not walk in the fields in bare feet. Others broke up the mud floors of their huts and their brick stoves and even pulled down their mud walls to use as fertilizer. Elsewhere people tried to turn ordinary soil into manure by heating and smoking it for ten days. Some tried to collect manure by dragging riverbeds for the rich mud and weeds. An article in the *People's Daily* explained that, thanks to the Communists, China was now no longer short of fertilizer:

> Chinese scientists have said that in the past, many people only considered the mineral plant nutrients, that is the amount of nitrogen, phosphorus and potassium in the fertilizer and their relative proportions. They neglected the experience of the Chinese peasants over thousands of years in using organic fertilizer whose application in massive quantities produces high yields. Agronomists proved last year that they could supply the nutrients continuously and improve the physical properties of the soil.[24]

The Research Institute of Hydrobiology also claimed to have invented 'an everlasting fertilizer', described as a blue-green algae which assimilates nitrogen. *China Pictorial* boasted that when planted in a paddy field 'it is the equivalent of a permanent nitrogenous fertilizer'. Peasant scientists such as He Wenyi, 'who could neither recognize chemical symbols, nor understand laboratory reports, nor remember lists of ingredients', were also said to have invented a method for producing fertilizer from bacteria.

The Innovation of Farm Tools

Some of these incredible Heath Robinson inventions made of wood instead of steel have already been described. China also experienced major setbacks when she tried to mass-produce and use machinery based on impractical designs. One example was a rice planter designed to automate the delicate and back-breaking task of planting rice shoots which proved useless because it could handle only one variety at a fixed spacing. Another was a special Soviet plough designed for deep ploughing. The Chinese version, the double-share plough, cost ten times as much as a traditional plough but proved unsuitable for the terraces and paddy fields of southern China: 700,000 had to be withdrawn from use and melted down again. In addition, the Chinese began to manufacture big, heavy Soviet tractors and rejected the small walking tractors which were then helping Japanese farmers to reap record yields on their small plots. In the 1980s, these small tractors were produced in large numbers and were credited with transforming the work of Chinese peasants.

Improved Field Management

Improved field management referred to the field rotation system advanced by Williams. A communiqué issued at a high-level meeting at Wuhan in 1958 summarized its aims: 'We should try to reduce the area sown to various crops to about one-third the present acreage. Part of the land so saved can be left fallow or used for pasturage and the growing of grass fertilizers: the rest can be used for afforestation, reservoirs and the extensive cultivation of flowers, shrubs and trees to turn the whole land with its plains, hills, and waters into a garden.[25]

Though most provinces were not so foolish as to remove two-thirds of their fields from production, Mao's slogan of 'Plant less, produce more, harvest less' could not be completely ignored. Henan province reported cutting the area sown to grain by 14 per cent and Inner Mongolia and Qinghai by 21 per cent, while Shaanxi stated that it was allowing a third of its arable land to lie fallow.[26]

At the same time, the intensive effort put into those areas which were sown with grain sometimes had disastrous results. In provinces such as Hunan which normally grows two crops of rice, peasants were ordered to grow three. Farmers who had poor land were ordered to switch to growing crops which promised a higher yield but exhausted the soil. As a result, in northern Anhui the peasants planted maize in the summer, and in Shaanxi they had to grow corn instead of millet. Since the only crop that mattered to Mao was grain, the acreage devoted to cash crops was in some places reduced. And in Fujian, where China's best tea is grown, tea bushes were ripped out to make way for grain.

Pest Control

In the interests of pest control a new campaign to exterminate the 'four evils'— birds, rats, insects and flies—was launched in 1958. The whole country was turned out to make a noise, beating drums and pans to prevent sparrows from landing anywhere until they fell down dead with exhaustion. The war against the sparrows, as it was termed, was only called off in April 1960 and the birds were replaced on the list by bedbugs.[27] Without the birds to prey on them, insects multiplied, causing damage to crops. Peasants tried to kill the insects at night by setting up huge lamps in the middle of the fields so that the insects would fly around them until they dropped down dead. Everywhere people were ordered to fulfil a quota by catching and killing flies. The same had to be done with rats and field mice. Since Tibetans regarded the killing of a living animal as a grave sin, some imprisoned lamas killed themselves rather than meet their daily quotas. This campaign was also accompanied by an intensive hygiene campaign. Even at the height of the famine people's houses were still being inspected for cleanliness.

Increased Irrigation

At the same time, every county in China was ordered to construct a water reservoir by building a dam and water channels. A series of gigantic schemes were also conceived and the construction of those already under way, like the Sanmenxia Dam on the Yellow River, was speeded up. Almost without exception, the engineering schemes of this period neither worked nor lasted. A senior Ministry of Agriculture official speaking in the 1990s simply dismissed all the small reservoirs as 'completely worthless'.[28] Most of the county dams had collapsed within two or three years and the dam on the Yellow River quickly filled up with silt, rendering it next to useless.[29] Even today it barely functions. A few medium-scale dams did survive, only to collapse later with terrible results. In the worst dam disaster in history, the Banqiao and Shimantan dams at Zhumadian in Henan province burst after heavy rainfall in August 1975, releasing a wall of water which killed 240,000 people.[30]

The labour put into the construction of these dams was stupendous. Nearly all the construction work was performed by people using the simplest tools who worked day and night in shifts, living in makeshift tents and being fed only when they worked. The peasant labourers were organized in military units and marched to work following flags, with martial music blaring from loudspeakers. On the larger projects, tens of thousands were conscripted as labourers and paid nothing.

To make room for the reservoirs, uncounted numbers of people were evicted from their villages and forcibly relocated. In 1958, when the Xin'anjiang reservoir was built in northern Zhejiang province, 300,000 people were transferred *en masse*, and from one county alone, Chun An, 137,000 people were evacuated:

> Along the road, many of the evacuated families had to eat and sleep in the open air or in rough tents. Freezing and starving, they ate uncooked grain to fend off hunger. People collapsed with illness on the roadside, some even died; pregnant women had to give birth during the journey. According to an old cadre who took part in the relocation work, the marching peasants resembled wartime columns of refugees.[31]

Inspired by the gigantic dams in the Soviet Union, such as that on the Dnieper, and schemes like the Volga-White Sea canal, the Chinese also planned 'the greatest construction undertaking in history'. This was a project to divert surplus water from the Yangtze to the Yellow River in the north. The water would be taken through a huge interlocking system of deep canals, dams, tunnels, ravines and lakes. Work began during the Great Leap Forward and it was envisaged that it would take millions of men seven years to complete it. As it was, the Xinhua News Agency reported that throughout China the peasants had shifted more rock and earth in a single day than had the builders of the Panama Canal in a whole decade: 'A total of 6,560 million cubic feet was excavated in the week ending December 12, 1959. This is more than 12 times the amount shifted for the building of the Panama Canal.'[32] The Party also planned to water the deserts of western China and plant millions of trees by melting the glaciers of the Tianshan mountains. Propaganda photographs even showed scientists dropping materials from aeroplanes to melt the ice.

In the countryside, the dams collapsed because they were made of earth not concrete, and were designed not by engineers but by untrained peasants. The Party took a peculiar pride in defying 'book learning'. One article in *China Pictorial* eulogized Le Heyun, a water conservancy engineer of peasant origin, as a 'bold innovator' and 'advanced worker': 'In 1959, when the construction of the county's Huangtan reservoir was in progress, he suggested that the culvert and conduit should be built of substitutes instead of reinforced concrete as originally planned, thereby saving 7,000 yuan.' Interviewees said concrete was rarely used and this explained why none of the dams lasted more than a year or two. Without a functioning reservoir, the canals and irrigation ditches were rendered equally useless. In later years a few were rebuilt using concrete and one in Sichuan now serves as a boating lake.

Even when the famine was over, Mao's faith in his agricultural methods does not appear to have been shaken in the slightest by their evident failure. On the contrary, in 1964, Mao established at Dazhai in Shanxi province a working model of his eight-point 'constitution'. Millions of visitors, both domestic and foreign, would be taken around Dazhai and told of the wonders of its amazing peasant scientists, their nitrogen-fixing bacteria, the splendid new varieties of plants, the home-made dams, and so on. Perhaps Mao's vanity prevented him from realizing what a fool he had made of himself.

Certainly, in 1958 and 1959, Mao seemed immune to any doubts, believing he had personally witnessed proof that his methods were succeeding beyond even *his* expectations. As a peasant song put it, the grain reached to the sky and paradise was at hand. For example, in 1958 he visited Xushui, one of the model communes, a convenient train ride away from the capital in Hebei province. As he was driven up to the commune centre, his car passed piles of vegetables, turnips, cabbages and carrots laid out for half a mile along the roadside.[33] Officials told him that the peasants had dumped the vegetables because they had grown so much food they did not know what to do with it. At the commune headquarters, the Party secretary told him that they were eating five meals a day free of charge and the autumn grain harvest had quadrupled to half a million tonnes. Mao was reportedly so staggered by this that he pushed up his cap and asked: 'How can you consume all this food? What are you going to do with the surplus?'

The *People's Daily* even started a debate on how China should cope with its food surplus.[34] Everywhere Mao went, Party officials told him of astounding successes: fields which did not produce 330 lbs of grain—the average before the Great Leap Forward—but 49,500 lbs or even 53,000 lbs per 0.17 acres. In fact, there was no way of knowing the real size of the harvest since the State Statistical Bureau had been dismantled and its local offices replaced by 'good news reporting stations'. Yet the propaganda machine churned out one triumphant claim after another. China had outstripped the United States in wheat and cotton production, she had beaten Japan in per unit yields of rice, and she had bettered the United Sates in cotton yields.

Mao was not alone in believing this nonsense. Liu Shaoqi, formerly an advocate of gradual progress, and his wife, Wang Guangmei, applied to join the Xushui model commune. Its 1958 harvest was double that of 1957, Liu asserted, and he urged the country to 'go right ahead and realize Communism. We must not think that Communism will only be realized very slowly. So long as we work properly, it will be very soon.'

Deng Xiaoping was equally optimistic. He expected per capita grain distribution in 1958 to be 1,375 lbs on the strength of a peasant's assurance that by using Mao's agricultural methods he had produced 77,000 lbs per 0.17 acres on an experimental field. Deng calculated that at this rate yields in 1959 would rise to 231,000 lbs per 0.17 acres and would by 1962 stand at 2.5 tonnes. 'We can all have as much as we want,' he concluded.[35] At Ya'an, in Deng's home province of Sichuan, people showed how much food they had to eat by leaving pots of cooked food on the roadside from which any passer-by could help himself.[36] Chen Boda, one of Mao's cronies, went so far as to declare that the time had come to abolish money; from now on not only should food be free but also clothing, haircuts and everything else.

Mao felt such achievements trumped those of the Soviet Union which had in 1957 launched the first satellite in space. The breaking of such records was therefore called 'launching a satellite' or 'launching a sputnik'. He also declared that China was achieving such success that she was overtaking the Soviet Union on the road to Communism. No one dared challenge these bogus claims directly and later every senior official would explain that, like Deng, they had been innocently duped by the peasants.

In the belief that China was awash with food, everyone in the autumn of 1958 was encouraged to eat as much as they wanted, and for free. In Jiangsu province the slogan was 'Eat as much as you can and exert your utmost in production'. In Guangdong, the Party Secretary Tao Zhu urged everyone to 'eat three meals a day'.[37] In Zengu village, peasants later told American anthropologists what it was like: 'Everyone irresponsibly ate whether they were hungry or not, and in 20 days they had finished almost all the rice they had, rich which should have lasted six months.'[38] In Shanxi, the American William Hinton heard the same thing: 'If there was one facet of the Great Leap Forward that everyone remembers, it was the food. "We lived well," said Wei-de. "We ate a lot of meat. It was considered revolutionary to eat meat. If you didn't eat meat, it wouldn't do . . . People even vied with each other to see who could eat the most . . . "'[39]

What was happening in China was almost identical to what had happened in the Soviet Union during Stalin's collectivization movement. In his semi-fictional novel *The Soil Upturned*, Sholokhov describes a similar scene: 'They ate until they could eat no more. Young and old suffered from stomach-ache. At dinner-time, tables groaned under boiled and roasted meat. At dinner-time everyone had a greasy mouth, everyone hiccupped as if at a wake. Everyone blinked like an owl as if drunk from eating.'

In China, where there had never been enough food for all, people ate so much that by the winter of 1958–9, the granaries were bare. Some far-sighted rural Party secretaries saved their communities by planting sweet potatoes but elsewhere people trusted that they, like the city folk, would under Communism be provided for out of the state granaries. Yet Mao refused to accept that there was a shortage and, since he was convinced that the peasants were hiding their grain, he refused to open the state granaries. Even worse, over the three years from 1958 China doubled her grain exports and cut her imports of food. Exports to the Soviet Union rose by 50 per cent and China delivered grain *gratis* to her friends in North Korea, North Vietnam and Albania.[40] This generosity spelt death to many in China.

The Chinese are still suffering from the greatest and most far-reaching consequence of Mao's illusions. Convinced that China had entered an era of unprecedented abundance, Mao rejected any thought of China limiting her population growth. The country's most prominent advocate of birth control was Ma Yinchu, the Chancellor of Beijing University. In 1958, he was dismissed and condemned as a Malthusian. Only a year earlier he had warned of the consequences if no limits were set on population growth. As with so many things, Mao took an orthodox Leninist view. From early on Communists had believed that modern science was the key to a limitless expansion of food supplies. In 1913 Lenin had declared that 'we are the implacable enemy of the neo-Malthusian theory' which he described as 'reactionary' and 'cowardly'. Mao repeatedly attacked the warnings not just of experts like Professor Ma but also of foreigners such as Professor Lossing Buck and the US Secretary of State, Dean Acheson, who feared that China's population growth would outpace any increase in her food supply. In the early 1960s, as China was starving, Mao wrote in yet another criticism of Acheson that: 'Among all things on earth man is the most precious. Under the leadership of the Communist Party miracles can be wrought as long as there are men. We are against Acheson's counter-revolutionary theory. We believe that revolution can change everything. China's big population is a very good thing.'[41]

Mao even feared that there would be a labour shortage. In December 1958, following a meeting of Chinese leaders at Wuchang, a communiqué was issued claiming that 'it will be found that the amount of arable land is not too little but quite a lot and it is not a question of overpopulation but rather a shortage of manpower'. So, from the start of the Great Leap Forward, the Chinese peasants were encouraged to have as many children as possible because, as Mao liked to remind listeners, 'with every stomach comes another pair of hands'. Within a generation, China's population would double to 1.2 billion.

In the winter of 1958–9, people in China began to starve in large numbers but another two years would pass before the Party would come to grips with the terrible disaster. Within the Party leadership, however, a struggle over Mao's policies was about to begin.

How Many Died?

'Any society that is alive is a society with a *history*.'

Vaclav Havel

China has never officially acknowledged that the famine took place nor published an estimate of the death toll. The results of any internal investigations are a state secret and no public discussion of the famine is permitted.

Western experts made the first estimates of the death toll in the early 1980s, nearly a quarter of a century after the famine had taken place, and these calculations are only educated guesses, carried out on the basis of limited information. Yet given that the number of victims of the Holocaust and the Ukrainian famine are still being debated even though far more is known about them, such uncertainty over the death toll in China is hardly surprising. Moreover, in China the Party responsible for the famine is still in power and venerates the memory of Mao. Even in Russia, where the Communists have lost power, it is still proving difficult to determine how many died in Stalin's purges, the famines or the Second World War. Nor have the internal records of Mao's regime been scrutinized by an occupying power in the way the Allies were able to examine those of Nazi Germany.

However, reaching a reliable figure about a famine which lasted for years and extended over such a large country would be difficult even if China were to open all her archives. Many records were lost during the Cultural Revolution and a great deal of other evidence has been deliberately destroyed. In addition, only three censuses were taken in China between 1949 and 1982, one in 1953, another in 1964 and the third in 1982. And, as will be seen, data from that of 1964 must be treated with considerable caution.

During the Great Leap Forward, the State Statistical Bureau, set up in 1952 and modelled on its Soviet equivalent, simply did not function. Professional statisticians were relegated to other work and were only reappointed in July 1961. And only in the following year, on the instructions of Liu Shaoqi and Zhou Enlai, were plans drawn up for the establishment of a powerful, centralized and unified statistics system. At the same time, Party and government departments were forbidden to change statistical figures.[1]

Provisional regulations governing statistical work were issued in 1963 but the newly reconstituted bureau functioned only for another four years or so. On the eve of the Cultural Revolution, Wang Sihua, head of the State Statistical Bureau, was arrested and accused of implementing a revisionist line, 'seizing power from the Party' and 'asserting his independence'. At the same time, large quantities of material from the bureau were burnt. Wang had been in charge of organizing China's second national population census completed in 1964. The census had been conducted amid such secrecy that the outside world was unaware of it, and Mao refused to publish the results. Details of the 1964 census were only published in 1980. Thus for nearly a quarter of a century there was an effective blackout on all Chinese population statistics.[2]

These circumstances parallel those during collectivization and the ensuing famine in the Soviet Union. Stalin had ordered a new census in 1937 but its results were never released and lay buried in the central national archives for half a century. The director of the Census Bureau, O.A. Kvitkin, was dismissed and later shot. Stalin had estimated that the Soviet Union had a population of around 170 million people. However, the census itself counted only 162 million people, clearly showing that 7 million or more people had starved to death in the Ukraine and the northern Caucasus.

The parallels with China do not end there. Researchers have discovered that the Soviet Central Office of Statistics produced two sets of demographic statistics, one for internal use and one for publication. During the Mao era, China appears to have done much the same, at least as far as meteorological data is concerned. During the Great Leap Forward, the Central Meteorological Office continued to function accurately but the information it produced was restricted to senior levels of the Party. The meteorologists reported that there was no unusually bad weather or natural disasters in 1959, 1960 or 1961; indeed the weather was rather good. However, the official media reported claims by Mao and others that China had in this period experienced the worst natural disasters for a century. Official news reports even quoted experts as saying that China's climate had changed. In fact, the worst years since 1949 have been 1954 and 1980–1 when there was neither a severe grain shortage nor a nationwide famine.[3]

However, even if one is prepared to accept that the statistics released by China after 1980 were undoctored, there are doubts as to whether in the midst of a ruthless political struggle, an accurate census was taken in 1964. The count must have been made at the provincial level with the co-operation of the local Party organization and the results passed on to the centre only with the approval of the provincial Party Secretaries. In many provinces, the same officials who were responsible for the famine were still in power and would have had every reason to censor damaging information. In Sichuan, for example, Li Jingquan was still in power in 1964: the census would have revealed his responsibility for 7–9 million deaths. Nonetheless, the data from the 1964 census is crucial to making a proper estimate of the death toll for, without it, one is faced with a gap of twenty-nine years between the first census in 1953 and the third in 1982.

China began to publish a flood of statistical and demographic data after 1980, when the State Statistical Bureau was re-established and the country's few remaining statisticians returned from long years of physical labour in the countryside. It is now possible, using the data from 1953, 1964 and 1982, to track the progress of each age cohort from census to census and therefore establish how many of those born in 1950 survived until 1964 and then 1982. However, two factors in particular hinder a demographer from making a definitive study of the death toll during the famine—internal migration and the number of children who were born and died between 1958 and 1962.

In a famine people flee their homes and often do not return, but a census count does not show whether they have starved to death or whether they have moved away and failed to register elsewhere. Census figures for Shanghai, for example, show that 950,000 people left Shanghai between 1953 and 1964, but they do not reveal what happened to these people or where they went. During the famine, uncounted numbers fled the worst-hit regions, over 10 million settling in Manchuria and Inner Mongolia alone.

The other great challenge is to try and guess how many children were born during the famine years and, of these, how many died. This is not revealed by the 1953 and 1964 censuses although experts can make educated guesses based on birth rates and infant mortality rates before and after the famine. On the other hand, pre-famine trends are not a strong guide because it is clear that fewer babies are born in a famine. Many women stop ovulating altogether, and if they do give birth, they produce less milk and infant mortality rises sharply. One expert has calculated that Anhui suffered a fertility crisis for as long as two years during the famine but obviously the scale of the crisis varied from province to province.[4] With a population the size of China's, the margin for error is fairly high. Under normal conditions, China might in the late 1950s and early 1960s have seen around 25 million births a year. Even in famine conditions, the number of births might still have been 14 million a year. Thus in the four years from 1958 to 1962, the number of births could have ranged from a low of 56 million to a maximum of 100 million.

The censuses are not the sole guide to calculating the death toll in China because the local authorities also maintain registers of births and deaths. Given the rationing system which existed during this period, a careful record would have been made at times of the number of mouths to feed. On the other hand, at the height of the famine in the countryside, no one was burying the dead, let alone recording the number of deaths. The births and deaths of small children, in particular, would often have passed almost unnoticed. Nor would officials have kept track of those who fled and managed to survive or of those who died on the roads. And there is another, final question-mark about Chinese figures: how were the inmates of the labour camps and prisons recorded? And the millions in the armed forces? Generally, both groups are excluded from provincial population figures but during the famine there were perhaps as many as 10 million prisoners and the death rate in the camps was exceptionally high, on average 20 per cent and often far higher.

In the early 1980s, Dr Judith Banister undertook a major investigation of China's population statistics which was published in *China's Changing Population*. Taking all the above factors into account, she reached the following conclusion:

> Assuming that without the Great Leap Forward policies and experiences China would have maintained its claimed 1957 death rate of 10.8 during the years 1958–1961, the official data imply that those four years saw over 15 million excess deaths attributable to the Great Leap Forward in combination with poor weather conditions. The computerized reconstruction of China's population trends utilized in this book, which assumes under-reporting of deaths in 1957,

as well as in all the famine years, results in an estimated 30 million excess deaths during 1958–1961.[5]

This figure, arrived at in 1984, is the most reliable estimate we have but it is not the only one.

While China has never formally rejected this total or put forward an alternative, a wealth of statistical information has been published which amounts to quasi-official recognition that millions did die of famine. One such work, *Contemporary Chinese Population* published in 1988, goes further by explicitly stating that the official data disguises the extent of the death toll. Official figures show that between 1959 and 1961, the population fell by 13.48 million but the authors say: 'The problem is that there are false figures and 6.03 million people during the three years of difficulty were not taken into account when the calculations were made . . . If we take this into account, the death rate in 1960 should be 1 per cent higher at 3.85 per cent. So out of a population of 500 million, there were 19.5 million deaths in the countryside.'[6]

The authors also substantiate anecdotal evidence that large numbers of girls were allowed to die or were killed during the famine. According to the 1964 census, 0.5 per cent more boys than girls aged 5–9 and 0.4 per cent more males than females aged 9–14 years survived the famine. Generally, even in normal times a higher proportion of male infants than female infants survive in China but the 1982 census indicates that the normal difference is only about 0.1 per cent. This means that during the famine 4.7 million fewer girls survived than would have done so in normal years. In other words, nearly a quarter of the 19.5 million famine victims were peasant girls, who appear to have been deliberately allowed to starve to death or were killed by their parents.

Articles published by some experts in China and by exiled dissidents claim that the death toll is far higher even than Banister's estimate. In 1993, a Chinese scholar writing under the pen-name Jin Hui published an article in a Shanghai academic journal, *Society*, which was later withdrawn. The author looked at inconsistencies in official statistics on birth and death rates, sex ratios, rural and urban populations and provincial and national figures, and concluded that the figures had been falsified to hide a death toll of at least 40 million. Unfortunately, it is also true that Chinese statistics about any subject are rarely internally consistent so it is hard to know how significant these discrepancies are. Whether or not this figure of 40 million is to be trusted, it is now used, almost casually, by various authors inside China who lump deaths and the reduction in births together. Cong Jin of the National Defence University writes in *China 1949– 1989: The Zig-zag Development Era* that 'From 1959 to 1961 the abnormal deaths plus the reduction of births reached about 40 million.'[7] Another book, *Leftism in China* by Wen Yu, published in 1993, claims that 'from 1959 to 1961, the abnormal deaths plus the reduction of births reached altogether more than 40 million with direct economic losses of 120 billion yuan'.[8]

The estimates of American demographers are also challenged by Chen Yizi, a senior Chinese Party official who fled to America after the crackdown that followed the 1989 Tiananmen pro-democracy demonstrations. After 1979, Chen played an important role in the rural reforms as a member of a think-tank called the *Tigaisuo* or System Reform Institute patronized by Zhao Ziyang, then Premier and later Party General Secretary. The new Chinese leadership wanted to find out what had really happened under Mao, and one of the institute's first tasks was to draw up a picture of rural China. Chen was part of a large team of 200 officials who visited every province and examined internal Party documents and records. The institute's report concluded that between 43 and 46 million people had died during the famine and several sources said that an even larger figure of 50 and 60 million deaths were cited at internal meetings of senior Party officials.

The institute's report has never been released but in an interview Chen recalled the death toll for a number of provinces:

Henan	7.8 million
Anhui	8 million
Shandong	7.5 million
Sichuan	9 million
Qinghai	900,000

Thus, in these five provinces alone, 33.2 million people died. Chen argues that these figures are reliable because each province compiled detailed statistics on its population. In normal times, Chinese local officials keep records of household registration and these were particularly important when the commune system operated because with all food rationed, great care was taken in counting the number of mouths.

That such detailed records were kept is clear from the report on Fengyang county in Anhui. Such figures were also used when the Party compiled reports on the famine in each province at the end of 1960; and in places like Gansu officials kept a record of famine deaths as well as the number of mouths to feed. However, while it is clear that Beijing was aware of the scale of the disaster, the reliability of such figures is hard to ascertain. In addition, there is an added complication, because evidence suggests that the Party often produced different versions of the same report. Lower figures were released to lower-ranking officials. Until these internal reports are made public, we cannot be sure that they exist or, if they do, whether they take into account such factors as internal migration or include normal deaths in the totals.

From a moral perspective, the debate is meaningless. Whether 30 or over 40 million perished, China managed to hide the largest famine in history for twenty years. In terms of sheer numbers, no other event comes close to this. Until the Great Leap Forward, the largest famine on record took place in China between 1876 and 1879 when 9–13 million died.

In other great historical famines, a higher proportion of the population died than in China in 1958–61. At the start of the great Irish potato famine in 1845, Ireland had a population of about 8.5 million of whom around 1 million died of hunger and 1.5 million emigrated. Most historians recognize that the Irish famine was caused by a blight which destroyed the potato harvest on which the population depended for most of its food. Relief efforts were undermined by the slowness of communications and transport, and when grain was shipped from North America it did not relieve the hunger. The Irish economy was so dependent on the potato that it was not equipped to process the grain for human consumption. Indeed, before the famine bread was seldom seen and ovens virtually unknown. Even so, the British government still stands accused of acting with indifference to a subject people.

In more recent times, except during war, famines have become rarer. China is often compared to India but in this century India has not suffered a famine of comparable dimensions. India's largest famine in modern times took place between 1896 and 1897 when drought led to 5 million deaths. The Bengal famine of 1942, when around 1.5 million died, was caused by the Japanese invasion of Burma which cut off rice imports.

What sets Mao's famine apart from those in Ireland and India is that it was entirely man-made. China was at peace. No blight destroyed the harvest. There were no unusual floods or droughts. The granaries were full and other countries were ready to ship in grain. And the evidence shows that Mao and the Chinese bureaucracy were in full control of the machinery of government.

The event which most resembles Mao's famine is that in the Ukraine in 1932–3 where circumstances were almost identical. A slightly larger proportion of China's population died in the Great Leap Forward than in the Soviet Union—4.6 per cent (if one accepts a figure of 30 million out of a total population of 650 million) compared to 4.11 per cent (7 million out of 170 million). In China, deaths were concentrated among the rural population, so out of a maximum 550 million peasants 5.45 per cent died, one in twenty. Around a quarter of the population of the Ukraine perished in the famine there, largely in one year, 1933. However, in parts of China such as Anhui, it is likely that a quarter of the rural population died just as in the Ukraine.[9]

One can also compare China with Cambodia under Pol Pot. Inspired by Mao, the Khmer Rouge collectivized the entire population in the 1970s and it is reckoned that out of 8 million people, 1 million died. However, this number also includes the victims of a civil war and a war with Vietnam, so the extent of deaths due to famine alone is unclear.

If we look at Mao's famine as a deliberate act of inhumanity, then his record can also be measured against that of Hitler and Stalin. Some 12 million died in the Nazi concentration camps and a further 30 million were killed during the Second World War. Stalin is thought to have allowed 20 million to die in the gulags and overall he is believed to have been responsible for between 30 and 40

million deaths. However, an investigation into Mao's record by Daniel Southerland in the *Washington Post* suggests that Mao exceeded even these ghastly
totals:

> While most scholars are reluctant to estimate a total number of 'unnatural
> deaths' in China under Mao, evidence shows that he was in some way responsi-
> ble for at least 40 million deaths and perhaps 80 million or more. This includes
> deaths he was directly responsible for and deaths resulting from disastrous
> policies he refused to change. One government document that has been inter-
> nally circulated and seen by a former Communist Party official now at Prince-
> ton University [Chen Yizi] says that 80 million died unnatural deaths—most of
> them in the famine following the Great Leap Forward.[10]

Notes for "False Science, False Promises"

1. Edward Friedman, Paul G. Pickowicz and Mark Selden, *Chinese Village, Socialist State*, pp. 216–217.
2. Quoted in Klaus Mehnert, *Peking and Moscow*, p. 356. Mehnert also describes how during the Great Leap Forward, Shanghai writers undertook to produce 3,000 literary works in two years. Soon they had far exceeded their plan: one single evening three thousand Shanghai workers and soldiers 'produced' 3,000 poems and 360 songs. One of the poems awarded a special prize was 'Ode to the Red Sun':
    'When Chairman Mao comes forth,
    The East shines Red.
    All living things prosper,
    The Earth is "red".
    Six hundred million, peony bright:
    Each one is "red".
    For all our beautiful hills and streams,
    Eternal time is "red".
3. Quoted from a Red Guard magazine in Roderick MacFarquhar, *The Origins of the Cultural Revolution*, p. 84.
4. Dawa Norbu, *Red Star over Tibet*, p. 129.
5. Zhou Libo, *Great Changes in a Mountain Village*, was translated by Derek Bryan and published by the Foreign Languages Press in 1961. Quoted in *A Chinese View of China* by John Gittings, p. 139.
6. John Byron and Robert Pack, *The Claws of the Dragon: Kang Sheng*, p. 234.
7. John Byron and Robert Pack, *The Claws of the Dragon: Kang Sheng*, p. 234.
8. Li Rui, *A True Account of the Lushan Meeting*, p. 8.
9. Mikhail Klochko, *Soviet Scientist in China*, pp. 139–140.
10. *People's Daily*, 1958.
11. *They Are Creating Miracles*, Foreign Languages Press, 1960. The Chinese edition appeared earlier.
12. For a detailed account of Lysenko see Zhores A. Medvedev, *The Rise and Fall of T.D. Lysenko*, translated by I. Michael Wermner, Columbia University Press, 1969; and David Joravsky, *The Lysenko Affair*, University of Chicago Press, 1970.
13. Nikita Khrushchev, *Khrushchev Remembers*, p. 13.
14. Roderick MacFarquhar, Timothy Cheek and Eugene Wu (eds.), *The Secret Speeches of Chairman Mao*, p. 450.
15. Denis Fred Simon and Merle Goldman (eds.), *Science and Technology in Post-Mao China*, p. 48.
16. Denis Fred Simon and Merle Goldman (eds.), *Science and Technology in Post-Mao China*, p. 53.
17. Interview with the author.
18. British United Press, printed in the *Guardian*, 24 March 1960.
19. Reported in the *Sunday Times* by Richard Hughes, June 1960.
20. Alfred L. Chan, 'The Campaign for Agricultural Development in the Great Leap Forward: A Study of Policy-making and Implementation in Liaoning', *China Quarterly*, No. 129 (March 1992), pp. 68–69.
21. Bo Yibo, *Retrospective of Several Big Decisions and Incidents*, Central Party School, 1993.
22. Interview with Chen Yizi.
23. *China Pictorial*, 1959.

24. *Far Eastern Economic Review*, February 1959.
25. *Far Eastern Economic Review*, 10 December 1958.
26. Roderick MacFarquhar, *The Origins of the Cultural Revolution*.
27. Reuters, 7 April 1960.
28. Interview with the author.
29. Vaclav Smil, *The Bad Earth: Environmental Degradation in China*.
30. *Human Rights Watch Asia Report*, February 1995, pp. 37–44.
31. Dai Qing (ed.), *Changjiang Yimin (Population Transfer on the Yangzi River)*, a documentary anthology.
32. Richard Hughes, *The Chinese Communes*, p. 69.
33. Interview with the author.
34. Jung Chang, *Wild Swans*, p. 226.
35. Roderick MacFarquhar, *The Origins of the Cultural Revolution*, p. 121.
36. Interview with the author.
37. Roderick MacFarquhar, *The Origins of the Cultural Revolution*, p. 139.
38. Jack Potter and Sulamith Heins Potter, *China's Peasants—The Anthropology of a Revolution*, p. 73.
39. William Hinton, *Shenfan*, p. 218.
40. Denis Twitchett and John K. Fairbank (eds.), *Cambridge History of China*, vol. 14, pp. 378–386.
41. *Far Eastern Economic Review*, 11 August 1960.

Notes for "How Many Died"

1. Judith Banister, *China's Changing Population*, p. 13.
2. Judith Banister, *China's Changing Population*, pp. 2–26.
3. Interview with Chinese officials. The worst fear for droughts and floods was 1954 according to tables produced by the Chinese Central Meteorological Centre. Both 1960 and 1961 had fewer floods and droughts than 1958 which was publicly hailed as an outstanding year.
4. Peng Xizhe, 'Demographic Consequences of the Great Leap Forward in China's Provinces', *Population and Development Review*, Vol. 3, No. 4, December 1987, p. 641.
5. Banister (p. 85) draws on work on Chinese population figures by John S. Aird, Ansley J. Coale and other authorities in the United States.
6. Wang Weizhi, *Contemporary Chinese Population*, edited by Xu Dixin, p. 9.
7. Cong Jin, *China, 1949–1989: The Zig-zag Development Era*, p. 272.
8. Wen Yu, *Disasters of Leftism in China*, p. 280.
9. See also Nicholas R. Lardy, 'The Chinese Economy under Stress, 1958–1965' in *The Cambridge History of China*, Vol. 14, which looks at mortality and compares China's famine with that in the Soviet Union.
10. Daniel Southerland in *Washington Post*, 18 July 1994. Chen Yizi is now President of the Center for Modern China at Princeton University.

Reading 7

WAITING FOR A JEW
Marginal Redemption at the Eighth Street Shul

Jonathan Boyarin

My story begins in a community, with an illusion of wholeness. I am between the age when consciousness begins and the age of ten, when my family leaves the community and my illusion is shattered. Our family lives on the edge of the Pine Barrens in Farmingdale, New Jersey, along with hundreds of other families of Jewish chicken farmers who have come from Europe and New York City in several waves, beginning just after World War I.

Among the farmers are present and former Communists, Bundists, Labor Zionists, German refugees who arrived in the 1930s, and Polish survivors of concentration camps. These, however, are not the distinctions I make among them as a child. Johannes Fabian has shown us that when we write ethnography we inevitably trap those about whom we write into a hypostatic, categorical, grammatical "present" (Fabian 1983). An autobiographer has the same power over the memory of himself and those he knew in prior times as the fieldworker who later obliterates the narrative aspect of his encounter with his subjects—the power to deny their autonomy in hindsight.[1] Those of the farming community whom I will later remember, I know therefore by their own names and places: my grandparents closer to Farmingdale proper; the Silbers off on Yellowbrook Road, with a tree nursery now instead of chickens; the Lindauers, stubbornly maintaining an egg-packing and -distribution business, while others find different ways to earn a living.

Boyarin, Jonathan. "Waiting for a Jew." *Thinking in Jewish.* Chicago: The U of Chicago P., 1996. 8–34.

My child's world is not exclusively Jewish, nor am I brought up to regard it as such. Across our road and down a few hundred yards is a tiny house built by Jewish farmers when they first came to settle here. It is now, incredibly, occupied by a black family of ten. Next to them lives an equally poor and large white family. Shortly before we leave Farmingdale, the old Jew in the farm next to ours passes away, and the property passes to a Japanese businessman. The young men he hires live in the farmhouse, growing oriental vegetables on the open field and bonsai in a converted chicken coop, and they introduce me to the game of Go. The nearest Jewish household is that of my great-uncle Yisroel and his wife Helen, the third house to the right of ours.

Yet we are near the heart of Jewish life in Farmingdale. Half a mile—but no, it must be less—down Peskin's Lane (the name my grandfather Israel Boyarin gave to what was a dirt road in the 1930s) is the Farmingdale Jewish Community Center, on the next plot of land after Uncle Yisroel's house. Just past the community center is the farm that once belonged to my father's uncle Peskin, the first Jew in Farmingdale. Fifteen years after Peskin's death, the bodies of two gangsters were found buried on the farm. The local papers noted: "Mr. Peskin was not available for comment."

Our own farm consists of eleven acres. Facing the road is the house my grandfather built, with a large front lawn and an apple tree in back. Farther back, four large chicken coops mark the slope of a hill ending in our field, behind which woods conceal the tiny Manasquan River. The field, well fertilized by chickens allowed to scratch freely on it during the day, is leased each summer by a dirt farmer who grows corn. My father has joined the insurance agency begun by my mother, and they have gotten rid of the birds. The coops stand empty by my fourth birthday. One day, though, while a friend and I chase each other through the coops in play, we are startled by a pair of chickens. Their presence in the stillness and the faint smell of ancient manure is inexplicable and unforgettable. Thus, on the abandoned farm, my first memories are tinged with a sense of traces, of mystery, of loss. Do all who eventually become anthropologists have this experience in some form, at some time in their early lives?

My mother's turn to business is wise: chicken farming as the basis for the community's livelihood is quickly becoming untenable. Nor is it surprising, as she had given up a career as a chemist to come live with my father on the farm—thus taking part in the process of Jewish dispersal from the immigrants' urban centers, which in the last quarter of the century would be mirrored by a shrinking of Jewish communities in small towns and a reconsolidation of the Orthodox centers. My mother's father, an Orthodox Jew from a leading Lithuanian rabbinical family, has struggled to learn English well and has gone into the insurance business himself. After his death, my mother tells me that he had originally resisted her desire to marry the son of a Jewish socialist, but he consented when he met my father's father's father, a Lubavitcher Hasid named Mordechai.

My grandfather's concern for his daughter's future as an observant Jew was well founded. The Sabbath is marked in our family only on Friday nights: by my mother's candle-lighting, and her chicken soup in winter; by the challah; by the presence of my grandfather. We do not keep kosher, nor do we go to shul on *shabbes*.

The Jewish Community Center—with its various functions as social and meeting hall, synagogue, and school—is nevertheless a focus of our family's life. Most of the ten or so other children in these classes I see at other times during the week as well, either in public school or playing at one another's homes. I am there three times each week, first for Sunday school, and then for Hebrew school on Tuesday and Thursday afternoons. This odd distinction is no doubt a practical one, since some parents do not choose to send their children three times a week. But since Sunday school was first a Christian institution, it also reflects an accommodation to Christian church patterns, as evidenced by the fact that Sundays are devoted to teaching stories of the Bible. One Sunday school teacher we have in our kindergarten year captivates me with his skill in making these stories come to life, as when he imitates the distress of an Egyptian waking up to find his bed covered with frogs.

Another teacher, a young woman with a severe manner and a heavy black wig, the wife of a member of the Orthodox yeshiva in Lakewood, later causes general misery because of her inability to understand children, although I will eventually appreciate the prayers she teaches us to read. One time I come in to Hebrew school immediately after yet another in a series of martyred family dogs has been run over in front of our house. Her attempt to comfort me is like some malicious parody of Talmudic reasoning: "You shouldn't be so upset about an animal. If a chicken and a person both fell down a well, which one would you save first?"

In addition to this somewhat haphazard religious training, there is the local chapter of Habonim, the Labor Zionist Youth Organization, to which my older brother and sister belong. I tag along and am tolerated by their peers. Once I am given a minor role in a stage performance by the chapter. Though I am too young to remember quite what it is about, the phrase *komets-aleph:aw* stands in my memory.

Later I will learn that this phrase occurs in a famous and sentimental Yiddish folksong. It is the first letter of the Hebrew alphabet, the first thing countless generations of Jewish children have been taught. Here is an unusual case in which a traditional lesson—how to pronounce the alphabet—is successfully inculcated in the secularized framework of a dramatic performance about the traditional setting. Perhaps this is because of the necessary rehearsals, in which I must have heard, as the song puts it, "once more, over and over again, *komets-aleph:aw*." The memory reinforces my later preference for this older, European pronunciation of the Hebrew vowels, my sense of the Israeli *kamets-aleph:ah* as inauthentic.

Also memorable at the Jewish Community Center is the annual barbecue run by the Young Couples' Club. Though my father will assure me in an interview years later that its association with the Fourth of July was purely a matter of convenience, the atmosphere is certainly one of festival, even including "sacrifices" and "altars": My father and his friends set up huge charcoal pits with cement blocks, and broil vast amounts of chicken; corn is boiled in aluminum garbage cans to go with it.[2] For the children, a Purim-like element of riotous excess is added: This one time each year, we are allowed to drink as much soda as we want. One year "wild," blond-haired Richie L., whose parents have a luncheonette booth for a kitchen table and an attic filled with antiques, claims to drink fourteen bottles, thus adding to the mystique he holds for me.

But it is the days when the Community Center becomes a synagogue that leave the strongest impression on my memory. There must be services every Saturday morning, but I am completely unaware of them. What I will remember are the holidays: Purim, Rosh Hashanah, Yom Kippur, Simchas Torah, and a crowd of people who just a few years later will never be there again. On the fall holidays, the shul is full of movement, impatience, noise, and warmth. Except for a few moments such as the shofar blowing, we children are free to come and go: By the steps in front, tossing the juicy, poisonous red berries of a yew that was planted, I am told, in memory of my brother Aaron, whom I never knew; inside the main doors, to look left at Walter Tenenbaum wrapped in a *tallis* that covers his head, standing at a lectern by the Ark of the Torah as he leads the service, or to look right, along the first long row of folding chairs for our fathers; thence a few rows back to where our mothers sit separately from the men, although unlike most synagogues that look and sound as traditional as this one, there is no *mekhitse*, no barrier between women and men; and finally out through the side door and down a flight of wooden steps to the monkey bars, into the ditch where one miraculous day we found and drank an intact bottle of orange soda, or into the kitchen, social room, and classroom in the basement. Once each year we children are the center of attention, as we huddle under a huge tallis in front of the Ark on Simchas Torah to be blessed.

In classic ethnographies of hunting-and-gathering groups, landscapes are described as personalized, integral elements of culture. This was true of the landscape of my childhood friendships, which today is as obliterated as any *shtetl* in Eastern Europe. Any marginal group in mass society may be subject without warning to the loss of its cultural landscape, and therefore those who are able to create portable landscapes for themselves are the most likely to endure.

The Jews have been doing so for thousands of years; the Simchas Torah tallis can stand in front of any Ark, and the original Ark, in the biblical account, was itself transported from station to station in the desert. Yet the members of a community are orphaned when the naïve intimacy of a living environment is torn away from them. Such a break appears often in Jewish literature—significantly with the emphasis not forward on the beginning of adulthood, as in the European *Bildungsroman*, but rather on the end of childhood.[3]

I suddenly discover the distance between the world and myself at the end of August in 1966. When my parents pick me up from camp, they take me to a new house. For the last time, we attend high holiday services in Farmingdale. It is the only time we will ever drive there, and our family's friends no longer join us during the afternoon break on Yom Kippur for a surreptitious glass of tea and a slice of challah. Farmingdale is no longer home, and though our new house is only ten miles away, it is another world.

We live now in an almost exclusively white, middle-class suburb with many Jews, but our older, brick house is isolated on a block of working-class cubes. While neighbors my age play football in our yard, I often retreat to my room and console myself with sports books for preadolescents. My new and bewildering sense of marginality leads me to develop an exquisite self-consciousness. It is manifested in an almost constant internal dialogue, which keeps me company and will interfere with my adolescent sexuality.

Ostracism is often the fate of a new kid on the block, and it may last longer when his family is Jewish and his home better than those on either side. There is a custom in this part of New Jersey of tolerating petty vandalism on "mischief night," the night before Halloween. Pumpkins are smashed, and we, along with other unpopular families on the block, have the windows of our cars and house smeared with soap. One Halloween I wake up to see graffiti chalked in bold letters on the sidewalk in front of our house: "Jon the Jew, a real one too." My father summons the kids next door—whom we suspect of being the authors—to scrape the words off the sidewalk, as I burn with shame.

He and I never discuss the incident, but later I will compare it with a memory of Freud's: As a child, he was walking with his father, when a gentile knocked his father's hat off. Rather than confronting the man, Freud's father meekly bent over to pick up the hat, and his son's humiliation persisted into adulthood (Bakan 1958; D. Boyarin 1997). The moral is that a victim is likely to view any response as adding insult to injury. In my case, as my father asserts the American principle of equality and "teaches a lesson" to my occasional and vindictive playmates by forcing them to erase what they have written, I feel as though he is inviting them to write the words again, this time making me watch my own degradation.

The new synagogue my parents join is only a partial refuge. It exemplifies the difference between a shul and a temple. Everything in Farmingdale had faced inward: little concern was paid for praying in unison, and though the *shammes* would bang his hand on the table for silence, he was seldom heeded; even the cantor was alone with God, facing away from everyone else, rather than performing for the congregation. Calling a synagogue a temple, by contrast, is doubly revealing. On the one hand, it indicates a striving for the majesty of the ancient House in Jerusalem. On the other hand, just like the English term used to designate it, its trappings are borrowed from the Christian world, down to the black robes worn by the rabbi and cantor.

These robes lack the warm mystery of Walter Tenenbaum's tallis. The responsive readings of Psalms in English seem ridiculously artificial to me from the first. And my mother, who still comes only on the holidays though I sometimes drag my father to temple on Friday nights, complains of the rabbi's long-winded sermons and yearns aloud for the intimate conversations along the back wall of the Farmingdale Jewish Community Center.

Unlike some, I do not leave the synagogue immediately after my bar mitzvah. I teach the blessings of the Haftorah to two reluctant boys a year younger than me. I briefly experience religious inspiration, and for perhaps two weeks put on *tefillin.* every morning. But the atmosphere is hollow, and the emptiness breeds cynicism in me in my teens.

The coldness of the building itself is symptomatic of the lack of sustenance I sense there. The pretense and bad taste of modern American synagogues are well-known yet puzzling phenomena that deserve a sociological explanation of their own. Even the walls of the temple are dead concrete blocks, in contrast to the wood of the Farmingdale Jewish Community Center. Services are held in a "sanctuary," unlike the room at the Community Center where activities as varied as dances and political meetings were conducted when services were not being held. Aside from any question of Jewish law, there is a loss of community marked by the fact that everyone drives to the temple rather than walking. It is a place separated from the home, without the strong and patient webs spun by leisurely strolling conversations to and from a shul.

Most generally, the temple is victim to the general alienation of the suburbs. What happens or fails to happen there is dependent on what the people who come there expect from each other. Those who belong (there are vastly more "members" than regular attendees) seem bound primarily by a vague desire to have Jewish grandchildren. The poor rabbi, typical of Conservative congregations, seems hired to be a stand-in Jew, to observe all the laws and contain all the knowledge they don't have the time for. They are not bound to each other by Jewish religious ways, nor do they share the common interests of everyday life—the same livelihood or language—that helped to make a complete community in Farmingdale.

I go off to college and slowly discover that my dismissal of Judaism leaves me isolated, with few resources. I had realized my individual difference on leaving Farmingdale. Now, much more removed from a Jewish environment than ever before, I become aware of my inescapable Jewishness. In the small northwestern college of my dreams, everyone around me seems "American" and different, though I have never thought of myself as anything but American. Even in the humanities curriculum on which the school prides itself, Jewish civilization is absent. It is as though Western cultural history were just a triumphant straight line from the Greeks to Augustine and Michelangelo (with his horned Moses and uncircumcised David), confusion setting in at last only with Marx and Freud.

Five years too late to benefit me, a Jewish Studies position will in fact be established at the college. Such positions are usually funded by Jewish individuals or organizations, and hence they represent the growing acculturation (not assimilation) of Jews into American academic life. The fact that they are regarded as legitimate by the academic community, however, is part of a reintegration of Jewish thought into the concept of Western humanities. Jewish ethnographers can contribute to this movement—for example, by elucidating the dialectic of tradition and change as worked out in communities facing vastly different historical challenges. We may then move beyond efforts to explain the explosive presence of Jews in post-Enlightenment intellectual life as a result of their "primitive" encounter with "civility" (Cuddihy 1974) to explore how the Jewish belief that "Creation as the (active) speech or writing of God posits first of all that the Universe is essentially intelligible" (Faur 1986:7) provided a pathway from Torah to a restless, unifying modern impulse in the natural and social sciences.

Such notions are far beyond me as an undergraduate. At my college in the 1970s, the social scientists in their separate departments strive to separate themselves from their "objects of study"; the humanists treasure the peace of their cloisters; the artists, knowing they are intellectually suspect, cultivate a cliquish sense of superiority; and there is none of the give-and-take between learning and everyday experience that I have come to associate with the best of Jewish scholarship.

I find a friend, a Jew from Long Island, and we begin to teach each other that we need to cultivate our Jewishness. We discuss the "Jewish mentality" of modern thinkers, and paraphrasing Lenny Bruce's category of the *goyish*, sarcastically reject all that is "white." "I am not 'white,' " my friend Martin proudly postures, "I am a Semite." Meanwhile, reflecting on my own dismissal of suburban Judaism, I decide not to end willingly an almost endless chain of Jewish cultural transmission. I stake my future on the assumption that a tradition so old and varied must contain the seeds of a worthwhile life for me, and decide to begin to acquire them through study.

Besides, my reading as a student of anthropology leads me to reason that if I concentrate on Jewish culture, no one will accuse me of cultural imperialism (see Gough 1968). No doubt others in my generation who choose to do fieldwork with Jews are motivated by similar considerations. Jewish anthropologists as a class are privileged to belong to the world of academic discourse, and to have an entrée into a variety of unique communities that maintain cultural frameworks in opposition to mass society.

Something deeper than Marxist critiques of anthropology draws me to Yiddish in particular. Before leaving Farmingdale, my best friend had been a child of survivors from Lemberg. I remember being at his house once, and asking with a sense of wonder: "Ralph, do you really know Yiddish?"

Ralph told me that although he understood the language—which his parents still spoke to him—he had never learned to speak it. Still, I was impressed that he knew this secret code. And now that I am finished with college and looking to find my own way home, Yiddish seems to be the nearest link to which I can attach myself. It is the key to a sense of the life of the shtetl, that Jewish dreamtime that I inevitably associate with my lost Farmingdale.

The Farmingdale community has, by this point, completely disintegrated: Virtually no Jews in that part of New Jersey earn their living as chicken farmers anymore. Many of those who have gone into business have moved to nearby towns like Lakewood. The Torah scrolls of the Community Center have been ceremoniously transferred to a new synagogue near housing developments on the highway between Farmingdale and Lakewood. I have never considered becoming a chicken farmer myself.

So, when I finish my college courses, without waiting for graduation, I flee back to New York. "Flee": No one chases me out of Portland, Oregon, God forbid! "Back": The city, though a magnet and a refuge, has never been my home before. Yet for three years I have shaped my identity in opposition to the "American" world around me, and I have reverted, along with my close friends, to what we imagine is an authentic New York accent—the "deses" and "doses" that were drilled out of my parents' repertoire in the days when New York public school teachers had to pass elocution exams.

Rejecting suburban Judaism, belatedly pursuing the image of the sixties' counterculture to the Pacific Northwest, and self-consciously affecting a "New York Jew" style were all successive attempts to shape a personal identity. In each case, the identity strategy was in opposition to the prevailing conventions of the immediate social order. Similarly, opposition to their parents' perceived bourgeois complacency may underlie the involvement of young people with Judaism. Yet as Dominique Schnapper has noted (1983), for young, intellectual Jews becoming involved in Jewish religion, politics, or culture, there can be no question of canceling out prior experience and "becoming traditional." In fact, this is true even of the most seemingly Orthodox and insular Jewish communities. There is a difference between learning about great rabbis of the past through meetings with Jewish graybeards who knew them, and through reading about their merits in the Williamsburg newspaper *Der Yid*.

Of course, not only Jews are in the position of reconstituting interrupted tradition (cf. Clifford 1986: 116 ff.). But since they have been in the business of reshaping tradition in a dialogue with written texts for thousands of years, Jews may benefit more directly than others from learning about what other Jews are doing with their common tradition. It is conceivable that individuals may choose to adopt traits from other communities or even join those communities based on what they read in ethnographies. Whether such cultural borrowings and recombinations are effected in an "authentic" manner will depend less on precedent than on the degree of self-confident cultural generosity that results.

Arriving in New York, I adopt a knitted yarmulke, although my hair still falls below my shoulders. I immediately begin a nine-week summer course in Yiddish at Columbia, and it seems as though the language were being brought out from deep inside me. When I go to visit my parents on weekends, my father remembers words he'd never noticed forgetting. When I take the IRT after class back down to the Village, it seems as if everybody on the train is speaking Yiddish. Most important for my sense of identity, phrases here and there in my own internal dialogue are now in Yiddish, and I find I can reflect on myself with a gentle irony that was never available to me in English.

Then, after my first year in graduate school, I am off to Europe the following summer, courtesy of my parents. I arrive at the Gare du Nord in Paris with the address of a friend and without a word of French. I am spotted wearing my yarmulke by a young North African Jew who makes me understand, in broken English, that he studies at the Lubavitch yeshiva in Paris. He buys me a Paris guidebook and sets me on my way in the Metro. At the end of the summer, this meeting will stand as the first in a set of Parisian reactions to my yarmulke which crystallize in my memory:

—The reaction of the generous young Trotskyist with whom my friend had grown close and with whom I stayed for two weeks: She could see the yarmulke only as a symbol of Jewish nationalism and argued bitterly that it was inherently reactionary;

—Of a young North African Jew, selling carpets at the flea market at Clignoncourt, who grabbed my arm and cried, "*Haver! Haver!* Brother Jew!";

—Of another young man, minding a booth outside one of the great department stores, who asked me if I were Orthodox, and interrupted my complicated response to explain that, although he was Orthodox himself, he was afraid to wear a yarmulke in the street;

—Of an old man at the American Express office who spoke to me in Yiddish and complained that the recent North African migrants dominated the Jewish communal organizations, and that there was no place for a Polish Jew to go.

Those first, fragmentary encounters are my fieldwork juvenilia. In assuming the yarmulke, I perhaps do not stop to consider that neither my actions nor my knowledge match the standards that it symbolically represents. But it works effectively, almost dangerously, as a two-way sensor, inducing Jews to present themselves to me and forcing me to try to understand how I am reflected in their eyes.

Externally, I learn many things about the situation of French Jewry. From the patent discomfort my non-Jewish Trotskyist friend feels at my display of Jewish specificity, I gain some sense of the conflicts young French Jews—coming out of the universalist, antihistorical revolutionary apogee of May 1968— must have felt years later when they first began to distinguish themselves from their comrades and view the world from the vantage point of their specific history. From the young street peddlers, I learn about how much riskier public proclamation of oneself as a Jew is perceived as being in Paris than in New York, and a concomitant depth of instant identification of one Jew with another. My meeting with the old Polish Jew at the American Express office hints at the dynamics of dominant and declining ethnic groups within the Jewish community, so vastly different from those dynamics in the United States.

Internally, I begin to understand that an identifiably Jewish headcovering places its own claims on the one who wears it. The longer it stays put, the more its power to keep him out of non-kosher restaurants grows. More important, people want to know who he is as a Jew. And if he does not know, the desire for peace of mind will spur further his effort to shape an identity.

Returning from Paris, I find an apartment at Second Avenue and Fifth Street in Manhattan. I tell people, "After three generations, my family has finally made it back to the Lower East Side." In fact, none of my grandparents lived on the East Side for a long time after immigrating, even though my mother tells me she regrets having missed the Yiddish theater on Second Avenue during her girlhood. By the time I move in, there is no Yiddish theater left. The former Ratner's dairy restaurant on Second Avenue, where, I'm told, Trotsky was a lousy tipper, is now a supermarket. Though sometimes one still sees a white newspaper truck with the word *Forverts* in lovely blue Hebrew letters on its side drive by late at night, this neighborhood has been the East Village since the sixties, and I think of it as such.

A new friend, who devotes his time to a frustrating effort to rescue Lower East Side synagogues, tells me of a shul still in use on an otherwise abandoned block east of Tompkins Square Park. Though my friend has never been inside, he is sure that I will be welcomed, since such an isolated congregation must be looking for new blood.

The place is called the Eighth Street Shul, but its full name is Kehilas Bnei Moshe Yakov Anshei Zavichost veZosmer—Congregation Children of Moses and Jacob, People of Zavichost and Zosmer. It is owned by a *landsmanshaft* (hometown society) founded by émigrés and refugees from two towns in south central Poland. No one born in either town prays regularly at the shul now, and only one or two of the congregants are actually members of the society.

The shul is located in the center of what New York Latinos call "Loisaida"—an area bounded by Avenue A on the east, Avenue D on the west, Houston Street on the south, and Fourteenth Street on the north. Once the blocks up to Tenth Street were almost exclusively Jewish, and on nearly every one stood a synagogue or a religious school. Now two of those former synagogues stand abandoned, several more have become churches, and the rest have disappeared.

Eighth Street is a typical and not especially distinguished example of turn-of-the-century Lower East Side synagogue architecture.[4] It consists of five levels. The lowest contains a cranky and inadequate boiler. The second is the *besmedresh* or study room, which was destroyed by a suspicious fire in August 1982. The third level is the main sanctuary, long and narrow like the tenements among which it was tucked when it was built. Two rows of simple pews are separated by an aisle, which is interrupted in the center of the room by the raised table from which the weekly Torah portion is read. At the very front is the Ark, surrounded by partially destroyed wooden carvings that are the most artistic aspect of the shul. The walls are decorated with representations of the traditional Jewish signs for the zodiac; the two in front on the left have been obliterated by water damage from the leaky roof. Covering most of this level, with roughly an eight-foot opening extending toward the back, is the women's gallery. The gallery is constructed in such a way that it is easier for women sitting on opposite sides of the opening to converse with one another than to see what the men are doing downstairs. Finally, upstairs from the women's gallery is an unused and cramped apartment that was once occupied by the shul's caretaker. In the roof behind it, an opening that was a skylight until there was a break-in is now covered with a solid wooden framework, allowing neither light nor vandals to enter.

Avenues B and C, which mark off the block, were once lively commercial streets with mostly Jewish storekeepers. There were also several smaller streets lined with tenements, right up to the edge of the East River. When the FDR Drive was built along the river, all the streets east of Avenue D disappeared, the tenements on the remaining available land were replaced by municipal housing, and the stores declined rapidly. During the same years, a massive middle-class housing cooperative, funded by a government mortgage, was built along Grand Street one mile to the south. Many of the remaining Jewish families moved into those houses, leaving virtually no Jews in the immediate area of the Eighth Street Shul.

Yet a minyan has continued to meet there every Saturday morning, with virtually no interruptions, throughout the years of the neighborhood's decline, while the block served as the Lower East Side's heaviest "shopping street" for hard drugs. It has lasted into the present, when buildings all around it are being speculated upon and renovated by both squatters and powerful real estate interests. It appears that until recently the main reason for this continuity was a felicitous rivalry between two men who were unwilling to abandon the synagogue because their fathers had both been presidents of it at one time. Perhaps if there had been only one, he would have given up and made peace with his conscience. Perhaps if the two men had naturally been friends they could have agreed to sell the building and officially merge their society with another still functioning further south in the neighborhood. If they had been able to agree on anything besides continuing to come to the shul, the shul might not have survived this long.

The first time I walk in, a clean-shaven, compact man in his sixties—younger than several of the congregants, who number perhaps seventeen in all—

hurries forward to greet me. What's my name? Where do I live? Where am I from originally? And where do I usually go to pray on shabbes? His name is Moshe Fogel, and he sees to it that I am called to the Torah, the honor accorded any guest who comes for the first time, without asking any questions as to his level of religious observance. Later, an older member explains to me: "Once upon a time, you wouldn't get called to the Torah unless you kept kosher and observed shabbes." Now, Moish prefers simply to leave those matters undiscussed.

The history of the East Side as a place where all types of Jews have lived together reinforces his discretion. Externalities such as proper or improper clothing are not essential criteria for participation. This is true of the entire Orthodox community on the East Side and has even become part of its mystique. Rabbi Reuven Feinstein, head of the Staten Island branch of the East Broadway-based yeshiva, Tifereth Jerusalem, noted in a recent speech the common reaction in Boro Park and other thriving Orthodox centers to the nonconformist dress of East Side visitors: "It's okay, you're from the East Side." The president at Eighth Street still wears a traditional *gartl* when he prays, a belt worn over his jacket to separate the pure from the base parts of his body, and no one has suggested that such old customs are out of place today. But partly because the older members at the Eighth Street Shul walked through the East Village in the 1960s and knew there were many young Jews among the longhairs—even if they were horrified at the thought—they were willing to include in the minyan a young man in the neighborhood who, when he first came, wore dreadlocks under a Rastafarian-style knitted cap. It is also doubtless true that at that time there was no other Orthodox synagogue anywhere that he would have contemplated entering.

By contrast, it is impossible for any Jew raised in the middle of secular society (including a Jewish anthropologist) to join a traditionalist community without giving up major parts of his or her identity. The ways in which a researcher of contemporary Hasidic life "becomes a Hasid" are much more dramatic than the way in which one becomes a regular at Eighth Street—but they are probably more transient as well. In order to gain the confidence of the traditionalist communities, the fieldworker has to give the impression, whether implicitly or explicitly, that he or she is likely eventually to accept their standards in all areas of life (Belcove-Shalin 1988). All one has to do at Eighth Street is agree to come back—"a little earlier next time, if possible."

Two things will draw me back to join this congregation, occasionally referred to as "those holy souls who *daven* in the middle of the jungle." The first pull is the memory of Farmingdale: the Ashkenazic accents and melodies (though here they are Polish, whereas Walter Tenenbaum had prayed in his native Lithuanian accent); the smell of herring on the old men's breath and hands; the burning sensation of whiskey, which I must have tasted surreptitiously at the conclusion of Yom Kippur one year in Farmingdale.

The second thing that draws me, though I do not come every week, is a feeling that I am needed and missed when I am absent. It's hard for me to get up early on Saturday mornings, after being out late Friday nights. It still seems like a sacrifice, as though I were stealing part of my weekend from myself. If I arrive in time for the *Shema*, about half an hour into the service, I congratulate myself on my devotion. The summer before I marry, in 1981, I hardly come at all. When I go with my brother to meet Moshe Fogel at the shul and give him the provisions for the kiddush I am giving to celebrate my upcoming wedding, I tell Dan that I usually arrive "around nine-thirty," to which Moish retorts: "Even when you used to come, you didn't show up at nine-thirty!" Though he says it with a smile, a message comes through clearly: If I want to claim to belong, I should attend regularly and arrive on time. Although I am always welcome, only if I can be counted on am I part of the minyan. The dependence of Jews on each other— a theme running through biblical and rabbinic literature—is pressingly literal at Eighth Street.

Meanwhile, my feelings about Paris coalesce into a plan. I know I want to live there for a time, but only if I will be among Jews. Since I am at the point in my graduate school career when I must find a dissertation topic, I decide to look for fieldwork situations with Jews in Paris. I make an exploratory visit with my fiancée, Elissa. Will she agree to a pause in her own career to follow me on this project? Will the organizations of Polish Jewish immigrants whom I have chosen to study be willing to have me study them?

The answer is yes to both questions. Speaking Yiddish and appearing as a nice young Jewish couple seem to be the critical elements in our success. We are invited to sit in on board meetings, negotiations aimed at the reunification of societies split by political differences for over half a century. I am struck by the fact that these immigrants seem so much more marked by their political identification than the East European Jews I've met in New York. Also, I am impressed at the number of societies remaining in a country that has suffered Nazi occupation and that historically has shown little tolerance for immigrant cultural identifications.

But I am drawn not so much by the differences between these Yiddish speakers and those I know in New York as by encountering them in an environment that is otherwise so foreign. Speaking Yiddish to people with whom I have no other common language confirms its legitimacy and reinforces the sense of a distinctive Jewish identity that is shared between generations. I go for a trial interview of one activist, who is disappointed that I didn't bring "the girl," Elissa, along with me. When he discovers to my embarrassment that I have been secretly taping the interview, he is flattered.

Just before leaving Paris, Elissa and I climb the steps of Sacré Coeur. The cathedral itself is an ungracious mass, and the city looks gray and undifferentiated below us. I experience a moment of vertigo, as if I could tumble off Montmartre and drown. Part of my dream of Paris, "capital of the nineteenth century," is an infantile fantasy of becoming a universal intellectual—to be free both of the special knowledge and of the limitations of my knowledge that follow on my personal history. Yet I know I cannot come to Paris and immediately move among its confident, cliquish intellectual elite. Even less will I ever have contact with that "quintessentially French" petite bourgeoisie typified by the stolid Inspector Maigret. My first place will be with the immigrants, whose appearance, strange language, and crowded quarters provided material for unkind portraits by Maigret's creator, Simenon, in the 1930s.[5] If I am unable to come to see Paris as they have seen it, if I cannot make out of a shared marginality a niche in the city for myself, I will be lost, as much as the "lost generation," and in a most unromantic way.

During the two years between our decision to spend a year in Paris and the beginning of that year, I attend the Eighth Street Shul more and more regularly, and Elissa occasionally joins me. Gradually, my feelings when I miss a week shift from guilt to regret. One shabbes, waking up late but not wanting to miss attending altogether, I arrive just in time for the kiddush, to the general amusement of the entire minyan. One February morning I wake up to see snow falling and force myself to go outside against my will, knowing that on a day like this I am truly needed.

Other incidents illustrate the gap in assumptions between myself and the other congregants. I try to bring friends into the shul, partly because it makes me more comfortable, and partly to build up the congregation. A friend whose hair and demeanor reflect his love of reggae music and his connections with Jamaican Rastafarians comes along one Yom Kippur. We reach the point in the service when pious men, remembering the priests in the days of the Temple, descend to their knees and touch their foreheads to the floor. Since no one wants to soil his good pants on the dirty floor, sheets of newspaper are provided as protection. Reb Simcha Taubenfeld, the senior member of the congregation, approaches my friend with newspaper in hand and asks in his heavy Yiddish accent: "Do you fall down?" The look of bewilderment on my friend's face graphically illustrates the term "frame of reference."

Another week, the same friend, failing to observe the discretion with regard to the expression of political opinions that I have learned to adopt at shul, gets into a bitter argument over the Palestinian question. Fishel Mandel, a social worker and one of the younger members of the congregation, calls me during the week to convey the message that "despite our political differences, your friend is still welcome."

After our wedding, I attend virtually every week. When Elissa comes, she is doubly welcome, since the only other woman who attends regularly is Goldie Brown, Moish Fogel's sister. Though Goldie doesn't complain about being isolated in the women's gallery one flight above the men, she seconds Elissa's suggestion that a mekhitse be set up downstairs. The suggestion gets nowhere, however: It would entail displacing one of the regular members of the congregation from his usual seat, and though there is no lack of available places (I myself wander from front to back during the course of the service), he refuses to consider moving.

I reason that I will have more of a voice concerning questions such as the seating of women if I formalize my relationship to the shul by becoming a member. My timid announcement that I would like to do so meets with initial confusion on the part of the older members of the society present. Then Fishel, ever the mediator and interpreter, explains to me that the shul is not organized like a suburban synagogue: "There's a *chevra*, a society, that owns the shul. In order to join, you have to be *shomer mitzves*, you have to keep kosher and strictly observe the Sabbath."

I drop my request. Shiye the president reassures me with a speech in his usual roundabout style to the effect that belonging to the chevra is a separate question from being a member of the minyan: "They send their money in from New Jersey and Long Island, but the shul couldn't exist without the people that actually come to pray here."

Meanwhile, our plans to go to Paris proceed. Our travel plans become a topic for discussion over kiddush at shul. One of the older, Polish-born members tell us for the first time that he lived in Paris for nine years after the war. We ask him why he came to America, and he answers, "*Vern a frantsoyz iz shver* [It's hard to become a Frenchman]," both to obtain citizenship and to be accepted by neighbors.

At the end of the summer, we expect to give a farewell kiddush at the shul. A few days before shabbes, I get a phone call from Moish Fogel: "Don't get things for kiddush. We won't be able to daven at Eighth Street for a while. There's been a fire. Thank God, the Torah scrolls were rescued, but it's going to take a while to repair the damage." It is two weeks after Tisha B'Av, the fast commemorating the destruction of the Temple in Jerusalem.

Leaving New York without saying goodbye to the shul and its congregation, we fly overnight to Brussels and immediately *shlep* (the word "drag" would not do the burden justice) our seven heavy suitcases onto a Paris train. Arriving again at the Gare du Nord, I think of the thousands of Polish Jews who were greeted at the station in the twenties and thirties by fellow immigrants eager to hire workers. As soon as we get off the train, Elissa immediately "gets involved," demanding the credentials of two men who claim to be policemen and attempt to "confiscate" a carpet two Moroccan immigrants are carrying. Upon Elissa's challenge, the "policemen" demur.

We practice our French on the cab driver: I explain to him why we've come to Paris. He warns us that we shouldn't tell strangers we're Jewish. It is only a few weeks since the terrorist attack on Goldenberg's restaurant, and no one knows when the next anti-Semitic attack may come. I reply that if I hadn't said we were Jewish, we wouldn't have found out he was a Jew as well, adding that in New York the names of taxi drivers are posted inside the cabs. He says he wouldn't like that at all.

So we receive an early warning that ethnicity in Paris is not celebrated publicly as it is in New York, nor are ethnic mannerisms and phrases so prevalent as a deliberate element of personal style. This is the repressive underside of marginality. It appears wherever the individual or community think it is better not to flaunt their distinctiveness, even if they cannot fully participate in the host culture. It leads to suspicion and silence, to the taxi driver's desire for anonymity.

Arriving at our rented apartment, we meet our neighbor Isabel, who will be our only non-Jewish friend during the year in Paris, and who later explains that meeting us has helped dispel her prejudices about Jews. Over the next few days, we introduce ourselves to Jewish storekeepers in the neighborhood: Guy, the Tunisian kosher butcher; Chanah, the Polish baker's wife; Leon, the deli man from Lublin, who insists he didn't learn Yiddish until he came to Paris.

We have a harder time finding a synagogue where we feel at home. For Rosh Hashanah and Yom Kippur, we have purchased tickets at one of the "official" synagogues run by the Consistoire, the recognized religious body of French Jewry set up under Napoleon. Most synagogues run by the Consistoire are named after the streets on which they're located. Meeting a Hasid on the street, I ask him whether he happens to know when Rosh Hashanah services begin at "Notre Dame de Nazareth." He grimaces and makes as if spitting: "Don't say that name, *ptu ptu ptu!*"

The synagogue is strange to us as well. Most of the crowd seems if anything more secular than most American Jews, who go to the synagogue only on the high holidays. Many teenagers wear jeans or miniskirts. Because of the fear of terrorism, everyone is frisked on entering. Inside, the synagogue is picturesque with its nineteenth-century pseudo-Moorish motifs; when it was built, Offenbach was the choirmaster. Yet it is as religiously dissatisfying as the suburban American temple I used to attend. The services seem to be conducted in a traditional manner, but it is hard to tell from among the noisy throng in back. The shammes, as a representative of the government, wears a Napoleonic hat, and the rabbi delivers his sermon from a high pulpit.

After Yom Kippur, I think idly about the need to find a more comfortable shul, and when I hear about an East European-style minyan within walking distance, I consider going on Simchas Torah. Watching television reports of terrorist attacks on Simchas Torah in other European capitals, I am consumed with shame at my own apathy, and thus I walk a kilometer or two to find the synagogue on the rue Basfroi the following shabbes.

Going in, I am first shown into a side room, where men are reciting incomprehensible prayers with strange and beautiful melodies. Eventually I realize that they are North African Jews, and I venture into the main room to ask, "Is there an Ashkenazic minyan here?"

The man I ask replies in French, "We're not racists here! We're all Jews!" at which his friend points out:

"The young man spoke to you in Yiddish!" Continuing in Yiddish, he explains that while everyone is welcome in the main synagogue, the services there are in fact Ashkenazic, and so some of the North African men prefer to pray in their own style in the smaller room.

Gradually I settle in, though I have trouble following the prayers in the beginning. Remembering a particular turn in the melody for the reader's repetition of the Amidah that the president at Eighth Street uses, I listen for it from the cantor here at the rue Basfroi, and hear a satisfying similarity in his voice. I feel like a new immigrant coming to his landsmanshaft's shul to hear the melodies from his town.

Throughout our year in Paris, I attend this synagogue about as frequently as I had gone to Eighth Street at first. Although the congregation is not unfriendly, no one invites me home for lunch, partly out of French reserve, and perhaps also because it is clear that I'm not very observant. I feel "unobservant" here in another sense: I do not register the vast store of information obviously available here about the interaction of religious Jews from different ethnic backgrounds. It escapes me, as though I were "off duty." In contrast to my feelings at Eighth Street, I am not motivated by the desire to make myself a regular here. And this is not my fieldwork situation: Nothing external moves me to push my way through socially, to find out who these people really are and let them see me as well.

The Jews I encounter in the course of my research belong to an entirely different crowd. The landsmanshaftn to which they belong are secular organizations. If I wanted to observe the Sabbath closely, it would be difficult for me to do my fieldwork. The immigrants hold many meetings on Saturdays, including a series of *shabbes-shmuesn*, afternoon discussions at which the main focus this year is the war in Lebanon.

I mention to one of my informants that I sometimes go to the synagogue. "I admire that," he responds. "I can't go back to the synagogue now. I've been away too long; it's too late for me." Toward the end of the year, we invite an autodidact historian of the immigrant community to dinner on Friday night and ask him to say the blessing over the challah. "I can't," he refuses, and will not explain further. Though his intellectual curiosity has led him to become friendly with us, and he is considering doing research on the resurgence of Orthodoxy among French Jews, his critical stance vis-à-vis his own secularist movement is insufficient to allow him to accept this religious honor. Enjoying the possibilities offered by marginality is sometimes impossible for those who are neither young nor well educated and who have often been deceived in their wholehearted commitments.

Throughout the year, Elissa has been growing stricter regarding *kashres*. She refuses to eat nonkosher meat and will order only fish in restaurants. She articulates our shared impression that Jewish secularism has failed to create everyday lifeways that can be transmitted from generation to generation, and that any lasting Judaism must be grounded in Jewish law and learning. Before parting for the summer—she to study Yiddish at Oxford, I to Jerusalem, to acquire the Hebrew that I will need to learn about Jewish law—we discuss the level of observance we want to adopt on our return to New York, but we come to no decision.

Elissa and I meet at the end of the summer in Los Angeles, for the bar mitzvah of her twin cousins. I am uncomfortable riding on shabbes; after spending an entire summer in Jerusalem, for the first time, it seems like a violation of myself. The roast beef sandwich I eat at the reception is the first nonkosher food I've eaten since leaving Paris.

Thus, without having made a formal declaration, I join Elissa in observing kashres (save for occasional lapses that I call my "*treyf* of the month club" and that become less and less frequent), and she joins me in keeping shabbes, albeit with some reluctance. Preparing to fulfill a promise made in a dream I had while in Paris, I take a further step: At the beginning of November, I begin attending daily services at another East Side shul and thus putting on tefillin again. One of my mother's cousins at the Telshe Yeshiva in Cleveland—whom I have never met—told me in the dream that I would always be welcome there, and I responded that if I got there, I would put on tefillin every day from then on. Later in November, Elissa and I fly to Cleveland for the weekend. Though we are welcomed warmly, it is clear that the rabbis and *rebetsins* at the yeshiva hoped for something more Jewish from me, the great-grandson of the Rosh Yeshiva's second wife, Miriam.

We return to the Eighth Street Shul as well, which has been secured and repaired sufficiently to make it usable once again. There are changes. Old Mr. Klapholz, with whom I hardly had exchanged a word, has passed away. Fishel's uncle Mr. Hochbaum, a congregant for half a century, no longer attends, since he is unable to walk all the way from Grand Street. On the other hand, my long-haired friend has moved into the neighborhood and attends regularly. Two of the younger members of the congregation have small children now, and they must go to a shul where there are other children for their son and daughter to play with. In February, our oldest member passes away, and after Shavuot, another member moves to Jerusalem. Two more young men eventually begin coming regularly and bring along their infant children. Now, in June 1986, the shul has thirteen regular male attendees. I am no longer free to sleep late on Saturday mornings, and fortunately I no longer want to.

All of this, to the extent it is of my own making, is the result of a search to realize that fragile illusion of wholeness which was destroyed when my family and almost all the others left Farmingdale. I will hazard a guess that Jewish anthropologists—perhaps anthropologists in general—are motivated by a sense of loss. Yet the seamless image of community is inevitably a child's image. We cannot regain what is lost, if only because it never existed as we remember it. Nothing in society is quite as harmonious as it seemed to me then, and I later learned about bitter political struggles that had taken place in Farmingdale, just as they had among the immigrants in Paris.

Our strategy, rather, should be to attempt to understand what it is we miss and need, which is available in still-living communities in another form. The image of wholeness which we share is foreshadowed by communities all of us stem from, however many generations back, and it can serve as a guide in the search for the reciprocal relationships of autonomous adulthood.

Anthropology is a tool for mediating between the self and the community. It has helped me to come to belong at the Eighth Street Shul: to withhold my opinions when it seems necessary, without feeling the guilt of self-compromise; to accept instruction and gentle reprimands with good humor; to believe it is worthwhile preserving something that might otherwise disappear. But belonging at Eighth Street does not mean that I have dissolved myself into an ideal Orthodox Jew. If I attempted to do so, I would be unable to continue being an anthropologist. If I fit into any category, it may be what my friend Kugelmass calls the "funky Orthodox": that is, those who participate in the community but whose interests and values are not confined to the Orthodox world. In fact, there are no ideal Orthodox Jews at Eighth Street; it is our respective quirks that provide the *raison d'être* of this haphazard but now intentional once-a-week community.

The fact that I have found a religious community that needs me because of its marginality and will tolerate me because of a generosity born of tradition is what I mean by the marginal redemption of one Jew. Likewise, if the shul survives, it will be because of its very marginality, because of the many individuals who have recognized the creative possibilities of a situation that demands that they create a new unity, while allowing each of them to retain their otherness. Isn't this the dream of anthropologists? Whether attempting to communicate knowledge between different Jewish communities, or between communities much more distant in tradition and empathy, we are messengers. We spend our own lives in moving back and forth among the worlds of others. As we do so, in order to avoid getting lost along the way we must become cultural pioneers, learning to "get hold of our *trans*cultural selves" (Wolff 1970: 40). Communities on the edge of mass society, or even on the fringes of ethnic enclaves, seem to be among the most congenial fields in which to do so.

Let me finish with a parable:

Two Jews can afford to be fastidious about the dress, comportment, and erudition of a third. It gives them something to gossip about and identify against. Ten healthy Jews can have a similar luxury; an eleventh means competition for the ritual honors. It's nine Jews who are the most tolerant, as I learned one forlorn shabbes at Eighth Street. It was almost ten o'clock, and there was no minyan. Since everyone seemed content to wait patiently, I assumed that someone else had promised to come, and asked, "Who are we waiting for?"

"A *yid*," our oldest member replied without hesitation.

Eventually a Jew came along.

Notes

1. Compare Pierre Bourdieu's critique of the structuralist theory of "reciprocal" gift exchange: "Even if reversibility [i.e., the assumption that gifts entail counter-gifts of equivalent value] is the objective truth of the discrete acts which ordinary experience knows in discrete form and calls gift exchanges, it is not the whole truth of a practice which could not exist if it were consciously perceived in accordance with the model. The temporal structure of gift exchange, which objectivism ignores, is what makes possible the coexistence of two opposing truths, which defines the full truth of the gift" (1977:6).

   Similarly, in a narrative such as this one, because I, as author, already know the ending, it may seem as though each successive element fits into those that precede and follow it in such a way that their necessity is perfectly known. Actually my aim is to show how the background that nurtured me shaped in part my unpredictable responses to situations that in themselves were historically rather than culturally determined. See my conclusion, where I refer to one of the communities I now participate in as "haphazard but intentional."

2. Even if it was no more than a matter of convenience, this annual event demonstrates Jonathan Woocher's point that American Jewish "civil religion expects Jews to take advantage of the opportunities which America provides, and to use them to help fulfill their Jewish responsibilities" (1985:161).

3. This may seem an outrageously loose claim, and I am quite willing to be proven wrong by literary scholars. But compare the conclusion of James Joyce's *Portrait of the Artist as a Young Man:*

   Mother is putting my new secondhand clothes in order. She prays now, she says, that I may learn in my own life and away from home and friends what the heart is and what it feels. Amen. So be it. Welcome, O life! I go to encounter for the millionth time the reality of experience and to forge in the smithy of my soul the uncreated conscience of my race. (1968:252–53)

   with the end of Moshe Szulsztein's memoir of a Polish Jewish childhood:

   When the truck was already fairly far along Warsaw Street and Kurow was barely visible, two more relatives appeared in a great rush, wanting to take their leave. These were my grandfather's pair of pigeons. The pigeons knew me, and I knew them. I loved them, and perhaps they loved me as well . . . But the truck is stronger than they are, it drives and drives further and further away from Kurow. My poor pigeons can't keep up, they remain behind . . . Before they disappear altogether from my view I still discern them within the distant evening cloud, two small flying silver dots, one a bit behind the other. That, I know, is the male, and the second, a bit in front, is the female. (1982:352)

4. For photographs of Eighth Street and other Lower East Side shuls, both surviving and abandoned, see Fine and Wolfe (1978).

5. "In every corner, in every little patch of darkness, up the blind alleys and the corridors, one could sense the presence of a swarming mass of humanity, a sly, shameful life. Shadows slunk along the walls. The stores were selling goods unknown to French people even by name" (Simenon 1963: 45).

Reading 8

LIVING TOGETHER
Psychic Space and the Demand for Sexual Equality

Drucilla Cornell

Equal Protection of Minimum Conditions of Individuation

In this [work], I defend a feminist view of legal equality that synchronizes[1] the distinct values of freedom and equality in the emotionally fraught sphere of life we call sex. Feminist legal theory has been plagued by the seemingly irreconcilable tension between these two values, particularly when it comes to issues like pornography and sexual harassment where they have been explicitly pitted against one another. When we demand equality for women, we are accused of being the sexual police trampling on the most intimate inner recesses of other people's lives. And, indeed, the question of exactly what the demand of equality means as legal intervention into the issues of pornography, abortion, and sexual harassment has created deep divisions within the feminist movement itself. In the case of abortion, feminist legal theory has also floundered over the question of the relationship between sexual difference and the claim that law should guarantee parity for women based on their equal personhood to men. Given the so-called realities of sexual difference, what and how are we to think of personhood in order to make coherent a claim of parity?

Cornell, Drucilla. "Living Together: Psychic Space and the Demand for Sexual Equality." *The Imaginary Domain.* New York: Routledge, 1995. 4–27. (Plus Notes.)

In this [work], I will develop a view of equality that provides us with a new perspective on the relationship of sexual difference to equality and of equality to freedom in the hotly contested issues of abortion, pornography, and sexual harassment. This view of equality entails the equal protection of certain minimum conditions of individuation. There are three conditions that insure a minimum degree of individuation which I defend as *necessary*[2] for the equivalent chance to transform ourselves into individuated beings who can participate in public and political life as equal citizens. They are as follows: 1) bodily integrity, 2) access to symbolic forms sufficient to achieve linguistic skills permitting the differentiation of oneself from others, and 3) the protection of the imaginary domain itself. The detailed elaboration and defense of these conditions takes place [here and elsewhere in my work]. The purpose of this introduction is to sketch the philosophical basis, always informed by a feminist purpose, on which the argument for equal protection of the minimum conditions of individuation is built.

The Possibility of the Person

What we think of as "individuality" and "the person" are not assumed as a given but respected as part of a project, one that must be open to each one of us on an equivalent basis. My argument is that without minimum conditions of individuation, we cannot effectively get the project of becoming a person off the ground. I am using the word "person" in a particular way. *Per-sona*, in Latin, means literally a shining-through. A person is what shines through a mask even though the concept of the "mask" is the usual association made with the word "persona." It is that which shines through. For a person to be able to shine through, she must first be able to imagine herself as whole even if she knows that she can never truly succeed in becoming whole or in conceptually differentiating between the "mask" and the "self." The equal worth of personhood of each one of us must be legally guaranteed, at least in part, in the name of the equivalent chance to take on that project.

A person is not something "there" on this understanding, but a possibility, an aspiration which, because it is that, can never be fulfilled once and for all. The person is, in other words, implicated in an endless process of working through personae. On this definition, the person is neither identical with the self or the traditional philosophical subject.

The argument that I develop through a psychoanalytic framework insists that the freedom to struggle to become a person is a chance or opportunity which depends on a prior set of conditions that I refer to as minimum conditions of individuation. This freedom will always be a chance. We must protect, as a legal matter of equality, the equivalent bases for this chance to transform ourselves into the individuated beings we think of as persons. My argument, then, is that we cannot assume as a given that a human creature is by definition a free person. And yet I refuse the other extreme that argues for a full substantive theory of equality that would attempt to fully elaborate the conditions of free personhood.[3] Given my understanding of the person as involving an endless process of working through, each one of us must have the chance to take on this struggle in his or her own unique way. It is under my definition a project that demands the space for the renewal of the imagination and the concomitant re-imagining of who one is and who one seeks to become. Hence, my insistence on the imaginary domain as crucial to the very possibility of freedom. The equal protection of minimum conditions of individuation can only insure that none of us is cut off from that chance of freedom. Freedom to transform oneself cannot be given, let alone guaranteed, and certainly not by law.

Sex vs. Gender

Since my focus in this book is on "sex," I am more specifically arguing that these conditions of minimum conditions of individuation are necessary for the chance of sexual freedom and the possibility of sexual happiness. But such freedom and happiness are not merely contingent, secondary virtues.

Sex is so basic to who we are that when we imagine ourselves, sex is always already in the picture. Most of us know that on some level. All of us live as sexed beings. And yet within political philosophy, sex, sexuality, and gender have traditionally not been considered formative of human personality as have other basic facts. Feminists have relentlessly struggled to have gender accorded proper recognition in political philosophy and in law. Unfortunately, this insistence on "gender" as if it were the category of legal analysis rather than "sex" has been conserving of the category at the expense of putting gays and lesbians outside the reach of discrimination law.[4] Making gender the "single axis"[5] of discrimination law has also failed to provide an analysis of the unique focus of discrimination endured by women of color *as* women of color. I will return to discuss the limits of the current competing legal theories of gender equality shortly.

In spite of the analytic shortcomings of the current legal analysis of gender equality for women, "sex," even if understood exclusively as gender hierarchy and the subordination of women, has been accorded a place in some political philosophy. Even so, this "place" is often reduced to a secondary category, or squeezed into schemes of equality tailored for some other subject such as class.[6] I am arguing, on the contrary, that sex cannot be analogized to some other category. Sex and sexuality are unique and formative to human personality and should be treated as such. Thus, in order to have an adequate feminist theory of legal equality we must explicitly recognize the sexuate bases of each one of us as a human creature. At the very heart of the struggle to work through imposed and assumed personae is the matter of sex and sexuality.

As sexuate beings, we cannot mark out an identity without implicating who we are through a set of culturally encoded fantasies about what it means to be a creature with a "sex." As "sexed beings," we assume personae through unconscious, encoded identifications. I am using the word "sex" to involve at least three dimensions of our common usage. Firstly, to have a "sex" marks us as the sexuate beings we are. Human beings are sexual creatures. One does not have to endorse any particular concept of a "sex drive" to recognize that human beings are sexuate beings involved in lives of pleasure as well as reproduction. Secondly, as part of their sexual activity, human beings "have sex." Sex here is understood not just as a set of identifications which we take on as personae but as an activity we engage in as sexual beings. Thirdly, sex is the internalized identity and the assumption of personae imposed by the gender divide.

There is an additional dimension to this idea of sex. Each one of us, as part of our unconscious identification of ourselves as beings who have been "sexed," has a sexual imago which implicates our sexual imaginary. In psychoanalytic theory, a sexual imago involves the idea that we do not see ourselves from the outside as men and women. Instead, we see ourselves so deeply and profoundly from the "inside" as men and women that we cannot easily, if at all, separate ourselves from this imago. This imago is the basis of our unconscious assumed persona.

Femininity as Masquerade

I argue throughout [this work] that in the case of those of us who are designated as women, the sexual imago is both encoded and symbolically enforced so as to split women off from themselves as sexual objects[7] and to re-impose the persona we associate with conventional femininity. This splitting off marks a women as her "sex" and thus rips her away from her identification of herself as a woman *and* as a person beyond the persona or masquerade of femininity.[8] This analysis, which I develop through the writings of Jacques Lacan,[9] helps us to understand the difficulties of affirming the feminine within sexual difference as other than the imposed masquerade. "The wound of femininity" is one way to describe this ripping of one's sex and sexual persona away from any affirmation of oneself as a person with power and creativity. *"Vive la différence"* too often translates as: "Let women remain within the stereotyped characteristics of the masquerade of femininity." Psychoanalysis offers an analysis of the symbolic underpinnings that govern many of our unconscious fantasies about sex. These symbolic underpinnings shape our reality to the extent that we are unable to truly envision the feminine as anything other than this persona of femininity. Consequently, it is difficult to view women as equal persons before the law. More generally, the psychoanalytic account of erotic life demands that we examine sexuality through underpinnings that are at least a-rational, if not irrational. It shows us that sex does not easily yield to discussion under the rubric of rational choice theory.[10]

But one need not agree on the usefulness of Lacan or accept feminist appropriation of Lacan's work to adopt the idea that we are profoundly immersed in a sexual identity with our assumed personae, which dictate the way we think of ourselves as having sex and having a sex.

Neither homosexuality nor heterosexuality, then, can be called a "choice" since they implicate an unconscious, or at least pre-conscious, sexual imago. Such an engagement with "sex" and having a "sex" is too fundamental to the person's identity to argue that it is assumed consciously. Thus, to deny a person their life as a sexuate being, as they have imagined it through their own sexual imago and lived it out as persona, is to deny them a fundamental part of their identity. This point is crucial to the project of ensuring lesbians and gay men, and any other form of sexuate being for that matter, their equality *as* sexuate beings.

The Imaginary Domain and the Degradation Prohibition

The imaginary domain illuminates more profoundly what traditional legal theory has dubbed sexual privacy. The notion of the imaginary domain recognizes that literal space cannot be conflated with psychic space and reveals that our sense of freedom is intimately tied to the renewal of the imagination as we come to terms with who we are and who we wish to be as sexuate beings. Since, psychoanalytically, the imaginary is inseparable from one's sexual imago, it demands that no one be forced to have another's imaginary imposed upon herself or himself in such a way as to rob him or her of respect for his or her sexuate being. Thus, what John Rawls has argued is a primary good, namely self-respect, is integrated into the very idea of the imaginary domain itself.[11] Rawls explicitly connects the denial of self-respect with crippling shame. The profound shame articulated by gays and lesbians that limits sexual life to the closet, directly countered by the notion of "pride," resonates with Rawls' own account of the shame imposed by the denial of the primary good of self-respect:

> When we feel that our plans are of little value, we cannot pursue them with pleasure or take delight in their execution. Nor plagued by failure and self-doubt can we continue in our endeavors. It is clear then why self-respect is a primary good. Without it nothing may seem worth doing, or if some things have value for us, we lack the will to strive for them. All desire and activity becomes empty and vain, and we sink into apathy and cynicism.[12]

[. . .] Rawls' compelling account of the toll of imposed shame through the denial of the primary good of self-respect can help us in re-thinking the wrong in sexual harassment. As a primary good, self-respect functions as a legitimate expectation that each one of us would demand for ourselves as a basic need in a society in which we are regarded as equal citizens. Thus, it is this primary good that we should use in assessing the legitimacy of women's claims of sexual harassment. But I am also insisting that the primary good of self-respect is fundamental to the freedom to transform oneself into a person. Thus, unlike Rawls, I would foreground the primary good of self-respect as fundamental to the very formation of what we think of personhood.[13] This foregrounding dovetails with my insistence that sex and sexuality are formative to one's being, and that the struggle to become a person is inseparable from the psychic space needed to truly play with imposed and assumed sexual personae.

Imposed sexual shame severely limits psychic space for free play with one's sexuality, if it does not cut it off altogether. The foregrounding of the primary good of self-respect is an aspect of the imaginary domain also helps to illuminate what legitimate constraints can be imposed upon any one of us in the expression of the sexual imaginary. The constraint I would like to argue for as consistent with the primary good of self-respect that can be legitimately imposed upon the free play with one's sexuality in *public* space is the "degradation prohibition."[14] I use the word "degradation" to specify what I mean by the primary good of self-respect for each one of us as a sexuate being. It should go without saying that hierarchical gradations of any of us as unworthy of personhood violates the postulation of each one of us as an equal person called for by a democratic and modern legal system. By "degradation," I mean a literal "grading down" because of one's sex or sexuality. By a "grading down," I mean that one has been "graded" as unworthy of personhood, or at least as a lesser form of being. The treatment of a person as a "dumb-ass woman" or a "stupid fag" violates the degradation prohibition because it creates hierarchical gradations of sexual difference that scar some of us as less than persons worthy of happiness.

We also need to have an analysis of the different kinds of public space. Thus, for example, I differentiate between the forms of regulation demanded by the equal protection of minimum conditions of individuation in the distribution of pornography and in the establishment of workplace equality for all of us as sexuate beings.

Given the importance of the freedom to play with and, indeed, to "act out" the personae of lived sexuality, I have tailored the degradation prohibition as narrowly as possible. Someone is degraded when they are reduced to stereotypes of their "sex" or have imposed upon them objectified fantasies of their "sex" so that they are viewed and treated as *unworthy* of equal citizenship. We are degraded, in other words, when our "sex" is defined, symbolized and treated as antithetical to equal personhood and citizenship. The purpose of specifically tailoring the degradation prohibition in this way is to ally ourselves with rather than pit ourselves against those who insist on their right to break out of the closet and "act up" in public. It is no coincidence that one of the most active militant gay rights organizations is called ACT UP. Certainly, gays and lesbians need the space to "act up"—to define their own sexual identity, in their own terms, and to do so in public. By the same token, we see at the very heart of the masquerade of femininity, the imposed demand that we be "ladylike," particularly in public. Therefore, as feminists, we have nothing to gain, and a lot to lose, by any attempt to sexually purify public space.

Transsexuals *should* be able to eat in peace in a restaurant. Gay men and lesbians *should* be able to joyously express their love on the streets. The presence of a transsexual in a restaurant does not deny equal personhood to anyone. Nor does a lesbian couple holding hands. The homophobic spectator may be offended, he may even find *his* restaurant contaminated by the presence of the transsexual. But the presence of a being whose "sex" violates his own sense of propriety of public space does not degrade him in his person. He is left in his freedom to be heterosexual. He can pursue his sex and his sexuality; he simply cannot control the sexuality of others. Thus, the degradation prohibition is consistent with at least the spirit of Kant's definition of freedom under law in two ways. To quote Kant:

> Man's *freedom* as a human being, as a principle for the constitution of a commonwealth, can be expressed in the following formula. No one can compel me to be happy in accordance with his conception of the welfare of others, for each may seek his happiness in whatever way he sees fit, so long as he does not infringe upon the freedom of others to pursue a similar end which can be reconciled with the freedom of everyone else within a workable general law—i.e. he must accord to others the same rights as he enjoys himself.[15]

I write "spirit" because if a heterosexual man's freedom to be heterosexual involves his belief that heterosexuality is normal, then he will be "infringed upon" in the pursuit of his happiness. If he, for example, feels that his sexuality is dependent on its power to reign as the norm, then the very acceptance of transsexuality and transvestitism attacks his conception of his sex and the exercise of his sexuality. His happiness is undermined. But his *worthiness* to be happy is not challenged. It is the challenge to the *worthiness* to be happy and to be regarded as equal in one's personhood that I describe as degradation. Thus, we need to replace "infringe" with "degrade." But to do so does not fundamentally undermine the spirit of the Kantian definition of freedom under law. The degradation prohibition demands that, as sexuate beings, we all be treated as worthy of the right to pursue sexual happiness. The message inherent in much anti-gay legislation is that lesbians and gay men are not worthy to pursue their happiness: not worthy to pursue satisfying jobs, not worthy to develop relationships, not worthy to live in peace and security with their children. And yet at the heart of Kant's conception of the dignity of the person and of the struggle to become a person, in my sense, is the idea that we are all worthy of happiness. Thus, the protection of the equivalent chance to become a person necessarily includes the refusal of the evaluation that just because of our sex, some of us are inherently unworthy of happiness. This rejection of the prior evaluation that some of us are inherently unworthy of happiness is also clearly in the spirit of Kant's postulation that all of us are equal as persons before the law. Indeed, my defense of legal equality proceeds through a revised version, specifically tailored to questions of sex and sexuality, of the Kantian test of the rightfulness of public law in a democratic and modern legal system.

We judge public law by the "as if" of a postulated original contract.[16] The rightfulness of a law is tested by the "as if" in the following way: a rightful law is one that all citizens, regarded as free and equal, *could* have agreed to if they were in a position to actually consent within the general will. This contract is an idea of reason with practical effect in that it can guide legislators with a test for rightfulness. To my mind, the most powerful representation of the original contract as an idea of reason is John Rawls' formulation of the veil of ignorance. The veil of ignorance is a representational device to guide us in the hypothetical experiment of the imagination demanded by the Kantian "as if." The veil of ignorance, according to Rawls, seeks to represent "some point of view, removed from and not distorted by the particular features and circumstances of the all-encompassing background framework, from which a fair agreement between persons regarded as free and equal can be reached."[17]

The veil of ignorance involves us in an experiment in the hypothetical imagination whose purpose is screening out the implications, at least in the realm of political justice, of our actual station in life. It does not purport to justify a pure view of practical reason; a "view from nowhere."[18] It is explicitly defended as a representational device as a view from somewhere, a view of those suitably represented, a definition which returns us to the fundamental idea that behind the veil of ignorance we are all to be regarded as free and equal persons and thus as symmetrically positioned. It is important to note the Rawls' conception of suitable representation behind the veil of ignorance leads to egalitarian conclusions that Kant himself clearly would have rejected as following from the recognition of the uniform equality of human beings as subjects of a state. Kant, for example, argues:

> This uniform equality of human beings as subjects of a state is, however, perfectly consistent with the utmost inequality of the mass in the degree of its possessions, whether these take the from of physical or mental superiority over others, or of fortuitous external property and of particular rights (of which there may be many) with respect to others.[19]

Rawls, in *A Theory of Justice*, argues that the opposite conclusion would be reached by persons suitably represented behind the veil of ignorance.[20]

In Defense of Reasonableness

My defense of minimum conditions of individuation is in alliance with Rawls' egalitarianism as opposed to Kant's more conservative conclusions. Like both Rawls and Kant, I also defend the idea of reasonableness and public reason.

Reasonableness and public reason depend on the demand of the "as if" itself. Judges and legislators are called upon to proceed through the "as if" because this is the test for the rightfulness of the law consistent with the evaluation of each one of us as a free and equal person. Rawls' account diverges with Kant's, however, and it is his conception of reasonableness that I defend in the chapter on sexual harassment. For Rawls, there are two basic aspects of reasonableness.

> The first basic aspect of the reasonable, then, is the willingness to propose fair terms of cooperation and to abide by them provided others do. The second basic aspect . . . is the willingness to recognize the burdens of judgement and to accept their consequences for the use of public reason in directing the legitimate exercise of political power in a constitutional regime.[21]

For Rawls, the reasonable is an element of the idea of a system of fair cooperation, meaning that a society's public institutions should be guided by the demand of the "as if," i.e., that they would be hypothetically agreed to by the citizens valued as free and equal in their personhood and suitably represented in accordance with that evaluation. For me, more specifically, reasonableness is the demand that judges and legislators use the "as if" as the test of the rightfulness of the law. Thus, in this book, my focus is on the acceptance of the burdens of judgements—what Rawls calls the second aspect of reasonableness—particularly as these are imposed on judges and legislators. This is firstly because this book focuses on a feminist theory of legal equality, and thus on standards of judgement for legislators and judges. Ultimately, it also reflects my difference with Rawls over whether the *concept* of justice can be fully realized in a *conception* of justice. My view is that is cannot. Feminism further demands much greater room for political contestation over the conception of justice than is left open in *A Theory of Justice*.[22]

To discuss this difference at length is obviously beyond the scope of this [work]. For my purposes here, I only want to emphasize that, like Kant, I believe that law has inherent limits because it is inevitably an arena of coercion. This is why I advocate a feminist theory of legal equality that is both universal and limited. But this does not mean that the "as if" can not guide as a test for rightfulness. I accept the argument that we must proceed through the "as if" even if our results would involve the synchronization[23] of basic values through the prudential considerations inseparable from the translation of legal principles into the arena of actual litigation. Still, my argument that the "as if" demands the recognition of reasonableness and of public reason represents a break with recent feminist critiques of reasonableness. Let me briefly explain why I think the feminist critique of reasonableness has been misguided.

As I explain [elsewhere], sexual harassment law calls for a inquiry into whether a reasonable person would recognize the complained-of behavior as sexual harassment. If the answer to the inquiry is yes, then the defendant is legally liable for the harms he caused. If not, he is not at fault.

Feminists have argued that the reasonable man standard, in its invocation of the reasonable *man*, is biased against women. The fault of the standard is found in its reliance on how men, rather than women, perceive their social world. The privileging of the masculine, so the argument goes, is the result of the rhetorical slippage between the concept of reasonableness and the concept of man that the standard legitimates. While the concept of man purportedly refers to all individuals, it also obviously is the word for individuals of the male sex. Feminists have argued that this slippage through which males are rhetorically identified with the universal idea of reasonableness leads to a relative association of the masculine as reasonable against the feminine, which is thereby inevitably coded as irrational. It is the corruption of the universal standard of reasonableness by the political hierarchicalization of masculinity that some feminists have called the hierarchical social construction of reasonableness.[24] Reasonableness is not natural and objective but rather socially and politically constructed through the identification of this supposedly neutral concept with masculinity.

This social construction of reasonableness as masculine is thought to create a series of problems for women and other individuals who do not conform to the normatively constructed ideal of reasonableness. For example, when a woman claims harassment or an African American claims racism and their claims are held not to meet the reasonable man standard by a judge or jury, their perception of reality is delegitimized as irrational. This, of course, is true as well for a white man whose claim is denied as unreasonable. But feminists have argued that because of the slippage between reasonableness and the masculine, the bias of the standard will more often than not favor those who sociologically conform to "normal" masculinity and disadvantage those who are identified as "other."

Feminist legal theorists have responded to this dilemma in various ways. Some argue that since law itself is inherently tainted with a masculine bias, legal reform is well-nigh impossible. Others seek a reversal by claiming that the "reasonable woman" standard should be adopted as the norm.[25] Following this line of thought, some feminists have argued that the perspective of the most oppressed groups in society should be adopted as a challenge to the current imbalance of power erased by the reasonable man standard.[26] However, the most dominant response to the perceived problem of the reasonable man standard among feminist—and other minority—critical legal reformers has been to assail the reasonable man standard and the ideal of universality in general. Since universality will always be constructed to the political advantage of some conception of the norm, feminists and critical scholars have advocated a move from universal to subjective standards. Thus, they recommend some version of the reasonable woman standard with varying degrees of specificity.

The flight from the universal towards the subjective has a political justification. Feminists have argued that the individualized standard of reasonableness is a necessary response to the universalist pretense that masks hierarchies and has denied the multiplicity of voices and therefore the multiplicity of socially con-structed conceptions of reasonableness.[27]

While the work of feminist legal scholars has been invaluable in giving voice to women's realities, the flight towards subjectivity is, nonetheless, mis-directed. If the problem is the conflation of the purported universal with the masculine, the proliferation of standards—even admittedly political standards—cannot be the solution. Just as women have attacked the masculinity of the rea-sonable man and women of color have exposed the whiteness of the reasonable woman, every group and indeed every individual can rightfully show that a nor-mative standard of reasonableness can never adequately account for the unique particularity of a person. Every standard is incapable, as an abstract generaliza-tion, of doing justice to individual persons judged under it.

This is not a condemnation of law as opposed to some other institutional ordering but an understanding of justice as a limit principle.[28] Justice is not something to be achieved, it is something to be struggled for. Substituting sub-jective for universal standards does not make the law more just; if anything, it turns the law away from the struggle for justice by embroiling the law in a myr-iad of formal an doctrinal disputes about the reasonable woman, the reasonable black woman, the reasonable lesbian, etc. Instead of focusing on the essential injustice of, and the need to continually transform the significance of, general normative standards, feminists have fostered debate about what *is* the reason-able woman or what *is* the reasonable black lesbian. Law, when it retreats from the universal concern of equivalent evaluation, ceases to struggle for justice and instead becomes an administrative institution charged with debating, construct-ing, and enforcing an exploding matrix of norms that purport to define reason-ableness for increasingly narrow categories of individuals.

Thus, against the grain of feminist thought, I argue that we must struggle to maintain the legal ideal of reasonableness, explicitly tailored by an appeal to the Kantian "as if," as the test for the rightfulness of the law with its explicit demand for the equivalent evaluation of all of us as worthy of personhood.

Practical Reason and Equivalent Evaluation

Rawls forcefully argues that articulating the standards of reasonableness and objectivity for his Kantian constructivist work on a conception of political liber-alism must proceed primarily through an appeal to practical and not theoretical reason. Rawls' articulation of the distinction between theoretical and practical reason is as follows:

> Following Kant's way of making this distinction, we say: practical reason is
> concerned with the production of objects according to a conception of those
> objects—for example, the conception of a just constitutional regime taken as

the aim of political endeavor while theoretical reason is concerned with the knowledge of given objects.[29]

Rawls develops conceptions of the person and of society as conceptions of practical reason. For Rawls, the conception of the person in both *A Theory of Justice* and *Political Liberalism* must address the question: "What must persons be like to engage in practical reason?" The answer for Rawls is to presume that human beings have two basic moral powers—a sense of justice and a capacity for the good. As equal and free citizens, we are all assumed, for the purpose of *A Theory of Justice* and *Political Liberalism*, to have these basic capacities to the degree that each of us can be full cooperating members of society. The fair terms of cooperation and the principles of justice are generated by persons so conceived and suitably represented in accordance with the representation of the original contract as an idea of reason.

Thus, Rawls does not address the question of what conditions are necessary for us to be able to symbolically pull ourselves together to the degree that would give us an equivalent chance of becoming persons in the first place. That question is "prior" to the beginning point of *A Theory of Justice*, which postulates each one of us as a person with the two capacities needed to engage in practical reason. Sex takes us back in time because it is foundational to human being. The need to ask the prior question stems in part from an explicit feminist recognition of just how precious and difficult the achievement of individuation sufficient to undertake the project of becoming a person actually is. The care involved in reproducing a human creature as a rudimentary self is an overwhelming task. That effort and that care performed by the primary care-taker is often "disappeared" in starting political philosophy with the assumption that we are persons from the beginning, rather than creatures whose equal worth is postulated as personhood. Asking this question facilitates the reappearance of the maternal not just as a function, but as a labor which actively brings us to the point of sufficient individuation after which we may begin to undertake the struggle to become a person.

My defense of minimum conditions of individuation, even if it is prior to the traditional starting point of a Kantian constructivist project, is still consistent with the development of the conception of the person as a conception of practical reason. We are conceived as needing the conditions necessary for the equivalent chance to become persons. This equivalent chance is simply assumed if we are postulated in advance as persons with the capacity to be fully cooperating members of society. My argument is that if we are to be regarded as of equivalent worth in our personhood, we must still confront the prior question, and yet address it through an appeal to practical and not theoretical reason. What must persons be like to engage in practical reason? They must be individuated enough to have the equivalent chance to become persons in the first place.[30] Minimum conditions of individuation are, admittedly, justified through an appeal to empirical practical reason since they demand some recognition of experience, i.e., the experience provided by psychoanalytic knowledge. But they are tailored broadly enough so that almost all psychological and psychoanalytical schools would agree that these conditions are necessary for the achievement of any sense of self. The defense of minimum conditions of individuation is also justified by the appeal to practical reason, in the sense that if one does not accept that we are to be regarded as free and equal citizens and thus worthy of happiness, one will not accept these conditions. They are understood as part of the equivalent evaluation of each one of us as equal persons and thus as beings worthy of happiness as well as capable of pursuing that happiness.

It should be noted that the appeal to minimum conditions of individuation is universal. The uniqueness of feminine sexual difference is not taken into account in the elaboration of the conditions themselves. As an appeal to practical reason, however, it turns on the assumption that as equal citizens and, moreover, as sexuate beings, we should all be equivalently evaluated as worthy of achieving the conditions of personhood. No form of sexuate being, in other words, can be evaluated as inherently antithetical to personhood since such an evaluation would be antithetical to the idea that we be regarded as free and equal persons for the purposes of the "as if" of an original contract. Nor do I emphasize the formal equality of women with men because the key to resolving the problem of how to think of sexual difference and equality simultaneously is to think through the facts of the *devaluation* or *degradation* of the feminine within our system of sexual difference. The demand for parity, then, is defended as the demand for the recognition of the equivalent value of the feminine within sexual difference. Thus, before practical reason, we assume that feminine sexual difference must be valued equivalently to that of other forms of sexuate being. It is not that we have to claim that women are equal to men in the sense that they are the same as men; rather, we have to claim that the feminine sex is of equivalent value to the masculine sex, in the name of women's equal personhood before the law.

The demand for equivalent evaluation, at least from within the dictates of practical reason, illustrates that it has not been so-called "real differences" that have denied women equality—the most obvious example being pregnancy—but the devaluation of those differences before the protection of minimum conditions of individuation. I use the phrase "the feminine within sexual difference" because the ultimate aspiration of feminism to undermine encoded structures of femininity cannot appeal to any current conception of our sex. Thus, the appeal to the equivalent evaluation of the feminine within sexual difference, as this evaluation is itself to be justified through recourse to an analysis of the protection of the minimum conditions of individuation, does not undermine our freedom. Rather, as I have already argued, it can be understood as providing the equivalent chance for freedom. Equal protection of minimum conditions of individuation, therefore, does not pit freedom against equality. Indeed, attempts by feminists such as Catharine MacKinnon to think of equality in a way that re-inscribes and conserves a stereotype of the feminine as reducible to a sexual object are incompatible with the notion of equivalence implied by equal protection of minimum conditions of individuation. In the area of sexual relations, this is particularly important because certain feminists have consistently maintained that it is precisely their sexual freedom as women that has been denied because they are forced to live under the projected fantasies of others.[31]

The ethical and political advantage of this call for minimum conditions of individuation is that it does not turn on gender comparison between men and women. It argues for equality for each one of us as a sexuate, and thus as a phenomenal, creature. Correspondingly, it allows us to be inclusive of the demands of lesbian and gay activists, transsexuals, and any other form of sexuate being because it insists on returning gender discrimination to sex discrimination.

The Competing Theories of Legal Equality

I now wish to put this preliminary formulation of a vision of equality based on minimum conditions of individuation into the context of the recent history of feminist attempts to answer the hard questions with which I opened this introduction. My aim is to delineate the tensions between feminists who have advocated formal equality and those who have advocated substantive equality. This tension, as I have argued, has divided feminists on two points: the first on difference and equality; the second on sexual freedom and equality. In legal feminism this latter tension has manifested itself most explicitly in the context of the pornography debate.

Throughout [this work], I argue that neither of the two theories of legal equality have been adequate to either sexual difference, freedom, or equality; all of which must be intertwined in an adequate feminist defense of an egalitarian vision.

Feminist Dilemmas in Theories of Formal and Substantive Equality

The theoretical argument made by Catharine MacKinnon, that femininity is nothing but the production of woman as "fuckees", has led to a theory of equality which insists that an egalitarian appeal must rest on the theoretical acceptance of the way in which gender hierarchy is perpetuated as domination.[32] This brand of feminism has argued that equality must be substantive in order to address the systematic subordination of women.

Such substantive theories of equality are not, strictly speaking, essentialist. But they do re-encode the unconscious structures of gender hierarchy as the basis of a theory of equality. This re-encoding is dangerous for feminists because it re-invests us in limited conceptions of femininity. Further, it undermines the full power of the appeal to equality itself by forcing us to make such an appeal based on an implicit comparison with men which seeks to bring women "up to" the position of men, rather than on an ethical conception of personhood that would demand a more egalitarian social order altogether. The combination of re-investing women in the structures of femininity associated with the gender hierarchy it contests, and the self-imposed limitation concerning what equality can demand, undermines the call for substantive equality as an adequate basis for a feminist legal reform program.[33] This brand of legal feminism, however, obviously finds its power in its ability to respond to the glaring inadequacies of an appeal to actual likeness as the basis for the claim of parity. The problem with the appeal to likeness as the basis for the claim of parity is that when there is a real difference—again, the obvious example is pregnancy—then the appeal to equality fails because women are not like men and, therefore, they cannot claim that they should legally be treated like men.

The failure of what has come to be called "formal equality" is twofold. First, such a theory fails to adequately address the real differences between women and men. Second, a theory such as the substantive theory of equality explicitly relies on a comparative standard of women and men. This comparative standard, as I have already argued, is incompatible with feminist aspirations since feminism seeks to challenge the use of "man" as a basis of interpersonal comparison. One practical legal result of the inability of formal equality to address questions of women's sexual difference in our time is that abortion is theorized under a privacy analysis rather than an equality analysis. Abortion is an example of the materiality of a real sexual difference, as it clearly implicates women's unique reproductive capacity.[34]

More generally, other questions of sexual difference as well as those of sex, such as pornography and sexual harassment, are out of the reach of gender comparison altogether because, at least hypothetically, men, as well as women, can be harassed and violated, for example, on porn sets. Thus, for the purposes of the law, a vulnerability to sexual harassment was not initially seen as a characteristic universal to women.[35] In order to proceed through the gender comparison model provided by formal equality, a claim of discrimination has to show that a characteristic is universal to women and, at the same time, not unique to them so that there can be a basis of comparison of women with men. Where there is no basis of comparison with men, no legal discrimination can be found, and when the characteristic is not universal to women, then there is no comparison between women and men because said comparison would only be within the class of women. If the comparison is only within the class of women, then there is also no legal discrimination that can be addressed. An infamous example of an attempt to use an intra-class comparison was Justice Rehnquist's distinction between pregnant and non-pregnant persons.[36] Rehnquist's conclusion was that since pregnancy is a characteristic unique though not universal to women, the absence of protection for pregnancy in an insurance plan was not discrimination. On this theory of equality, then, sexual harassment could easily be viewed as an intra-class claim: some women get harassed, some do not. For MacKinnon, on the other hand, sexual harassment is at the very heart of the subordination of women because it reflects the behavioral patterns of men towards those they view as "fuckees."[37]

In her pathbreaking work on sexual harassment, MacKinnon develops her own substantive theory of equality to show that it is possible to make the claim that sexual harassment is gender discrimination against women.[38] Pornography, on the other hand, seems to be beyond the reaches of equality analysis altogether, implicating as it does the value of free speech and of sexual expression. Again, it is Catharine MacKinnon, through her own substantive theory of equality, who shows that pornography can be analyzed under an egalitarian vision. Pornography, for MacKinnon, is the ultimate reality of woman's being as the "fuckee."

On this account, the only view of equality that seems capable of addressing the questions of sexual harassment and pornography, and indeed to construct these questions as involving claims of right and wrong, is the substantive view which turns on an analysis of how women are subordinated. This theoretical analysis is then incorporated into the view of equality as the new basis for a comparison between women and men. If the practice can be found to perpetuate the domination of women by enforcing their reality as the "fuckee," then it is discriminatory. The question of what constitutes domination turns, for MacKinnon, on her analysis of femininity as absolutely reducible to its production of women as objects of desire for men: "fuckees."

Gender subordination and sexual domination are analyzed as necessarily inseparable. We have a sex, we are "women," according to MacKinnon, because we have sex in and through the structures of heterosexual domination. These structures must, therefore, be undone by the law through an appeal to substantive equality. This in turn will render women's chances for an equal life something other than a mere fantasy or a replication of the structures of denial that make the perpetuation of gender hierarchy possible. Thus, it is not at all surprising that it was MacKinnon—whose position was that a theory of equality must take into account women's sexual damage—who first articulated an understanding of both pornography and of sexual harassment as questions of equality; questions of equality that should be addressed by the law.

The response, both from those feminists that embrace formal equality as the basis of their analysis of gender discrimination, and from more libertarian feminists who insist on their rights of sexual freedom,[39] has been to condemn

MacKinnon's substantive theory of gender subordination as a return to protectionism and indeed a fundamentalist conservatism that is, itself, part of the encoding of the wounds of femininity. MacKinnon's substantive view of equality has been challenged by feminists as well as more traditional legal scholars who endorse the comparative gender analysis of formal equality.

Lesbian and gay activists, as well as feminists who wish to challenge the strictures of femininity that have separated them from their sexuality,[40] argue that MacKinnon reinscribes the very gender identities she is seeking to contest.[41] The seemingly unsurpassable barrier between the recognition of sexual difference and the value of liberty, including sexual liberty on the one hand and the legal appeal to a substantive theory of equality on the other, has led feminists outside of law to question whether or not discrimination law itself may not be part of the problem.[42]

Feminism, particularly legal feminism, has been torn apart by deeply contested ideas about how the values of liberty and equality are best expressed in terms of feminist aspirations and, more particularly, as these two values are implicated in "sex" and erotic life. But questions of sex do seem to demand a substantive theory of equality if they are to be addressed as discrimination. Thus, we seem to need an account of the asymmetry of men and women before sexually harassing behavior in order to indict it or construct it as a wrong that can be legally addressable through an appeal to equality.

Theoretical appeals to asymmetry as the basis of claims to equality, however, undermine their own appeal by reinscribing themselves in the language of the repudiation of femininity that has informed, throughout history, the denial of women's parity with men.[43] On the other hand, the appeal to the likeness of women to men, as if they were already similarly situated before, for example, sexually harassing behavior, seems to implicate a form of denial of the real suffering of women. The very word "gender" as it is appropriated in law carries its own conservative overtones not only by, once again, refusing to recognize the value of the feminine within sexual difference, but also by trying to separate feminism from the "mess" of sex. Within what has been called "the second wave of feminism," this mess of sex was forcefully felt in splits that took place in the early 1970s between those feminists who sought a life or a fundamental political alliance with those who positioned themselves outside of the rigid dictates of normalized heterosexuality, and those who argued that if feminism was to achieve actual power in our society, it had to be wary of such sexual "radicals."[44] Note here that the focus on gender comparison is implicated by both these theories of substantive and formal equality, and these divergent theories share much in common in virtue of this focus.

My purpose in [my work] is to analyze three of the most difficult issues facing feminists—abortion, pornography, and sexual harassment—through the new theory of equality I have defended. These issues are difficult to the extent that

they demand that we look at the intertwining of sex, gender, and sexual difference as these are necessarily implicated in any construction of the right and
wrong characteristics that would make abortion, pornography, and sexual
harassment addressable as legal wrongs. We must not, however, respond to this
difficulty by *directly* incorporating a theoretical appeal to an analysis of how and
why women are asymmetrically positioned, and their sexual differences systematically devalued, into the elaboration of the ideal of equality itself.

In more philosophical terms, we should delineate as precisely as possible
the role that theoretical reason plays in the elaboration of the ideal of equality. I
do not deny that feminism needs a theoretical account of the asymmetry of the
masculine and feminine. But, as I've argued elsewhere, this asymmetry should
not be identified in any simplistic manner with those who are actually identified
as men and women. In other words, it is perfectly possible for a woman to take
up the place of the masculine as well as for a man to take the place of the side of
the feminine. But this ability to move between positions in a field of significance
does not deny that there exist parameters of that field of significance which produce powerful social and political effects. Still, this analysis of the masculine
and feminine does not turn on the re-inscription, even on a theoretical plane, of
how we are rigidly produced as either men or women in a way that absolutely
forecloses the crossing over from one position to the other or, indeed, more profoundly, prevents the slippage in meaning of either the masculine or the feminine itself. Thus, ethical feminism must paradoxically turn on the philosophical
elaboration of a limit to any theoretical analysis that claims to have the last word
on what it means to be a woman. It involves the elaboration of the limit of theoretical reason, understood as capable of a full analysis of the system of gender
that makes truth claims in the traditional sense.[45]

But whether or not one is sympathetic to an analysis of the limit of theoretical reason, or, more specifically, to how the limit of theoretical reason plays out
in the redefinition of feminism, one can still endorse the need to rely primarily
on practical reason to elaborate the idea of equality.[46]

The primary reliance on practical reason in the elaboration and defense of
an egalitarian vision for all forms of sexuate being through minimum conditions
of individuation does not deny that feminism needs a theoretical account of the
abjection, the simultaneous repudiation and making-other, of the feminine.[47]
But the argument here is that this account should not be directly incorporated
into any ideal of equality. Politically, this reliance on practical reason allows us
to create legal alliances with those who are not feminists and who would reject
any comprehensive and general feminist analysis. Rawls' conception of an overlapping consensus[48] stems from the possibility of an agreement about fundamental political values within and alongside the public culture's understanding
that there will always be considerable disagreement on the theoretical bases
about those shared political values. In other words, citizens who are not femi-

nists could still endorse feminist positions in the public sphere without justifying them on any special basis of a feminist position.[49] To reiterate: minimum conditions of individuation are proposed primarily to develop an adequate conception of a legal theory of equality for feminist purposes. But this account recognizes the severe limits of any legal project, indeed of law in general, as a field of coercion, for the more far-reaching aspects of feminism, as these necessarily imply an endless process of contesting the imposed definitions of what it means to be a woman. Feminism must not entrench itself in the realm of legal struggle as the primary arena of its political and personal aspirations to change the social world and our form of life.

A Feminist Understanding of the Limits of Law

The feminist theory of legal equality presented here then meets a civic duty to ally with others who could endorse a theory of justice and feminist legal reform—but not necessarily feminism per se—and at the same time remains true to the radical implications of ethical feminism that must reach far beyond the scope of law and what has traditionally been thought of as public life.[50] For example, I endorse self-organization and self-representation as the heart of the matter for the feminist program for reform within the pornography industry. This is a feminist re-statement of why we should prioritize justice over the good. We do not wish law, as it inevitably implicates accommodation to our current forms of social and symbolic life, to stamp and limit our own explorations with a fully developed conception of the good. Such a conception can be used as much against us as for us as we attempt to contest the cultural and psychical limits imposed upon our sexual imagination which all of us have, at least to some extent, internalized. Feminism, as it demands that we return to the very question of the relationship of sexuality to civilization, inevitably challenges us to re-think the very basis of civilization and its discontents.[51] But this process of re-thinking as well as contesting the order of civilization as it is predicated upon psychical laws governing our sexuality and its possibilities, takes us beyond the parameters of public political life and of legal reform. As feminists, then, we want to understand both the role of law *and* its limit in the course of our most profound challenges to what we think of as human life. The protection of minimum conditions of individuation allows us an equivalent chance for freedom. Feminism is ultimately about politically taking that chance to create new worlds.

Notes

1. I discuss the concept of "synchronization" in my book *Transformations:* "The goal of the modern legal system is synchronization and not rational coherence. Synchronization recognizes that there are competing rights situations and real conflicts between the individual and the community, which may not be able to yield a "coherent" whole. The conflicts may be mediated and synchronized but not eradicated. In reality, a complex differentiated community can never be reduced to a single voice. Synchronization recognizes the inevitable complexity of the modern state and the imperfection of all our attempted solutions." Please see Drucilla Cornell, "Pragmatism, Recollective Imagination, and Transformative Legal Interpretation," in *Transformations: Recollective Imagination and Sexual Difference* (New York: Routledge, 1993).

2. Please note that I defend these conditions as necessary but not sufficient.

3. A crucial aspect of my legal theory of equality is the move beyond the dichotomy between positive and negative liberty, inherited from Isaiah Berlin's famous essay, "On Positive and Negative Freedom,' in *Four Essays on Liberty* (London: Oxford University Press, 1969), as this divide has limited the way in which we think about rights. On the one hand, minimum conditions of individuation clearly bows to Hegel's insight that what we think of as the free person is constituted and not just given. Thus, minimum conditions of individuation provide us with freedom *to*, and not just freedom against. Please see G.W.F. Hegel, *Hegel's Science of Logic*, trans. A.V. Miller (Atlantic Highlands, NJ: Humanities Press International, 1969). It is also important, for the sake of keeping the philosophical record straight, to remember that Hegel did not reject what has to come to be thought of as rights based on negative freedom, but rather to explain philosophically how these rights have come to be realized in history. Please see Drucilla Cornell, "The Ethical Message of Negative Dialectics," in *Philosophy of the Limit* (New York: Routledge, 1992). My intention here is not to defend my reading of Hegel's understanding of rights, which I have done extensively elsewhere. However, there are two problems in Hegel that we do have to note which inform my own philosophical justification for minimum conditions of individuation. The first is that Hegel argued that there had been an historically achieved philosophical closure between theoretical and practical reason in Absolute Knowledge. I justify minimum conditions of individuation through an appeal to practical and not theoretical reason.

   The second problem is closely related to the first. For Hegel, the free person, or legal subject, was to be valued on the basis of a constitutive theory of human being that had come to be objectified in history and, indeed, served as the ethical truth of history. In Rawlsian terms, Hegel offers us a general and comprehensive theory of human being. I reject that such a philosophical conception of human being is either philosophically justifiable or politically and ethically desirable. My claim for the protection of minimum conditions of individuation as a matter of right is more modest since it is in accord with the dictates of practical reason. In this manner, it remains consistent with the privileging of the right over the good, specifically in the sphere of law. Thus, although I am profoundly sympathetic to Amartya Sen and Martha Nussbaum's inclusion of differentiation and individuation in their conception of human flourishing and equality of well-being and capability, I want to specifically tailor my defense of minimum conditions of individuation in accordance with the demand for justice and not a vision of the good life. Please see Martha C. Nussbaum and Amartya Sen, ed., *The Quality of Life*, (Oxford: Clarendon Press, 1993).

Hence, my argument is for the placement of minimum conditions of individuation as prior to, yet ultimately justified by, a Kantian constructivist conception of the equivalent worth of our personhood. Still, I want to recognize the importance for this entire project of Sen and Nussbaum's pathbreaking work.

4. Please see Drucilla Cornell, "Sex-Discrimination Law and Equivalent Rights," in *Transformations: Recollective Imagination and Sexual Difference* (New York: Routledge, 1993), pp. 147–155.

5. Please see Kimberlé Williams Crenshaw, "Race, Reform and Retrenchment: Transformation and Legitimation in Anti-Discrimination Law," *Harvard Law Review*, vol. 101 (May 1988), and "Mapping the Margins: Intersectionality, Identity Politics and Violence against Women of Color," *Stanford Law Review*, vol. 43 (July 1991).

6. Let me give an example of what I mean. Although I clearly argue for a feminist alliance with Rawls' Kantian constructivism, this appropriation has to be rethought fundamentally in terms of sex, rather than simply forcing questions of sex and sexuality into a theory of justice primarily addressed to class. Thus, for example, I reject the idea that questions of sex can be addressed through Rawls' difference principle.

7. I use the word "object" in the Kantian sense.

8. Please see Joan Riviere, "Womanliness as a Masquerade," in Victor Burgin, James Donald & Cora Kaplan, ed., *Formations of Fantasy* (London: Methuen, 1986).

9. See Jacques Lacan, *Feminine Sexuality: Jacques Lacan and the école freudienne*, ed. Juliet Mitchell and Jacqueline Rose, trans. Jacqueline Rose (New York: Pantheon Books, 1982), Lacan, "Le stade de miroir comme formateur de la function du Je," in *Ecrits* (Paris: Editions du Seuil, 1966), and Lacan, *Encore*, Le Séminare XX, Paris, 1975.

10. This is my fundamental disagreement, for example, with Richard Posner. See Richard Posner, *Sex and Reason* (Cambridge, MA: Harvard University Press, 1992).

11. John Rawls, *A Theory of Justice* (Cambridge, MA: The Belknap Press of Harvard University Press, 1971), pp. 440–446.

12. Rawls, *A Theory of Justice*, p. 440.

13. I am aware that foregrounding the primary good of self-respect as an aspect of minimum conditions of individuation internalizes these conditions in a manner that is at odds with Rawls' understanding of the primary goods. For a more extensive discussion of this problem as it relates to my theory of the primary good, please refer to Chapter 3 of [Cornell, *The Imaginary Domain*, pp 95-166,] "Pornography's Temptation." Obviously, a full discussion of the tensions produced in Rawls' analysis of the primary goods deserves more space.

14. I borrow this phrase from Henry Shue's *Basic Rights Subsistence, Affluence, and U.S. Foreign Policy* (Princeton: Princeton University Press, 1980), p. 119. Shue writes: "There are types of inequality that are morally unacceptable, namely, inequalities that are degrading. This principle I call the degradation prohibition."

15. Please see *Kant: Political Writings*, ed. Hans Reiss, trans. H.B. Nisbet (Cambridge: Cambridge University Press, 1970), p. 74.

16. Although I am relying on Kant's postulation of an original contract as an idea of reason, my formulation is not strictly "contractarian," if one means, by contractarian, the use of a contract theory in a liberal way as a "moral or justice proof procedure." I am explicitly using the idea of the original contract as a heuristic device. More traditional contractarians, such as T.M. Scanlon, have also not relied on contract theory to provide a "moral or justice proof procedure" for what is right or wrong. Please see T.M. Scanlon, "The Structure of Contractualism" in *What Do We Owe Each*

Other (unpublished manuscript on file with author. Department of Philosophy, Harvard University). I have gone at least one step beyond Scanlon in delimiting the original contract as a heuristic device. Ultimately, I agree with Jean Hampton when she argues that, "animating the contract test is a certain very Kantian conception of human worth. To say that a policy must be 'agreed to' by all is to say that in formulating a just policy, we must recognize that none of us can take only herself to 'matter' such that she can dictate the solution alone, and also that none of us is allowed to ignore or disregard her own importance in the formulation of the right policy." Please see Jean Hampton, "Feminist Contractarianism," in *A Mind of One's Own: Feminist Essays on Reason & Objectivity*, ed. Louise M. Antony and Charlotte Witt (Boulder, Colorado: Westview Press, 1993), p. 241. The Kantian construction of the equal worth of personhood animates the entire cause of my argument in this book.

Yet the idea of minimum conditions of individuation also explodes the image that Hampton argues informs contractarian theory, particularly in its Hobbesian variety. Hampton points out that, "Advocates of this approach ask us to imagine a group of people sitting around a bargaining table; each person is interested only in himself. This group is to decide answers to moral or political questions by determining what they can all agree to or what they would all be unreasonable to reject." See Hampton, *Feminist Contractarianism*, p. 232. Obviously, this image pictures the participants as adults, with no available account of how they achieved that maturation, at least as relevant to the theory itself.

17. Please see John Rawls, *Political Liberalism* (New York: Columbia University Press, 1993), p. 23.
18. I borrow this phrase from Tom Nagel. See, generally, Thomas Nagel, *The View from Nowhere* (New York: Oxford University Press, 1986).
19. Please see Immanuel Kant, *Kant: Political Writings*, ed. Hans Reiss (Cambridge, U.K.: Cambridge University Press, 1970), p. 75.
20. See Rawls, *A Theory of Justice*, pp. 136–148.
21. Rawls, *Political Liberalism*, p. 54.
22. I want to be as clear as possible over what I mean by "political contestation over the conception of justice." First, my argument is that a concept of justice cannot be realized in a conception of justice that successfully resolves the tension between fundamental values such as freedom and equality in and through a Kantian constructivist conception of the person. For me, there will always be tension between freedom and equality, even as we rely on the hypothetical contract in an attempt to synchronize those values. As a result, there can always be political contestation over the manner in which those values are synchronized.

    But I am not arguing that the concept of justice, now understood to include minimum conditions of individuation as a matter of right, should downplay right in the name of a concept of justice that turns over such matters to politics, discursive or otherwise. For example, I want discussion on the right to abortion *ended*. I justify ending the discussion in my defense of the equal protection of minimum conditions of individuation as a matter of right. Thus, I want to distinguish my position from the discursive concept of justice promoted by Jürgen Habermas, which would do just that: put the question of abortion back into the political fray.
23. Supra note 1.
24. See Mary Elizabeth Bartholomew for an analysis of the social construction of reasonableness.
25. For a comprehensive account of all these standards of reasonableness, see Mary Elizabeth Bartholomew, "The Reasonable Woman Standard in the Law of Sexual

Harassment: Imagining Title VII," manuscript on file with the author. See also Martha Fineman's "The Neutered Mother" for an excellent analysis of how patriarchal ideology limits the possibility of legal reform. Martha Fineman, *The Neutered Mother, the Sexual Family and Other Twentieth–Centruy Tragedies* (New York: Routledge, 1995).

26. See Bartholomew, "The Reasonable Woman Standard," for an excellent defense of the reasonable woman standard as the appropriate legal standard for Title VII.

27. Feminists are not the only scholars to argue that conceptions of reasonableness and rationality are differentiated by cultural and historical circumstances. See, for example, Alasdair MacIntyre, *Whose Justice: Which Rationality* (Notre Dame: University of Notre Dame Press, 1988).

28. Cornell, *Philosophy of the Limit*, pp. 117–169.

29. Rawls, *Political Liberalism*, p. 93.

30. See Amartya Sen, "Well-Being, Agency and Freedom" in *Philosophy and Public Affairs*, Vol. 19 (April, 1985), and "Equality of What?" in *Choice, Welfare and Measurement* (Cambridge, Mass.: MIT Press, 1982). See also Isaiah Berlin, *Four Essays on Liberty* (London: Oxford University Press, 1969).

31. See Deborah Rhode, *Justice and Gender* (Cambridge, Mass.: Harvard University Press, 1989).

32. "Fuckee" is my own term, derived from MacKinnon's famous dictum, "Man fucks woman; subject, verb, object." See Catharine MacKinnon, *Toward a Feminist Theory of the State* (Cambridge, M.A.: Harvard University Press, 1989), p. 124 and *passim*.

33. Ibid. See also Catharine MacKinnon, *Only Words* (1993 by Catharine MacKinnon).

34. See *Roe v. Wade*, 410 U.S. 113 (1973). See also Norma McCorvey with Andy Meisler, *I am Roe* (New York: Harper Collins, 1994).

35. For an excellent history of how sexual harassment came to be legalized as gender discrimination, please see Catharine MacKinnon, *Sexual Harassment of Working Women* (New Haven: Yale University Press, 1979), pp. 57–99.

36. *Geduldig v. Aiello*, 417 U.S. 484, 94 S. Ct. 2485, 41 L. Ed. 256 (1974).

37. MacKinnon, *Sexual Harassment of Working Women*.

38. Ibid.

39. See, generally, *Sex Exposed: Sexuality and the Pornography Debate*, ed. Lynne Segal and Mary McIntosh (New Brunswick, NJ: Rutgers University Press, 1993).

40. See Marcia Pally, *Sex and Sensibility: Reflections on Forbidden Mirrors and the Will to Censor* (Hopewell, NJ: The Ecco Press, 1994).

41. See Wendy Brown, "The Mirror of Pornography: Catharine MacKinnon's Social Theory of Gender," in *States of Injury: Essays on Power and Freedom in Late Modernity* (Princeton, NJ: Princeton University Press, 1995).

42. See Kristin Bumiller, *The Civil Rights Society* (Baltimore: John Hopkins University, 1988), and Wendy Brown, *States of Injury*.

43. See Drucilla Cornell, *Beyond Accommodation* (New York: Routledge, 1991).

44. See Betty Friedan, *The Second Stage* (New York: Dell, 1991) or Friedan, *The Feminine Mystique* (New York: Norton, 1963).

45. See Drucilla Cornell, "What is Ethical Feminism?" in *Feminist Contentions: A Philosophical Exchange* (New York: Routledge, 1995), Drucilla Cornell, *Beyond Accommodation* (New York: Routledge, 1991), and Cornell, *The Philosophy of the Limit*.

46. See Cornell, *The Philosophy of the Limit*.

47. For instance, I devoted an entire book to developing such an account of the abjection of the feminine. The question turns not on whether we need an analysis, but

what kind of philosophical judgement we give for making that analysis. This is the relationship between philosophy and feminism as it helps us think through the limits of theoretical reason as these are implicated even in our attempts to provide feminism with an account of the abjection of the feminine. See Cornell, *The Philosophy of the Limit*.

48. See Rawls, *Political Liberalism*, pp. 15, 133–172.
49. Ibid.
50. Please see *Transformations*, specifically "Gender Hierarchy, Equality, and the Possibility of Democracy." Definitions of public life have all too often turned on the re-incorporation of the abjection of the feminine.
51. See Sigmund Freud, *Civilization and its Discontents*, trans. and ed. James Strachey (New York: W.W. Norton & Co., 1961).

Reading 9

THE WRECK OF TIME
Taking Our Century's Measure

Annie Dillard

Ted Bundy, the serial killer, after his arrest, could not fathom the fuss. What was the big deal? David Von Drehle quotes an exasperated Bundy in *Among the Lowest of the Dead*: "I mean, there are *so* many people."

One R. Houwink, of Amsterdam, uncovered this unnerving fact: The human population of earth, arranged tidily, would just fit into Lake Windermere, in England's Lake District.

Recently in the Peruvian Amazon a man asked the writer Alex Shoumatoff, "Isn't it true that the whole population of the United States can be fitted into their cars?"

How are we doing in numbers, we who have been alive for this most recent installment of human life? How many people have lived and died?
"The dead outnumber the living, in a ratio that could be as high as 20 to 1," a demographer, Nathan Keyfitz, wrote in a 1991 letter to the historian Justin Kaplan. "Credible estimates of the number of people who have ever lived on the earth run from 70 billion to over 100 billion." Averaging those figures puts the total persons ever born at about 85 billion. We living people now number 5.8 billion. By these moderate figures, the dead outnumber us about fourteen to one. The dead will always outnumber the living.

Dillard, Annie. "The Wreck of Time." *Harper's* Jan. 1998: 51–56.

Dead Americans, however, if all proceeds, will not outnumber living Americans until the year 2030, because the nation is young. Some of us will be among the dead then. Will we know or care, we who once owned the still bones under the quick ones, we who spin inside the planet with our heels in the air? The living might well seem foolishly self-important to us, and overexcited.

We who are here now make up about 6.8 percent of all people who have appeared to date. This is not a meaningful figure. These our times are, one might say, ordinary times, a slice of life like any other. Who can bear to hear this, or who will consider it? Are we not especially significant because our century is—our century and its nuclear bombs, its unique and unprecedented Holocaust, its serial exterminations and refugee populations, our century and its warming, its silicon chips, men on the moon, and spliced genes? No, we are not and it is not.

Since about half of all the dead are babies and children, we will be among the longest-boned dead and among the dead who grew the most teeth—for what those distinctions might be worth among beings notoriously indifferent to appearance and all else.

In Juan Rulfo's novel *Pedro Páramo*, a dead woman says to her dead son, "Just think about pleasant things, because we're going to be buried for a long time."

II

On April 30, 1991—on that one day—138,000 people drowned in Bangladesh. At dinner I mentioned to my daughter, who was then seven years old, that it was hard to imagine 138,000 people drowning.

"No, it's easy," she said. "Lots and lots of dots, in blue water."

The paleontologist Pierre Teilhard de Chardin, now dead, sent a dispatch from a dig. "In the middle of the tamarisk bush you find a red-brick town, partially exposed. . . . More than 3,000 years before our era, people were living there who played with dice like our own, fished with hooks like ours, and wrote in characters we can't yet read."

Who were these individuals who lived under the tamarisk bush? Who were the people Ted Bundy killed? Who was the statistician who reckoned that everybody would fit into Lake Windermere? The Trojans likely thought well of themselves, one by one; their last settlement died out by 1,100 B.C.E. Who were the people Stalin killed, or any of the 79.2 billion of us now dead, and who are the 5.8 billion of us now alive?

"God speaks succinctly," said the rabbis.

Is it important if you have yet died your death, or I? Your father? Your child? It is only a matter of time, after all. Why do we find it supremely pertinent, during any moment of any century on earth, which among us is topsides? Why do we concern ourselves over which side of the membrane of topsoil our feet poke?

"A single death is a tragedy, a million deaths is a statistic." Joseph Stalin, that connoisseur, gave words to this disquieting and possibly universal sentiment.

How can an individual count? Do we individuals count only to us other suckers, who love and grieve like elephants, bless their hearts? Of Allah, the Koran says, "Not so much as the weight of an ant in earth or heaven escapes from the Lord." That is touching, that Allah, God, and their ilk care when one ant dismembers another, or note when a sparrow falls, but I strain to see the use of it.

Ten years ago we thought there were two galaxies for each of us alive. Lately, since we loosed the Hubble Space Telescope, we have revised our figures. There are nine galaxies for each of us. Each galaxy harbors an average of 100 billion suns. In our galaxy, the Milky Way, there are sixty-nine suns for each person alive. The Hubble shows, says a report, that the universe "is at least 15 billion years old." Two galaxies, nine galaxies . . . sixty-nine suns, 100 billion suns—

These astronomers are nickel-and-diming us to death.

III

What were you doing on April 30, 1991, when a series of waves drowned 138,000 people? Where were you when you first heard the astounding, heartbreaking news? Who told you? What, seriatim, were your sensations? Who did you tell? Did you weep? Did your anguish last days or weeks?

All my life I have loved this sight: a standing wave in a boat's wake, shaped like a thorn. I have seen it rise from many oceans, and I saw it rise from the Sea of Galilee. It was a peak about a foot high. The standing wave broke at its peak, and foam slid down its glossy hollow. I watched the foaming wave on the port side. At every instant we were bringing this boat's motor, this motion, into new water. The stir, as if of life, impelled each patch of water to pinch and inhabit this same crest. Each crest tumbled upon itself and released a slide of white foam. The foam's bubbles popped and dropped into the general sea while they were still sliding down the dark wave. They trailed away always, and always new waters peaked, broke, foamed, and replenished.

What I saw was the constant intersection of two wave systems. Lord Kelvin first described them. Transverse waves rise abaft the stern and stream away perpendicular to the boat's direction of travel. Diverging waves course out in a V shape behind the boat. Where the waves converge, two lines of standing crests persist at an unchanging angle to the direction of the boat's motion. We think of these as the boat's wake. I was studying the highest standing wave, the one nearest the boat. It rose from the trough behind the stern and spilled foam. The curled wave crested over clear water and tumbled down. All its bubbles broke, thousands a second, unendingly. I could watch the present; I could see time and how it works.

On a shore, 8,000 waves break a day. James Trefil, a professor of physics, provides these facts. At any one time, the foam from breaking waves covers between 3 and 4 percent of the earth's surface. This acreage of foam is equal to the entire continent of North America. By coincidence, the U.S. population bears nearly the same relation to the world population: 4.6 percent. The U.S. population, in other words, although it is the third largest population among nations, is as small a portion of the earth's people as breaking waves' white foam is of the sea.

"God rises up out of the sea like a treasure in the waves," wrote Thomas Merton.

We see generations of waves rise from the sea that made them, billions of individuals at a time; we see them dwindle and vanish. If this does not astound you, what will? Or what will move you to pity?

IV

One tenth of the land on earth is tundra. At any time, it is raining on only 5 percent of the planet's surface. Lightning strikes the planet about a hundred times every second. The insects outweigh us. Our chickens outnumber us four to one.

One fifth of us are Muslims. One fifth of us live in China. And every seventh person is a Chinese peasant. Almost one tenth of us live within range of an active volcano. More than 2 percent of us are mentally retarded. We humans drink tea—over a billion cups a day. Among us we speak 10,000 languages.

We are civilized generation number 500 or so, counting from 10,000 years ago, when we settled down. We are *Homo sapiens* generation number 7,500, counting from 150,000 years ago, when our species presumably arose; and we are human generation number 125,000, counting from the earliest forms of *Homo*.

Every 110 hours a million more humans arrive on the planet than die into the planet. A hundred million of us are children who live on the streets. Over a hundred million of us live in countries where we hold no citizenship. Twenty-

three million of us are refugees. Sixteen million of us live in Cairo. Twelve million fish for a living from small boats. Seven and a half million of us are Uygurs.
One million of us crew on freezer trawlers. Nearly a thousand of us a day commit suicide.

HEAD-SPINNING NUMBERS CAUSE MIND TO GO SLACK, the *Hartford Courant*
says. But our minds must not go slack. How can we think straight if our minds
go slack? We agree that we want to think straight.

Anyone's close world of family and friends composes a group smaller than
almost all sampling errors, smaller than almost all rounding errors, a group
invisible, at whose loss the world will not blink. Two million children die a year
from diarrhea, and 800,000 from measles. Do we blink? Stalin starved 7 million
Ukrainians in one year, Pol Pot killed 1 million Cambodians, the flu epidemic of
1918 killed 21 or 22 million people . . . shall this go on? Or do you suffer, as
Teilhard de Chardin did, the sense of being "an atom lost in the universe"? Or do
you not suffer this sense? How about what journalists call "compassion
fatigue"? Reality fatigue? At what limit for you do other individuals blur? Vanish? How old are you?

V

Los Angeles airport has 25,000 parking spaces. This is about one space for every
person who died in 1985 in Colombia when a volcano erupted. This is one space
for each of the corpses of more than two years' worth of accidental killings from
leftover land mines of recent wars. At five to a car, almost all the Inuit in the
world could park at LAX. Similarly, if you propped up or stacked four bodies to a
car, you could fit into the airport parking lot all the corpses from the firestorm
bombing of Tokyo in March 1945, or the corpses of Londoners who died in the
plague, or the corpses of Burundians killed in civil war since 1993. But you could
not fit America's homeless there, not even at twenty to a car.

Since sand and dirt pile up on everything, why does the world look fresh
for each new crowd? As natural and human debris raises the continents, vegetation grows on the piles. It is all a stage—we know this—a temporary stage
on top of many layers of stages, but every year a new crop of sand, grass, and
tree leaves freshens the set and perfects the illusion that ours is the new
and urgent world now. When Keats was in Rome, I read once, he saw pome-
granate trees overhead; they bloomed in dirt blown onto the Colosseum's broken walls. How can we doubt our own time, in which each bright instant probes
the future? In every arable soil in the world we grow grain over tombs—sure,
we know this. But do not the dead generations seem to us dark and still as
mummies, and their times always faded like scenes painted on walls at
Pompeii?

How can we see ourselves as only a new, temporary cast for a long-running show when a new batch of birds flies around singing and new clouds move? Living things from hyenas to bacteria whisk the dead away like stagehands hustling between scenes. To help a living space last while we live on it, we brush or haul away the blowing sand and hack or burn the greenery. We are mowing the grass at the cutting edge.

IV

In northeast Japan, a seismic sea wave killed 27,000 people on June 15, 1896. Do not fail to distinguish this infamous wave from the April 30, 1991, waves that drowned 138,000 Bangladeshi. You were not tempted to confuse, conflate, forget, or ignore these deaths, were you?

On the dry Laetoli plain of northern Tanzania, Mary Leakey found a trail of hominid footprints. The three barefoot people—likely a short man and woman and child *Australopithecus afarensis*—walked closely together. They walked on moist volcanic tuff and ash. We have a record of those few seconds from a day about 3.6 million years ago—before hominids even chipped stone tools. More ash covered their footprints and hardened. Ash also preserved the pockmarks of the raindrops that fell beside the three who walked; it was a rainy day. We have almost ninety feet of the three's steady footprints intact. We do not know where they were going or why. We do not know why the woman paused and turned left, briefly, before continuing. "A remote ancestor," Leakey said, "experienced a moment of doubt." Possibly they watched the Sadiman volcano erupt, or they took a last look back before they left. We do know we cannot make anything so lasting as these three barefoot ones did.

After archeologists studied this long strip of record for several years, they buried it again to save it. Along one preserved portion, however, new tree roots are already cracking the footprints, and in another place winds threaten to sand them flat; the preservers did not cover them deeply enough. Now they are burying them again.

Jeremiah, walking toward Jerusalem, saw the smoke from the Temple's blaze. He wept; he saw the blood of the slain. "He put his face close to the ground and saw the footprints of sucklings and infants who were walking into captivity" in Babylon. He kissed the footprints.

Who were these individuals? Who were the three who walked together and left footprints in the rain? Who was that eighteenth-century Ukrainain peasant the Baal Shem Tov, the founder of modern Hasidism, who taught, danced, and dug clay? He was among the generations of children of Babylonian exiles whose footprints on the bare earth Jeremiah kissed. Centuries later the Emperor Hadrian destroyed another such son of exile in Rome, Rabbi Akiba. Russian Christians and European Christians tried, and Hitler tried, to wipe all those survivors of children of exile from the ground of the earth as a man wipes a plate—survivors of exiles whose footprints on the ground I kiss, and whose feet.

Who and of what import were the men whose bones bulk the Great Wall, the 30 million Mao starved, or the 11 million children under five who die each year now? Why, they are the insignificant others, of course; living or dead, they are just some of the plentiful others. And you?

Is it not late? A late time to be living? Are not our current generations the important ones? We have changed the world. Are not our heightened times the important ones, the ones since Hiroshima? Perhaps we are the last generation—there is a comfort. Take the bomb threat away and what are we? We are ordinary beads on a never-ending string. Our time is a routine twist of an improbable yarn.

We have no chance of being here when the sun burns out. There must be something ultimately heroic about our time, something that sets it above all those other times. Hitler, Stalin, Mao, and Pol Pot made strides in obliterating whole peoples, but this has been the human effort all along, and we have only enlarged the means, as have people in every century in history. (That genocides recur does not mean that they are similar. Each instance of human evil and each victim's death possesses its unique history and form. To generalize, as Cynthia Ozick points out, is to "befog" evil's specificity.)

Dire things are happening. Plague? Funny weather? Why are we watching the news, reading the news, keeping up with the news? Only to enforce our fancy—probably a necessary lie—that these are crucial times, and we are in on them. Newly revealed, and I am in the know: crazy people, bunches of them! New diseases, sways in power, floods! Can the news from dynastic Egypt have been any different?

As I write this, I am still alive, but of course I might well have died before you read it. Most of the archeologists who reburied hominid footprints have likely not yet died their deaths; the paleontologist Teilhard is pushing up daisies.

Chinese soldiers who breathed air posing for 7,000 individual clay portraits—twenty-two centuries ago—must have thought it a wonderful difference that workers buried only their simulacra then so that their sons could bury their flesh a bit later. One wonders what they did in the months or years they gained. One wonders what one is, oneself, up to these days.

IV

Was it wisdom Mao Tse-tung attained when—like Ted Bundy—he awakened to the long view?

"The atom bomb is nothing to be afraid of," Mao told Nehru. "China has many people. . . . The deaths of ten or twenty million people is nothing to be afraid of." A witness said Nehru showed shock. Later, speaking in Moscow, Mao displayed yet more generosity: he boasted that he was willing to lose 300 million people, half of China's population.

Does Mao's reckoning shock me really? If sanctioning the death of strangers could save my daughter's life, would I do it? Probably. How many others' lives would I be willing to sacrifice? Three? Three hundred million?

An English journalist, observing the Sisters of Charity in Calcutta, reasoned: "Either life is always and in all circumstances sacred, or intrinsically of no account; it is inconceivable that it should be in some cases the one, and in some the other."

One small town's soup kitchen, St. Mary's, serves 115 men a night. Why feed 115 individuals? Surely so few people elude most demographics and achieve statistical insignificance. After all, there are 265 million Americans, 15 million people who live in Mexico City, 16 million in greater New York, 26 million in greater Tokyo. Every day 1.5 million people walk through Times Square in New York; every day almost as many people—1.4 million—board a U.S. passenger plane. And so forth. We who breathe air now will join the already dead layers of us who breathed air once. We arise from dirt and dwindle to dirt, and the might of the universe is arrayed against us.

Reading 10

THE CORE OF ART
Making Special

Ellen Dissanayake

When contemporary philosophers of art make the radical and rather astonishing statement that art has existed for only two centuries,[1] they are referring to the insufficiently appreciated fact that the abstract concept "art" is a construction of Western culture and in fact has a discernible historical origin.[2] It was only in the late eighteenth century—in Enlightenment England and Germany–and subsequently, that the subject of aesthetics was named and developed, that " the aesthetic" came to be regarded as a distinctive kind of experience, and that an art world of academies, museums, galleries, dealers, critics, journals, and scholars arose to address a type of human artifact that was made primarily and often specifically for acquisition and display. At the same time ideas of genius, creative imagination, self-expression, originality, communication, and emotion, having originated in other contexts, became increasingly and even primarily or exclusively associated with the subject of "art." The concepts "primitive" and "natural" that I referred to briefly in the preceding chapters also developed at this time to become part of modern Western cultural consciousness.

Previously, the sorts of objects that in the post-eighteenth century West came to be called art—paintings, sculptures, ceramics, music, dance, poetry, and so forth—were made to embody or to reinforce religious or civic values, and rarely, if ever, for purely aesthetic purposes. Paintings and sculptures served as portraits, illustrations, interior or exterior decoration; ceramics were vessels for use; music and dance were part of a ceremonial or special social occasion;

Dissanayake, Ellen. "The Core of Art: Making Special." *Homo Aestheticus: Where Art Comes From and Why.* New York: The Free Press. 39–63.

poetry was storytelling or praise or oratory to sway an audience. Even when beauty, skill, or ostentation were important qualities of an object, they did not exist "for their own sake," but as an enhancement of the object's ostensible if not actual use. This enhancement would be called beautification or adornment, not art. The word *art* as used before the late eighteenth century meant what we would today call "craft" or "skill" or "well-madeness," and could characterize any object or activity made or performed by human (rather than natural or divine) agency—for example, the art of medicine, of retailing, of holiday dining.

It may be a surprise to realize how peculiar our modern Western notion of art really is—how it is dependent on and intertwined with ideas of commerce, commodity, ownership, history, progress, specialization, and individuality—and to recognize the truth that only a few societies have thought of it even remotely as we do (Alsop 1982). Of course, in the preindustrial West and elsewhere, people had and continue to have "aesthetic" ideas—notions of what makes something beautiful or excellent-of-its-kind—but such ideas can be held without tacitly assuming that there is a superordinate abstract category, Art, to which belong *some* paintings, drawings, or carvings and not *other* paintings, drawings, or carvings.[3]

As Western aesthetics developed, something was assigned to the category of genuine art if it was deemed capable of providing and sustaining genuine aesthetic experience. Genuine aesthetic experience was defined as something one experienced when contemplating genuine art. Note the circularity of this argument. Moreover, difficulties arose in specifying the cause or location of this genuineness (in the face of differences of opinion about the validity of individual works or responses). People should have recognized that these difficulties threw the concept of a pure or singular art itself into doubt.

To be sure, philosophers and artists in the past (for example, Aristotle, Saint Thomas Aquinas, Leonardo da Vinci) had proposed criteria for beauty or excellence, for example, fitness, clarity, harmony, radiance, a mirror held up to nature. Nineteenth- and twentieth-century thinkers proposed other criteria, such as truth, order, unity in variety, and significant form, as being the defining feature of this mysterious entity "Art."

But, as every first-year student of Western aesthetics learns, determining what is beauty or truth, not to mention significance or harmony, is no less difficult than defining art in the first place. And in any case, since the romantic period artists themselves (influenced by the ever-growing Western cultural emphasis on individualism and originality) have deliberately flouted and contradicted the canonic aesthetic features, as they were described or proposed by philosophers, critics, and other thinkers, as if to demonstrate that art, whatever its essence or validity, is protean, undefinable, and irreducible.

Hence the search for a common denominator, some quality or feature that characterizes all instances of art, that *makes* something "Art," gradually became both outmoded and a lost cause. Today's philosophers of art have totally abandoned trying to define the word or the concept. Looking at the plural and radical nature of the arts in our time, aware of the economic ramifications where canvases may be "worth" millions of dollars and where critics, dealers, and museum directors rather than artists or publics largely decide this value, philosophers concerned with art have concluded that art no longer exists (if it ever did) in a vacuum or ideal realm for its own sake, with its sacred essence waiting to be discovered, but must be considered as it appears in and is dependent on a particular social context. In a postindustrial, postmodern society, an art world (or "artworld") determines what "Art" is and what is "Art." It exists, if at all, only as a socially and historically conditioned label.

The reader must recognize, however, that this position arises from contemporary postmodern Western society, which despite our natural ethnocentrism [. . .] is not, of course, the apogee of humankind's enterprise and wisdom nor its ultimate destiny. We must not forget that although "Art" as a concept seems to have been born of and continues to be sustained by a commercial society, is therefore only roughly two centuries old, and hence is relative, even discardable, *the arts* have always been with us. And so have ideas of beauty, sublimity, and transcendence, along with the verities of the human condition: love, death, memory, suffering, power, fear, loss, desire, hope, and so forth. These have been the subject matter of and occasion for the arts throughout human history. Thus when contemporary theory accepts that art is contingent and dependent on "a particular social context," the mistake should not be made of assuming that the abiding human concerns and the arts that have immemorially been their accompaniment and embodiment are themselves contingent and dependent.

The species-centric view of art recognizes and proclaims as valid and intrinsic the association between what humans have always found to be important and certain ways—called "the arts"—that they have found to grasp, manifest, and reinforce this importance. That the arts in postmodern society do not perform these functions, at least to the extent that they do in premodern societies, is not because of some deficiency or insubstantiality of an abstract concept but because their makers inhabit a world—unprecedented in human history—in which these abiding concerns are artificially disguised, denied, trivialized, ignored, or banished.

An ethological view of art, then, departs from the entrenched position of contemporary aesthetics and reinstates the search for a "common denominator," although in a manner never dreamed of by philosophers of art. In order to show that a behavior of art is universal and indelible, *it is necessary to identify a core behavioral tendency upon which natural selection could act.*

In trying to uncover this deep marrow of a behavior of art, we will not be primarily concerned with contemporary society, not even with earlier civilizations or with traditional or what used to be called "primitive" societies. Rather, we must look for a behavioral tendency that could have been possessed by protohumans, the early hominids who existed one to four million years ago.

These, our ancestors, were creatures who walked on two legs and lived in small, nomadic bands on the African savannah. They hunted, foraged, scavenged, and gathered their food, as hominids did until about 10,000 B.C. when settled agricultural communities began to establish themselves in certain parts of the world. Somewhere in this continuum of hominid evolution will have arisen a behavioral tendency that helped individuals who possessed it (and by extension a social group whose members had it) to survive better than individuals and groups who lacked the tendency. This core or common denominator of art will, however, be a behavioral tendency that is not incompatible with art today and elsewhere, yet can also characterize creatures such as these, our hominid ancestors.

The Extra-Ordinary

In my view, the biological core of art, the stain that is deeply dyed in the behavioral marrow of humans everywhere, is something I have elsewhere called "making special." Like other key phrases used to name or summarize a complex concept ("pleasure principle," "survival of the fittest"), "making special" can without elaboration or context sound trivial or woolly. Before describing it in more detail, [. . .] I would like to recount briefly the background of my search for this core tendency that I believe lies behind or within what is today considered to be the impulse toward (the behavioral tendency of) art.

Play and Ritual

My own earliest attempts to approach art as a behavior began when I first read ethological accounts of play. Play in animals (including humans) is an appealing and quite mysterious behavior. It occurs in many species in which animals play naturally, without being taught. Yet, unlike other behaviors, play seems to be, at the time of playing at least, biologically purposeless and even disadvantageous. The players do not gain a life-serving goal, as they do in other behaviors where they find food, mate, repel an intruder, rest, and so on. In fact, animals at play seem to expend a lot of energy for no useful purpose and risk hurting themselves, attracting predators, or otherwise decreasing their chances of survival. Yet young animals will play indefatigably. They seem to play for play's sake, for sheer enjoyment and intrinsic reward. Thus it would seem that play has hidden survival benefits that outweigh the costs of its energy expenditure and risks.

In play, novelty and unpredictability are actively sought, whereas in real life we do not usually like uncertainty. Wondering whether an untried shortcut will take us to the bank before it closes on the day before a holiday is different from choosing an unknown path just to see where it will lead while on holiday.

Play can be said to be "extra," something outside normal life. At least normal constraints do not hold. At play, you can be a princess, a mother, or a horse. You can be strong and invincible. You can act *like*, be *like*, a desperado or a soldier. You pretend to fight or pretend to have a tea party, but these are "not for real." Real weapons (like loaded guns or unsheathed claws) are not used; the teacups may be empty.

But play is marked by constraints nevertheless. One generally finds, even in animals, "rules" of play: special signals (such as wagging the tail or not using claws), postures, facial expressions, and sounds that mean "This is make-believe." Often special places are set aside for playing: a stadium, a gymnasium, a park, a recreation room, a ring or circle. There are special times, special clothes, a special mood for play—think of holidays, festivals, vacations, weekends.

As I read about play, its similarities to art became obvious. Art, as I knew it from aesthetics and art history classes, is "nonutilitarian," "for its own sake": Cellini's saltcellar was art, but not because it held salt better than a clay or glass container. Art, like play, was not "real" but pretend: the actor playing Hamlet did not really stab the actor playing Polonius. Art made exquisite use of surprise and ambiguity. There were special places like museums and concert halls set aside for art, special times, even special clothes for it—such as dark attire for symphony musicians. And there was especially a special mood, which I had learned to describe as "disinterested contemplation": one *did not* rush up on stage to help the hero overcome the villain, one *did* contemplate the skill and subtlety of the actors, the craft and language of the playwright. Art, like play, was something extra, an embellishment, an enhancement to life.

As I looked further into the subject, I discovered I was only the latest in a long lineage to have noticed the resemblance between play and art and to have gone on to conclude that art was a derivative of play.[4] The new contribution I hoped to offer was making this conclusion plausible by means of ethological (rather than, as others had done, from psychological or historical or metaphysical) evidence. I thought that the "metaphorical" nature of both art and play, the make-believe aspect where something is, in reality, something else, was the salient core feature.

For an ethologist, the apparent absence of evolutionary purpose is a problem both for play and for art. Because humans everywhere avidly engage in both playful and artistic pursuits, these must serve some purpose, even if it is not immediately evident.

With regard to play, it is generally agreed that although there might not be immediate survival benefits associated with play, young animals in play are practicing (in situations that are not yet "for keeps") skills that eventually enable them to find food, defend themselves, and mate, among other adult necessities.

Also—importantly—in play, they learn how to get along with others. Individuals who play, and thereby learn practical and social skills, survive better than individuals who are not inclined to play or who are deprived of play and therefore lack practice with these essential things. As with an insurance policy, the benefits of play are deferred.

Looking at art, I was aware that it consisted of more than exercise, practice, or socialization. But what? Freud claimed that the function of both play and art was therapy. They allowed for fantasy, for the sublimation or fulfillment of hidden wishes that in real life were denied or tabooed: if you can't get the girl, dream or fantasize or write a story or paint a picture about getting her. As I considered the problem from an ethological point of view, I concluded that art in human evolution must have done something more than give fantasy free rein. How much fantasy did our hominid ancestors practice anyway? Did they need more make-believe than they acquired from play? (It is almost certain that early hominids, like all primates, must have played.) Was it not more important that they accept and comply with *reality:* the daily "business" of meals, safety, cooperation?[5] Fantasy and make-believe may well be important safety valves for modern humans mired in the discontents of civilization, but I hoped to find a more plausible reason to explain why early hominids would have developed art *as well as* or in addition to play. Practice, socialization, recreation, wish-fulfillment—these goals could have been satisfied by play without necessitating another sort of behavior that accomplished the same ends. Unless I were willing to accept the idea that art was simply a variety of play, which seemed an inadequate explanation, I had to look further into the matter of its ethological origin, nature, and probable selective value.

During the years that I lived in Sri Lanka, the small Buddhist country formerly known as Ceylon, I became acquainted with what sociologists call a traditional society. In such societies, modern technology is still relatively undeveloped: at building sites, for example, scaffoldings are made of bamboo tied together, and people rather than backhoes and bulldozers move the earth. Many families still live on the land and are relatively self-sufficient; village houses and utensils are largely made by hand from local materials and food is grown in the family garden. Custom and authority continue to provide the boundaries within which people lead their lives and find their satisfactions—most marriages are arranged by parents or other relatives, for example, and it is not considered unusual for important decisions to be made only after consulting an astrologer.

People living in traditional societies seem much closer to the verities of life than people living in highly technological societies like our own. Because they have known each other's families for generations, events like weddings and funerals—matters of life and death—are important occasions for socializing. I attended my first funeral and saw a dead body for the first time while in Sri

Lanka, and I was initially amazed that babies and small children were also in attendance.

Traditional ceremony and custom thus play a much larger part in the life of a Sri Lankan than in ours. After a person dies in Sri Lanka, the mourners arrive during the course of the day at the home where the deceased is lying in an open coffin on a table in the living room, surrounded by flowers. The bereaved family members greet each visitor at the door, breaking down in sobs with each new arrival as they talk about the circumstances of the death and the merits of the deceased. The guest enters the house and joins other guests; they chat quietly with each other about any subject (I heard discussions about movies, business, and political matters); and after a decent interval they leave. Eventually the family and close friends go to the place of cremation or burial where Buddhist monks join them and recite the appropriate Pali texts—reflections on birth, death, decay, and reincarnation. Three days after the disposition of the body the family and priests hold an almsgiving ceremony; other almsgivings in memory of the deceased occur after three months, one year, and at yearly intervals thereafter.

I realized that this kind of formalized handling of grief, with regular, community-sanctioned opportunities to weep and express one's loss at greater and greater intervals of time, gave to the bereaved a sort of patterned program to follow, a form that could shape and contain their feelings. Instead of having to suppress their grief and sense of loss in the interests of being brave or "realistic," or having to release it haphazardly or in solitude, the bereaved is enabled—compelled—by the ritual of mourning to acknowledge and express it publicly, over and over again, within a preordained structure. The temporal structure of the mourning ritual, simple as it is, assures that thoughts and feelings about one's loss will be reiterated at prescribed times. Even if one might not consciously have proper mournful feelings, the custom of successive almsgivings ensures that these feelings are elicited. The prescribed formal ceremonies become the occasion for and even the cause of individuals feeling and publicly expressing their sorrow.[6]

It occurred to me that in a very similar way, the arts also are containers for, molders of feeling. The performance of a play, a dance, or a musical composition manipulates the audience's response: expands, contracts, excites, calms, releases. The rhythm and form of a poem do the same thing. Even nontemporal arts, like painting, sculpture, and architecture, structure the viewer's response and give a form to feeling.

It is well known that in most societies the arts are commonly associated with ceremonial contexts, with rituals. So next I began to try to discover what art and ritual had in common. It was intriguing to learn that "ritualized behavior" in animals, like play, was an important ethological subject and that at least some anthropologists noted real, not just superficial, parallels between ritualized behavior in animals and ceremonial rituals in humans (Huxley 1966; Turner 1983). Perhaps like ritual (and play), one could call art "a behavior" also.

As I had suspected and hoped, the similarities between ceremonial ritual and art were provocative. For example, both ritual and art are *compelling*. They use various effective means to arouse, capture, and hold attention. Both are fashioned with the intent to affect individuals emotionally—to bring their feelings into awareness, to display them. A large part of the compelling nature of rituals and art is that they are deliberately *nonordinary*. In Sri Lankan—and our own— funeral services, for example, unusual language is used: ancient religious works with their archaic and poetic vocabulary and word order serve as texts for the services, and these texts are intoned or chanted in a voice unlike that employed in normal discourse. Other nonordinary devices for making ritual (and art) compelling include exaggeration (the rhythm of funeral processions may be unusually slow and deliberate), repetition (the Sri Lankan funeral ritual punctuates time with repeated almsgivings), and elaboration (the profusion of flowers, the wearing of special clothing, other extravagances like the gathering of unusually large numbers of people).

The *stylization* of ritual and art also adds to their nonordinary aspect. They are self-consciously performed as if acted. During the ceremonial signing of a bill, the president of the United States speaks highly rhetorical phrases sanctified by use reaching back two hundred years, things like "Thereunto I set this seal." The ballerina or opera singer makes a ritualized—exaggerated, elaborated, formalized—series of bows to acknowledge the applause at the end of her performance (which itself was composed of exaggerated, elaborated, and formalized movements or vocalizations).

Thus, in general, both rituals and art are *formalized*. Movements—what people do—are prescribed, the order of events is structured, and the individual participants' perceptions, emotions, and interpretations are thereby shaped.

Ritual ceremonies and the arts are *socially reinforcing,* uniting their participants and their audiences in one mood. They both provide an occasion for feelings of individual transcendence of the self—what Victor Turner (1969) calls *communitas* and Mihaly Csikszentmihalyi (1975) calls "flow"—as everyone shares in the same occasion of patterned emotion. For a time, the hard edges of their customary isolation from each other are softened or melted together or their everyday taken-for-granted comradeship is reinforced.

Rituals and the arts are *bracketed,* set off from real or ordinary life. A stage of some kind—a circle, a demarcated area, a museum, or platform—sets off the holy from the profane, the performers from the audience, the extra-ordinary from the everyday. And both rituals and the arts make conspicuous *use of symbols:* things have hidden or arcane meanings, reverberations beyond their apparent surface significance.

Ritual ceremonies are universal, found in every human society. They serve numerous social purposes: they state and publicly reinforce the values of a group of people; they unite it in common purpose and belief; they "explain" the inexplicable—birth, death, illness, natural disaster—and attempt to control it and make it bearable. From the ethological perspective, people in social groups that did not have ceremonial rituals would not survive as well as those who did have them. They would be less cohesive and cooperative; they would respond to adversity in individualized, fragmented, unfocused, and ultimately less satisfactory ways.

Apart from the many similarities that ritual and art share as general "behaviors," they are virtually always linked together in practice. During ritual ceremonies one invariably finds the arts: the use of beautiful or arresting objects, the wearing of specially decorated attire, music, visual display, poetic language, dance, performances. It seemed nondebatable to me that an understanding of ceremonial ritual was relevant, even critical, to an ethological understanding of art.

Because of the many close connections between art and ritual, I first wondered whether art could be considered as a derivative of ritual, much as I had earlier thought of art as a kind of play.[7] After struggling to make sense of how and why this might have happened, an idea came to me: art was not a variety of play or ritual, but like them it was concerned with a special order, realm, mood, state of being. In play, ritual, *and* art things were not ordinary—they are less real or more real than everyday reality. I decided to try looking there for the behavioral core of art.

Differentiating Ordinary from Extra-Ordinary

My thesis that the evolution and selective value of a behavior of art arises from a tendency to make special rests on the claim that humans everywhere, in a manner that is unlike that of other animals, differentiate between an order, realm, mood, or state of being that is mundane, ordinary, or "natural," and one that is unusual, extra-ordinary, or "super-natural."

But is this a justifiable claim? In some premodern societies the former and the latter appear to interpenetrate. According to Robert Tonkinson (1978, 96), the Mardudjara, an Australian aboriginal group, make no clear distinction between natural and spiritual realms, considering themselves and nonhuman entities and forces to be all equally real inhabitants of their cosmic order.[8] Other peoples, in Australia and elsewhere, similarly find "natural" and "spiritual" to be more continuous than we do—to consider the spiritual *as* natural. One might wonder whether an "obvious" separation between ordinary and extra-ordinary, like that between profane and sacred, natural and super-natural, nature and culture, body and soul, flesh and spirit, is to be traced to the discontents and artificialities of civilization.

I am prepared to claim, however, that making such a distinction is a characterizing universal predisposition of human behavior and mentality. Moreover, I would argue that it is in this predisposition that we are to look for the core of a behavior of art. Even in human groups that do not articulate an explicit separation between extra-ordinary and ordinary, their actions demonstrate such an awareness. Tonkinson himself says of the Mardudjara: "the Dreamtime [the spiritual dimension or domain in which ancestral beings have their existence] is crucial because it is held to be the source of all power, given in response to ritual performance, but also available to individuals when they are able *briefly to transcend their humanity and tap this reservoir (for example, during dance, trance, visions, dreams, and heightened emotional and religious states."* (Tonkinson 1978, 16; my italics).

Many anthropological studies describe "other worlds": the mysterious permanent dimension of reality that the Yoruba call *iron* (Drewal and Drewal 1983); the spirit of the forest of the Ituri forest pygmies (Turnbull 1961); the *engang,* or unseen world of dead spirits, of the Fang of Gabon (Fernandez 1973); the Eskimo *sila* or "life force" (Birket-Smith 1959); the *kore* ("wilderness") of the Gimi, otherworldly compared to *dusa,* the domesticated forms of plants and animals and the constraints of human social existence (Gillison 1980, 144); the transcendent reality of the Umeda which is grasped only through rituals that are the antithesis or opposite of what usually is (Gell 1975); the "underneath" side of things and words of the Kaluli (Feld 1982); the hyperanimacy of the powerful beings that the Kalapalo communally sing into being (Basso 1985); the *kia* experience of Bushmen (Katz 1982)—one would be hard-pressed to find an anthropological monograph about a people that did not recognize or manifest by their actions the recognition of a nonordinary if not sacred dimension along with everyday reality.

How and why would evolving humans perceive or create "other worlds" apart from the everyday? As I pointed out in the pervious section, the penchant for acknowledging an extra-ordinary realm is inherent in the behavior of play, where actions are "not for real." The "as-ifness" of play, then, can be thought of as a reservoir from which more flexible, imaginative, innovative behaviors can arise—as when we "play around with" an idea. And in ritual also (both the ritualized behaviors of animals and human ritual ceremonies), ordinary behavior is formalized and exaggerated, thereby (particularly in humans) acquiring a meaning and weight that makes it different from what it usually is: it becomes extraordinary. It seems undeniable that at some point, evolving hominids, being acquainted in their daily lives with play and ritual, would have been predisposed (as individuals and eventually as a species) to recognize and even create "meta-" or "as-if" realities.

Yet it must be admitted that at the most fundamental level, being able to distinguish between ordinary and extra-ordinary is not a particularly remarkable ability at all. Every animal is equipped to differentiate the normal from the abnormal, the neutral from the extreme. A salamander or mosquito, as well as more complex forms of life, will know when there is a change that suggests something out of the ordinary might occur: a sudden shadow, a sharp noise, an unexpected movement. Life, after all, depends on reacting (or being ready to react) to changes in habitual existence. Moreover, many nonhuman animals also play, but did not go on to invent arts or imaginative works of any kind. And formalized, ritualized behaviors, analogous to ritual ceremonies in humans in their use of rare and extra-ordinary postures, odors, sounds, and movements (Geist 1978), are also widespread in other animals but have not given rise in them to anything we can justifiably call art. What was it about humans that provoked or permitted them to recognize and then proceed to further elaborate "other" worlds, special fanciful worlds like those invented in play, invoked in ritual, or fabricated in the arts?

The evolving hominids we are concerned with—say, a quarter of a million years ago—were more intelligent and resourceful than other animals. Their brains were larger and more intricately composed, and the mental and emotional complexity this endowment permitted led to a wider range of thought and feeling. Whereas other animals can be assumed to inhabit a continuous present, generally unconcerned with what happened yesterday and what might happen tomorrow, gradually during the Middle or Early Upper Paleolithic, humans must have become, as Walter Burkert (1987; 172) has remarked with regard to the biological origins of religion, "painfully aware of past and future."

I suggest that the standard and unexceptional animal inclination to differentiate ordinary from extra-ordinary, to recognize specialness, would have been developing over tens of thousands of years, along with other higher-level cognitive abilities that were also evolving, such as planning ahead or assessing causes and their consequences.[9] At some point in their evolution, humans began deliberately to set out to *make things special* or extra-ordinary, perhaps for the purpose of influencing the outcome of important events that were perceived as uncertain and troubling, requiring action beyond simple fight or flight, approach or avoidance.[10]

A Closer Look at Making Special

In *What Is Art For?* I proposed that we could understand the arts ethologically by considering them as ways of making important things and activities "special." That is to say, I emphasized the "behavior" or activity [. . .] rather than, as other art theorists have done, the results: the things and activities themselves as "works of art."

I suggested that elements of what we today call the arts (e.g., pattern, vividness) would have existed first in nonaesthetic contexts. But because these elements were inherently gratifying (perceptually, emotionally, cognitively) to humans, humans who had an inherent proclivity for making special would use them—not for their own sake, but instead, in ethological terms, as "enabling mechanisms"—in the performance of other selectively valuable behaviors.

To begin with, I thought that the reason making special first occurred might have been to persuade oneself and others that what was being done was worthwhile and effective. This is a reason for embellishment in other species—notably, songbirds, who elaborate their songs much more than is necessary simply to advertise their presence or individuality. My reasoning went something like this. If you are an early human who wants to achieve a goal—to kill an animal, for example, or to cure a sickness—you will take pains, take the activity seriously. If you accidentally or deliberately say or do something extra, and are successful, you may well remember to do the extra something again the next time, just in case, as when a baseball player touches his cap and ear in a certain way before throwing a pitch, or a performer or pilot always carries a particular trinket that has in the past brought her or him good luck.

It is clear that taking serious and important activities seriously should be of immense survival value. Every bit of psychological reinforcement would count, for yourself as well as for the others who observe you. (As I pointed out, people who spent time and trouble to reinforce and elaborate deleterious things would not have survived.)

The idea of making special as persuasion or rhetoric seemed promising. Making life-serving implements (tools, weapons) special both expressed and reinforced their importance to individuals and would have assured their more careful manufacture and use. But equally or more important would have been the contribution of making special to ritual ceremonies. When language was used poetically (with stress, compelling rhythm, rhyme, noteworthy similes or word choice); when costumes or decor were striking and extravagant; when choruses, dances, and recitations allowed vicarious or actual audience participation, the content of the ceremonies would have been more memorable than when left "untreated." Whatever message the ceremony intended to communicate ("In union is strength"; Death is an end and a beginning"; "We are the best"; "Transitions are scary but unavoidable"; "We need food for the coming season") would be first engendered and then reinforced, acquiring special import by virtue of the special effort and attention expended upon it. At the same time, the fellow-feeling arising from the mutual participation and shared emotion was a microcosmic acting out of the general cooperation and coordination that was essential for small groups to survive in a violent, unpredictable world.[11] Groups whose individual members had the tendency to make things special would have had more unifying ritual ceremonies, and thus these individuals and groups would have survived better than individuals and groups that did not.

In ritual ceremonies, then, one can see that making special could acquire even more important than in individual occurrences. Because it is used to articulate substantive and vital concerns, it is drawn from, expresses, and engages one's deepest and strongest feelings.[12] [. . .]

The Relationship of Making Special and Art

[. . .] I was first led to develop the concept of making special because of my dissatisfaction with Western culture's general perplexity surrounding the notion of art and, reflecting this confusion, the inadequacy of the available speculations about the role of the arts in human evolution. It seemed to me that if evolutionists did not recognize *Homo aestheticus,* that is, could not satisfactorily explain how and why art was a human universal and could view it only as an epiphenomenon, their concept of art itself must be aberrant. Something so widespread, pleasurable, and obviously important to those who did it should not be so inexplicable.

Trapped in the confines and presuppositions of my culture's concepts and attitudes regarding art, I too floundered and took circuitous detours around the subject, as when I tried for a time to derive art from play or art from ritual. I continually returned to the quality in the arts of all times and places of being *extraordinary,* outside the daily routine and not strictly utilitarian (in a materialistic, ultimate sense)—even when considered "necessary" to their practitioners. That was where evolutionary explanations always broke down because something "nonutilitarian" should not have been selected for. Yet nonetheless it existed.

The best word for this characteristic of the arts seemed to be *special. Extraordinary* with a hyphen might have served, but it is too easily read as "astonishing" or "remarkable"—that is, as a synonym for nonhyphenated *extraordinary. Unnecessary* and *nonutilitarian* emphasize what the arts are not, and also smack too much of Western ideas of art-for-art's-sake. *Elaboration* used alone disregards the importance of shaping, and like *enhance* suggests, in Western culture at least, the superficial or merely added. While "special" might seem too imprecise and naively simple, or suggest mere decoration, it easily encompassed an array of what is done in making the arts that is generally different from making nonarts: embellishing, exaggerating, patterning, juxtaposing, shaping, and transforming.

"Special" also denotes a positive factor of care and concern that is absent from the other words. It thus suggests that the special object or activity appeals to emotional as well as perceptual and cognitive factors—that is, to all aspects of our mental functioning. Even though all three are inseparable, [. . .] the usual aesthetic nomenclature ("for its own sake," "beauty," "harmony," "contemplation") tends to emphasize calm or abstract intellectual satisfactions at the expense of sensory/emotional/physical/pleasurable ones. Hence "special" can indicate that not only are our senses arrested by a thing's perceptual strikingness (specialness), and our intellects intrigued and stimulated by its uncommonness (specialness), but that we make something special because doing so gives us a way of expressing its positive emotional valence for us, and the ways in which we accomplish this specialness not only reflect but give unusual or special gratification and pleasure (i.e., are aesthetic).

It is important to recognize that the elements used for making something aesthetically special are normally themselves inherently pleasing and gratifying to humans and thus can be called "aesthetic" or "protoaesthetic" even when they occur naturally in nonaesthetic contexts. These pleasing characteristics are those that would have been selected-for in human evolution as indicating that something is wholesome and good: for example, visual signs of health, youth, and vitality such as smoothness, glossiness, warm or true colors, cleanness, fineness, or lack of blemish, and vigor, precision, and comeliness of movement.

Thus we find that most, if not all, societies value agility, endurance, and grace in dance; sonority, vividness, and rhythmic or phonic echoing (rhyme and other poetic devices) in language; and resonance and power in percussion. The Wahgi of Papua New Guinea's Western Highlands, for example, explicitly judge body decoration, dancing, drumming, and ensemble performance in terms of their being rich, glossy, glinting, fiery, slashing, shining, flaming, that is, as the converse of dull, dry, flaky, matte, and lusterless (O'Hanlon 1989).

In the arts of the West, high value has also been given to skillfully made polished marble statuary, implements and ornaments of burnished metal, vivid glowing tempera and oil paintings, and ornately sumptuous or softly diaphanous textiles. Indeed, it is the obvious lack of these inherently pleasurable or "beautiful" features that has made it so difficult for unsophisticated people to accept certain works of art made during the past century or so as "art," for the artists' deliberate choices to defy traditional expectations regarding pleasing characteristics have set their works outside the pale of "recognizable" art.

In addition to elements that appeal to the senses, particularly vision and hearing, there are others that are pleasing to the cognitive faculties: repetition, pattern, continuity, clarity, dexterity, elaboration or variation of a theme, contrast, balance, proportion. These qualities have to do with comprehension, mastery, and hence security, and thus they are recognized as "good," when used outside a utilitarian context, to make something special. Visual prototypes (e.g., fundamental geometric shapes such as circles or other mandala forms like diagonal or upright crosses) also clarify and control untidiness and are thought and felt to be satisfying and good. [. . .]

The responses to "specialness" in the aesthetic sense—"This is (sensorily and emotionally as well as intellectually) gratifying and special"—presumably evolved alongside other responses to "specialness"—"This is dangerous, unprecedented, needs to be dealt with." As I suggested in speaking of salamanders and mosquitoes, not all specialness engenders or results from gratifying "aesthetic" acts or responses.

"Marking" of any kind for utilitarian identification, for example, the X's made by Hindus on the doors of railway cars that carried Moslems during the Indian-Pakistani conflicts after independence, is, strictly speaking, making something special, as is the construction by a state security police department of a special room, in a special place, without windows and with unusual equipment, in which to extract confessions from prisoners. But these unpleasant examples of "specialness" should not be included in the notion I am developing here of aesthetic specialness: the intention to appeal to (that is, to attract and, if successful, to satisfy) another's faculty for apprehending and appreciating a specialness that is more than what is necessary to fulfill a practical end. Additionally, the "artist" takes the protoaesthetic elements out of their "natural" context of indicating vitality and goodness, and "domesticates" them—deliberately using them in aesthetic making special. [. . .]

Thus, in order to be "aesthetically special," the X's made by the Hindus would have to have been made with care as to their proportion, color, and spatial relationship to the size of the door; and the room constructed by the security police would have to be arranged with an eye for visual relationship among the objects in the room, color coordination, or accent—that is, with a sensory/emotional component that originally evolved for enhancement, pleasure, and gratification over and above (or along with) the sheerly informational or purposeful aspects which, in an academic or analytic sense, we can isolate and separate out.

To evolving humans, as to those living in premodern societies today, the "aesthetic pleasure" derived from making special is not perhaps so easily separated from the "message" it packages as it has become in Western art today. Although contemporary aesthetic (and evolutionary) theory considers making and responding to aesthetic specialness to be nonutilitarian or "more than necessary" (hence not understandable as a selectively valuable behavioral tendency in human evolution), in its original context it *was* necessary and utilitarian. To adapt an anthropological truism, the obligatory was converted—by making it special—into the desirable, and hence it was willingly done.[13]

But even after establishing that aesthetic making special (in the sense of being sensorily and emotionally gratifying and more than strictly necessary) can be differentiated from nonaesthetic making special such as marking or intimidating, it still remains true that even though all art can be included as aesthetic making special, not all aesthetic making special is art. In ritual and play everyday reality is transformed, as in art, in emotionally and sensorily gratifying ways, and thus can be appreciated apart from use or practical function. I have not always been able to separate instances of making special in "art" from those in "ritual" and "play," as from X's on doors or torture chambers.

I do not think, however, that this difficulty seriously jeopardizes the attempt to treat art—in the sense of making special—as a human behavior. For if we step outside our blinkered Western modernist and post-modernist paradigms where art is either grand, rare, and intimidating, or socially constructed, slick, and provocative, it should be possible to accept the larger, more inclusive entity, making special (including art, ritual, and play) as a universal behavior. That is, by expanding our notion from "art" or even "art as making special" to "the faculty for making and expressing specialness," we can understand in a humanly grounded and relevant way how "the arts" (instances of making special) originally arose and why they not only enhance our individual lives as *Homo aestheticus,* but have been essential for our evolution as a species.

The radical position that I offer here as a species-centered view of art is that *it is not art (with all its burden of accreted connotations from the past two centuries) but making special that has been evolutionarily or socially and culturally important.* That is to say, until recent times in the West, what has been of social, cultural, and individual evolutionary importance in any art or "work of art" has been its making something special that is important to the species, society, or culture.

There is no need to decide whether a theater or concert performance is "play," "ritual" or "art." The three often interpenetrate, since "metareality" and "specialness" generally presuppose the freedom, unpredictability, make-believe, imagination, and delight that are associated with play (and art), or the formality, stylization, elaboration, and entrancement that characterize ritual (and art).

In *What Is Art for?* (59) I likened the modern Western concept of art to the Victorian notion of "vapours," an ambiguous ailment that has long since disappeared, or rather has been replaced by a number of particular named maladies: depression, premenstrual syndrome, hypochondria, flu, bad cold, and so forth. The analogy may have appeared to be merely an amusing aside, but I think it deserves further attention. Indeed, I think our understanding of art as a human behavior would improve if we altogether banned the word *art* in its singular, conceptual form, just as we no longer find it useful to invoke a broad term, *vapours,* for diverse complaints that gain nothing by being clumped together.

Postmodernists, who claim that art is in any case only two centuries old, should have little theoretical difficulty abandoning the word *art,* although to be sure it has permeated our thought from a practical point of view and is probably impossible to eliminate. The reader should try to remember, however, that henceforth in this book, reference to a "behavior of art" means "aesthetic making special" as elucidated in this section, which is a broader concept of "art" than is usual.

[Elsewhere], I will describe in more detail how a behavior of art could have developed from the tendency to recognize an extra-ordinary dimension of experience—that is, I will examine what circumstances in the human evolutionary environment could have called forth and refined such a behavioral tendency and hence why it should have been selected-for. Before ending the discussion of making special, however, I think it would be useful to summarize some of its implications for aesthetic theory today.

Implications of Making Special

The concept of making special, in the biobehavioral view of its being the core defining feature of a behavior of art, casts a new light on previously troublesome questions about the nature, origin, purpose, and value of art, and its place in human life.

1. It explains how a concept of art can comprise such variety, even contradiction. Art may be rare and restricted, as modernists believed, or liberating and problematizing, as postmodernists argue. It may be well or poorly done; it may be an individual original creation or a manifestation of a codified historical or regional tradition. It may require talent and long specialized training or be something everyone does naturally much as they learn to swim or cook or hunt. It may be used for anything, and anything can become an occasion for art. It may or may not be beautiful; although making special often results in "making beautiful," specialness also may consist of strangeness, outrageousness, or extravagance. As making special is protean and illimitable, so is art.

2. If the essential behavioral core is making special, a concern about whether one or another example of it is or is not "art" becomes irrelevant. One can, of course, ask whether one personally wants to take the time and trouble to appreciate or attempt to appreciate its specialness. Funding agencies will no doubt continue to debate whether certain Robert Mapplethorpe photographs, for example, are or are not "art" in some restricted culture-centered sense. But from the species-centered perspective with which this book is concerned, what is relevant is that *Homo aestheticus* "needs" to make special and appreciate specialness. Humans and their societies provide the means and parameters within which to do (or not do) this and within which to evaluate the results.

3. At the same time, the idea of making special would not allow the loose declaration (sometimes heard from postmodernist artists, composers, and critics) that art is everything and everything is art. It may be the case that anything is *potentially* art, but in order to *be* art, there is a requirement, first, of aesthetic intention or regard and secondly, of fashioning in some way—actively making special or imaginatively treating as special. If art is everything and everything is art, or sound is music and music is sound, as I have heard it said, why distinguish these activities by calling them "art" or "music"?

4. Making special emphasizes the idea that the arts, biologically endowed predispositions, have been physically, sensuously, and emotionally satisfying and pleasurable to humans. By using elements that pleased and gratified human senses—elements that themselves arose in nonaesthetic contexts: bright colors; appealing shapes and sounds; rhythmic movement; aural, gestural, and visual contours with emotional significance[14]—and arranging and patterning these elements in unusual, "special" ways, early humans assured the willing participation in, and accurate performance of, ceremonies that united them. The arts "enabled" ceremonies because they made ceremonies feel good. Before they were ever consciously used to make things special, the satisfactions of rhythm, novelty, order, pattern, color, bodily movement, and moving in synchrony with others were fundamental animal pleasures, essential ingredients of life. Using

these bodily pleasurable elements to make ceremonies special—elaborating and shaping them—the arts, and art, were born.

5. My theory recognizes that art, or, more accurately, the desire to make some things special, is a biologically endowed need. The impetus to mark as "special" an expression or artifact, even our bodies, is deep-seated and widespread. Quite naturally we exaggerate, pattern, and otherwise alter our movements or voices or words to indicate that what we are doing is set apart from ordinary movement, intonation, and speech.[15] More essential than the result (the "work of art," which can be striking or dull, achieved or abandoned) is the behavior or the activity, and more interesting, for our purposes, is the impetus that animates the behavior or activity. Not all things are made special and those that are chosen are usually made special for a reason. That reason throughout our unrecorded evolutionary history, and also for most of recorded human history, was different, more serious and emotionally involving, than the reason or reasons involved with making special in the modern, industrialized, Western or Western-influenced world.

6. My theory reminds us that the desire or need to make special has been throughout human history, until quite recently, primarily in the service of abiding human concerns—ones that engage our feelings in the most profound ways. Until recently, the arts—when they were not play or entertainment (which are legitimate and age-old ways of making human life more than ordinary)—were used to address or at least to suggest or intimate serious and vital concerns. We moderns feel "art" to be a private compulsion, a personal desire to mold or make something out of one's individual experience. But art actually originated and thrived for most of human history as a communal activity: in the smaller and more interdependent and like-minded societies in which humans evolved, the need to make sense of experience was satisfied in communally valued and validated activities. Much art today is rather like the display of a captive, lone peacock vainly performed for human (not peahen) spectators, or the following by baby geese of a bicycle wheel instead of their mother. When an animal is removed from its natural milieu and deprived of the cues and circumstances to which it is designed by nature to respond, it will respond and behave as best it can but probably in aberrant ways or with reference to aberrant cues and circumstances.

The principal evolutionary context for the origin and development of the arts was in activities concerned with survival. As we look back through the eons, we see abundant evidence of humans making things or experience special. Overwhelmingly what was chosen to be made special was what was considered important: objects and activities that were parts of ceremonies having to do with important transitions, such as birth, puberty, marriage, and death; finding food, securing abundance, ensuring fertility of women and of the earth; curing the sick; going to war or resolving conflict; and so forth. In the past things were made special because they were perennially important, while today we consider something (anything) momentarily important because it has been made flashily if transiently special.

This is an important difference and points up, I think, why in the contemporary West we have been so preoccupied with and confused about art, seduced by it, expecting miracles from it, alternately feeling elevated or dispirited by it, feeling somewhat betrayed if not altogether scorned by it.

In Wallace Stevens's poem "Anecdote of the Jar" a round jar is placed on a hill in Tennessee and the "slovenly wilderness" surrounding it immediately seems to fall into place. The jar becomes a kind of focus or center—"it took dominion everywhere"—that gives meaning or relevance to what before was wild, haphazard, and insignificant. In my ethological terms, placing the jar in that unlikely place was "making it special": an instance, if you will, of artistic behavior. Stevens's poem that tells the story also makes the deed (real or imagined) special by choosing unusual word order ("and round it was upon that hill"), strange phrases ("and of a port in air," "it did not give of bird or bush"), and rhyme (round/ground; air/bare/where) for the telling. A beautiful and successful poem in the high modernist tradition, "Anecdote of the Jar" is an exemplum of what a modern or postmodern painter or sculptor does when she or he chooses a subject and material and shapes and elaborates them, making special what before her or his action and vision would have been ordinary and unremarkable.

Yet in premodern society, the hill, though slovenly and wild, would most likely have been already somehow important: it would have been the abode of a spirit, or the place where a valued person was killed, or the site where a vision had occurred. Or perhaps the jar itself would have been important—because of some sacredness involved in its making or some magical marks added to its surface—so that placing it on the hill would have been a way of bringing human or divine presence to the hill or imparting a power to it. While such motives may still be the impetus behind some artistic acts today, they need not be. The act alone, for its own sake, is enough and we have learned to respond to the act and its result quite apart from the intention or idea that gave rise to the act.

Human evolution may have involved gratuitous acts of making special, but it is difficult to see how these would have made sufficient difference to the survival of individuals or groups to have been retained by natural selection as a genetic predisposition (except perhaps insofar as they are considered part of the general behavior of play, whose motivation is quite different from acknowledging or creating or celebrating importance). I admit that making special manifested as playfulness or idiosyncrasy can be pleasurable and rewarding, but I doubt whether in themselves they would have led before modern times to the creations that have been enshrined as our most representative examples of "art."

7. To suggest that making important things special was the original impetus for a "behavior of art" accounts for the close association in historic times as well

as in prehistory between the arts and religion—more accurately, the ritual expression of religion.

The earliest anthropological observers noted the importance of religion in human societies everywhere. Emile Durkheim, the great French founder of sociology, called religion a unified system of beliefs and practices related to sacred things—things set apart and forbidden (1964, 62). These beliefs, practices, and things belong to a realm called by different authors the numinous (Dodds 1973), the serious (Shils 1966), the supernatural—all suggesting the extra-ordinary, outside ordinary life.

[Elsewhere,] I will show that the origins of religious beliefs and practices and the arts must have been inseparable and that the ceremonies that have arisen in every human society for the purpose of dealing with vital, emotionally significant, archetypal concerns expressed these by means of arts. Yet before doing this I should remind the reader that today in the modern West very little is, in Durkheim's words, set apart or forbidden. Indeed, being considered forbidden or taboo seems cause and justification for being openly discussed and displayed.[16]

What is more, in the modern world, as Kaplan (1978, 86) has pithily remarked, the interesting is no longer important, and the important is no longer interesting. It seems worth asking whether the confusing and unsatisfying state of art in our world has anything to do with the fact that we no longer care about important things. In our predominantly affluent and hedonistic society survival is no longer paramount for most of us, and spiritual concerns, while perhaps given public lip service, are less and less privately validated. Our experience of the extra-ordinary tends to be an ever-growing involvement with such things as gambling, violent films, and mood-altering drugs. Caring deeply about vital things is out of fashion, and, in any case, who has the time (or allows the time) to care and to mark one's caring?[17] Human history has demonstrated that people can endure surprising amounts of hardship and suffering—conditions that usually elicit a serious and religious attitude toward life. Whether people are as well equipped to thrive under conditions of unprecedented leisure, comfort, and plenty is a question that is being tested on a large scale in our present circumstances: the answer does not appear to be promising.

Notes

1. Paul Mattick, comment made during presentation in panel entitled "The Institutions of Art/2" (forty-seventh Annual Meeting of the American Society for Aesthetics, 25–28 October 1989, New York City).
2. My account concerns Western aesthetics and does not attempt to address aesthetic concepts in other civilizations or how they relate to those in the West.
3. While my discussion in the text uses examples primarily from the visual arts, the history, criticism, and theory of the other arts are much the same. For example, Lydia Goehr (1989) makes a point similar to mine in her analysis of the development of an abstract concept of a musical "work."
4. "Play" theories of art are most commonly associated with Friedrich Schiller (1795/1967), Herbert Spencer (1880–82), Sigmund Freud (1908/1959), and Johan Huizinga (1949).
5. Richard Alexander (1989) explains human social play as leading "to an expanding ability and tendency to elaborate and internalize social-intellectual-physical scenarios," which itself underlies the evolutionary development of the human psyche—a neat combination of the human appreciation of fantasy and reality. [. . .]
6. Radcliffe-Brown (1922/1948) in his monograph on the Andaman Islanders, stresses that ceremonies produce changes in or structure feelings. They "maintain and transmit from one generation to another the *emotional dispositions on which the society depends for its existence*" (234, my italics). Being obligatory, they compel participants to act as though they felt certain emotions and thereby to some extent actually serve to induce those emotions in them. [. . .]
7. It was also intriguing for me to realize that play is often ritualized, as in sport, with its special arena, costumes, ways of behaving, structure in time. In rituals people often pretend (play or act "as if"): Australian aborigines, for example, imitate animals or pretend to kill them, and the Yanomamo Indians of South America do battle with spirits. Our "plays," and performances in general, can be considered simultaneously as art, as ritual, and as play.
8. Peter Sutton (1988, 18–19) also states that in traditional Aboriginal thought, there is no nature without culture. He quotes W. E. H. Stanner (*On Aboriginal Religion* [1963, 227]): "Anyone who . . . has moved in the Australian bush with Aboriginal associates becomes aware . . . [that he] moves not in a landscape but in a humanized realm saturated with significations."
9. Evidence of deliberate foresight and planning has been claimed for Middle Paleolithic early *sapiens* hominids more than 100,000 years ago in their cooperative hunting strategies (Chase 1989); in their hafting of stone tools, which implies the ability to predict the likelihood of recurring tasks requiring a particular tool (Shea 1989); and in their transporting artifactual material from afar to be used at home (Deacon 1989). Hayden and Bonifay (1991, 6) marshal data that "provide overwhelming support for the notion that Neanderthals were curating lithic tools, exhibiting planning and foresight similar to upper Paleolithic people, and acting in economically rational fashions."
10. The earliest archaeological evidence for body ornaments seems to date from the transition from the Middle Paleolithic to the Upper Paleolithic, that is, from around 35,000 B.P. It is interesting that these ornaments were made primarily from exotic (i.e., "special") materials, such as shell, soft stone, teeth, and tusks, that had been brought sometimes from hundreds of kilometers away from where they were

excavated. Randall White (1989) suggests that the ornaments were used for social display and were perhaps symbolic of social distinctions. Whatever their use or significance, it is interesting to see that when making themselves special, individuals also used special materials.

11. In *The Creative Explosion* (1982), John Pfeiffer presented a similar reconstruction of art and ceremony in the Upper Paleolithic. His concern was to elucidate the remarkable flowering of cultural behavior at that time, and not to address ethologically art's earlier origins and putative selective value.

12. It was both amusing and gratifying to later discover that Arthur Danto (1986, 21), who was not concerned with selective value or ethology, argued that "the structure of artworks is of a piece with the structure of rhetoric," and that "it is the office of rhetoric to modify the minds and then the actions of men and women by coopting their feelings." Danto's idea of "the transfiguration of the commonplace" in contemporary Western art (1981) is also congruent with a notion of making the ordinary extra-ordinary or "making special."

13. See note 6. In his classic monograph (1922/1948), Radcliffe-Brown explicitly states that ceremonies (in which, of course, objects and activities are made special) transmit feelings. More recent anthropologists have been generally concerned with ceremonies primarily as a means of transmitting information, traditions, and symbols.

14. See Eibl-Eibesfeldt (1989a, 1989b) for additional and fascinating examples of appealing and arresting bioaesthetic elements arising from human perception and behavior.

15. Even in the gestural sign language of the deaf, poetic statements are signed in a different manner than everyday conversation. Rather than using a dominant hand, the two hands are balanced; a smoothness of movement is imposed on the signs; and they are given a rhythmic temporal pattern and an enlarged "designed" spatial pattern, with exaggerations of representational or pantomime aspects (Klima and Bellugi 1983).

16. In some areas of modern life disclosure and open discussion are still frowned upon—e.g., military, government, and industrial affairs—but the information associated with these realms does not really correspond to the kinds of information formerly considered numinous. Revealing military or industrial secrets is considered far more deplorable than exposing personal emotional or spiritually significant matters.

17. It is not only that we are too "busy" or sated to care. Caring usually involves acting upon what one cares about. In our pluralistic and impersonal society, we cannot usually affect change, or by trying to do so we may at the same time be going against other important personal or group interests. Thus not caring is self-protective and a way of coping with impotence.

Reading 11

THE AGE OF SOCIAL TRANSFORMATION

Peter F. Drucker

A survey of the epoch that began early in this century, and an analysis of its latest manifestations: an economic order in which knowledge, not labor or raw material or capital, is the key resource; a social order in which inequality based on knowledge is a major challenge; and a polity in which government cannot be looked to for solving social and economic problems

No century in recorded history has experienced so many social transformations and such radical ones as the twentieth century. They, I submit, may turn out to be the most significant events of this, our century, and its lasting legacy. In the developed free-market countries—which contain less than a fifth of the earth's population but are a model for the rest—work and work force, society and polity, are all, in the last decade of this century, qualitatively and quantitatively different not only from what they were in the first years of this century but also from what has existed at any other time in history: in their configurations, in their processes, in their problems, and in their structures.

Far smaller, and far slower social changes in earlier periods triggered civil wars, rebellions, and violent intellectual and spiritual crises. The extreme social transformations of this century have caused hardly any stir. They have proceeded with a minimum of friction, with a minimum of upheavals, and, indeed, with a minimum of attention from scholars, politicians, the press, and the public. To be sure, this century of ours may well have been the cruelest and most violent in history, with its world and civil wars, its mass tortures, ethnic cleansings, genocides, and holocausts. But all these killings, all these horrors inflicted on the human race by this century's murderous "charismatics," hindsight clearly

Drucker, Peter. "The Age of Social Transformation." *The Atlantic Monthly.* Nov. 1994. 53–69.

shows, were just that: senseless killings, senseless horrors, "sound and fury, sig- nifying nothing." Hitler, Stalin, and Mao, the three evil geniuses of this century, destroyed. They created nothing.

Indeed, if this century proves one thing, it is the futility of politics. Even the most dogmatic believer in historical determinism would have a hard time explaining the social transformations of this century as caused by the headline- making political events, or the headline-making political events as caused by the social transformations. But it is the social transformations, like ocean currents deep below the hurricane-tormented surface of the sea, that have had the lasting, indeed the permanent, effect. They, rather than all the violence of the political surface, have transformed not only the society but also the economy, the com- munity, and the polity we live in. The age of social transformation will not come to an end with the year 2000—it will not even have peaked by then.

The Social Structure Transformed

Before the First World War, farmers composed the largest single group in every country. They no longer made up the population everywhere, as they had from the dawn of history to the end of the Napoleonic Wars, a hundred years earlier. But farmers still made up a near-majority in every developed country except England and Belgium—in Germany, France, Japan, the United States—and, of course, in all underdeveloped countries, too. On the eve of the First World War it was considered a self-evident axiom that developed countries—the United States and Canada being the only exceptions—would increasingly have to rely on food imports from nonindustrial, nondeveloped areas.

Today only Japan among major developed free-market countries is a heavy importer of food. (It is one unnecessarily, for its weakness as a food producer is largely the result of an obsolete rice-subsidy policy that prevents the country from developing a modern, productive agriculture.) And in all developed free- market countries, including Japan, farmers today are at most five percent of the population and work force—that is, one tenth of the proportion of eighty years ago. Actually, productive farmers make up less than half of the total farm popu- lation, or no more than two percent of the work force. And these agricultural producers are not "farmers" in most senses of the word; they are "agribusiness," which is arguably the most capital-intensive, most technology-intensive, and most information-intensive industry around. Traditional farmers are close to extinction even in Japan. And those that remain have become a protected species kept alive only by enormous subsidies.

The second-largest group in the population and work force of every devel- oped country around 1900 was composed of live-in servants. They were con- sidered as much a law of nature as farmers were. Census categories of the time defined a "lower middle class" household as one that employed fewer than three servants, and as a percentage of the work force domestics grew steadily up to the First World War. Eighty years later live-in domestic servants scarcely exist in developed countries. Few people born since the Second World War—that is, few people under fifty—have even seen any except on the stage or in old movies.

In the developed society of 2000 farmers are little but objects of nostalgia, and domestic servants are not even that.

Yet these enormous transformations in all developed free-market countries were accomplished without civil war and, in fact, in almost total silence. Only now that their farm population has shrunk to near zero do the totally urban French loudly assert that theirs should be a "rural country" with a "rural civilization."

The Rise and Fall of the Blue-Collar Workers

One reason why the transformations caused so little stir (indeed, the main reason) was that by 1900 a new class, the blue-collar worker in manufacturing industry—Marx's "proletarian"—had become socially dominant. Farmers were loudly adjured to "raise less corn and more hell," but they paid little attention. Domestic servants were clearly the most exploited class around. But when people before the First World War talked or wrote about the "social question," they meant blue-collar industrial workers. Blue-collar industrial workers were still a fairly small minority of the population and work force—right up to 1914 they made up an eighth or a sixth of the total at most—and were still vastly outnumbered by the traditional lower classes of farmers and domestic servants. But early twentieth-century society was obsessed with blue-collar workers, fixated on them, bewitched by them.

Farmers and domestic servants were everywhere. But as classes, they were invisible. Domestic servants lived and worked inside individual homes or on individual farms in small and isolated groups of two or three. Farmers, too, were dispersed. More important, these traditional lower classes were not organized. Indeed, they could not be organized. Slaves employed in mining or in producing goods had revolted frequently in the ancient world—though always unsuccessfully. But there is no mention in any book I ever read of a single demonstration or a single protest march by domestic servants in any place at any time. There have been peasant revolts galore. But except for two Chinese revolts in the nineteenth century—the Taiping Rebellion, in midcentury, and the Boxer Rebellion, at the century's end, both of which lasted for years and came close to overturning the regime—all peasant rebellions in history have fizzled out after a few bloody weeks. Peasants, history shows, are very hard to organize and do not stay organized—which is why they earned Marx's contempt.

The new class, industrial workers, was extremely visible. This is what made these workers a "class." They lived perforce in dense population clusters and in cities—in St. Denis, outside Paris; in Berlin's Wedding and Vienna's Ottakring; in the textile towns of Lancashire; in the steel towns of America's Monongahela Valley; and in Japan's Kobe. And they soon proved eminently organizable, with the first strikes occurring almost as soon as there were factory workers. Charles Dickens's harrowing tale of murderous labor conflict, *Hard Times,* was published in 1854, only six years after Marx and Engels wrote *The Communist Manifesto.*

By 1900 it had become quite clear that industrial workers would not become the majority, as Marx had predicted only a few decades earlier. They therefore would not overwhelm the capitalists by their sheer numbers. Yet the most influential radical writer of the period before the First World War, the French ex-Marxist and revolutionary syndicalist Georges Sorel, found widespread acceptance for his 1906 thesis that the proletarians would overturn the existing order and take power by their organization and in and through the violence of the general strike. It was not only Lenin who made Sorel's thesis the foundation of his revision of Marxism and built around it his strategy in 1917 and 1918. Both Mussolini and Hitler—and Mao, ten years later—built their strategies on Sorel's thesis. Mao's "power grows out of the barrel of a gun" is almost a direct quote from Sorel. The industrial worker became the "social question" of 1900 because he was the first lower class in history that could be organized and could stay organized.

No class in history has ever risen faster than the blue-collar worker. And no class in history has ever fallen faster.

In 1883, the year of Marx's death, "proletarians" were still a minority not just of the population but also of industrial workers. The majority in industry were then skilled workers employed in small craft shops, each containing twenty or thirty workers at most. Of the anti-heroes of the nineteenth century's best "proletarian" novel, *The Princess Casamassima,* by Henry James—published in 1886 (and surely only Henry James could have given such a title to a story of working-class terrorists!)—one is a highly skilled bookbinder, the other an equally skilled pharmacist. By 1900 "industrial worker" had become synonymous with "machine operator" and implied employment in a factory along with hundreds if not thousands of people. These factory workers were indeed Marx's proletarians—without social position, without political power, without economic or purchasing power.

The workers of 1900—and even of 1913—received no pensions, no paid vacation, no overtime pay, no extra pay for Sunday or night work, no health or old-age insurance (except in Germany), no unemployment compensation (except, after 1911, in Britain); they had no job security whatever. Fifty years later, in the 1950s, industrial workers had become the largest single group in every developed country, and unionized industrial workers in mass-production industry (which was then dominant everywhere) had attained upper-middle-class income levels. They had extensive job security, pensions, long paid vacations, and comprehensive unemployment insurance or "lifetime employment." Above all, they had achieved political power. In Britain the labor unions were considered to be the "real government," with greater power than the Prime Minister and Parliament, and much the same was true elsewhere. In the United States, too—as in Germany, France, and Italy—the labor unions had emerged as the country's most powerful and best organized political force. And in Japan they had come close, in the Toyota and Nissan strikes of the late forties and early fifties, to overturning the system and taking power themselves.

Thirty-five years later, in 1990, industrial workers and their unions were in retreat. They had become marginal in numbers. Whereas industrial workers who make or move things had accounted for two fifths of the American work force in the 1950s, they accounted for less than one fifth in the early 1990s—that is, for no more than they had accounted for in 1900, when their meteoric rise began. In the other developed free-market countries the decline was slower at first, but after 1980 it began to accelerate everywhere. By the year 2000 or 2010, in every developed free market country, industrial workers will account for no more than an eighth of the work force. Union power has been declining just as fast.

Unlike domestic servants, industrial workers will not disappear—any more than agricultural producers have disappeared or will disappear. But just as the traditional small farmer has become a recipient of subsidies rather than a producer, so will the traditional industrial worker become an auxiliary employee. His place is already being taken by the "technologist"—someone who works both with hands and with theoretical knowledge. (Examples are computer technicians, x-ray technicians, physical therapists, medical-lab technicians, pulmonary technicians, and so on, who together have made up the fastest-growing group in the U.S. labor force since 1980.) And instead of a class—a coherent, recognizable, defined, and self-conscious group—industrial workers may soon be just another "pressure group."

Chroniclers of the rise of the industrial worker tend to highlight the violent episodes—especially the clashes between strikers and the police, as in America's Pullman strike. The reason is probably that the theoreticians and propagandists of socialism, anarchism, and communism—beginning with Marx and continuing to Herbert Marcuse in the 1960s—incessantly wrote and talked of "revolution" and "violence." Actually, the rise of the industrial worker was remarkably nonviolent. The enormous violence of this century—the world wars, ethnic cleansings, and so on—was all violence from above rather than violence from below; and it was unconnected with the transformations of society, whether the dwindling of farmers, the disappearance of domestic servants, or the rise of the industrial worker. In fact, no one even tries anymore to explain these great convulsions as part of "the crisis of capitalism," as was standard Marxist rhetoric only thirty years ago.

Contrary to Marxist and syndicalist predictions, the rise of the industrial worker did not destabilize society. Instead it has emerged as the century's most stabilizing social development. It explains why the disappearance of the farmer and the domestic servant produced no social crises. Both the flight from the land and the flight from domestic service were voluntary. Farmers and maids were not "pushed off" or "displaced." They went into industrial employment as fast as they could. Industrial jobs required no skills they did not already possess, and no additional knowledge. In fact, farmers on the whole had a good deal more skill than was required to be a machine operator in a mass-production plant—and so did many domestic servants. To be sure, industrial work paid poorly until the First World War. But it paid better than farming or household work. Industrial workers in the United States until 1913—and in some countries, including Japan, until the Second World War—worked long hours. But they worked shorter hours than farmers and domestic servants. What's more, they worked specified hours: the rest of the day was their own, which was true neither of work on the farm nor of domestic work.

The history books record the squalor of early industry, the poverty of the industrial workers, and their exploitation. Workers did indeed live in squalor and poverty, and they were exploited. But they lived better than those on a farm or in a household, and were generally treated better.

Proof of this is that infant mortality dropped immediately when farmers and domestic servants moved into industrial work. Historically, cities had never reproduced themselves. They had depended for their perpetuation on constant new recruits from the countryside. This will still true in the mid-nineteenth century. But with the spread of factory employment the city became the center of population growth. In part this was a result of new public-health measures: purification of water, collection and treatment of wastes, quarantine against epidemics, inoculation against disease. These measures—and they were effective mostly in the city—counteracted, or at least contained, the hazards of crowding that had made the traditional city a breeding ground for pestilence. But the largest single factor in the exponential drop in infant mortality as industrialization spread was surely the improvement in living conditions brought about by the factory. Housing and nutrition became better, and hard work and accidents came to take less of a toll. The drop in infant mortality—and with it the explosive growth in population—correlates with only one development: industrialization. The early factory was indeed the "Satanic Mill" of William Blake's great poem. But the countryside was not "England's green and pleasant Land" of which Blake sang; it was a picturesque but even more satanic slum.

For farmers and domestic servants, industrial work was an opportunity. It was, in fact, the first opportunity that social history had given them to better themselves substantially without having to emigrate. In the developed free-market countries over the past 100 or 150 years every generation has been able to expect to do substantially better than the generation preceding it. The main reason has been that farmers and domestic servants could and did become industrial workers.

Because industrial workers are concentrated in groups, systematic work on their productivity was possible. Beginning in 1881, two years before Marx's death, the systematic study of work, tasks, and tools raised the productivity of manual work in making and moving things by three to four percent compound on average per year—for a fiftyfold increase in output per worker over 110 years. On this rest all the economic and social gains of the past century. And contrary to what "everybody knew" in the nineteenth century—not only Marx but all the conservatives as well, such as J.P. Morgan, Bismarck, and Disraeli—practically all these gains have accrued to the industrial worker, half of them in the form of sharply reduced working hours (with the cuts ranging from 40 percent in Japan to 50 percent in Germany), and half of them in the form of a twenty-five fold increase in the real wages of industrial workers who make or move things.

There were thus very good reasons why the rise of the industrial worker was peaceful rather than violent, let alone revolutionary. But what explains the fact that the fall of the industrial worker has been equally peaceful and almost entirely free of social protest, of upheaval, of serious dislocation, at least in the United States?

The Rise of the Knowledge Worker

The rise of the class succeeding industrial workers is not an opportunity for industrial workers. It is a challenge. The newly emerging dominant group is "knowledge workers." The very term was unknown forty years ago. (I coined it in a 1959 book, *Landmarks of Tomorrow.*) By the end of this century knowledge workers will make up a third or more of the work force in the United States—as large a proportion as manufacturing workers ever made up, except in wartime. The majority of them will be paid at least as well as, or better than, manufacturing workers ever were. And the new jobs offer much greater opportunities.

But—and this is a big but—the great majority of the new jobs require qualifications the industrial worker does not possess and is poorly equipped to acquire. They require a good deal of formal education and the ability to acquire and to apply theoretical and analytical knowledge. They require a different approach to work and a different mind-set. Above all, they require a habit of continuous learning. Displaced industrial workers thus cannot simply move into knowledge work or services the way displaced farmers and domestic workers moved into industrial work. At the very least they have to change their basic attitudes, values, and beliefs.

In the closing decades of this century the industrial work force has shrunk faster and further in the United States than in any other developed country—while industrial production has grown faster than in any other developed country except Japan.

The shift has aggravated America's oldest and least tractable problem: the position of blacks. In the fifty years since the Second World War the economic position of African-Americans in America has improved faster than that of any other group in American social history—or in the social history of any country. Three fifths of America's blacks rose into middle class incomes; before the Second World War the figure was one twentieth. But half that group rose into middle-class incomes and not into middle class jobs. Since the Second World War more and more blacks have moved into blue-collar unionized mass-production industry—that is, into jobs paying middle-class and upper-middle-class wages while requiring neither education nor skill. These are precisely the jobs, however, that are disappearing the fastest. What is amazing is not that so many blacks did not acquire an education but that so many did. The economically rational thing for a young black in postwar America was not to stay in school and learn; it was to leave school as early as possible and get one of the plentiful mass-production jobs. As a result, the fall of the industrial worker has hit America's blacks disproportionately hard—quantitatively, but qualitatively even more. It has blunted what was the most potent role model in the black community in America: the well-paid industrial worker with job security, health insurance, and a guaranteed retirement pension—yet possessing neither skill nor much education.

But, of course, blacks are a minority of the population and work force in the United States. For the overwhelming majority—whites, but also Latinos and Asians—the fall of the industrial worker has caused amazingly little disruption and nothing that could be called an upheaval. Even in communities that were once totally dependent on mass-production plants that have gone out of business or have drastically slashed employment (steel cities in western Pennsylvania and eastern Ohio, for instance, or automobile cities like Detroit and Flint, Michigan), unemployment rates for nonblack adults fell within a few short years to levels barely higher than the U.S. average—and that means to levels barely higher than the U.S. "full-employment" rate. Even in these communities there has been no radicalization of America's blue-collar workers.

The only explanation is that for the nonblack blue-collar community the development came as no surprise, however unwelcome, painful, and threatening it may have been to individual workers and their families. Psychologically—but in terms of values, perhaps, rather than in terms of emotions—America's industrial workers must have been prepared to accept as right and proper the shift to jobs that require formal education and that pay for knowledge rather than for manual work, whether skilled or unskilled.

In the United States the shift had by 1990 or so largely been accomplished. But so far it has occurred only in the United States. In the other developed free-market countries, in western and northern Europe and in Japan, it is just beginning in the 1990s. It is, however, certain to proceed rapidly in these countries from now on, perhaps faster than it originally did in the United States. The fall of the industrial worker in the developed free-market countries will also have a major impact outside the developed world. Developing countries can no longer expect to base their development on their comparative labor advantage—that is, on cheap industrial labor.

It is widely believed, especially by labor-union officials, that the fall of the blue-collar industrial worker in the developed countries was largely, if not entirely, caused by moving production "offshore" to countries with abundant supplies of unskilled labor and low wage rates. But this is not true.

There was something to the belief thirty years ago. Japan, Taiwan, and, later, South Korea did indeed (as explained in some detail in my 1993 book *Post-Capitalist Society*) gain their initial advantage in the world market by combining, almost overnight, America's invention of training for full productivity with wage costs that were still those of a pre-industrial country. But this technique has not worked at all since 1970 or 1975.

In the 1990s only an insignificant percentage of manufactured goods imported into the United States are produced abroad because of low labor costs. While total imports in 1990 accounted for about 12 percent of the U.S. gross personal income, imports from countries with significantly lower wage costs accounted for less than three percent—and only half of those were imports of manufactured products. Practically none of the decline in American manufacturing employment from some 30 or 35 percent of the work force to 15 or 18 percent can therefore be attributed to moving work to low-wage countries. The main competition for American manufacturing industry—for instance, in automobiles, in steel, and in machine tools—has come from countries such as Japan and Germany, where wage costs have long been equal to, if not higher than, those in the Untied States. The comparative advantage that now counts is in the application of knowledge—for example, in Japan's total quality management, lean manufacturing processes, just-in-time delivery, and price-based costing, or in the customer service offered by medium-sized German or Swiss engineering companies. This means, however, that developing countries can no longer expect to base their development on low wages. They, too, must learn to base it on applying knowledge—just at the time when most of them (China, India, and much of Latin America, let alone black Africa) will have to find jobs for millions of uneducated and unskilled young people who are qualified for little except yesterday's blue-collar industrial jobs.

But for the developed countries, too, the shift to knowledge-based work poses enormous social challenges. Despite the factory, industrial society was still essentially a traditional society in its basic social relationships of production. But the emerging society, the one based on knowledge and knowledge workers, is not. It is the first society in which ordinary people—and that means most people—do not earn their daily bread by the sweat of their brow. It is the first society in which "honest work" does not mean a callused hand. It is also the first society in which not everybody does the same work, as was the case when the huge majority were farmers or, as seemed likely only forty or thirty years ago, were going to be machine operators.

This is far more than a social change. It is a change in the human condition. What it means—what are the values, the commitments, the problems of the new society—we do not know. But we do know that much will be different.

The Emerging Knowledge Society

Knowledge workers will not be the majority in the knowledge society, but in many if not most developed societies they will be the largest single population and work-force group. And even where outnumbered by other groups, knowledge workers will give the emerging knowledge society its character, its leadership, its social profile. They may not be the ruling class of the knowledge society, but they are already its leading class. And in their characteristics, social position, values, and expectations, they differ fundamentally from any group in history that has ever occupied the leading position.

In the first place, knowledge workers gain access to jobs and social position through formal education. A great deal of knowledge work requires highly developed manual skill and involves substantial work with one's hands. An extreme example is neurosurgery. The neurosurgeon's performance capacity rests on formal education and theoretical knowledge. An absence of manual skill disqualifies one for work as a neurosurgeon. But manual skill alone, no matter how advanced, will never enable anyone to be a neurosurgeon. The education that is required for neurosurgery and other kinds of knowledge work can be acquired only through formal schooling. It cannot be acquired through apprenticeship.

Knowledge work variers tremendously in the amount and kind of formal knowledge required. Some jobs have fairly low requirements, and others require the kind of knowledge the neurosurgeon possesses. But even if the knowledge itself is quite primitive, only formal education can provide it.

Education will become the center of the knowledge society, and the school its key institution. What knowledge must everybody have? What is "quality" in learning and teaching? These will of necessity become central concerns of the knowledge society, and central political issues. In fact, the acquisition and distribution of formal knowledge may come to occupy the place in the politics of the knowledge society which the acquisition and distribution of property and income have occupied in our politics over the two or three centuries that we have come to call the Age of Capitalism.

In the knowledge society, clearly, more and more knowledge, and especially advanced knowledge, will be acquired well past the age of formal schooling and increasingly, perhaps, through educational processes that do not center on the traditional school. But at the same time, the performance of the schools and the basic values of the schools will be of increasing concern to society as a whole, rather than being considered professional matters that can safely be left to "educators."

We can also predict with confidence that we will redefine what it means to be an educated person. Traditionally, and especially during the past 300 years (perhaps since 1700 or so, at least in the West, and since about that time in Japan as well), an educated person was somebody who had a prescribed stock of formal knowledge. The Germans called this knowledge *allgemeine Bildung,* and the English (and, following them, the nineteenth century Americans) called it the liberal arts. Increasingly, an educated person will be somebody who has learned how to learn, and who continues learning, especially by formal education, throughout his or her lifetime.

There are obvious dangers to this. For instance, society could easily degenerate into emphasizing formal degrees rather than performance capacity. It could fall prey to sterile Confucian mandarins—a danger to which the American university is singularly susceptible. On the other hand, it could overvalue immediately usable, "practical" knowledge and underrate the importance of fundamentals, and of wisdom altogether.

A society in which knowledge workers dominate is under threat from a new class conflict: between the large minority of knowledge workers and the majority of people, who will make their living traditionally, either by manual work, whether skilled or unskilled, or by work in services, whether skilled or unskilled. The productivity of knowledge work—still abysmally low—will become the economic challenge of the knowledge society. On it will depend the competitive position of every single country, every single industry, every single institution within society. The productivity of the nonknowledge, services worker will become the social challenge of the knowledge society. On it will depend the ability of the knowledge society to give decent incomes, and with them dignity and status, to non-knowledge workers.

No society in history has faced these challenges. But equally new are the opportunities of the knowledge society. In the knowledge society, for the first time in history, the possibility of leadership will be open to all. Also, the possibility of acquiring knowledge will no longer depend on obtaining a prescribed education at a given age. Learning will become the tool of the individual—available to him or her at any age—if only because so much skill and knowledge can be acquired by means of the new learning technologies.

Another implication is that how well an individual, an organization, an industry, a country, does in acquiring and applying knowledge will become the key competitive factor. The knowledge society will inevitably become far more competitive than any society we have yet known—for the simple reason that with knowledge being universally accessible, there will be no excuses for non-performance. There will be no "poor" countries. There will only be ignorant countries. And the same will be true for companies, industries, and organizations of all kinds. It will be true for individuals, too. In fact, developed societies have already become infinitely more competitive for individuals than were the societies of the beginning of this century, let alone earlier ones.

I have been speaking of knowledge. But a more accurate term is "knowledges," because the knowledge of the knowledge society will be fundamentally different from what was considered knowledge in earlier societies—and, in fact, from what is still widely considered knowledge. The knowledge of the German *allgemeine Bildung* or of the Anglo-American liberal arts had little to do with one's life's work. It focused on the person and the person's development, rather than on any application—if, indeed, it did not, like the nineteenth-century liberal arts, pride itself on having no utility whatever. In the knowledge society knowledge for the most part exists only in application. Nothing the x-ray technician needs to know can be applied to market research, for instance, or to teaching medieval history. The central work force in the knowledge society will therefore consist of highly specialized people. In fact, it is a mistake to speak of "generalists." What we will increasingly mean by that term is people who have learned how to acquire additional specialities rapidly in order to move from one kind of job to another—for example, from market research into management, or from nursing into hospital administration. But "generalists" in the sense in which we used to talk of them are coming to be seen as dilettantes rather than educated people.

This, too, is new. Historically, workers were generalists. They did whatever had to be done—on the farm, in the household, in the craftsman's shop. This was also true of industrial workers. But knowledge workers, whether their knowledge is primitive or advanced, whether there is a little of it or a great deal, will by definition be specialized. Applied knowledge is effective only when it is specialized. Indeed, the more highly specialized, the more effective it is. This goes for technicians who service computers, x-ray machines, or the engines of fighter planes. But it applies equally to work that requires the most advanced knowledge, whether research in genetics or research in astrophysics or putting on the first performance of a new opera.

Again, the shift from knowledge to knowledges offers tremendous opportunities to the individual. It makes possible a career as a knowledge worker. But it also presents a great many new problems and challenges. It demands for the first time in history that people with knowledge take responsibility for making themselves understood by people who do not have the same knowledge base.

How Knowledges Work

That knowledge in the knowledge society has to be highly specialized to be productive implies two new requirements: that knowledge workers work in teams, and that if knowledge workers are not employees, they must at least be affiliated with an organization.

There is a great deal of talk these days about "teams" and "teamwork." Most of it starts out with the wrong assumption—namely, that we have never before worked in teams. Actually people have always worked in teams; very few people ever could work effectively by themselves. The farmer had to have a wife, and the farm wife had to have a husband. The two worked as a team. And both worked as a team with their employees, the hired hands. The craftsman also had to have a wife, with whom he worked as a team—he took care of the craft work, and she took care of the customers, the apprentices, and the business altogether. And both worked as a team with journeymen and apprentices. Much discussion today assumes that there is only one kind of team. Actually there are quite a few. But until now the emphasis has been on the individual worker and not on the team. With knowledge work growing increasingly effective as it is increasingly specialized, teams become the work unit rather than the individual himself.

The team that is being touted now—I call it the "jazz combo" team—is only one kind of team. It is actually the most difficult kind of team both to assemble and to make work effectively, and the kind that requires the longest time to gain performance capacity. We will have to learn to use different kinds of teams for different purposes. We will have to learn to understand teams—and this is something to which, so far, very little attention has been paid. The understanding of teams, the performance capacities of different kinds of teams, their strengths and limitations, and the trade-offs between various kinds of teams will thus become central concerns in the management of people.

Equally important is the second implication of the fact that knowledge workers are of necessity specialists: the need for them to work as members of an organization. Only the organization can provide the basic continuity that knowledge workers need in order to be effective. Only the organization can convert the specialized knowledge of the knowledge worker into performance.

By itself, specialized knowledge does not yield performance. The surgeon is not effective unless there is a diagnosis—which, by and large, is not the surgeon's task and not even within the surgeon's competence. As a loner in his or her research and writing, the historian can be very effective. But to educate students, a great many other specialists have to contribute—people whose specialty may be literature or mathematics, or other areas of history. And this requires that the specialist have access to an organization.

The access may be as a consultant, or it may be as a provider of specialized services. But for the majority of knowledge workers it will be as employees, full-time or part-time, of an organization, such as a government agency, a hospital, a university, a business, or a labor union. In the knowledge society it is not the individual who performs. The individual is a cost center rather than a performance center. It is the organization that performs.

What is an Employee?

Most knowledge workers will spend most if not all of their working lives as "employees." But the meaning of the term will be different from what it has been traditionally—and not only in English but in German, Spanish, and Japanese as well.

Individually, knowledge workers are dependent on the job. They receive a wage or salary. They have been hired and can be fired. Legally each is an employee. But collectively they are the capitalists; increasingly, through their pension funds and other savings, the employees own the means of production. In traditional economics—and by no means only in Marxist economics—there is a sharp distinction between the "wage fund," all of which goes into consumption, and the "capital fund," or that part of the total income stream that is available for investment. And most social theory of industrial society is based, one way or another, on the relationship between the two, whether in conflict or in necessary and beneficial cooperation and balance. In the knowledge society the two merge. The pension fund is "deferred wages," and as such is a wage fund. But it is also increasingly the main source of capital for the knowledge society.

Perhaps more important, in the knowledge society the employees—that is, knowledge workers—own the tools of production. Marx's great insight was that the factory worker does not and cannot own the tools of production, and therefore is "alienated." There was no way, Marx pointed out, for the worker to own the steam engine and to be able to take it with him when moving from one job to another. The capitalist had to own the steam engine and to control it. Increasingly, the true investment in the knowledge society is not in machines and tools but in the knowledge of the knowledge worker. Without that knowledge the machines, no matter how advanced and sophisticated, are unproductive.

The market researcher needs a computer. But increasingly this is the researcher's own personal computer, and it goes along wherever he or she goes. The true "capital equipment" of market research is the knowledge of markets, of statistics, and of the application of market research to business strategy, which is lodged between the researcher's ears and is his or her exclusive and inalienable property. The surgeon needs the operating room of the hospital and all its expensive capital equipment. But the surgeon's true capital investment is twelve or fifteen years of training and the resulting knowledge, which the surgeon takes from one hospital to the next. Without that knowledge the hospital's expensive operating rooms are so much waste and scrap.

This is true whether the knowledge worker commands advanced knowledge, like a surgeon, or simple and fairly elementary knowledge, like a junior accountant. In either case it is the knowledge investment that determines whether the employee is productive or not, more than the tools, machines, and capital furnished by an organization. The industrial worker needed the capitalist infinitely more than the capitalist needed the industrial worker—the basis for Marx's assertion that there would always be a surplus of industrial workers, an "industrial reserve army," that would make sure that wages could not possibly rise above the subsistence level (probably Marx's most egregious error). In the knowledge society the most probable assumption for organizations—and certainly the assumption on which they have to conduct their affairs—is that they need knowledge workers far more than knowledge workers need them.

There was endless debate in the Middle Ages about the hierarchy of knowledges, with philosophy claiming to be the "queen." We long ago gave up that fruitless argument. There is no higher or lower knowledge. When the patient's complaint is an ingrown toenail, the podiatrist's knowledge, not that of the brain surgeon, controls—even though the brain surgeon has received many more years of training and commands a much larger fee. And if an executive is posted to a foreign country, the knowledge he or she needs, and in a hurry, is fluency in a foreign language—something every native of that country has mastered by age three, without any great investment. The knowledge of the knowledge society, precisely because it is knowledge only when applied in action, derives its rank and standing from the situation. In other words, what is knowledge in one situation, such as fluency in Korean for the American executive posted to Seoul, is only information, and not very relevant information at that, when the same executive a few years later has to think through his company's market strategy for Korea. This, too, is new. Knowledges were always seen as fixed stars, so to speak, each occupying its own position in the universe of knowledge. In the knowledge society knowledges are tools, and as such are dependent for their importance and position on the task to be performed.

Management in the Knowledge Society

One additional conclusion: Because the knowledge society perforce has to be a society of organizations, its central and distinctive organ is management.

When our society began to talk of management, the term meant "business management"—because large-scale business was the first of the new organizations to become visible. But we have learned in this past half century that management is the distinctive organ of all organizations. All of them require management, whether they use the term or not. All managers do the same things, whatever the purpose of their organization. All of them have to bring people—

each possessing different knowledge—together for joint performance. All of them have to make human strengths productive in performance and human weaknesses irrelevant. All of them have to think through what results are wanted in the organization—and have then to define objectives. All of them are responsible for thinking through what I call the theory of the business—that is, the assumptions on which the organization bases its performance and actions, and the assumptions that the organization has made in deciding what not to do. All of them must think through strategies—that is, the means through which the goals of the organization become performance. All of them have to define the values of the organization, its system of rewards and punishments, its spirit and its culture. In all organizations managers need both the knowledge of management as work and discipline and the knowledge and understanding of the organization itself—its purposes, its values, its environment and markets, its core competencies.

Management as a practice is very old. The most successful executive in all history was surely that Egyptian who, 4,500 years or more ago, first conceived the pyramid, without any precedent, designed it, and built it, and did so in an astonishingly short time. That first pyramid still stands. But as a discipline management is barely fifty years old. It was first dimly perceived around the time of the First World War. It did not emerge until the Second World War, and then did so primarily in the United States. Since then it has been the fastest-growing new function, and the study of it the fastest-growing new discipline. No function in history has emerged as quickly as has management in the past fifty or sixty years, and surely none has had such worldwide sweep in such a short period.

Management is still taught in most business schools as a bundle of techniques, such as budgeting and personnel relations. To be sure, management, like any other work, has its own tools and its own techniques. But just as the essence of medicine is not urinalysis (important though that is), the essence of management is not techniques and procedures. The essence of management is to make knowledges productive. Management, in other words, is a social function. And in its practice management is truly a liberal art.

The Social Sector

The old communities—family, village, parish, and so on—have all but disappeared in the knowledge society. Their place has largely been taken by the new unit of social integration, the organization. Where community was fate, organization is voluntary membership. Where community claimed the entire person, organization is a means to a person's ends, a tool. For 200 years a hot debate has been raging, especially in the West: are communities "organic" or are they simply extensions of the people of which they are made? Nobody would claim that the new organization is "organic." It is clearly an artifact, a creation of man, a social technology.

But who, then, does the community tasks? Two hundred years ago whatever social tasks were being done were done in all societies by a local community. Very few if any of these tasks are being done by the old communities anymore. Nor would they be capable of doing them, considering that they no longer have control of their members or even a firm hold over them. People no longer stay where they were born, either in terms of geography or in terms of social position and status. By definition, a knowledge society is a society of mobility. And all the social functions of the old communities, whether performed well or poorly (and most were performed very poorly indeed), presupposed that the individual and the family would stay put. But the essence of a knowledge society is mobility in terms of where one lives, mobility in terms of what one does, mobility in terms of one's affiliations. People no longer have roots. People no longer have a neighborhood that controls what their home is like, what they do, and, indeed, what their problems are allowed to be. The knowledge society is a society in which many more people than ever before can be successful. But it is therefore, by definition, also a society in which many more people than ever before can fail, or at least come in second. And if only because the application of knowledge to work has made developed societies so much richer than any earlier society could even dream of becoming, the failures, whether poor people or alcoholics, battered women or juvenile delinquents, are seen as failures of society.

Who, then, takes care of the social tasks in the knowledge society? We cannot ignore them. But the traditional community is incapable of tackling them.

Two answers have emerged in the past century or so—a majority answer and a dissenting opinion. Both have proved to be wrong.

The majority answer goes back more than a hundred years, to the 1880s, when Bismarck's Germany took the first faltering steps toward the welfare state. The answer: the problems of the social sector can, should, and must be solved by government. This is till probably the answer that most people accept, especially in the developed countries of the West—even though most people probably no longer fully believe it. But it has been totally disproved. Modern government, especially since the Second World War, has everywhere become a huge welfare bureaucracy. And the bulk of the budget in every developed country today is devoted to *Entitlements*—to payments for all kinds of social services. Yet in every developed country society is becoming sicker rather than healthier, and social problems are multiplying. Government has a big role to play in social tasks—the role of policymaker, of standard setter, and, to a substantial extent, of paymaster. But as the agency to run social services, it has proved almost totally incompetent.

In my *The Future of Industrial Man* (1942), I formulated a dissenting opinion. I argued then that the new organization—and fifty years ago that meant the large business enterprise—would have to be the community in which the individual would find status and function, with the workplace community becoming the one in and through which social tasks would be organized. In Japan (though quite independently and without any debt to me) the large employer—government agency or business—has indeed increasingly attempted to serve as a community for its employees. Lifetime employment is only one affirmation of this. Company housing, company health plans, company vacations, and so on all emphasize for the Japanese employee that the employer, and especially the big corporation, is the community and the successor to yesterday's village—even to yesterday's family. This, however, has not worked either.

There is need, especially in the West, to bring the employee increasingly into the government of the workplace community. What is now called empowerment is very similar to the things I talked about fifty years ago. But it does not create a community. Nor does it create the structure through which the social tasks of the knowledge society can be tackled. In fact, practically all these tasks—whether education or health care; the anomies and diseases of a developed and, especially, a rich society, such as alcohol and drug abuse; or the problems of incompetence and irresponsibility such as those of the underclass in the American city—lie outside the employing institution.

The right answer to the question Who takes care of the social challenges of the knowledge society? is neither the government nor the employing organization. The answer is a separate and new social sector.

It is less than fifty years, I believe, since we first talked in the United States of the two sectors of a modern society—the "public sector" (government) and the "private sector" (business). In the past twenty years the United States has begun to talk of a third sector, the "nonprofit sector"—those organizations that increasingly take care of the social challenges of a modern society.

In the United States, with its tradition of independent and competitive churches, such a sector has always existed. Even now churches are the largest single part of the social sector in the United States, receiving almost half the money given to charitable institutions, and about a third of the time volunteered by individuals. But the nonchurch part of the social sector has been the growth sector in the United States. In the early 1990s about a million organizations were registered in the United States as nonprofit or charitable organizations doing social-sector work. The overwhelming majority of these, some 70 percent, have come into existence in the past thirty years. And most are community services concerned with life on this earth rather than with the Kingdom of Heaven. Quite a few of the new organizations are, of course, religious in their orientation, but for the most part these are not churches. They are "parachurches" engaged in a specific social task, such as the rehabilitation of alcohol and drug addicts, the rehabilitation of criminals, or elementary school education. Even within the church segment of the social sector the organizations that have shown the capacity to grow are radically new. They are the "pastoral" churches, which focus on the spiritual needs of individuals, especially educated knowledge workers, and then put the spiritual energies of their members to work on the social challenges and social problems of the community—especially, of course, the urban community.

We still talk of these organizations as "nonprofits." But this is a legal term. It means nothing except that under American law these organizations do not pay taxes. Whether they are organized as nonprofit or not is actually irrelevant to their function and behavior. Many American hospitals since 1960 or 1970 have become "for-profits" and are organized in what legally are business corporations. They function in exactly the same way as traditional "nonprofit" hospitals. What matters is not the legal basis but that the social-sector institutions have a particular kind of purpose. Government demands compliance; it makes rules and enforces them. Business expects to be paid; it supplies. Social-sector institutions aim at changing the human being. The "product"of a school is the student who has learned something. The "product"of a hospital is a cured patient. The "product" of a church is a churchgoer whose life is being changed. The task of social-sector organizations is to create human health and well being.

Increasingly these organizations of the social sector serve a second and equally important purpose. They create citizenship. Modern society and modern polity have become so big and complex that citizenship—that is, responsible participation—is no longer possible. All we can do as citizens is to vote once every few years and to pay taxes all the time.

As a volunteer in a social-sector institution, the individual can again make a difference. In the United States, where there is a long volunteer tradition because of the old independence of the churches, almost every other adult in the 1990s is working at least three—and often five—hours a week as a volunteer in a social-sector organization. Britain is the only other country with something like this tradition, although it exists there to a much lesser extent (in part because the British welfare state is far more embracing, but in much larger part because it has an established church—paid for by the state and run as a civil service). Outside the English-speaking countries there is not much of a volunteer tradition. In fact, the modern state in Europe and Japan has been openly hostile to anything that smacks of volunteerism—most so in France and Japan. It is ancien regime and suspected of being fundamentally subversive.

But even in these countries things are changing, because the knowledge society needs the social sector, and the social sector needs the volunteer. But knowledge workers also need a sphere in which they can act as citizens and create a community. The workplace does not give it to them. Nothing has been disproved faster than the concept of the "organization man," which was widely accepted forty years ago. In fact, the more satisfying one's knowledge work is, the more one needs a separate sphere of community activity.

Many social-sector organizations will become partners with government—as is the case in a great many "privatizations," where, for instance, a city pays for street cleaning and an outside contractor does the work. In American education over the next twenty years there will be more and more government-paid vouchers that will enable parents to put their children into a variety of different schools, some public and tax supported, some private and largely dependent on the income from the vouchers. These social-sector organizations, although partners with government, also clearly compete with government. The relationship between the two has yet to be worked out—and there is practically no precedent for it.

What constitutes performance for social-sector organizations, and especially for those that, being nonprofit and charitable, do not have the discipline of a financial bottom line, has also yet to be worked out. We know that social-sector organizations need management. But what precisely management means for the social-sector organization is just beginning to be studied. With respect to the management of the nonprofit organization we are in many ways pretty much where we were fifty or sixty years ago with respect to the management of the business enterprise: the work is only beginning.

But one thing is already clear. The knowledge society has to be a society of three sectors: a public sector of government, a private sector of business, and a social sector. And I submit that it is becoming increasingly clear that through the social sector a modern developed society can again create responsible and achieving citizenship, and can again give individuals—especially knowledge workers—a sphere in which they can make a difference in society and re-create community.

The School as Society's Center

Knowledge has become the key resource, for a nation's military strength as well as for its economic strength. And this knowledge can be acquired only through schooling. It is not tied to any country. It is portable. It can be created everywhere, fast and cheaply. Finally, it is by definition changing. Knowledge as the key resource is fundamentally different from the traditional key resources of the economist—land, labor, and even capital.

That knowledge has become the key resource means that there is a world economy, and that the world economy, rather than the national economy, is in control. Every country, every industry, and every business will be in an increasingly competitive environment. Every country, every industry, and every business will, in its decisions, have to consider its competitive standing in the world economy and the competitiveness of its knowledge competencies.

Politics and policies still center on domestic issues in every country. Few if any politicians, journalists, or civil servants look beyond the boundaries of their own country when a new measure such as taxes, the regulation of business, or social spending is being discussed. Even in Germany—Europe's most export-conscious and export-dependent major country—this is true. Almost no one in the West asked in 1990 what the government's unbridled spending in the East would do to Germany's competitiveness.

This will no longer do. Every country and every industry will have to learn that the first question is not Is this measure desirable? but What will be the impact on the country's, or the industry's, competitive position in the world economy? We need to develop in politics something similar to the environmental-impact statement, which in the United States is now required for any government action affecting the quality of the environment: we need a competitive-impact statement. The impact on one's competitive position in the world economy should not necessarily be the main factor in a decision. But to make a decision without considering it has become irresponsible.

Altogether, the fact that knowledge has become the key resource mans that the standing of a country in the world economy will increasingly determine its domestic prosperity. Since 1950 a country's ability to improve its position in the world economy has been the main and perhaps the sole determinant of performance in the domestic economy. Monetary and fiscal policies have been practically irrelevant, for better and, very largely, even for worse (with the single exception of governmental policies creating inflation, which very rapidly undermines both a country's competitive standing in the world economy and its domestic stability and ability to grow).

The primacy of foreign affairs is an old political precept going back in European politics to the seventeenth century. Since the Second World War it has also been accepted in American politics—though only grudgingly so, and only in emergencies. It has always meant that military security was to be given priority over domestic policies, and in all likelihood this is what it will continue to mean, Cold War or no Cold War. But the primacy of foreign affairs is now acquiring a different dimension. This is that a country's competitive position in the world economy—and also an industry's and an organization's—has to be the first consideration in its domestic policies and strategies. This holds true for a country that is only marginally involved in the world economy (should there still be such a one), and for a business that is only marginally involved in the world economy, and for a university that sees itself as totally domestic. Knowledge knows no boundaries. There is no domestic knowledge and no international knowledge. There is only knowledge. And with knowledge becoming the key resource, there is only a world economy, even though the individual organization in its daily activities operates within a national, regional, or even local setting.

How Can Government Function?

Social tasks are increasingly being done by individual organizations, each created for one, and only one, social task, whether education, health care, or street cleaning. Society, therefore, is rapidly becoming pluralist. Yet our social and political theories still assume that there are no power centers except government. To destroy or at least to render impotent all other power centers was, in fact, the thrust of Western history and Western politics for 500 years, from the fourteenth century on. This drive culminated in the eighteenth and nineteenth centuries, when, except in the United States such early institutions as still survived—for example, the universities and the churches—became organs of the state, with their functionaries becoming civil servants. But then, beginning in the mid nineteenth century, new centers arose—the first one, the modern business enterprise, around 1870. And since then one new organization after another has come into being.

The new institutions—the labor union, the modern hospital, the mega church, the research university—of the society of organizations have no interest in public power. They do not want to be governments. But they demand—and, indeed, need—autonomy with respect to their functions. Even at the extreme of Stalinism the managers of major industrial enterprises were largely masters within their enterprises, and the individual industry was largely autonomous. So were the university, the research lab, and the military.

In the "pluralism" of yesterday—in societies in which control was shared by various institutions, such as feudal Europe in the Middle Ages and Edo Japan in the seventeenth and eighteenth centuries—pluralist organizations tried to be in control of whatever went on in their community. At least, they tried to prevent any other organization from having control of any community concern or community institution within their domain. But in the society of organizations each of the new institutions is concerned only with its own purpose and mission. It does not claim power over anything else. But it also does not assume responsibility for anything else. Who, then, is concerned with the common good?

This has always been a central problem of pluralism. No earlier pluralism solved it. The problem remains, but in a new guise. So far it has been seen as imposing limits on social institutions—forbidding them to do things in the pursuit of their mission, function, and interest which encroach upon the public domain or violate public policy. The laws against discrimination—by race, sex, age, educational level, health status, and so on—which have proliferated in the United States in the past forty years all forbid socially undesirable behavior. But we are increasingly raising the question of the social responsibility of social institutions: What do institutions have to do—in addition to discharging their own functions—to advance the public good? This, however, though nobody seems to realize it, is a demand to return to the old pluralism, the pluralism of feudalism. It is a demand that private hands assume public power.

This could seriously threaten the functioning of the new organizations, as the example of the schools in the United States makes abundantly clear. One of the major reasons for the steady decline in the capacity of the schools to do their job—that is, to teach children elementary knowledge skills—is surely that since the 1950s the United States has increasingly made the schools the carriers of all kinds of social policies: the elimination of racial discrimination, of discrimination against all other kinds of minorities, including the handicapped, and so on. Whether we have actually made any progress in assuaging social ills is highly debatable; so far the schools have not proved particularly effective as tools for social reform. But making the school the organ of social policies has, without any doubt, severely impaired its capacity to do its own job.

The new pluralism has a new problem: how to maintain the performance capacity of the new institutions and yet maintain the cohesion of society. This makes doubly important the emergence of a strong and functioning social sector. It is an additional reason why the social sector will increasingly be crucial to the performance, if not to the cohesion, of the knowledge society.

Of the new organizations under consideration here, the first to arise, 120 years ago, was the business enterprise. It was only natural, therefore, that the problem of the emerging society of organizations was first seen as the relationship of government and business. It was also natural that the new interests were first seen as economic interests.

The first attempt to come to grips with the politics of the emerging society of organizations aimed, therefore, at making economic interests serve the political process. The first to pursue this goal was an American, Mark Hanna, the restorer of the Republican Party in the 1890s and, in many ways, the founding father of twentieth-century American politics. His definition of politics as a dynamic disequilibrium between the major economic interests—farmers, business, and labor—remained the foundation of American politics until the Second World War. In fact, Franklin D. Roosevelt restored the Democratic Party by reformulating Hanna. And the basic political position of this philosophy is evident in the title of the most influential political book written during the New Deal years—*Politics: Who Gets What, When, How* (1936), by Harold D. Lasswell.

Mark Hanna in 1896 knew very well that there are plenty of concerns other than economic concerns. And yet it was obvious to him—as it was to Roosevelt forty years later—that economic interests had to be used to integrate all the others. This is still the assumption underlying most analyses of American politics—and, in fact, of politics in all developed countries. But the assumption is no longer tenable. Underlying Hanna's formula of economic interests is the view of land, labor, and capital as the existing resources. But knowledge, the new resource for economic performance, is not in itself economic.

It cannot be bought or sold. The fruits of knowledge, such as the income from a patent, can be bought or sold; the knowledge that went into the patent cannot be conveyed at any price. No matter how much a suffering person is willing to pay a neurosurgeon, the neurosurgeon cannot sell to him—and surely cannot convey to him—the knowledge that is the foundation of the neurosurgeon's performance and income. The acquisition of knowledge has a cost, as has the acquisition of anything. But the acquisition of knowledge has no price.

Economic interests can therefore no longer integrate all other concerns and interests. As soon as knowledge became the key economic resource, the integration of interests—and with it the integration of the pluralism of a modern polity—began to be lost. Increasingly, non-economic interests are becoming the new pluralism—the special interests, the single-cause organizations, and so on. Increasingly, politics is not about "who gets what, when, how" but about values, each of them considered to be an absolute. Politics is about the right to life of the embryo in the womb as against the right of a woman to control her own body and to abort an embryo. It is about the environment. It is about gaining equality for groups alleged to be oppressed and discriminated against. None of these issues is economic. All are fundamentally moral.

Economic interests can be compromised, which is the great strength of basing politics on economic interests. "Half a loaf is still bread" is a meaningful saying. But half a baby, in the biblical story of the judgment of Solomon, is not half a child. No compromise is possible. To an environmentalist, half an endangered species is an extinct species.

This greatly aggravates the crisis of modern government. Newspapers and commentators still tend to report in economic terms what goes on in Washington, in London, in Bonn, or in Tokyo. But more and more of the lobbyists who determine governmental laws and governmental actions are no longer lobbyists for economic interests. They lobby for and against measures that they—and their paymasters—see as moral, spiritual, cultural. And each of these new moral concerns, each represented by a new organization, claims to stand for an absolute. Dividing their loaf is not compromise; it is treason.

There is thus in the society of organizations no one integrating force that pulls individual organizations in society and community into coalition. The traditional parties—perhaps the most successful political creations of the nineteenth century—can no longer integrate divergent groups and divergent points of view into a common pursuit of power. Rather, they have become battlefields between groups, each of them fighting for absolute victory and not content with anything but total surrender of the enemy.

The Need for Social and Political Innovation

The twenty-first century will surely be one of continuing social, economic, and political turmoil and challenge, at least in its early decades. What I have called the age of social transformation is not over yet. And the challenges looming ahead may be more serious and more daunting than those posed by the social transformations that have already come about, the social transformations of the twentieth century.

Yet we will not even have a chance to resolve these new and looming problems of tomorrow unless we first address the challenges posed by the developments that are already accomplished facts, the developments reported in the earlier sections of this essay. These are the priority tasks. For only if they are tackled can we in the developed democratic free market countries hope to have the social cohesion, the economic strength, and the governmental capacity needed to tackle the new challenges. The first order of business—for sociologists, political scientists, and economists; for educators; for business executives, politicians, and nonprofit-group leaders; for people in all walks of life, as parents, as employees, as citizens—is to work on these priority tasks, for few of which we so far have a precedent, let alone tested solutions.

We will have to think through education—its purpose, its values, its content. We will have to learn to define the quality of education and the productivity of education, to measure both and to manage both.

We need systematic work on the quality of knowledge and the productivity of knowledge—neither even defined so far. The performance capacity, if not the survival, of any organization in the knowledge society will come increasingly to depend on those two factors. But so will the performance capacity, if not the survival, of any individual in the knowledge society. And what responsibility does knowledge have? What are the responsibilities of the knowledge worker, and especially of a person with highly specialized knowledge?

Increasingly, the policy of any country—and especially of any developed country—will have to give primacy to the country's competitive position in an increasingly competitive world economy. Any proposed domestic policy needs to be shaped so as to improve that position, or at least to minimize adverse impacts on it. The same holds true for the policies and strategies of any institution within a nation, whether a local government, a business, a university, or a hospital.

But then we also need to develop an economic theory appropriate to a world economy in which knowledge has become the key economic resource and the dominant, if not the only, source of comparative advantage.

We are beginning to understand the new integrating mechanism: organization. But we still have to think through how to balance two apparently contradictory requirements. Organizations must competently perform the one social function for the sake of which they exist—the school to teach, the hospital to cure the sick, and the business to produce goods, services, or the capital to provide for the risks of the future. They can do so only if they single-mindedly concentrate on their specialized mission. But there is also society's need for these organizations to take social responsibility—to work on the problems and challenges of the community. Together these organizations are the community. The emergence of a strong, independent, capable social sector—neither public sector nor private sector—is thus a central need of the society of organizations. But by itself it is not enough—the organizations of both the public and the private sector must share in the work.

The function of government and its functioning must be central to political thought and political action. The megastate in which this century indulged has not performed, either in its totalitarian or in its democratic version. It has not delivered on a single one of its promises. And government by countervailing lobbyists is neither particularly effective—in fact, it is paralysis—nor particularly attractive. Yet effective government has never been needed more than in this highly competitive and fast-changing world of ours, in which the dangers created by the pollution of the physical environment are matched only by the dangers of worldwide armaments pollution. And we do not have even the beginnings of political theory or the political institutions needed for effective government in the knowledge-based society of organizations.

If the twentieth century was one of social transformations, the twenty first century needs to be one of social and political innovations, whose nature cannot be so clear to us now as their necessity.

Reading 12

MAID TO ORDER
The politics of other women's work

Barbara Ehrenreich

In line with growing class polarization, the classic posture of submission is making a stealthy comeback. "We scrub your floors the old-fashioned way," boasts the brochure from Merry Maids, the largest of the residential-cleaning services that have sprung up in the last two decades "on our hands and knees." This is not a posture that independent "cleaning ladies" willingly assume—preferring, like most people who clean their own homes, the sponge mop wielded from a standing position. In her comprehensive 1999 guide to homemaking, *Home Comforts,* Cheryl Mendelson warns: "Never ask hired housecleaners to clean your floors on their hands and knees; the request is likely to be regarded as degrading." But in a society in which 40 percent of the wealth is owned by 1 percent of households while the bottom 20 percent reports negative assets, the degradation of others is readily purchased. Kneepads entered American political discourse as a tool of the sexually subservient, but employees of Merry Maids, The Maids International, and other corporate cleaning services spend hours every day on these kinky devices, wiping up the drippings of the affluent.

I spent three weeks in September 1999 as an employee of The Maids International in Portland, Maine, cleaning, along with my fellow team members, approximately sixty houses containing a total of about 250 scrubbable floors—bathrooms, kitchens, and entryways requiring the hands-and-knees treatment. It's a different world down there below knee level, one that few adults voluntarily enter. Here you find elaborate dust structures held together by a scaffolding of dog hair; dried bits

Ehrenreich, Barbara. "Maid to Order: The politics of other women's work." *Harper's* April 2000. 59–70.

of pasta glued to the floor by their sauce; the congealed remains of gravies, jellies, contraceptive creams, vomit, and urine. Sometimes, too, you encounter some fragment of a human being: a child's legs, stamping by in disgust because the maids are still present when he gets home from school; more commonly, the Joan & David—clad feet and electrolyzed calves of the female homeowner. Look up and you may find this person staring at you, arms folded, in anticipation of an overlooked stain. In rare instances she may try to help in some vague, symbolic way, by moving the cockatoo's cage, for example, or apologizing for the leaves shed by a miniature indoor tree. Mostly, though, she will not see you at all and may even sit down with her mail at a table in the very room you are cleaning, where she would remain completely unaware of your existence unless you were to crawl under that table and start gnawing away at her ankles.

Housework, as you may recall from the feminist theories of the Sixties and Seventies, was supposed to be the great equalizer of women. Whatever else women did—jobs, school, child care—we also did housework, and if there were some women who hired others to do it for them, they seemed too privileged and rare to include in the theoretical calculus. All women were workers, and the home was their workplace—unpaid and unsupervised, to be sure, but a workplace no less than the offices and factories men repaired to every morning. If men thought of the home as a site of leisure and recreation—a "haven in a heartless world"—this was to ignore the invisible female proletariat that kept it cozy and humming. We were on the march now, or so we imagined, united against a society that devalued our labor even as it waxed mawkish over "the family" and "the home." Shoulder to shoulder and arm in arm, women were finally getting up off the floor.

In the most eye-catching elaboration of the home-as-workplace theme, Marxist feminists Maria Rosa Dallacosta and Selma James proposed in 1972 that the home was in fact an economically productive and significant workplace, an extension of the actual factory, since housework served to "reproduce the labor power" of others, particularly men. The male worker would hardly be in shape to punch in for his shift, after all, if some woman had not fed him, laundered his clothes, and cared for the children who were his contribution to the next generation of workers. If the home was a quasi-industrial workplace staffed by women for the ultimate benefit of the capitalists, then it followed that "wages for housework" was the obvious demand.

But when most American feminists, Marxist or otherwise, asked the Marxist question *cui bono?* they tended to come up with a far simpler answer—men. If women were the domestic proletariat, then men made up the class of domestic exploiters, free to lounge while their mates scrubbed. In consciousness-raising groups, we railed against husbands and boyfriends who refused to pick up after themselves, who were unaware of housework at all, unless of course it hadn't been done. The "dropped socks," left by a man for a woman to gather up and launder, joined lipstick and spike heels as emblems of gender oppression. And if, somewhere, a man had actually dropped sock in the calm expectation that his wife would retrieve it, it was a sock heard round the world. Wherever second-wave feminism took root, battles broke out between lovers and spouses over sticky countertops, piled-up laundry, and whose turn it was to do the dishes.

The radical new idea was that housework was not only a relationship between a woman and a dust bunny or an unmade bed; it also defined a relationship between human beings, typically husbands and wives. This represented a marked departure from the more conservative Betty Friedan, who, in *The Feminine Mystique,* had never thought to enter the male sex into the equation, as either part of the housework problem or part of an eventual solution. She raged against a society that consigned its educated women to what she saw as essentially janitorial chores, beneath "the abilities of a woman of average or normal human intelligence," and, according to unidentified studies she cited, "peculiarly suited to the capacities of feeble-minded girls." But men are virtually exempt from housework in *The Feminine Mystique*—why drag them down too? At one point she even disparages a "Mrs. G.," who "somehow couldn't get her housework done before her husband came home at night and was so tired then that he had to do it." Educated women would just have to become more efficient so that housework could no longer "expand to fill the time available."

Or they could hire other women to do it—an option approved by Friedan in *The Feminine Mystique* as well as by the National Organization for Women, which she had helped launch. At the 1973 congressional hearings on whether to extend the Fair Labor Standards act to household workers, NOW testified on the affirmative side, arguing that improved wages and working conditions would attract more women to the field, and offering the seemingly self-contradictory prediction that "the demand for household help inside the home will continue to increase as more women seek occupations outside the home." One NOW member added, on a personal note: "Like many young women today, I am in school in order to develop a rewarding career for myself. I also have a home to run and can fully conceive of the need for household help as my free time at home becomes more and more restricted. Women know [that] housework is dirty, tedious work, and they are wiling to pay to have it done. . . . " On the aspirations of the women paid to do it, assuming that at least some of them were bright enough to entertain a few, neither Friedan nor these members of NOW had, at the time, a word to say.

So the insight that distinguished the more radical, post-Friedan cohort of feminists was that when we talk about housework, we are really talking, yet again, about power. Housework was not degrading because it was manual labor as Friedan thought, but because it was embedded in degrading relationships and inevitably served to reinforce them. To make a mess that another person will have to deal with—the dropped socks, the toothpaste sprayed on the bathroom mirror, the dirty dishes left from a late-night snack—is to exert domination in one of its more silent and intimate forms. One person's arrogance—or indifference, or hurry—becomes another person's occasion for toil. And when the person who is cleaned up after is consistently male, while the person who cleans up is consistently female, you have a formula for reproducing male domination from one generation to the next.

Hence the feminist perception of housework as one more way by which men exploit women or, more neutrally stated, as "a symbolic enactment of gender relations." An early German women's liberation cartoon depicted a woman scrubbing on her hands and knees while her husband, apparently excited by this pose, approaches from behind, unzipping his fly. Hence, too, the second-wave feminists' revulsion at the hiring of maids, especially when they were women of color: At a feminist conference I attended in 1980, poet Audre Lorde chose to insult the all-too-white audience by accusing them of being present only because they had black housekeepers to look after their children at home. She had the wrong crowd; most of the assembled radical feminists would no sooner have employed a black maid than they would have attached Confederate flag stickers to the rear windows of their cars. But accusations like hers, repeated in countless conferences and meetings, reinforced our rejection of the servant option. There already were at least two able-bodied adults in the average home—a man and a woman—and the hope was that, after a few initial skirmishes, they would learn to share the housework graciously.

A couple of decades later, however, the average household still falls far short of that goal. True, women do less housework than they did before the feminist revolution and the rise of the two-income family: down from an average of 30 hours per week in 1965 to 17.5 hours in 1995, according to a July 1999 study by the University of Maryland. Some of that decline reflects a relaxation of standards rather than a redistribution of chores; women still do two thirds of whatever housework—including bill paying, pet care, tidying, and lawn care—gets done. The inequity is sharpest for the most despised of household chores, cleaning: in the thirty years between 1965 and 1995, men increased the time they spent scrubbing, vacuuming, and sweeping by 240 percent—all the way up to 1.7 hours per week—while women decreased their cleaning time by only 7 percent, to 6.7 hours per week. The averages conceal a variety of arrangements, of course, from minutely negotiated sharing to the most clichéd division of labor, as described by one woman to the *Washington Post:* "I take care of the inside, he takes care of the outside." But perhaps the most disturbing finding is that almost the entire increase in male participation took place between the 1970s and the mid-1980s. Fifteen years after the apparent cessation of hostilities, it is probably not too soon to announce the score: in the "chore wars" of the Seventies and Eighties, women gained a little ground, but overall, and after a few strategic concessions, men won.

Enter then, the cleaning lady as *dea ex machina,* restoring tranquility as well as order to the home. Marriage counselors recommend her as an alternative to squabbling, as do many within the cleaning industry itself. A Chicago cleaning woman quotes one of her clients as saying that if she gives up the service, "my husband and I will be divorced in six months." When the trend toward hiring out was just beginning to take off, in 1988, the owner of a Merry Maids franchise in Arlington, Massachusetts, told the *Christian Science Monitor,* "I kid some women. I say, 'We even save marriages. In this new eighties period you expect more from the male partner, but very often you don't get the cooperation you would like to have. The alternative is to pay somebody to come in. . . . ' " Another Merry Maids franchise owner has learned to capitalize more directly on housework-related spats; he closes between 30 and 35 percent of his sales by making follow-up calls Saturday mornings, which is "prime time for arguing over the fact that the house is a mess." The micro-defeat of feminism in the household opened a new door for women, only this time it was the servants' entrance.

In 1999, somewhere between 14 and 18 percent of households employed an outsider to do the cleaning, and the numbers have been rising dramatically. Mediamark Research reports a 53 percent increase, between 1995 and 1999, in the number of households using a hired cleaner or service once a month or more, and Maritz Marketing finds that 30 percent of the people who hired help in 1999 did so for the first time that year. Among my middle-class, professional women friends and acquaintances, including some who made important contributions to the early feminist analysis of housework, the employment of a maid is now nearly universal. This sudden emergence of a servant class is consistent with what some economists have called the "Brazilianization" of the American economy: We are dividing along the lines of traditional Latin American societies— into a tiny overclass and a huge underclass, with the latter available to perform intimate household services for the former. Or, to put it another way, the home, or at least the affluent home, is finally becoming what radical feminists in the Seventies only imagined it was—a true "workplace" for women and a tiny, though increasingly visible, part of the capitalist economy. And the question is: As the home becomes a workplace for someone else, is it still a place where you would want to live?

Strangely, or perhaps not so strangely at all, no one talks about the "politics of housework" anymore. The demand for "wages for housework" has sunk to the status of a curio, along with the consciousness-raising groups in which women once rallied support in their struggles with messy men. In the academy, according to the feminist sociologists I interviewed, housework has lost much of its former cachet—in part, I suspect, because fewer sociologists actually do it. Most Americans, over 80 percent, still clean their homes, but the minority who do not include a sizable fraction of the nation's opinion-makers and culture-producers—professors, writers, editors, politicians, talking heads, and celebrities of all sorts. In their homes, the politics of housework is becoming a politics not only of gender but of race and class—and these are subjects that the opinion-making elite, if not most Americans, generally prefer to avoid.

Even the number of paid houseworkers is hard to pin down. The Census Bureau reports that there were 549,000 domestic workers in 1998, up 9 percent since 1996, but this may be a considerable underestimate, since so much of the servant economy is still underground. In 1995, two years after Zoe Baird lost her chance to be attorney general for paying her undocumented nanny off the books, the *Los Angeles Times* reported that fewer than 10 percent of those Americans who paid a housecleaner reported those payments to the IRS. Sociologist Mary Romero, one of the few academics who retain an active interest in housework and the women who do it for pay, offers an example of how severe the under-counting can be: the 1980 Census found only 1,063 "private household work-ers," in El Paso, Texas, though the city estimated their numbers at 13,400 and local bus drivers estimated that half of the 28,300 daily bus trips were taken by maids going to and from work. The honesty of employers has increased since the Baird scandal, but most experts believe that household workers remain, in large part, uncounted and invisible to the larger economy.

One thing you can say with certainty about the population of household workers is that they are disproportionately women of color: "lower" kinds of people for a "lower" kind of work. Of the "private household cleaners and ser-vants" it managed to locate in 1998, the Bureau of Labor Statistics reports that 36.8 percent were Hispanic, 15.8 percent black, and 2.7 percent "other." Cer-tainly the association between housecleaning and minority status is well estab-lished in the psyches of the white employing class. When my daughter, Rosa, was introduced to the wealthy father of a Harvard classmate, he ventured that she must have been named for a favorite maid. And Audre Lorde can perhaps be forgiven for her intemperate accusation at the feminist conference mentioned above when we consider an experience she had in 1967: "I wheel my two-year-old daughter in a shopping cart through a supermarket . . . and a little white girl riding past in her mother's cart calls out excitedly, 'Oh look, Mommy, a baby maid.' " But the composition of the household workforce is hardly fixed and has changed with the life chances of the different ethnic groups. In the late nine-teenth century, Irish and German immigrants served the northern upper and middle classes, then left for the factories as soon as they could. Black women replaced them, accounting for 60 percent of all domestics in the 1940s, and dominated the field until other occupations began to open up to them. Similarly, West Coast maids were disproportionately Japanese American until that group, too, found more congenial options. Today, the color of the hand that pushes the sponge varies from region to region: Chicanas in the Southwest, Caribbeans in New York, native Hawaiians in Hawaii, whites, many of recent rural extraction, in Maine.

The great majority—though again, no one knows exact numbers—of paid housekeepers are freelancers, or "independents," who find their clients through

agencies or networks of already employed friends and relatives. To my acquaintances in the employing class, the freelance housekeeper seems to be a fairly
privileged and prosperous type of worker, a veritable aristocrat of labor—sometimes paid $15 an hour or more and usually said to be viewed as a friend or
even treated as "one of the family." But the shifting ethnic composition of the
workforce tells another story: this is a kind of work that many have been trapped
in—by racism, imperfect English skills, immigration status, or lack of education—but few have happily chosen. Interviews with independent maids collected by Romero and by sociologist Judith Rollins, who herself worked as a
maid in the Boston area in the early Eighties, confirm that the work is undesirable to those who perform it. Even when the pay is deemed acceptable, the hours
may be long and unpredictable; there are usually no health benefits, no job security, and, if the employer has failed to pay Social Security taxes (in some cases
because the maid herself prefers to be paid off the books), no retirement benefits. And the pay is often far from acceptable. The BLS found full-time "private
household cleaners and servants" earning a median annual income of $12,220 in
1998, which is $1,092 below the poverty level for a family of three. Recall that
in 1993 Zoe Baird paid her undocumented household workers about $5 an hour
out of her earnings of $507,000 a year.

At the most lurid extreme there is slavery. A few cases of forced labor pop
up in the press every year, most recently—in some nightmare version of globalization—of undocumented women held in servitude by high-ranking staff members of the United Nations, the World Bank, and the International Monetary
Fund. Consider the suit brought by Elizabeth Senghor, a Senegalese woman
who alleged that she was forced to work fourteen-hour days for her employers in
Manhattan, without any regular pay, and was given no accommodations beyond
a pull-out bed in her employers' living room. Hers is not a particularly startling
instance of domestic slavery; no beatings or sexual assaults were charged, and
Ms. Senghor was apparently fed. What gives this case a certain rueful poignancy
is that her employer, former U.N. employee Marie Angelique Savane, is one of
Senegal's leading women's rights advocates and had told *The Christian Science
Monitor* in 1986 about her efforts to get the Senegalese to "realize that being a
woman can mean other things than simply having children, taking care of the
house."

Mostly, though, independent maids—and sometimes the women who
employ them—complain about the peculiar intimacy of the employer-employee
relationship. Domestic service is an occupation that predates the refreshing
impersonality of capitalism by several thousand years, conditions of work being
still largely defined by the idiosyncrasies of the employers. Some of them seek
friendship and even what their maids describe as "therapy," though they are usually quick to redraw the lines once the maid is perceived as overstepping. Others
demand deference bordering on servility, while a growing fraction of the nou-
veau riche is simply out of control. In August 1999, the *New York Times* reported

on the growing problem of dinner parties being disrupted by hostesses scream-ing at their help. To the verbal abuse add published reports of sexual and physi-cal assaults—a young teenage boy, for example, kicking a live-in nanny for refusing to make sandwiches for him and his friends after school.

But for better or worse, capitalist rationality is finally making some headway into this weird preindustrial backwater. Corporate cleaning services now control 25 to 30 percent of the $1.4 billion housecleaning business, and perhaps their greatest innovation has been to abolish the mistress-maid relationship, with all its quirks and dependencies. The customer hires the service, not the maid, who has been replaced anyway by a team of two to four uniformed people, only one of whom—the team leader—is usually authorized to speak to the customer about the work at hand. The maids' wages, their Social Security taxes, their green cards, backaches, and child-care problems—all these are the sole concern of the company, meaning the local franchise owner. If there are complaints on either side, they are addressed to the franchise owner; the customer and the actual workers need never interact. Since the franchise owner is usually a middle-class white person, cleaning services are the ideal solution for anyone still sensitive enough to find the traditional employer-maid relationship morally vexing.

In a 1997 article about Merry Maids, *Franchise Times* reported tersely that the "category is booming, [the] niche is hot, too, as Americans look to outsource work even at home." Not all cleaning services do well, and there is a high rate of failure among informal, mom-and-pop services. The "boom" is concentrated among the national and international chains—outfits like Merry Maids, Molly Maids, Mini Maids, Maid Brigade, and The Maids International—all named, curiously enough, to highlight the more antique aspects of the industry, though the "maid" may occasionally be male. Merry Maids claimed to be growing at 15 to 20 percent a year in 1996, and spokesmen for both Molly Maids and The Maids International told me that their firms' sales are growing by 25 percent a year; local franchisers are equally bullish. Dan Libby, my boss at The Maids, confided to me that he could double his business overnight if only he could find enough reliable employees. To this end, The Maids offers a week's paid vaca-tion, health insurance after ninety days, and a free breakfast every morning con-sisting—at least where I worked—of coffee, doughnuts, bagels, and bananas. Some franchises have dealt with the tight labor market by participating in wel-fare-to-work projects that not only funnel employees to them but often subsidize their paychecks with public money, at least for the first few months of work (which doesn't mean the newly minted maid earns more, only that the company has to pay her less). The Merry Maids franchise in the city where I worked is conveniently located a block away from the city's welfare office.

Among the women I worked with at The Maids, only one said she had pre-viously worked as an independent, and she professed to be pleased with her new status as a cleaning-service employee. She no longer needed a car to get her from house to house and could take a day off—unpaid of course—to stay home with a sick child without risking the loss of a customer. I myself could see the advantage of not having to deal directly with the customers, who were sometimes at home while we worked and eager to make use of their supervisory skills: criticisms of our methods, and demands that we perform unscheduled tasks, could simply be referred to the franchise owner.

But there are inevitable losses for the workers as any industry moves from the entrepreneurial to the industrial phase, probably most strikingly, in this case, in the matter of pay. At Merry Maids, I was promised $200 for a forty-hour week, the manager hastening to add that "you can't calculate it in dollars per hour" since the forty hours include all the time spent traveling from house to house—up to five houses a day—which is unpaid. The Maids International, with its straightforward starting rate of $6.63 an hour, seemed preferable, though this rate was conditional on perfect attendance. Miss one day and your wage dropped to $6 an hour for two weeks, a rule that weighed particularly heavily on those who had young children. In addition, I soon learned that management had ways of shaving off nearly an hour's worth of wages a day. We were told to arrive at 7:30 in the morning, but our billable hours began only after we had been teamed up, given our list of houses for the day, and packed off in the company car at about 8:00 A.M. At the end of the day, we were no longer paid from the moment we left the car, though as much as fifteen minutes of work— refilling cleaning-fluid bottles, etc.—remained to be done. So for a standard nine-hour day, the actual pay amounted to about $6.10 an hour, unless you were still being punished for an absence, in which case it came out to $5.50 an hour.

Nor are cleaning-service employees likely to receive any of the perks or tips familiar to independents—free lunches and coffee, cast-off clothing, or a Christmas gift of cash. When I asked, only one of my coworkers could recall ever receiving a tip, and that was a voucher for a free meal at a downtown restaurant owned by a customer. The customers of cleaning services are probably no stingier than the employers of independents; they just don't know their cleaning people and probably wouldn't even recognize them on the street. Plus, customers probably assume that the fee they pay the service—$25 per person-hour in the case of The Maids franchise I worked for—goes largely to the workers who do the actual cleaning.

But the most interesting feature of the cleaning-service chains, at least from an abstract, historical perspective, is that they are finally transforming the home into a fully capitalist-style workplace, and in ways that the old wages-for-housework advocates could never have imagined. A house is an innately difficult workplace to control, especially a house with ten or more rooms like so many of those we cleaned; workers may remain out of one another's sight for as much as an hour at a time. For independents, the ungovernable nature of the home-as-workplace means a certain amount of autonomy. They can take breaks (though this is probably ill-advised if the homeowner is on the premises); they can ease the monotony by listening to the radio or TV while they work. But cleaning services lay down rules meant to enforce a factorylike—or even conventlike—discipline on their far-flung employees. At The Maids, there were no breaks except for a daily ten-minute stop at a convenience store for coffee or "lunch"—meaning something like a slice of pizza. Otherwise, the time spent driving between houses was considered our "break" and the only chance to eat, drink, or (although this was also officially forbidden) smoke a cigarette. When the houses were spaced well apart, I could eat my sandwich in one sitting; otherwise it would have to be divided into as many as three separate, hasty snacks.

Within a customer's house, nothing was to touch our lips at all, not even water—a rule that, on hot days, I sometimes broke by drinking from a bathroom faucet. TVs and radios were off-limits, and we were never, ever, to curse out loud, even in an ostensibly deserted house. There might be a homeowner secreted in some locked room, we were told, ear pressed to the door, or, more likely, a tape recorder or video camera running. At the time, I dismissed this as a scare story, but I have since come across ads for devices like the Tech-7 "incredible coin-sized camera" designed to "get a visual record of your babysitter's actions" and "watch employees to prevent theft." It was the threat or rumor of hidden recording devices that provided the final capitalist-industrial touch—supervision.

What makes the work most factorylike, though, is the intense Taylorization imposed by the companies. An independent, or a person cleaning his or her own home, chooses where she will start and, within each room, probably tackles the most egregious dirt first. Or she may plan her work more or less ergonomically, first doing whatever can be done from a standing position and then squatting or crouching to reach the lower levels. But with the special "systems" devised by the cleaning services and imparted to employees via training videos, there are no such decisions to make. In The Maids' "healthy touch" system, which is similar to what I saw of the Merry Maids' system on the training tape I was shown during my interview, all cleaning is divided into four task areas—dusting, vacuuming, kitchens, and bathrooms—which are in turn divided among the team members. For each task area other than vacuuming, there is a bucket containing rags and the appropriate cleaning fluids, so the biggest decision an employee has to make is which fluid and scrubbing instrument to deploy on which kind of surface; almost everything else has been choreographed in advance. When vacuuming, you begin with the master bedroom; when dusting, with the first room off of the kitchen; then you move through the rooms going left to right. When entering each room, you proceed from left to right and top to bottom, and the same with each surface—top to bottom, left to right. Deviations are subject to rebuke, as I discovered when a team leader caught me moving my arm from right to left, then left to right, while wiping Windex over a French door.

It's not easy for anyone with extensive cleaning experience—and I include myself in this category—to accept this loss of autonomy. But I came to love the

MAID TO ORDER 259

system: First, because if you hadn't always been traveling rigorously from left to right it would have been easy to lose your way in some of the larger houses and omit or redo a room. Second, some of the houses were already clean when we started, at least by any normal standards, thanks probably to a housekeeper who kept things up between our visits; but the absence of visible dirt did not mean there was less work to do, for no surface could ever be neglected, so it was important to have "the system" to remind you of where you had been and what you had already "cleaned." No doubt the biggest advantage of the system, though, is that it helps you achieve the speed demanded by the company, which allots only so many minutes per house. After a week or two on the job, I found myself moving robotlike from surface to surface, grateful to have been relieved of the thinking process.

The irony, which I was often exhausted enough to derive a certain malicious satisfaction from, is that "the system" is not very sanitary. When I saw the training videos on "Kitchens" and "Bathrooms," I was at first baffled, and it took me several minutes to realize why: There is no water, or almost no water, involved. I had been taught to clean by my mother, a compulsive housekeeper who employed water so hot you needed rubber gloves to get into it and in such Niagaralike quantities that most microbes were probably crushed by the force of it before the soap suds had a chance to rupture their cell walls. But germs are never mentioned in the videos provided by The Maids. Our antagonists existed entirely in the visible world—soap scum, dust, counter crud, dog hair, stains, and smears—and were attacked by damp rag or, in hardcore cases, by a scouring pad. We scrubbed only to remove impurities that might be detectable to a customer by hand or by eye; otherwise our only job was to wipe. Nothing was ever said, in the videos or in person, about the possibility of transporting bacteria, by rag or by hand, from bathroom to kitchen or even from one house to the next. Instead, it is the "cosmetic touches" that the videos emphasize and to which my trainer continually directed my eye. Fluff out all throw pillows and arrange them symmetrically. Brighten up stainless steel sinks with baby oil. Leave all spice jars, shampoos, etc., with their labels facing outward. Comb out the fringes of Persian carpets with a pick. Use the vacuum to create a special, fernlike pattern in the carpets. The loose ends of toilet paper and paper towel rolls have to be given a special fold. Finally, the house is sprayed with the service's signature air freshener—a cloying floral scent in our case, "baby fresh" in the case of the Mini Maids.

When I described the "methods" employed to housecleaning expert Cheryl Mendelson, she was incredulous. A rag moistened with disinfectant will not get a countertop clean, she told me, because most disinfectants are inactivated by contact with organic matter—i.e., dirt—so their effectiveness declines with each swipe of the rag. What you need is a detergent and hot water, followed by a rinse. As for floors, she judged the amount of water we used—one half of a small bucket—to be grossly inadequate, and, in fact, the water I wiped around on floors was often an unsavory gray. I also ran The Maids' cleaning methods by Don Aslett, author of numerous books on cleaning techniques and self-styled "number one cleaner in America." He was hesitant to criticize The Maids directly, perhaps because he is, or told me he is, a frequent speaker at conventions of cleaning-service franchise holders, but he did tell me how he would clean a countertop: first, spray it thoroughly with an all-purpose cleaner, then let it sit for three to four minutes of "kill time," and finally wipe it dry with a clean cloth. Merely wiping the surface with a damp cloth, he said, just spreads the dirt around. But the point at The Maids, apparently, is not to clean so much as it is to create the appearance of having been cleaned, not to sanitize but to create a kind of stage setting for family life. And the stage setting Americans seem to prefer is sterile only in the metaphorical sense, like a motel room or the fake interiors in which soap operas and sitcoms take place.

But even ritual work takes its toll on those assigned to perform it. Turnover is dizzyingly high in the cleaning-service industry, and not only because of the usual challenges that confront the working poor—child-care problems, unreliable transportation, evictions, and prior health problems. As my long-winded interviewer at Merry Maids warned me, and my coworkers at The Maids confirmed, this is a physically punishing occupation, something to tide you over for a few months, not year after year. The hands-and-knees posture damages knees, with or without pads; vacuuming strains the back; constant wiping and scrubbing invite repetitive stress injuries even in the very young. In my three weeks as a maid, I suffered nothing more than a persistent muscle spasm in the right forearm, but the damage would have been far worse if I'd had to go home every day to my own housework and children, as most of my coworkers did, instead of returning to my motel and indulging in a daily after-work regimen of ice packs and stretches. Chores that seem effortless at home, even almost recreational when undertaken at will for twenty minutes or so at a time, quickly turn nasty when performed hour after hour, with few or no breaks and under relentless time pressure.

So far, the independent, entrepreneurial housecleaner is holding her own, but there are reasons to think that corporate cleaning services will eventually dominate the industry. New users often prefer the impersonal, standardized service offered by the chains, and, in a fast-growing industry, new users make up a sizable chunk of the total clientele. Government regulation also favors the corporate chains, whose spokesmen speak gratefully of the "Zoe Baird effect," referring to customers' worries about being caught paying an independent off the books. But the future of housecleaning may depend on the entry of even bigger players into the industry. Merry Maids, the largest of the chains, has the advantage of being a unit within the $6.4 billion ServiceMaster conglomerate, which includes such related businesses as TruGreen-ChemLawn, Terminix, Rescue Rooter, and Furniture Medic. Swisher International, best known as an industrial toilet-cleaning service, operates Swisher Maids in Georgia and North

Carolina, and Sears may be feeling its way into the business. If large multinational firms establish a foothold in the industry, mobile professionals will be able to find the same branded and standardized product wherever they relocate. For the actual workers, the change will, in all likelihood, mean a more standardized and speeded-up approach to the work—less freedom of motion and fewer chances to pause.

The trend toward outsourcing the work of the home seems, at the moment, unstoppable. Two hundred years ago women often manufactured soap, candles, cloth, and clothing in their own homes, and the complaints of some women at the turn of the twentieth century that they had been "robbed by the removal of creative work" from the home sound pointlessly reactionary today. Not only have the skilled crafts, like sewing and cooking from scratch, left the home but many of the "white collar" tasks are on their way out, too. For a fee, new firms such as the San Francisco-based Les Concierges and Cross It Off Your List in Manhattan will pick up dry cleaning, baby-sit pets, buy groceries, deliver dinner, even do the Christmas shopping. With other firms and individuals offering to buy your clothes, organize your financial files, straighten out your closets, and wait around in your home for the plumber to show up, why would anyone want to hold on to the toilet cleaning?

Absent a major souring of the economy, there is every reason to think that Americans will become increasingly reliant on paid housekeepers and that this reliance will extend ever further down into the middle class. For one thing, the "time bind" on working parents shows no sign of loosening; people are willing to work longer hours at the office to pay for the people—housecleaners and baby-sitters—who are filling in for them at home. Children, once a handy source of household help, are now off at soccer practice or SAT prep classes; grandmother has relocated to a warmer climate or taken up a second career. Furthermore, despite the fact that people spend less time at home than ever, the square footage of new homes swelled by 33 percent between 1975 and 1998, to include "family rooms," home entertainment rooms, home offices, bedrooms, and often bathrooms for each family member. By the third quarter of 1999, 17 percent of new homes were larger than 3,000 square feet, which is usually considered the size threshold for household help, or the point at which a house becomes unmanageable to the people who live in it.

One more trend impels people to hire outside help, according to cleaning experts such as Aslett and Mendelson: fewer Americans know how to clean or even to "straighten up." I hear this from professional women defending their decision to hire a maid: "I'm just not very good at it myself" or "I wouldn't really know where to begin." Since most of us learn to clean from our parents (usually our mothers), any diminution of cleaning skills is transmitted from one generation to another, like a gene that can, in the appropriate environment, turn out to be disabling or lethal. Upper-middle-class children raised in the servant economy of the Nineties are bound to grow up as domestically incompetent as their parents and no less dependent on people to clean up after them. Mendelson sees this as a metaphysical loss, a "matter of no longer being physically centered in your environment." Having cleaned the rooms of many overly privileged teenagers in my stint with The Maids, I think the problem is a little more urgent than that. The American overclass is raising a generation of young people who will, without constant assistance, suffocate in their own detritus.

If there are moral losses, too, as Americans increasingly rely on paid household help, no one has been tactless enough to raise them. Almost everything we buy, after all, is the product of some other person's suffering and miserably underpaid labor. I clean my own house (though—full disclosure—I recently hired someone else to ready it for a short-term tenant), but I can hardly claim purity in any other area of consumption. I buy my jeans at the Gap, which is reputed to subcontract to sweatshops. I tend to favor decorative objects no doubt ripped off, by their purveyors, from scantily paid Third World craftspersons. Like everyone else, I eat salad greens just picked by migrant farm workers, some of them possibly children. And so on. We can try to minimize the pain that goes into feeding, clothing, and otherwise provisioning ourselves—by observing boycotts, checking for a union label, etc.—but there is no way to avoid it altogether without living in the wilderness on berries. Why should housework, among all the goods and services we consume, arouse any special angst?

And it does, as I have found in conversations with liberal-minded employers of maids, perhaps because we all sense that there are ways in which housework is different from other products and services. First, in its inevitable proximity to the activities that compose "private" life. The home that becomes a workplace for other people remains a home, even when that workplace has been minutely regulated by the corporate cleaning chains. Someone who has no qualms about purchasing rugs woven by child slaves in India or coffee picked by impoverished peasants in Guatemala might still hesitate to tell dinner guests that, surprisingly enough, his or her lovely home doubles as a sweatshop during the day. You can eschew the chain cleaning services of course, hire an independent cleaner at a generous hourly wage, and even encourage, at least in spirit, the unionization of the housecleaning industry. But this does not change the fact that someone is working in your home at a job she would almost certainly never have chosen for herself—if she'd had a college education, for example, or a little better luck along the way—and the place where she works, however enthusiastically or resentfully, is the same as the place where you sleep.

It is also the place where your children are raised, and what they learn pretty quickly is that some people are less worthy than others. Even better wages and working conditions won't erase the hierarchy between an employer and his or her domestic help, because the help is usually there only because the employer has "something better" to do with her time, as one report on the growth of cleaning services puts it, not noticing the obvious implication that the cleaning person herself has nothing better to do with her time. In a merely middle-class home, the message may be reinforced by a warning to the children that that's what they'll end up doing if they don't try harder in school. Housework, as radical feminists once proposed, defines a human relationship and, when unequally divided among social groups, reinforces preexisting inequalities. Dirt, in other words, tends to attach to the people who remove it—"garbagemen" and "cleaning ladies." Or, as cleaning entrepreneur Don Aslett told me with some bitterness—and this is a successful man, chairman of the board of an industrial cleaning service and frequent television guest—"The whole mentality out there is that if you clean, you're a scumball."

One of the "better" things employers of maids often want to do with their time is, of course, spend it with their children. But an underlying problem with post-nineteenth-century child-raising, as Deirdre English and I argued in our book *For Her Own Good* years ago, is precisely that it is unmoored in any kind of purposeful pursuit. Once "parenting" meant instructing the children in necessary chores; today it's more likely to center on one-sided conversations beginning with "So how was school today?" No one wants to put the kids to work again weeding and stitching; but in the void that is the modern home, relationships with children are often strained. A little "low-quality time" spent washing dishes or folding clothes together can provide a comfortable space for confidences—and give a child the dignity of knowing that he or she is a participant in, and not just the product of, the work of the home.

There is another lesson the servant economy teaches its beneficiaries and, most troublingly, the children among them. To be cleaned up after is to achieve a certain magical weightlessness and immateriality. Almost everyone complains about violent video games, but paid housecleaning has the same consequence-abolishing effect: you blast the villain into a mist of blood droplets and move right along; you drop the socks knowing they will eventually levitate, laundered and folded, back to their normal dwelling place. The result is a kind of virtual existence, in which the trail of litter that follows you seems to evaporate all by itself. Spill syrup on the floor and the cleaning person will scrub it off when she comes on Wednesday. Leave *The Wall Street Journal* scattered around your airplane seat and the flight attendants will deal with it after you've deplaned. Spray toxins into the atmosphere from your factory's smokestacks and they will be filtered out eventually by the lungs of the breathing public. A servant economy breeds callousness and solipsism in the served, and it does so all the more effectively when the service is performed close up and routinely in the place where they live and reproduce.

Individual situations vary, of course, in ways that elude blanket judgment. Some people—the elderly and disabled, parents of new babies, asthmatics who require an allergen-free environment—may well need help performing what nursing-home staff call the "ADLs," or activities of daily living, and no shame should be attached to their dependency. In a more generous social order, housekeeping services would be subsidized for those who have health-related reasons to need them—a measure that would generate a surfeit of new jobs for the low-skilled people who now clean the homes of the affluent. And in a less gender-divided social order, husbands and boyfriends would more readily do their share of the chores.

However we resolve the issue in our individual homes, the moral challenge is, put simply, to make work visible again: not only the scrubbing and vacuuming but all the hoeing, stacking, hammering, drilling, bending, and lifting that goes into creating and maintaining a livable habitat. In an ever more economically unequal culture, where so many of the affluent devote their lives to such ghostly pursuits as stock-trading, image-making, and opinion-polling, real work—in the old-fashioned sense of labor that engages hand as well as eye, that tires the body and directly alters the physical world—tends to vanish from sight. The feminists of my generation tried to bring some of it into the light of day, but, like busy professional women fleeing the house in the morning, they left the project unfinished, the debate broken off in midsentence, noble intentions unfulfilled. Sooner or later, someone else will have to finish the job.

Reading 13

THE NAKED CITADEL

By Susan Faludi

A visit behind the walls of the military academy called The Citadel reveals an isolated, relentless, and sometimes brutal male culture, and yields an unexpected explanation of why the cadets, and their administrative mentors, so fear the presence of one female student.

Along the edges of the quad, in the gutters, the freshman cadets were squaring their corners. The "knobs," as they are called for their nearly hairless doorknob pates, aren't allowed to step on the lawn of the broad parade ground, which is trimmed close, as if to match their shorn heads. Keeping off the grass is one of many prohibitions that obtain at The Citadel, a public military college on Charleston's Ashley River. Another is the rule that so many of the cadets say brought them to this Moorish-style, gated campus: Girls keep out.

The campus has a dreamy, flattened quality, with its primary colors, checkerboard courtyards, and storybook-castle barracks. It feels more like an architect's rendering of a campus—almost preternaturally clean, orderly, antiseptic—than the messy real thing. I stood at the far end of the quad, at the academic hall's front steps, and watched the cadets make their herky-jerky perpendicular turns as they drew closer for the first day of class. They walked by stiffly, their faces heat-blotched and vulnerable, and as they passed each in turn shifted his eyes downward. I followed one line of boys into a classroom, a Western Civ class—except, of course, they weren't really boys at all. These were college men, manly recruits to an elite military college whose virile exploits were mythicized in best-selling novels by Calder Willingham and Pat Conroy, both Citadel alumni. So why did I expect their voices to crack when

Faludi, Susan. "The Naked Citadel." *The New Yorker.* Sept 5, 1994. 62–81.

they spoke for the first time? Partly, it was the grammar-schoolish taking of attendance, compulsory at The Citadel. Multiple absences can lead to "tours," hours of marching back and forth in the courtyard with a pinless rifle over one shoulder; or to "cons," confinement to one's room.

But mostly it was the young men themselves, with their doughy faces and twitching limbs, who gave me the urge to babysit. Despite their enrollment in a college long considered "the big bad macho school" (as a former R.O.T.C. commander, Major General Robert E. Wagner, once put it), the cadets lacked the swagger and knowingness of big men on campus. They perched tentatively on their chairs, their hands arranged in a dutiful clasp on their desktops, as if they were expecting a ruler slap to the knuckles. A few dared to glance over at the female visitor, but whenever they made eye contact they averted their gaze and color stained their cheeks.

"As many of you probably know," their teacher said, "this was almost the day the first woman joined The Citadel." The cadets continued to study their polished shoes. "How do you, in fact, feel about whether women should be allowed to attend?"

Silence reigned. Maybe the cadets felt the question put them in an awkward spot. Not only was their teacher in favor of admitting women to The Citadel's Corps of Cadets, the teacher *was* a woman. Indeed, Professor Jane Bishop seemed to be in the strange situation of calling in an air strike on her own position. It was the first day of fall classes in the 1993–94 academic year at The Citadel, and she was broaching the question of the hour. But this incongruity wasn't limited to her classroom. From the moment I stepped onto the school's campus, I had been struck by an unexpected circumstance: though an all-male institution—an institution, moreover, whose singular mission was "making men"—The Citadel was by no means free of women. Female teachers were improving cadets' minds, female administrators were keeping their records, and an all-female (and all-black) staff served the meals in the mess hall. There was also the fact that female students made up seventy-seven per cent of the enrollment of the evening school, and many other female students attended summer school with the cadets. What about them? Of course, summer school and evening school aren't part of the military college proper. Cadets don't attend the evening school; and as Major Rick Mill, The Citadel's public-relations director, notes, those cadets who attend the summer school "aren't wearing their uniforms."

Today they were, and so was their teacher. All permanent instructors, regardless of their sex (about fifteen per cent are women), wear uniforms as part of their required affiliation with a largely ceremonial outfit once known as the South Carolina Unorganized Militia, and still called by the unfortunate acronym SCUM. Bishop wore hers with what seemed like a deliberate air of disarray.

The cadets' uniforms were considerably tidier—testament to the efficacy of the famous cadet shirt tuck, a maneuver akin to hospital-corners bedmaking and so exacting a cadet cannot perform it without assistance. Even so, the gray cadet uniform, with the big black stripe down the side of the pants and the nametag above the left breast, is the sort more often seen on high-school band members than on fighting soldiers.

"Remember," Bishop prodded them, "speech is free in the classroom."

At last, a cadet unclasped and raised a hand. "Well, I'd have no problem with her in the day program, but she can't join the Corps."

"She," as everyone there knew, was Shannon Faulkner, the woman who had challenged the school's hundred-and-fifty-year-old all-male policy by omitting reference to her sex from her application and winning acceptance to the Corps of Cadets earlier that year—acceptance that was rescinded once the administrators discovered their error. Faulkner's attempt to gain entrance then shifted from the admissions office to the courts. She was allowed under court order to attend day classes during the spring semester of 1994, the first woman to do so. On July 22nd, a United States District Court ruled that The Citadel must admit Faulkner into the Corps of Cadets proper; three weeks later, the Fourth United States Circuit Court of Appeals granted The Citadel a stay pending appeal.

Yet why shouldn't she be permitted into the Corps, Bishop pressed. One of her students recited the fitness requirement—forty-five pushups and fifty-five sit-ups in two-minute sets, and a two-mile run in sixteen minutes. But the administration made passing the fitness test a requirement for graduation only *after* Shannon Faulkner filed suit. An alumnus recounted in court that many upperclassmen he knew who had failed the test skipped the punitive morning run and "sat around and ate doughnuts." Another of Bishop's students cited the shaved-head rule. But this, too, seemed a minor point. A woman cadet could conceivably get a buzz cut. Sinead O'Connor had done it, Bishop pointed out, without undue injury to her career. And, anyway, after freshman year the men no longer get their heads shaved. Other deprivations of freshman year were invoked: having to "brace" on demand—that is, assume a stance in which a knob stands very erect and tucks in his chin until it puckers up like a rooster's wattle—and having to greet every upperclassman's bellowed command and rebuke with "Sir, yes sir!" or "Sir, no sir!" or "Sir, no excuse sir!" But women, obviously, aren't incapable of obeisance; one might even say they have a long history of it.

Weighing heaviest on the cadets' minds, it turned out, was the preservation of the all-male communal bathroom. The sharing of the stall-less showers and stall-less toilets is "at the heart of the Citadel experience," according to more than one cadet. The men bathe as a group; they walk to the shower down the open galleries, in full view of the courtyard below, and do so, one cadet said, in "nothing but our bathrobes" or "even without any clothes." Another cadet said, "I know it sounds trivial, but all of us in one shower, it's like we're all one, we're all the same, and—I don't know—you feel like you're exposed, but you feel safe. You know these guys are going to be your friends for life." His voice trailed off. "I just can't explain it but when they take that away, it's over. This place will be ruined."

"If women come here, they'll have to put up window shades in all the rooms," a cadet said. "Think of all the windows in the barracks. That could be eight thousand, nine thousand dollars. You've got to look at the costs."

At the end of the hour, the cadets filed out and resumed their double-time jog along the gutters—and their place in the "fourth-class system." This "system" is a nine-month regimen of small and large indignities intended to "strip" each young recruit of his original identity and remold him into the "Whole Man," a vaguely defined ideal, half Christian soldier, half Dale Carnegie junior executive. As a knob explained it to me, "We're all suffering together. It's how we bond." Another knob said, "It's a strange analogy, but it's almost like a P.O.W. camp."

One cadet dawdled, glancing nervously around, then sidled up to me. He spoke in an ear whisper, and what he had to say had nothing to do with lavatory etiquette or military tradition. "The great majority of the guys here are very misogynistic," he said. "All they talk about is how girls are pigs and sluts."

I asked him to explain at greater length. He agonized, "I have to keep quiet," he said, but he finally agreed to meet me later, in an out-of-the-way spot on the upper floor of the student-activities center. He rejoined his classmates with that distinctive knob march, "the march of the puppets," as a professor described it to me later. It was a gait caused in some cases, I was told, by the most conscientious cadets' efforts to keep their shirts perfectly straight with the help of garters—one end of the garter clipped to the shirttail, the other end to the socks.

As I waited for my cadet informant, I decided to kill an hour on the vast parade ground, where the Corps of Cadets marches every Friday afternoon in full dress uniforms, and where, according to an old school brochure, "manhood meets mastery." This is a paramilitary display, not a military one. Despite the regalia and officer ranks, and despite its notoriously fierce military discipline ("To discipline is to teach" is the motto emblazoned on one of the school's books of regulations), this is a military academy by self-designation only. Unlike the federal service academies—West Point, Annapolis, the Air Force Academy—The Citadel has no connection with the United States Armed Forces (other than its R.O.T.C. program and its employment of some active and retired officers). Its grounds are adorned with dusty and decommissioned military hardware—a Sherman tank, a submarine's torpedo-loading hatch, a Phantom jet named Annette, two cannons named Betsy and Lizzie. In most cases, the weapons, including the pinless M-14s the cadets carry, are inoperative. The mouths of the various cannons are stuffed with cement—all except those of Betsy and Lizzie, which are fired during parades, but carefully aimed high enough so that their powder does not dust the crenellated barracks. The over-all effect is that of a theme park for post-Cold War kids.

The hokeyness and childlike innocence of the scene—the stage-prop artillery, the toy-soldier clip-clop of the cadets as they squared their corners—were endearing, in a Lost Boys sort of way, and I strolled over to the

student-activities center for my rendezvous with my cadet informant thinking
that The Citadel's version of martial culture was not so menacing after all. The
cadet was not in evidence. I spent the next thirty minutes prowling the halls,
which were lined with portraits of stern-faced "generals" (I couldn't tell which
were United States military and which were SCUM), and examining ads on the
student bulletin board for items like "Save the Males" bumper stickers. I tried to
reach the cadet's room by phone—women aren't admitted into the barracks—
but he was not there. A bit thoughtlessly, I left a message with an upper-class-
man and headed toward town.

propaganda

At my hotel, the receptionist handed me a message from my vanished cadet.
"Please, don't ever call here again!" it read. The phone clerk peered at me curiously. "Sorry about that exclamation mark, but he seemed quite distraught," she
said. "His voice was shaking."

What brought a young man to an all-male preserve in the last decade of the
twentieth century, anyway? What was going on outside the academy gates that
impelled thousands of boys, Southern and Northern alike (about a fifth of its student body of about two thousand are Yankees), to seek refuge behind a pair of
corroding cannons?

"The forces arrayed against us," an attorney named Robert Patterson declared in
a February, 1994, court hearing, consider his military academy to be "some big-
game animal to be hunted down, tracked, caught, badgered, and killed so that
some lawyer or some organization can go back up and hang a trophy on a wall in
an office." Patterson was defending not The Citadel but the Virginia Military Institute, which is the only other public military academy in the United States that
does not admit women, and which was involved in a similar sex-discrimination
suit. (Three months later, Patterson, a V.M.I. alumnus, returned to court to defend The Citadel.) "I will say this, Your Honor," he went on. "This quest by these
people constitutes the longest and most expensive publicly financed safari in the
annals of big-game hunting."

The Citadel's administration has fought the female hunters with a legal
arsenal of nearly a million dollars and with dour, tight-lipped determination,
which has only increased with time. The Citadel's president, Claudius Elmer
(Bud) Watts III, who is a retired Air Force lieutenant general and a second-
generation Citadel alumnus, views Shannon Faulkner's legal efforts as an enemy
invasion, placing his young troops "under attack." "The Citadel is in this to the
end," he pronounced at a press conference held in the spring of 1994 on the
parade ground, his feet planted between Betsy and Lizzie, his uniform decked
with ribbons, and his chin tucked in, as is his custom, as if in a permanent brace
position.

Later, in his living room, surrounded by coffee-table books on football,
Watts told me firmly, "You cannot put a male and a female on that same playing
field," though he couldn't say exactly why. Of his own Citadel years he

conceded, "I've not the foggiest notion if it would have been different" had women attended. He was just glad there were no female cadets then; otherwise, he said, the cadets would have faced "a different form of intimidation—not wanting to be embarrassed in front of a girl."

Faulkner has been opposed not only by many Citadel staff and alumni but— at least, publicly—by almost all the current cadets. They say that her presence in the Corps would absolutely destroy a basic quality of their experience as Citadel men. She would be what one Citadel defender called in his court deposition "a toxic kind of virus." Tellingly, even before the United States District Court judge enjoined The Citadel to admit Faulkner to the Corps of Cadets for the fall of 1994, and before the injunction was set aside, the administration announced its selection of her living quarters; the infirmary.

Cadets cite a number of reasons that women would have a deleterious effect on the Corps of Cadets, and the reasons are repeated so often as to be easily predictable, though their expression can be novel. "Studies show—I can't cite them, but studies show that males learn better when females aren't there," one cadet explained to me (a curious sentiment at a school where a knob motto about grades is "2.0 and Go"). "If a girl was here, I'd be concerned not to look foolish. If you're a shy student, you won't be as inhibited." Another cadet said, "See, you don't have to impress them here. You're free." From a third: "Where does it end? Will we have unisex bathrooms?" But among the reasons most frequently heard for repelling Faulkner at the gate is this: "She would be destroying a long and proud tradition."

The masculine traditions of West Point and Annapolis were also closely guarded by their male denizens, but the resistance to women joining their ranks was nowhere near as fierce and filled with doomsday rhetoric as The Citadel's efforts to repel feminine interlopers. At Norwich University, a private military college in Northfield, Vermont, that voluntarily opened its barracks to women in 1974, two years before the federal service academies, the administration actually made an effort to recruit and accommodate women. "There was no storm of protest," said a Norwich spokeswoman, Judy Clauson. But then, "it was a time when there were so many rules that were being loosened." The Air Force veteran Linnea Westberg, who was one of the eight women in Norwich's first coed class, recalled, of her integration into its corps, that "ninety-five per cent of the male cadets were fine, especially the freshmen, who didn't know any different." Westberg said she was baffled by the intensity of The Citadel's opposition to women in its corps. "It's hard for me to believe it's still an issue."

"The Citadel is a living museum to the way things used to be," John Drennan, a Citadel graduate and a public defender in Charleston, told me one day during The Citadel's legal proceedings. But how, exactly, did things use to be? The cadets and the alumni of the school, along with those protesting against its exclusionary policies, envision its military tradition above all. And The Citadel once did have a strong military aspect: it was formed as an arsenal in 1822 in response to a slave revolt purportedly planned by the freed Charleston slave Denmark Vesey, which, though it was foiled, aroused widespread alarm in the region. Yet twenty years later the guns and the gold braid became mere adornment as The Citadel turned into an industrial school of domestic and practical skills. Union troops shut down The Citadel at the end of the Civil War, but it was reinvented and reopened in 1882, after the Union's Reconstruction officials had thoroughly stripped the school of all military muscle. Its new mission was to reinvigorate the masculinity of the South by showing its men how to compete with the business and industrial skills of the Yankee carpetbaggers, who were believed to be much better prepared than the sons of Dixie to enter the Darwinian fray of modern commerce. John Peyre Thomas, who ran The Citadel from 1882 to 1885, wrote of the need to teach spoiled plantation boys the rudiments of self-reliance. "It must be admitted that the institution of African slavery in many respects, affected injuriously the white youth of the South," he wrote. "Reared from infancy to manhood with servants at his command to bring his water, brush his shoes, saddle his horse, and, in fine, to minister to his personal wants, the average Southern boy grew up in some points of character dependent, and lazy, and inefficient. He was found, too, wanting in those habits of order and system that come from the necessity, in man, to economize time and labor."

What makes the school's Reconstruction-era mission important is that in so many ways it remains current; the masculine and industrial culture of our age and that of the conquered South may have more in common than we care to imagine. Again, we are at a psychic and economic crisis point for manhood. And, again, the gun issues hide the butter issues: the bombast masks a deep insecurity about employment and usefulness in a world where gentleman soldiers are an anachronism and a graduate with gentleman's C's may find himself busing tables at Wendy's.

The uncertain prospects of Citadel graduates are worsened by military downsizing. Only about a third of recent graduates entered the military—a figure that has fallen steeply since the mid-seventies, when half of The Citadel's graduating class routinely took a service commission. News of Shannon Faulkner's court case competed in the Charleston *Post & Courier* with news of the shutting down of the local shipyards and decommissionings from the local military installations.

The night before the closing arguments in Faulkner's suit, I had dinner at the on-campus home of Philippe and Linda Ross, who have both taught at The Citadel. Philippe, the head of the Biology Department, had just completed his first round of moonlighting as a "retraining" instructor at the Charleston Naval Shipyard. He had been prepping laid-off nuclear engineers to enter one of the few growth industries in the area—toxic-waste management. Facing a room filled with desperate men each day had been a dispiriting experience, he said. He recalled the plea of a middle-aged engineer, thrust out of the service after twenty-six years:

"All I want to do is work." Linda Ross, who was then teaching psychology at The Citadel, looked across the table with a pained expression. "That whole idea that if a young man went to college he could make a decent living and buy a house, and maybe even a boat, just does not hold anymore," she said softly. "There's a Citadel graduate working as a cashier at the grocery store. And the one thing these young men felt they could count on was that if things got hard they could always go into the military. No more. And they are bitter and angry."

In the fall of 1991, Michael Lake, a freshman, decided to leave The Citadel. He had undergone weeks of bruising encounters with upperclassmen—encounters that included being knocked down with a rifle butt and beaten in the dark by a pack of cadets. Incidents of hazing became so violent that, in a school where publicly criticizing the alma mater is virtually an act of treason, several athletes told their stories to *Sports Illustrated.* Much of the violence was aimed at star freshman athletes: a member of the cycling team was forced to hang by his fingers over a sword poised two inches below his testicles; a placekicker had his head dunked in water twenty times until he was unconscious; a linebacker was forced to swallow his chewing tobacco and tormented until, he said later, "I was unable even to speak clearly in my classes." It was a time when the Churchill Society, a literary club reportedly containing a white-supremacist faction, was organized on campus. It was a time when the local chapter of the National Association for the Advancement of Colored People urged a federal investigation into a pair of racial incidents on the school's campus: the appearance of a noose over the bed of a black freshman who had earlier refused to sing "Dixie," and the shooting and wounding of a black cadet by a sniper who was never identified. (A few years earlier, upperclassmen wearing Klan-like costumes left a charred paper cross in the room of a black cadet.) And it was a time when a leader of the Junior Sword Drill, a unit of cadet sword-bearers, leaped off a five-foot dresser onto the head of a prostrate cadet, then left him in a pool of blood in a barracks hall. According to one cadet, a lacrosse-team member returning from an away game at three in the morning stumbled upon the victim's unconscious body, his face split open, jaw and nose broken, mouth a jack-o'-lantern of missing teeth.

One night, at about 2 A.M., high-ranking cadets trapped a raccoon in the barracks and began to stab it with a knife. Beau Turner, a student at the school, was awakened by the young men's yelling. "My roommate and I went out there to try and stop it," Turner recalled, "but we were too late." Accounts of the episode vary. In a widely circulated version (which was referred to in a faculty member's testimony), the cadets chanted, "Kill the bitch! Kill the bitch!" as they tortured the raccoon to death.

In October, 1993, two upperclassmen burst into the room of two freshmen and reportedly kneed them in the genitals, pulled out some of their chest hair, and beat them up. They were arrested on charges of assault and battery, and agreed to a program of counselling and community service, which would wipe clean their records. They withdrew from The Citadel, in lieu of expulsion, the spokesman Major Rick Mill said.

One of the offending cadets, Adrian Baer, told me that he and the other accused sophomore, Jeremy Leckie, did indeed come back from drinking, burst into the knobs' room after 10 P.M., and "repeatedly struck them in the chest and stomach" and bruised one of them in the face, but he denied having kicked them in the groin and yanked out chest hair. He said that what he did was common procedure—and no different from the "motivational" treatment he had received as a knob at the hands of a senior who came into *his* room. They entered the freshmen's room, Baer explained, because they viewed one of the occupants as "a problem" knob who "needed some extra motivation." Baer elaborated: "His pinkie on his right hand wouldn't completely close when he went to salute. He caught a lot of heat for that, of course, because it's a military school; it's important to salute properly." The strict rule that upperclassmen not fraternize with knobs, he said, meant that they couldn't simply counsel the freshman kindly. "If we just sat down and said, 'Listen, guy, we have a little problem,' that would be fraternization. And more important, knobs would lose respect for upperclassmen. It's a lot of denial on the part of officials at The Citadel about hazing," Baer said. "They don't want to believe it goes on." Leckie's father, Timothy Rinaldi, said that while he believed his son "was definitely in the wrong," he felt The Citadel's fourth-class system bred such behavior. "They help build this monster," he said of The Citadel, "the monster gets up off the table and starts walking through town—and now Dr. Frankenstein wants to shoot it."

Needless to say, not every cadet embraces the climate of cruelty; the nocturnal maulings likely frighten as many cadets as they enthrall. But the group mentality that pervades The Citadel assures that any desire on the part of a cadet to speak out about the mounting violence will usually be squelched by the threat of ostracism and shame. While group rule typifies many institutions, military and civilian, that place a premium on conformity, the power and authoritarianism of the peer group at The Citadel is exceptional, because the college gives a handful of older students leave to "govern" the others as they see fit. (A lone officer provided by the military, who sleeps in a wing off one of the dorms, seldom interferes.) This is a situation that, over the years, an occasional school official has challenged, without success. A former assistant commandant for discipline, Army Lieutenant Colonel T. Nugent Courvoisie, recalled that he "begged" the school's president back in the sixties to place more military officers—and ones who were most mature—in the barracks, but his appeals went unheeded. Discipline and punishment in the dorms is in the hands of the student-run regimental command, and ascendancy in this hierarchy is not always predicated on compassion for one's fellow-man. In consequence, the tyranny of the few buys the silence of the many.

This unofficial pact of silence could, of course, be challenged by the Citadel officialdom. On a number of occasions over the past three decades—most recently when some particularly brutal incidents found their way into the media—The Citadel has commissioned "studies." But when the administration does go on the offensive, its animus is primarily directed not at miscreant cadets but at the "unfair" media, which are "victimizing" the institution by publicizing the bad behavior of its boys.

In recent years, enough bad news leaked out locally to become a public-relations nightmare, and the school appointed a committee of Citadel loyalists to assess the situation. Even the loyalists concluded, in a January, 1992, report, that the practice of physical abuse of freshmen, along with food and sleep deprivation, had got out of hand. As a result, Major Mill told me, The Citadel ordered upperclassmen to stop using pushups as a "disciplinary tool" on individual cadets. "That was the most important one" of the reforms prompted by the report, Mill said. Other reforms were adopted: for example, freshmen would no longer be compelled to deliver mail to upperclassmen after their evening study hours, thus reducing opportunities for hazing; freshmen would—at least officially—no longer be compelled to "brace" in the mess hall. At the same time, the report declared that it "wholeheartedly endorses the concept of the fourth-class system," which it called "essential to the attainment of college objectives and the development of the Citadel man."

Institutions that boast of their insularity, whether convents or military academies, are commonly pictured in the public imagination as static, unchanging abstractions, isolated from the ebb and flow of current events. But these edifices are rarely as otherworldly as their guardians might wish; indeed, in the case of The Citadel, its bricked-off culture has functioned more as a barometer of national anxieties than as a garrison against them. The militaristic tendencies within the Corps seem to vary inversely with the esteem in which the American soldier is held in the larger society. In times when the nation has been caught up in a socially acceptable conflict, one in which its soldiers return as heroes greeted by tickertape parades, The Citadel has loosened its militaristic harness, or even removed it altogether. Thus, during perhaps the most acceptable war in American history, the Second World War, the fourth-class system of knob humiliation was all but discontinued. Upperclassmen couldn't even order a knob to brace. The changes began largely in response to the demands of the real military for soldiers they could use in a modern war. "The War Department and the Navy Department were asking R.O.T.C. to do less drilling, more calculus," Jamie Moore, a professor of history at The Citadel and a former member of the Untied States Army's Historical Advisory Committee, told me. "The Citadel dismantled its fourth-class system because it was getting in the way of their military training." The changes didn't seem to interfere with the school's production of Whole Men; on the contrary, an extraordinary percentage of The Citadel's most distinguished graduates come from these years, among them United States Senator Ernest (Fritz) Hollings; Alvah Chapman, Jr., the former chief executive of Knight-Ridder; and South Carolina's former governor John C. West.

The kinder, gentler culture of the Second World War-era Citadel survived well into the next decade. Although a new fourth-class system was soon established, it remained relatively benign. "We didn't have the yelling we have today," Colonel Harvey Dick, class of '53 and now a member of The Citadel's governing body, recalled. "They didn't even shave the freshmen's heads."

The postwar years also brought the admission of women to the summer program, and without the hand-wringing provoked by Shannon Faulkner's application. "WOMEN INVADE CITADEL CLASSES FIRST TIME IN SCHOOL'S HISTORY," the Charleston daily noted back on page 16 of its June 21, 1949, edition. "Most male students took the advent of the 'amazons' in their stride," the paper reported cheerfully. "Only the younger ones seemed at all uneasy. Professors and instructors were downright glad to see women in their classes."

The Vietnam War, needless to say, did not inspire the same mood of relaxation on campus. "The fourth-class system was very physical," Wallace West, the admissions director, who was an undergraduate at The Citadel during the Vietnam War years, said. "When I was there, there was no true emphasis on academics, or on positive leadership. It was who could be worked to physical exhaustion." Alumni from those years recounted being beaten with sticks, coat hangers, and rifle butts. That was, of course, the era that inspired Pat Conroy's novel "The Lords of Discipline," a tale of horrific hazing, directed with special virulence against the school's first African-American cadet. "They just tortured us," Conroy recalled from his home, in Beaufort, South Carolina. "It taught me the exact kind of man I didn't want to be," he added.

In 1968, the administration appointed a committee to investigate the violence. The committee issued a report that, like its 1992 successor, concluded "there have been significant and extensive abuses to the [fourth-class] system." And, with its strong recommendation that hazing result in expulsion, the report seemed to promise a more pacific future on campus.

In the past decade and a half, however, the record of violence and cruelty at The Citadel has attracted increasing notice, even as the armed forces have been racked by downsizing and scandal. The Citadel president during much of this era, Major General James A. Grimsley, Jr., declined to discuss this or any other aspect of campus life during his tenure. "I don't do interviews," he said. "Thank you for calling, young lady." He then hung up. Others have been less reticent.

Thirteen years before Vice-Admiral James B. Stockdale consented to be Ross Perot's running mate, he took on what turned out to be an even more thankless task: fighting brutal forms of hazing at The Citadel. In 1979, Stockdale, who had graduated from Annapolis, was chosen to be The Citadel's president because of his status as a genuine military hero: he had survived eight years as a P.O.W. in Vietnam. This hero failed to see the point of manufactured adversity.

In an afterword to the book "In Love and War," a collaboration between Stock-dale and his wife, Sybil, he wrote that there was "something mean and out of control about the regime I had just inherited."

On his first day in the president's office, Stockdale opened a desk drawer and discovered "what turned out to be Pandora's box," he wrote. "From the top down, what was written on the papers I took out of the desk drawers—and conversations with some of their authors—was enough to break anybody's heart." Among them was a letter from an infuriated father who wanted to know what had happened to his son "to change him from a levelheaded, optimistic, aggressive individual to a fatigued, irrational, confused and bitter one." He also found copies of memos from The Citadel's staff physician complaining repeatedly of (as Stockdale recalled) "excessive hospitalization"—such as the case of a knob who had suffered intestinal bleeding and was later brought back to the infirmary, having been exercised to unconsciousness. Stockdale sought to reform the system, but he was stymied at every turn. He clashed with The Citadel's powerful Board of Visitors an eleven-member committee of alumni that sets school policy. The Board of Visitors, overruled his expulsion of a senior cadet who had reportedly been threatening freshmen with a pistol. A year into his presidency, Stockdale submitted his resignation. After he left, the board reinstated an avenging friend of the senior cadet who, according to Stockdale, had attempted to break into his house one evening. (The then chairman of the Board of Visitors maintains that the cadet was drunk and looking for the barracks.)

"They thought they were helping people into manhood," Stockdale recalled, from a more serene post, in Palo Alto, California, where he is a scholar at Stanford's Hoover Institution on War, Revolution, and Peace. "But they had no idea what that meant—or who they were."

After Watts became president, in 1989, some faculty members began to observe a creeping militarization imposed by the administration upon the Corps's already drill-heavy regimen. Four special military days were added to the academic year. At the beginning of one semester, President Watts held a faculty meeting in a room above the mess hall. "Watts had these soldiers standing around the room with their hands behind them," Gardel Feurtado, a political-science professor and one of only two African-American professors, recalled. Watts, he said, lectured the faculty for about three hours. "He didn't talk about academics or educational goals. He just talked about cadets' training, and he showed us a film of it," Feurtado told me. According to Feurtado, Watts told the faculty to line up in groups behind the soldiers for a tour of the barracks. "I said, 'Enough of this,' and I started to walk out. And this soldier stopped me and said, 'Where do you think you're going, sir?' and I said, 'You do realize that I am not in the military?' " Feurtado had to push by him to leave.

When Michael Lake looked back on the abuse he suffered during his abbreviated knob year of '91, he could now see before him, like the emergence of invisible ink on what appeared to be a blank piece of paper, the faint outlines of another struggle. What he saw was a submerged gender battle, a bitter but definitely fixed contest between the sexes, concealed from view by the fact that men played both parts. The beaten knobs were the women, "stripped" and humiliated, and the predatory upperclassmen were the men, who bullied and pillaged. If they couldn't re-create a male-dominant society in the real world, they could restage the drama by casting male knobs in all the subservient feminine roles.

"They called you a 'pussy' all the time," Lake recalled. 'Or a 'fucking little girl.' " It started the very first day they had their heads shaved, when the upperclassmen stood around and taunted. 'Oh, you going to get your little girlie locks cut off?" When they learned that Lake would be playing soccer that fall, their first response was "What is that, a girl's sport?" Another former cadet said that he had withstood "continual abuse," until he found himself thinking about jumping out the fourth-story window of the barracks—and quit. He reported an experience similar to Lake's. Virtually every taunt equated him with a woman: whenever he showed fear, they would say, "You look like you're having an abortion," or "Are you menstruating?" The knobs even experienced a version of domestic violence. The upperclassmen, this cadet recalled, "would go out and get drunk and they would come home and haze, and you just hoped they didn't come into your room."

"According to the Citadel creed of the cadet," Lake said, "women are objects, they're things that you can do with whatever you want to." In order to maintain this world view, the campus has to be free of women whose status might challenge it—a policy that, of course, is rarely enunciated. The acknowledged policy is that women are to be kept at a distance so they can be "respected" as ladies. Several months before Faulkner's lawsuit came to trial, I was sitting in the less than Spartan air-conditioned quarters of the senior regimental commander, Norman Doucet, the highest-ranking cadet, who commanded the barracks. Doucet, who was to be The Citadel's star witness at the Faulkner trial, was explaining to me how excluding women had enhanced his gentlemanly perception of the opposite sex. "The absence of women makes us understand them better," Doucet said. "In an aesthetic kind of way, we appreciate them more—because they are not there."

Women at less of a remove fare less well. In The Citadel's great chain of being, the "waitees"—as many students call that all-black, all-female mess-hall staff—rate as the bottom link. Some upperclassmen have patted them on their rear ends, tried to trip them as they pass the tables, or hurled food at their retreating backs. Cadets have summoned them with "Come here, bitch," or addressed one who dropped a plate or forgot an order as "you stupid whore." The pages of the *Brigadier,* the school's newspaper, bear witness to the cadets' contempt for these women. Gary Brown, now the editor-in-chief of the *Brigadier,* once advised fellow-cadets to beware of "waitee" food contamination—"the germ filled hands, the hair follicles, and other unknown horrors." Not only was he dismayed by "wavy little follicles in my food" but he found the women insufficiently obedient. "Duty is certainly not the sublimest word in the Waitee language," he wrote. In a letter to the editor, Jason S. Pausman, class of '94, urged fellow-cadets to demand "waitees without chronic diseases that involve sneezing, coughing or wiping of body parts. . . . The reality is simple, we CAN-NOT sit by and let the waitees of this school control us."

Some women faculty members report similarly resentful responses to their presence, despite—or because of—their positions of authority. Angry messages on a professor's door are one tactic. When Jane Bishop recently posted on her office door a photocopy of a New York *Times* editorial supporting women's admission to the Corps of Cadets, she found it annotated with heated rejoinders in a matter of days. "Dr. Bishop, you are a prime example of why women should not be allowed here," one scribble read. Another comment:"Women will destroy the world."

The Citadel men's approach to women seems to toggle between extremes of gentility and fury. "First, they will be charming to the women to get their way," Linda Ross said. "But if that doesn't work they don't know any other way. So then they will get angry." It's a pattern that is particularly evident in some cadets' reaction to younger faculty women.

December Green joined The Citadel's Political Science Department in 1988, the first woman that the department had ever hired for a tenure-track position. She was twenty-six and attractive—"someone the cadets might fantasize about," a colleague recalled. They were less enchanted, however, by her left-leaning politics. She soon found herself getting obscene phone calls in the middle of the night. Then obscenities began appearing on her office door. "Pussy" is the one that sticks in her mind.

Though Green's work at The Citadel was highly praised—she received an award for teaching, research, and service—she said that no one in the administration tried to stop her when she left in 1992, in despair over her inability to contain the cadets' fury. Nor, apparently, had anyone responded to her appeals to correct the situation. "A lot of terrible things happened to me there," Green, who is now teaching in Ohio, said, reluctant to revisit them. The hostility ranged from glowering group stares in the hallway to death threats some of which appeared on the cadets' teacher-evaluation forms. The male faculty offered little support. Green recalls the department chairman instructing her to "be more maternal toward the students" when a cadet lodged a complaint about her (she had challenged his essay in which he praised apartheid). And a professor who stood by one day while his students harassed her and another woman informed her, "You get what you provoke."

Green said she eventually had to get an unlisted number to stop the obscene calls, and also moved, in part out of fear of the cadets' vengeance. The last straw, however, came when she submitted the written threats she had received to her chairman, who passed them on to the dean of undergraduates studies, in hopes of remedial action. The dean, she said, did nothing for some months, then, after she inquired, said he had "misplaced" the offending documents.

The dean, Colonel Isaac (Spike) Metts, Jr., told me he didn't recall saying he misplaced the documents but "I might have said it's not on my desk at that time and I don't know where it is." He added that Green was a "very valuable" professor. "I don't know what else we could've done," Metts said. In any event, soon after submitting the threatening notes to the dean Green gave up. At her exit interview, she recalled, President Watts told her he didn't understand why she had been upset by the cadet harassment. "It's just a bunch of kid stuff," another male colleague said. (Lewis Spearman, the assistant to the president, said that, because of federal privacy law, Watts would have no response to Green's version of events.)

The remaining category of women that cadets have to deal with is "the dates," as the young women they socialize with are generally called. (There are no wives; Citadel policy forbids cadets to marry, and violators are expelled.) In some respects, these young women are the greatest challenge to the cadet's sense of gender hierarchy. While the "waitees" can be cast as household servants and the female teachers as surrogate mothers, the dates are more difficult to place. Young women their age are often college students, with the same aspirations as the cadets, or even greater ones. The cadets deal with young women's rising ambitions in a number of ways. One is simply to date high-school girls, an option selected by a number of cadets. Another strategy, facilitated by The Citadel, is to cast the young women who are invited on campus into the home-coming-queen mold. The college holds a Miss Citadel contest each year, and Anne Poole, whose husband, Roger, is the vice-president of academic affairs and the dean of the college, has sat on the judging panel. Each cadet company elects a young woman mascot from a photograph competition, and their faces appear in the yearbook.

The school also sends its young men to an in-house etiquette-training seminar, in which the Citadel "hostess," a pleasant woman in her forties named Susan Bowers, gives them a lecture on how "to act gentlemanly with the girls." She arms cadets with "The Art of Good Taste," a do's-and-don'ts manual with a chapter entitled "Helping the Ladies." The guidebook outlines the "correct way of offering an arm to a lady . . . to help her down the steps," and the best method for assisting "a lady in distress." (The example of distress provided involves an elderly woman trying to open a door when her arms are full of shopping bags.) Such pointers are illustrated with pictures of fifties-style coeds sporting Barbie-doll hair flips and clinging to the arms of their cadets, who are escorting them to "the Hop." The manual's preface states emphatically, "At all times [ladies] must be sheltered and protected not only from the elements and physical harm but also from embarrassment, crudity, or coarseness of any sort."

Susan Bowers explained the duties of her office: "At the beginning of the year, we do 'situation cards' for the freshmen. And we'll bring in cheerleaders and use them as props. . . . We show cadets how to go through the receiving line, how to introduce your date, and what to say to them. In the past, we didn't have the cheerleaders to use, so they dressed up some of the guys as girls." Bowers said she felt bad for the cadets, who often come to her seeking maternal consolation. "They are very timid—afraid, almost," she said. "They are so lost, and they need a shoulder."

"The Art of Good Taste" is silent on the subject of proper etiquette toward women who require neither deference nor rescue. And, as Linda Ross observed, when the gentlemanly approach fails them cadets seem to have only one fallback—aggression. Numerous cadets spoke to me of classmates who claimed to have "knocked around" uncompliant girlfriends. Some of those classmates, no doubt, were embellishing to impress a male audience, but not always. "I know lots of stories where cadets are violent toward women," a 1991 Citadel graduate named Ron Vergnolle said. He had witnessed cadets hitting their girlfriends at a number of Citadel parties—and observed one party incident in which two cadets held down a young woman while a third drunken cadet leaned over and vomited on her. Vergnolle, a magna-cum-laude graduate of the Citadel class of '91, recounted several such stories to me, and added that bragging about humiliating an ex-girlfriend is a common practice—and the more outrageous the humiliation, the better the story, as far as many cadets are concerned. Two such cadet storytellers, for example, proudly spread the word of their exploits on Dog Day, a big outdoor party sponsored by The Citadel's senior class. The two cadets told about the time they became enraged with their dates, followed them to the Portosans, and, after the women had entered, pushed the latrines over so they landed on the doors, trapping the occupants. The cadets left them there. Another cadet told Vergnolle that he had tacked a live hamster to a young woman's door. There was also the cadet who boasted widely that, as vengeance against an uncooperative young woman, he smashed the head of her cat against a window as she watched in horror. "The cat story," Vergnolle noted, "that was this guy's calling card."

Something of these attitudes shows up even in the ditties the cadets chant during their daily runs. Many of the chants are the usual military "jodies," well known for their misogynistic lyrics. But some are vintage Citadel, and include lyrics about gouging out a woman's eyes, lopping off body parts, and evisceration. A cadence remembered by one Citadel cadet, sung to the tune of "The Candy Man," begins, "Who can take two jumper cables/Clip 'em to her tit/Turn on the battery and watch the bitch twitch." Another verse starts with "Who can take an ice pick . . . " and so on.

The day after last Thanksgiving, the phone rang at one-thirty in the morning in the home of Sandy and Ed Faulkner, in Powdersville, South Carolina, a tiny community on the outskirts of Greenville. The caller was a neighbor. They had better come outside, he said—a car had been circling their block. Sandy and Ed, the parents of Shannon Faulkner, went out on their front lawn and looked around. At first, they saw nothing. Then, as they turned back to the house, they saw that across the white porch columns and along the siding of the house, painted in gigantic and what Sandy later recalled as "blood-red" letters, were the words, "Bitch," "Dyke," "Whore," and "Lesbo." Ed got up again at 6 A.M. and, armed with a bucket of white paint, hurried to conceal the message from his daughter.

A few days after the judge ordered The Citadel to admit Faulkner to the Corps of Cadets, morning rush-hour drivers in Charleston passed by a huge portable sign that read "Die Shannon." At least this threat wasn't home delivered. In the past year, instances of vandalism and harassment have mounted at the Faulkner home. Someone crawled under the house and opened the emergency exhaust valve on the water heater. The gas tank on Sandy's car was pried open. Someone driving a Ford Bronco mowed down the mailbox. Another motorist "did figure-eights through my flower bed," Sandy said. "This year, I didn't even plant flowers, because I knew they would just tear them up." And someone with access to Southern Bell's voice-mail system managed, twice, to tap into their voice mail and change their greeting, both times to a recording featuring rap lyrics about a "bitch" with a "big butt." Callers phoned in the middle of the night with threatening messages. Sandy called the county sheriff's department about the vandalism, but in Anderson county, which has been home to many Citadel's graduates, the deputy who arrived was not particularly helpful. He told them, Sandy recalled, "Well, if you;re going to mess with The Citadel, you're just going to have to expect that."

Every trial has its rare moments of clarity, when the bramble of admissibility arguments and technicalities is cut away and we see the actual issue in dispute. One such moment came toward the end of the Faulker-Citadel trial, when Alexander Astin, the director of the Higher Education Research Institute at the University of California at Los Angeles, took the stand. Astin, who is widely viewed as a leading surveyor of college-student performance and attitudes, found no negative effects on male students in nineteen all-male colleges he had studied which had gone coeducational.

"Can you tell me what kind of woman you would think would want to attend a coeducational Citadel? Robert Patterson, the Citadel attorney who had previously represented V.M.I, asked Astin, his voice full of unflattering insinuation about the kind of woman he imagined her to be.

ASTIN: I suppose the same as the kind of men who want to go there.

PATTERSON: Would it be a woman that would not be all that different from men?

ASTIN: Yes.

To Patterson, this was a triumphant moment, and he closed on it: he had forced the government's witness to admit that a woman like Shannon Faulkner would have to be a mannish aberration from her gender. But in fact Astin's testimony expressed the precise point that the plaintiff's side had been trying to make all along, and that The Citadel strenuously resisted: that the sexes were, in the end, not all that different.

"I was considered the bitch of the band," Shannon Faulkner said, without embarrassment, of her four years in her high school's marching band—just stating a fact. She was lounging on the couch in her parents' living room, comfortable in an old T-shirt and shorts, one leg swung over an arm of the couch. "That's because I was the one who was mean and got it done." The phone range, for the millionth time—another media call. "I'm not giving statements to the press right now," she said efficiently into the phone, and hung up. She did not apologize for her brusqueness, as I was half expecting her to do, after she put down the receiver. There is nothing of the good girl about her. Not that she is disagreeable; Shannon Faulkner just doesn't see the point in false deference. "I never let anyone push me around, male or female," Faulkner said, and that fact had been exasperatingly obvious to reporters who covered the trial: they found that all the wheedling and cheap flatteries that usually prompt subjects to say more than they should didn't work with Faulkner.

One could scrounge around in Faulkner's childhood for the key to what made her take on The Citadel. You could say that it was because she was born six weeks premature, and her fierce struggle to live forged a "survivor." You could cite her memory that as a small child she preferred playing outside with the boys to playing with certain girls whom she deemed "too prissy." You could point to her sports career in high school and junior high: she lettered in softball for four years and kept stats for three of the schools' four basketball teams. You could note her ability to juggle tasks: she edited the yearbook, wrote for the school paper, and graduated with a 3.48 grade-point average. And you could certainly credit the sturdy backbone and outspokeness of both her mother and her maternal grandmother; this is a family where the women talk and the men keep a low profile. Her father, Ed, owns a small fence-building business. At thirty, a few years after Shannon's birth, Sandy returned to college to get her degree, a double major in psychology and education, and became a high-school teacher of psychology, sociology, United States history, and minority cultures. When a male professor had complained about certain "older women" in his class who asked "too many questions," Sandy hurled one of her wedge-heeled sandals at him. "I said, 'I'm paying for this class, and don't you ever tell me what I can ask.'" Shannon's maternal grandmother sixty-seven-year-old Evelyn Richey, was orphaned at six and worked most of her life in textile factories, where, she noted, "women could do the job and men got the pay." Of her granddaughter's suit she said, "Women have got to come ahead. I say, let's get on with the show."

But there's little point in a detailed inspection of family history, because there's no real mystery here. What is most striking about Shannon herself is that she's not particularly unusual. She reads novels by Tom Clancy and John Grisham, has worked in a local day-care center, is partial to places like Bennigan's. She wants a college education so she can support herself and have a career as a teacher or a journalist—she hasn't yet decided which. She might do a stint in the military, she might not. She is in many ways representative of the average striving lower-middle-class teenage girl, circa 1994, who intends to better herself and does not intend to achieve that betterment through a man—in fact, she has not for a moment entertained such a possibility.

Throughout the trial, cadets and Citadel alumni spoke of a feminist plot: she is "a pawn" of the National Organization for Women, or—a theory repeatedly posited to me by cadets—"Her mother put her up to it." Two Citadel alumni asked me in all seriousness if feminist organizations were paying Shannon Faulkner to take the stand. In truth, Shannon makes an unlikely feminist poster girl. She prefers to call herself "an individualist" and seems almost indifferent to feminist affairs; when I mentioned Gloria Steinem's name once in conversation, Shannon asked me, "Who's that?" After the judge issued his decision to admit her to the Corps, she told the New York *Times* that she didn't consider the ruling a victory "just for women"—only a confirmation of her belief that if you want something, "go for it." Shannon Faulkner's determination to enter The Citadel's Corps of Cadets was fuelled not so much by a desire to trailblaze as by a sense of amazement and indignation that this trail was barricaded in the first place. She had never, she told the court, encountered such a roadblock in all her nineteen years—a remark that perhaps only a young woman of her fortunate generation could make without perjuring herself.

Shannon Faulkner got the idea of attending The Citadel back in December of 1992. She was taking a preparatory education course at Wren High School, the local public school. Mike Hazel, the teacher, passed out articles for them to read and discuss, and Faulkner picked the article in *Sports Illustrated* about hazing at The Citadel. "It was almost as accidental as Rosa Parks," Hazel recalled. "I just held up *Sports Illustrated* and asked, 'Who wants to do this? "

Faulkner told me she'd selected the article because "I had missed that issue." During the ensuing discussion, the class wandered off the subject of hazing and onto the question of what, exactly, a public state institution was doing barring women from its classrooms. After a while, Faulkner got up and went down to the counselor's office, and returned with an application form from The Citadel. "I said, 'Hey, it doesn't even say 'Male/Female,'" she recalled. While she was sitting in class, she filled it out. "I didn't really make a big to-do about it."

Two weeks after Faulkner received her acceptance letter, The Citadel got word she was a woman and revoked her admission, and in August of 1993 she went off to spend a semester at the University of South Carolina at Spartanburg while the courts thrashed out the next move. As the lawyers filed papers, The Citadel's defenders delivered their own increasingly agitated personal beliefs to the plaintiff herself. Faulkner worked evenings as a waitress in a local bar called Chiefs Wings and Firewater until the nightly tirades from the many drunk Citadel-graduate customers got to be too much. Actually, Faulkner said, she wouldn't have quit if some of her male college friends hadn't felt the need to defend her honor. "I didn't want them getting hurt," she said. Her manner of dealing with the Citadel crowd was more good-humored. One day at the bar, she recalled, "a guy came up to me. 'Are you Shannon Faulkner?' he asked, and I said, 'Why?—very casual. Then he got real huffy-puffy, madder and madder." Finally, she said, he stuck his ring in her face, then slammed his hand down on the table. "You will never wear *that!* " he yelled. Shannon saw him a few times in the bar after that, scowling at her from a far table. To lighten the mood, she once had the bartender send him a beer. He wouldn't drink it.

"I never show my true emotions in public," Shannon said. "I consider that weak." She can laugh at the cadets' threats, even when they turn ugly, because she doesn't see the reason for all the fuss. Whenever she is asked to sign the latest T-shirt inspired by the controversy, which depicts a group of male bulldogs (The Citadel's mascot) in cadet uniforms and one female bulldog in a red dress, above the caption "1,952 Bulldogs and 1 Bitch," Faulkner told me, "I always sign under the 'Bitch' part."

The first day that Shannon Faulkner attended classes, in January, 1994, the cadets who had lined up by the academic building told the media the same thing over and over. "We were trained to be gentlemen, and that's what we'll be." But in Shannon's first class, biology, all three cadets assigned to sit in her row changed their seats. The teacher, Philippe Ross, had to threaten to mark them absent to get them to return to their places. (More than twenty unexcused absences a semester is grounds for failure). Shortly thereafter, a rumor began to circulate that Faulkner was using a fake I.D. in the local bars. This summer, talk of a plot against Faulkner surfaced—to frame her, perhaps by planting drugs in her belongings. The threat seemed real enough for Faulkner to quit her summer job, in the Charleston area, and return home.

The *Brigadier's* column "Scarlet Pimpernel" took up the anti-Shannon cause with a vengeance. The columnist dubbed her "the divine bovine," likening her to a plastic revolving cow at a nearby mall (the mounting of which is a cadet tradition). The "Pimpernel" comments on an incident that occurred on Faulkner's first day were particularly memorable. An African-American cadet named Von Mickle dared to shake her hand in front of the media and say, "It's time for women," and compared the exclusion of women to that of blacks. For this lone act, he was not only physically threatened by classmates but derided in the "Pimpernel." "The PIMP doth long to tame the PLASTIC COW on this most wondrous of nights," the anonymous author wrote, with the column's unusual antique-English flourishes and coded references. "But it seems that we will have a live specimen, a home grown DAIRY QUEEN from the stables of Powerville. Perhaps NON DICKLE will be the first to saddle up. He is DIVINE BOVINE's best friend after all."

More disturbing were cadet writings on Faulkner that were not for public consumption. Tom Lucas, a graduate student in The Citadel's evening program, told me about some "very harsh" graffiti that he'd found over one of the men's rooms in The Citadel's academic building. the inscription that most stuck in his mind: "Let her in—then fuck her to death."

On the whole, the Citadel administrators to whom I spoke were defensive, evasive, or dismissive of the cadet's hostile words and deeds toward Faulkner. When I asked Citadel officials to respond to reports of barracks violence, harrassment of women on staff, or verbal abuse of Faulkner, the responses were dismaying. Cases of violence and abuse were "aberrations"; cadets who spoke up were either "troublemakers" or "mama's boys"; and each complaint by a female faculty member was deemed a "private personnel matter" that could not be discussed further.

Certainly the administrators and trustees themselves are less than enthusiastic about Faulkner's arrival. William F. Prioleau, Jr., until recently a member of the Board of Visitors, implied in a radio talk show that abortions would go up as a result of the female invasion, as he claimed had happened at West Point. Meanwhile, in The Citadel's Math Department, all that was going up as a result of Shannon Faulkner's presence was the grade-point average. Faulkner's highest mark at the semester's end was in calculus, where she earned an A (prompting a surprised Dean Poole to comment to her that she was "certainly not a stereotypical woman"). The Math Department has in recent years invited A students to an annual party. But rather than include Faulkner, the department limited the guest list to math majors. Math professor David Trautman, who was in charge of invitations to the party, explained in an E-mail message to colleagues, "Her presence would put a damper on the evening."

Linda Ross, then a professor at The Citadel, was speaking one day with a seventy-six-year-old alumnus, and the talk turned to Faulkner's lawsuit. He asked her if she thought it possible that this young woman might prevail. "Well, it's probably an inevitable turning of the tide," Ross said, shrugging. To her amazement, the alumnus began to cry.

"I have the worst chance in society of getting a job, because I'm a white male," William H. Barnes, the senior platoon leader, shouted at me over the din in The Citadel's mess hall, a din created by the upperclassmen's tradition of berating knobs at mealtime. "And that's the major difference between me and my father." In a society where, at least since the Second World War, surpassing one's father has been an expected benchmark of American manhood, Barnes's point is a plangent one. But it's hard to say which Citadel generation is more undone by the loss of white male privilege—the young men who will never partake of a dreamed world of masculine advantage or the older men who are seeing that lived world split apart, shattered.

"I was in Vietnam in '63, and I'll defy you or Shannon or anyone else to hike through the rice paddies," the usually genial Colonel Harvey Dick, sixty-seven, a Board of Visitors member, an ex-marine, and an Army lieutenant colonel, was practically shouting from his recliner armchair in his Charleston home. He popped a Tums in his mouth. "There's just no way you can do that. . . . You can't pick up a ninety-five-pound projectile. There are certain things out there that are differences." On the wall above his head were seven bayonets. He was wearing his blue Citadel T-shirt, which matched the Citadel mementos that overwhelmed his den—Citadel mugs, hats, footballs, ceramic bulldogs. It was a room known in the Dick household as "Harvey's 'I Love Me' Room." Dick treated it as his command post—whenever the phone rang, he whipped it off the cradle and barked "Colonel Dick!"—but what he was commanding was unclear; he retired in 1993 from a sixteen-year stint as The Citadel's assistant comman- dant. Still, he at least knew that he was once in charge, that he once enjoyed life- time job security as a career military man. This was something his son couldn't say: Harvey Dick II, a nuclear pipe fitter, had recently been laid off at the Charleston Naval Shipyard.

Colonel Dick wanted it known that he wasn't "one of those male-chauvinist pigs"; in fact, he believes that women are smarter than men. "Women used to let the men dominate," he said. "Maybe we need a male movement, since evidently we're coming out second on everything." He slipped another Tums from an almost empty roll. The sun was dropping as we spoke, and shadows fell across the Citadel hats and figurines in his room. "Go back and look at your Greek and Roman empires and why they fell," he said.

His wife cleared her throat. "This doesn't have anything to do with male- female," she said.

"I see a decline in this great nation of ours," Dick said. He crossed his arms and stared into the gathering darkness of the late summer afternoon. After a while, he said, "I guess I sound like a buffoon."

Unlike the cadets, the older male Citadel officials often have to face dissent from wives or daughters whose views and professional aspirations or accomplish- ments challenge their stand on women's proper place. Lewis Spearman, the assistant to the president, recently remarried, and his wife is a feminist paralegal who is now getting her master's degree in psychology. She says she engaged for more than a year in "shriekfests" with him over the Shannon Faulkner ques- tion before she halfheartedly came around to the Citadel party line on barring women. And, while the wife of Dean Poole may have sat on the Miss Citadel judging panel, their daughter, Mindy, had loftier ambitions. Despite the fact that she suffered from cystic fibrosis, she was an ardent skier, horseback rider, and college athlete, rising at 5 A.M. daily with her crew-team members at the Univer- sity of Virginia. And, despite a double lung transplant during her junior year, she graduated in 1991 with honors and won a graduate fellowship. "She was an out- standing young lady," Poole said. "I was very proud of her." His eyes clouding over at the memory, he recalled that she had made him promise to take her to the big Corps Day parade on The Citadel's sesquicentennial. The day the father and daughter were to attend the parade was the day she died. "Sort of an interesting footnote," he said, wiping at his moist eyes. What if she had wanted to go to The Citadel? Well, actually, Poole said, she *had* talked about it. If she had persisted he would have tried to change her mind, he said, but he added, "I would never have stopped her from doing something she wanted to do."

One of the biggest spousal battles over Shannon Faulkner is waged nightly at the home of a man who might seem the least likely figure at The Citadel to wind up with a feminist wife. Probably The Citadel's most legendary elder, thanks to Pat Conroy's thinly veiled and admiring portrait of him in "The Lords of Discipline," is Lieutenant Colonel T. Nugent Courvoisie, who, as an assistant commandant in the sixties, oversaw the admission of the first African-American cadet to The Citadel. A gravelly-voiced and cigar-chomping tender tyrant, Courvoisie—or the Boo, as he is known, for obscure reasons—was a fixture at the school for more than two decades. There are two Citadel scholarships in his family name, and his visage peers down from two portraits on campus.

A courtly man, and still dapper at seventy-seven, the Boo, who has since given up cigars, insisted on picking me up at my hotel and driving me to his home, though I had a rental car sitting in the parking lot. On the drive over, he ticked off the differences between the sexes which he believed made it impossible for The Citadel to admit women—differences such as that "the average female is not as proficient athletically as the average male." When we were settled in the living room, the Boo on his recliner and his second wife, Margaret, who is also seventy-seven, in a straight-back chair, the subject of Shannon Faulkner was revisited. The first words out of Margaret's mouth were "The Citadel wants to chop the head off women." A low growl emanated from the Boo's corner. He lowered the recliner a notch. "We don't talk about it here," Margaret said—an obvious untruth. "We haven't come to blows yet, but—"

The Boo interrupted, "I have the correct view."

She retorted, "No one has the *correct* view." She turned and addressed me. "You have to understand him," she said of her husband of nine years. "This is a man who went to military prep schools and a church that was male-dominated, naturally."

The Boo interrupted, "J.C. picked twelve *men* as his disciples," he said.

Margaret rolled her eyes. "See? He even takes it into the church—and he's on such familiar ground with Christ he calls him J.C."

The Boo said, "J.C. never picked a woman, except his mother."

Margaret said, "Oh God, see, this is why we don't go into it."

But, as usual, go into it they did. As the words got batted back and forth, with Margaret doing most of the batting, the Boo levered his recliner progressively lower, until all I could see of him were the soles of his shoes.

MARGARET: You had plenty of good women soldiers in Saudi Arabia.

BOO: Plenty of pregnant ones . . .

MARGARET: What, do you think [the cadets] didn't get girls pregnant before? There've been plenty of abortions. And I know of a number of cases that, by the time [a cadet] graduated, there were four or five kids.

BOO: That's an exaggeration. Maybe two or three . . . With women, there's going to be sexual harassment.

MARGARET: Oh, honey, those cadets are harassing each other right now, all the time.

BOO: That's different. That's standard operating procedure.

In the nineteen-sixties, Margaret worked in the library at The Citadel, where she would often see Charles Foster, the first African-American cadet (who died a few years ago) alone at one of the library desks. "He would just come to the library and sit there a lot. It's hard to be the only one, to be the groundbreaker. That's why I admire this girl."

Boo's voice boomed from the depths of his recliner: "But there's no need for her. She's ruining a good thing."

Margaret gave a mock groan. "This is the last vestige of male bastionship," she said, "and it's going to kill 'em when it crumbles." Boo raised his chair halfway back up and considered Margaret. "She has a good mind," he told me after a while.

Margaret smiled. "I'm a new experience for him. He's always been military. People didn't disagree with him."

The Boo showed the way upstairs, to the attic, where he has his own "Citadel room"—a collection of Citadel memorabilia vaster than but almost identical to Dick's. Around the house, there were sketches of Boo at various points in his Citadel career. He told me that, before he retired, the cadets commissioned a portrait of him that hangs in Jenkins Hall. "Man, I looked good in that," he said. "Like a man. A leader."

Margaret didn't think so. "No, it was horrible," she said. "It didn't look like you."

"If Shannon were in my class, I'd be fired by March for sexual harassment," Colonel James Rembert, an English professor, was saying as we headed toward his classroom. He had a ramrod bearing and a certain resemblance to Ted Turner (who, it happens, sent all three of his sons to The Citadel—Beau Turner among them—and donated twenty-five million dollars to the school earlier this year). The Colonel identifies himself as one of "the last white Remberts" in South Carolina, the Remberts being a Huguenot family of sufficiently ancient lineage to gain him admission to the St. John's Hunting Club, of South Carolina—an all-male society chaired by a Citadel alumnus. Rembert, who has a Cambridge University doctorate and wrote a book on Jonathan Swift, said he preferred the company of men, in leisure and in learning. "I've dealt with young men all my life," he went on. "I know how to play with them. I have the freedom here to imply things I couldn't with women. I don't want to have to watch what I say."

The literary work under discussion that day was "Beowulf," and the cadets agreed that it was all about "brotherhood loyalty" and, in the words of one student, "the most important characteristics of a man—glory and eternal fame." Then they turned to their papers on the topic.

"Mr. Rice," Rembert said in mock horror. "You turned in a single-spaced paper." This was a no-no. Rembert instructed him to take a pencil and "pen-e-trite"—Rembert drew the syllables out—the paper with the point. He shook his head. "What a pansy!" Rembert said. "Can't catch, can't throw, can't write." Another student was chastised for the use of the passive voice. "Never use the passive voice—it leads to effeminacy and homosexuality," Rembert told the class. "So next time you use the passive voice I'm going to make you lift up your limp wrist." Literary pointers concluded, Rembert floated the subject of Shannon Faulkner. The usual objections were raised. But then the class wandered into more interesting territory, provoked by a cadet's comment that "she would change the relationship between the men here." Just what is the nature of that relationship?"

"When we are in the showers, it's very intimate," a senior cadet said. "We're one mass, naked together, and it makes us closer. . . . You're shaved, you're naked, you're afraid together. You can cry." Robert Butcher, another senior, said that the men take care of each classmate. "They'll help dress him, tuck in his shirt, shine his shoes." You mean like a mother-child relationship? I asked.

"That *is* what it is," another cadet said. "It's a family, Even the way we eat—family style." A fourth cadet said, "Maybe it's a Freudian thing, but males feel more affection with each other when women are not around. Maybe we're all homosexuals."

The class groaned. "Speak for yourself, buddy," a number of cadets said, almost in a chorus.

Rembert said, "With no women, we can hug each other. There's nothing so nurturing as an infantry platoon."

The hooted-down cadet weighted in again: "when I used to wrestle in high school, we had this great tradition. Right before the game, the coach, he'd slap us really hard on the butt."

Rembert, a onetime paratrooper, said he and his skydiving buddies did that, too, right before they jumped. "First man out gets a pat right there."

Over lunch, Rembert returned to the theme of manly nurturance among Citadel men. "We hug each other," he said. One of his colleagues, "always kisses me on the cheek," he went on. "It's like a true marriage. There's an affectionate intimacy that you will find between cadets. With this security they can, without being defensive, project tenderness to each other."

Months later, I was sitting in court watching Norman Doucet, the cadet regimental commander, testify. He was showing the judge a video of the Citadel experience and explaining the various scenes. First we were shown "one of the great parts" of a knob's first day—the mothers looking weepy at the gate as their sons were led away. Doucet lingered over the head-shaving science. "this is what does it, right here," he said. "Mother's can't even tell their sons apart after this." Thus shielded from the prying maternal eye, the cadets began their new life, and the video action shifted to a typical day in the life of the Corps. But the editing made it a day as heavy on early-morning domestic chores as it was on martial activity. Much of the film was devoted to housekeeping: scenes of cadets making beds, dressing each other, sweeping, taking out the trash, all of which Doucet described as "like some kind of a ballet or a dance that's going on." This is a dance where the most important moves took place before the show, in the dressing room. "What they are doing here is the Citadel shirt tuck," Doucet said. The tuck requires that a cadet unzip his pant halfway and fold down his waistband, then stand still while his helper approaches him from the back, puts his arms around the cadet's waist, pulls the loose shirt material firmly to the back, jams it as far down in the pants as he can, and then pulls the cadet's pants up. "If you watch closely right here, this is what the fourth-class system is all about," Doucet continued. "In order to get a proper shirt tuck, you can't do it yourself—you need your classmates to do it for you. There's really a lot of dependence upon your classmates." But, as Doucet's account suggested, cadets can experience that dependence only in concealment, away from mothers, away from all women.

When a Citadel attorney asked Doucet why female cadets would pose a problem on the campus, the only issue he raised was the humiliation that cadets feel if women observed the cadets' on-campus interactions. He spoke of the shame that knobs feel when, on occasion, a woman happened to be on the parade ground while upperclassmen were disciplining them. The cadets observing in the courtroom nodded in agreement.

It may seem almost paradoxical that the fourth-class system should be so solicitous of the emotional vulnerability of its wards—the same wards it subjects to such rigors. And yet the making of Whole Men evidently requires an initial stage of infantilization. Indeed, the objective of recapitulating childhood development is plainly spelled out in The Citadel's yearbook, known as "the Sphinx." The 1990 "Sphinx" explained, "As a freshman enters, he begins to release his childhood and takes the first steps to becoming a 'Citadel Man.' . . . As a 'knob,' every aspect of life is taught, a new way to walk. . . . Knobs are told how, where, and when to walk." Reëntrance into manhood for the toddling knobs occurs on Recognition Day, when the upper-classmen force the knobs to do calisthenics until they drop, then gently lift up their charges and nurse them with cups of water. At that moment, for the first time in nine months, the older cadets call the knobs by their first names and embrace them.

The relationship between knobs and upperclassmen following Recognition Day, as they are integrated into the Corps, shifts from maternal to matrimonial. The yearbooks of the last several years picture Citadel men spending a lot of time embracing and kissing. Of course, this impulse, when it is captured on film, is always carefully disarmed with a jokey caption.

One afternoon, a group of cadets recounted for me the campus's many "nudity rituals," as they jokingly called them. There's "Senior Rip-Off Day," a spring rite in which three hundred seniors literally rip each other's clothes off, burn them in a bonfire, and hug and wrestle on the ground. There's "Nude Platoon," in which a group of juniors, unclad except for their cross-webbing, run around the quad yelling, "We love the Nude Platoon!" And there's the birthday ritual, in which the birthday boy is stripped, tied to a chair, and covered with shaving cream, while his groin is coated in liquid shoe polish.

During the fall semester before graduation, the seniors receive their "band of gold" (as it is called) in the Ring Ceremony. The chaplain blesses each class ring. (Receiving the ring, which I was constantly reminded is "the biggest class ring of any college," is a near-sacrament, and the yearbooks are filled with pictures of young men holding up their rings in fervor, as if clutching a crucifix before a vampire.) Then each senior walks through a ten-foot replica of the class ring with his mother on one arm and his "date" on the other. In a sort of reverse marriage ceremony, the mother gives the cadet away. Mother and date accompany him through the towering ring; then he kisses Mother farewell and marches under the arched swords of the Junior Sword Drill, a new bride of the Corps. Several cadets and alumni told me that when a Citadel graduate marries, it is a tradition to slide the class ring over the wedding band. Indeed, I saw such an ordering of priorities on the fingers of a number of Citadel men in the courtroom.

In the late-twentieth-century setting of The Citadel, in a time when extreme insecurity and confusion about masculinity's standing run rampant, the Corps of Cadets once again seeks to obscure a domestic male paradise with an intensifying of virile showmanship and violence. The result is a ruthless intimacy, in which physical abuse stands in for physical affection, and every display of affection must be counterbalanced by a display of sadism. Knobs told me that they were forced to run through the showers while the upperclassmen "guards" knocked the soap out of their hands and, when the knobs leaned over to retrieve it the upperclassmen would unzip their pants and yell, "Don't pick it up, don't pick it up! We'll use you like we used those girls!" A former Citadel Halloween tradition, of upper-classmen dressing up—mostly in diapers and women's clothes—and collecting candy treats from knobs, has given way to "tricks" of considerable violence. (One upperclassman told me of cadets who knocked dressers over on candy-dispensing cadets and then walked on top of them.) The administration tried, unsuccessfully, to put a stop to the whole affair; too many freshmen were getting injured. And the playful pat on the butt that served to usher cadets into the brotherhood has degenerated into more invasive acts. According to a recent graduate one company of cadets recently devised a regimen in which the older cadets tested sophomores nightly with increasingly painful treatments—beatings and stompings and so forth. The process, which they dubbed "Bananarama," culminated on a night in which an unpeeled banana was produced—and shoved into a cadet's anus.

Given this precarious dynamic, it is not surprising that in the past few years at The Citadel social rage has been directed toward any men who were perceived to be gay. Several young men who were suspected of homosexual inclinations were hounded out of the school. One cadet, Herbert Parker, who said that he was falsely accused of having a sexual encounter with a male janitor, recalled a year of total isolation—cadets refused to sit near him in the mess hall or in classes—and terror; incessant threatening phone calls and death threats. The cadets and the administration—which had responded to the report of his encounter by sending out a campus-security police car with lights flashing to question him—acted "like I had murdered someone."

The scapegoating reached such brutal proportions that the counselling center recently set up a sort of group-therapy session for the targeted young men, who are known as It, as in the game of tag.

One evening after the trial, I went over to the Treehouse, a "mixed" bar in Charleston, with an upstairs gay bar and nightly drag shows on the weekends. My intention was to ask about cadet violence against gay men. I presumed that on a campus where every second epithet was "faggot" such hate crimes were all but inevitable. There were indeed a few such cases, I learned, but the circumstances were different from what I had imagined. Nor were those cases the essence of my findings that evening.

"The proper terminology for The Citadel," a customer at the bar named Chris said, "is The Closet." Up and down the bar, heads bobbed in agreement. "They love faggots like me." What he meant by "like me," however, was not that he was gay. That night, he looked like a male model—sleek black hair and a handsome, chiselled face. But on the nights he was dressed for a performance he could pass for a woman. Arching an eyebrow, Chris said, "The cadets go for the drag queens."

Chris's observation was echoed in ensuing conversations in the bar. There are thousands of cadets, presumably, who have not dated drag queens, but in two visits to the Treehouse I could find only two drag queens, out of maybe a dozen, who did not tell me of dating a cadet—and that was only because these two found Citadel men "too emotional." Cadets can also occasionally be dangerous, Chris told me. "You can get the ones who are violent. They think they want it, then afterwards they turn on you, like you made them do it." Nonetheless, a drag queen who called himself Holly had been happily involved with a cadet for three years now. Marissa, another drag queen, the reigning "Miss Treehouse, 1993–94," had gone out with one cadet, broken up, and was now in the throes of a budding romance with another. A third drag queen, who asked to be identified as Tiffany, was known to be a favorite of cadets.

As Chris and I were talking that first night, a drag queen called Lownie wandered in and settled on a bar stool. Lownie delighted in the Corps of Cadets pageantry—especially the Friday dress parades. "The parades are a big thing with the queers in Charleston," he said. "We'll have a cocktail party and go over and watch the boys. It's a very Southern-'lady' thing to do." Years ago, Lownie had been a student at the College of Charleston when he met *his* Citadel lover, and they had begun covert assignations—communicating through notes slipped in little-used books in the Citadel library. The only drawback, Lownie said, was dealing with his lover's constant emotional anxiety over making the grade at The Citadel. He was, in fact, a model macho cadet: a Junior Sword Drill member, a regimental officer, and a "hang king," who could dangle interminably from a closet rack by his fingertips. Lownie, who found such records more amusing than impressive, grinned, and said, "I used to make him wear his shako."—The Citadel's military cap—"when we were having sex. It's manhood at its most."

Lownie said he could begin to fathom his cadet's intense attachment to The Citadel—an emotion that he likened to a love affair—because he himself had spent four years in the Air Force. "The day-to-day aspect of being in a military environment is that you run around in a little bit of clothing and you are being judged as to how good a man you are by doing women's work—pressing pants, sewing, polishing shoes. You are a *better* man if you have mastery of womanly arts. . . . The camaraderie doesn't get any stronger than when you are in the barracks, sitting around at the end of the day in your briefs and T's and dogtags—like a bunch of hausfraus, talking and gossiping." The military stage set offers a false front and a welcome trapdoor—an escape hatch from the social burdens of traditional masculinity. Behind the martial backdrop, Lownie said, "you don't have to be a breadwinner. You don't have to be a leader. You can play back seat. It's a great relief. You can act like a human being and not have to act like a man."

"You know what the [cadet] I'm seeing now said to me?" Tiffany said. We were sitting in the dressing room a couple of hours before the night's performance, and as Tiffany spoke he peered into an elaborate mirror set illuminated with miniature movie-star lights, applying layer after layer of mascara and eyeliner with expert precision. "He said, 'You're more of a woman than a woman is.' And that's an exact quote." Tiffany stood up and struck a Southern-belle pose by way of illustration. "I overexemplify everything a female is—my breasts, my hair, the way I hold myself." And who could better complete the hoopskirts picture than a fantasy gentleman in uniform?

Marissa, Miss Treehouse, looked up from his labors, painting row after row of fake nails with pink polish. "I love how they wear their caps slung low so you can't quite see their eyes," he said. "It's like all of us are female illusionists and they are male illusionists. A man in a uniform is a kind of dream."

Tiffany said, "For Halloween, you know what my cadet boyfriend wanted to dress as? A cadet."

The dressing-room scene before me, of a group of men tenderly helping each other get ready for the evening—an elaborate process of pinning and binding and stuffing—was not very different, in its way, from the footage in Norman Doucet's video of the cadets tucking in each other's shirts. As the drag queens conversed, they tossed stockings and Ace bandages and cosmetic bags back and forth. "Has anyone seen my mascara wand?" "O.K., who has the blush?" There was a homey comfort that reminded me of slumber parties when I was a girl, where we would put big pink spongy rollers in each other's hair and screech with laughter at the results. And suddenly it became obvious to me what was generating that void, that yearning, in the cadets' lives—and maybe in the lives of many American men. What was going on here was play—a kind of freedom and spontaneity that, in this culture, only women are permitted.

No wonder men found their Citadels, their Treehouses, where the rules of gender could be bent or escaped. For the drag queens of the Treehouse, the distinctions between the sexes are a goof, to be endlessly manipulated with funhouse-mirror glee. For cadets, despite the play set of The Citadel and the dress-up braids and ribbons, the guarding of their treehouse is a dead-serious business. Still, undercover at The Citadel, the cadets have managed to create for themselves a world in which they get half the equation that Lownie described: they can "act like human beings" in the safety of the daily domestic life of the barracks. But, in return, the institution demands that they never cease to "act like a man"—a man of cold and rigid bearing, a man no more male than Tiffany's Southern belle is female, a man that no one, humanly, can be. That they must defend their inner humanity with outer brutality may say as much about the world outside The Citadel walls as about the world within them. The cadets feel called to defend those walls. Never mind that their true ideal may not be the vaunted one of martial masculinity, just as their true enemy is not Shannon Faulkner. The cadets at The Citadel feel that something about their life and routine is worthy on its merits and is endangered from without. And in that they may be right.

Reading 14

RECONCEIVING CENTRAL ASPECTS OF THE HOLOCAUST

Daniel Goldhagen

Captain Wolfgang Hoffmann was a zealous executioner of Jews. As the commander of one of the three companies of Police Battalion 101, he and his fellow officers led their men, who were not SS men but ordinary Germans, in the deportation and gruesome slaughter in Poland of tens of thousands of Jewish men, women, and children. Yet this same man, in the midst of his genocidal activities, once stridently disobeyed a superior order that he deemed morally objectionable.

The order commanded that members of his company sign a declaration that had been sent to them. Hoffmann began his written refusal by saying that upon reading it, he had thought that an error had been made, "because it appeared to me a piece of impertinence to demand of a decent German soldier to sign a declaration in which he obligates himself not to steal, not to plunder, and not to buy without paying . . . " He continued by describing how unnecessary such a demand was, since his men, of proper ideological conviction, were fully aware that such activities were punishable offenses. He also pronounced to his superiors his judgment of his men's character and actions, including, presumably, their slaughtering of Jews. He wrote that his men's adherence to German norms of morality and conduct "derives from their own free will and is not caused by a craving for advantages or fear of punishment." Hoffmann then declared defiantly: "As an officer I regret, however, that I must set my view against that of the battalion commander and am not able to carry out the order, since I feel injured in my sense of honor. I must decline to sign a general declaration."[1]

Goldhagen, Daniel. "Reconceiving Central Aspects of the Holocaust." *Hitler's Willing Executioners: Ordinary Germans and the Holocaust.* New York: Alfred Knopf, 1996.

Hoffmann's letter is astonishing and instructive for a number of reasons. Here is an officer who had already led his men in the genocidal slaughter of tens of thousands of Jews, yet who deemed it an effrontery that anyone might suppose that he and his men would steal food from Poles! The genocidal killer's honor was wounded, and wounded doubly, for he was both a soldier and a German. His conception of his obligations that Germans owed the "subhuman" Poles must have been immeasurably greater than those owed Jews. Hoffmann also understood his parent institution to be so tolerant that he was willing to refuse a direct order and even to record his brazen insubordination in writing. His judgment of his men—a judgment based, no doubt, on the compass of their activities, including their genocidal ones—was that they acted not out of fear of punishment, but with willing assent; they acted from conviction, according to their inner beliefs.

Hoffmann's written refusal sets in sharp relief important, neglected aspects of the Holocaust—such as the laxness of many of the institutions of killing, the capacity of the perpetrators to refuse orders (even orders to kill), and, not least of all, their moral autonomy—and provides insight into the unusual mind-set of the perpetrators, including their motivation for killing. It should force us to ask long-ignored questions about the sort of worldview and the institutional context that could produce such a letter which, though on a tangential subject and seemingly bizarre, reveals a host of typical features of the Germans' perpetration of the Holocaust. Understanding the actions and mind-set of the tens of thousands of ordinary Germans who, like Captain Hoffmann, became genocidal killers is the subject of this book.

During the Holocaust, Germans extinguished the lives of six million Jews and, had Germany not been defeated, would have annihilated millions more. The Holocaust was also the defining feature of German politics and political culture during the Nazi period, the most shocking event of the twentieth century, and the most difficult even to understand in all of German history. The Germans' persecution of the Jews culminating in the Holocaust is thus the central feature of Germany during the Nazi period. It is so not because we are retrospectively shocked by the most shocking event of the century, but because of what it meant to Germans at the time and why so many of them contributed to it. It marked their departure from the community of "civilized peoples.[2] " This departure needs to be explained.

Explaining the Holocaust is the central intellectual problem for understanding Germany during the Nazi period. All the other problems combined are comparatively simple: How the Nazis came to power, how they suppressed the left, how they revived the economy, how the state was structured and functioned, how they made and waged war are all more or less ordinary, "normal" events, easily enough understood. But the Holocaust and the change in sensibilities that it involved "defies" explanation. There is no comparable event in the twentieth century, indeed in modern European history. Whatever the remaining debates, every other major event of nineteenth- and twentieth-century Germany history and political development is, in comparison to the Holocaust, transparently clear in its genesis. Explaining how the Holocaust happened is a daunting task empirically and even more so theoretically, so much so that some have argued, in my view erroneously, that it is "inexplicable." The theoretical difficulty is shown by its utterly new nature, by the inability of social theory (or what passed for common sense) preceding it to provide a hint not only that it would happen but also that it was even possible. Retrospective theory has not done much better, shedding but modest light in the darkness.

The overall objective of this book is to explain why the Holocaust occurred, to explain how it could occur. The success of this enterprise depends upon a number of subsidiary tasks, which consist fundamentally of reconceiving three subjects: the perpetrators of the Holocaust, German antisemitism, and the nature of German society during the Nazi period.

Foremost among the three subjects that must be reconceived are the perpetrators of the Holocaust. Few readers of this book will have failed to give some thought to the question of what impelled the perpetrators of the Holocaust to kill. Few have neglected to provide for themselves an answer to the question, an answer that necessarily derives usually not from any intimate knowledge of the perpetrators and their deeds, but greatly from the individual's conception of human nature and social life. Few would probably disagree with the notion that the perpetrators should be studied.

Yet until now the perpetrators, the most important group of people responsible for the slaughter of European Jewry, excepting the Nazi leadership itself, have received little concerted attention in the literature that describes the events and purports to explain them. Surprisingly, the vast literature on the Holocaust contains little on the people who were its executors. Little is known of who the perpetrators were, the details of their actions, the circumstances of many of their deeds, let alone their motivations. A decent estimate of how many people contributed to the genocide, of how many perpetrators there were, has never been made. Certain institutions of killing and the people who manned them have been hardly treated or not at all. As a consequence of this general lack of knowledge, all kinds of misunderstandings and myths about the perpetrators abound. These misconceptions, moreover, have broader implications for the way in which the Holocaust and Germany during the Nazi period are conceived and understood.

We must therefore refocus our attention, our intellectual energy, which has overwhelmingly been devoted elsewhere, onto the perpetrators, namely the men and women who in some intimate way knowingly contributed to the slaughter of Jews.[3] We must investigate their deeds in detail and explain their actions. It is not sufficient to treat the institutions of killing collectively or singly as internally uncomplicated instruments of the Nazi leadership's will, as well-lubricated machine that the regime activated, as if by the flick of a switch, to do its bidding, whatever it might have been. The study of the men and women who collectively gave life to the inert institutional forms, who peopled the institutions of genocidal killing must be set at the focus of scholarship on the Holocaust and become as central to investigations of the genocide as they were to its commission.

These people were overwhelmingly and most importantly Germans. While members of other national groups aided the Germans in their slaughter of Jews, the commission of the Holocaust was primarily a German undertaking. Non-Germans were not essential to the perpetration of the genocide, and they did not supply the drive and initiative that pushed it forward. To be sure, had the Germans not found European (especially, eastern European) helpers, then the Holocaust would have unfolded somewhat differently, and the Germans would likely not have succeeded in killing as many Jews. Still, this was above all a German enterprise; the decisions, plans, organizational resources, and the majority of its executors were German. Comprehension and explanation of the perpetration of the Holocaust therefore requires an explanation of the *Germans'* drive to kill Jews. Because what can be said bout the Germans cannot be said about any other nationality or about all of the other nationalities combined—namely no Germans, no Holocaust—the focus here is appropriately on the German perpetrators.

The first task in restoring the perpetrators to the center of our understanding of the Holocaust is to restore to them their identities, grammatically by using not the passive but the active voice in order to ensure that they, the actors, are not absent from their own deeds (as in, "five hundred Jews were killed in city X on date Y"),[4] and by eschewing convenient, yet often inappropriate and obfuscating labels, like "Nazis" and "SS men," and calling them what they were, "Germans." The most appropriate, indeed the only appropriate *general* proper name for the Germans who perpetrated the Holocaust is "Germans."[5] They were Germans acting in the name of Germany and its highly popular leader, Adolf Hitler. Some were "Nazis," either by reason of Nazi Party membership or according to ideological conviction; some were not. Some were SS men; some were not. The perpetrators killed and made their other genocidal contributions under the auspices of many institutions other than the SS. Their chief common denominator was that they were all Germans pursuing German national political goals—in this case, the genocidal killing of Jews.[6] To be sure, it is sometimes appropriate to use institutional or occupational names or roles and the generic terms "perpetrators" or "killers" to describe the perpetrators, yet this must be done only in the understood context that these men and women were Germans first, and SS men, policemen, or camp guards second.

A second and related task is to reveal something of the perpetrators' backgrounds, to convey the character and quality of their lives as genocidal killers, to bring to life their *Lebenswelt*. What *exactly* did they do when they were killing? What did they do during their time as members of institutions of killing, while they were not undertaking killing operations? Until a great deal is known about the details of their actions and lives, neither they nor the perpetration of their crimes can be understood. The unearthing of the perpetrators' lives, the presentation of a "thick," rather than the customary paper-thin, description of their actions, as important and necessary as it is for its own sake, lays the foundation for the main task of this book's consideration of them, namely to explain their actions.[7]

It is my contention that this cannot be done unless such an analysis is embedded in an understanding of German society before and during its Nazi period, particularly of the political culture that produced the perpetrators and their actions. This has been notably absent from attempts to explain the perpetrators' actions, and has doomed these attempts to providing situational explanations, ones that focus almost exclusively on institutional and immediate social psychological influences, often conceived of as irresistible pressures. The men and women who became the Holocaust's perpetrators were shaped by and operated in a particular social and historical setting. They brought with them prior elaborate conceptions of the world, ones that were common to their society, the investigation of which is necessary for explaining their actions. This entails, most fundamentally, a reexamination of the character and development of antisemitism in Germany during its Nazi period and before, which in turn requires a theoretical reconsideration of the character of antisemitism itself.

Studies of the Holocaust have been marred by a poor understanding and an under-theorizing of antisemitism. Antisemitism is a broad, typically imprecisely used term, encompassing a wide variety of phenomena. This naturally poses enormous obstacles for explaining the perpetration of the Holocaust because a central task of any such attempt is to evaluate whether and how antisemitism produced and influenced its many aspects. In my view, our understanding of antisemitism and of the relationship of antisemitism to the (mal)treatment of Jews is deficient. We must begin considering these subjects anew and develop a conceptual apparatus that is descriptively powerful and analytically useful for addressing the ideational causes of social action. The first chapter is devoted to initiating such a theoretical reconsideration.

The study of the perpetrators further demands a reconsideration, indeed a reconceiving, of the character of Germany society during its Nazi period and before. The Holocaust was the defining aspect of Nazism, but not only of Nazism. It was also the defining feature of German society during its Nazi period. No significant aspect of Germany society was untouched by anti-Jewish policy; from the economy, to society, to politics, to culture, from cattle farmers, to merchants, to the organization of small towns, to lawyers, doctors, physicists, and professors. No analysis of German society, no understanding or characterization of it, can be made without placing the persecution and extermination of the Jews at its center. The program's first parts, namely the systematic exclusion of Jews from German economic and social life, were carried out in the open, under approving eyes, and with the complicity of virtually all sectors of German society, from the legal, medical, and teaching professions, to the churches, both Catholic and Protestant, to the gamut of economic, social, and cultural groups and associations.[8] Hundreds of thousands of Germans contributed to the genocide and the still larger system of subjugation that was the vast concentration camp system. Despite the regime's half-hearted attempts to keep the genocide beyond the view of most Germans, millions knew of the mass slaughters.[9] Hitler announced many times, emphatically, that the war would end in the extermination of the Jews.[10] The killings met with general understanding, if not approval. No other policy (of similar or greater scope) was carried out with more persistence and zeal, and with fewer difficulties, than the genocide, except perhaps the war itself. The Holocaust defines not only the history of Jews during the middle of the twentieth century but also the history of Germans. While the Holocaust changed Jewry and Jews irrevocably, its commission was possible, I argue, because Germans had *already* been changed. The fat of the Jews may have been a direct, which does not, however, mean an inexorable, outgrowth of a worldview shared by the vast majority of the German people.

Each of these reconceivings—of the perpetrators, of German antisemitism, and of German society during the Nazi period—is complex, requires difficult theoretical work and the marshaling of considerable empirical material, and, ultimately, is deserving of a separate book in its own right. While the undertaking of each one is justifiable on its own theoretical and empirical grounds, each, in my view, is also strengthened by the others, for they are interrelated tasks. Together the three suggest that we must substantially rethink important aspects of German history, the nature of Germany during the Nazi period, and the perpetration of the Holocaust. This rethinking requires, on a number of subjects, the turning of conventional wisdom on its head, and the adoption of a new and substantially different view of essential aspects of this period, aspects which have generally been considered settled. Explaining why the Holocaust occurred requires a radical revision of what has until now been written. This book is that revision.

This revision calls for us to acknowledge what has for so long been generally denied or obscured by academic and non-academic interpreters alike: Germans' antisemitic beliefs about Jews were the central causal agent of the Holocaust. They were the central causal agent not only of Hitler's decision to annihilate European Jewry (which is accepted by many) but also of the perpetrators' willingness to kill and to brutalize Jews. The conclusion of this book is that antisemitism moved many thousands of "ordinary" Germans—and would have moved millions more, had they been appropriately positioned—to slaughter Jews. Not economic hardship, not the coercive means of a totalitarian state, not social psychological pressure, not invariable psychological propensities, but ideas about Jews that were pervasive in Germany, and had been for decades, induced ordinary Germans to kill unarmed, defenseless Jewish men, women, and children by the thousands, systematically and without pity.

* * *

For what developments would a comprehensive explanation of the Holocaust have to account? For the extermination of the Jews to occur, four principal things were necessary:

1. The Nazis—that is, the leadership, specifically Hitler—had to decide to undertake the extermination.[11]
2. They had to gain control over the Jews, namely over the territory in which they resided.[12]
3. They had to organize the extermination and devote to it sufficient resources.[13]
4. They had to induce a large number of people to carry out the killings.

The vast literature on Nazism and the Holocaust treats in great depth the first three elements, as well as others, such as the origins and character of Hitler's genocidal beliefs, and the Nazis' ascendancy to power.[14] Yet, as I have already indicated, it has treated the last element [. . .] perfunctorily and mainly by assumption. It is therefore important to discuss here some analytical and interpretive issues that are central to studying the perpetrators.

Owing to the neglect of the perpetrators in the study of the Holocaust, it is no surprise that the existing interpretations of them have been generally produced in a near empirical vacuum. Until recently, virtually no research has been done on the perpetrators, save on the leaders of the Nazi regime. In the last few years, some publications have appeared that treat one group or another, yet the state of our knowledge about the perpetrators remains deficient.[15] We know little about many of the institutions of killing, little about many aspects of the perpetration of the genocide, and still less about the perpetrators themselves. As a consequence, popular and scholarly myths and misconceptions about the perpetrators abound, including the following. It is commonly believed that the Germans slaughtered Jews by and large in the gas chambers,[16] and that without gas chambers, modern means of transportation, and efficient bureaucracies, the Germans would have been unable to kill millions of Jews. The belief persists that somehow only technology made horror on this scale possible.[17] "Assembly-line killing" is one of the stock phrases in discussions of the event. It is generally believed that gas chambers, because of their efficiency (which is itself greatly overstated), were a necessary instrument for the genocidal slaughter, and that the Germans chose to construct the gas chambers in the first place because they needed more efficient means of killing the Jews.[18] It has been generally believed by scholars (at least until very recently) and non-scholars alike that the perpetrators were primarily, overwhelmingly SS men, the most devoted and brutal Nazis.[19] It has been an unquestioned truism (again until recently) that had a German refused to kill Jews, then he himself would have been killed, sent to a concentration camp, or severely punished.[20] All of these views, views that fundamentally shape people's understanding of the Holocaust, have been held unquestioningly as though they were self-evident truths. They have been virtual articles of faith (derived from sources other than historical inquiry), have substituted for knowledge, and have distorted the way in which this period is understood.

The absence of attention devoted to the perpetrators is surprising for a host of reasons, only one of which is the existence of a now over-ten-year-long debate about the genesis of the *initiation* of the Holocaust, which has come to be called by the misnomer the"intentionalist-functionalist" debate.[21] For better or worse, this debate has become the organizing debate for much of the scholarship on the Holocaust. Although, it has improved our understanding of the exact chronology of the Germans' persecution and mass murder of the Jews, it has also, because of the terms in which it has been cast, confused the analysis of the causes of the Germans' policies [. . .], and it has done next to nothing to increase our knowledge of the perpetrators. Of those who defined this debate and made its central early contributions, only one saw fit to ask the question, Why, once the killing began (however it did), did those receiving the orders to kill do so?[22] It appears that for one reason or another, all the participants in the debate assumed that executing such orders was unproblematic for the actors, and unproblematic for historians and social scientists. The limited character of our knowledge, and therefore our understanding, of this period is highlighted by the simple fact that (however the category of "perpetrator" is defined) the number of people who were perpetrators is unknown. No good estimate, virtually no estimate of any kind, exists of the number of people who knowingly contributed to the genocidal killing in some intimate way. Scholars who discuss them, inexplicably,neither attempt such an estimate nor point out that this, a topic of such great significance, is an important gap in our knowledge.[23] If ten thousand Germans were perpetrators, then the perpetration of the Holocaust, perhaps the Holocaust itself, is a phenomenon of another kind, perhaps the deed of a select, unrepresentative group. If five hundred thousand or one million Germans were perpetrators, then it is a phenomenon of another kind, best conceived as a German national project. Depending on the number and identity of the Germans who contributed to the genocidal slaughter, different sorts of questions, inquiries, and bodies of theory might be appropriate or necessary in order to explain it.

This dearth of knowledge, not only about the perpetrators but also about the functioning of their host institutions has not stopped some interpreters from making assertions about them—although the most striking fact remains how few even bother to address the subject, let alone take it up at length. Still, from the literature a number of conjectured explanations can be distilled, even if they are not always clearly specified or elaborated upon in a sustained manner. (In fact, strands of different explanations are frequently intermingled without great coherence.) Some of them have been proposed to explain the actions of the German people generally and, by extension, they would apply to the perpetrators as well. Rather than laying out what each interpreter has posited about the perpetrators, an analytical account is provided here of the major arguments, with references to leading exemplars of each one. The most important of them can be classified into five categories:

One explanation argues for external compulsion: the perpetrators were coerced. They were left, by the threat of punishment, with no choice but to follow orders. After all, they were part of military or police-like institutions, institutions with a strict chain of command, demanding subordinate compliance to orders, which should have punished insubordination severely, perhaps with death. Put a gun to anyone's head, so goes the thinking, and he will shoot others to save himself.[24]

A second explanation conceives of the perpetrators as having been blind followers of orders. A number of proposals have been made for the source or sources of this alleged propensity to obey: Hitler's charisma (the perpetrators were, so to speak, caught in his spell),[25] a general human tendency to obey authority,[26] a peculiarly German reverence for and propensity to obey authority,[27] or a totalitarian society's blunting of the individual's moral sense and its conditioning of him or her to accept all tasks as necessary.[28] So a common proposition exists, namely that people obey authority, with a variety of accounts of why this is so. Obviously, the notion that authority, particularly state authority, tends to elicit obedience merits consideration.

A third explanation holds the perpetrators to have been subject to tremendous social psychological pressure, placed upon each one by his comrades and/or by the expectations that accompany the institutional roles that individuals occupy. It is, so goes the argument, extremely difficult for individuals to resist pressures to conform, pressures which can lead individuals to participate in acts which they on their own would not do, indeed would abhor. And a variety of psychological mechanisms are available for such people to rationalize their actions.[29]

A fourth explanation sees the perpetrators as having been petty bureaucrats, or soulless technocrats, who pursued their self-interest or their technocratic goals and tasks with callous disregard for the victims. It can hold for administrators in Berlin as well as for concentration camp personnel. They all had careers to make, and because of the psychological propensity among those who are but cogs in a machines to attribute responsibility to others for overall policy, they could callously pursue their own careers or their own institutional or material interests.[30] The deadening effects of institutions upon the sense of individual responsibility, on the one hand, and the frequent willingness of people to put their interests before those of others, on the other, need hardly be belabored.

A fifth explanation asserts that because tasks were so fragmented, the perpetrators could not understand what the real nature of their actions was; they could not comprehend that their small assignments were actually part of a global extermination program. To the extent that they could, this line of thinking continues, the fragmentation of tasks allowed them to deny the importance of their own contributions and to displace responsibility for them onto others.[31] When engaged in unpleasant or morally dubious tasks, it is well known that people have a tendency to shift blame to others.

The explanations can be reconceptualized in terms of their accounts of the actors' capacity for volition: The first explanation (namely coercion) says that the killers could not say "no." The second explanation (obedience) and the third (situational pressure) maintain that Germans were psychologically incapable of saying "no." The fourth explanation (self-interest) contends that Germans had sufficient personal incentives to kill in order not to want to say "no." The fifth explanation (bureaucratic myopia) claims that it never even occurred to the perpetrators that they were engaged in an activity that might make them responsible for saying "no."

Each of these conventional explanations may sound plausible, and some of them obviously contain some truth, so what is wrong with them? While each suffers from particular defects, [. . .] they share a number of dubious *common* assumptions and features worth mentioning here.

The conventional explanations *assume* a neutral or condemnatory attitude on the part of the perpetrators towards their actions. They therefore premise their interpretations on the assumption that it must be shown how people can be brought to commit acts to which they would not inwardly assent, acts which they would not agree are necessary or just. They either ignore, deny, or radically minimize the importance of Nazi and perhaps the perpetrators' ideology, moral values, and conception of the victims, for engendering the perpetrators' willingness to kill. Some of these conventional explanations also caricature the perpetrators, and Germans in general. The explanations treat them as if they had been people lacking a moral sense, lacking the ability to make decisions and take stances. They do not conceive of the actors as human agents, as people with wills, but as beings moved solely by external forces or by transhistorical and invariant psychological propensities, such as the slavish following of narrow "self-interest." The conventional explanations suffer from two other major conceptual failings. They do not sufficiently recognize the extraordinary nature of the deed: the mass killing of people. They *assume* and imply that inducing people to kill human beings is fundamentally no different from getting them to do any other unwanted or distasteful task. Also, none of the conventional explanations deems the *identity* of the victims to have mattered. The conventional explanations imply that the perpetrators would have treated any other group of intended victims in exactly the same way. That the victims were Jews—according to the logic of these explanations—is irrelevant.

I maintain that any explanation that fails to acknowledge the actors' capacity to know and to judge, namely to understand and to have views about the significance and the morality of their actions, that fails to hold the actors' beliefs and values as central, that fails to emphasize the autonomous motivating force of Nazi ideology, particularly its central component of antisemitism, cannot possibly succeed in telling us much about why the perpetrators acted as they did. Any explanation that ignores either the particular nature of the perpetrators' actions—the systematic, large-scale killing and brutalizing of people—or the identity of the victims is inadequate for a host of reasons. All explanations that adopt these positions, as do the conventional explanations, suffer a mirrored, double failure of recognition of the human aspect of the Holocaust: the humanity of the perpetrators, namely their capacity to judge and to choose to act inhumanely, and the humanity of the victims, that what the perpetrators did, they did to these people with their specific identities, and not to animals or things.

My explanation—which is new to the scholarly literature on the perpetrators[32]—is that the perpetrators,"ordinary Germans," were animated by antisemitism, by a particular *type* of antisemitism that led them to conclude that the Jews *ought to die*.[33] The perpetrators' beliefs, their particular brand of antisemitism, though obviously not the sole source, was, I maintain, a most significant and indispensable source of the perpetrators' actions and must be at the center of any explanation of them. Simply put, the perpetrators, having consulted their own convictions and morality and having judged the mass annihilation of Jews to be right, did not *want* to say "no."

Because studying the perpetration of the Holocaust is a difficult task interpretively and methodologically, it is necessary to address a number of issues openly and directly. Consequently, I layout here central features of my approach to the subject, and specify clearly the gamut of perpetrators' actions that needs to be explained. [. . .]

Interpreters of this period make a grave error by refusing to believe that people could slaughter whole populations—especially populations that are by any objective evaluation not threatening—out of conviction. Why persist in the belief that "ordinary" people could not possibly sanction, let alone partake in wholesale human slaughter? The historical record, from ancient times to the present, amply testifies to the ease with which people can extinguish the lives of others, and even take joy in their deaths.[34]

No reason exists to believe that modern, western, even Christian man is incapable of holding notions which devalue human life, which call for its extinction, notions similar to those held by peoples of many religious, cultural, and political dispensations throughout history, including the crusaders and the inquisitors, to name but two relevant examples from twentieth-century Christian Europe's forebears.[35] Who doubts that the Argentine or Chilean murderers of people who opposed the recent authoritarian regimes thought that their victims deserved to die? Who doubts that the Tutsis who slaughtered Hutus in Burundi or the Hutus who slaughtered Tutsis in Rwanda, that one Lebanese militia which slaughtered the civilian supporters of another, that the Serbs who have killed

Croats or Bosnian Muslims, did so out of conviction in the justice of their actions? Why do we not believe the same for the German perpetrators?

The manifold problems in writing about the Holocaust begin with the choice of assumptions that are brought to the study of Germany. [. . .] Perhaps the most important is whether or not it is assumed, as the rule has been for most interpreters of this period, that Germany was more or less a "normal" society operating according to rules of "common sense" similar to our own. For people to be *willing* to slaughter others, in this view, they must be moved by a cynical lust for power or riches or they must be in the grip of a powerful ideology that is so self-evidently false that only the disturbed few could actually succumb to it (aside from those who cynically exploit it for power). The majority of modern people, simple and decent, may be pushed around by these few—but not won over.

Alternatively, this period can be approached without such assumptions, and instead with the critical eye of an anthropologist disembarking on unknown shores, open to meeting a radically different culture and conscious of the possibility that he might need to devise explanations not in keeping with, perhaps even contravening his own common-sense notions, in order to explain the culture's constitution, its idiosyncratic patterns of practice, and its collective projects and products. This would admit the possibility that large numbers of people, in this case Germans, might have killed or been willing to kill others, in this case Jews, in good conscience. Such an approach would not predetermine the task, as virtually all previous studies have done, to be the explanation of what could have forced people to act against their will (or independent of any will, namely like automatons). Instead, it might be necessary to explain how Germans came to be such potential willing mass killers and how the Nazi regime tapped this disastrous potentiality. This approach, which rejects the anthropologically and social-scientifically primitive notion of the universality of our "common sense,"[36] guides this inquiry.[37]

Central and generally unquestioned methodological and substantive assumptions that have guided virtually all scholarship on the Holocaust and its perpetrators are jettisoned here, because such assumptions are theoretically and empirically unsustainable. In contrast to previous scholarship, this book takes the actors' cognition and values seriously and investigates the perpetrators' actions in light of a model of choice. This approach, particularly with regard to the Holocaust, raises a set of social theoretical issues that, however briefly, must be addressed.

The perpetrators were working within institutions that prescribed roles for them and assigned them specific tasks, yet they individually and collectively had latitude to make choices regarding their actions. Adopting a perspective which acknowledges this requires that their choices, especially the patterns of their choices, be discerned, analyzed, and incorporated into any overall explanation or interpretation. Ideal data would answer the following questions:

What did the perpetrators actually do?

What did they do in excess of what was "necessary"?

What did they refuse to do?

What could they have refused to do?

What would they not have done?[38]

What was the manner in which they carried out their tasks?

How smoothly did the overall operations proceed?

In examining the pattern of the perpetrators' actions in light of the institutional role requirements and incentive structure, two directions beyond the simple act of killing must be explored. First, in their treatment of Jews (and other victims), the Germans subjected them to a wide range of acts other than the lethal blow. It is important to understand the *gamut* of their actions towards Jews, if the genocidal slaughter is to be explicated. This is discussed in more detail presently. Second, the perpetrators' actions when they were *not* engaged in genocidal activities also shed light on the killing; the insights that an analysis of their non-killing activities offers into their general character and disposition to action, as well as the general social psychological milieu in which they lived might be crucial for understanding the patterns of their genocidal actions.

All of this points to a fundamental question: Which of the gamut of perpetrators' acts constitute the universe of the perpetrators' actions that need to be explained? Typically, the interpreters of the perpetrators have focused on one facet of the Germans' actions: the killing. This tunnel-vision perspective must be broadened. Imagine that the Germans had not undertaken to exterminate the Jews but had still mistreated them in all the other ways that they did, in concentration camps, in ghettos, as slaves. Imagine if, in our society today, people perpetrated against Jews or Christians, Whites or Blacks anything approaching one one-hundredth of the brutality and cruelty that Germans, independent of the killing, inflicted on Jews. Everyone would recognize the need for an explanation. Had the Germans not perpetrated a genocide, then the degree of privation and cruelty to which the Germans subjected Jews would in itself have come into focus and have been deemed an historic outrage, aberration, perversion that requires explanation. Yet these same actions have been lost in the genocide's shadow and neglected by previous attempts to explain the significant aspects of this event.[39]

The fixation on the mass killing to the exclusion of the other related actions of the perpetrators has led to a radical misspecification of the explanatory task. The killing should be, for all the obvious reasons, at the center of scholarly attention. Yet it is not the only aspect of the Germans' treatment of the Jews that demands systematic scrutiny and explication. Not only the killing but also *how* the Germans killed must be explained. The "how" frequently provides great insight into the "why." A killer can endeavor to render the deaths of others—whether he thinks the killing is just or unjust—more or less painful, both physically and emotionally. The ways in which Germans, collectively and individually, sought in their actions, or merely considered, to alleviate or intensify their victims' suffering must be accounted for in any explanation. An explanation that can seemingly make sense of Germans putting Jews to death, but not of the manner in which they did it, is a faulty explanation.

If analytical clarity is to be achieved, then the actions that need to be explained must be stated clearly. A classificatory scheme that specifies four types of actions can be mapped in two dimensions. One dimension denotes whether or not a German's action was a consequence of an order to perform *that* action or was taken on his own initiative. The other dimension characterizes whether a German perpetrated cruelty.[40]

THE PERPETRATORS' ACTIONS

Ordered by Authority

		Yes	No
Cruelty	Yes	Organized and "Structured" Cruelty	"Excesses" Such as Torture
	No	Killing Operations and Individual Killings	"Acts of Initiative" Such as Individually Initiated Killings

Acts committed under orders, such as rounding up, deporting, and killing Jews, which were devoid of "excess" or "surplus" cruelty, are acts that in the German context of the times were utilitarian in intent. They were the deeds that the proverbial (mythical) good German who merely slavishly "followed orders" is alleged to have committed. "Acts of initiative" and "excesses" are really both acts of initiative, not done as the mere carrying out of superior orders. Crucially, both are acts of voluntarism on the part of the individual perpetrators. They differ in the dimension of cruelty—the "acts of initiative" having been the actions of the cool executioner, the "excesses" that of the German who, presumably, took special pleasure in the suffering that he inflicted. The final category of action comprises those actions that Germans undertook under orders, the sole purpose of which was to inflict suffering on the Jews. Such actions are interesting, and some of them are discussed in the case chapters, because they cast doubt on the perpetrators' retrospective rationales for their actions which they have typically proffered after the war. Although the sorts of sham reasons that were ordinarily offered to the men at the time (and by them after the war) for killing Jews (for example, that the Jews threatened Germany, that they were "partisans" and "bandits," or that they spread disease) could perhaps have been believed by a Nazified mind in search of some utilitarian reason for the genocidal slaughter, orders to torture victims should have cast doubt on the "legality" and "reasonableness" of the alleged rationale for their overall treatment of the Jews.

The perpetrators' treatment of Jews, even the act of killing, consisted of different actions, or variables, each of which requires explanation. Any general explanation of Germans' contribution to genocidal slaughter must account for all of them. Large in number, the sorts of actions that need to be explained include those specified by the two dimensions of actions done with or without authoritative directive, and actions which were or were not cruel:

1. All perpetrator actions carried out under orders without surplus cruelty, the most important of these having been those that contributed to genocidal killing.
2. Perpetrator cruelties committed by dint of authority's directives. Institutional, structured cruelties are more important than those carried out on an *ad hoc* basis by individuals or small groups.
3. Perpetrator actions that required initiative beyond what was strictly ordered or required by authority, but which were not marked by "excessive" cruelty.
4. Perpetrator cruelties performed on the perpetrator's own initiative.

This kind of objective characterization of the perpetrators' actions, as useful as it is, remains insufficient either for adequate description and classification, or as the complete basis for explanation. Unless further qualified, this analytical scheme, like previous interpretations of the perpetrators, suggests that "order following" is an unproblematic category. Yet it must be recognized that other actions—such as an individual's disobeyal of other orders, although he carries out the lethal ones—may shed light on the meaning of "order following" in this specific context. In other words, if Germans discriminated among the orders that they chose to follow or in how well they chose to execute them, then the mere obeying of orders, as well as the manner of their execution, needs to be investigated and explained. This action classification also ignores the potential opportunities that perpetrators had to extract themselves from situations or institutions where they were likely to receive tasks that they deemed undesirable.[41] In short, these naïve characterizations of "obeying orders" or of "acting under orders" shear the perpetrators' actions out of their broader social, political, and institutional context. It is necessary to recapture this context if the actors' willingness to obey orders is to become intelligible.

In light of this discussion, the following must be considered: The first category of action or variable, obeying orders, is not itself unproblematic. German perpetrators had available to them the options of trying to avoid killing duty or to lessen the suffering of the victims. Why did they exercise these options as they did, not more and not less? Knowledge of the second type of action, authoritative cruelties, should lead us to pose the question of why large-scale institutions in the middle of twentieth-century Europe came to be structured in a manner that would purposely promote, to whatever extent they did, enormous misery for their inhabitants. All the institutions were, for their nature and functioning, dependent upon their personnel. The third type of action, initiative or voluntarism, to the extent that it characterized German conduct, obviously needs to be explained, for it might be supposed that those who opposed mass murder would have done no more than the minimum required of them. The fourth type of action, individual cruelty, must, it goes without saying, be explained.[42]

An explanation must account for two more aspects of the perpetrators' actions. The first is the manner in which the perpetrators carried out their assignments, whether half-heartedly or zealously. Even those acts that Germans undertook because of orders should be assessed for their zeal of implementation. An actor can perform a job with various degrees of dedication, thoroughness, and accomplishment. When Germans were searching for hidden Jews, they could have done their utmost to uncover them or could have sought them out in a dilatory, half-hearted manner. The Germans' zeal of implementation both provides insight into their motivation and itself needs to be explained. A second additional feature that requires explanation relates to the horror of their deeds. Why did the horror, brutality, and frequent gruesomeness of the killing operations fail to stay the perpetrators' hands or at least substantially daunt them? The horrific nature of the operations was, of course, not a type of action on the part of the perpetrators, but one of the conditions of their actions that might be thought to have been so revolting and off-putting that its failure to have affected the perpetrators significantly is itself in need of explanation.[43]

Even with these qualifications, this approach must be broadened beyond being an objective categorization of actions to include an investigation of the motives of those Germans performing acts in a given category, particularly among the "order followers." No matter what category of action a person's act is properly classified as, the person's attitude towards his act, and his motivation to undertake it, is still important, for it renders the act itself one thing or another.[44] This "objective" categorization needs to be supplemented by a subjective one of motivation. A variety of motives is compatible with acting under orders, with showing initiative, with committing "excesses," or with doing a job well or badly. Most important is the question of whether or not the perpetrators believed their treatment of the Jews to be just and, if so, why.[45]

The motivational dimension is the most crucial for explaining the perpetrator' willingness to act, and to a great extent is a product of the social construction of knowledge.[46] The types of actions that a person is wiling to carry out— whether only those directly ordered, those that take initiative, those that are excessive, and those that are the product of zealousness—are derived from a person's motivation; but the person's actions do not *necessarily* correspond to his motivations, because his actions are influenced by the circumstances and opportunities for action. Obviously, without opportunity, a person's motivation to kill or to torture cannot be acted upon. But opportunity alone does not a killer or torturer make.

To say that every (socially significant) action must be motivated does not mean that all acts are merely the result of the actor's prior beliefs about the desirability and justice of the action. It simply means that a person must decide to undertake the action and that some mental calculation (even if he does not conceive of it in such terms) leads him to decide not to refrain from undertaking the action. The mental calculation can include a desire to advance one's career, not to be ridiculed by comrades, or not to be shot for insubordination. A person might kill another without believing in the justice of the death if, despite the understood injustice, he is sufficiently motivated to act by other considerations, such as his own well-being. Wanting to protect one's life is a motive. As such, structures, incentives, or sanctions, formal or informal, can themselves never be motives; they only provide inducements to act or not to act, which the actor might consider when deciding what he will do.[47] Now, of course, certain situations are such that the vast majority of people will act in the same manner, seemingly regardless of their prior beliefs and intentions. Instances of this sort have tempted many to conclude, erroneously, that "structures" cause action.[48] The structures, however, are always interpreted by the actors, who, if they share similar cognitions and values (preserving one's life is a value, as is wanting to live in a "racially pure" society, or wanting to succeed in one's career, or seeking monetary gain, or wanting to be like others at all costs), will respond to them in a like manner. Not every person will place his own well-being over principle; not every person will violate deeply held moral positions because his comrades do not share them. If people do, then the values—which are not universal values and certainly not universal social psychological dispositions—that lead them to do so must be seen as a crucial part of the explanation. Some people will risk their lives for others, renounce the advancement of their careers, dissent in word and deed from their comrades. Inanimate objects do not independently produce cognition and values; all new cognition and values depend upon a preexisting framework of cognition and value that lends meaning to the material circumstances of people's lives. And it is cognition and values, and only cognition and values, that in the last instant move someone willfully to pick up his hand and strike another.

Whatever the cognitive and value structures of individuals may be, changing the incentive structure in which they operate might, and in many cases will certainly, induce them to alter their actions, as they calculate the desired course of action in light of what they know and value, and the possibilities of realizing them in differing mixes. This, it must be emphasized, does not mean that the incentive structure itself is causing people to act, but only that it *in conjunction with the cognitive and value structures* are together producing the action.

Explaining the perpetrators' actions demands, therefore, that the perpetrators' phenomenological reality be taken seriously. We must attempt the difficult enterprise of imagining ourselves in their places, performing their deeds, acting as they did, viewing what they beheld.[49] To do so we must always bear in mind the essential nature of their actions as perpetrators: they were killing defenseless men, women, and children, people who were obviously of no martial threat to them, often emaciated and weak, in unmistakable physical and emotional agony, and sometimes begging for their lives or those of their children. Too many interpreters of this period, particularly when they are psychologizing, discuss the Germans' actions as if they were discussing the commission of mundane acts, as if they need explain little more than how a good man might occasionally shoplift.[50] They lose sight of the fundamentally different, extraordinary, and trying character of these acts. The taboo in many societies, including western ones, against killing defenseless people, against killing children, is great. The psychological mechanisms that permit "good" people to commit minor moral transgressions, or to turn a blind eye even to major ones committed by others, particularly if they are far away, cannot be applied to people's perpetration of genocidal killing, to their slaughter of hundreds of others before their own eyes—without careful consideration of such mechanisms' appropriateness for elucidating such actions.

Explaining this genocidal slaughter necessitates, therefore, that we keep two things always in mind. When writing or reading about killing operations, it is too easy to become insensitive to the numbers on the page. Ten thousand dead in one place, four hundred in another, fifteen in a third. Each of us should pause and consider that ten thousand deaths meant that Germans killed ten thousand individuals—unarmed men, women, and children, the old, the young, and the sick—that Germans took a human life ten thousand times. Each of us should ponder what that might have meant for the Germans participating in the slaughter. When a person considers his or her own anguish, abhorrence, or revulsion, his or her own moral outrage at the murder of one person, or of a contemporary "mass murder" of, say, twenty people—whether by a serial killer, or by a semiautomatic-toting sociopath in a fast food outlet—that person gains some perspective on the reality that these Germans confronted. The Jewish victims were not the "statistics" that they appear to us on paper. To the killers whom they faced, the Jews were people who were breathing one moment and lying lifeless, often before them, the next. All of this took place independent of military operations.

The second item to bear in mind, always, is the horror of what the Germans were doing. Anyone in a killing detail who himself shot or who witnessed his comrades shoot Jews was immersed in scenes of unspeakable horror. To present mere clinical descriptions of the killing operations is to misrepresent the phenomenology of killing, to eviscerate the emotional components of the acts, and to skew any understanding of them. The proper description of the events under discussion, the re-creation of the phenomenological reality of the killers, is crucial for any explication. For this reason, I eschew the clinical approach and try to convey the horror, the gruesomeness, of the events *for the perpetrators* (which, of course, does not mean that they were always horrified). Blood, bone, and brains were flying about, often landing on the killers, smirching their faces and staining their clothes. Cries and wails of people awaiting their imminent slaughter or consumed in death throes reverberated in German ears. Such scenes—not the antiseptic descriptions that mere reportage of a killing operation presents—constituted the reality for many perpetrators. For us to comprehend the perpetrators' phenomenological world, we should describe for ourselves every gruesome image that they beheld, and every cry of anguish and pain that they heard.[51] The discussion of any killing operation, of any single death, should be replete with such descriptions. This, of course, cannot be done, because it would make any study of the Holocaust unacceptably lengthy, and also because few readers would be able to persevere in reading through the gruesome accounts—such inability itself being a powerful commentary on the extraordinary phenomenology of the perpetrators' existence and the powerful motivations that must have impelled Germans to silence such emotions so that they could kill and torture Jews, including children, as they did.

Abbreviations

BAK	Bundesarchiv Koblenz
Buchs	ZStL 205 AR-Z 20/60
Dörr	Investigation and trial of Alois Dörr, StA Hof 2 Js 1325/62
Grünberg	ZStL 410 AR 1750/61
HG	Investigation of H.G. et al., StA Hamburg 141 Js 128/65
HGS	*Holocaust and Genocide Studies*
Hoffmann	Investigation and trial of Wolfgang Hoffmann et al., StA Hamburg 141 Js 1957/62
HSSPF	Higher SS and Police Leader
IMT	*Trials of the Major War Criminals Before the International Military Tribunal,* vols. 1–42
JK	ZStL 206 AR-Z 6/62
Kdo	Commander of the Order Police
KR	ZStL 208 AR 967/69
Nazism	J. Noakes and G. Pridham, eds., *Nazism: A History in Documents and Eyewitness*

	Accounts, 1919–1945 (New York: Schocken Books, 1988)
SSPF	SS and Police Leader
SSPF Lublin	Investigation Against the *SSPF* Lublin, ZStL 208 AR-Z 74/60
StA	Office of the State Prosecutor
StAH	Hamburg State Archive
Streckenbach	Indictment Against Streckenbach, ZStL 201 AR-Z 76/59
TWC	*Trials of War Criminals before the Nürnberg Military Tribunals under Control Council Law No. 10. Nürnberg, October 1946–April 1949*, vols. 1–15
VfZ	*Vierteljahrshefte für Zeitgeschichte*
YVS	*Yad Vashem Studies*
ZStL	Zentrale Stelle der Landesjustizverwaltungen zur Aufklärung nationalsozialistische Verbrechen in Ludwigsburg

Notes

1. See letter of Jan. 30, 1943, StA Hamburg 147 Js 1957/62, pp. 523–524.
2. They departed from this admittedly vague standard, both in the ordinary language sense of being civilized and in Norbert Elias' social theoretical sense of imposing external and especially internal controls over emotional displays, including outbursts of destructive violence. See *The Civilizing Process,* 2 vols., (New York: Pantheon, 1978).
3. Definitional and substantive issues pertaining to the category of "perpetrators" are discussed in Chapter 5 of *Hitler's Willing Executioners.*
4. The literature's neglect of the perpetrators takes more subtle form than a mere failure to focus on them. Through conscious, half-conscious, and unconscious linguistic usage, the perpetrators often, and for some authors, typically, disappear from the page and from the deeds. The use of the passive voice removes the actors from the scene of carnage, from their own acts. It betrays the authors' understanding of the events and forms the public's comprehension of them, an understanding robbed of human agency. See Martin Broszat and Saul Friedländer, "A Controversy about the Historicization of National Socialism," in Peter Baldwin, ed. *Reworking the Past: Hitler, the Holocaust, and the Historians' Debate* (Boston: Beacon Press, 1990), pp. 102–134, for a discussion of this tendency in the work of Martin Broszat, one of the most influential interpreters of the Holocaust and of Germany during the Nazi period.
5. We do not hesitate to refer to the citizens of the United States who fought in Vietnam to achieve the aims of their government as "Americans," and for good reason. The reason is just as good in the case of Germans and the Holocaust. The perpetrators were Germans as much as the soldiers in Vietnam were Americans, even if not

all people in either country supported their nation's efforts. Customary usage for analogous cases, as well as descriptive accuracy and rectitude, not only permit but also mandate the use of "Germans" as the term of choice. Moreover, the Jewish victims conceived of the German perpetrators and referred to them overwhelmingly not as Nazis but as Germans. This usage does not mean that all Germans are included when the term "Germans" is employed (just as the term "Americans" does not implicate every single American), because some Germans opposed and resisted the Nazis as well as the persecution of the Jews. That they did so does not alter the identity of those who were perpetrators, or what we should properly call them.

A real terminological problem exits when discussing "Germans, because "Germans," particularly when contrasted to "Jews," seems to imply that the Jews of Germany were not also Germans. I have, with some misgivings, decided to call Germans simply "Germans" and not to use some cumbersome locution like "non-Jewish Germans." Thus, whenever German Jews are referred to as "Jews," their Germanness is implicit.

6.   Many non-Germans contributed to the genocidal slaying of Jews, particularly various formations of eastern European auxiliaries who worked in conjunction with Germans under German supervision. Perhaps the most notable of these were the so-called Trawnikis, the mainly Ukrainian auxiliaries who contributed greatly to the decimation of the Jews living in the *Generalgouvernement,* by being parties to deportations and mass shootings and working in the extermination centers of Treblinka, Belzec, and Sobibór. The Germans found willing helpers in Lithuania, Latvia, in the various regions of the conquered Soviet Union, in other countries of eastern and central Europe, and in western Europe as well. Generally speaking, these perpetrators have been neglected in the literature on this period. Their comparative study should be undertaken (and is discussed briefly in Chapter 15), yet it is not an integral part of this book, for two reasons. The first, already mentioned, is that the Germans and not the non-Germans were the prime movers and executors of the Holocaust. The second is a practical consideration. This book is already ambitious in scope, so its purview had to be restricted so as to be manageable. The study of non-German perpetrators, which would include a large number of people of many nationalities, is the fitting subject for another project. For a discussion of the disposition of ethnic Germans during the war, see Valdis O. Lumans, *Himmler's Auxiliaries: The Volksdeutsche Mittelstelle and the German National Minorities of Europe, 1933–1945* (Chapel Hill: University of North Carolina Press, 1993); for the contributions of the "Trawnikis," the east European auxiliaries who manned the extermination camps of Belzec, Treblinka, and Sobibór, and who killed and brutalized tens of thousands of Jews while deporting them from the ghettos of Poland or while shooting them themselves, see Judgment Against Karl Richard Streibel et al., Hamburg 147 Ks 1/72; for the Soviet Union,see Richard Breitman, "Himmler's Police Auxiliaries in the Occupied Soviet Territories," *Simon Wiesenthal Annual* 7(1994): pp. 23–39.

7.   See Clifford Geertz, "Thick Description: Toward an Interpretive Theory of Culture," in *The Interpretation of Cultures: Selected Essays* (New York: Basic Books, 1973), pp. 3–30.

8.   This is discussed in Chapter 3 of *Hitler's Willing Executioners.*

9.   See Hans-Heinrich Wilhelm, "The Holocaust in National-Socialist Rhetoric and Writings: Some Evidence against the Thesis that before 1945 Nothing Was Known about the 'Final Solution,' " *YVS* 16 (1984): pp. 95–127; and Wolfgang Benz, "The Persecution and Extermination of the Jews in the German Consciousness," in John

Milfull, ed., *Why Germany? National Socialist Anti-Semitism and the European Context* (Providence: Berg Publishers, 1993), pp. 91–104, esp. 97–98.

10. See, for example, Max Domarus, *Hitler: Speeches and Proclamations, 1932–1945* (London: I. B. Tauris, 1990), vol. 1, p. 41; and C. C. Aronsfeld, *The Text of the Holocaust: A Study of the Nazis' Extermination Propaganda, from 1919–1945* (Marblehead, Mass.: Micah Publications, 1985), pp. 34–36.

11. This is the subject of the "intentionalist-functionalist" debate discussed below. On the motivation for the decision to exterminate European Jewry, see Erich Goldhagen, "Obsession and *Realpolitik* in the 'Final Solution,' " *Patterns of Prejudice* 12, no. 1 (1978): pp. 1–16; and Eberhard Jäckel, *Hitler's World View: A Blueprint for Power* (Cambridge: Harvard University Press, 1981).

12. This was a consequence of Germany's military expansion.

13. This is a major focus of Raul Hilberg, *The Destruction of the European Jews* (New York: New Viewpoints, 1973).

14. Naturally, it is the biographers of Hitler who wrestle most with this question. See, for example, Allan Bullock, *Hitler: A Study in Tyranny* (Harmondsworth: Penguin, 1974); Robert G. L. Waite, *The Psychopathic God: Adolf Hitler* (New York: Signet Books, 1977); Joachim C. Fest, *Hitler* (New York: Vintage, 1975); see also Hitler's own account in Adolf Hitler, *Mein Kampf* (Boston: Houghton Mifflin, 1971). For two treatments of the Nazis' ascent to power, see Karl Dietrich Bracher, *Die Auflösung der Weimarer Republik* (Villingen: Schwarzwald Ring Verlag, 1964); and William Sheridan Allen, *The Nazi Seizure of Power: The Experience of a Single German Town, 1922–1945,* rev. ed. (New York: Franklin Watts, 1984).

15. These are discussed in Chapter 5 of *Hitler's Willing Executioners.*

16. The focus on the gassing, to the exclusion of other features of the Holocaust, with the exception of a fair amount of attention that has been devoted to the *Einsatzgruppen,* justified the title of Wolfgang Scheffler's article "The Forgotten Part of the 'Final Solution': The Liquidation of the Ghettos," *Simon Wiesenthal Center Annual* 2 (1985): pp. 31–51.

17. This is a common notion, whose most prominent exponent is Hilberg, *The Destruction of the European Jews.*

18. See Uwe Dietrich Adam's recent discussion, "The Gas Chambers," in François Furet, ed., *Unanswered Questions: Nazi Germany and the Genocide of the Jews* (New York: Schocken Books, 1989), pp. 134–154. He opens the essay appropriately: "Even today certain false ideas and abusive generalizations about the existence, placement, functioning, and 'efficiency' of the gas chambers continue to circulate even in reputable historical works, and these lead to confusion and errors" (p. 134).

19. This is demonstrated by the literature's general, overwhelming failure to discuss the perpetrators in a manner which indicates clearly that many were not SS men; had this been understood, then it would have been emphasized as an important feature of the genocide.

20. It is astonishing how readily available material on this has been ignored; it is not even mentioned in virtually all of the standard works on the Holocaust, including the most recent treatments. This subject is taken up at length during the discussion of police battalions in Part III and in Chapter 15 of *Hitler's Willing Executioners.*

21. For the positions of the major protagonists, see Tim Mason, "Intention and Explanation: A Current Controversy about the Interpretation of National Socialism," in Gerhard Hirschfeld and Lothar Kettenacker, eds., *Der "Führerstaat": Mythos and Realität* (Stuttgart: Klett-Cotta, 1981), pp. 23–40; Ian Kershaw, *The Nazi Dictatorship: Problems and Perspectives of Interpretation,* 3d ed. (London, Edward

Arnold, 1993), pp. 80–107; and Michael R. Marrus, *The Holocaust in History* (Hanover: University Press of New England, 1987), pp. 31–51.

22. Hans Mommsen, "The Realization of the Unthinkable: The 'Final Solution of the Jewish Question' in the Third Reich," in Gerhard Hirschfeld, ed., *The Policies of Genocide: Jews and Soviet Prisoners of War in Nazi Germany* (London: Allen & Unwin, 1986), pp. 98–99.

23. *Encyclopedia of the Holocaust,* 4 vols., ed. Israel Gutman (New York: Macmillan, 1990), for example, which attempts to summarize and codify the state of knowledge about the Holocaust, and which provides statistics on an enormous array of matters, as far as I can tell, neither addresses the subject nor provides an estimate.

24. This is obviously a widely shared belief among the public that the perpetrators had the choice either to kill or to be killed. Few recent scholarly interpreters have made this assertion so baldly. For one, see Sarah Gordon, *Hitler, Germans and the "Jewish Question"* (Princeton: Princeton University Press, 1984), who says as much about the German army's cooperation in the genocide (p. 283).

25. See Saul Friedländer, *History and Psychoanalysis: An Inquiry into the Possibilities and Limits of Psychohistory* (New York: Holmes & Meier, 1978).

26. See Stanley Milgram, *Obedience to Authority: An Experimental View* (New York: Harper Colophon, 1969). See also Herbet C. Kelman and V. Lee Hamilton, *Crimes of Obedience: Toward A Social Psychology of Authority and Responsibility* (New Haven: Yale University Press, 1989).

27. This propensity is sometimes conceived of as having been historically formed. See Erich Fromm, *Escape from Freedom* (New York: Avon Books, 1965); and G.P. Gooch et al., *The German Mind and Outlook* (London: Chapman & Hall, 1945).

28. See Hannah Arendt, *The Origins of Totalitarianism* (New York: Meridian, 1971). Hans Mommsen, in "The Realization of the Unthinkable," pp. 98–99, 128–129, follows a related line of reasoning, as does Rainer C. Baum, *The Holocaust and the German Elite: Genocide and National Suicide in Germany, 1871–1945* (Totawa, N.J.: Rowman & Littlefield, 1981).

29. The most recent and most considered account of this sort is Christopher R. Browning, *Ordinary Men: Reserve Police Battalion 101 and the Final Solution in Poland* (New York: HarperCollins, 1992). Essentially, this is also Hilberg's position in *The Destruction of the European Jews*. Robert Jay Lifton, who has studied the German doctors at Auschwitz in *The Nazi Doctors: Medical Killing and the Psychology of Genocide* (New York: Basic Books, 1986), provides a psychoanalytic explanation for how professional healers could become killers, how otherwise decent men could perpetrate such evil. It too depends on situational factors and psychological mechanisms, and its psychoanalytical bearing notwithstanding, falls into this category.

30. Mommsen, "The Realization of the Unthinkable"; Götz Aly and Susanne Heim, *Vordenker der Venichtung: Auschwitz und die deutschen Pläne für eine neue europäische Ordnung* (Hamburg: Hoffmann and Campe, 1991); also Gordon, *Hitler, Germans and the "Jewish Question," p. 312.*

31. This explanation is so untenable in the face of what the actual killers were doing, such as shooting defenseless people at point-blank range, that it need be mentioned only because some have seen fit to put it forward. Marrus, an exponent of this view, writes with unwarranted certitude: "As students of the Holocaust have long understood, the extensive division of labor associated with the killing process helped perpetrators diffuse their own responsibility." See *The Holocaust in History,* p. 47. To the (small) extent that this is true, it is a tiny part of the story and not, as Marrus appears to be contending, almost the whole of it.

32. A partial exception is the acknowledgement by Herbert Jäger, *Verbrechen unter totalitärer Herrschaft: Studien zur nationalsozialitischen Gewaltkriminalität* (Olton: Walter-Verlag, 1967), that some percentage of the perpetrators acted out of ideological conviction (pp. 62–64). Jäger, however, does not believe that it was ideological conviction that moved most of the perpetrators (see pp. 76–78). On the whole, as the book's title, "Crimes under Totalitarian Domination," suggests, Jäger accepts the 1950s totalitarian model of Germany during the Nazi period (see pp. 186–208), employing concepts such as "totalitarian mentality" (*totalitäre Geisteshaltung*) (p. 186). This model—wrong in the most fundamental of ways and which continues to obscure for many the substantial freedom and pluralism that actually existed within German society—consistently misdirects Jäger's analysis, which in many ways is rich and insightful. For revisions and critiques of the totalitarian model's applicability to Germany during the Nazi period and of the general issues and debates in classifying Nazism, see Kershaw, *The Nazi Dictatorship*, pp. 17–39. Hans Safrian, in the introduction to his recent study of those who worked under Adolf Eichmann to deport European Jewry to their deaths, has also called into question the historical consensus that antisemitism did not motivate the perpetrators, though he fails to develop this a notion much beyond asserting it. See *Die Eichmann-Männer* (Vienna: Europaverlag, 1993), pp. 17–22.

33. Others have of course recognized and emphasized the importance of political ideology and antisemitism for the Nazi *leadership's* decision to undertake the total extermination of the Jews. For a wide-ranging discussion of this issue, see Eberhard Jäckel and Järgen Rohwer, eds., *Der Mord an den Juden im Zweiten Weltkrieg: Entschlussbildung und Verwirklichung* (Stuttgart: Deutsche Verlags-Anstalt, 1985); Lucy Dawidowicz, *The War Against the Jews, 1933–1945* (New York: Bantam Books, 1975); Gerald Fleming, *Hitler and the Final Solution* (Berkeley: University of California Press, 1984), and Saul Friedländer's introduction to the book; and Klaus Hildebrand, *The Third Reich* (London: Allen & Unwin, 1984). Those who do take this position, however, either have not looked at the perpetrators or have denied that the perpetrators as a group were themselves moved by similar cognitions. Marrus, citing approvingly Hans Mommsen, speaks for the historical consensus in his historiographic *The Holocaust in History:* "Antisemitic indoctrination is plainly an insufficient answer, for we know [*sic*] that many of the officials involved in the administration of mass murder did not come to their tasks displaying intense antisemitism. In some cases, indeed, they appear to have had no history of anti-Jewish hatred and to have been coldly uninvolved with their victims" (p. 47). Erich Goldhagen is an exception to this general consensus, and although he has not published on the subject, he has emphasized in his course lectures and in our many conversations precisely the point being made here. Thus, while my claim might not sound so novel to some, it actually stands in contradiction to the existing literature.

34. For an overview of a number of cases from the recent and distant past, see Frank Chalk and Kurt Jonassohn, *The History and Sociology of Genocide: Analyses and Case Studies* (New Haven: Yale University Press, 1990).

35. See Cecil Roth, *The Spanish Inquisition* (New York: W.W. Norton, 1964); and Malise Ruthven, *Torture: the Grand Conspiracy* (London: Weidenfeld & Nicolson, 1978). The Spanish in the New World were genocidally murderous towards the indigenous inhabitants, usually in the name of Jesus; see Bartolome de las Casa, *The Devastation of the Indies: a Brief Account* (New York: Seabury Press, 1974).

36. See Clifford Geertz, "Common Sense as a Cultural System," in *Local Knowledge: Further Essays in Interpretive Anthropology* (New York: Basic Books, 1983).

37. The crucial subject of how different starting assumptions bias conclusions by requiring different kinds of falsifying evidence is discussed in Chapter 1 of *Hitler's Willing Executioners*. Generally speaking, the fewer data that exist on a given subject, the more prejudicial the assumptions will be. And since interpretations of the issue at hand often depend on readings of the actors' cognitions, for which the data is far from ideal, particular attention must be given to justifying the assumptions being used; incompatible assumptions about, say, the attitudes of Germans may *each* be "unfalsifiable"; data that allows for generalizing with confidence about large groups of Germans is often hard to come by, so most data can be deemed by someone holding a given assumption to be anecdotal and therefore not sufficient to *falsify* the initial assumption.

38. This is obviously hypothetical, yet thinking about it—particularly if the conclusion drawn is that boundaries did exist which the perpetrators would not have crossed—should lead to a consideration of the nature of the limits of their willingness to act.

39. Primo Levi, *The Drowned and the Saved* (New York: Summit Books, 1986), is one who attempts, not entirely successfully, to understand the Germans' cruelty (pp. 105–126).

40. Discussing and delimiting "cruelty" for the phenomena that collectively compose the Holocaust, or, more broadly, the Germans' persecution of European Jewry, is always difficult. The Germans' actions were so "out of this world" that they skew our frames of reference. Killing innocent people might be justly conceived of as being an act of cruelty, as would forcing people who are emaciated and debilitated to perform taxing manual labor. Still, these were ordinary—"normal" in the German context of the times—utilitarian parts of the Germans' jobs, so it makes sense to distinguish them from acts (in this context) of gratuitous cruelty, such as beating, mocking, torturing Jews or forcing them to perform senseless, debilitating labor for the sole purpose of immiserating them further.

41. Jäger, *Verbrechen unter totalitärer Herreschaft,* is aware of these issues, the discussion of which he pioneered in the published literature. See pp. 76–160. For another discussion of this issue, see Hans Buchheim, "Command and Compliance," in Helmut Krausnick et al., *Anatomy of the SS State* (London: Collins, 1968), pp. 303–396.

42. German cruelty towards Jews occurred not only during the killing operations. This is another reason why cruelty (and the other actions) are best conceptualized as variables and analytically distinct from the killing itself.

43. The horror is significant for still another reason. Since Hannah Arendt, a dominant strand of interpretation has assumed or explicitly held that the perpetrators were "affectively neutral," devoid of emotion towards the Jews. All explanations which deny the importance of the identity of the victims, at least potentially imply that the perpetrators' views about the victims, whatever they were, were not causally important. As if the wholesale killing of people alone were not sufficient to force the perpetrators to examine their views of their actions, having to confront the horror of their deeds would have made it virtually impossible for them to have no view of the desirability of the slaughter. The notion that the perpetrators were totally neutral towards the Jews is, I am willing to assert, a psychological impossibility. And if not neutral, then what did they think of Jews, what emotions did they bring to the mass slaughters? Whatever these cogitations and emotions were, how did they influence the perpetrators' actions? This line of thinking is meant merely to emphasize the need to investigate as thoroughly as possible the cognitions of the perpetrators, indeed their shared cognitions; for once it is admitted that they could not have been

neutral towards their actions and the victims, then their thoughts and feelings must be taken seriously as sources of their actions.

44. See Max Weber, *Economy and Society,* eds. Guenther Roth and Claus Wittich (Berkeley: University of California Press, 1978), pp. 8–9.

45. Categorizing the killings and the killers is difficult. One question to ask in thinking about them is: What would an enabling order such as "Do what you can to kill Jews," which carried no sanctions and promised no rewards, have spurred each German to have done and why? Would he have sat immobile? Would he have worked towards their deaths in a perfunctory manner? Killed with efficiency? Or zealously pursued, with body and soul, the extermination of as many Jews as possible?

46. Obviously, in order to answer the questions guiding this inquiry, it is not enough to explicate the motivations of those who set policy or of those who worked at the pinnacle of the genocidal institutions. The elite's motivations and actions are, of course, important, so it is good that we know already a fair amount about many of them. For a few examples, see Waite, *The Psychopathic God;* Richard Breitman, *The Architect of Genocide: Himmler and the Final Solution* (New York: Alfred A. Knopf, 1991); Matthias Schmidt, *Albert Speer: The End of a Myth* (New York: St. Martin's Press, 1984); and Ruth Bettina Birn, *Die Höheren SS- und Polizeiführer: Himmlers Vertreter im Reich und in den besetzten Gebieten* (Düsseldorf: Droste Verlag, 1986).

47. Anthony Giddens, *The Constitution of Society: Outline of the Theory of Structuration* (Berkeley: University of California Press, 1984), writes: "Structural constraint is not expressed in terms of the implacable causal forms which structural sociologists have in mind when they emphasize so strongly the association of 'structure' with 'constraint.' Structural constraints do not operate independently of the motives and reasons that agents have for what they do. They cannot be compared with the effect of, say, an earthquake which destroys a town and its inhabitants without their in any way being able to do anything about it. The only moving objects in human social relations are individual agents, who employ resources to make things happen, intentionally or otherwise. The structural properties of social systems do not act, or 'act on,' anyone like forces of nature to 'compel' him or her to behave in a particular way" (pp. 180–181).

48. For an example of this kind of reasoning, see Theda Skocpol, *States and Social Revolutions: A Comparative Analysis of France, Russia, and China* (Cambridge: Cambridge University Press, 1979).

49. This recommendation follows in the tradition of Weber's demand for achieving "*Verstehen.*" See Weber, *Economy and Society,* pp. 4–24.

50. See Marrus, *The Holocaust in History,* p. 51.

51. Part of the reason that many have failed to understand the killers and the moving forces behind the Holocaust is likely that they have systematically, if not self-consciously, avoided coming to grips with the phenomenological horror of the genocidal killings. Reading most of the "explanations" reveals few gruesome scenes; when presented, they are typically followed by little analysis, the horror remaining unexplored, mute, as the discussion turns to other (often logistical) matters. When ghetto roundups and deportations, mass slaughters, and gassings are mentioned, they are frequently merely recorded as having happened. The horror of specific killing operations is not adequately conveyed, which makes it difficult to comprehend the compass of the horror for the perpetrators, the frequency of their immersion in it, and its cumulative toll on them.

Those who do take into account the horrors are the survivors and the scholars who focus on them. These people, however, have as a rule not concerned themselves with explaining the perpetrators' acts, except impressionistically and in passing. An interesting feature of scholarship on the Holocaust is how little overlap and intersection there has been between those who write about the perpetrators and those who write about the victims. My work is not much of an exception in this respect.

52 Jäger, *Verbrechen unter totalitärer Herrschaft,* is an obvious exception to this, as is, to a lesser extent, Browning, *Ordinary Men;* Hermann Langbein, *Menschen in Auschwitz* (Frankfurt/M: Ullstein, 1980), also takes cognizance of the varieties of the perpetrators' actions.

53. Those who, like Browning in *Ordinary Men,* have failed to integrate their investigations adequately with the two higher levels of analysis.

Reading 15

WHAT DOES THE DREADED "E" WORD MEAN, ANYWAY?
A Reverie for the Opening of the New Hayden Planetarium

Stephen Jay Gould

Evolution posed no terrors in the liberal constituency of New York City when I studied biology at Jamaica High school in 1956. But our textbooks didn't utter the word either—a legacy of the statues that had brought William Jennings Bryan and Clarence Darrow to legal blows at Tennessee's trial of John Scopes in 1925. The subject remained doubly hidden within my textbook—covered only in chapter 63 (of 66) and described in euphemism as "the hypothesis of racial development."

The antievolution laws of the Scopes era, passed during the early 1920s in several southern and border states, remained on the books until 1968, when the Supreme Court declared them unconstitutional. The laws were never strictly enforced, but their existence cast a pall over American education, as textbook publishers capitulated to produce "least common denominator" versions acceptable in all states—so schoolkids in New York got short shrift because the statutes of some distant states had labeled evolution dangerous and unteachable.

Ironically, at the very end of this millennium (I am writing this essay in late November 1999), demotions, warnings, and anathemas have again come into vogue in several regions of our nation. The Kansas school board has reduced evolution, the central and unifying concept of the life sciences, to an optional subject within the state's biology curriculum—an educational ruling akin to stating

Gould, Stephen Jay. "What does the dreaded 'E' word *mean* anyway? A Reverie for the Opening of the New Hayden Planetarium." *Natural History.* 2/00. 28–44.

that English will still be taught but that grammar may henceforth be regarded as a peripheral frill, permitted but not mandated as a classroom subject. Two states now require that warning labels be pasted (literally) into all biology textbooks, alerting students that they might wish to consider alternatives to evolution (although no other well-documented scientific concept evokes similar caution). Finally, at least two states have retained all their Darwinian material in official pamphlets and curricula but have replaced the dreaded "e" word with a circumlocution, thus reviving the old strategy of my high school text.

As our fight for good (and politically untrammeled) public education in science must include our forceful defense of a key word—for inquisitors have always understood that an idea can be extinguished most effectively by suppressing all memory of a defining word or an inspirational person—we might consider an interesting historical irony that, properly elucidated, might even aid us in our battle. We must not compromise *our* showcasing of the "e" word, for we give up the game before we start if we grant our opponents control over basic terms. But we should also note that Darwin himself never used the word "evolution" in his epochal book of 1859. In *Origin of Species,* he calls this fundamental biological process "descent with modification." Darwin, needless to say, did not shun "evolution" from motives of fear, conciliation, or political savvy but rather for an opposite and principled reason that can help us appreciate the depth of the intellectual revolution that he inspired and some of the reasons (understandable if indefensible) for the persistent public unease.

Pre-Darwinian terminology for evolution—a widely discussed, if unorthodox, view of life in early nineteenth-century biology—generally used such names as transformation, transmutation, or the development hypothesis. In choosing a label for his own, very different account of genealogical change, Darwin would never have considered "evolution" as a descriptor, because that vernacular English word implied a set of consequences contrary to the most distinctive features of his proposed revolutionary mechanism of change.

"Evolution," from the Latin *evolvere,* literally means "an unrolling"—and clearly implies an unfolding in time of a predictable or prepackaged sequence in an inherently progressive, or at least directional, manner (the "fiddlehead" of a fern unrolls and expands to bring forth the adult plant—a true evolution of preformed parts). The *Oxford English Dictionary* traces the word "evolution" to seventeenth-century English poetry. Here the word's key meaning—the sequential exposure of prepackaged potential—inspired the first recorded usages in our language. For example, Henry More (1614–87), the British philosopher responsible for several of the seventeenth-century citations in the *OED* entry, stated in 1664, "I have not yet evolved all the intangling superstitions that may be wrapt up."

The few pre-Darwinian English citations of genealogical change as "evolution" all employ the word as a synonym for predictable progress. For example, in describing Lamarch's theory for British readers (in the second volume of his

Principles of Geology, 1832), Charles Lyell generally uses the neutral term "transmutation"—except in one passage, where he wishes to highlight a claim for progress: "The testacea of the ocean existed first, until some of them by gradual evolution were improved into those inhabiting the land."

Although the word "evolution" does not appear in the first edition of *Origin of Species,* Darwin does use the verbal form "evolved," clearly in the vernacular sense and in an especially crucial spot: the very last word of the book! Most students have failed to appreciate the incisive and intended "gotcha" of these closing lines, which have generally been read as a poetic reverie, a harmless linguistic flourish essentially devoid of content, however rich in imagery. In fact, the canny Darwin used this maximally effective location to make a telling point about the absolute glory and comparative importance of natural history as a calling.

We usually regard planetary physics as the paragon of rigorous science, while dismissing natural history as a lightweight exercise in dull, descriptive cataloging that any person with sufficient patience might accomplish. But Darwin, in his closing passage, identified the primary phenomenon of planetary physics as a dull and simple cycling to nowhere, in sharp contrast with life's history, depicted as a dynamic and upwardly growing tree. The Earth *revolves* in uninteresting sameness, but life *evolves* by unfolding its potential for ever expanding diversity along admittedly unpredictable, but wonderfully various, branchings:

> *Whilst this planet has gone cycling on according to the fixed law of gravity, from so simple a beginning endless forms most beautiful and most wonderful have been, and are being, evolved.*

But Darwin could not have described the process regulated by his mechanism of natural selection as "evolution" in the vernacular meaning then conveyed by the word. For the mechanism of natural selection yields only increasing adaptation to changing local environments, not predictable progress in the usual sense of cosmic or general betterment expressed as growing complexity, augmented mentality, or whatever. In Darwin's causal world, an anatomically degenerate parasite, reduced to a formless clump of feeding and reproductive cells within the body of a host, may be just as well adapted to its surroundings, and just as well endowed with prospects for evolutionary persistence, as is the most intricate creature, exquisitely adapted in all parts to a complex and dangerous external environment. Moreover, since natural selection can adapt organisms only to local circumstances, and since local circumstances change in an effectively random manner through geological time, the pathways of adaptive evolution cannot be predicted.

Thus, on these two fundamental grounds—lack of inherent directionality and lack of predictability—the process regulated by natural selection could scarcely have suggested, to Darwin, the label "evolution," an ordinary English word for sequences of predictable and directional unfolding. We must then, and obviously, ask how "evolution" achieved its coup in becoming the name for Darwin's process—a takeover so complete that the word has now almost (but not quite, as we shall soon see) lost its original English meaning of "unfolding" and has transmuted (or should we say "evolved"?) into an effective synonym for biological change through time.

This interesting shift, despite Darwin's own reticence, occurred primarily because a great majority of his contemporaries, while granting the overwhelming evidence for evolution's factuality, could not accept Darwin's radical views about the causes and patterns of biological change. Most important, they could not bear to surrender the comforting and traditional view that human consciousness must represent a predictable (if not a divinely intended) summit of biological existence. If scientific discoveries enjoined an evolutionary reading of human superiority, then one must bow to the evidence. But Darwin's contemporaries (and many people today as well) would not surrender their traditional view of human domination, and therefore could conceptualize genealogical transmutation only as a process defined by predictable progress toward a human acme—in short, as a process well described by the term "evolution" in its vernacular meaning of "unfolding an inherent potential."

Herbert Spencer's progressivist view of natural change probably exerted the greatest influence in establishing "evolution" as the general name for Darwin's process, for Spencer held a dominating status as Victorian pundit and grand panjandrum of nearly everything conceptual. In any case, Darwin had too many other fish to fry and didn't choose to fight a battle about words rather than things. He felt confident that his views would eventually prevail, even over the contrary etymology of a word imposed upon his process by popular will. (He knew, after all, that meanings of words can transmute within new climates of immediate utility, just as species transform under new local environments of life and ecology!) Darwin never used the "e" word extensively in his writings, but he did capitulate to a developing consensus by referring to his process as evolution for the first time in *Descent of Man,* published in 1871. (Still, Darwin never used the word "evolution" in the title of any book—and he chose, in his book on human history, to emphasize the genealogical "descent" of our species, not our "ascent" to higher levels of consciousness.)

When I was a young boy, growing up on the streets of New York City, the American Museum of Natural History became my second home and inspiration. I loved two exhibits most of all—the *Tyrannosaurus* skeleton on the fourth floor and the star show at the adjacent Hayden Planetarium. I juggled these two passions for many years and eventually became a paleontologist; Carl Sagan, my near-contemporary from the neighboring neverland of Brooklyn (I grew up in Queens) weighed the same two interests in the same building but opted for astronomy as a calling. (I have always suspected a basic biological determinism behind our opposite choices. Carl was tall and looked up toward the heavens; I am shorter than average and tend to look down at the ground.)

My essays may be known for their tactic of selecting odd little tidbits as illustrations of general themes. But why, to take the reopening of the Hayden Planetarium, would I highlight such a quirky and apparently irrelevant subject as the odyssey of the term "evolution" in scientific, and primarily biological, use—thus seeming, once again, to reject the cosmos in favor of the dinosaurs? Method does inhere in my apparent madness (whether or not I succeed in conveying this reasoning to my readers). I am writing about the term "evolution" in the domain I know in order to explicate its strikingly different meaning in the profession that I put aside but still love avocationally. A discussion of the contrast between biological evolution and cosmological evolution might offer some utility as a commentary about alternative worldviews and as a reminder that many supposed debates in science arise from confusion engendered by differing uses of words and not from deep conceptual muddles about the nature of things.

Interdisciplinary unification represents a grand and worthy goal of intellectual life, but greater understanding can often be won by principled separation and mutual respect, based on clear definitions and distinctions among truly disparate processes, rather than by false unions forged with superficial similarities and papered over by a common terminology. In our understandable desire to unify the sciences of temporal change, we have too often followed the Procrustean strategy of enforcing a common set of causes and explanations upon the history of a species and the life of a star—partly, at least, for the very bad reason that both professions use the term "evolution" to denote change through time. In this case, the fundamental differences trump the superficial similarities—and true unity will be achieved only when we acknowledge the disparate substrates that, taken together, probe the range of possibilities for theories of historical order.

The Darwinian principle of natural selection yields temporal change—evolution in the biological definition—by the twofold process of producing copious and undirected variation within a population and then passing along only a biased (selected) portion of this variation to the next generation. In this manner, the variation within a population at any moment can be converted into differences in mean values (average size, average braininess) among successive populations through time. For this fundamental reason, we call such theories of change *variational* as opposed to the more conventional, and more direct, models of *transformational* change imposed by natural laws that mandate a particular trajectory based on inherent (and therefore predictable) properties of substances and environments. (A ball rolling down an inclined plane does not reach the bottom because selection has favored the differential propagation of moving versus stable elements of its totality but because gravity dictates this result when round balls roll down smooth planes.)

To illustrate the peculiar properties of variational theories like Darwin's in an obviously caricatured, but not inaccurate, description: Suppose that a population of elephants inhabits Siberia during a warm interval before the advance of an ice sheet. The elephants vary, at random and in all directions, in their amount of body hair. As the ice advances and local conditions become colder, elephants with more hair will tend to cope better, by the sheer good fortune of their superior adaptation to changing climates—and they will leave more surviving offspring on average. (This differential reproductive success must be conceived as broadly statistical and not guaranteed in every case: in any generation, the hairiest elephant of all may fall into a crevasse and die.) Because offspring inherit their parents' degree of hairiness, the next generation will contain a higher proportion of more densely clad elephants (who will continue to be favored by natural selection as the climate becomes still colder). This process of increasing average hairiness may continue for many generations, leading to the evolution of woolly mammoths.

This little fable can help us understand how peculiar and how contrary to all traditions of Western thought and explanation of the Darwinian theory of evolution, and variational theories of historical change in general, must sound to the common ear. All the odd and fascinating properties of Darwinian evolution—the sensible and explainable but quite unpredictable nature of the outcome (dependent upon complex and contingent changes in local environments), the nonprogressive character of the alteration (adaptive only to these unpredictable local circumstances and not inevitably building a "better" elephant in any cosmic or general sense)—flow from the variational basis of natural selection.

Transformational theories work in a much simpler and more direct manner. If I want to go from A to B, I will have so much less conceptual (and actual) trouble if I can postulate a mechanism that will just push me there directly than if I must rely upon the selection of "a few good men" from a random cloud of variation about point A, then constitute a new generation around an average point one step closer to B, then generate a new cloud of random variation about this new point, then select "a few good men" once again from this new array—and then repeat this process over and over until I finally reach B.

When one adds the oddity of variational theories in general to our strong cultural and psychological resistance against their application to our own evolutionary origin (as an unpredictable and not necessary progressive little twig on life's luxuriant tree), then we can better understand why Darwin's revolution surpassed all other scientific discoveries in reformatory power and why so many people still fail to understand, and may even actively resist, its truly liberating content. (I must leave the issue of liberation for another time, but once we recognize that the specification of morals and the search for a meaning to our lives cannot be accomplished by scientific study in any case, then Darwin's variational mechanism will no longer seem threatening and may even become liberating in teaching us to look within ourselves for answers to these questions and to abandon a chimerical search for the purpose of our lives, and for the source of our ethical values, in the external workings of nature.)

These difficulties in grasping Darwin's great insight became exacerbated when our Victorian forebears made their unfortunate choice of a defining word—"evolution"—with its vernacular meaning of "directed unfolding." We would not face this additional problem today if "evolution" had undergone a complete transformation to become a strict and exclusive definition of biological change—with earlier and etymologically more appropriate usages then abandoned and forgotten. But important words rarely undergo such a clean switch of meaning, and "evolution" still maintains its original definition of "predictable unfolding" in several nonbiological disciplines—including astronomy.

When astronomers talk about the evolution of a star, they clearly do not have a variational theory like Darwin's in mind. Stars do not change through time because mama and papa stars generate broods of varying daughter stars, followed by the differential survival of daughters best adapted to their particular region of the cosmos. Rather, theories of stellar "evolution" could not be more relentlessly transformational in positing a definite and predictable sequence of changes unfolding as simple consequences of physical laws. (No biological process operates in exactly the same manner, but the life cycle of an organism certainly works better than the evolution of a species as a source of analogy.)

Ironically, astronomy undeniably trumps biology in faithfulness to the etymology and the vernacular definition of "evolution"—even though the term now holds far wider currency under the radically altered definition of the biological sciences. In fact, astronomers have been so true to the original definition that they confine "evolution" to historical sequences of predictable unfolding and resolutely shun the word when describing cosmic changes exhibiting the key features of biological evolution—unpredictability and lack of inherent directionality.

As an illustration of this astronomical usage, consider the most standard and conventional of all sources—the *Encyclopedia Britannica* article "Stars and Star Clusters" (15th edition, 1990 printing). The section entitled "Star Formation and Evolution" begins by analogizing stellar "evolution" to a preprogrammed life cycle, with the degree of evolution defined as the position along the predictable trajectory:

> *Throughout the Milky Way Galaxy . . . astronomers have discovered stars that are well evolved or even approaching extinction, or both, as well as occasional stars that must be very young or still in the process of formation. Evolutionary effects on these stars are not negligible.*

The fully predictable and linear sequence of stages in a stellar lifetime (evolution, to astronomers) records the consequences of a defining physical process in the construction and history of stars: the conversion of mass to energy by nuclear reactions deep within stars, leading to the transformation of hydrogen into helium.

> *The spread of luminosities and colors of stars within the main sequence can be understood as a consequence of evolution . . . As the stars evolve, they adjust to the increase in the helium-to-hydrogen ratio in their cores . . . When the core fuel is exhausted, the internal structure of the star changes rapidly; it quickly leaves the main sequence and moves towards the region of giants and super-giants.*

The same basic sequence unfolds through stellar lives, but the rate of change (evolution, to astronomers) varies as a predictable consequence of differences in mass:

> *Like the rate of formation of a star, the subsequent rate of evolution on the main sequence is proportional to the mass of the star; the greater the mass, the more rapid the evolution.*

More complex factors may determine variation in some stages of the life cycle, but the basic directionality (evolution, to astronomers) does not alter, and predictability from natural law remains precise and complete:

> *The great spread in luminosities and colors of giant, supergiant, and subgiant stars is also understood to result from evolutionary events. When a star leaves the main sequence, its future evolution is precisely determined by its mass, rate of rotation (or angular momentum), chemical composition, and whether or not it is a member of a close binary system.*

In the most revealing verbal clue of all, the discourse of this particular scientific culture seems to shun the word "evolution" when historical sequences become too meandering, too nondirectional, or too complex to explain as simple consequences of controlling laws—even though the end result may be markedly different from the beginning state, thus illustrating significant change through time. For example, the same *Britannica* article on stellar evolution notes that one can often reach conclusions about the origin of a star or a planet from the relative abundance of chemical elements in its present composition.

Earth, however, has become so modified during its geological history that we cannot use this inferential method to reconstruct the initial state of our own planet. Because the current configuration of Earth's surface developed through complex contingencies and could not have been predicted from simple laws, this style of change apparently does not rank as evolution—but only, in astronomical parlance, as being "affected."

The relative abundances of the chemical elements provide significant clues regarding their origin. The Earth's crust has been affected severely by erosion, fractionation, and other geologic events, so that its present varied composition offers few clues as to its early stages.

I don't mention these differences to lament, to complain, or to criticize astronomers in any way. After all, their use of "evolution" remains more faithful to etymology and the original English definition, whereas our Darwinian reconstruction has virtually reversed the original meaning. In this case, since neither side will or should give up its understanding of "evolution" (astronomers because they have retained an original and etymologically correct meaning, and evolutionists because their redefinition expresses the very heart of their central and revolutionary concept of life's history), our best solution lies simply in exposing the legitimate differences and explaining the good reasons behind the disparity in usage.

In this way, at least, we may avoid confusion and also the special frustration generated when prolonged wrangles arise from misunderstandings of words rather than from genuine disputes about things and causes in nature. We evolutionary biologists must remain especially sensitive to this issue, because we still face considerable opposition, based on conventional hopes and fears, to our insistence that life evolves in unpredictable directions, with no inherent goal. Since astronomical evolution upholds both contrary positions—predictability and directionality—evolutionary biologists need to emphasize their own distinctive meaning, especially since the general public feels much more comfortable with the astronomical sense and will therefore impose this more congenial definition upon the history of life if we do not clearly explain the logic, the evidence, and the sheer fascination of our challenging conclusion.

Two studies published within the past month led me to this topic, because each discovery confirms the biological, variational, and Darwinian "take" on evolution while also, and quite explicitly, refuting a previous, transformational interpretation—rooted in our culturally established prejudices for the more comforting, astronomical view—that had blocked our understanding and skewed our thoughts about an important episode in life's history.

1. *Vertebrates "all the way down."* In one of the most crucial and enigmatic episodes in the history of life—and a challenge to the older, more congenial idea that life has progressed in a basically stately, linear manner through the ages—nearly all animal phyla made their first appearance in the fossil record at essentially the same time, an interval of some 5 million years (about 525 million to 530 million years ago) called the Cambrian explosion. (Geological firecrackers have long fuses when measured by the inappropriate scale of human time.) Only one major phylum with prominent and fossilizable hard parts did not appear in

this incident or during the Cambrian period at all—the Bryozoa, a group of colonial marine organisms unknown to most nonspecialists today (although still relatively common in shallow oceanic waters) but prominent in the early fossil record of animal life.

One other group, until last month, also had no record within the Cambrian explosion, although late Cambrian representatives (well after the explosion itself) have been known for some time. Whereas popular texts have virtually ignored the Bryozoa, the absence of this other group has been prominently showcased and proclaimed highly significant. No vertebrates had ever been recovered from deposits of the Cambrian explosion, although close relatives within our phylum (the Chordata), if not technically vertebrates, had been collected (the Chordat includes three major subgroups: the tunicates, *Amphioxus* and its relatives, and the vertebrates proper).

This absence of vertebrates from strata bearing nearly all other fossilizable animal phyla provided a strong ray of hope for people who wished to view our own group as "higher" or more evolved in a more predictable direction. If evolution implies linear progression, then later is better—and uniquely later (or almost uniquely, given those pesky bryozoans) can only enhance the distinction. But the November 4, 1999, issue of *Nature* includes a persuasive article ("Lower Cambrian Vertebrates from South China," by D-G. Shu, H-L. Luo, S. Conway Morris, X-L. Zhang, S-X. Hu, L. Chen, J. Han, M. Zhu, Y. Li, and L-Z. Chen) reporting the discovery of two vertebrate genera wtihin the Lower Cambrian Chengjiang formation of southern China, right within the temporal heart of the Cambrian explosion. (The Burgess shale of western Canada, the celebrated site for most previous knowledge of early Cambrian animals, postdates the actual explosion by several million years. The recently discovered Chengjiang fauna, with equally exquisite preservation of soft anatomy, has been yielding comparable or even greater treasures for more than a decade. See "On Embryos and Ancestors," *Natural History,* July–August 1998.)

These two creatures—each only an inch or so in length and lacking both jaws and a backbone and in fact possessing no bony skeleton at all—might not strike a casual student as worthy of inclusion within our exalted lineage. But these features, however much they may command our present focus, arose later in the history of vertebrates and do not enter the central and inclusive taxonomic definition of our group. The vertebrate jaw, for example, evolved from hard parts that originally fortified the gill openings and then moved forward to surround the mouth. All early fishes—and two modern survivors of this initial radiation, the lampreys and the hagfishes—lacked jaws.

The two Chengjiang genera possess all the defining features of vertebrates: the stiff dorsal supporting rod, or notochord (subsequently lost in adults after the vertebal column evolved); the arrangement of flank musculature in a series of zigzag elements from front to back; the set of paired openings piercing the pharynx (operating primarily as respiratory gills in later fishes but used mostly for filter feeding in ancestral vertebrates). In fact, the best reconstruction of branching order on the vertebrate tree places the origin of these two new genera after the inferred ancestors of modern hagfishes but before the presumed forebears of lampreys. If this inference holds, then vertebrates already existed in substantial diversity within the Cambrian explosion. In any case, we now have two distinct and concrete examples of vertebrates "all the way down"—that is, in the very same strata that include the first known fossils of nearly all phyla of modern multicellular animals. We vertebrates do not stand higher and later than our invertebrate cousins, for all "advanced" animal phyla made their first appearance in the fossil record at essentially the same time. The vaunted complexity of vertebrates did not require a special delay to accommodate a slow series of progressive steps, predictable from the general principles of evolution.

2. *An ultimate parasite, or "how are the mighty fallen."* The phyla of complex multicellular animals enjoy a collective designation as Metazoa (literally, "higher animals"). Mobile, single-celled creatures bear the name Protozoa ("first animals"—actually a misnomer, since many of these creatures, in terms of genealogical branching, rank as close to multicellular plants and fungi as to multicellular animals). In a verbal in-between stand the Mesozoa ("middle animals"). Many taxonomic and evolutionary schemes for the organization of life rank the Mesozoa by the literal implication of their name—that is, as a persistently primitive group intermediate between the single-celled and the multicellular animals and illustrating a necessary transitional step in a progressivist reading of life's history.

But the Mesozoa have always been viewed as enigmatic, primarily because they live as parasites within truly multicellular animals, and parasites often adapt to their protected surroundings by evolving an extremely simplified anatomy, sometimes little more than a glob of absorptive and reproductive tissue cocooned within the body of a host. Thus, the extreme simplicity of parasitic anatomy could represent the evolutionary degeneration of a complex, free-living ancestor rather than the maintenance of a primitive state.

The major group of mesozoans, the Dicyemida, live as microscopic parasites in the renal organs of squid and octopuses. Their adult anatomy could hardly be simpler: a single axial cell (which generates the reproductive cells) in the center, enveloped by a single layer of ciliated outer cells (some ten to forty in number) arranged in a spiral around the axial cell, except at the front end [. . .].

The zoological status of the dicyemids has always been controversial. Some scientists, including Libbie H. Hyman, who wrote the definitive, multivolume text on invertebrate anatomy for her generation, regarded their simplicity as primitive and their evolutionary status as intermediate in the rising complexity of evolution. As she noted in 1940, "Their characters are in the main primitive and not the result of parasitic degeneration." But even those researchers who viewed the dicyemids as parasitic descendants of more complex free-living ancestors never dared to derive these ultimately simple multicellular creatures from a *very* complex metazoan. For example, Horace W. Stunkard, the leading student of dicyemids in the generation of my teachers, thought that these mesozoans had descended from the simplest of all Metazoa above the grade of sponges and corals—the platyhelminth flatworms.

Unfortunately, the anatomy of dicyemids has become so regressed and specialized that no evidence remains to link them firmly with other animal groups, so the controversy of persistently primitive versus degeneratively parasitic could never be settled until now. But newer methods of gene sequencing can solve this dilemma, because even though visible anatomy may fade or transform into something unrecognizable, evolution can hardly erase all traces of complex gene sequences. If genes known only from advanced Metazoa—and known to operate only in the context of organs and functions unique to Metazoa—also exist in dicyemids, then these creatures are probably degenerated metazoans. But if, after extensive search, no sign of distinctive metazoan genomes can be detected in dicyemids, then the Mesozoa may well be intermediate between single and multicelled life after all.

In the October 21, 1999, issue of *Nature,* M. Kobayashi, H. Furuya, and P.W.H. Holland present an elegant solution to this old problem ("Dicyemids Are Higher Animals"). These researchers located a *Hox* gene—a member of a distinctive subset known only from metazoans and operating in the differentiation of body structures along the antero-posterior (front to back) axis—in *Dicyema orientale.* These particular *Hox* genes occur only in triploblastic, or "higher," metazoans with body cavities and three cell layers, and not in any of the groups (such as the Porifera, or sponges, and the Cnidaria, or corals and their relatives) traditionally placed "below" triploblasts. Thus, the dicyemids are descended from "higher," triploblastic animals and have become maximally simplified in anatomy by adaptation to their parasitic lifestyle. They do not represent primitive vestiges of an early stage in the linear progress of life.

In short, if the traditionally "highest" of all triploblasts—the vertebrate line, including our exalted selves—appears in the fossil record at the same time as all other triploblastic phyla in the Cambrian explosion, and if the most anatomically simplified of all parasites can evolve (as an adaptation to local ecology) from a free-living lineage within the "higher," triploblastic phyla, then the biological, variational, and Darwinian meaning of "evolution" as unpredictable and nondirectional gains powerful support from two cases that, in a former and now disproven interpretation, once bolstered an opposite set of transformational prejudices.

As a final thought to contrast the predictable unfolding of stellar evolution with the contingent nondirectionality of biological evolution, I should note that Darwin's closing line about "this planet . . . cycling on according to the fixed law of gravity," while adequate for now, cannot hold for all time. Stellar evolution will, one day, enjoin a predictable end, at least to life on Earth. Quoting one more time from *Britannica:*

> *The Sun is destined to perish as a white dwarf. But before that happens, it will evolve into a red giant, engulfing Mercury and Venus in the process. At the same time, it will blow away the earth's atmosphere and boil its oceans, making the planet uninhabitable.*

The same predictability also allows us to specify the timing of this catastrophe—about 5 billion years from now! A tolerably distant future, to be sure, but consider the issue another way, in comparison with the very different style of change known as biological evolution. Earth originated about 4.6 billion years ago. Thus, half of our planet's potential history unfolded before contingent biological evolution produced even a single species with consciousness sufficient to muse over such matters. Moreover, this single lineage arose within a marginal group of mammals—the primates, which include about 200 of the 4,000 or so mammalian species. By contrast, the world holds at least half a million species of beetles. If a meandering process consumed half of all available time to build such an adaptation even once, then mentality at a human level certainly doesn't seem to rank among the "sure bets," or even the mild probabilities, of history.

We must therefore contrast the good fortune of our own evolution with the inexorable evolution of our nurturing Sun toward a spectacular climax that might make our further evolution impossible. True, the time may be too distant to inspire any practical concern, but we humans do like to muse and to wonder. The contingency of our evolution offers no guarantees against the certainties of the Sun's evolution. We shall probably be long gone by then, perhaps taking a good deal of life with us and perhaps leaving those previously indestructible bacteria as the highest mute witnesses to a stellar expansion that will finally unleash a unicellular Armageddon. Or perhaps we, or our successors, will have colonized the universe by then and will shed only a brief tear for the destruction of a little cosmic exhibit entitled "the museum of our geographic origins." Somehow I prefer the excitement of wondering and cogitation—not to mention the power inherent in acting upon things that *can* be changed—to the certainty of distant dissolution.

Reading 16

PLACE

Susan Griffin

We know not where we are.
—HENRY DAVID THOREAU, *Walden*

Forgetting occurs when all information of a
particular kind or mode about a situation is
suppressed.
—BRIAN ROTMAN, *Ad Infinitum—*
The Ghost in Turing's Machine

Little fleece of my flesh
that I wove in my womb,
little shivering fleece,
sleep close to me!
—GABRIELA MISTRAL, "Close to Me"

The great mythos here in the country of my birth is movement. Ships filled with pilgrims, or protestants, or immigrants. The passages are almost abstract, as if all that lies over the waters is freedom. The release is from a corrupt world, from oppression, persecution. But of course there is another story, too, the underside of the ideal. The hellish middle passage, men, women, and children chained in the holds of ships, packed so tightly movement was all but impossible, drowning less often in the open sea than in the fluid of their own bodies. This passage was to slavery. And then there were the forced marches, the Trail of Tears of the Cherokee, the forced migration of Navajo, repeated all over the continent as one people after another were severed from their lands.

Griffin, Susan. "Place," *The Eros of Everyday Life: Essays on Ecology, Gender, and Society.* New York: Doubleday, 1995. 73–96.

The dream was and still is forked. In one direction the movement is toward democracy. The underground railroad during the Civil War. The labor movement. The movement for civil rights. For women's liberation. The metaphor holds. More often than not, in this dream the pilgrim and the protester come to or from a place of meeting. Not only with each other but with existence, manifested intensely and freshly, newly revealed by a land less marked by familiar structures, a slate of assumptions wiped clean. The chance for a new start and the rhetoric of beginnings echo in the words of Thoreau, Whitman, Frederick Douglass, Margaret Fuller.

But this dream too takes another fork. The desire to be free of the necessities of place and the limitations of earthly life. Streets paved with gold. Robber barons. Vast wealth and lives of leisure built on the labor of slaves and indentured servants. The inventions of machines to replace every task. Gravity no longer a restraint; the American flag planted on the moon. Businessmen with cellular phones and powerbooks, no longer tied to the body, extending themselves electronically all over the world. Yearly migrations to better jobs, better economies; the search for cheaper labor, new markets. The freedom to grow endlessly. An infinity of power suspended in a space defined by no location, no settling ground, even if all the time the ground is here, and no one, except in these mad dreams, is apart.

Where does one leave off and the other begin? My hand curled around the pen. Paper and ink. Heavy gray clouds massing over the hills, and the wet air. Everywhere an exchange takes place. One can make out differences, perceive outlines, boundaries, discover distinguishing marks. But the exchange continues at such a rate that the conclusion is clear. One cannot exist without the other. In the arc of existence, each being is wholly dependent on the matrix we all make.

One speaks of living *on* the earth but in truth life is held within the earth. An atmosphere woven from life circles the planet. Every movement, every breath, every response, the least thought is shaped to the curve of this mass. Even time and space bend to it. Like a child in a womb, all we know exists inside this outer body. And all is dependent on it.

But my mind was schooled differently. I remember being mystified in my childhood by the words "For dust thou art, and unto dust shalt thou return." So little else in my Christian cosmology pointed to that meaning. By every other lesson, I was taught to think of myself as somehow apart from soil and dust. Very little in my culture taught me that my existence depends on the existence of earth.

When in a dream of himself as a child Freud asked his mother where he came from, and she showed him bits of soil on the palm of her hand, he was terrified. The knowledge must have evoked fear, not only of death but of dependency. Because, if death is at a remove in time, dependency is always present.

Perhaps that is why a dialogue over dependency is built so solidly into the discourse of gender. In the Western tradition independence has been configured as masculine, dependence as feminine. Seeking liberation from traditional female roles, a woman is said to gain her independence. And as if her dependence prevented his liberation, a man calls his wife "a ball and chain."

But this pattern of thought conceals a reversal. Though men may complain about the dependence of women and children, what goes unmentioned is a man's dependence on female labor to meet the humble needs of his daily sustenance. That such a dependence embarrasses masculinity is clear even in the idealized trajectory of male development, which requires first that a man free himself from his mother's apron strings and then from his wife's. This is no simple story of autonomy. It has a subtext: the process requires mastery of women (which is to say of nature). Nor does the story allow for the ambiguity that shapes every relationship and always contains a mixture of give and take, complementarily and mutuality. To need is a form of trust and love.

But need is nothing but an enemy in this story. Yawning at night, hungering in the morning, a little cold in the afternoon.

Perhaps it is this too that inspires a fear of homosexuality. The image of a man's body curled into the arms of another man, letting his vulnerability be seen or even exist in the company of men, corrupting the masculine realm of independence with want. To recognize the necessity of earthly sustenance for male survival would strike an alarm. The whole scaffolding of male independence rests on the invisibility of a female foundation, a feminine world turned toward a masculine world ready to give what enables a man to produce the illusion of autonomy.

In this scheme, the private realm of domestic life becomes a place to hide dependency. The humiliation and vulnerability of nakedness and need can be hidden at home away from the public world. This is as true for society as it is for the individual psyche. In order to conceal the dependency of Western *man* on earthly process, private life must be carefully bifurcated from public life. For this life holds the secret of need.

Perhaps this is why a woman's body seems so threatening to the masculine psyche. Along with the home, this body has become the repository for an abandoned knowledge of dependency. One can read this fear in the traditional masculine hatred of women. Women know that men are dependent and with this knowledge they hold the power, either to reveal the secret or not. This revelation would bring with it a humiliation of cataclysmic proportions, one that holds within it the memory of a childhood fragility and the mother's power to erase one's own existence.

It is a fear that comes to play dramatically in the current angry debate over abortion. Intense arguements laid before both courts and public audiences attempt to prove that the fetus has separate rights as a human being. That even before the fetus can exist outside the womb independently, it is an independent being. So in the unconscious recesses of a psyche which imagines itself impervious to earthly frailty, to make abortion against the law would also banish any felt memory of union with a greater, enclosing, nourishing body.

But the union is all about us. It cannot even be separated from the progression of our thoughts. Here in this room I can hear water falling outside, see moisture on the ground in the garden, feel the dampness in the air and in a certain heaviness of mind that overtakes me in the rain. Yet this is not how I have been trained to see thought. I was taught to think of the mind as independent from place. Among all the fantasies of independence that are part of the Western mythos, the adventurer, the pioneer alone in the wilderness, the sailor on the open seas, the crusading knight, the heroic marine, perhaps the most enduring and profound in its influence has been the idea of a mind autonomous from any surrounding.

The concept that consciousness is separate from physical existence is deeply worn into the crevices of the European mind. This dividedness provides the metaphor through which an elevation over earthly process can be imagined. Only by considering itself independent of the earth can consciousness believe in its own transcendence.

Just as the natural process of human birth is reversed in Genesis to make woman born of man, so mental process has been reversed in the mythos of this civilization so that the physical universe is depicted as proceeding from abstractions. Plato's idea of earthly existence as a poor shadow of eternal ideas not only permeates the dominant traditions of Western philosophy but also reflects a fundamental posture toward existence, a hierarchy of values in which abstractions, theories, principles, ideas, mathematical equations, logic, and analysis are elevated above what is called concrete, corporeal, sensible, palpable, tangible, solid, physical, material, and contextual.

In the theology that preceded and yet still shapes modern scientific thought, the realm of the abstract was said to reflect the mind of God more accurately than a corrupt earthly life. The heresy of science was to observe the things of this earth. Science made a break from pure deductive logic by inserting experiment into the process by which truth is discovered. And to a certain degree, through experiment, what is palpable has been given value again. Yet, by an odd twist of mind, what is palpable has also been robbed of credence. Now what one perceives directly is no longer trusted without the intervention of the scientific method.

By what almost amounts to a kind of psychological sleight of hand, science has by one stroke seized authority over both concrete and abstract realms of knowledge. In this fabulous rendering of the scientific method, the scientist brings reality into his laboratory and returns with truth. This story gains strength through a subtle heritage which partakes of religion, philosophical assumptions, and the intrinsic authority of direct sensual experience. And so we do not notice that even scientific conjecture remains conjecture still. So inured have we become to the authority of science that when one "proven" scientific portrait of the world, such as Newtonian physics, is refuted by other portraits, such as relativity or quantum mechanics, we never question the scientific method itself, nor do we understand that all along scientific thought, like religious abstraction, is not the same as reality.

An experiment conducted in a laboratory is subject to many different kinds of influence and that is why experiments must be replicated in more than one laboratory to be taken seriously. But even what is taken as proof by the scientific community is not conclusive. A condition in one laboratory may be replicated in almost all laboratories because this condition is part of the ethos of a whole civilization. One of these conditions, a mostly unquestioned part of the scientific method, is the practice of studying any being in isolation from the environment in which it lives. But, as ecologists have shown, to study a creature outside of its surroundings is to study another animal altogether, one that does not exist in nature.

And as the philosopher and historian of science Paul Feyerabend has made clear in *Against Method,* no theory accounts for all of the facts in its domain. There are always seemingly stray aspects of reality that remain outside every theory's capacity to explain phenomena. There are even occurrences and test results that appear to contradict what becomes in the end an agreement about what is truth. Facts, whether from the laboratory or the field, do not make theory by themselves. They must be interpreted, and in science as in other fields this interpretation is not immune to diverse influences including political bias. And finally, as Feyerabend makes clear, even what is called a fact is constituted by scientific effort; it is *made.* Theory is implicit in the language of science, the method, the attitudes by which "facts" are discerned and shaped.

One of these prejudices is the enshrinement of numbers as the most reliable kind of data. Yet, as descriptions of the material universe, mathematical calculations must always be tried and proven by experiment. During the Manhattan Project, numerous mathematical calculations were done before the first experimental explosion of the atomic bomb. These calculations were partly based on smaller experiments such as the small chain reaction Enrico Fermi had created in the Chicago Metallurgy Laboratory, partly on conjecture, partly on mathematical theory. But, as the physicist Hans Bethe pointed out, no calculation can be relied upon to produce predictable consequences. Some early calculations, which were later "disproved," suggested that an atomic explosion could set off an endless chain reaction that would destroy the earth. In fact, the calculations which closely preceded the first experimental explosion of the bomb at Alamogordo were in error. The power of the blast was underestimated. The bomb destroyed the instrument designed to measure its force.

From hindsight, one might say that those earlier calculations which were dismissed had in them a grain of truth which was concealed by the limits scientific tradition places on knowledge. For the study of the bomb's effect was done by physicists, who were uneducated in botany, biology, and physiology. That infinitely small but also infinitely destructive nuclear explosions are still occurring in the bodies of those exposed years ago to ionizing radiation is a consequence which was not discernible in their calculations.

I am not immune to the great appeal of numbers. They have about them a kind of coolness which makes for relief from the chaos of need and desire, anguish or anger, the flood of words, not to speak of loud sounds, unpleasant sensations of any kind. When I think of numbers proceeding in orderly sequence, or balanced carefully into equations, my mind arranges itself into a kind of calm. I am reminded of Bach. Of quiet. Reason. This realm of the mind is as real as any place on the universe. But in the history of Western science, mathematics has taken on a specific metaphysical meaning. Identified by Kepler, among others, with the mind of God, the world of numbers not only claims to be real but to be more real than any other place.

The metaphysic continues but now transcendent truth is wrought from specimens of earth. If in the public mind, scientific knowledge rests on *hard* facts conjured from incontrovertible calculations and dense material evidence alike, this would appear to be a union of spirit and matter. But science is subtly arranged around an opposition between the two. Even if modern science no longer bifurcates matter and energy, by the scientific method, theory has been elevated above the realm of matter, as if scientific intelligence, like all intelligence, were not of the earth.

Yet, in the actual processes of thought, scientific or otherwise, no absolute division between material and theoretical or concrete and abstract actually exists. Thought not only moves continually back and forth on a continuum the West describes as abstract and concrete, but the human experience of knowledge can never at any instant be wholly one or the other. Even theory itself has a materiality rarely acknowledged in a culture still aiming toward transcendence. Ideas as well as poems, narratives of any kind as well as stories, sounds of words, even alphabets, certainly numbers, exist as physical entities, not only becoming flesh as they affect the thinker, the reader, or speaker, listener, acting as a kind of mortar for communities, families, peoples, but themselves emanating from, and participating in an ecology of mind that is as much of nature as are rocks and trees.

But in the West this commingling is veiled. If by means of duality Western culture has secured the illusion of transcendence, the culture is also blind to the order and pattern, the memory and intelligence, all the qualities of abstract thought, that exist *in* nature. By that hubris which in Western culture characterizes most thought about human intelligence, the ability to perceive pattern and order in nature has been elevated above nature while pattern and order are not perceived as qualities of a profound analytical intelligence in nature. Even the most abstract concepts of science, those which belong to mathematics, exist in nature. One has only to slice open an apple to find symmetry. Birth certainly contains a kind of division and multiplication at the same time, as do cell mitosis, DNA, the future lives within a seed pod, a copse of birch trees, splitting and reproducing even as they appear in repose.

Nor was sequence invented by the human mind but exists as a significant principle of order within all nature, most clearly perhaps with seasons, the progress of the earth circumnavigating the sun, or human growth and aging. Even the concept of the integer exists in nature, in beings and things which have a discernible integrity, a wholeness within themselves, such as one day, or, as the astronomer Caroline Herschel called them, "the integer days." And computations made possible by the use of Arabic numerals, with their crucial use of position, can be observed in the meaningful arrangements of chromosomes which also change significance through where they are placed and in what sequence.

Gregory Bateson was famous for beginning his classes by throwing a crab on his desk and asking his students to describe the qualities of life, using the crab as an example. The symmetrical order is so clear. Near the end of his life Bateson argued that the capacity to symbolize, basic not only to all mathematics but also to what is called abstract thought, is also deeply embedded in natural process. In an interview taped for a Lindisfarne Fellows meeting, Bateson described metaphor as the "logic upon which the biological world" has been built, "the main characteristic organizing glue . . ." of what he calls elsewhere the mental world of organisms.

The manner of symbolic thinking he describes is not the symbolic representation of logos but the metaphor of poets. He compares two syllogisms, the famous example of "good" thinking:

Men die
Socrates is a man
Socrates will die

and the equally famous example of "bad" thinking:

Grass dies
Men die
Men are grass

Because the first example depends on the likeness of subjects rather than verbs it is a kind of logic not found in biology. For billions of years there has been no separation of subject and verb in living organisms. To extend the implications of his insight, one can see in the very insistence that the subject be separated from *this* verb a separation from the natural world and natural process. A human death is made distinct from the death of grass. And the biological cycle of participation and transmutation at the heart of being, by which men and women are grass and grass is fed by and becomes animal life, is obscured.

But of course what is equally obscured and for the same reasons is the idea of thought as an attribute of the natural world. The possibility certainly exists that human beings have the capacity for and have invented forms of thought which are unique in the universe. But the assertion that what is considered the highest form of thought, namely abstract thought, is uniquely human has an emotional valence. This assertion takes the human thinker in the direction of a mythical world of ideas outside the biosphere. "For most mathematicians (and, one can add, most scientists)," Brian Rotman writes, "mathematics is a Platonic science, the study of timeless entities, *pure forms* that are somehow or other simply 'out there,' preexistent objects independent of human volition or of any conceivable human activity . . ." and, I might add, of any biological or earthly activity too.

If with arithmetic, algebra, geometry, calculus scientists are able to measure and begin to describe and in some ways even understand the abundant complex patterns in nature, this is an astonishing accomplishment. It is a mirror of human nature and of the dimensions of human intelligence, including the human desire to know. Yet in every aspect this accomplishment is also a mirror of the complexity and the vast intelligence which belong to natural existence. Human intelligence is woven from *this* complexity, the complexity of the universe.

But with the concealment of nature the full dimension of human intelligence is also sacrificed. Those forms of human knowledge associated with materiality suffer invisibility and marginalization. It is thus not only the natural world that is mechanized but one's own experience of the natural world. Sensual knowledge, seeing, tasting, smelling, feeling, hearing, crucial abilities through which the human species has survived for millennia in balance with other life forms, have been made subject to distrust, given a lower value, and hence, outside of a handful of artists and healers who are also marginalized, these capacities have been left underdeveloped in Western culture.

And what suffers equally in the estimation of modern science is what Pascal described as the reason of the heart. Human emotional knowledge, which has also evolved in community with natural existence, has been reduced to a problem that gets in the way of objectivity. By this method what is lost is the human experience of the beauty of a river, the trees along its side, the mountains rising behind it, rocks washed, polished by waves of water, silvery fish leaping within it, leaves falling on its surface, shining, illuminated by a setting sun, an experience central to what we would call any question of truth.

I can remember the intensity with which as a child I entered the Sierra Mountains, the deserts outside Los Angeles, the ocean just over the hills ringing the valley where I lived. Were I to put language to these experiences now I would describe them as meetings, transformational exchanges which touched me and through which I learned the nature of existence. I was taught. But I had no way to explain such lessons. The cosmology I had been given by my culture, its philosophies, would not embrace this knowledge. In the world view I have inherited, if nature seems to have meaning, this meaning is just an appearance, a sentimental overlay, one which only the naive, children, the uneducated, or those from lesser cultures, take at face value. If the child sees heaven in a wildflower, her innocent vision must later yield to a higher but severing wisdom which would have it that heaven exists on earth only in the eye of the human beholder.

What is sacrificed with the elevation of human consciousness above natural process is not only the idea of the intelligence of nature, but one's experience of being immersed in a larger whole. A deep and continuing relationship with all other forms of existence is an ancient aspect of human consciousness. One encounters it in children who delight in plants and animals. And this knowledge is kept alive in the myths and stories children learn about the natural world.

But the child becomes an adult. Culture schools her to imagine her own intelligence as unique and isolated in the universe. An older sense of participation in a world of meaning is traded for a mental world that, however dry and abstract, has the virtue of independence. To know is no longer erotic, no longer relational, but becomes instead a means of escape from enmeshment in material existence. By an incremental process of separation from the body, from emotions, from the direct experience of nature, nature becomes alien. Now independence from nature is supposed to provide safety from an increasingly menacing earthbound fate. Knowledge, which has become a form of power rather than intimacy, works a kind of magic in the psyche. Though, in this habit of mind, understanding and analysis bear with them the illusion of having captured the material world and bent it to submission, ironically the mind that imagines itself to be independent from the physical universe becomes more fearful. Because the fact of natural power is unavoidable. And in a withering cycle that is as inescapable as the fact of the human dependence on the biosphere, this fear grows more and more terrible if only because in the Western mind existence has become meaningless. To be swallowed by such a universe would be a preternaturally cold and lonely fate.

Yet the mind is already swallowed. Just as in any ecosystem the existence of each species or life form is dependent on the existence of the whole, so too human knowledge is dependent on the matrix in which it exists. As Hans Blumenberg writes of the Copernican revolution, the air we inhabit is just dense enough to allow us to draw breath and shield us from cosmic rays and yet thin enough to allow us to see the stars. Or, less sanguinely, one might imagine a nuclear winter in which the sky is darkened, polluted air stings the eyes, a lack of oxygen and the effects of radiation, not to speak of the trauma of events, affects the brain; since the smell of ash expunges every other scent, food cannot be smelled to know if it has gone bad; because buildings, trees, shrubs, rocks no longer exist as markers of a familiar landscape, one cannot find one's way. Without the other and without otherness, knowledge is limited to the point of extinction.

But any number of less dramatic examples might be drawn from the history of scientific discourse. Within the history of physics, two simple examples spring to mind. One is from the written work of Galileo. As Italo Calvino points out, whether he is describing a dialogue, the process of thought, or physical motion, he is likely to use the image of a horse, racing, dragging sacks of grain, performing elaborate feats. The other example I use is more famous. That is Einstein's description of relativity, which at times he likens to the operations of an elevator and at other times a train. These concrete metaphors are not just illustrations. Human perspicacity is literally constituted by what can be perceived on earth and in the universe. Thought is impossible without such images.

The interdependency of human thought and the environment is a vast topic which has not been explored with anywhere near the same passion as the assertion of independence. But this mutuality goes back to the very origins of a human consciousness that evolved with the rest of nature. Answering Bishop Berkeley's famous epistemological question, If a tree falls in the forest and no one is present to hear it, does it make a sound? one might pose another question: If sound does not exist can there be such a thing as a human ear? For the ear and human knowledge evolved in community with other life forms and with the physical properties of an audible universe. Human knowledge, if nothing else, is a testament to the connectedness and interdependence of life. There can be no subject apart from an object. This understanding should transform our epistemologies by embedding not only being but the capacity to know in an earth imbued with intrinsic significance.

A return to what is a birthright of meaning is more than a philosophical journey. Something changes in the mood. An atmosphere of nihilism dissolves. Certainly I notice this shift when, turning away from the page or the computer screen, the living world is suddenly present.

When I rise and walk under the trees in my neighborhood, the russet color of their leaves burnishes my mind. Even turning in my chair, opening the window, feeling a cold wind against my face, my mind is joined, taken up, educated. This simple experience is one that most of us regard as an emotional necessity. A room, an enclosure, must have a window. Yet out of the mentality of this civilization we have made a windowless room.

What is at stake is sanity. There is a mad arrogance that flows from the diminishment of meaning in nature, one that approaches megalomania. A presumption of omniscience accompanies every dangerous attempt to control and dominate nature. Again and again disasters are created because human knowledge has been imagined as having no limits. A substance is given to young pregnant women because scientific tests indicate it can prevent miscarriage. Decades later this substance is shown to have no effect on miscarriage, but it causes cancer in the daughters born of this experiment. Fields are saturated with another chemical because this substance kills certain pests. But this substance finds its way into the bodies of birds and causes a silent spring. And then men, women, and children begin to grow ill and die too. But the lesson is never learned. With each new invention, a claim for safety is made that is founded on an idea of infallible knowledge.

In his beautiful accounts of peasant life in Alpine France, John Berger describes a very different attitude toward knowledge. The peasant farmer lives and works daily with an understanding of scarcity. This understanding, he writes, diverges from both the "bourgeois and Marxist ideals of equality" which "presume a world of plenty . . . They demand equal rights before a cornucopia . . . to be constructed by science and the advancement of knowledge . . ." But the peasant ideal of equality is different. It "recognizes a world of scarcity, and its promise is for mutual fraternal aid in struggling against this scarcity and a just sharing of what the work produces."

The experience of scarcity delivers a dramatic lesson in dependency on the earth. Not only the dependency of the body but of the mind too. Closely "connected with the peasant's recognition, as a survivor, of scarcity is his recognition of man's relative ignorance," Berger writes. "He may admire knowledge and the fruits of knowledge but he never supposes that advance of knowledge reduces the extend of the unknown. . . . The unknown can only be eliminated within the limits of a laboratory experiment. Those limits seem to him to be naive."

It is these limits that are ignored when, in the case of possible pollution, from ionizing radiation, or one of hundreds of thousands of man-made chemicals released into the environment every day, no margin is made for the limits of human knowledge. If an effect cannot be measured by modern scientific and statistical means, it is presumed not to exist.

In an ironic footnote to both the history of mathematics, and also the history of a certain hubris, the symbol for zero, z, which came from the Hindu tradition, stands for the unknown. It was the adoption of this symbol and its use to occupy space that so radically advanced mathematical knowledge. Now, an older understanding of zero is crucial to human life, and that is the limitation before which we must learn to stand in respect as well as wonder.

Yet zero is also a circle. One is in fact encircled by the inutterable. And the edges of the unknown are closer than one would think. Behind every expression of belief in unlimited knowledge and power one can detect an earlier scene. In a half-forgotten, probably hazy, hardly focused memory an infant lies on his mother's lap. Everything he learns, he learns from her, from her body. He is learning even before he has words. Even if he fails to remember his early studies, his body will always remember them.

But as he grows to an adult and learns to equate power with independence, what his body remembers will threaten to humiliate him. Because what his body knows is not only that dependency is inextricable from his own existence, but that tracing the origins of his own knowledge back in time, to the body of his mother, and to the larger power of the cosmos he has met in her body, he arrives at the limits of his own understanding.

Is this why infancy is so often described in Western culture as telluric and primitive? The derision is ostensibly aimed at what the infant does not know. But in the guise of derogation, an old fear expresses itself. A fear of what the infant *does* know, including his knowledge of the limits of human knowledge.

Even now, that in the course of a day one holds within oneself not only the memory of infancy, but the same state of being, is wholly erased from consciousness. In the English language, except for pejorative descriptions, such as *regressed,* there are no words for this state of mind which is so much a part of human experience.

And if what is considered regressed is repressed, in the territory of mental exile to which this memory is banished, it mingles with other memories, all forbidden and frightening. The same social structure which creates a fictional divide between masculine and feminine, private and public, infant and adult experience, has also made of childhood a history of betrayal, trespasses, wounds. And it has produced a social amnesia about these events. Not only sexual abuse but emotional and physical abuses of many kinds are so common in childhood in Western society that such misery is more ordinary than a happy childhood. The memories of these traumas, whether conscious or not, contribute to the desire to forget the experience of infancy altogether.

Yet the erasure is not simple. Julia Kristeva explores the unacknowledged longing for the body of the mother as a source of melancholy. A closeness that has been forsaken even in memory. Within the very knowledge of dependency lies a sweetness. Here is an unparalleled intimacy and trust, the first knowledge of love, of belonging to a larger existence, merged with otherness. And this loss is also the loss of a matrix of meaning.

What results in the breech is a kind of paralysis. The psyche is cast into an arrested state, frozen between longing and fear, unable to carry the knowledge of infancy forward into adult consciousness. So that the state of being which is the birthright of the infant and has its own profundity, never ages, never matures, is never allowed to shape and illuminate an adult knowledge of who we are and what is the nature of the universe.

The dislocation is profound. In grief for himself, feeling at the core of himself an inner anomie, Western *man* has projected his inner state of mind onto the world. Because the world has no meaning for him he says it has no meaning at all. He invents a philosophy of nihilism. And in an atmosphere of denial and false sentiments, this philosophy has a ring of truth. Bearing the shock of honesty, cynicism at least approaches the emptiness that lies in the wake of the universe that has been abandoned.

By this chain of reactions, the fear of dependency creates an even deeper dependency. Were it allowed to become, to develop, the state of mind that the infant experiences with the mother would become part of an adult self. But the cost of adulthood in Western society, especially for men, is to lose the knowledge of infancy. Instead of developing this knowledge, the Western psyche replaces it with another kind of knowledge, not knowledge as intimacy but knowledge as power. And even here a disappointed, abandoned infant is concealed, one who in an adult body has become "infantile," and through power tries to extract limitless demands from others, society, the earth.

Paradoxically and yet predictably, primary among these demands is the wish for an earlier sense of knowledge, intimate, embedded, connected. By the same stroke with which it was severed from the self, this knowledge has been projected onto a woman's body. She possesses what he no longer has. And so once again he finds himself dependent on her for what he needs. But this time the need is exaggerated, even unmanageable, for what he imagines he desires really belongs to him, *is* him. He is not himself without it.

To regain a sense of himself, he may attempt to take possession of a woman's body, but erotic feeling can only intensify his sense of loss. Every effort only makes him feel more fragmented and without substance. If through the illusion of transcendence he achieves a certain sense of safety, this is only palliative. He may fantasize, along with Descartes, that his cognitive skills preceded not only his own infancy but birth itself, *Cogito ergo sum,* but his body knows that his thought followed. The existence of his own body. The existence of his mother. The existence of the earth. Unaware, his mind longs for its own lineage, wanders like an orphan seeking a substantial home.

In other, older cultures, perhaps at one time in the earlier history of most European and Mediterranean cultures, and even in the minds of the very young who are born into modern societies that have lost the sense of participation in a larger natural world, identity has been less an assertion of independence than an experience of interdependence. One is dependent for coming into existence not only on a mother and father but on an intricate web of life: one is born from the ground, the tree, the bird in the tree, the body of water feeding the roots, hence the rain, and the sun, and the air of course, the coolness of the mountain, indeed on all that one sees. Others in the family, each of whom contributes daily to make one's life what it is, neighbors, villagers, the farmers, the baker, the potters (for each thing used is made by someone one knows), are part of one's existence. In this matrix one defines oneself finally not by opposition to dependency but by a layered complexity that includes the process of exchange, of giving and getting, by which one's life comes into being and continues.

This is a rich identity. One that is not lonely, for it includes the great worlds to which we are all heir by birth, not as masters, but as participants, as members. And if perhaps we are small under the swirling clouds of the cosmos, as we cast our eyes over the night sky, or across the horizon when we awaken, knowing we are part of this vast, astonishing pattern, we are also large, as large at least as our own awe at what surrounds us and is at the same time who we are.

But along with the mourning one feels over a lost sense of connectedness, of immersion and placement, when this connection to the larger matrix of existence is sacrificed for the illusion of independence, one must also feel confusion. Who am I when I am separated from the ground of my being? It is here, at this psychological moment, that one can witness the birth of fierce nationalisms and fundamentalisms of all kinds.

In place of a widening circle, through which the self is both defined and extended, beginning with one's own body, the body of one's mother, father, family, community, tribe or village, the land on which one walks, where one's food is grown, where water can be found, where hills or mountains, a stream, an ocean, a forest nearby, provide markers, orientation, something else is substituted. A nation. A religion. A set of ideas which one comes to believe and to which one must *belong*. So a man calls himself American, or German, or Serbian, or French. And in time to be devoutly patriotic or religious is to embrace violence.

No one in modern society can be entirely immune to the anguish that must lie mute behind this state of mind. Severed from a world of meaning, one hangs on as if for dear life to an ideology. Belief is no longer an experience but a frail hope. One that must be fed continually by large and small evidence. And as this promise of fulfillment suffers the inevitable diminishment of groundless expectations, enlarging the boundaries of its purview would seem to be imperative. Only such aggressive growth makes the whole system seem alive. The doubt that must live daily underneath fanaticism can be projected on whoever resists conversion. Now there is a clear enemy to battle, to vanquish, to convince if even by force.

But knowledge by itself can be a form of force. The experience is as close to rape as one can imagine: the psyche penetrated by ideas, a way of thinking, a way of perceiving that is not one's own. If women are in many ways socialized into submissiveness from the earliest age by rape and the threat of rape, whole peoples can be trained to intellectual passivity through invasive systems of knowledge. In the twentieth century particularly one has witnessed and is still witnessing many kinds of mental tyranny. I am thinking here not only of fundamentalist campaigns against homosexuality, or the fascist and anti-Semitic propaganda of the Third Reich, but of a modern culture that seems to spin itself out of almost nothing, extending into nameless space by wires and waves, producing dazzling images, and a resemblance to truth that is as monolithic as it is, by virtue of the very power of the medium, intoxicating.

That in the Western habit of mind knowledge is conceived as above life has led to a habit of dissociation which is also a dislocation. Wisdom has been separated from any particular place. In the modern sensibility knowledge is being severed from any earthly context as never before. Earlier in the century, Walter Benjamin had this to say about the mechanical reproduction of art: "Even the most perfect reproduction of a work of art is lacking in one element: its presence in time and space, its unique existence at the place where it happens to be." As he writes of patina, and more invisible marks, of a "sphere of authenticity" outside the capability of technical reproduction, he laments what he calls the liquidation of traditions which occurs as a result of the loss of context.

Within a wide range of cultural traditions—painting in Siena in the fifteenth century, the ninth-century bronze sculptures of the Yoruba on the Ivory Coast, the basket weaving of Pomo Indian women of California, Catalan music of western France and eastern Spain—one finds a wedding of place and art. That valleys of Tuscany appear as background in a portrait, or that Pomo baskets are woven from a grass that grows only in one area, is part of a process of rendering through which a mirror of a whole world, a specific moment in time and space is created. By these mirrors a story is told through which one can behold the coherence of self, society, and nature.

The contrast between these traditions and the new cyberspace is often difficult to discern. I am happy to walk across my room and slide a compact disc into a machine that will at one instant play back the reproduced sounds of a Beethoven quartet and at the next reproduce a choir of Buddhist monks singing traditional chants. My life is made richer; yet the relative lack in my own life of such a tradition is obscured by this seeming abundance. I do not know what it would be to be a Buddhist in a small village in which these chants have echoed for hundreds of years.

And what is also lost when knowledge is removed from place is a basic form of democracy. One which in the past has in many ways been able to elude tyrannous governments. This is the democracy of knowledge. A king or a dictator or the lord of the manor may pronounce that it will rain on Friday. But when I walk out of my house I can see for myself that it is not raining. Human knowledge and wisdom, the capacities to see, estimate, judge, make choices, decisions, have evolved over time together with all life in context, in particular places. Taken in this way, the capacity to know diminishes with distance.

But in the West the power to pronounce the truth grows with distance. As institutions of all kinds are increasingly centralized, authority is almost always elsewhere. And by this removal not only are citizens stripped of the most basic right, the right to perceive—but because those authorities who claim the exclusive right to determine truth are acting at a distance, they have become capable of the most monumental foolishness. Everyone can cite examples. American generals after World War II giving up a huge stretch of Eastern Europe to the Soviet Union because they were unfamiliar with the region. Soviet planners shipping tons of Georgian pine across thousands of miles and then shipping it back again for building projects in Georgia.

Once when I was teaching drama to a group of students whose families lived largely on small means and in run-down urban housing projects, I encountered a sociological "study" ordered by some funding agency. The study argued that this particular neighborhood of children had every middle-class advantage. One of the questions that the sample of children who were interviewed were asked was how many hours they spent a week mowing the grass in front of their homes. In this neighborhood I knew of only one plot of grass, and that was in the small city park where I taught. But the children had answered the question, imagining perhaps that they would like to mow a lawn sometime, or that they were supposed to have mowed lawns to pass the test, or just to jive the interviewer. That so many children had mowed lawns for several hours a week was cited in the study as proof of the neighborhood's middle-class status.

Increasingly, whether one is trained as a business executive, a teacher, an accountant, a doctor, or a lawyer, social power is derived from various kinds of such dissociated knowledge. One becomes dependent on this knowledge to survive, to rise in society, to earn enough money to feed oneself and one's children. Survival has been recast as primarily a social drama in which any collaboration with nature becomes nearly irrelevant. In this phantasmagoric atmosphere, to save the environment, the earth, and the complex processes by which we survive on earth is considered a luxury. For the knowledge of place that is being all but erased in the new technological consciousness is also a knowledge of the necessities and limitations of natural existence.

And yet even more is lost. The paradox is sad. The myth that ideas are independent from material existence promises to yield a ken of meaning beyond the petty and mundane considerations of daily life. Yet it is the habit of separating thought from place and the considerations of natural existence that makes daily life petty and mundane. And it is finally one within scarcity, in the smallest limitation, or through the most painful necessity of nature, that one begins to glimpse what lies beyond, a larger coherence to which we all belong. Dying or birthing, awareness opens and the heart is pierced with an unreasoned love that is also knowledge. The rounds of birth and death from which life emanates, the rising and setting of the sun, the course of seasons, every need of the body, all partake of the infinity of natural cycles and so can enlarge consciousness to infinite domains. They are there. Immense landscapes of the mind, just past that familiar pretense of power which is also a veil of ignorance.

Reading 17

A POLITICS FOR GENERATION X

Ted Halstead

Everett Carll Ladd, a political scientist, once remarked, "Social analysis and commentary has many shortcomings, but few of its chapters are as persistently wrong-headed as those on the generations and generational change. This literature abounds with hyperbole and unsubstantiated leaps from available data." Many of the media's grand pronouncements about America's post-Baby Boom generation—alternatively called Generation X, Baby Busters, and twentysomethings—would seem to illustrate this point.

The 1990s opened with a frenzy of negative stereotyping of the roughly 50 million Americans born from 1965 to 1978: they were slackers, cynics, whiners, drifters, malcontents. A *Washington Post* headline captured the patronizing attitude that Baby Boomers apparently hold toward their successors: "THE BORING TWENTIES: GROW UP, CRYBABIES." Then books and articles began to recast young Americans as ambitious, savvy, independent, pragmatic, and self-sufficient. For instance, *Time* magazine described a 1997 article titled "Great Xpectations" this way: "Slackers? Hardly. The so-called Generation X turns out to be full of go-getters who are just doing it—but their way."

Stereotyping aside, some disquieting facts jump out regarding the political practices and political orientation of young Americans. A wide sampling of surveys indicates that Xers are less politically or civically engaged, exhibit less social trust or confidence in government, have a weaker allegiance to their country or to either political party, and are more materialistic than their predecessors. Why are so many young people opting out of conventional politics, and what does this mean for the future of American democracy? Might it be that today's political establishment is simply not addressing what matters to the nation's young? And if so, what *is* their political agenda?

Halstead, Ted. "A Politics for Generation X." *Atlantic Monthly* Aug. 1999: 33–42.

The Disengaged Generation

Although political and civic engagement began to decrease among those at the tail end of the Baby Boom, Xers appear to have enshrined political apathy as a way of life. In measurements of conventional political participation the youngest voting-age Americans stand out owing to their unprecedented levels of absenteeism. This political disengagement cannot be explained away as merely the habits of youth, because today's young are markedly less engaged than were their counterparts in earlier generations.

Voting rates are arrestingly low among post-Boomers. In the 1994 midterm elections, for instance, fewer than one in five eligible Xers showed up at the polls. As recently as 1972 half those aged eighteen to twenty-four voted; in 1996, a presidential-election year, only 32 percent did. Such anemic participation can be seen in all forms of traditional political activity: Xers are considerably less likely than previous generations of young Americans to call or write elected officials, attend candidates' rallies, or work on political campaigns. What is more, a number of studies reveal that their general knowledge about public affairs is uniquely low.

The most recent birth cohort to reach voting age is also rejecting conventional partisan demarcations: the distinction between Democrats and Republicans, which has defined American politics for more than a century, doesn't resonate much with the young, who tend to see more similarities than differences between the two parties. Even those young adults who are actively engaged in national politics see partisan boundaries blurring into irrelevance. Gary Ruskin, an Xer who directs the Congressional Accountability Project, a public-policy group in Washington, D.C., puts it this way: "Republicans and Democrats have become one and the same—they are both corrupt at the core and behave like children who are more interested in fighting with each other than in getting anything accomplished."

Surveys suggest that no more than a third of young adults identify with either political party, and only a quarter vote a straight party ticket. Xers are the group least likely to favor maintaining the current two-party system, and the most likely to favor candidates who are running as independents. Indeed, 44 percent of those aged eighteen to twenty-nine identify themselves as independents. Not surprisingly, young adults gave the strongest support to Ross Perot in 1992 and to Jesse Ventura in 1998.

More fundamental, Xers have internalized core beliefs and characteristics that bode ill for the future of American democracy. This generation is more likely to describe itself as having a negative attitude toward America, and as placing little importance on citizenship and national identity, than its predecessors. And Xers exhibit a more materialistic and individualistic streak than did their parents at a similar age. Moreover, there is a general decline in social trust among the young, whether that is trust in their fellow citizens, in established institutions, or in elected officials. These tendencies are, of course, related: heightened individualism and materialism, as Alexis de Tocqueville pointed out, tend to isolate people from one another, weakening the communal bonds that give meaning and force to notions of national identity and the common good.

Explanation X

Many explanations have been advanced for the political apathy of Generation X, but none seems to tell the entire story. One theory holds that television, which the average child now watches for forty hours a week, is to blame for the cynicism and lack of civic education among the young. Another is that growing up during the Reagan and Bush presidencies, when government-bashing was the norm, led many Xers to internalize a negative attitude toward politics and the public sector. A third theory blames the breakdown of the traditional family, in which much of a child's civic sensitivity and partisan orientation is said to develop. And, of course, the incessant scandals in contemporary politics deserve some blame for driving young people into political hiding. Each of these theories undoubtedly holds some truth, but a simpler and more straightforward explanation is possible—namely, that young Americans are reacting in a perfectly rational manner to their circumstances, at least as they perceive them.

As they enter adulthood, this explanation goes, Xers are facing a particularly acute economic insecurity, which leads them to turn inward and pursue material well-being above all else. They see the outlines of very real problems ahead—fiscal, social, and environmental. But in the nation's political system they perceive no leadership on the issues that concern them; rather, they see self-serving politicians who continually indenture themselves to the highest bidders. So Xers have decided, for now, to tune out. After all, they ask, what's the point?

To be sure, today's young have a great deal to be thankful for. Xers have been blessed to come of age in a time of peace and relative material prosperity—itself a significant historical aberration. And the positive legacy they are inheriting goes much deeper: Generation X enjoys the fruits of the civil-rights, women's-rights, and environmental-conservation battles waged by its parents. Finally, who could deny that today's young are benefiting from significant leaps in technology, science, and medicine? But for all these new opportunities, the world being passed on to young Americans is also weighed down by truly bedeviling problems. Prevailing ideologies have proved incapable of accommodating this seeming contradiction.

Ever since the pioneering work on generational theory by the German sociologist Karl Mannheim, in the 1920s, political generations have been thought to arise from the critical events that affect young people when they are most malleable. "Early impressions," Mannheim wrote, "tend to coalesce into a *natural view* of the world." At the very heart of the Xer world view is a deep-seated economic insecurity. In contrast to Baby Boomers, most of whom came of age during the period of unparalleled upward mobility that followed the Second World War, Xers grew up in a time of falling wages, shrinking benefits, and growing economic inequality.

Since 1973, while the earnings of older Americans have mostly stagnated, real median weekly earnings for men aged twenty to thirty-four have fallen by almost a third. In fact, Xers may well be the first generation whose lifetime earnings will be less than their parents'. Already they have the weakest middle class of any generation born in this century.

Falling wages and rising inequality have affected all young Americans, regardless of educational achievement. During the said-to-be economically strong years 1989–1995 earnings for recent college graduates fell by nearly 10 percent—representing the first time that a generation of graduates has earned less than the previous one. And circumstances are far worse for the roughly 67 percent of Xers aged twenty-five to thirty-four who don't have a college degree. In 1997 recent male high school graduates earned 28 percent less (in dollars adjusted for inflation) than did the comparable group in 1973, and recent female high school graduates earned 18 percent less. When politicians and the media continually extol the economy's performance, many Xers just scratch their heads in disbelief.

The economic hardship facing today's young cannot be overstated: America's rate of children in poverty—the highest in the developed world—rose by 37 percent from 1970 to 1995. During the same period the old notions of lifetime employment and guaranteed benefits gave way to the new realities of sudden downsizing and contingent, or temporary, employment. Forty-four million Americans lack basic health insurance today, and Xers—many of whom are part of the contingent work force—are the least insured of all. To compound these problems, many Xers received a poor education in failing public schools, which left them especially ill-prepared to compete in an ever more demanding marketplace.

A Legacy of Debt

Besides struggling against downward economic mobility, Generation X is inheriting a daunting array of fiscal, social, and environmental debts. Although most media reports focus on the national debt and the likely future insolvency of Social Security, the real problem is actually much broader. When they envision their future, Xers don't just see a government drifting toward the political equivalent of Chapter 11; they also see a crippled social structure, a dwindling middle class, and a despoiled natural habitat.

Despite bipartisan fanfare about balancing the federal budget, the fiscal outlook remains quite bleak for young adults—and for reasons seldom discussed.

Long before Social Security and Medicare go insolvent under the burden of Boomer retirement, entitlement payments will have crowded out the public investments that are essential to ensuring a promising future. Government spending on infrastructure, education, and research has already lessened over the past twenty-five years, from 24 percent to 14 percent of the federal budget, and the downward squeeze will only worsen. In other words, Xers will be forced to pay ever higher taxes for ever fewer government services.

Financially most frightening, however, are the nation's skyrocketing levels of personal debt and international debt. With all the focus on balancing the federal budget, not enough attention has been paid to the fact that American families, and Xers in particular, are increasingly unable to balance their own books. Xers carry more personal debt than did any other generation at their age in our nation's history; in fact, a full 60 percent of Xers carry credit-card balances from month to month. In addition, those who attend college face the dual burden of soaring tuition bills and shrinking federal education grants. From 1977 to 1997 the median student-loan debt has climbed from $2,000 to $15,000. The combination of lower wages and overleveraged lifestyles is doubly worrisome to a generation that wonders if it will ever collect Social Security.

Then there is America's ballooning international debt. For the past two decades the nation as a whole has consumed more than it has produced, and has borrowed from abroad to cover the difference—nearly $2 trillion by the end of this decade, or more than a fifth of the total annual output of the U.S. economy. In the short life-span to date of most Xers, America has gone from being the world's largest creditor to being its largest debtor. At some point in the future, especially as interest on our international debt accumulates, investors in other countries will become reluctant to keep bankrolling us. When they do, we will have no choice but to tighten our belts by cutting both investment and consumption. In other words, just as Xers start entering their prime earning years, with their own array of debts and demographic adversities awaiting them, they may well find themselves having to pay off the international debt that Boomers accumulated in the 1980s and 1990s.

Despite the penumbra of long-term debt, the U.S. economy remains the envy of the world; U.S. social conditions, however, are certainly not. America has some of the worst rates of child poverty, infant mortality, teen suicide, crime, family breakup, homelessness, and functional illiteracy in the developed world. In addition, many of our inner cities have turned into islands of despair, a frightening number of our public schools are dangerous, and almost two million of our residents are behind bars.

Many Xers sense that the basic fabric of American society is somehow fraying. Traditional civic participation, community cohesion, and civility are in decline, and not just among the young. The long-held belief in the value of hard work is under assault, as many Americans work longer hours for less pay, watch the gap between rich and poor grow ever wider, and see their benefits cut by corporations with little allegiance to people or place. The result is a fundamental loss of trust: between citizens and elected officials, between employees and employers, and, ultimately, between individuals and their neighbors. Yet trust and civility are the pillars on which any well-functioning democracy and free-market economy depend.

Finally, Xers face large environmental debts that stem from the use and abuse of our natural resources. Well over half of the world's major fisheries are severely depleted or overfished; loss of species and habitat continues at an unprecedented rate, with some 50,000 plant and animal species disappearing each year; freshwater tables across the globe, including parts of America, are falling precipitously; each year America alone loses more than a million acres of productive farmland to sprawl; and emissions of carbon dioxide and other greenhouse gases continue to rise, threatening to raise global temperatures by two to six degrees within the next century.

Global warming is a revealing case study from the perspective of Generation X. There is nearly unanimous scientific agreement on the problem, and a consensus among economists that the nation could reduce its greenhouse-gas emissions without harming its economy. In addition, there is ample evidence— ranging from temperature increases to abnormally frequent weather disturbances to icebergs breaking off from the poles—to warrant deep concern. Yet our political establishment has resigned itself to virtual inaction. Why act now, politicians appear to reason, when we can just pass the problem on to our kids?

How, Xers have every right to ask, can one generation justify permanently drawing down the financial, social, and natural capital of another?

But whining will do no good. The only way for Xers to reverse their sad situation—and to realize the promise of the economic opportunities and technological innovations of the next century—is by entering the political arena that they have every reason to loathe. After all, collective problems require collective solutions. Xers cannot reasonably expect the political establishment to address, let alone fix, the sobering problems they are to inherit unless they start participating in the nation's political process, and learn to flex their generational muscle. Whether or not they do so will depend on two more immediate questions: Does this generation share a set of political beliefs? And if so, how might these translate into a political agenda?

"Balanced-Budget Populism"

Three quarters of Generation X agree with the statement "Our generation has an important voice, but no one seems to hear it." Whatever this voice may be, it does not fit comfortably within existing partisan camps. "The old left-right paradigm is not working anymore," according to the novelist Douglas Coupland, who coined the term "Generation X." Neil Howe and William Strauss, who have written extensively on generational issues, have argued in these pages that from the Generation X perspective "America's greatest need these days is to clear out the underbrush of name-calling and ideology so that simple things can work again." If Xers have any ideology, it is surely pragmatism.

In an attempt to be more specific Coupland has claimed, "Coming down the pipe are an extraordinarily large number of fiscal conservatives who are socially left." The underlying assumption here is that the Xer political world view stems simplistically from a combination of the 1960s social revolution and the 1980s economic revolution. This kind of thinking has led some to describe young adults as a generation of libertarians, who basically want government out of their bedrooms and out of their pocketbooks. As it turns out, however, the political views of most Xers are more complex and more interesting than that.

To say that Xers are fiscal conservatives is to miss half the economic story; the other and equally powerful force at play can best be described as economic populism. In fact, the Xer consensus represents a novel hybrid of two distinct currents of economic thought that have rarely combined in the history of American politics. It might well be called "balanced-budget populism."

On the one hand, many Xers are worried about the debts being loaded onto their future, and therefore support fiscal prudence, balanced budgets, and a pay-as-you-go philosophy. On the other hand, Xers are more concerned than other generations about rising income inequality, and are the most likely to support government intervention to reverse it. The majority believe that the state should do more to help Americans get ahead.

What makes the Generation X economic agenda so surprising is that its two main components have thus far proved to be mutually exclusive in contemporary politics. Fiscal conservatism, widely viewed as the economic philosophy of the Republican right, has generally been accompanied by calls for lower taxes, smaller government, and reduced assistance to the neediest. Meanwhile, concern about the distribution of wealth and helping low-income workers, customarily a pillar of the Democratic left, has been associated with notions of tax-and-spend liberalism and big government. Xers appear to be calling for a new economic synthesis. Like conservatives, they favor fiscal restraint—but unlike the conservative leadership in Congress, only 15 percent believe that America should use any budget surplus to cut taxes. Like Democrats, they want to help the little guy—but unlike traditional Democrats, they are unwilling to do it by running deficits.

The Generation X social synthesis is no more conventional. Although the young are presumed to be more tolerant and socially permissive than their elders, today's young are returning to religion, have family-oriented aspirations, and are proving to be unsupportive of some traditional liberal programs, among them affirmative action. There are numerous indications that Xers—many of whom grew up without a formal religion—are actively searching for a moral compass to guide their lives, and a recent poll suggests that the highest priority for the majority of young adults is building a strong and close-knit family.

Wade Clark Roof, a professor of religion and society at the University of California at Santa Barbara, who studies the religious life of Generation X, says, "It is too early to predict whether today's young adults will form lasting commitments to particular religious denominations or institutions, but it is quite clear that there is a renewed level of interest in religion and spirituality among the post–Baby Boom generation. Many, in fact, have embarked upon a spiritual quest." As if they were spiritual consumers, young adults are shopping around among a wide range of religious traditions. In the process they are finding new ways to incorporate religion into their daily lives: for instance, church socials are rapidly becoming the new singles scene for Xers who want to combine their devotional and romantic ambitions. A clear majority of older Americans believe that a more active involvement of religious groups in politics is a bad idea, but Xers are divided on the issue.

This revival of spiritual and family-oriented aspirations represents a partial repudiation of the moral relativism that took hold in the 1960s and has since become a mainstay of American pop culture. In essence, many Xers are struggling to find a new values consensus that lies somewhere between the secular permissiveness of the left and the cultural intolerance of the right.

When it comes to race relations, Xers are particularly difficult to categorize. They are the cohort most likely to say that the civil-rights movement has not gone far enough. Yet, like Americans of all ages, they register a high level of opposition to job- and education-related affirmative-action programs. The American National Election Survey has reported that 68 percent of Xers oppose affirmative action at colleges. This seeming paradox can be explained in part by the fact that most Xers—though genuinely concerned about improving race relations—are among the first to have felt the actual (or perceived) bite of the affirmative-action programs that their parents and grandparents put into place.

Improving public education is one of the highest policy priorities for Xers. In fact, when asked what should be done with any future budget surplus, nearly half favor increased education spending. They seem to understand that knowledge will be the key to success in the information- and service-based economy of the twenty-first century. Their strong emphasis on education betokens a larger belief in the importance of investing in the future. Rather than maintaining the social-welfare state, the Xer philosophy would favor the creation of a social-investment state.

Although Xers have forsaken conventional political participation en masse, it would be a mistake to assume, as many do, that they are wholly apolitical. There is considerable evidence to suggest that volunteerism and unconventional forms of political participation have increased among young adults. Local voluntary activities, demonstrations, and boycotts all seem to be on the rise within their ranks. Heather McLeod, a Generation X co-founder of *Who Cares* magazine, has provided the following explanation: "We can *see* the impact when we volunteer. We know the difference is real." The implication, of course, is that the conventional political system has become so ineffectual and unresponsive that young people can make a positive difference only by circumventing it.

Xers may be poorly informed when it comes to public affairs, but they know enough to believe that our political system is badly in need of reform. At a very basic level they recognize that the political system is rigged against their interests. For one thing, Xers continually see a large gap between the issues they care most about and the ones that politicians choose to address. For another, they understand that Democrats and Republicans, despite an appearance of perpetual partisan infighting, collude to favor upper-income constituencies and to prevent a range of issues (including campaign-finance reform) from being acted on. Seeing themselves as the "fix-it" generation, Xers long for leaders who will talk straight and advocate the shared sacrifices necessary to correct the long-term problems that preoccupy them most. But today's elected officials are far too deeply trapped in a politics of short-term convenience to deliver anything of the sort. Not surprisingly, then, Xers are eager to do away with the two-party system. They register particularly strong support for third parties, for campaign-finance reform, and for various forms of direct democracy.

The final core belief that helps to define the political views of today's young adults is their commitment to environmental conservation. Thanks to the advent of environmental education and the spread of environmental activism, Xers grew up experiencing recycling as second nature; many actually went home and lobbied their parents to get with the program. In fact, the environment is one of the rare public-policy arenas in which Xers are fairly aware. Many have incorporated their environmental values into their lifestyles and career choices. For instance, a 1997 *Harvard Business Review* article titled "Tomorrow's Leaders: The World According to Generation X" revealed that most current MBA students believed that corporations have a clear-cut responsibility to be environment-friendly in their practices. This generation does not believe that a tradeoff is necessary between a strong economy and a healthy environment.

Fiscal prudence, economic populism, social investment, campaign reform, shared sacrifice, and environmental conservation—this constellation of beliefs transcends the existing left-right spectrum. It should be immediately apparent that this generation's voice is not represented by any of the established leaders or factions in the political mainstream. And Xers seem to recognize as much— 61 percent agree with the statement "Politicians and political leaders have failed my generation." So how would American politics change if the voice of Generation X were suddenly heard?

A New Political Agenda

Despite its feeble rates of political participation, Generation X has already—if unwittingly—exerted an influence on the substance of our politics. This may seem counterintuitive, but who would deny that young Americans were a major force in pushing the balanced-budget cause to the fore? In part this is owing to the large number of Xer votes cast in 1992 for Ross Perot, the candidate who staked much of his campaign on balancing the federal books. Though Perot lost, his pet issue gained momentum as candidates from both parties scrambled to win over Reform Party voters, and the young ones in particular. Recognizing that Generation X makes up a large and particularly unpredictable voting bloc, candidates from across the spectrum have gone out of their way to woo the youth vote, usually by paying lip service to some of young people's more obvious concerns, including, most recently, Social Security reform. Over time, however, Xer support for issues such as balancing the budget and saving Social Security will turn out to be only part of a much broader agenda, one that could come to challenge the status quo on everything from taxes to social policy to political reform.

For years the nation's tax debate has revolved around the question of how much to tax, with the left arguing for more and the right for less. In keeping with the concept of balanced-budget populism, the Xer economic agenda would start with the assumption that the government's share of national income should remain roughly constant. It would focus instead on a far more profound set of questions: What should be taxed? Who should be taxed? What should we invest in? and Who should get the benefits? Over the past several decades the tax burden has crept further and further down the income and age ladder, with the benefits going increasingly to the elderly and the well-to-do—the government now spends nine times as much on each elderly person as it does on each child. If Xers had their way, the collection of taxes would become more progressive and the distribution of benefits more widespread.

One would never know it from partisan skirmishes over income-tax cuts, but the payroll tax actually constitutes the largest tax burden borne by 70 percent of working families and by a full 90 percent of working Americans under age thirty. It is also the most regressive of all taxes, because it kicks in from the first dollar earned, falls exclusively on wages, and is capped at $72,600. An appealing solution to this problem would be to replace payroll taxes with pollution taxes, thereby boosting wages, promoting jobs, and cleaning up the environment, all without raising the deficit. Taxing waste instead of work is precisely the kind of innovative and pragmatic proposal that could help to galvanize the members of Generation X, who have been put to sleep by the current tax debate.

Sooner or later Xers will figure out that America could raise trillions of dollars in new public revenues by charging fair market value for the use of common assets—the oil and coal in the ground, the trees in our national forests, the air-waves and the electromagnetic spectrum—and the rights to pollute our air. We currently subsidize the use of these resources in a number of ways, creating a huge windfall for a small number of industries and a significant loss for all other Americans. The idea of reversing this trend by charging fair market value for the use of common assets and returning the proceeds directly to each American citizen plays to a number of Xer political views—it is populist, equitable, libertarian, and pro–environment all at once.

The populist economic leanings of young adults will also lead them to rethink various other elements of the social contract between citizens, government, and business. For one thing, ending corporate welfare would appeal to a generation weaned on the principle of self-sufficiency. The hidden welfare state, composed of corporate subsidies and tax loopholes that overwhelmingly benefit the well-to-do, has grown several times as large as the hotly debated social-welfare state that benefits the disadvantaged through means-tested programs. Yet today's politicians are too much indebted to the beneficiaries of this governmental largesse to do anything about it. Here, then, may be the key to keeping the budget balanced while funding the social investments that are so important to Xers: all of the money raised or saved by charging for the use of common assets, ending corporate welfare, and closing unproductive tax loopholes could be used to make a topnotch education affordable and accessible to all and, just as important, to make every American child a "trust-fund" baby from birth.

Making economic incentives more progressive and redirecting budgetary priorities is only one part of an Xer economic agenda. Today's young adults, more than any other group at a comparable age, are concerned about their economic outlook and their ability to balance the conflicting demands of work and family. If such problems worsen as a result of economic globalization, then the populism of Generation X, which up to this point has been relatively mild, may suddenly become more pronounced. For instance, the 2030 Center, an advocacy group concerned about the economic well-being of Generation X, is launching a campaign to promote a contingent workers' bill of rights, which calls on employers to provide health care and other benefits to more of their workers.

Even as they were being told that education is the key to a promising future, many Xers were learning the hard way how bad our urban schools have become, and how inequitable is the access to a high-quality education. Neither party is providing a palatable solution: Republicans are all but writing off public schools by emphasizing vouchers that favor private schools, and Democrats are perpetuating many of the worst public-school problems by refusing to challenge the teachers' unions. There are no simple solutions to the predicament, but an obvious starting point would be to sever the traditional link between public-school funding and local property taxes, which only exacerbates existing socioeconomic inequalities. (Several states have already begun moving in this direction.)

Another significant improvement would be to increase the skill level of our public-school teachers by imposing stricter standards and offering more-competitive salaries.

Xers would support enacting new policies to advance racial integration and civil rights in America—policies that avoid the divisiveness and unintended consequences of race-based affirmative action. Although such policies made sense when they were introduced, many Xers believe, race is no longer the determining factor in who gets ahead. In the twenty-first century poor black Americans will have more in common with poor white Americans than they will with upper-middle-class blacks. If the goal is to help those most in need, it would make a lot more sense to pursue class-based affirmative-action programs. Doing so would enable all those at the bottom—regardless of race—to get the help they need, in a way that promoted national unity and racial integration. Another promising alternative to race-based affirmative action is the Texas Ten Percent Plan, whereby all students graduating in the top tenth of their high school classes—whether in inner-city schools or in elite private ones—are automatically accepted into the state's public universities.

Fundamental campaign and political reform is the sine qua non of a Generation X political agenda. Like most Americans, Xers would like to see bold steps taken to get money out of politics. But persuading America's young that their individual votes matter is likely to require reforms far more radical than any currently under consideration.

Until recently most political-reform movements in the United States were based on the assumption that the problem was not the two-party system itself but rather its corruption by special interests and incumbency (hence the proposed cures of campaign-finance reform and term limits). But neither the reduction of private campaign contributions nor the implementation of term limits for elected officials will alter what seems to alienate Xers most of all: the political duopoly of Democrats and Republicans. The rules of today's two-party system actively discourage a third or a fourth party. Consequently, there is growing interest among the young in replacing our archaic electoral process (itself a remnant from eighteenth-century England) with a modern multiparty system. With three or four parties contesting many races, politics might become exciting enough to draw in disenchanted Xers who believe, correctly, that in most elections today their votes do not count.

As the vanguard of the digital age, Xers will also be inclined to support experiments with electronic democracy. For instance, one Xer has launched an effort to make information about the sources of campaign contributions immediately available to the public and the media over the Internet. But the full potential of digital democracy runs much deeper. Already groups are experimenting with electronic town-hall meetings and various forms of deliberative democracy, in which individuals are provided with a full range of information on a particular issue and can register their opinions with the push of a button. It is not hard to imagine a day when citizens will be able to register and vote online, and to monitor the performance of their elected officials with electronic scorecards.

The introduction of electronic communication within corporate America has helped to flatten organizational hierarchies, boost information flows, increase decision-making speed, and, most of all, empower workers. It is at least conceivable that the introduction of electronic forms of democracy could serve to re-engage a generation that has been alienated by today's money-, spin-, and celebrity-dominated politics. And if Xers do eventually enter the fray, their agenda will transform America's political landscape.

The Future of American Politics

Republicans and Democrats will be tempted to dismiss the Xer agenda, because it threatens their electoral coalitions and the politics of short-term convenience. But both parties will do so at their peril, because many of the issues that Xers care most about are already rising to the political surface.

A glimpse of the future may come, strangely enough, in the election of Jesse Ventura as governor of Minnesota. Much of Ventura's support came from young adults, who took advantage of Minnesota's same-day registration law and stormed the polls, helping to create a record turnout. This suggests that if a political candidate can somehow capture the passion of young adults, they will do their part. Ventura offered young Minnesotans something refreshing: a clear alternative to Democrats and Republicans, and a willingness to take on the status quo. But Jesse Ventura is no figurehead for Xers; he is just an early beneficiary of their pent-up political frustration.

As the Xer political agenda starts to take hold, it will further strain existing loyalties. On the Republican side, the odd-bedfellow coalition of social conservatives and economic libertarians that has defined the party for the past two decades is coming apart as a result of the Clinton impeachment saga, whose most lasting legacy may be that it dealt a coup de grace to the political aspirations of the religious right. The Democratic coalition is just as fragile, particularly since it has been losing its base of working-class white men, and the potential retreat of the religious right may deprive Democrats of an obvious opponent against which to rally. As these de-alignments unfold, major shifts in the makeup and core agendas of both parties become almost inevitable.

The stability of today's political consensus is also contingent on the promise of an economy that continues to expand. Take that away, and the props of the status quo—a balanced budget and the novelty of a budgetary surplus, a booming stock market and stable price structures, low unemployment and rising wages, falling welfare rolls and crime rates, and the illusion of a painless fix to Social Security—all topple at once. No business cycle lasts forever, and the global economic crisis of 1998 should come as a warning of what may lie ahead. The prospect of a significant recession leaves the future of American politics wide open.

Turning points in our nation's political history, occasioned by the collapse of an existing civic and political consensus, have usually been accompanied by rampant individualism, weakened institutions, and heightened levels of political alienation. On these scores Xers are playing out their historic role remarkably well. But such periods of civic unrest have also stimulated new political agendas, which eventually force one or both parties to remake themselves around new priorities and coalitions. Could the Generation X political agenda serve as the basis of America's next political consensus?

Balanced-budget populism, social investment, no-nonsense pragmatism, and shared sacrifice could resonate quite strongly with Americans of all ages—particularly the increasing number who are fed up with conventional politics. What is more, the Xer synthesis of a middle-class economic agenda with a moderate social one could remake the powerful alliance between progressives and populists that dominated national politics (and brought widespread upward mobility) from the 1930s to 1960s, when it was ripped apart by the cultural upheaval of the Baby Boom. In practical terms this new politics—based on fiscal prudence, economic populism, family-friendly morality, social investment, campaign reform, environmental conservation, and technological innovation—could eventually take hold in either of the major parties, both of which are now searching for a coherent agenda and a lasting voter base. For Democrats it could mark a return to the party's New Deal roots, and for Republicans it could give substance to heretofore vague calls for a "compassionate conservatism."

Since this new politics could speak to many of those who are alienated by the current political order, Xers and older Americans alike, it could give birth to our nation's next majoritarian coalition. Such a coalition could do a great deal to reinvigorate our nation's democracy, benefit the majority of its citizens, and restore legitimacy to our political system.

When history books are written at the end of the twenty-first century, it is unlikely that the post–Baby Boom generation will still be referred to as a nondescript "X." One way or another, this generation will be judged and labeled by its legacy. Today's young adults will be remembered either as a late-blooming generation that ultimately helped to revive American democracy by coalescing around a bold new political program and bringing the rest of the nation along with them, or as another silent generation that stood by as our democracy and society suffered a slow decline.

The great question of twenty-first-century politics is whether a critical mass of Xers will eventually recognize the broader potential of their agenda, and outgrow their aversion to politics.

Reading 18

THE CYBERSPACE DIALECTIC

Michael Heim

Cyberspace floats now in a cultural limbo. The limbo is a zigzag holding pattern that professional philosophers call "the dialectic." This dialectic is a social fever characterized by wide mood swings between utopian fantasy and hateful cynicism. Hyperbole alternates with attack, and the status of cyberspace hovers undertain: commercial jukebox? neodemocracy? the end of broadcasting? monster information swamp?

Cyberspace has always been provocative, but it has not always been controversial. The word, and the concepts it came to represent, burst on the scene like gangbusters in William Gibson's 1984 science-fiction novel *Neuromancer,* and then gained academic gravity in the early 1990s through conferences and books like Michael Benedikt's anthology, *Cyberspace: First Steps.*[1] Then in the mid 1900s, cyberspace became celebrated in daily newspapers and television spots, and the tenth edition (revised) of Merriam-Webster's *Collegiate Dictionary* confidently defined it as "the on-line world of computer networks." Politicians sought to extend legislative power over "the information highway" be dredging up on-line obscenities, pursuing hacker felons, and declaring cyberspace a federal "superhighway" where the speed of telecommunication would fall under congressional jurisdiction. Today, näive questions like What is it? and How do I connect to it? have evolved into trickier questions like Am I for or against cyberspace? What position do I take regarding its social benefits? Now that we have crossed the electronic frontier, how does our society measure cyberspace? This is where most of us could learn from the dialectic.

Originally, the word circulated among the ancient Greeks, who used *dialektikē (tekhnē)* to mean the art of debate and conversation. *Dialegesthai* means

Heim, Michael, "The Cyberspace Dialectic," *The Digital Dialectic : New Essays on New Media.* Peter Lunenfeld, ed. Cambridge, Mass.: MIT Press, 1999. 25–45.

"talking something through" or "organizing a subject matter." In other words, transformational dynamics first appeared as part of the art of conversation. The ancient Greeks gave dialectic its classical expression in written dialogues. There, in the Greek language, the workd "dialectic" was born, and its twin sibling was the word "dialogue."

Jumping ahead several millennia, the idea of dialectic in modern times has come, through G. F. W. Hegel and Karl Marx, to signify the transformational dynamics of social history. Hegel developed his notion of the dialectic to include the back-and-forth process of social movements where one advance in freedom evokes its opposite reaction, which in turn calls forth another and opposite reaction, and so forth. Dialectic was not simply an abstract template of "thesis-antithesis-synthesis" to be applied in a doctrinaire manner to politics. Dialectic was, rather, the concrete movement of social history itself. Marx, the next signpost in the development of the dialectic, identified history with the history of civil wars and violent revolutions, but Hegel's dialectic originally included the more subtle shifting forces of social change that propel human evolution.

In those systems that adopted Marx's philosophy, the dialectic became the cornerstone of official ideology. In the Soviet Union, for example, millions of students in Communist schools carried textbooks bearing the stamp "DIAMAT," short for "Dialectical Materialism." The dialectic in its Marxist-Leninist form belonged to materialistic philosophy as a rigid set of doctrines defining the socioeconomic struggle between capital and labor. The straight party line of communism largely eroded the original meaning of "dialectic" as a term to describe historical dynamics. This was particularly ironic, for, as we have seen, dialectic resists stability, finding its form in the unsettling, the changing, the shifting.

Both historical and critical discussion of the dialectic runs through this paper, but it is important to acknowledge that the present taint of the word "dialectic" is due to its centrality to Marxist thought and policies. As a result, many people automatically recoil against dialectic and fail to see its usefulness in weighing the new reality layer. It is true that networked computer media have launched an information space that ill befits the materialistic mold of Marxism, based as it was in the reading of early industrial capitalism. I believe, nonetheless, that we can still use dialectic as a tool to move beyond the polarity of fear and fascination that characterizes the continuum binding the fans of the anti-technology Unabomber to the millions who use computers to surf the Internet.

The dialectic I have in mind is that which preceded Marxism and can be clearly described. I want to show that dialectic can indeed illuminate the paradoxes of the current debate about the value of cyberspace. Though bound by an underlying ontology, the dialectic can still illuminate the confusion and tension created by new media. There is something of the joke or paradox that propels all dialectical thinking. We live in a most appropriate era to savor the dialectical joke. An appropriate joke, indeed, for an era when people express their support for anarchist-inspired attacks on technology by posting messages to the World Wide Web.

Unabomber Backlash

The figure of the Unabomber (and the concerns he came to represent) is one side of the cyberspace dialectic.[2] An extreme provokes the full force of its opposite. To be sure, the Unabomber's fervor cannot be understood in isolation from the one-sided enthusiasm that pervades a commercial culture that sells millions of computers every year. The Unabomber's extremism became clear to the public in September 1995, when the *Washington Post* published his 56-page, 35,000-word manifesto, "Industrial Society and Its Future."[3] Under the pressure of bomb threats against airline passengers, the newspaper carried the manifesto in its morning edition. By evening on the East coast, you could not find a single copy of the *Post* with its 8-page manifesto insert. The next day, however, the 200-kilobyte text of the manifesto turned up on the Internet. It appeared on a World Wide Web site sponsored by the Federal Bureau of Investigation. Desperate to be published, the Unabomber now had his own "home page," illustrated with "wanted" posters and maps pinpointing the series of explosions he had caused, all in a high-tech, HTML format.

Search the Unabomber Manifesto and you find the word "computer" frequently used in conjunction with "control" and "technology." The serial bomber blames technology, especially computers, for a vast variety of social ills: the invasion of privacy, genetic engineering, and "environmental degradation through excessive economic growth." The Unabomber Manifesto borrows from an older school of social critics who followed the French writer Jacques Ellul. Ellul's *Technological Society,* a bible in the 1960s, demonized an all-pervasive technology monster lurking beneath the "technological-industrial system."[4] Ellul took a snapshot of technology in the 1960s, then projected and expanded that single frozen moment in time onto a future where he envisioned widespread social destruction. Ellul's approach—what economists and futurists call "linear trend extrapolation"—takes into account neither social evolution nor economic transformation. Ellul did not take into account the possibility that economics of scale could develop that would redistribute certain forms of technological power, allowing individuals, for instance, to run personal computers from domestic spaces and, in turn, publish content on an equal footing with large corporations.

The dark future portrayed by Ellul appears throughout the Unabomber Manifesto, but the Unabomber goes further by linking the technology threat specifically to computers. This killer-critic sees computers as instruments of control to oppress human beings either by putting them out of work or by altering how they work. The manifesto states:

It is certain that technology is creating for human beings a new physical and social environment radically different from the spectrum of environments to which natural selection has adapted the human race physically and psychologically. If man does not adjust to this new environment by being artificially re-engineered, then he will be adapted to it through a long and painful process of natural selection. The former is far more likely than the latter.[5]

The dilemma outlined by the Unabomber can be found in writings of other extremist critics. Many share the Unabomber's views without harboring his pathological desperation. The no-win dilemma they see is either to permit evolution to wreck millions of lives or to use technology to forcibly reengineer the population. Laissez-faire evolution or artificial engineering seem to be the sole options: Either manipulate humans to fit technology, or watch technology bulldoze the population until all that remains is a techno-humanoid species of mutants. The Ellul school of criticism posits a monolithic steamroller "technology" that flattens every activity, and the Ellulian view allows only a static fit between technology and society. Recent alumni of this school, like Jean Baudrillard, nationalize the alien technology monster and call it "Americanization."[6] They fear the ghostly "representations of representations" that inject Disneylike simulacra into every facet of cultural life. Cultural life floats on a thin sea of representations that represent other representations whose active content has been exploited until they are empty images without meaning.

We need not look outside the borders of the United States, of course, to find antitechnological, Luddite theory. The Unabomber Manifesto reveals concerns raised by American critics. Some authors—Kirkpatrick Sale, for instance—felt compelled to distance themselves from the Unabomber Manifesto because they in fact use many of the same arguments to reject technology and they share with the Unabomber some common critical sources like Ellul. While agreeing in principle with what the Unabomber says, they want to distance themselves from terrorist practices. Such critics grew in numbers during the early 1990s, when information technology extended into every area of life, spawning a multimedia industry and virtual reality companies. Computer networks like the Internet came into general use in the early 1990s, and economic forecasts indicated that the computerized infrastructure was transforming the national economy as well as the American culture. Not surprisingly, critics took a look.

The computer's impact on culture and the economy mutated from a celebration into what I call the cyberspace backlash. A cultural pendulum swings back and forth, both feeding off and being fed to a sensation-hungry media.[7] The media glom onto hype and overstatement culled from marketers and true believers. When the media assess the technoculture, a trend climbs in six months from obscurity to one of the Five Big Things—complete with magazine covers, front-page coverage in newspapers, and those few minutes on television that now constitute the ultimate in mass appeal. After the buildup, the backlash begins. The process is as follows: (1) simplify an issue; (2) exaggerate what was simplified; (3) savage the inadequacies of the simplification. Cyberspace was no exception, and the reverse swing against cyberspace was inevitable.

The backlash is not simply the product of a fevered media economy; it taps into people's real attitudes toward an ever more technologized culture. This runs from those who are frustrated by the frequent need to upgrade software to those who experience "future shock" as a personal, existential jolt. While futurologists Alvin and Heidi Toffler preach "global trends" from an economist's overview, the individual suffers painful personal changes in the workplace and the market-place. Waves of future shock may intrigue forward-looking policy makers, but those same swells look scary to someone scanning the horizon from a plastic board adrift in the ocean. The big picture of evolutionary trends often over-whelms and silences the personal pain of living people. Those people will eventually find their voices in a backlash against the confident soothsayers in business suits.

A streak of the Unabomber's Luddite passion weaves through the cyber-space backlash. The titles of several books published in the past few years give a glimpse of the breadth of the backlash. Among the books are *Resisting the Vir-tual Life,* by James Brook and Iain Boal; *Rebels Against the Future: The Lud-dites and Their War on the Industrial Revolution,* by Kirkpatrick Sale; *Silicon Snake Oil: Second Thoughts on the Information Highway,* by Clifford Stoll; *The Age of Missing Information,* by Bill McKibben; *The Gutenberg Elegies,* by Sven Birkerts; *War of the Worlds: Cyberspace and the High-Tech Assault on Reality,* by Mark Slouka; and *The Future Does Not Compute,* by Steve Talbott. Obvi-ously, these books show infinitely more grace than the Unabomber's crude, coercive manifestos, but they all reject, to varying degrees, the movement of life into electronic environments.[8]

These critics tend toward what I call "naïve realism." Many naïve realists take reality to be that which can be immediately experienced, and they align computer systems with the corporate polluters who dump on the terrain of unmediated experience. The elaborate data systems we are developing still exist outside our primary sensory world. The systems do not belong to reality but con-stitute instead, in the eyes of the naïve realist, a suppression of reality. The sup-pression comes through "the media," which are seen to function as vast, hegemonic corporate structures that systematically collect, edit, and broadcast packaged experience. The media infiltrate and distort nonmediated experience, compromising and confounding the immediacy of experience. Computers accel-erate the process of data gathering and threaten further, in their eyes, what little remains of pure, immediate experience. The naïve realist believes that genuine experience is as endangered as clean air and unpolluted water.

The purity of experience was defended by the New England transcendental-ists in the nineteenth-century. Thinkers like Henry David Thoreau, backed by the publicity skills of Ralph Waldo Emerson, proclaimed a return to pure,

unmediated experience.[9] Thoreau left city life to spend weeks in a rustic cabin in
the woods at Walden Pond, near Concord, Massachusetts, so he could "confront
the essential facts of life." Far from the social and industrial hubbub, he spent
two years contemplating the evils of railroads and industrialization. Although
railroad tracks and freeways now circumscribe Walden Pond, many contemporary critics, such as Wendell Berry, seek to revive the Thoreauvian back-to-
nature ethic and take up the cause represented by his Walden retreat.[10]

In the eyes of the naïve realist, computer networks add unnecessary frills to
the real world while draining blood from real life. Reality, they assert, is the
physical phenomena we perceive with our bodily senses: what we see directly
with our eyes, smell with our noses, hear with our ears, taste with our tongues,
and touch with our own skin. From the standpoint of this empirically perceived
sensuous world, the computer system is at best a tool, at worst a mirage of dis-
tracting abstractions from the real world. The mountains, rivers, and great planet
beneath our feet existed long before computers, and the naïve realist sees in the
computer an alien intruder defiling God's pristine earth. The computer, say the
naïve realists, should remain a carefully guarded tool, if indeed we allow computers to continue to exist. The computer is a subordinate device that tends to
withdraw us from the primary world. We can and should, if the computer ener-
vates us, pull the plug or even destroy the computer.

The naïve realist speaks from fear. There is fear of abandoning local community values as we move into a cyberspace of global communities. There is
fear of diminishing physical closeness and mutual interdependence as electronic
networks mediate more and more activities. There is fear of crushing the spirit
by replacing bodily movement with smart objects and robotic machines. There
is fear of losing the autonomy of our private bodies as we depend increasingly
on chip-based implants. There is fear of compromising integrity of mind as we
habitually plug into networks. There is fear that our own human regenerative
process is slipping away as genetics transmutes organic life into manageable
strings of information. There is fear of the sweeping changes in the workplace
and in public life as we have known them. There is fear of the empty human
absence that comes with increased telepresence. There is fear that the same
power elite who formerly "moved atoms" as they pursued a science without conscience will now "move bits" that govern the computerized world. By voicing
such fears, the naïve realist sounds alarms that contrast sharply with the idealistic good cheer of futurists like Alvin and Heidi Toffler.

Naïve Realists vs. Network Idealists

Futurists describe and advise a culture shaken by future shock. But the shock
they describe comes in macroeconomic waves, not in personal, existential distress. In this sense, futurists like the Tofflers are idealists. Idealists take the mea-

sure of individuals by placing them within the larger economic or political contexts to which they belong. Most futurists look to the economically and politically global, not to the individually existential. Their big idea absorbs
individuals. The "digerati" celebrated by *Wired* magazine welcome the digital
revolution and offer a central warning: you had better join soon, or be crushed
by the wheels of history. Many of the celebrated digerati come from institutions
of technology that are dedicated to advancing the cybernetic control systems of
society. Such institutions came to prominence not by educating through the liberal arts but by subordinating education to the advancement of government-
sponsored technical research. When Alvin Toffler writes about a "powershift,"
he uses a prophetic style that underlines the assumptions of the power group to
which his futurist rhetoric belongs.[11] Drowning the individual in the "waves" of
social development has been a consistent theme in the history of idealism, from
the conservative F. H. Bradley in England to the liberal-monarchic idealism of
Hegel in Germany.[12]

Such idealism goes back to the early pioneers of computing. Seventeenth-
century rationalists like Gottfried W. Leibniz and René Descartes pushed com-
putation and mathematical physics far ahead of ethics and feelings. The
Cartesian revolution in philosophy put mathematical physics at the top of the list
of priorities while ethics became the incidental victim of skeptical reasoning.
The Cartesian faith in progress relied on the reduction of thinking to systems of
rational logic. So great was the optimism of seventeenth-century rationalists that
they became easy targets for satirists like Voltaire, the French philosopher and
writer whose works epitomize the Age of Enlightenment. In his novel *Candide*
(1759), Voltaire caricatured Leibniz in the character of Professor Pangloss. Pangloss's tortured young student Candide meditates: "My Master said, 'There is a
sweetness in every woe.' It must be so. It must be so."[13]

The idealist points to evolutionary gains for the species and glosses over the
personal sufferings of individuals. Idealists are optimists, or, on bad days, they
are happy worriers. The optimist says, "This is the best of all possible worlds, and
even the pain is a necessary component." In the eyes of naïve realists, the idealist
is selling snake oil. No accident that Leibniz, who was caricatured in Pangloss,
was the same Leibniz who worked on the protocomputer and pioneered the
binary logic that was to become the basis for computers and digital culture.

The cyberspace backlash strikes at idealistic—futurist flimflam as much as it
reacts to felt personal—existential changes. Postmodern theory, with its often
glib talk of "cyborgs," "software cities," and "virtual communities," provokes its
opponents by flashing a brand of intellectually sophisticated terror. Postmodern
rhetoric, lacking a compassionate basis in shared experience and common practices, aims to frighten the insecure and to train commandos who attack common
sense. After all, linguistics, semiology, and structuralism combined to make it
virtually impossible to see language as anything but a code or system, never as a
living event through which we are all responsible to one another. Since Ferdinand

de Saussure, the communicative power of language, its ability to build community, has become suspect to the point of ridicule for sophisticated theoreticians.[14]

And what of those who ignore the theoreticians and insist on building a community around the new words, the new structures thrown up by the computer's wake? There is, of course, a certain jaded idealism that also enjoys poking common sense in the eye with hot purple hair, revolutionary verbiage, and cyberpunk affectations. A cybervocabulary promotes confusion as a fashion statement. Wave the banner of confusion, however, and you provoke a return to basics. Naïveté then seems a blessing. Yet the dialectical story does not end so simply, because the futurist vision is not without cogency. What the futurist sees is precisely what frightens others.

Nerds in the Noosphere

The futurist sees the planet Earth converging. Computer networks foster virtual communities that cut across geography and time zones. Virtual community seems a cure-all for isolated people who complain about their isolation. Locked in metal boxes on urban freeways, a population enjoys socializing with fellow humans through computer networks. Shopping, learning, and business are not far away once we enhance our telepresence abilities. The prospect seems so exciting that you see the phrase "virtual communities" mentioned in the same breath as McLuhan's "global village" or Teilhard's "Omega Point."

Pierre Teilhard de Chardin, a French Jesuit paleontologist, envisioned the convergence of humans into a single massive "noosphere" or "mind sphere" (Ionian Greek *noos*, "mind").[15] This giant network would surround Earth to control the planet's resources and shepherd a world unified by Love. Teilhard's catholic vision ranged from evolutionary physics to world religion (though his views received more suspicion than support from Church orthodoxy). He saw in the physical world an inner drive for all substance to converge into increasingly complex units. Material atoms merge to create higher-level units. Matter eventually converges to form organisms. The convergence of organic life in turn produces higher-level complexities. The most complex units establish a new qualitative dimension where consciousness emerges. On the conscious level, the mind—and then the networking of minds—gives birth to a new stage of spirit.

As in Hegel's nineteenth-century philosophy, Teilhard sees the birth of spirit as the inner meaning or cosmic purpose of the entire preceding evolution. Convergence toward greater complexity, even on the subatomic material level, exemplifies the principle of Love (agapic rather than erotic love). Only later, with the dawn of intelligence, does Love come into full consciousness and self-awareness. For Teilhard, this is the Christ principle that guides the universe. "In the beginning was the Logos." Only at its culminating point does history reveal its full meaning as the mental sphere becomes dominant. Teilhardians see ultimate convergence as the Omega or End Point of time, the equivalent of the Final Coming of Christ.

Teilhard, like Marx before him, absorbed much about evolutionary dynamics from Hegel, the father of German idealism. Hegel's centrality to the discourse of Western philosophy is such that his work on the dialectic deserves another telling in this context. Hegel applied the Christian notion of Divine Providence to the recorded events of civilized history in order to show a rational progression. His elaborate encyclopedias and multi-volume histories of Western civilization affirmed a hidden evolutionary will driving with purpose toward a single culmination. The fulfillment of history, according to Hegel, was a unity harmonized in diversity, a oneness that later interpreters described as a "classless society" (as with Marx) or as "social progress" (as with William Torrey Harris and the American Hegelians).[16]

Hegel's genius was to see a divine Idea unfold in the material world of historical events—even to the point of squeezing all recorded history into a Procrustean logic of progress. The famous "Hegelian dialectic" changed from its original meaning of logical conversation to its new meaning of social movements and improvements. The motor that powered the movement of history was a series of internal civil wars, each bringing the entire society a little closer to perfection. The culmination of all revolutions, for Hegel, produced Western constitutional democracies where the individual and the individual's rights are recognized by the social collective. Just what this heavenly harmony looks like in practice appeared differently to the various proponents of Hegelian idealism. While Marx's advocates dressed in the worker's garb of political economy or in the revolutionary's guerrilla fatigues, Teilhard's vision blended synthetic physics with Christian communitarianism. It is especially the communitarianism that attracts network idealists.

This link between the communitarian impulse and the cult of technology may seem incongruous at first glance, but we must not forget that the organized, durational community is itself a by-product of agricultural technology, of the development of machines. At first, and for millennia, machines functioned as stand-alone tools under supervision of a single human operator—the hoe, the plow. With larger-scale projects and manufacturing, machines increasingly functioned in an ensemble—the mill, the boatyard. The shift from isolated work tools to the components of larger systems became one of the defining characteristics of the industrial era, with railroads, fuel distribution, and highway systems being the obvious examples. The interconnection of one machine with another extended into the sphere of human society and cultural production with networks: first radio, then television, and now computers. The recent convergence of all three media has created a situation in which a vast variety of machines plug into seemingly limitless networks, all with the computer as the controller switch.

The network idealist builds collective beehives. The idealist sees the next century as an enormous communitarian buzz. The worldwide networks that cover the planet form a global beehive where civilization shakes off individual controls and electronic life steps out on its own. In that networked world, information circulates freely through the planetary nervous system, and intellectual property vanishes as a concept. Individuals give and take freely. Compensation is automated for the heavenly, disembodied life. Electronic angels distribute credit. Private territory and material possessions no longer divide people. Digital mediation does away with the battle of the books, and proprietary ideas give way to free exchange and barter. Cooperative intelligence vanquishes private minds. Extropian idealists (who define themselves as the enemies of entropy) encourage their members to entrust their deceased bodies to cryonic storage until scientists can one day either revive the repaired body or upload the brain-encased mind into silicon chips. The Teilhardian Internet is optimism gone ballistic.

Realists remain unimpressed. They are uneasy with the idealists who celebrate an electronic collective. I know people in rural communities who hear wishful thinking in the phrase "virtual community." It sticks in their craw. For many, real community means a difficult, never-resolved struggle. It is a sharing that cannot be virtual because its reality arises from the public places that people share physically—not the artificial configurations you choose but the spaces that fate allots, complete with the idiosyncrasies of local weather and a mixed bag of family, friends, and neighbors. For many, the "as-if community" lacks the rough interdependence of life shared. And here is where the naïve realist draws the line. The direct, unmediated spaces we perceive with our senses create the places where we mature physically, morally, and socially. Even if modern life shrinks public spaces by building freeways, and even if the "collective mind" still offers much interaction among individuals through computers, the traditional meeting places still foster social bonds built on patience and on the trust of time spent together. Here is the bottom line for realists.

No surprise, then, for realists when they hear the Internet Liberation Front is bringing down the Internet's pipeline for six hours, when anti-Semitic hate groups pop up on Prodigy, when *Wired* magazine gets letter-bombed, or when neo-Nazis work their way into the German Thule Network. The utopian *communitas* exists as an imagined community, as the Mystical Body. Real community exists, on the contrary, where people throw their lot together and stand in face-to-face ethical proximity. Computer hardware may eventually allow us to transport our cyberbodies, but we are just learning to appreciate the trade-offs between primary and virtual identities. Put the New Jerusalem on hold until we phone security.

Reclaiming the Idea of Dialectic

Both network idealism and naïve realism belong to the cyberspace dialectic. They are two sides of the same coin, binary brothers. One launches forth with unreserved optimism; the other lashes back with a longing to ground us outside technology. Some enthusiastically embrace the commercial development of the Internet, while others vehemently oppose it. While everyone agrees that information technology is transforming postmodern society, not everyone agrees that we can make any sense out of the transformation at the present moment. A third group insists that cyberspace is going through a confusing birth process, like every other important earlier technology, and they believe that all attempts at understanding the process, no matter how intelligent, remain pointless. This third group regards the cyberspace dialectic as irrational guesswork and hyperbole. All bets are off, as far as they are concerned. They support their skepticism by pointing to the histories of other media, like television and film, illustrating their viewpoint with the scribblings of critics of yore who attacked prior technologies but whose screeds are now amusing because they failed utterly to understand how the future would choose to use the technology.[17] This skeptical view results in a let's-wait-and-see attitude because rational criticism has, according to this view, never worked in the past. Such skepticism kills dialectic by rejecting social evaluation as baseless futurism.

Skepticism cannot guide us through a dialectical situation. We must make some sense of the future as we make decisions in the present. Cyberspace is contested territory, and those who reject the contest will not meet the challenge of the present. The battle between the telecommunications legislators and the Electronic Frontier Foundation confirms the fact that cyberspace is contested territory.[18] The cultural struggle over cyberspace signals the need to rethink dialectic so that we can enter it properly.

The cyberspace debate reveals a subtle groundswell presaging the pulse of the next century. Some historians, in fact, gauge the twentieth century as one of the shorter centuries, one of those epochs that ends before its official centennial birthday. They mark the end of the twentieth century with the 1989 fall of the Berlin Wall. Many historians count the advent of personal computers and worldwide information systems among the causative factors leading to the overthrow of Marxism—Leninism and the changes in world history that are ushering in the twenty-first century.

If Marxism has expired as a political and economic model, its characteristic dialectic has evinced an intellectual afterlife in the work of German-influenced French thinkers and their American disciples. From structuralism to semiotics to hermeneutics to poststructuralism and deconstruction, the dialectic of Marxism persists as an unspoken model of how correct-thinking and postmodern people should regard society. Critical theory has often been just another name for Marxian analysis incognito. Through virtuoso verbalism, critical theory often refuses to submit its covert social assumptions to clear argumentation. Earlier variants—the Frankfurt School with Max Horkheimer and Theodor Adorno's "negative dialectics,"[19] and Jürgen Habermas's theory of ideal communication[20]—were willing and able to address their Marxian roots. When Horkheimer and Adorno spelled out what they called the "dialectic of the Enlightenment," or Herbert Marcuse continued their work by advocating the "No" or Great Refusal ("drop out") in the face of the industrial-technological system, they were engaged in an avowedly Marxian critique of the West's capitalist society.[21] But the obscurantism of recent French theory conceals under its narcotic smoke screen a whole host of Marxist assumptions about social revolution that do not spell their meaning clearly in this era of information.[22] We need to know more explicitly what kind of dialectic we move in, if we are moving in a dialectic at all. Once the dialectic no longer swings between the socially oppressed and the power of big capital, we must ask where and how dialectic comes into play. If our social developments begin to manifest outside the mode of material production, what does the mode of information mean for social change?

We keep returning to the same core questions: What is dialectic? How does the dialectic apply to the struggle over cyberspace? While we definitely need to recognize the cyberspace dialectic, we do not want a replay of the violent civil wars that attach to Marxist dialectical materialism. Perhaps we need to return to the earliest incarnation of the dialectic, starting with its appearance in the *Dialogues of Plato,* which are actually the dialogues of Socrates written down and polished by Plato (with "dialogue" having its root in the Greek *dia logou,* "through words or argument"). The dialectic—the "working through words or argument" of the *dialegesthai*—was an integral part of Plato's *Dialogues.* Dialectic refers to the logical side of what occurs in the *Dialogues.* Dialectic emphasizes the oppositions found within dialogue. Dialogues between people achieve more than mutual recognition and shared feelings; dialogues also expose conceptual and attitudinal differences as they apply to the issues under consideration. The interplay of differences about issues constitutes the original meaning of dialectic. It is this meaning of dialectic—an ongoing exchange between polar positions—that I wish to emphasize for and in cyberspace.

You could say, then, that dialectic is the conceptual exchange that happens in dialogue. Dialogues can contain banter, jokes, irony, and shared feelings, but any serious, sustained dialogue will sooner or later reveal a dialectic in play. Dialectic is the inner logic of differences exposed over an extended period of interchange. We should not, in other words, associate dialectic exclusively with conflict and flat-out contradiction. Dialectic comes from human differences as they become articulate—not from the confrontation that breeds revolution and civil war. What more fitting support to dialectic could we have than the technological medium we call cyberspace?

Hegel would have appreciated a mutual opposition while betting on an eventual synthesis. Right now, a cyberspace synthesis is not in sight, certainly not in the near future. But a collision or the collapse of one of the sides may not be the only end point to look for. We may have to learn to live with the dialectic as the art of permanent exchange. We might learn to balance the idealist's enthusiasm for computerized life with the need to ground ourselves more deeply in the felt earth that the realist affirms to be our primary reality. This uneasy balance I have elsewhere called "virtual realism."[23] Virtual realism is the middle path between naïve realism and network idealism. On the middle path, the dialectic becomes electric. The cyberspace dialectic sustains opposition as the polarity that continually sparks the dialogue, and the dialogue is the life of cyberspace.

Virtual Realism

Virtual realism walks a tightrope. The delicate balancing act sways between the idealism of unstoppable Progress and the Luddite resistance to virtual life. The Luddite falls out of sync with the powerful human push that has been promoting rationality for three centuries, and that now seems ready either to blossom or to blow up in the next century. The idealist falls for the Progress of tools without content, of productivity without satisfaction, of ethereal connections without corporeal discipline. Both inclinations—naïve realism and futurist idealism—belong to the current of our time. The long, thin rope stretches across the chasm of change and permits no return. Indifferent standstill is even more dangerous. The challenge is not to end the oscillation between idealism and realism but to find the path that goes through them. It is not a synthesis in the Hegelian sense of a result achieved through logic. Neither is it a synthesis arising from the warfare of the two sides. Rather, virtual realism is an existential process of criticism, practice, and conscious communication.

What is the path of virtual realism? Virtual realism parts with realism pure and simple. Realism often means lowered expectations. "Being realistic" often implies reducing or compromising ideals. Historically, in fact, realism often follows periods of high idealism. The pendulum swings back because it had swung so high in the first place. No movement of history begins, however, without an initial affirmation, without a first postulate affirming that it has cleared the mist and found reality. Realism begins as a sober criticism of overblown, high-flown ideals. Yet at the core of realism is an affirmation of what is real, reliable, functional. Today we must be realistic about virtual reality, untiringly suspicious of the airy idealism and commercialism surrounding it, and we must keep an eye on the weeds of fiction and fantasy that threaten to stifle the blossom.

At the same time, we have to affirm those entities that virtual reality presents as our culture begins to inhabit cyberspace.[24] Virtual entities are indeed real, functional, and even central to life in coming eras. Part of work and leisure life will transpire in virtual environments. Thus it is important to find a balance that swings neither to the idealistic blue sky where primary reality disappears, nor to the mundane indifference that sees just another tool, something that can be picked up or put down at will. The balancing act requires a view of life as a mixed bag, as a series of trade-offs that we must discern and then evaluate. Balancing means walking a pragmatic path of involvement and critical perception.

In *Electric Language: A Philosophical Study of Word Processing,* I developed a theory of cultural trade-offs as they happen during ontological shifts.[25] There I describe in detail the trade-offs between the computerized and the traditional ways of doing things. For *Electric Language,* this meant the specific trade-offs between electronic and printed texts. The method used was phenomenology, a way of describing the first-person modes in which we read and write, specifically to contrast reading and writing with computers and with traditional books. Such descriptions highlight the psychic frameworks of two very different modes of reading and writing—not from the viewpoint of economic, or social, or legal products but from the viewpoint of living through the activity itself.

These trade-offs belong to what I called "the ontological shift." This ontological shift has been referred to by others in shorthand as a move from "managing atoms to managing bits." But I would argue against this pat reduction. Our practical use of symbols never did move in the element of atoms, for atoms are scientific abstractions. The abstractions of science about the atomic level have, of course, had an enormous impact on history, but that impact came not from a change at the core of culture but from the pressure that bore down on the surface of politics, warfare, and energy production. Culture took the atomic age into account only slowly. Atoms are abstractions, just as bits and bytes are abstractions. But while bits and bytes abstract from a computational process, they touch information, and information reaches to the core of culture.

The ontological shift described in *Electric Language* occurs in what I called "the tectonic plates of culture," the unnoticed cultural element that supports—at different times, in different ways—the symbols of language. No longer papyrus or paper, the new element is digital information. The element belongs to the psychic framework of life, not to the abstractions of physics or the sciences. The symbol element is where much of practical culture transpires. It is where we store our memory, where we record our history, and where the sacred things are preserved. Most important to virtual realism is the sense of history behind the ontological shift. We need the large perspective on cultural change and the way symbolic elements mutate in history. The big picture is crucial for virtual realism, for only from that broad perspective can we envision the trade-offs that occur in historical drift.[26]

An important component of virtual realism is what I call *technalysis.* Technalysis—as the term suggests—is the analysis of technologies, and the analysis proceeds from a critical but practical standpoint. It is a critical strategy for describing specific technologies, a style of thinking appropriate for walking the fissures of a culture in transition. Technalysis accepts the ontological fact that we move in a new layer of electronic reality. In the technologized West, fewer and fewer discussions or oppositions occur without leaving traces in cyberspace. Today, the Unabomber's fans as well as the network idealists meet on-line. The dialectic of cyberspace is happening *in cyberspace.* This dialectic, if sustained, can become technalysis, a new kind of social self-awareness.

Whether right or wrong in its conclusions, each attempt at technalysis brings to language the human encounter with specific technologies. Detailed analysis of specific technologies has major advantages over the wholesale rejection of technology found in writers from Ellul and Baudrillard to the Unabomber. The wholesale suspicion of technology as a monstrous Leviathan supposes that we can extricate ourselves sufficiently from automobiles, telephones, and computers in order to arrive at a negative assessment and eventual disengagement. The suspicion directs its gaze at a monster whose features must remain vague and remote. Fear of the giant technology monster blinds the critic to detail in daily life as we install technologies and as we install ourselves in technological environments. Blind to details, such critics close off the possibility that their analysis might contribute something of value to the concrete planning of future systems. Instead, they must maintain a posture of hostility—a posture that requires considerable effort but delivers no constructive dividend.

The advantage of technalysis—the detailed phenomenology of specific technologies—resides in its working alongside "human factors" engineering, which, however remote from its participants, places the human being at the center of technology.

Virtual realism, then, seeks to support the cyberspace dialectic as an ongoing exchange, as a mutual penetration of the opposite poles of discussion. Virtual realism meets destiny without being blind to the losses of progress. It strives to enrich the unfolding future from a personal standpoint by referring to moments when we have been at our best. It explores the need to ground ourselves in the earth, not naïvely, but in a way that draws on the growing knowledge we are obtaining from a global garden of human practices, from the body energy cultivation of Taoism and yoga to the new green therapy that insists on our spending time outdoors. As we look beyond alphabetic writing, increasingly away from symbolic processes and toward virtualized processes, our path must be one of virtual realism.

Notes

1. William Gibson, *Neuromancer* (New York: Ace Books, 1984); and Michael Benedikt, ed., *Cyberspace: First Steps* (Cambridge, MA: MIT Press, 1991).
2. Theodore J. Kaczynski, a Montana recluse who once taught mathematics at the University of California, Berkeley, has confessed to the Unabomber's crimes. The merits of my arguments are predicated on a different set of criteria than the adjudication of this particular case. To browse the many variants of the Unabomber Manifesto, the reader can begin at the Yahoo Internet site (www.yahoo.com) and look under "Society and Culture." Then click on "Crime," then "Crimes" and "Homicides," then "Serial Killers," under which are "Unabomber" and "Unabomber Manifesto." Along the way, the reader will also find many satirical and not-so-satirical Web sites devoted to the mythos of the Unabomber.
3. The Unabomber Manifesto appeared in the *Washington Post* on September 19, 1995. The name "Unabomber" came from the Federal Bureau of Investigation code for "university—airlines bomber," since the majority of the twenty-three bomb targets were people who worked at universities or traveled on the airlines.
4. Jacques Ellul, *The Technological Society,* trans. John Wilkinson (New York: Vintage, 1964).
5. Unabomber Manifesto, "Industrial Society and Its Future," para. 178. The paragraph numbering I use belongs to the CoE/Bono version, revision 2, which corrects most, if not all, of the known errors in the *Washington Post* version, including the omission of para. 116. The CoE/Bono version is on the Web in a hypertext version at <www.envirolink.org/orgs/coe/resources/fc/unabetoc.html>. A search via Yahoo will turn up several other versions.
6. See Mark Poster's perceptive treatment of Baudrillard in Poster's *The Second Media Age* (Cambridge, MA: Blackwell, 1995), pp. 95–117.
7. I am using the term "media" here as a kind of shorthand for an admittedly vast segment of society whose components are often at odds with each other, and sometimes even with themselves.
8. James Brook and Iain Boal, eds., *Resisting the Virtual Life* (San Francisco: City Lights Books, 1995); Kirkpatrick Sale, *Rebels Against the Future: The Luddites and Their War on the Industrial Revolution* (Reading, MA: Addison-Wesley, 1995); Clifford Stoll, *Silicon Snake Oil: Second Thoughts on the Information Highway* (New York: Doubleday, 1995); Bill McKibben, *The Age of Missing Information* (New York: Plume, 1992); Sven Birkerts, *The Gutenberg Elegies* (Boston: Faber & Faber, 1994); Mark Slouka, *War of the Worlds: Cyberspace and the High-Tech Assault on Reality* (New York: Basic Books, 1995); Stephen L. Talbott, *The Future Does Not Compute: Transcending the Machines in Our Midst* (Sebastopol, CA: O'Reilly & Associates, 1995).
9. Thoreau spent two years on the shore of Walden Pond (1845–1847). His essays on the topic appear in his book *Walden* (1854).
10. See Wendell Berry, *A Continuous Harmony: Essays Cultural and Agricultural* (New York: Harcourt Brace Jovanovich, 1970).
11. See Alvin Toffler, *Powershift: Knowledge, Wealth, and Violence in the 21st Century* (New York: Bantam Books, 1990).
12. See F. H. Bradley, *Ethical Studies* (Oxford: Oxford University Press, 1926 [orig. 1876]).
13. This line actually comes from the libretto to Leonard Bernstein's musical version of Voltaire's *Candide.* The libretto was put into lyric verse by the poet Richard Wilbur.

14. Ferdinand de Saussure, *Course on General Linguistics*, trans. Wade Baskin (New York: McGraw-Hill, 1966 [orig. 1915]).

15. See Pierre Teilhard de Chardin, *The Future of Man*, trans. Norman Denny (New York: Harper & Row, 1964), and *The Phenomenon of Man*, trans. Bernard Wall (New York: Harper & Row, 1959).

16. William Torrey Harris (1835–1909) was the American philosopher and Hegel translator who in 1873 established the first public-school kindergarten in the United States; he later served as U.S. commissioner of education from 1889 to 1906. Hegelians in St. Louis and in Ohio took seriously Hegel's view that the Absolute Spirit (citizenship under a free constitution) had emigrated from Europe to America. These social reformers rejected Marx's revolutionary violence while promoting public-spirited projects like national parks, public libraries, and the 1904 International Exhibition that invoked "the Spirit of St. Louis." See William H. Goetzmann, ed., *The American Hegelians: An Intellectual Episode in the History of Western America* (New York: Knopf, 1973); Loyd David Easton, ed., *Hegel's First American Followers: The Ohio Hegelians* (Athens: Ohio University Press, 1966); and Paul Russell Anderson, *Platonism in the Midwest* (New York: Columbia University Press, 1963). To understand the break between the Hegelians and Karl Marx, see Harold Mah, *The End of Philosophy and the Origin of "Ideology": Karl Marx and the Crisis of the Young Hegelians* (Berkeley: University of California Press, 1987). Classic Hegelian idealism differs in its historical depth and breadth from the network idealism described in this paper. But that is another story in itself.

17. See Carolyn Marvin, *When Old Technologies Were New: Thinking About Electric Communication in the Late Nineteenth Century* (New York: Oxford University Press, 1988).

18. The Electronic Frontier Foundation, founded in 1990, is a civil liberties advocacy group for the Internet at <www.eff.org>. It offers legal counsel for members of the on-line community regarding issues of privacy, intellectual property, and telecommunications legislation. The EFF sometimes joins with the American Civil Liberties Union in representing "netizens" involved in litigation.

19. See Max Horkheimer and Theodor W. Adorno, *Dialectic of Enlightenment*, trans. John Cumming (New York: Continuum Books, 1987, © 1972). See also Theodor W. Adorno, *Negative Dialectics*, trans. E. B. Ashton (New York: Seabury Press, 1973).

20. See Jürgens Habermas, *The Theory of Communicative Action*, trans. Thomas McCarthy (Boston: Beacon Press, 1984).

21. See especially Herbert Marcuse, *The Aesthetic Dimension: Toward a Critique of Marxist Aesthetics* (Boston: Beacon Press, 1978). See also Marcuse's *Negations: Essays in Critical Theory*, trans. Jeremy J. Shapiro (Boston: Beacon Press, 1968). For Marcuse's treatment of his roots in Marxian and Hegelian dialectic, see his *Reason and Revolution: Hegel and the Rise of Social Theory* (London and New York: Oxford University Press, 1941).

22. See Mark Poster's three studies: *Critical Theory and Poststructuralism: In Search of a Context* (Ithaca, NY: Cornell University Press, 1989); *Existential Marxism in Postwar France: From Sartre to Althusser* (Princeton: Princeton University Press, 1975); and *Foucault, Marxism, and History: Mode of Production Versus Mode of Information* (Cambridge and New York: Blackwell, 1984).

23. Michael Heim, *Virtual Realism* (New York: Oxford University Press, 1997). Chapter 2 takes up the idea of dialectic from another angle.

24. I make the argument for virtual entities in cyberspace in ibid. Here I want to emphasize the pragmatic nature of virtuality and of the status of virtual entities, because I

base virtual realism on pragmatism as the middle between naïve realism and network idealism.

25. *Electric Language: A Philosophical Study of Word Processing* (New Haven: Yale University Press, 1987; rev. ed. 1999); for more on the notion of balance, see my *The Metaphysics of Virtual Reality* (New York: Oxford University Press, 1993).

26. This essay is not the place to go further into these notions, and in the first three chapters of *Electric Language* the reader can find one approach to that larger history with its ontological shifts.

Reading 19

SELECTIONS FROM:

EDUCATED IN ROMANCE: WOMEN, ACHIEVEMENT AND COLLEGE CULTURE.

Dorothy C. Holland and Margaret A. Eisenhart

Schoolwork for What?

Ostensibly, women and men go to college to further their educations and to acquire the credentials necessary for future careers.[1] But there is more to college life than classes, studying, and examinations. When the women in our study got to college, they found themselves in a world of peers in which, whether at Bradford or SU, schoolwork was relatively unimportant. As far as the peer culture was concerned, the women could excel or not in schoolwork, and have or not have serious career plans. These areas were viewed as matters of individual capability, effort, and preference. In this chapter, we address the place of academics in the peer culture and the women's attitudes toward their schoolwork. In the next chapter, we describe how these attitudes, in combination with the women's other experiences during college, affected their entry into the workforce after graduation.

The Place of Academics in the Peer Culture

Amid all their talk about romantic relationships, our informants offered relatively little about the content of courses, the value of different majors, or the viability of

Holland, Dorothy C. and Margaret A. Eisenhart. "Schoolwork for What?" and "Pathways to Marginal Careers." *Educated in Romance: Women, Achievement, and College Culture.* Chicago: U of Chicago P, 1990. 163–201.

various careers. When they did talk with their peers about schoolwork, they tended to complain: classes required too much work, professors were "unfair," or there was not enough time to study properly for a test. They seemed not to know or care very much about the coursework or future career plans of their friends. For example, in our life-history interviews each woman was asked to describe how her high-school friends would have responded if she had experienced trouble with her schoolwork. Almost without exception, the women said that their friends would have done very little, because either they would not have known about the trouble or they would have pretended not to know about it. Most felt that this response was appropriate. Paula said, "I felt like it was none of their business."

When Paula was asked directly whether she and her friends from high school ever talked about why they chose their majors, she said, "No. . . . It's just that we all picked things that we did well in in school." When Della was asked whether she and her high-school friends ever got together and talked about schoolwork, she said, "No, no; schoolwork didn't play with our minds."

In general, schoolwork and career decisions seemed to be conceived by the peer culture as matters of individual choice, not for group discussion or debate. The women made repeated references to "making my own decision" and "making up my own mind" about what field to pursue or what major to choose. Aleisha, who spent hours talking with her girlfriends about her many romantic interests, said when asked what her girlfriends were majoring in, "I don't know; I never asked them."

The evidence for women's inclination to think about academic matters in individual terms was corroborated by our survey. When asked to rate thirteen academic or career-related activities and relationships that had been identified by members of the ethnographic sample, the surveyed women rated individual academic achievements as more important than peer relationships oriented to academic or career interests. Overall, it appeared that the women, although immersed in a world of peers, tended to deal with academic matters on their own.

Correspondingly, status in the peer system was not determined by academic success—in fact, somewhat the contrary. Occasional references were made to "brains" and "intellectuals," but the women were quick to disassociate themselves from these labels, indicating that they were not interested in having such terms applied to them and that they would not gain any status from them. One woman said: "People thought that I studied a lot more than I did and that was always looked on negatively: the brain syndrome." Another said something similar: "Some of my friends . . . and my father call me 'the brain,' but they're just kidding. I'm glad they don't take it too far." And Paula spoke disparagingly about a "guy with a 4.0 [a perfect grade-point average] who wanted to go to Harvard Medical School" but couldn't get in because "all he did was study."

People in math and science courses, especially, were sometimes considered "weird," at least in part because they were so serious about schoolwork. Paula presented the following picture of science students when she was looking for someone to talk to about getting into medical school:

> I need to talk to somebody who knows what's going on . . . all the people I know are business majors . . . except, I guess, the people in chemistry class. And I don't want to get into a detailed conversation [with them] . . . half the people in chemistry are weird. . . . They could be mad scientists, . . . hunchbacks, running around with their lab coats on.

Struggles to Manage Schoolwork and Peers

Although schoolwork was deemphasized in the peer group system, doing schoolwork could not be relegated to a secondary place as easily as some other aspects of life, such as female/female relationships. No system existed to propel women into close female/female relationships, but the academic system did exert pressure, because it was necessary to pay some attention to schoolwork in order to stay in school. The dynamic between the peer and academic systems produced a tension on the two campuses of which most of the women spoke. During the course of our ethnographic study, all of our informants struggled— some more, some less—with what they perceived to be the conflicting demands of schoolwork and peers.

For most, schoolwork and peer activities were viewed as competing domains: time spent studying was time spent away from peers, and time with peers accomplished little schoolwork. One SU woman described the situation as a choice: one could be a "bookworm" or a person who liked to "have fun." Della, at Bradford, described the same dichotomy in another way: "The ones that did all the book studying, they had no social life; the ones that didn't do no book work, they had a lot [of social life]."

None of the women wished to be viewed as one or the other of these extreme types. When they arrived at college, they all wanted and expected to be successful in both schoolwork and the peer system. Almost from the beginning though, they talked about needing to study more and "party" less. Most were surprised to find that schoolwork took more time than they had given it in high school, and they struggled to complete it and do other things as well. One woman at SU had this to say:

> I always liked school, ever since I was very young . . . but here I haven't done anything for enjoyment in so long. . . . All I do is work. . . . It always came so easy for me in high school, and now I've got to compete with somebody just to get a spot [in medical school], so I almost never have time to do anything with my friends . . . I'm going crazy.

The struggle with the demands of schoolwork was evident in our survey responses too. One of the survey questions asked about people and activities that had taken more time than expected over the semester and hence had caused the respondent to cut back on other things she normally did. Schoolwork was felt to be extraordinarily demanding by the largest percentage: more than 80 percent of the women surveyed on both campuses felt that schoolwork took an unexpectedly large amount of their time. Jobs and peer relationships were much less likely to be seen as taking up an undue amount of time.

The women in our ethnographic study seemed to agree that peers complained when they devoted too much time to schoolwork. One Bradford woman put it this way:

> Guys will tell you, "Come on, let's go out." And if you tell him you have to study, he'd probably be upset. . . . Some of my friends tell me I'm a party-pooper . . . 'cause I usually have to study. A lot of times when [my two closest friends] have somewhere to go, they won't ask me. . . . This sort of bothered me 'cause they were having a good time and I wasn't.

Jobs, in contrast to schoolwork and peers, could be ignored. One woman described her typical day as follows:

> Go to class, go to work, go out to dinner with some friends, . . . relax and watch TV [with friends] . . . study.

When she got a couple of Cs on tests, she decided:

> Work's [the job's] the bother; there's no time left for studying. . . . I think I'm going to have to quit work. You think I'm gonna let that work bother me? Nah!

Occasionally, the women spoke admiringly of other women who could keep peer activities from getting out of control. For example, Della described an older student on her hall as follows:

> She's a girl that sets a good example as a very studious person. . . . I see her studying all the time. . . . She lets you know that studying is very important . . . that you can't just all the time have a bunch of friends over or go out all the time. There's a time for everything; she lets you know.

And Della knew that failure to manage both could have long-term implications:

> My sister . . . has messed up her life along the way, and she's still messing up . . . having so many men until she don't even have [time] to work.

The women's comments about the need to study more often included irritation at the thought of devoting even more time to schoolwork. Perhaps not surprisingly, the women frequently let themselves be drawn into impromptu peer activities. One student explained what happened as she and her suitemates were preparing to leave her room for a night of studying for the next day's exams:

> We had a spontaneous party . . . everyone was here . . . till two in the morning. We made all kinds of daiquiris . . . . My parents called [during the party] and I never knew it. They couldn't believe we partied the night before exams. *I* can't believe we did. I've never done anything like that in my life.

Another said:

> I've been doing a lot of things with guys. I know my grades are going to suffer. . . . I guess I'll have to buckle down one of these days.

And a third had this to say:

> If I do homework every night and on the weekends, I can probably do a good job in my courses . . . [but] during the week I'm pretty lazy. . . . I try to study but I just go to sleep . . . or, you know, somebody'll come along and want to do something.

The survey indicated that peer-related factors affected attention to academics, particularly at SU. One variable, "extraordinary demands from peers," was negatively correlated for students at both Bradford and SU with "energy available for schoolwork." That is, the relationship was inverse: women who said that demands from peers were high also said that energy available for schoolwork was low (and vice versa), but only at SU was the correlation statistically significant (Holland and Eisenhart 1981:96).

It appears that although the women at Bradford and SU wanted and expected to do well both in schoolwork and with their peers, schoolwork seemed to interfere with peer activities by demanding a lot of time. Peer-related activities, on the other hand, were viewed as more fun and potentially more rewarding. Thus, they threatened to overwhelm schoolwork.

The Women's Answers to "Schoolwork for What?"

Weiler (1988:34) states that schooling is contradictory for women in a patriarchal society. Although she does not explain exactly what she is referring to, we assume she means that schools, especially universities, are generally regarded as a pathway to upward social mobility, that is, to more elite and better-paying jobs. Yet women have traditionally faced job ceilings and the likelihood of working in jobs that are lower-paying than those of men. Given that the peer system pays virtually no attention to schoolwork, given the job ceilings, and given the likelihood of low-paying jobs, why do women do schoolwork? Do they want an education simply for the pleasure of having one? Do they want to build their own lives by having at least some career—which, as Gaskell (1985) reminds us, has been the traditional view of what women can do with their schooling? Are they seeking husbands who are likely to be of a more advantaged class than the boyfriends they left behind in their hometown high schools?

Among the women in our study, we found three major cultural interpretations of schoolwork.[2] These "developing understandings" of the academic work of college life (see Holland and Eisenhart 1988b) were alternative views of the purpose of schoolwork and also of the women as students. Although we believe that these cultural interpretations were learned before college, they were susceptible to challenges and revision during college, primarily because college schoolwork was more demanding than high-school work had been and because the competing demands of the college peer system were more intense. The combination of forces derailed some of the women but not others, and some sooner than others, depending on which interpretation the individual woman had of schoolwork.

The three interpretations were organized around motives for doing schoolwork: (1) work in exchange for "getting over," that is, finishing college and thereby obtaining college credentials;[3] (2) work in exchange for "doing well," that is, receiving good grades and other academic accolades; and (3) work in exchange for "learning from experts." These orientations to schoolwork affected the women's interpretations of grades, evaluations of teachers, decisions about studying, choices of courses and majors, and feelings about their own performance. During the three-semester period of our main study, each woman seemed to hold one interpretation as a dominant one. Some, however, were aware of the alternative interpretations and sometimes entertained them, if only partially or fragmentarily.

Work for "Getting Over"

Ten of the women in our ethnographic study (nine at Bradford and one at SU) viewed the work they did at college as a means of finishing up their schooling— what Rosalind referred to as "getting over." From this perspective, "going to college" and "getting through" the work there was what mattered. Going to college and getting through were important because they led to a degree that could be used to get a good job later. Another way to say this is that attending and completing college and receiving a degree was a means of moving up in life. Cynthia, for example, said,

> I felt like going to college would bring me a good job . . . and I wanted to become something . . . I didn't want to just get out of high school and just set up and just wait for somebody to bring me some money.

Later, Cynthia made it clearer that she viewed simply getting through college as a step toward achieving her goals.

If I can just pass, I'll feel all right . . . I have to pass to get out of here. It's going to have to be done in order to get myself somewhere in life. It's just a step higher.

Associated with this interpretation was the idea that the work and requirements of college were somewhat arbitrary and simply tasks that somehow had to be completed. The work had no particular significance in and of itself to the students, except as a collection of activities that had to be done or procedures that had to be followed in order to finish. This view was reflected in the women's statements about the kinds of things that instructors required. For example, Rosalind, in talking about what her algebra instructor was like, said,

She's teaching a whole different way from the way I learned it. I'm used to taking shortcuts and in her class you cannot take a shortcut. You have to go from one step to the next. If you miss a step, the problem is wrong even if you come up with the right answer.

Later she made a similar remark about a history exam.

You have to write everything in order. You couldn't put one part here, at the top, and another part at the bottom.

And, finally, about a health exam, she complained,

It was a smoking exam. Half the things we covered in class weren't even on the exam. You really had to know something about health to pass that exam!

When the tasks associated with getting the work done became especially bothersome, doing them might simply not be worth the trouble. Because tasks were perceived as arbitrary, with little future return, there was no point in enduring a great deal of hardship to accomplish them. Rosalind likewise expressed this position:

I studied two weeks for that exam . . . I forgot three things which I didn't care to remember because it was just too hard to keep writing.

These obstacles to getting finished were described for most courses and professors. The strategy adopted was simply to persist in order to get the degree. Rosalind, who was asked by her interviewer on numerous occasions whether she might consider changing her major or not completing college, always answered with a resounding "No!"

I wasn't gonna change . . . I want my degree in biology, then I want my master's in physical therapy . . . I wouldn't be satisfied with a bachelor's [or less].

Cynthia, who experienced considerable difficulty in the math courses required for her degree in business, was also determined to continue:

> I see myself as a person that knows that if I want this fulfilled in my major, then it's [the math's] going to have to be done. . . . I'm gonna have to get used to seeing it. I'm just hoping I can cope.

For Cylene, buying the books she needed for classes became too much of a burden. She explained that purchasing books took a large share of the meager financial resources she had for college, was difficult to transact because she had problems in getting a ride to the bookstore, and was not likely to do her much good anyway because people in the dorm "borrowed" her books right before the tests. Furthermore, buying books allowed "the white man" at the bookstore to get her hard-earned money. After one semester of buying books, she had seen little return on her investment and decided not to buy them again; she proceeded without the books.

Cylene's feelings about buying books reflected another aspect of the "getting over" interpretation: that the costs of getting an education had to be weighed against the potential return. For the women at Bradford, going to college required financial sacrifice, especially for their parents or the other adults who helped with their expenses. When the costs became too high relative to the anticipated return, some of the women decided to drop out of school. A number of the Bradford women did make the decision to drop out, at least for a semester or two (cf. Weis 1985).

The women at Bradford who adopted the "getting over" interpretation all recognized that going to class, buying books, studying, taking tests, and writing papers—however the requirements were defined by the school or by individual instructors—had to be done. But one could "get over," or get through, without completing all the tasks individually or fully. For example, some students "traded up on notes," meaning that one student took notes for another who for whatever reason decided not to attend a class. Some students regularly took turns trading up on notes with each other. Some students shared books, and some bought papers that they turned in as their own work.

These women saw themselves as "getting" grades, not "making" grades. Primarily, grades were viewed as tokens that had to be accumulated to get through courses and, eventually, college. They were important because they were necessary for finishing college and obtaining a degree. From this view, "passing" grades, as Cynthia indicated earlier, were what was needed. A grade of C was described as "fine," and a C+ average as "doing real good." Only an F was a problem, because it meant that the course had to be repeated, which meant falling behind and delaying progress toward completion of the degree.

The women were not unaware that grades could be indications of the quality of one's performance. Cylene worried about her mother's disappointment if her grades did not measure up to her cousin's. Rosalind talked about wanting to bring up her 2.8 average. However, getting high grades seemed to be of only secondary importance to the women in this group. As Cynthia suggested, in talking about getting passing grades in order to get out of college and get a good job, grades were only tokens of how well one had adhered to an arbitrary set of requirements; they did not indicate anything about one's future performance in a field of work.

Grades were "given" by teachers in exchange for work completed. Teachers were evaluated in terms of how well they made clear their requirements for grades. Rosalind's dismay about a health teacher's test that did not cover the material discussed in class contrasts with her assessment of two other teachers:

> She told us each and every thing that was going to be on that exam. . . . She gave us an eleven-page outline. . . . She gave us a chance to pass. My English teacher is pretty nice. . . . He repeats the material two or three times to make sure everyone understands, and at the end of the class, he'll say, "If there's anyone who does not understand, you're welcome to come to my desk." So, I like him.

Teachers were also evaluated on the fairness of their grading, which was determined according to the principle that effort expended should be recognized with an appropriate grade. For Cylene, an appropriate grade was one that reflected the amount of work that one had put in; equal amounts of work should receive equal rewards. Cylene criticized one teacher for giving higher grades to students who had previously taken a course from her, despite the quality of their work relative to Cylene's, and another teacher for giving Cylene and others the same grade, despite the fact that Cylene had turned in more work. For Rosalind, an appropriate grade was one that reflected the time one had put in and not necessarily the skill one had acquired. She made her view clear in responding to the interviewer's surprise that she had made an A in swimming without learning to swim: "He grades you on your time in the pool, coming to class, and how hard you are trying. He grades pretty fairly."

All the women who held this interpretation of schoolwork seemed to be quite certain about their majors. They had come to college with majors chosen in high school or earlier, said they fully intended to pursue those majors, and kept them as long as they remained in college. These women did not believe that they needed to make outstanding grades or otherwise demonstrate special mastery in academic areas. They were simply trying to make grades good enough to finish school and get the credentials they believed necessary to be eligible for the future jobs they envisioned. They did not find the content of schoolwork compelling. Della's comment was typical: "I just did enough [schoolwork] to get over; hey, that's all."

Work for "Doing Well"

Seven of the women—six at SU and one at Bradford—viewed the work they did in college as a way of gaining recognition for their natural abilities and skills.

All seven talked about wanting to do well in school for their parents, but they also all had the goal of doing well as their own. One of them, Linda, put it this way:

> I always wanted to achieve the best, to be the best that I could academically. I always wanted to make As . . . if I made a B, I felt I was a failure within; that if I had pushed a little harder, I could have made an A.

This idea of doing well was related to the idea of being good at, or having a natural ability for, schoolwork in general and at least one subject area in particular. Linda said,

> I'm just not a business mind, [so] econ. is hard for me. My suitemate, she's a business mind, and she whizzed right through econ. I'm just more like science, natural science. It's easier for me. The whole concept seems real easy. It just comes naturally to me.

The ideas about schoolwork held by the women with this interpretation also seemed to have been formed before coming to college. In high school or earlier, they had come to believe in their own academic ability, and they had learned that they did not have to work very hard to do well in school. Kelly said about her high school experience: "I really didn't have to work much to get a good grade." And Susan was able to make very good grades in high school with what she considered to be a minimum of work: "It wasn't the amount of effort you put into it, [what was important was] the grade that comes out of the little bit of effort you [do] put into it."

According to this interpretation, doing well in college should be easy for those who are naturally good at the kinds of tasks or the subject matter of school. That is, good grades should be attainable, and without a lot of hard work. All the women in this group talked about "making" grades in college. For them, good grades were made by combining ability with some, but not too much, work.

Very good grades, preferably A's and certainly no more than a few B's, were the paramount indicators of success. High grades validated that one was "good at schoolwork"; on the other hand, lower grades undermined the valued identity. High grades in a subject area also signified to a woman that she was "suited" for that field as a career. It was assumed that if a woman was naturally good at something in school, then she would also be naturally good at it later in a job or career.

The women selected courses with an eye to demonstrating their ability to do well. Whenever possible, they avoided courses in areas where they were not naturally adept or courses that were known to be hard. When difficult courses had to be taken, the women tried to stagger them across semesters and "balance them out" with easier courses, in order to maintain high grade-point averages.

Teachers were sometimes evaluated in terms of how easy or hard they were, and this information was used by the women to balance their course selections. Teachers were also described as good or bad lecturers; some were funny, and others were hard to get along with because they wanted the work done in quirky ways. However, success in a class was determined primarily by natural ability in the subject area and by willingness to work to make a good grade.

When the women with this interpretation of schoolwork went to college, they expected to be able to make high grades, especially in the subject area chosen for a major. Except for Natalie, they found that making high grades was not as easy as they had expected. It meant working harder in classes and taking a lot more time for studying than had been necessary in high school. The increased difficulty of making good grades led the women to question their natural ability for schoolwork or for their majors. Having to work hard to make high grades suggested that they were not suited for academic work after all, or at least not for the course of study they had initially chosen to pursue. They began to look around for new courses in which they could do better. They considered switching their majors to fields in which they thought they could make the high grades they valued. Five of the seven did change their majors to something they considered easier. Velma, the Bradford woman in this group, gave up on schoolwork and dropped out of school. Only Natalie was able to maintain the valued identity as a good student that she had brought from high school.

Consistent with their "doing well" interpretation, the five women saw changing their majors as a process of "finding themselves," that is, of identifying their natural talents. Since they chose majors they considered easier, they felt they had to forfeit their claims to being good students. They began to search for alternative ways to prove themselves in college and, as a consequence, became even more vulnerable than they had been to pressures to succeed in the peer system.

Work for "Learning from Experts"

The world of college was very different from the perspective of work in exchange for learning from experts. The five women—two at Bradford and three at SU—who had this interpretation of schoolwork saw college as an environment in which skills could be acquired from experts.[4] They were quite explicit in their expectation that college should provide experts to help students learn. Valecia, an English major who hoped to become a broadcaster some day, organized her view of work in college around the idea that she needed to learn "good English" from her instructors.

> I love speech and English. I like writing and I like talking about what I write, but it's the proper way of [doing it] that I have trouble comprehending. I want to major in [English] and I want to get it down solid. . . . In high school, I was

> neglected of an English background, so English, it's a lot to learn. But since I got to college . . . the instructor now . . . he's an expert and I'm an amateur. . . . He's published five or six books and he knows every corner of a good paper. . . . I always wanted an instructor that was real strict on the way I write and he is. . . . He's been critiquing me hard. That's why if I get a good grade, I'll feel like I've accomplished something.

Correspondingly, as a self-diagnosed "amateur," Valecia expected the development of good skills to be difficult and to take some time.

> I like English, but I'm having so much trouble. . . . Well, who said it would be easy? Everybody have their problems the first year. . . . I like English. Isn't that part of a major? Something you enjoy doing? . . . Freshmen start out just like a baby . . . having to learn a whole lot of new things. I just can't get downcouraged now because I'm a freshman. I have three more years to go.

Although Valecia was aware that other students had ways of completing their work more quickly, she sounded determined to take the time to learn the material really well:

> When I rush through, I do a bum job. Kids told me ways I can get it out easier, but I don't want to. I want to get the best grade and I want to put forth my best effort.

Karla, who began college tentatively saying she would major in journalism but soon began to contemplate a major in art or physics, was seeking a "broad-based education." (Valecia also mentioned "wanting to have some knowledge" in other subjects, but this aspect of college was overshadowed by her ambition to become good in English.) Karla was primarily interested in exploring different majors as possible careers:

> I'm here to gain a really broad-based education and learn as much as I can. . . . I would like to look at [lots of] different fields and job opportunities. . . . I would like it if you could just take courses without having to worry about degree requirements.

Karla expected to find knowledgeable professors who could evaluate her talents in a particular field—"When it comes to college, one expects a professor to be a demigod"—but she was sometimes disappointed. Some teachers' level of mastery of their subject was too low for them to be of much help to her. This was a special problem in art.

> I never had an art teacher I felt was really talented or good enough where their opinion would mean much as far as whether I should be an artist.

Peers likewise were not adequate sources of information or help because their skill level was no higher than Karla's. Also a problem were teachers who knew the subject matter but whose testing or grading procedures did not provide Karla with accurate feedback about her growing mastery of a subject. She complained about a French teacher who did not seem to comprehend the mathematics necessary to give partial credit and thus obscured the extent of her progress in French. She also complained about a zoology professor whose tests in a survey course covered "picky things" rather than the "basic" or fundamental knowledge that Karla had learned and believed was most important to have learned. She also believed that some professors, particularly in science, had to be convinced that the women in their classes should be taken seriously before they would make an effort to teach them what they knew.

Valecia described professors whose classes were a waste of her time because she did not learn anything new and professors whose grading and testing procedures obscured how much she had learned. The second was a problem even with the respected "strict" English teacher, who once informed the class members that if he felt a student had improved, he would give the grade deserved, but if he felt a student had not improved, he would give an F. When Valecia got an F, after working very hard in the class and believing that she was improving, she did not want to accept the grade as an indicator of her progress and complained to the dean about the grading procedure. Her response to what seemed an unfair grade echoed Cylene's, described earlier, but with one important difference: the issue here was not simply the hard work and time spent, but the student's perception that she had really improved her grasp of the subject.

Grades were important to Valecia and Karla because they were signs of learning and developing skills. Valecia hoped desperately to get a good grade from her English professor because it would signal progress toward getting English "down solid." Valecia decided to take a course that she had placed out of, but with a low score, in order to learn the material better. Later, when she discovered she was making a C- in a course, she decided to drop it and take it again for a better grade, even though doing so meant she would fall behind her classmates. For Karla, grades in each of the fields she was considering as a potential major were particularly important as indicating her level of mastery and thus something about her chances for a successful career in that field. Grades in these fields were also important because of how they would look on her transcript when she applied to graduate school for further, more advanced study.

Kandace, Aleisha, and Stephanie searched for a somewhat different type of expert at college. These women each had a "cause" that directed their search for experts, most of whom they found outside the university classroom. Kandace came to SU with memories of a drug-dependent relative who had poisoned her family life while she was growing up. She wanted college to be a place of experts who could help her make sense of her experiences and learn from them. Kandace found what she was looking for in some of the extracurricular and religious activities at the university. For her, classwork had some pertinence in providing a theoretical perspective on her situation, but the "real experts" she found at college were other people who had suffered from the same problems. Aleisha was active in causes to advance the position of blacks in U.S. society. She expected to find more accomplished political activists in the university community, as well as in the larger community of which Bradford was a part. Stephanie came to college primarily interested in learning how to create a self-sufficient lifestyle; thus she searched for people, usually older, who had some real-life experience with self-sufficiency.

Four of the five women with the "learning from experts" interpretation changed or added to their majors during college.[5] They did so not so much to "find themselves" as to pursue interests they had and wanted to extend. Aleisha increased the number of requirements she had to meet by choosing a double major, and Karla decided on marine science because it was "more of a challenge" to her. Kandace seemed to find all the challenge she needed in her original major and in her experiences meeting and learning from others she encountered outside the classroom.

Summary

The three distinctive interpretations of schoolwork that we found among our informants can be summarized as work in exchange for "getting over," for "doing well," and for "learning from experts." These interpretations had different implications for the facets of college work, affecting the meaning of grades, evaluations of teachers, allocations of time, decisions about majors, and even decisions about buying or not buying books.

The women with the "getting over" interpretation thought of their school careers in instrumental terms. The work was something that had to be done in order to finish college, even though it apparently had little intrinsic relevance to future work and later life. Their personal identities were not expressed in academic work. The women with the "doing well" interpretation began college with very different expectations. They saw academic work as an opportunity to demonstrate their identities as talented students.

The women with either of these two interpretations tended to end up with what Valli (1983:232) has called a "marginalization" of the worker identity. By the time the study ended, they had little of themselves invested in an identity as a full-time or serious worker, or learner, in school. Although we do not know when in their student careers the "getting over" interpretation first developed, the women having that interpretation appeared to have brought it with them to college. Their life-history interviews made it clear that they had held a "getting over" interpretation of high-school work too. They may have had to work harder in college, but their college experiences apparently did not challenge them to revise their view of what schoolwork was all about.

In contrast, we watched the women with the "doing well" interpretation become discouraged by their experiences in college and reconsider their commitment to identities as workers in school. Then developing understandings led them to a position similar to that of the women with the "getting over" interpretation: little investment in a strong worker identity.

We do not mean to imply that the two groups of women became entirely alike because of their marginalized worker identities with respect to schoolwork. They had taken different routes to arrive at a deemphasis of schoolwork as an important part of themselves. Among other differences, the women with the "doing well" interpretation had experienced a loss of self-esteem while those with a "getting over" interpretation had not. However, despite their different orientations to college, by the end of their sophomore year, all except two (Maureen and Natalie) had deemphasized academic pursuits as a crucial part of their personal identity. Performance in school had remained or had become instrumental, a means to an end, and not especially expressive of themselves as individuals.

Some have suggested to us that the "getting over" interpretation of college could be categorized in cultural Marxist terms as an accurate insight about the nature of the system, a "penetration" of how society works (see the discussion in Willis 1977:119–44). If the work required in college truly is irrelevant and arbitrary, if anything beyond a passing performance in college has little to do with later life, then one could say that a view that discredits the importance of schoolwork beyond its pragmatic, instrumental value constitutes an important insight. At the least the women with the "getting over" interpretation avoided the loss of self-esteem experienced by those with a "doing well" interpretation. But the value of the insight in helping the women to achieve their career goals is open to question.

The analysis of "getting over" as a penetration of the system is reminiscent of Ogbu's (1974, 1987) argument that black Americans accurately perceive that success in school will not, at least alone, permit them to surmount the obstacles blocking their access to societal rewards. In response, they develop "often in collective struggle, . . . a variety of 'survival strategies' . . . to compensate for apparent lack of equal opportunity for equal and fair competition in mainstream economic and other institutions" (1987:325). Perhaps the "getting over" interpretation is a survival strategy that the Bradford women had learned with their black compatriots in high school or even earlier.

Unfortunately for the women at Bradford who hoped for careers in the legitimate sector of the economic system, such survival strategies may turn out to be of limited value. Ogbu argues that when blacks and other "involuntary minorities" discredit the importance of school success for career success, they tend not to recognize that school work habits and attitudes are associated not only with school success but also with occupational success. The analogous limitations of the "getting over" view of work are revealed when it leads students to drop out of school or to take jobs that rank far below their original aspirations. As will be seen in the next chapter, the women with the "getting over" interpretation often inadvertently derailed their own stated ambitions to obtain "good jobs" or to pursue "careers."

A few of the women, those with the "learning from experts" interpretation, arrived at college ready to engage with their work in a way different from that of the others. They saw the work as relevant to acquiring knowledge and skills they wished to have, and they saw mastery of this knowledge as directly important to their self-definition and to their future success. These women were the most likely to seriously pursue careers beyond college.

Pathways to Marginal Careers

We conducted follow-up interviews with most of the women in the ethnographic study in 1983 and in 1987. Though brief, the interviews gave us some idea of what had happened to them during their last two years of college and their first four years after college. We found that the outcomes differed depending upon their interpretation of schoolwork ("getting over," "doing well," "learning from experts") and involvement in the world of romance and attractiveness. Two of the interpretations of schoolwork, combined with other experiences during college, led to an increasing marginalization of the women's identification with the world of work (see also Eisenhart and Holland n.d.).

Paula was one of the women who began college with the "doing well" interpretation. After experiencing difficulty in making good grades and maintaining interest in her coursework, she revised her view of herself as naturally good at schoolwork and scaled down her career aspirations. By 1987 she had married and had subordinated any career ambitions remaining from college to those of her husband.

The outcome of Paula's college career illustrates what happened to fourteen of the seventeen women who held a "getting over" or "doing well" interpretation of schoolwork. The other women also had come to college with strong academic records. They said they wanted to have careers but did not have much of a notion of themselves in a career. By the time they had been out of college for four years, only three—Maureen, Linda, and Natalie—were pursuing careers, in the sense of being engaged in a job sequence that requires a high degree of commitment and promises continuous professional development (see Rapoport and Rapoport 1976:9).[1] For the most part, we found that the other fourteen women had made career "decisions" that had led them into "traditional" roles for women in work settings and in families.[2]

In this chapter we first describe what happened to the women who held each interpretation of schoolwork as they progressed through college, entered the workplace, and started their own families. The educational, occupational, and social outcomes described are those that had been realized by nineteen (83 percent) of the women in 1983 and seventeen (74 percent) in 1987. We found that as the women progressed through the first two years of college, the majority seemed to have had unrewarding or disappointing experiences with schoolwork and to have turned increasingly to the peer culture for rewarding experiences. That is, for most the world of schoolwork remained or became of limited importance, and the world of social activity, romance, and attractiveness became more central. There were some important differences between the black and white women that obliged us to refine the concept of "marginalized worker identity" into two parts: marginalized identification with career and marginalized identification of self as a significant breadwinner. Much about marginalized career identities should become clear as we review our findings within the framework of the three interpretations of schoolwork and peers.

"Getting Over" and Enjoying Peers

We have already observed that the women with the "getting over" interpretation of schoolwork brought with them to college marginalized identities as workers in school, or in other words, as learners. As we followed these women through their first two years of college and afterwards, we found that they did not become any more interested in or identified with schoolwork. On the other hand, their views of themselves as romantic partners to men were, in consonance with the peer culture, important for all but one (Sandy, at SU). All of the Bradford women in this group had steady boyfriends or a series of romantic relationships with men during their freshmen and sophomore years. They all devoted considerable time to managing and maintaining these relationships. Sandy also seemed to be affected, but in a different way; she felt rejected by the peer culture and had rejected it. She became involved in a close and time-consuming relationship with a woman friend.

With two exceptions, the women with the "getting over" interpretation had no serious trouble doing "well enough" in their schoolwork and having time enough for friends. For them, only minor adjustments were necessary to participate in both worlds. One woman in this group put it this way: "I like Biology; it wasn't hard at all. I came out with a B. . . . I didn't ever go to class. . . . I was doing a lot of things with my friends. . . . I didn't learn anything, but I passed all my tests." Another said, "I never did bad to where I needed to change my ways." When Della started to have some trouble in her classes, she decided to quit her part-time job, with no regrets, in order to have more time to study and to preserve her "free time" with her friends and boyfriends.

Others decided to spend more time at the library or in their rooms in order to get their studying done, but without seriously disrupting their peer relationships. Usually, extra studying was done in the company of friends or boyfriends or was timed to coincide with the schedules of others the women wanted to be with. Della, who had always studied at home alone during high school, excitedly told the researcher one day during the middle of her freshman year: "I found a new way to study—with my friends."

In fact, the women in this group found schoolwork so boring and unrewarding in and of itself that they had to rely on their friends to keep them at it. Some reported that they stayed in school only because of pressure or encouragement from others. At one point Della said, "I was thinking of quitting school and [my boyfriend] told me, 'If you quit,' he was gonna whip my butt. . . . So, I can't quit." In another case a Bradford woman reported that she had avoided flunking out only because her friends insisted she study more so that she would not have to go home and be separated from them.

In the cases of Deidre and Sandy, friends pulled the women in other directions, and the women's interpretations of schoolwork were not motivating enough to keep them in school. These women dropped out of school before the end of the ethnographic study. Deidre came to believe that her goal of "getting a good job" could be better achieved elsewhere. "It's boring here . . . studying for four years. And most of the two-year colleges will find you a job. It's like guaranteed employment, and here it's not." Being at Bradford also interfered with Deidre's relationships with her hometown boyfriend and some close girlfriends from high school who attended the community college in her hometown. Before the end of her second semester in college, she had stopped going to class or studying. She stayed until the end of the semester only because another "home girl" was struggling to complete her courses and wanted Deidre's company. As a friend, Deidre thought it was her "obligation" to attend the other woman's classes with her and to help her with homework.

Sandy dropped out of school apparently because she wanted to devote as much time as possible to her developing relationship with her woman friend. About this she said, "[T]here's probably not gonna be another time in my life when I can just sit down and just be friends."

Immersed in a peer-dominated system that paid little attention to academic work or career preparation, and holding a cultural interpretation of schoolwork that focused on getting credentials in order to get a job, some women found insufficient incentives for staying in school. Even those who did remain in school often wondered if the distant goal of finishing a degree was worth even the limited effort they expended on schoolwork. At one point Della said, "I'm here for an education . . . [but it isn't very important to me] because if I can get a job in my field, where I want to be, . . . school would have no value." These women found no support in university life for developing or further elaborating their views of themselves in future careers, regardless of their majors, grades, or announced aspirations for future jobs.

It is not surprising, then, that of the ten, four left school without graduating, and that of those we contacted who were working in 1983, all but one held clerical or low-level technical jobs. When we talked to Rosalind in 1983, after she had dropped out of school, she said she had not been able to keep going to school in the face of what to her were arbitrary courses. She had not returned to Bradford for the 1982–83 school year because she was tired of "going to the same classes over and over." She was thinking of enrolling in a technical school. When asked what was the most satisfying aspect of her college experience, Rosalind said, "Nothing."

In 1987, when we talked to others who had held the "getting over" interpretation, we found that most had held a series of short-term and sometimes part-time jobs. They had not found these jobs very rewarding, but they needed money. Phyllis's case is illustrative. In college she had majored in business administration. The job she got afterwards was as a keypuncher.

> The first job I had was [at] a keypunch company, and the only thing I did was enter data. . . . [I took the job] because I was anxious. I wanted to get started and make some money as soon as possible. I worked there for six months and then I got hired [as] a computer . . . equipment operator. Then I was promoted to . . . a regular computer operator . . . . I would like for my career to be more prosperous . . . right now I'm in a position where I feel like I'm kinda standing at one point. I wish I really liked what I did.

There was one thing that Phyllis was pleased about. Unlike most of the others with the "getting over" interpretation, who were already or almost married when they graduated, she had not married until recently. About this, she said, "Right now, I'm just happy with the idea of having a husband."

Cynthia, who married before she graduated, had held clerical positions in four companies. Her first job was part-time. She moved when full-time work became available elsewhere, and she moved again for more money. She also had a baby.

Sybil, who had majored in social work, wanted a full-time job in her major but could not find one, so she first took a part-time, short-term job in social work and at the same time worked as a sales clerk "so I could pay off my debt for college." She enjoyed the social work, but when her job was completed, no additional work was available. She found work as a receptionist; she said simply, "I needed a job; that's why I took that one."

Charlotte married right after college graduation and soon had a baby. Like the others, she needed income, and she accepted a job as a sales clerk. "I had the baby and we needed the money," she said, "and the job came open. [So when it came open,] I just took it."

Maureen proved to be an exception among the women with the "getting over" interpretation of schoolwork. Although she had entertained the idea of dropping out of college ("because it's so boring"), she had decided against it. Her decision seemed to be motivated by a desire to avoid having to get a job ("I've never had one") and by the fact that she found college coursework "easy."

She also felt pressure from her parents, both of whom had college degrees, who had agreed to support her fully as long as she stayed in school. They had also convinced her that a Ph.D. was the credential necessary for a "good job" in psychology, her field of special interest. Maureen did graduate (although three years late and from a different school) with a degree in psychology and at the time of the last follow-up interview had applied for a doctoral program in psychology.

Our ethnographic material about the "getting over" interpretation of schoolwork tended to be confirmed by our survey data from Bradford, although the survey was not designed to determine cultural interpretations of college work. In fact, we had trouble interpreting the survey results from Bradford until we realized that the women there tended to view the university as arbitrary. According to the survey results, the Bradford women tended to stick with their original majors and to be certain about the careers they wished to pursue. What ambivalence they had was, like that of their fellow Bradford students in the ethnographic study, focused on the worth of the credential relative to its costs. Costs included time, energy, anxiety, money, and the sacrifice of other interests (such as competing peer relationships and activities). Survey respondents who felt that the costs were unfair or not relevant indicated less commitment to pursuing training in their majors (Holland and Eisenhart 1981:89).

"Doing Well" and Succumbing to Peers

The seven women who held the "doing well" interpretation of schoolwork were the most vulnerable to reducing career commitment as they tried to handle the demands of both peer and academic systems. Their experiences with schoolwork at college were more than boring and unrewarding: they were disappointing and discouraging.

From the vantage point of this interpretation, doing well in college should be easy for those who are naturally good at the tasks or the subject matter of school. Good grades should be attainable without a lot of hard work; it should be possible to make high grades and have time left over to be with friends and do other enjoyable things.

All of the women in this group, like most of the others, faced the situation of having to work harder in college to make the same grades they made in high school. In general, those with the "getting over" interpretation chose not to work harder and so made lower grades. But those whose major interpretation was "doing well" had a more worrisome problem. Not being able to do well was a challenge to their identity of being good at schoolwork. Not doing well in the chosen major was a blow to the idea of why one was in college—to study a subject at which one was naturally good.

Five of the seven women with the "doing well" interpretation responded to the demands of college work by reconsidering what courses to take and what to major in. Their difficulties led them to question what coursework and, by extension, what types of occupation, they were best suited for. One woman, who was having a great deal of trouble deciding on a major, put it this way: "I really don't know what I'm going to get into. I guess I should start talking to somebody. It makes me nervous so I always keep pushing it back in my mind."

Eventually, all five of these women scaled down their ambitions and notions of self. They came to see themselves as "average" rather than "good" at schoolwork and before the end of their sophomore year switched to what they believed were less demanding courses and majors. Kelly, like Paula, was faced with reconciling herself to a lower rank after only a few weeks of college. She dropped her goal of becoming a doctor, dropped her premed major, and switched to international studies before the end of her first semester. Kelly said, "I came from a background of good grades, tops in the class, never really worrying about it, [but in college] I'm just a face in the crowd . . . just average here. . . . It's a lot harder than I thought. . . . I wish I could have done a lot better." Linda, another SU woman who scaled down her commitment to schoolwork and switched her major from physical therapy to nursing, which she perceived as less demanding, also talked about the problem of "being average" at college: "I don't want to be average. . . . But, right now, I guess that's just what I'll have to content myself with because I don't know if I can do any better."

By the end of her freshman year, Kelly seemed to have resigned herself to a diminished commitment to doing well academically, at least at SU. She stated that the next year she planned to get more involved in extracurricular activities "because I wouldn't use this time any better." That is, she did not believe that more time spent studying was likely to help her make better grades: "It's just like [the time] would be wasted." Consistent with this statement, Kelly began her sophomore year by accepting a job as manager of the men's hockey team. She had no particular interest in hockey and knew nothing about the game or the players; she simply responded to an ad for the position because she wanted to use her time "more productively" to make some money. The job required her to work every afternoon and to take numerous out-of-town trips during the hockey season, for which she missed classes. When we attempted to contact Kelly in the spring of 1983, we were not able to talk directly to her, but we found out that she had dropped out of school.

Kelly's difficulties with schoolwork seemed to bring her to question whether she really was good at academic work. Her statements and eventual decision to allocate less time to her studies suggested that she had relinquished her identity as a good student—an identity that had been important to her in high school. Concomitantly, her investment of herself in her career as a student, as a school worker, had been attenuated. In this sense Kelly's experiences led her to a marginalization of her worker identity. Like the female clerical workers in Valli's (1983, 1986) study, Kelly did not seem very much attached to an identity as a full-time, serious worker. By 1987 she had returned to SU and graduated.

She had gotten married almost immediately after graduation and had started working in a series of part-time clerical positions. She explained that "there's not a whole lot else to do around here" (where her husband's job was). She also had two children.

Linda had a similar experience and response. Like Kelly, Linda realized that she would have to work harder in college to make the good grades she had come to expect in high school. Linda rethought her ideas of herself in light of her orientation toward doing well. She decided that she did not have what it took; she talked about herself as lacking mental and physical stamina, as being lazy, and as not having the intellect to do the work. Although the process was painful, she too adjusted her ideas of herself and "accepted" a view of herself as being average.

> I'm just very disappointed with myself. I wanted to do so much better than this. You can't be average and get into the medical field. And I don't want to be average. . . . But, right now, I guess that's just what I'll have to content myself with because I don't know if I can do any better.

One part of Linda's scaling down was to switch her major from physical therapy to nursing, because nursing required a lower grade-point average. Both Donny, Linda's boyfriend since high school, and his mother, also a nurse, encouraged Linda to enter nursing. Although Linda scaled down her aspirations and her view of herself, she worked to obtain her nursing degree and she took a nursing job immediately after graduating. She was working at the same job in 1987. By that time she had been married and divorced from Donny and was about to marry a doctor. On the basis of what she told us about her plans, we wondered whether her statement of many years earlier, that she would leave her job for a family or her husband's career "with no qualms", was about to come true.

Compared to Kelly and Linda, Susan came up with a more novel solution. She modified and eventually switched her view of schoolwork. In high school Susan had made good grades with little effort. She had been considered good at math and science. It soon became clear to her that at SU more work was necessary to make good grades, and she encountered a chemistry course that required more studying than she felt motivated to do. She received a D in the course and became convinced that she did not want to take another chemistry course ever again, although up until the end of her first semester she had spoken of chemistry as a possible major. Susan portrayed her poor performance as stemming from lack of interest. She described herself as being "slack" and "lazy," and the work as boring and uninteresting. She resorted to doing only the bare minimum because she did not know what she "wanted to do." The work had no meaning for her, and doing well had lost significance for her. By the end of her third semester, she was saying, "Right now I'm at this point in my life where I don't talk about schoolwork a lot cause I don't know what I want to do, but . . . I always have got so much work to do . . . for nothing." She daydreamed about taking a semester off.

Meanwhile Susan was spending a great deal of time with friends she described as "mellow"—who got together a lot to drink, do drugs, and listen to music. They were less like her socialite friends from high school, who worried about their social reputations and pursued expensive leisure activities, and more like her friends from a male prep school, who were not so reputation-conscious and were more caring toward others. Her search for and her talk about friends seemed to reflect an effort to sort out the kind of person she wanted to be.

As Susan proceeded through school, she rejected a concern with social reputation and getting rich. She moved toward a definition of herself as a "hippie . . . a peaceful deadhead." But she still did not know what she wanted to do in life. Without knowing exactly what she wanted to achieve, without having a worthwhile goal for future work, the work of college did not seem compelling. She preferred to spend time with her friends, and she would have liked to quit school and "go skiing out west."

Susan still had trouble giving up her image of herself as being good at schoolwork. Her sister was also in college and doing well:

> [She's] real smart. Well, she's not real smart, she's as smart as me, but she's more responsible and she studies more. . . . She just got her license to operate the [special equipment associated with her major]. . . . Mom and Dad, like if she got that, it's like . . . "Yes, Susan, [and] what are you going to do?" [I think] "Oh, shut up! I don't want to hear about that right now."

In the spring of her freshman year, Susan went to see a counselor:

> I was really getting bummed out about school, because I—I still kind of worry about not doing anything, you know. . . . I do what I have to do . . . the bare minimum . . . my grades aren't bad, they're about . . . a B or C average, . . . I'm just used to, well Mom and Dad are used to me having As and Bs, and so I was, you know, just kind of bummed out about it.

Susan did not scale down her ambitions or even her view of herself as smart. Instead she questioned the goal of working for grades: one must know what one wants to do or achieve, or the work is a waste of time. She did believe that a college degree would lead her to a better-paying job than she might get otherwise. In fact she often talked about the "paths" that one must take to get to various jobs. By the end of her sophomore year, she had settled for working for a degree in exchange for a job that would "pay more than being a waitress," but she was still searching for a more important goal.

By the end of her senior year, Susan had quit school for a semester. She still had not found a goal, but had come back to SU to work for a math degree, because it was the easiest to finish in the fewest semesters. She had reoriented to a "getting over" perspective. In our follow-up interview a few weeks before her graduation in 1983, she said: "Yeah, [I did] well enough. It doesn't take that high grades to get out of here. You just got to stick with it for a while."

Susan still had not found something she considered worth doing in a larger sense, although one of her courses in her last semester, an introductory course in education, had provoked her interest. The teacher happened to be upset about the mistreatment of the lower classes in the American educational system. Susan was impressed by his concern and thought perhaps she could make a difference. She considered going into math education.

Instead, Susan worked as a waitress and seasonal employee at various resorts, traveling along with the tourist business. The outcome of her struggles with schoolwork, at least by 1987, seemed to be a marginalization of her worker identity. She had come to view work instrumentally, primarily as a means of making money. Even had she become a teacher and invested herself in an education career, she still would have been a case of what Deem refers to as "leakage": the loss of a woman from the pool of those with abilities in math and science—specifically, the loss of a woman who majored in one of those subjects in college but failed to continue to graduate school or to obtain a high-paying, high-status "nontraditional" job (Deem 1978: 100).

Although Susan did not have much invested in herself as a worker in 1987, she was excited about one thing: she finally had a boyfriend. She had taken longer than the others who had held the "doing well" or "getting over" interpretations to find a romantic relationship, but she finally seemed to have managed it and sounded very happy about it.

As they reduced their commitment to schoolwork, most of the SU women with the "doing well" interpretation began to devote more time and energy to romantic and other peer relationships. They all spent more and more time during their freshmen and sophomore years worrying about finding the right man with whom to share a romantic relationship. All of them had relationships with high-school boyfriends when they first came to college, but for one reason or another all but Linda decided they were not satisfied with these relationships and looked, ever more urgently as time went on, for better prospects. Linda, who "broke up" with her high-school boyfriend during her freshman year, began dating others; after she and her boyfriend got back together, she spent more and more time away from SU with him at his school.

In sum, it appears that as these women divested themselves of strong student or schoolwork-related identities, they invested more of themselves in romantic identities. In contradistinction to the popular idea that women who cannot find husbands have careers, these women, who could not do as well as they wanted to at schoolwork, had boyfriends.

Lisa's interpretation of schoolwork at SU was difficult to categorize. She may have originally held a "doing well" interpretation, but we were not able confidently to place her in this group because her views about schoolwork were so affected by her boyfriend. Lisa's interest in maintaining her romantic relationship seemed completely to overwhelm her own ideas about her career and future. Although she was exceptional in our study, her orientation toward schoolwork and a future career, like some of her other experiences at college, seemed to presage what some of the other women, especially in the "doing well" group, would face as they become more heavily involved in and committed to their romantic relationships.

Lisa had an older steady boyfriend who had entered SU before she did. When asked why she selected SU, she said: "I always wanted to go here because [my boyfriend] was here." In most things that Lisa did at college, including her academic work, she followed her boyfriend's lead.

> He has a lot to do with the way I am. . . . He is the main person who . . . I imitate—not imitate, I wouldn't say, but base my behavior. That's it: base my behavior. . . . He's like a big brother who really cares a lot. . . . You know, the big brother is all the time [saying], "Well, I don't think you should do this," or "That guy's just taking advantage of you," or something like that . . . just pointing out situations I wasn't aware of at the time . . . because they were, you know, new to me or something.

One specific decision that Lisa based on her boyfriend's advice was her reconsideration and eventual choice of a college major. She had begun college planning to major in art but soon came to feel, after some questioning by her boyfriend, that she would need to find something else—a field in which she could hope to get a job. At first she thought about art therapy, but her interest was really captured by a course she was taking in her boyfriend's major. Her boyfriend convinced her that she was not suited for that field. He also pointed out to her that if she majored in it they would have to find two jobs in that field later. Lisa abandoned that idea and settled on a major in speech pathology, with her boyfriend's approval, saying: "He probably knows best. . . . He knows me so well." Lisa also noted that she did not expect to be well-paid as a speech pathologist, but at least she would be able to find work: "There are a lot of jobs in that, even around here."

Thus it appears that Lisa was letting her boyfriend take the lead in determining how she would think about her coursework and her job prospects. As she envisioned her future with him, she allowed him to set the parameters of her occupational life.

Velma, at Bradford, at first seemed to escape the difficulties associated with the "doing well" interpretation. In contrast to the women described above, she seemed to be able to make the grades she wanted and to resist, though just barely, the temptation to join in more peer activities:

> I know one night I had a biology exam the next day, and I came so close to that campus dance, but something was saying, "No, you stay and study for your

biology exam." And I did well on that exam and I was so glad I stayed. . . . I think I still could have went to the party and took my exam too, but I probably wouldn't have made as high.

At the same time, she claimed to have a boyfriend at home and to be very shy around men on campus.

> I have a hard time to look in a [man's] face. I play with my nails, anything. It happened this past weekend. This guy said, "All I could see was your ear." I'm going to try to do better. . . . I think I'm nervous if I look in their face. I start trembling, heart beating fast. If I'm turned the other way, it's ok. . . . It's just the opposite sex. If it's a female, [I'm] ok.

It became evident by her sophomore year that Velma was not going to be able to maintain her momentum. She became more and more popular with men and dropped out of college before 1983.

Of the women in this group, only one, Natalie at SU, was able to continue to do as well in college as she had in high school. She did not change her major, and she did not feel that she had to sacrifice time spent with friends in order to accomplish her academic goals. She also did not become very much involved in romantic relationships. She never had a boyfriend during the time of our ethnographic study, although she participated actively in campus social activities like parties and mixers. Natalie, unlike the others with the "doing well" interpretation, seemed to have a special kind of support from her family. She had ongoing help and assistance in learning about her specific career choice—to become an insurance specialist—from her father, who introduced her to the insurance specialists he knew and arranged for her to visit several firms. She also got advice about courses and professors from her older brother, who had attended SU and had also majored in math.

Everyone in this group except Velma graduated from college. In 1987 Linda had become a nurse, Lisa (whom we will discuss with this group) had taken a job in education, and Natalie had become an insurance specialist. The others were working in clerical or other low-paying jobs, like waitressing or cleaning. Two of the ones with better jobs, including Lisa, described themselves as "following" their husbands or husbands-to-be, that is, choosing their jobs or residences according to their husbands' careers. Linda seemed poised to follow suit. Only Natalie, who still had no serious romantic relationships, was pursuing her own career.

The women in our survey at SU were, as a group, similar to those in the ethnographic sample who held the "doing well" interpretation of schoolwork. Many were not certain whether their declared majors were the best ones for them.[3] Many were still in the process of winnowing their best subject from among their perceived abilities. They were sensitive to experiences and indications that could be taken as either confirming or disconfirming their talents for a particular major. For them, "comparative evaluation of major"—the balance of rewards, perceived ability to succeed, and costs associated with the major—was the main predictor of "commitment to pursue training in the chosen major" (see Holland and Eisenhart 1981:89). They did not seem to question the legitimacy of the costs of college training, as did the women at Bradford who saw much of the coursework as arbitrary. Not surprisingly, their assessment of the legitimacy of the costs was not associated with their commitment to pursue training, as it was for the women at Bradford. Concerning career path, the SU women appeared in the survey to be uncertain as to which aspects of themselves they should develop; the Bradford women were more likely to be uncertain whether the costs of college were worth the benefits of following the chosen paths. Although the SU women also expressed pragmatic concerns, they were less likely than the Bradford women to view college primarily as a place where one goes to obtain the credentials needed to pursue a career.

The survey data also suggested that for SU women peer activities and relationships affected commitment to pursue majors, through the intervening variable of "energy available for studies." "Extraordinary demands from peers" was inversely related and "indirect help/happiness from others" was positively correlated with "energy available for studies." At Bradford, none of the peer-related variables was strongly associated with "energy available for studies" (Holland and Eisenhart 1981:94).

"Learning from Experts" and Managing Peers

The women with the "learning from experts" interpretation believed that the purpose of doing academic work at college was to master an area of expertise for use in the future. Although concerned about good grades and obtaining their degrees, these women were more interested in finding "experts" in the university setting, especially in subjects they wished to pursue. For them, low grades were setbacks, but they were taken as indicating lack of mastery, not lack of ability. Professors were sought out not because they were easy or entertaining but because they could teach a subject of interest. Some viewed college as a place to get to know, and to talk at length with, a variety of more experienced people— professors, older students, townspeople—who could help them develop the special expertise they desired to have.

These women also participated in campus peer activities and romantic relationships, but they had a sense of wanting to contain these activities so they could pursue their other interests. One of the women in this group, Karla, chose a boyfriend who already had extraordinary demands on his own time. Because he could only go out occasionally and she was not very much interested in the activities of her other peers, she managed to be free, in comparison to women in the other groups, to pursue her career interests at college. Similarly, Stephanie's boyfriend lived in another city and was busy with his own interests there; they saw each other only infrequently, and she was free to do other things.

Karla and Stephanie were the only women with the "learning from experts" interpretation who had boyfriends while at college. The two Bradford women in this group refused to let their relationships with men become "too close." When a relationship started to become intense, they "cooled off" the relationship and did not jeopardize the time they devoted to academic interests. One said, "I don't believe in getting serious with guys; I think I'm too young. They have a lot on their hands . . . to get an education. And so do I."

Thus, with an interpretation that made schoolwork important to them and the ability or luck to keep their romantic and other peer relationships from taking too much time away from school-related interests, these women were able to maintain a commitment to themselves as career-oriented. All of them graduated from college, and all but Stephanie pursued their final college majors into graduate work or jobs in their fields of study. (Stephanie pursued her interests, but not her major, after college.)

To sum up: only a few (18 percent) of the women in our ethnographic study with a "getting over" or "doing well" interpretation of schoolwork pursued their college career interests after graduation; a much larger proportion (80 percent) of the women with a "learning from experts" interpretation pursued theirs.

Routes to Marginalization of Career

Overall, these outcomes suggest that the majority of women in our ethnographic study did not finish college with a clear or strong sense of themselves as future or potential career women. By default, most seemed to be falling into a reliance on men and marriage for economic support.

The women who held the "getting over" and "doing well" interpretations of schoolwork differed in some of their specific views, in their particular struggles with schoolwork, and in their insights about their own experiences. They also differed in the degree to which cross-gender attachments became more important in self-definition than work activities. But by and large, sixteen of the eighteen women in these two groups (seventeen plus Lisa) either saw or grew to see romantic relationships as closer to the core of their interests than careers. Significantly, as the women's career identities became marginalized their romantic relationships became more central.[4] For the remaining two, and for the five women with the "learning from experts" interpretation of schoolwork, the two areas were more equal in importance. By balancing romantic relationships more conservatively against schoolwork, these women left themselves freer to pursue strong career interests in college—and usually managed the transition to a career in the world of work.

Routes to Identification of Self as Future Breadwinner

Adrienne Rich (1980:643) has written that long-term relationships with men, marriage in particular, are unequal contractual arrangements in which the woman's position is considered low-status, and without a means of gaining power. We found that many of the women in our study ended up, by 1987, married and with jobs that were relatively low-paying, low-status, that they did not particularly value, and that they saw as secondary or supplemental to their husbands' careers. We have already suggested that these outcomes occurred at least in part because of their unrewarding and disappointing experiences with their schoolwork and their subsequent increased participation in the peer culture. These outcomes were also linked, we believe, to the women's ways of thinking about their economic futures, that is, to their ways of thinking about being breadwinners.

To a degree, the thinking of the black women at Bradford and the white women at SU about their futures as breadwinners differed in ways consistent with black and white patterns in the U.S. population as a whole. Although existing research, including the present study, is not sufficient to account for the similarities and differences we found at Bradford and SU, the women were undoubtedly heirs to the themes heard in their families and communities of subcultural traditions reflecting different, though related, experiences. No one can adequately distinguish the contribution of the shared structural position of gender from the contributions of cultural tradition, social class, and race, until additional case studies become available, particularly case studies of historical depth. However, we can tentatively address the differences here.

The women at Bradford tended to be from lower-middle-class families living in communities in the South where family farms and manufacturing have declined, especially in the recent past (see, for example, Heath 1983; Wood 1986). Black men in particular have experienced difficulty in securing other sources of economic stability. Nationwide and in the South, perhaps as a result of economic pressure, there has been a marked increase in the number of families—both black and white, but more so for black—headed by women (Farley 1984; Rodgers-Rose 1980:39). Black women from communities with increasing economic instability for black men, including our informants from Bradford, may grow up with the realization that they will have to provide financially for themselves and their children. They probably do not expect that they will ever be fully supported by a man. A look around them would suggest that a man may not be able to provide enough for the family, but that a man and a woman who both work can provide a higher family standard of living.

Southern white women, especially those of the middle and upper classes (whose mothers and grandmothers might have attended the women's college associated with SU before it became coeducational), are more likely to have anticipated considerable support from men which would relieve them from the necessity of working outside the home. Because of societal favoritism, white men could bring home significantly more money than women. Through marriage, white women traditionally have had access to more resources than through the job market.

The different orientations of the Bradford and the SU women should be interpreted in light of these historical and contemporary inequalities in access to economic resources. In 1979–81, when we conducted the main portion of the ethnographic study, our informants at SU did not mention the possibility that marriage might not be a lifelong means of support (cf. Weis 1988, on high school students). The business of being attractive to men and maintaining a relationship with a man was salient to them, as it probably had been for their mothers and grandmothers. They seemed to take for granted that their husbands would or could be the primary breadwinners. The Bradford women valued boyfriends and potential husbands, too, but they often stated explicitly that although men might be of economic assistance in the future, having to rely upon them for continuous financial support was not wise. This difference existed between the black and white women in our study despite rumors of improvement in the relative earning power of women to men and blacks to whites in the recent past, and despite the overall increased instability of American marriages.

Women's View of the Future at SU

While they were in college, the women at SU implied in numerous ways that they could expect men to support them in the future. When Linda said that she would give up her "job" in favor of her husband's "career" or in order to raise a family, with "no qualms at all," and when Lisa said that she knew her future job as a speech pathologist would not pay well, it was pretty clear that they were counting on men for substantial economic support. Karla, who could not understand why her roommate wanted to work so hard in school when she was planning to marry someone who did not want his wife to work, evidently accepted that in some typical marriages the woman stayed home while the man worked to support her. Susan, as she cast about for a goal for her life, suggested that marriage might be a fallback to work. In describing her plans for supporting herself in the future she said, "Five years is enough time to goof off. I'll be twenty-six by then and that's not that old. I can get married or something."

Two of the women at SU—Natalie and Stephanie—were exceptions to the rule. We have already quoted Natalie as she talked about her childhood dream of "marrying rich" and her eventual disillusionment with the dream. Her sister's difficult experience with a husband who could not hold a job made an impression on Natalie. Her desire not to repeat her sister's experience, together with her expectation that someday she would fall in love and want to marry, led Natalie to think about how she could do both. Her solution was to develop her own career as an insurance specialist and to look for a romantic partner who would not "bankrupt" her. Interestingly, she had not found anyone by 1987, when she was progressing through the steps of her apprenticeship as an insurance specialist, but she hoped that she would soon.

Stephanie also questioned the idea that men should provide economic support for their wives. She seemed to believe in a marriage partnership in which both people pursued their own interests and contributed roughly equally to household maintenance. For her, this idea went along with a desire to have both partners acquire the skills necessary for a self-sufficient household. She had come to believe, along with her high-school boyfriend and a group of older women who were his friends and later hers, that self-sufficiency was desirable in a world of environmental poisoning and nuclear weaponry.

It is likely that ideas about men's economic support of their wives had surrounded the SU women all of their lives. Many expressed positive feelings about their mothers who had stayed home while their children were young. Several mentioned that their fathers, in particular, thought that they and other women were going to college primarily to find husbands who would support them. Paula reported her father's response when she called home to tell her parents about her bad grades during her first semester as a sophomore:

> He has decided that when I meet somebody, . . . I'll get married quickly. I said, "You mean I'm up here doing all this for nothing . . . to find a man and stay home and raise a family?" I don't know . . . but that's what my father thinks.

Importantly, Paula was not angry at her father's response; she seemed pleased that he thought she was attractive enough to draw a man quickly.

Most of the SU women, like Paula, seemed to take for granted that a woman married in exchange for support from a man. This source of support was considered reliable, as long as one found the right man, and could be seen as a fallback, as it was for Lisa and Susan, if one's own career or earning power did not turn out well. Even Karla and Natalie, who had some difficulties accepting the pattern, did not really object to it, if it worked.

The View at Bradford

At Bradford the view was somewhat different. Men were seen as potential, and certainly desirable, economic contributors, but so were the women themselves. Men were also seen as possible financial drains. Velma captured the ideal of most of the Bradford women in the study when she listed what she wanted in a husband:

> Well-disciplined, well-educated, stable background, good-paying job, ready to play the father role: see that everyone is comfortable [financially]—the wife,

child, and himself. [The mother role] . . . the same things and listen to everyone's problems and take care of the house.

The possibility that a man might totally support a woman had its appeal for some women. One said, "I'll take a man to support me . . . he'll have to pay me half of his money." The interviewer then asked about the woman's desire for emotional ties with a man.

I have to look out for other ties first. . . . I don't never want to be poor again. . . . I don't really want to work. . . . For financial reasons I [will], but otherwise I don't want to.

And several of the Bradford women reported, with some pride, that their parents and friends noticed how many gifts and other financial benefits they were able to get from romantic partners.

But women at Bradford also voiced fear that men could drain away resources. They believed it was important to protect oneself from such situations. Della expressed this sentiment in describing why she was not ready to marry the man to whom she was about to be engaged.

He expects us to be engaged [this summer] and married by the first of the year. . . . I don't want to be his wife yet, 'cause I want to have my own money. I . . . don't want him always getting my money. . . . He already asked me to get a savings account with him cause he knows I got a hunk in the bank. . . . But I'm not going to do it because he'll spend $150 on one suit. . . . I ain't gonna do it and then be broke. . . . He wants me to put enough in so [he can buy a car]. But then he thinks he gonna take my car . . . but I'm gonna put it in my name. . . . He can't do nothing about it; it'll just be in my name. You just got to think of the tricks for these guys. . . . You just got to watch that you're prepared for them.

This view, which is reminiscent of Natalie's response to her sister's situation, was prevalent at Bradford: men were nice to have around, especially if they could provide economic benefits, but a woman had to protect herself from men who might wreck her own financial position.

It is likely that the women at Bradford had been surrounded all their lives with these ideas about the economic relationship of men and women. Although the Bradford women recognized much more of a need to look out for their own economic position, they, like the women at SU, did have hopes for romantic partners who would provide them with some economic benefits they did not expect to be able to obtain by themselves.[5]

Summary

For a majority of the women, their developing interpretations of schoolwork, together with their unrewarding and disappointing academic experiences and the availability—not to mention the pressure—of the peer culture, led to a marginalization of or a failure to develop their ideas of themselves as having careers in the future. They either were content for a career to be marginal or nonexistent in their lives or did not notice what was happening.

Most of the white women did not expect to be primary breadwinners in the future. At least they did not spend much time thinking about what would happen to their lifestyles or their potential families if they became the main money-earners. Only one talked about economic independence in the future and planned for it. The rest, except for Stephanie, who envisioned an equal partnership, were either silent on the subject or voiced some expectation of being part of a couple in which the man earned most of the money.

The black women were much less sanguine about the likelihood of being supported by a man. A number of them had originally come to Bradford in order to improve their earning potential and thereby their economic futures. For them, Adrienne Rich's predicted future of economic dependency on a husband was not a likely option, whether they wanted it or not.

Despite the differences between the women at Bradford and SU, many of them ended up at roughly the same place relative to the world of work and careers: with very little solid identification with a career, with lower academic *and* career achievement than they had intended, and with lesser credentials and training than they had expected. As we have seen, over the first two years of their college careers many of the women shifted more and more of their interests and energy away from college work and toward the peer group, with its emphasis on romance. It may not be surprising, then, that the discontents they voiced were generally with men, rather than with the university and what they might have seen, given their original goals, as disappointing educational outcomes.

Notes to "Schoolwork for What?"

1. Segments of this chapter were originally published in an article by Dorothy Holland and Margaret Eisenhart, "Women's Ways of Going to School: Cultural Reproduction of Women's Identities as Workers," in *Class, Race, and Gender in U.S. Education,* edited by Lois Weis (Buffalo: State University of New York Press, 1988). The segments are reprinted with the permission of the publisher.

2. In the terminology of cognitive anthropology these cultural interpretations are much like the "cultural models" described in Holland and Quinn (1987; see also Holy and Stuchlik 1981). The three interpretations were understandings of school and schoolwork that the women had learned from others, much as they had learned the cultural model of romance from others. The three interpretations were identified using the same methods of discourse analysis described in Quinn and Holland (1987) for the uncovering of cultural models. We refrain here from calling them "cultural models" because they seem to be portions of more encompassing models that subsume schoolwork, such as models of success or perhaps of survival. Additional analysis would be necessary to identify the larger models.

3. We use the term "getting over" to mean the process of completing something that consists of a challenging set of hurdles or obstacles. The term itself was used by the Bradford women in our study, and the contexts of its use suggested this meaning to us.

4. The observant reader will notice that our discussion of the women's orientations to schoolwork has accounted for 22 of the 23 women in our ethnographic study. The orientation of the last woman was considered an exception—a very telling one. Her situation is described in chapter 13 of *Educated in Romance.*

5. Table 3, in *Educated in Romance,* which shows changes in college majors, implies only three changes in the "learning from experts" group. Stephanie, the fourth change counted in the text, changed her major within the category listed in the table.

Notes to "Pathways to Marginal Careers"

1. All three of these women were pursuing careers, but only two—Maureen and Natalie—had maintained a strong worker identity. Lisa, although categorized as an exception in her interpretation of schoolwork and so not part of the seventeen discussed in this section, showed a pattern similar to Linda's.

2. We use the term "traditional" to refer loosely to the general pattern of female preference for and choice of certain college majors, occupations, and other adult activities. Correspondingly, "nontraditional" is applied to majors, occupations, and other activities conventionally associated with men and usually considered to be higher-status, more lucrative, and more career-oriented than those associated with women.

3. The reader should recall that we surveyed random samples of *sophomore* women.

4. As summarized earlier, the ethnographic and survey samples both revealed a preponderance of the "doing well" orientation at SU and of the "getting over" orientation at Bradford. If the processes revealed by the ethnographic data can be generalized—and the survey results give some assurance that they can—this marginalization is the predominant pattern.

5. Perhaps some at Bradford were beginning to give up on these hopes. A number of the Bradford women with the "getting over" interpretation mentioned when we talked in 1987 their interest in returning to school as a means of improving their earning potential, but none had yet done so.

Reading 20

SELECTIONS FROM:

INTO THE WILD

Jon Krakauer

The Alaksa Interior

I wished to acquire the simplicity, native feelings, and virtues of savage life; to divest myself of the factitious habits, prejudices and imperfections of civilization; . . . and to find, amidst the solitude and grandeur of the western wilds, more correct views of human nature and of the true interests of man. The season of snows was preferred, that I might experience the pleasure of suffering, and the novelty of danger.

Estwick Evans,
*A Pedestrious Tour, of Four Thousand Miles,
Through the Western States and Territories,
During the Winter and Spring of 1818*

Wilderness appealed to those bored or disgusted with man and his works. It not only offered an escape from society but also was an ideal stage for the Romantic individual to exercise the cult that he frequently made of his own soul. The solitude and total freedom of the wilderness created a perfect setting for either melancholy or exultation.

Roderick Nash,
Wilderness and the American Mind

On April 15, 1992, Chris McCandless departed Carthage, South Dakota, in the cab of a Mack truck hauling a load of sunflower seeds: His "great Alaskan odyssey" was under way. Three days later he crossed the Canadian border at Roosville, British Columbia, and thumbed

Krakauer, Jon. "The Alaska Interior" and "The Stampede Trail," *Into the Wild*. New York: Random House, 1996. 157–199.

north through Skookumchuck and Radium Junction, Lake Louise and Jasper, Prince George and Dawson Creek—where, in the town center, he took a snapshot of the signpost marking the official start of the Alaska Highway. MILE "0," the sign reads, FAIRBANKS 1,523 MILES.

Hitchhiking tends to be difficult on the Alaska Highway. It's not unusual, on the outskirts of Dawson Creek, to see a dozen or more doleful-looking men and women standing along the shoulder with extended thumbs. Some of them may wait a week or more between rides. But McCandless experienced no such delay. On April 21, just six days out of Carthage, he arrived at Liard River Hotsprings, at the threshold of the Yukon Territory.

There is a public campground at Liard River, from which a boardwalk leads half a mile across a marsh to a series of natural thermal pools. It is the most popular way-stop on the Alaska Highway, and McCandless decided to pause there for a soak in the soothing waters. When he finished bathing and attempted to catch another ride north, however, he discovered that his luck had changed. Nobody would pick him up. Two days after arriving, he was still at Liard River, impatiently going nowhere.

At six-thirty on a brisk Thursday morning, the ground still frozen hard, Gaylord Stuckey walked out on the boardwalk to the largest of the pools, expecting to have the place to himself. He was surprised, therefore, to find someone already in the steaming water, a young man who introduced himself as Alex.

Stuckey—bald and cheerful, a ham-faced sixty-three-year-old Hoosier— was en route from Indiana to Alaska to deliver a new motor home to a Fairbanks RV dealer, a part-time line of work in which he'd dabbled since retiring after forty years in the restaurant business. When he told McCandless his destination, the boy exclaimed, "Hey, that's where I'm going, too! But I've been stuck here for a couple of days now, trying to get a lift. You mind if I ride with you?"

"Oh, jiminy," Stuckey replied. "I'd love to, son, but I can't. The company I work for has a strict rule against picking up hitchhikers. It could get me canned." As he chatted with McCandless through the sulfurous mist, though, Stuckey began to reconsider: "Alex was clean-shaven and had short hair, and I could tell by the language he used that he was a real sharp fella. He wasn't what you'd call a typical hitchhiker. I'm usually leery of 'em. I figure there's probably something wrong with a guy if he can't even afford a bus ticket. So anyway, after about half an hour I said, 'I tell you what, Alex: Liard is a thousand miles from Fairbanks. I'll take you five hundred miles, as far as Whitehorse; you'll be able to get a ride the rest of the way from there.'"

A day and a half later, however, when they arrived in Whitehorse—the capital of the Yukon Territory and the largest, most cosmopolitan town on the Alaska Highway—Stuckey had come to enjoy McCandless's company so much that he changed his mind and agreed to drive the boy the entire distance. "Alex didn't come out and say too much at first," Stuckey reports. "But it's a long, slow drive. We spent a total of three days together on those washboard roads, and by the end he kind of let his guard down. I tell you what: He was a dandy kid. Real courteous, and he didn't cuss or use a lot of that there slang. You could tell he came from a nice family. Mostly he talked about his sister. He didn't get along with his folks too good, I guess. Told me his dad was a genius, a NASA rocket scientist, but he'd been a bigamist at one time—and that kind of went against Alex's grain. Said he hadn't seen his parents in a couple of years, since his college graduation."

McCandless was candid with Stuckey about his intent to spend the summer alone in the bush, living off the land. "He said it was something he'd wanted to do since he was little," says Stuckey. "Said he didn't want to see a single person, no airplanes, no sign of civilization. He wanted to prove to himself that he could make it on his own, without anybody else's help."

Stuckey and McCandless arrived in Fairbanks on the afternoon of April 25. The older man took the boy to a grocery store, where he bought a big bag of rice, "and then Alex said he wanted to go out to the university to study up on what kind of plants he could eat. Berries and things like that. I told him, 'Alex, you're too early. There's still two foot, three foot of snow on the ground. There's nothing growing yet.' But his mind was pretty well made up. He was champing at the bit to get out there and start hiking." Stuckey drove to the University of Alaska campus, on the west end of Fairbanks, and dropped McCandless off at 5:30 P.M.

"Before I let him out," Stuckey says, I told him, 'Alex, I've driven you a thousand miles. I've fed you and fed you for three straight days. The least you can do is send me a letter when you get back from Alaska.' And he promised he would.

"I also begged and pleaded with him to call his parents. I can't imagine anything worse than having a son out there and not knowing where he's at for years and years, not knowing whether he's living or dead. 'Here's my credit card number,' I told him. '*Please* call them!' But all he said was 'Maybe I will and maybe I won't.' After he left, I thought, 'Oh, why didn't I get his parents' phone number and call them myself?' But everything just kind of happened so quick."

After dropping McCandless at the university, Stuckey drove into town to deliver the RV to the appointed dealer, only to be told that the person responsible for checking in new vehicles had already gone home for the day and wouldn't be back until Monday morning, leaving Stuckey with two days to kill in Fairbanks before he could fly home to Indiana. On Sunday morning, with time on his hands, he returned to the campus. "I hoped to find Alex and spend another day with him, take him sightseeing or something. I looked for a couple of hours, drove all over the place, but didn't see hide or hair of him. He was already gone."

After taking his leave of Stuckey on Saturday evening, McCandless spent two days and three nights in the vicinity of Fairbanks, mostly at the university. In the campus book store, tucked away on the bottom shelf of the Alaska section, he came across a scholarly, exhaustively researched field guide to the region's edible plants, *Tanaina Plantlore/Dena'ina K'et'una: An Ethnobotany of the Dena'ina Indians of Southcentral Alaska* by Priscilla Russell Kari. From a postcard rack near the cash register, he picked out two cards of a polar bear, on which he sent his final messages to Wayne Westerberg and Jan Burres from the university post office.

Perusing the classified ads, McCandless found a used gun to buy, a semiautomatic .22-caliber Remington with a 4-x-20 scope and a plastic stock. A model called the Nylon 66, no longer in production, it was a favorite of Alaska trappers because of its light weight and reliability. He closed the deal in a parking lot, probably paying about $125 for the weapon, and then purchased four one-hundred-round boxes of hollow-point long-rifle shells from a nearby gun shop.

At the conclusion of his preparations in Fairbanks, McCandless loaded up his pack and started hiking west from the university. Leaving the campus, he walked past the Geophysical Institute, a tall glass-and-concrete building capped with a large satellite dish. The dish, one of the most distinctive landmarks on the Fairbanks skyline, had been erected to collect data from satellites equipped with synthetic aperture radar of Walt McCandless's design. Walt had in fact visited Fairbanks during the start-up of the receiving station and had written some of the software crucial to its operation. If the Geophysical Institute prompted Chris to think of his father as he tramped by, the boy left no record of it.

Four miles west of town, in the evening's deepening chill, McCandless pitched his tent on a patch of hard-frozen ground surrounded by birch trees, not far from the crest of a bluff overlooking Gold Hill Gas & Liquor. Fifty yards from his camp was the terraced road cut of the George Parks Highway, the road that would take him to the Stampede Trail. He woke early on the morning of April 28, walked down to the highway in the predawn gloaming, and was pleasantly surprised when the first vehicle to come along pulled over to give him a lift. It was a gray Ford pickup with a bumper sticker on the back that declared, I FISH THEREFORE I AM. PETERSBURG, ALASKA. The driver of the truck, an electrician on his way to Anchorage, wasn't much older than McCandless. He said his name was Jim Gallien.

Three hours later Gallien turned his truck west off the highway and drove as far as he could down an unplowed side road. When he dropped McCandless off on the Stampede Trail, the temperature was in the low thirties—it would drop into the low teens at night—and a foot and a half of crusty spring snow covered the ground. The boy could hardly contain his excitement. He was, at long last, about to be alone in the vast Alaska wilds.

As he trudged expectantly down the trail in a fake-fur parka, his rifle slung over one shoulder, the only food McCandless carried was a ten-pound bag of long-grained rice—and the two sandwiches and bag of corn chips that Gallien had contributed. A year earlier he'd subsisted for more than a month beside the Gulf of California on five pounds of rice and a bounty of fish caught with a cheap rod and reel, an experience that made him confident he could harvest enough food to survive an extended stay in the Alaska wilderness, too.

The heaviest item in McCandless's half-full backpack was his library: nine or ten paperbound books, most of which had been given to him by Jan Burres in Niland. Among these volumes were titles by Thoreau and Tolstoy and Gogol, but McCandless was no literary snob: He simply carried what he thought he might enjoy reading, including mass-market books by Michael Crichton, Robert Pirsig, and Louis L'Amour. Having neglected to pack writing paper, he began a laconic journal on some blank pages in the back of *Tanaina Plantlore.*

The Healy terminus of the Stampede Trail is traveled by a handful of dog mushers, ski tourers, and snow-machine enthusiasts during the winter months, but only until the frozen rivers begin to break up, in late March or early April. By the time McCandless headed into the bush, there was open water flowing on most of the larger streams, and nobody had been very far down the trail for two or three weeks; only the faint remnants of a packed snow-machine track remained for him to follow.

McCandless reached the Teklanika River his second day out. Although the banks were lined with a jagged shelf of frozen overflow, no ice bridges spanned the channel of open water, so he was forced to wade. There had been a big thaw in early April, and breakup had come early in 1992, but the weather had turned cold again, so the river's volume was quite low when McCandless crossed— probably thigh-deep at most—allowing him to splash to the other side without difficulty. He never suspected that in so doing, he was crossing his Rubicon. To McCandless's inexperienced eye, there was nothing to suggest that two months hence, as the glaciers and snowfields at the Teklanika's headwater thawed in the summer heat, its discharge would multiply nine or ten times in volume, transforming the river into a deep, violent torrent that bore no resemblance to the gentle brook he'd blithely waded across in April.

From his journal we know that on April 29, McCandless fell through the ice somewhere. It probably happened as he traversed a series of melting beaver ponds just beyond the Teklanika's western bank, but there is nothing to indicate that he suffered any harm in the mishap. A day later, as the trail crested a ridge, he got his first glimpse of Mt. McKinley's high, blinding-white bulwarks, and a day after that, May 1, some twenty miles down the trail from where he was dropped by Gallien, he stumbled upon the old bus beside the Sushana River. It was outfitted with a bunk and a barrel stove, and previous visitors had left the improvised shelter stocked with matches, bug dope, and other essentials. "Magic Bus Day," he wrote in his journal. He decided to lay over for a while in the vehicle and take advantage of its crude comforts.

He was elated to be there. Inside the bus, on a sheet of weathered plywood spanning a broken window, McCandless scrawled an exultant declaration of independence:

TWO YEARS HE WALKS THE EARTH. NO PHONE, NO POOL, NO PETS, NO CIGARETTES. ULTIMATE FREEDOM. AN EXTREMIST. AN AESTHETIC VOYAGER WHOSE HOME IS <u>THE ROAD</u>. ESCAPED FROM ATLANTA. THOU SHALT NOT RETURN, 'CAUSE "THE WEST IS THE BEST." AND NOW AFTER TWO RAMBLING YEARS COMES THE FINAL AND GREATEST ADVENTURE. THE CLIMACTIC

BATTLE TO KILL THE FALSE BEING WITHIN AND VICTORIOUSLY CONCLUDE THE SPIRITUAL PILGRIMAGE. TEN DAYS AND NIGHTS OF FREIGHT TRAINS AND HITCHHIKING BRING HIM TO THE GREAT WHITE NORTH. NO LONGER TO BE POISONED BY CIVILIZATION HE FLEES, AND WALKS ALONE UPON THE LAND TO BECOME LOST IN THE WILD.

Alexander Supertramp
May 1992

Reality, however, was quick to intrude on McCandless's reverie. He had difficulty killing game, and the daily journal entries during his first week in the bush include "Weakness," "Snowed in," and "Disaster." He saw but did not shoot a grizzly on May 2, shot at but missed some ducks on May 4, and finally killed and ate a spruce grouse on May 5; but he didn't shoot anything else until May 9, when he bagged a single small squirrel, by which point he'd written "4th day famine" in the journal.

But soon thereafter his fortunes took a sharp turn for the better. By mid-May the sun was circling high in the heavens, flooding the taiga with light. The sun dipped below the northern horizon for fewer than four hours out of every twenty-four, and at midnight the sky was still bright enough to read by. Everywhere but on the north-facing slopes and in the shadowy ravines, the snowpack had melted down to bare ground, exposing the previous season's rose hips and lingonberries, which McCandless gathered and ate in great quantity.

He also became much more successful at hunting game and for the next six weeks feasted regularly on squirrel, spruce grouse, duck, goose, and porcupine. On May 22, a crown fell off one of his molars, but the event didn't seem to dampen his spirits much, because the following day he scrambled up the nameless, humplike, three-thousand-foot butte that rises directly north of the bus, giving him a view of the whole icy sweep of the Alaska Range and mile after mile of uninhabited country. His journal entry for the day is characteristically terse but unmistakably joyous: "CLIMB MOUNTAIN!"

McCandless had told Gallien that he intended to remain on the move during his stay in the bush. I'm just going to take off and keep walking west," he'd said. I might walk all the way to the Bering Sea." On May 5, after pausing for four days at the bus, he resumed his perambulation. From the snapshots recovered with his Minolta, it appears that McCandless lost (or intentionally left) the by now indistinct Stampede Trail and headed west and north through the hills above the Sushana River, hunting game as he went.

It was slow going. In order to feed himself, he had to devote a large part of each day to stalking animals. Moreover, as the ground thawed, his route turned into a gauntlet of boggy muskeg and impenetrable alder, and McCandless belatedly came to appreciate one of the fundamental (if counterintuitive) axioms of the North: winter, not summer, is the preferred season for traveling overland through the bush.

Faced with the obvious folly of his original ambition, to walk five hundred miles to tidewater, he reconsidered his plans. On May 19, having traveled no farther west than the Toklat River—less than fifteen miles beyond the bus—he turned around. A week later he was back at the derelict vehicle, apparently without regret. He'd decided that the Sushana drainage was plenty wild to suit his purposes and that Fairbanks bus 142 would make a fine base camp for the remainder of the summer.

Ironically, the wilderness surrounding the bus—the patch of overgrown country where McCandless was determined "to become lost in the wild"— scarcely qualifies as wilderness by Alaska standards. Less than thirty miles to the east is a major thoroughfare, the George Parks Highway. Just sixteen miles to the north, beyond an escarpment of the Outer Range, hundreds of tourists rumble daily into Denali Park over a road patrolled by the National Park Service. And unbeknownst to the Aesthetic Voyager, scattered within a six-mile radius of the bus are four cabins (although none happened to be occupied during the summer of 1992).

But despite the relative proximity of the bus to civilization, for all practical purposes McCandless was cut off from the rest of the world. He spent nearly four months in the bush all told, and during that period he didn't encounter another living soul. In the end the Sushana River site was sufficiently remote to cost him his life.

In the last week of May, after moving his few possessions into the bus, McCandless wrote a list of housekeeping chores on a parchmentlike strip of birch bark: collect and store ice from the river for refrigerating meat, cover the vehicle's missing windows with plastic, lay in a supply of firewood, clean the accumulation of old ash from the stove. And under the heading "LONG TERM" he drew up a list of more ambitious tasks: map the area, improvise a bathtub, collect skins and feathers to sew into clothing, construct a bridge across a nearby creek, repair mess kit, blaze a network of hunting trails.

The diary entries following his return to the bus catalog a bounty of wild meat. May 28: "Gourmet Duck!" June 1: "5 Squirrel." June 2: "Porcupine, Ptarmigan, 4 Squirrel, Grey Bird." June 3: "Another Porcupine! 4 Squirrel, 2 Grey Bird, Ash Bird." June 4: "A THIRD PORCUPINE! Squirrel, Grey Bird." On June 5, he shot a Canada goose as big as a Christmas turkey. Then, on June 9, he bagged the biggest prize of all: "<u>MOOSE</u>!" he recorded in the journal. Overjoyed, the proud hunter took a photograph of himself kneeling over his trophy, rifle thrust triumphantly overhead, his features distorted in a rictus of ecstasy and amazement, like some unemployed janitor who'd gone to Reno and won a million-dollar jackpot.

Although McCandless was enough of a realist to know that hunting game was an unavoidable component of living off the land, he had always been ambivalent about killing animals. That ambivalence turned to remorse soon after he shot the moose. It was relatively small, weighing perhaps six hundred or seven hundred pounds, but it nevertheless amounted to a huge quantity of meat. Believing that it was morally indefensible to waste any part of an animal that has been shot for food, McCandless spent six days toiling to preserve what he had killed before it spoiled. He butchered the carcass under a thick cloud of flies and mosquitoes, boiled the organs into a stew, and then laboriously excavated a burrow in the face of the rocky stream bank directly below the bus, in which he tried to cure, by smoking, the immense slabs of purple flesh.

Alaskan hunters know that the easiest way to preserve meat in the bush is to slice it into thin strips and then air-dry it on a makeshift rack. But McCandless, in his naïveté, relied on the advice of hunters he'd consulted in South Dakota, who advised him to smoke his meat, not an easy task under the circumstances. "Butchering extremely difficult," he wrote in the journal on June 10. "Fly and mosquito hordes. Remove intestines, liver, kidneys, one lung, steaks. Get hindquarters and leg to stream."

June 11: "Remove heart and other lung. Two front legs and head. Get rest to stream. Haul near cave. Try to protect with smoker."

June 12: "Remove half rib-cage and steaks. Can only work nights. Keep smokers going."

June 13: "Get remainder of rib-cage, shoulder and neck to cave. Start smoking."

June 14: "Maggots already! Smoking appears ineffective. Don't know, looks like disaster. I now wish I had never shot the moose. One of the greatest tragedies of my life."

At that point he gave up on preserving the bulk of the meat and abandoned the carcass to the wolves. Although he castigated himself severely for this waste of a life he'd taken, a day later McCandless appeared to regain some perspective, for his journal notes, "henceforth will learn to accept my errors, however great they be."

Shortly after the moose episode McCandless began to read Thoreau's *Walden*. In the chapter titled "Higher Laws," in which Thoreau ruminates on the morality of eating, McCandless highlighted, "when I had caught and cleaned and cooked and eaten my fish, they seemed not to have fed me essentially. It was insignificant and unnecessary, and cost more than it came to."

"THE MOOSE," McCandless wrote in the margin. And in the same passage he marked,

> The repugnance to animal food is not the effect of experience, but is an instinct. It appeared more beautiful to live low and fare hard in many respects; and though I never did so, I went far enough to please my imagination. I believe that every man who has ever been earnest to preserve his higher or poetic faculties in the best condition has been particularly inclined to abstain from animal food, and from much food of any kind. . . .
>
> It is hard to provide and cook so simple and clean a diet as will not offend the imagination; but this, I think, is to be fed when we feed the body; they should both sit down at the same table. Yet perhaps this may be done. The fruits eaten

temperately need not make us ashamed of our appetites, nor interrupt the wor-
thiest pursuits. But put an extra condiment into your dish, and it will poison you.

"YES," wrote McCandless and, two pages later, "<u>Consciousness</u> of food. Eat and cook with <u>concentration</u>. . . . Holy Food." On the back pages of the book that served as his journal, he declared:

> *I am reborn. This is my dawn. <u>Real</u> life has just begun.*
> <u>*Deliberate Living*</u>*: Conscious attention to the basics of life, and a constant attention to your immediate environment and its concerns, example → A job, a task, a book; anything requiring efficient concentration (Circumstance has no value. It is how one <u>relates</u> to a situation that has value. All true meaning resides in the personal relationship to a phenomenon, what it means to you).*
> *The Great Holiness of* **<u>FOOD</u>**, *The Vital Heat.*
> <u>*Positivism*</u>*, the Insurpassable Joy of the Life Aesthetic.*
> *Absolute Truth and Honesty.*
> *Reality.*
> *Independence.*
> *Finality—Stability—Consistency.*

As McCandless gradually stopped rebuking himself for the waste of the moose, the contentment that began in mid-May resumed and seemed to continue through early July. Then, in the midst of this idyll, came the first of two pivotal setbacks.

Satisfied, apparently, with what he had learned during his two months of solitary life in the wild, McCandless decided to return to civilization: It was time to bring his "final and greatest adventure" to a close and get himself back to the world of men and women, where he could chug a beer, talk philosophy, enthrall strangers with tales of what he'd done. He seemed to have moved beyond his need to assert so adamantly his autonomy, his need to separate himself from his parents. Maybe he was prepared to forgive their imperfections; maybe he was even prepared to forgive some of his own. McCandless seemed ready, perhaps, to go home.

Or maybe not; we can do no more than speculate about what he intended to do after he walked out of the bush. There is no question, however, that he intended to walk out.

Writing on a piece of birch bark, he made a list of things to do before he departed: "Patch Jeans, Shave!, Organize pack. . . ." Shortly thereafter he propped his Minolta on an empty oil drum and took a snapshot of himself brandishing a yellow disposable razor and grinning at the camera, clean-shaven, with new patches cut from an army blanket stitched onto the knees of his filthy jeans. He looks healthy but alarmingly gaunt. Already his cheeks are sunken. The tendons in his neck stand out like taut cables.

On July 2, McCandless finished reading Tolstoy's "Family Happiness," having marked several passages that moved him:

*He was right in saying that the only certain happiness in life is to live for others. . . .
I have lived through much, and now I think I have found what is needed for
happiness. A quiet secluded life in the country, with the possibility of being
useful to people to whom it is easy to do good, and who are not accustomed to
have it done to them; then work which one hopes may be of some use; then rest,
nature, books, music, love for one's neighbor—such is my idea of happiness.
And then, on top of all that, you for a mate, and children, perhaps—what more
can the heart of a man desire?*

Then, on July 3, he shouldered his backpack and began the twenty-mile hike
to the improved road. Two days later, halfway there, he arrived in heavy rain at
the beaver ponds that blocked access to the west bank of the Teklanika River. In
April they'd been frozen over and hadn't presented an obstacle. Now he must
have been alarmed to find a three-acre lake covering the trail. To avoid having to
wade through the murky chest-deep water, he scrambled up a steep hillside,
bypassed the ponds on the north, and then dropped back down to the river at the
mouth of the gorge.

When he'd first crossed the river, sixty-seven days earlier in the freezing
temperatures of April, it had been an icy but gentle knee-deep creek, and he'd
simply strolled across it. On July 5, however, the Teklanika was at full flood,
swollen with rain and snowmelt from glaciers high in the Alaska Range, running
cold and fast.

If he could reach the far shore, the remainder of the hike to the highway
would be easy, but to get there he would have to negotiate a channel some one
hundred feet wide. The water, opaque with glacial sediment and only a few
degrees warmer than the ice it had so recently been, was the color of wet concrete. Too deep to wade, it rumbled like a freight train. The powerful current
would quickly knock him off his feet and carry him away.

McCandless was a weak swimmer and had confessed to several people that
he was in fact afraid of the water. Attempting to swim the numbingly cold torrent or even to paddle some sort of improvised raft across seemed too risky to
consider. Just downstream from where the trail met the river, the Teklanika
erupted into a chaos of boiling whitewater as it accelerated through the narrow
gorge. Long before he could swim or paddle to the far shore, he'd be pulled into
these rapids and drowned.

In his journal he now wrote, "Disaster. . . . Rained in. River look impossible. Lonely, scared." He concluded, correctly, that he would probably be swept
to his death if he attempted to cross the Teklanika at that place, in those conditions. It would be suicidal; it was simply not an option.

If McCandless had walked a mile or so upstream, he would have discovered
that the river broadened into a maze of braided channels. If he'd scouted carefully, by trial and error he might have found a place where these braids were
only chest-deep. As strong as the current was running, it would have certainly

knocked him off his feet, but by dog-paddling and hopping along the bottom as he drifted downstream, he could conceivably have made it across before being carried into the gorge or succumbing to hypothermia.

But it would still have been a very risky proposition, and at that point McCandless had no reason to take such a risk. He'd been fending for himself quite nicely in the country. He probably understood that if he was patient and waited, the river would eventually drop to a level where it could be safely forded. After weighing his options, therefore, he settled on the most prudent course. He turned around and began walking to the west, back toward the bus, back into the fickle heart of the bush.

The Stampede Trail

Nature was here something savage and awful, though beautiful. I looked with awe at the ground I trod on, to see what the Powers had made there, the form and fashion and material of their work. This was that Earth of which we have heard, made out of Chaos and Old Night. Here was no man's garden, but the unhandselled globe. It was not lawn, nor pasture, nor mead, nor woodland, nor lea, nor arable, nor waste land. It was the fresh and natural surface of the planet Earth, as it was made forever and ever,—to be the dwelling of man, we say,—so Nature made it, and man may use it if he can. Man was not to be associated with it. It was Matter, vast, terrific,—not his Mother Earth that we have heard of, not for him to tread on, or to be buried in,—no, it were being too familiar even to let his bones lie there,—the home, this, of Necessity and Fate. There was clearly felt the presence of a force not bound to be kind to man. It was a place of heathenism and superstitious rites,—to be inhabited by men nearer of kin to the rocks and to wild animals than we. . . . What is it to be admitted to a museum, to see a myriad of particular things, compared with being shown some star's surface, some hard matter in its home! I stand in awe of my body, this matter to which I am bound has become so strange to me. I fear not spirits, ghosts, of which I am one,—that my body might,—but I fear bodies, I tremble to meet them. What is this Titan that has possession of me? Talk of mysteries! Think of our life in nature,—daily to be shown matter, to come in contact with it,—rocks, trees, wind on our cheeks! the solid *earth! the* actual *world! the* common *sense!* Contact! Contact! Who *are we? where are we?*

Henry David Thoreau, "Ktaadn"

A year and a week after Chris McCandless decided not to attempt to cross the Teklanika River, I stand on the opposite bank—the eastern side, the highway side—and gaze into the churning water. I, too, hope to cross the river. I want to visit the bus. I want to see where McCandless died, to better understand why.

It is a hot, humid afternoon, and the river is livid with runoff from the fast-melting snowpack that still blankets the glaciers in the higher elevations of the Alaska Range. Today the water looks considerably lower than it looks in the photographs McCandless took twelve months ago, but to try to ford the river here, in thundering midsummer flood, is nevertheless unthinkable. The water is too deep, too cold, too fast. As I stare into the Teklanika, I can hear rocks the size of bowling balls grinding along the bottom, rolled downstream by the powerful current. I'd be swept from my feet within a few yards of leaving the bank and pushed into the canyon immediately below, which pinches the river into a boil of rapids that continues without interruption for the next five miles.

Unlike McCandless, however, I have in my backpack a 1:63,360-scale topographic map (that is, a map on which one inch represents one mile). Exquisitely detailed, it indicates that half a mile downstream, in the throat of the canyon, is a gauging station that was built by the U.S. Geological Survey. Unlike McCandless, too, I am here with three companions: Alaskans Roman Dial and Dan Solie and a friend of Roman's from California, Andrew Liske. The gauging station can't be seen from where the Stampede Trail comes down to the river, but after twenty minutes of fighting our way through a snarl of spruce and dwarf birch, Roman shouts, "I see it! There! A hundred yards farther."

We arrive to find an inch-thick steel cable spanning the gorge, stretched between a fifteen-foot tower on our side of the river and an outcrop on the far shore, four hundred feet away. The cable was erected in 1970 to chart the Teklanika's seasonal fluctuations; hydrologists traveled back and forth above the river by means of an aluminum basket that is suspended from the cable with pulleys. From the basket they would drop a weighted plumb line to measure the river's depth. The station was decommissioned nine years ago for lack of funds, at which time the basket was supposed to be chained and locked to the tower on our side—the highway side—of the river. When we climbed to the top of the tower, however, the basket wasn't there. Looking across the rushing water, I could see it over on the distant shore—the bus side—of the canyon.

Some local hunters, it turns out, had cut the chain, ridden the basket across, and secured it to the far side in order to make it harder for outsiders to cross the Teklanika and trespass on their turf. When McCandless tried to walk out of the bush one year ago the previous week, the basket was in the same place it is now, on his side of the canyon. If he'd known about it, crossing the Teklanika to safety would have been a trivial matter. Because he had no topographic map, however, he had no way of conceiving that salvation was so close at hand.

Andy Horowitz, one of McCandless's friends on the Woodson High cross-country team, had mused that Chris "was born into the wrong century. He was looking for more adventure and freedom than today's society gives people." In coming to Alaska, McCandless yearned to wander uncharted country, to find a blank spot on the map. In 1992, however, there were no more blank spots on the map—not in Alaska, not anywhere. But Chris, with his idiosyncratic logic, came up with an elegant solution to this dilemma: He simply got rid of the map. In his own mind, if nowhere else, the *terra* would thereby remain *incognita*.

Because he lacked a good map, the cable spanning the river also remained incognito. Studying the Teklanika's violent flow, McCandless thus mistakenly concluded that it was impossible to reach the eastern shore. Thinking that his escape route had been cut off, he returned to the bus—a reasonable course of action, given his topographical ignorance. But why did he then stay at the bus and starve? Why, come August, didn't he try once more to cross the Teklanika, when it would have been running significantly lower, when it would have been safe to ford?

Puzzled by these questions, and troubled, I am hoping that the rusting hulk of Fairbanks bus 142 will yield some clues. But to reach the bus, I, too, need to cross the river, and the aluminum tram is still chained to the far shore.

Standing atop the tower anchoring the eastern end of the span, I attach myself to the cable with rock-climbing hardware and begin to pull myself across, hand over hand, executing what mountaineers call a Tyrolean traverse. This turns out to be a more strenuous proposition than I had anticipated. Twenty minutes after starting out, I finally haul myself onto the outcrop on the other side, completely spent, so wasted I can barely raise my arms. After at last catching my breath, I climb into the basket—a rectangular aluminum car two feet wide by four feet long—disconnect the chain, and head back to the eastern side of the canyon to ferry my companions across.

The cable sags noticeably over the middle of the river; so when I cut loose from the outcrop, the car accelerates quickly under its own weight, rolling faster and faster along the steel strand, seeking the lowest point. It's a thrilling ride. Zipping over the rapids at twenty or thirty miles per hour, I hear an involuntary bark of fright leap from my throat before I realize that I'm in no danger and regain my composure.

After all four of us are on the western side of the gorge, thirty minutes of rough bushwhacking returns us to the Stampede Trail. The ten miles of trail we have already covered—the section between our parked vehicles and the river—were gentle, well marked, and relatively heavily traveled. But the ten miles to come have an utterly different character.

Because so few people cross the Teklanika during the spring and summer months, much of the route is indistinct and overgrown with brush. Immediately past the river the trail curves to the southwest, up the bed of a fast-flowing creek. And because beavers have built a network of elaborate dams across this creek, the route leads directly through a three-acre expanse of standing water. The beaver ponds are never more than chest deep, but the water is cold, and as we slosh forward, our feet churn the muck on the bottom into a foul-smelling miasma of decomposing slime.

The trail climbs a hill beyond the uppermost pond, then rejoins the twisting, rocky creek bed before ascending again into a jungle of scrubby vegetation. The going never gets exceedingly difficult, but the fifteen-foot-high tangle of alder pressing in from both sides is gloomy, claustrophobic, oppressive. Clouds of mosquitoes materialize out of the sticky heat. Every few minutes the insects' piercing whine is supplanted by the boom of distant thunder, rumbling over the taiga from a wall of thunderheads rearing darkly on the horizon.

Thickets of buckbrush leave a crosshatch of bloody lacerations on my shins. Piles of bear scat on the trail and, at one point, a set of fresh grizzly tracks—each print half again as long as a size-nine boot print—put me on edge. None of us has a gun. "Hey, Griz!" I yell at the undergrowth, hoping to avoid a surprise encounter. "Hey, bear! Just passing through! No reason to get riled!"

I have been to Alaska some twenty times during the past twenty years—to climb mountains, to work as a carpenter and a commercial salmon fisherman and a journalist, to goof off, to poke around. I've spent a lot of time alone in the country over the course of my many visits and usually relish it. Indeed, I had intended to make this trip to the bus by myself, and when my friend Roman invited himself and two others along, I was annoyed. Now, however, I am grateful for their company. There is something disquieting about this Gothic, overgrown landscape. It feels more malevolent than other, more remote corners of the state I know—the tundra-wrapped slopes of the Brooks Range, the cloud forests of the Alexander Archipelago, even the frozen, gale-swept heights of the Denali massif. I'm happy as hell that I'm not here alone.

At 9:00 P.M. we round a bend in the trail, and there, at the edge of a small clearing, is the bus. Pink bunches of fireweed choke the vehicle's wheel wells, growing higher than the axles. Fairbanks bus 142 is parked beside a coppice of aspen, ten yards back from the brow of a modest cliff, on a shank of high ground overlooking the confluence of the Sushana River and a smaller tributary. It's an appealing setting, open and filled with light. It's easy to see why McCandless decided to make this his base camp.

We pause some distance away from the bus and stare at it for a while in silence. Its paint is chalky and peeling. Several windows are missing. Hundreds of delicate bones litter the clearing around the vehicle, scattered among thousands of porcupine quills: the remains of the small game that made up the bulk of McCandless's diet. And at the perimeter of this boneyard lies one much larger skeleton: that of the moose he shot, and subsequently agonized over.

When I'd questioned Gordon Samel and Ken Thompson shortly after they'd discovered McCandless's body, both men insisted—adamantly and unequivocally—that the big skeleton was the remains of a caribou, and they derided the greenhorn's ignorance in mistaking the animal he killed for a moose. "Wolves had scattered the bones some," Thompson had told me, "but it was obvious that the animal was a caribou. The kid didn't know what the hell he was doing up here."

"It was definitely a caribou," Samel had scornfully piped in. "When I read in the paper that he thought he'd shot a moose, that told me right there he wasn't no Alaskan. There's a big difference between a moose and a caribou. A real big difference. You'd have to be pretty stupid not to be able to tell them apart."

Trusting Samel and Thompson, veteran Alaskan hunters who've killed many moose and caribou between them, I duly reported McCandless's mistake in the article I wrote for *Outside,* thereby confirming the opinion of countless readers that McCandless was ridiculously ill prepared, that he had no business heading into any wilderness, let alone into the big-league wilds of the Last Frontier. Not only did McCandless die because he was stupid, one Alaska correspondent observed, but "the scope of his self-styled adventure was so small as to ring pathetic—squatting in a wrecked bus a few miles out of Healy, potting jays and squirrels, mistaking a caribou for a moose (pretty hard to do). . . . Only one word for the guy: incompetent."

Among the letters lambasting McCandless, virtually all those I received mentioned his misidentification of the caribou as proof that he didn't know the first thing about surviving in the back country. What the angry letter writers didn't know, however, was that the ungulate McCandless shot was exactly what he'd said it was. Contrary to what I reported in *Outside,* the animal was a moose, as a close examination of the beast's remains now indicated and several of McCandless's photographs of the kill later confirmed beyond all doubt. The boy made some mistakes on the Stampede Trail, but confusing a caribou with a moose wasn't among them.

Walking past the moose bones, I approach the vehicle and step through an emergency exit at the back. Immediately inside the door is the torn mattress, stained and moldering, on which McCandless expired. For some reason I am taken aback to find a collection of his possessions spread across its ticking: a green plastic canteen; a tiny bottle of water-purification tablets; a used-up cylinder of Chap Stick; a pair of insulated flight pants of the type sold in military-surplus stores; a paperback copy of the bestseller *0 Jerusalem!,* its spine broken; wool mittens; a bottle of Muskol insect repellent; a full box of matches; and a pair of brown rubber work boots with the name Gallien written across the cuffs in faint black ink.

Despite the missing windows, the air inside the cavernous vehicle is stale and musty. "Wow," Roman remarks. "It smells like dead birds in here." A moment later I come across the source of the odor: a plastic garbage bag filled with feathers, down, and the severed wings of several birds. It appears that McCandless was saving them to insulate his clothing or perhaps to make a feather pillow.

Toward the front of the bus, McCandless's pots and dishes are stacked on a makeshift plywood table beside a kerosene lamp. A long leather scabbard is expertly tooled with the initials R. F.: the sheath for the machete Ronald Franz gave McCandless when he left Salton City.

The boy's blue toothbrush rests next to a half-empty tube of Colgate, a packet of dental floss, and the gold molar crown that, according to his journal, fell off his tooth three weeks into his sojourn. A few inches away sits a skull the size of a watermelon, thick ivory fangs jutting from its bleached maxillae. It is a bear skull, the remains of a grizzly shot by someone who visited the bus years before McCandless's tenure. A message scratched in Chris's tidy hand brackets a cranial bullet hole: ALL HAIL THE PHANTOM BEAR, THE BEAST WITHIN US ALL. ALEXANDER SUPERTRAMP. MAY 1992.

Looking up, I notice that the sheet-metal walls of the vehicle are covered with graffiti left by numerous visitors over the years. Roman points out a message he wrote when he stayed in the bus four years ago, during a traverse of the Alaska Range: NOODLE EATERS EN ROUTE TO LAKE CLARK 8/89. Like Roman, most people scrawled little more than their names and a date. The longest, most eloquent graffito is one of several inscribed by McCandless, the proclamation of joy that begins with a nod to his favorite Roger Miller song: TWO YEARS HE WALKS THE EARTH. NO PHONE, NO POOL, NO PETS, NO CIGARETTES. ULTIMATE FREEDOM. AN EXTREMIST. AN AESTHETIC VOYAGER WHOSE NAME IS THE ROAD. . . .

Immediately below this manifesto squats the stove, fabricated from a rusty oil drum. A twelve-foot section of a spruce trunk is jammed into its open doorway, and across the log are draped two pairs of torn Levi's, laid out as if to dry. One pair of jeans—waist thirty, inseam thirty-two—is patched crudely with silver duct tape; the other pair has been repaired more carefully, with scraps from a faded bedspread stitched over gaping holes in the knees and seat. This latter pair also sports a belt fashioned from a strip of blanket. McCandless, it occurs to me, must have been forced to make the belt after growing so thin that his pants wouldn't stay up without it.

Sitting down on a steel cot across from the stove to mull over this eerie tableau, I encounter evidence of McCandless's presence wherever my vision rests. Here are his toenail clippers, over there his green nylon tent spread over a missing window in the front door. His Kmart hiking boots are arranged neatly beneath the stove, as though he'd soon be returning to lace them up and hit the trail. I feel uncomfortable, as if I were intruding, a voyeur who has slipped into McCandless's bedroom while he is momentarily away. Suddenly queasy, I stumble out of the bus to walk along the river and breathe some fresh air.

An hour later we build a fire outside in the fading light. The rain squalls, now past, have rinsed the haze from the atmosphere, and distant, backlit hills stand out in crisp detail. A stripe of incandescent sky burns beneath the cloud base on the northwestern horizon. Roman unwraps some steaks from a moose he shot in the Alaska Range last September and lays them across the fire on a blackened grill, the grill McCandless used for broiling his game. Moose fat pops and sizzles into the coals. Eating the gristly meat with our fingers, we slap at mosquitoes and talk about this peculiar person whom none of us ever met, trying to get a handle on how he came to grief, trying to understand why some people seem to despise him so intensely for having died here.

By design McCandless came into the country with insufficient provisions, and he lacked certain pieces of equipment deemed essential by many Alaskans: a large-caliber rifle, map and compass, an ax. This has been regarded as evidence not just of stupidity but of the even greater sin of arrogance. Some critics have even drawn parallels between McCandless and the Arctic's most infamous tragic figure, Sir John Franklin, a nineteenth-century British naval officer whose smugness and hauteur contributed to some 140 deaths, including his own.

In 1819, the Admiralty assigned Franklin to lead an expedition into the wilderness of northwestern Canada. Two years out of England, winter overtook his small party as they plodded across an expanse of tundra so vast and empty that they christened it the Barrens, the name by which it is still known. Their food ran out. Game was scarce, forcing Franklin and his men to subsist on lichens scraped from boulders, singed deer hide, scavenged animal bones, their own boot leather, and finally one another's flesh. Before the ordeal was over, at least two men had been murdered and eaten, the suspected murderer had been summarily executed, and eight others were dead from sickness and starvation. Franklin was himself within a day or two of expiring when he and the other survivors were rescued by a band of métis.

An affable Victorian gentleman, Franklin was said to be a good-natured bumbler, dogged and clueless, with the naïve ideals of a child and a disdain for acquiring backcountry skills. He had been woefully unprepared to lead an Arctic expedition, and upon returning to England, he was known as the Man Who Ate His Shoes—yet the sobriquet was uttered more often with awe than with ridicule. He was hailed as a national hero, promoted to the rank of captain by the Admiralty, paid handsomely to write an account of his ordeal, and, in 1825, given command of a second Arctic expedition.

That trip was relatively uneventful, but in 1845, hoping finally to discover the fabled Northwest Passage, Franklin made the mistake of returning to the Arctic for a third time. He and the 128 men under his command were never heard from again. Evidence unearthed by the forty-odd expeditions sent to search for them eventually established that all had perished, the victims of scurvy, starvation, and unspeakable suffering.

When McCandless turned up dead, he was likened to Franklin not simply because both men starved but also because both were perceived to have lacked a requisite humility; both were thought to have possessed insufficient respect for the land. A century after Franklin's death, the eminent explorer Vilhjalmur Stefansson pointed out that the English explorer had never taken the trouble to learn the survival skills practiced by the Indians and the Eskimos—peoples who had managed to flourish "for generations, bringing up their children and taking care of their aged" in the same harsh country that killed Franklin. (Stefansson conveniently neglected to mention that many, many Indians and Eskimos have starved in the northern latitudes, as well.)

McCandless's arrogance was not of the same strain as Franklin's, however. Franklin regarded nature as an antagonist that would inevitably submit to force, good breeding, and Victorian discipline. Instead of living in concert with the land, instead of relying on the country for sustenance as the natives did, he attempted to insulate himself from the northern environment with ill-suited military tools and traditions. McCandless, on the other hand, went too far in the opposite direction. He tried to live entirely off the country—and he tried to do it without bothering to master beforehand the full repertoire of crucial skills.

It probably misses the point, though, to castigate McCandless for being ill prepared. He was green, and he overestimated his resilience, but he was sufficiently skilled to last for sixteen weeks on little more than his wits and ten pounds of rice. And he was fully aware when he entered the bush that he had given himself a perilously slim margin for error. He knew precisely what was at stake.

It is hardly unusual for a young man to be drawn to a pursuit considered reckless by his elders; engaging in risky behavior is a rite of passage in our culture no less than in most others. Danger has always held a certain allure. That, in large part, is why so many teenagers drive too fast and drink too much and take too many drugs, why it has always been so easy for nations to recruit young men to go to war. It can be argued that youthful derring-do is in fact evolutionarily adaptive, a behavior encoded in our genes. McCandless, in his fashion, merely took risk-taking to its logical extreme.

He had a need to test himself in ways, as he was fond of saying, "that mattered." He possessed grand—some would say grandiose—spiritual ambitions. According to the moral absolutism that characterizes McCandless's beliefs, a challenge in which a successful outcome is assured isn't a challenge at all.

It is not merely the young, of course, who are drawn to hazardous undertakings. John Muir is remembered primarily as a no-nonsense conservationist and the founding president of the Sierra Club, but he was also a bold adventurer, a fearless scrambler of peaks, glaciers, and waterfalls whose best-known essay includes a riveting account of nearly falling to his death, in 1872, while ascending California's Mt. Ritter. In another essay Muir rapturously describes riding out a ferocious Sierra gale, by choice, in the uppermost branches of a one-hundred-foot Douglas fir:

> [N]ever before did I enjoy so noble an exhilaration of motion. The slender tops fairly flapped and swished in the passionate torrent, bending and swirling backward and forward, round and round, tracing indescribable combinations of vertical and horizontal curves, while I clung with muscles firm braced, like a bobolink on a reed.

He was thirty-six years old at the time. One suspects that Muir wouldn't have thought McCandless terribly odd or incomprehensible.

Even staid, prissy Thoreau, who famously declared that it was enough to have "traveled a good deal in Concord," felt compelled to visit the more fearsome wilds of nineteenth-century Maine and climb Mt. Katahdin. His ascent of the peak's "savage and awful, though beautiful" ramparts shocked and frightened him, but it also induced a giddy sort of awe. The disquietude he felt on Katahdin's granite heights inspired some of his most powerful writing and profoundly colored the way he thought thereafter about the earth in its coarse, undomesticated state.

Unlike Muir and Thoreau, McCandless went into the wilderness not primarily to ponder nature or the world at large but, rather, to explore the inner country of his own soul. He soon discovered, however, what Muir and Thoreau already knew: An extended stay in the wilderness inevitably directs one's attention outward as much as inward, and it is impossible to live off the land without developing both a subtle understanding of, and a strong emotional bond with, that land and all it holds.

The entries in McCandless's journal contain few abstractions about wilderness or, for that matter, few ruminations of any kind. There is scant mention of the surrounding scenery. Indeed, as Roman's friend Andrew Liske points out upon reading a photocopy of the journal, "These entries are almost entirely about what he ate. He wrote about hardly anything except food."

Andrew is not exaggerating: The journal is little more than a tally of plants foraged and game killed. It would probably be a mistake, however, to conclude thereby that McCandless failed to appreciate the beauty of the country around him, that he was unmoved by the power of the landscape. As cultural ecologist Paul Shepard has observed,

> The nomadic Bedouin does not dote on scenery, paint landscapes, or compile a nonutilitarian natural history. . . . [H]is life is so profoundly in transaction with nature that there is no place for abstraction or esthetics or a "nature philosophy" which can be separated from the rest of his life. . . . Nature and his relationship to it are a deadly-serious matter, prescribed by convention, mystery, and danger. His personal leisure is aimed away from idle amusement or detached tampering with nature's processes. But built into his life is awareness of that presence, of the terrain, of the unpredictable weather, of the narrow margin by which he is sustained.

Much the same could be said of McCandless during the months he spent beside the Sushana River.

It would be easy to stereotype Christopher McCandless as another boy who felt too much, a loopy young man who read too many books and lacked even a modicum of common sense. But the stereotype isn't a good fit. McCandless wasn't some feckless slacker, adrift and confused, racked by existential despair. To the contrary: His life hummed with meaning and purpose. But the meaning he wrested from existence lay beyond the comfortable path: McCandless distrusted the value of things that came easily. He demanded much of himself—more, in the end, than he could deliver.

Trying to explain McCandless's unorthodox behavior, some people have made much of the fact that like John Waterman, he was small in stature and may have suffered from a "short man's complex," a fundamental insecurity that drove him to prove his manhood by means of extreme physical challenges. Others have posited that an unresolved Oedipal conflict was at the root of his fatal odyssey. Although there may be some truth in both hypotheses, this sort of posthumous off-the-rack psychoanalysis is a dubious, highly speculative enterprise that inevitably demeans and trivializes the absent analysand. It's not clear that much of value is learned by reducing Chris McCandless's strange spiritual quest to a list of pat psychological disorders.

Roman and Andrew and I stare into the embers and talk about McCandless late into the night. Roman, thirty-two, inquisitive and outspoken, has a doctorate in biology from Stanford and an abiding distrust of conventional wisdom. He spent his adolescence in the same Washington, D.C., suburbs as McCandless and found them every bit as stifling. He first came to Alaska as a nine-year-old, to visit a trio of uncles who mined coal at Usibelli, a big strip-mine operation a few miles east of Healy, and immediately fell in love with everything about the North. Over the years that followed, he returned repeatedly to the forty-ninth state. In 1977, after graduating from high school as a sixteen-year-old at the top of his class, he moved to Fairbanks and made Alaska his permanent home.

These days Roman teaches at Alaska Pacific University, in Anchorage, and enjoys statewide renown for a long, brash string of backcountry escapades: He has—among other feats—traveled the entire 1,000-mile length of the Brooks Range by foot and paddle, skied 250 miles across the Arctic National Wildlife Refuge in subzero winter cold, traversed the 700-mile crest of the Alaska Range, and pioneered more than thirty first ascents of northern peaks and crags. And Roman doesn't see a great deal of difference between his own widely respected deeds and McCandless's adventure, except that McCandless had the misfortune to perish.

I bring up McCandless's hubris and the dumb mistakes he made—the two or three readily avoidable blunders that ended up costing him his life. Sure, he screwed up," Roman answers, "but I admire what he was trying to do. Living completely off the land like that, month after month, is incredibly difficult. I've never done it. And I'd bet you that very few, if any, of the people who call McCandless incompetent have ever done it either, not for more than a week or two. Living in the interior bush for an extended period, subsisting on nothing except what you hunt and gather—most people have no idea how hard that actually is. And McCandless almost pulled it off.

"I guess I just can't help identifying with the guy," Roman allows as he pokes the coals with a stick. "I hate to admit it, but not so many years ago it could easily have been me in the same kind of predicament. When I first started coming to Alaska, I think I was probably a lot like McCandless: just as green, just as eager. And I'm sure there are plenty of other Alaskans who had a lot in common with McCandless when they first got here, too, including many of his critics. Which is maybe why they're so hard on him. Maybe McCandless reminds them a little too much of their former selves."

Roman's observation underscores how difficult it is for those of us preoccupied with the humdrum concerns of adulthood to recall how forcefully we were once buffeted by the passions and longings of youth. As Everett Ruess's father mused years after his twenty-year-old son vanished in the desert, "The older person does not realize the soul-flights of the adolescent. I think we all poorly understood Everett."

Roman, Andrew, and I stay up well past midnight, trying to make sense of McCandless's life and death, yet his essence remains slippery, vague, elusive. Gradually, the conversation lags and falters. When I drift away from the fire to find a place to throw down my sleeping bag, the first faint smear of dawn is already bleaching the rim of the northeastern sky. Although the mosquitoes are thick tonight and the bus would no doubt offer some refuge, I decide not to bed down inside Fairbanks 142. Nor, I note before sinking into a dreamless sleep, do the others.

Reading 21

RETHINKING QUESTIONS OF CONTROL
Lessons from McDonald's

Robin Leidner

One consequence of the ongoing shift in employment from manufacturing to services (Mills 1986; Noyelle 1987; Smith 1984) is that hamburgers have taken their place alongside guns and butter as the staples of political discourse about economics, with politicians and commentators questioning whether the United States is becoming "a nation of hamburger-flippers" (Kirkland 1985; also see Wildavsky 1989). Somewhat surprisingly, service work has not assumed an equally important place in sociological theorizing about work. Although scholars have acknowledged the growing importance of service jobs, they have failed to recast models of work that were derived from manufacturing. This failure is especially striking with regard to workplace control, since several excellent studies have demonstrated that service work raises distinctive problems of control (e.g., Benson 1986; Biggart 1989; Hochschild 1983). Examination of the case of McDonald's shows why we must reconceptualize workplace control in order to illuminate the dynamics of service work. Because the greatest challenge to accepted understandings of work comes from what I call "interactive service work"—work that involves direct interaction between workers and service recipients —I will focus not on hamburger-flippers, but on hamburger-servers.

Like many factory and office jobs, McDonald's jobs have been "routinized." Management has specified in advance almost all aspects of the work, so workers repeat a set of relatively simple tasks over and over again, with little opportunity for decision-making. In Braverman's (1974) term, the jobs have been "deskilled."

Leidner, Robin. "Rethinking Questions of Control: Lessons from McDonald's." *Working in the Service Society.* MacDonald, Cameron Lynne and Carmen Sirianni, eds. Philadelphia: Temple U P, 1996. 29–49.

Historians and sociologists of work have devoted considerable attention to struggles over control of the workplace. Studies of manufacturing and clerical work have focused on employers' and workers' ongoing attempts to take or maintain as much control as possible over the work, which puts the interests of these two groups directly at odds.[1] Since routinization limits the control that workers have over many aspects of their jobs, writers on the subject have typically assumed that workers will make every effort to resist it. How do the distinctive aspects of interactive service work affect how routinization is imposed and how workers respond to it?

In important ways, routinization affects service jobs much as it affects other kinds of jobs: it makes workers relatively easy to replace, it minimizes their autonomy, and it lowers their wages. In other ways, though, working behind the counter at McDonald's puts different demands on workers than, say, assembly-line work does. Instead of having just one boss issuing instructions, McDonald's workers literally take orders from anyone who comes into the restaurant. Instead of being held accountable only for their physical exertions, workers' moods, facial expressions, and words are subject to supervision.

McDonald's is hardly a "typical" service sector organization: its size, success, and visibility are all extraordinary. However, all interactive service work, ranging from sales to teaching to psychotherapy, shares certain characteristics. By definition, nonemployees are a part of the work process of interactive services. Their presence decisively changes the dynamics of workplace control, since service recipients may both try to exert control themselves and be the target of workers' and managers' control efforts. Also, because the quality of the interaction is frequently part of the service being delivered, there are no clear boundaries between the worker, the work process, and the product in interactive service work. For this reason, employers often feel entitled to extend their control efforts to more and more aspects of workers' selves. Workers' looks, words, personalities, feelings, thoughts, and attitudes may all be treated by employers as legitimate targets of intervention. Controlling interactive service work can therefore require techniques and induce responses that are not typical in other kinds of workplaces.[2]

While opinions differ on whether McDonald's jobs are worth having, they are well worth analyzing. Given the growing dominance of service sector employment, social scientists should take even low-level service work as seriously as they have taken manufacturing, managerial, and professional work. Since McDonald's has the virtue of almost universal familiarity, it provides a convenient starting place for a discussion of how our understanding of workplace control needs to be expanded if it is to accommodate the range of experiences of interactive service workers. It is important to keep in mind, however, that although McDonald's approach to controlling service work—strict standardization—has been emulated by many businesses, strategies for resolving the dilemmas of control peculiar to service work vary considerably.

I collected data at McDonald's through participant observation and interviewing during the spring through fall of 1986. I attended classes at McDonald's main management training facility, Hamburger University, in Oakbrook, Illinois. At a local franchise, I was trained to serve customers (to "work window" in McDonald's phrasing) and worked half a dozen shifts. I conducted twenty-seven interviews with crew people and interviewed or spoke informally with management trainers, the managers of the franchise and its owner, and a former McDonald's executive who had been in charge of employee research. I also spent a great deal of time hanging around the franchise's crew room, listening to and talking with workers. Because my research was part of a larger project on the routinization of service interactions, my worker interview sample was limited to the window crew, the people who deal with customers most directly. While I did not investigate the experiences of grill workers and other crew people as systematically, I got to know some of these workers and heard about their reactions to their jobs through informal conversations and observation. All of my informants were aware that I was conducting research on McDonald's, although customers were not.

In the sections that follow I show how McDonald's instituted control mechanisms that allowed the company to overcome difficulties inherent in the application of the principles of routinization to interactive service work. It has extended organizational control in several ways: in scope, by subjecting customers to standardization; in depth, by subjecting more aspects of workers' selves to regulation; and in intensity, by using multiple forms of constraint and supervision to standardize every detail of the work. Next, I turn to the outcomes of McDonald's control efforts, showing that we can understand these outcomes only by applying a more complex model of workplace dynamics than the literature provides. The interests and resources of workers and management remain crucial determinants of workplace practices, but the interests of service recipients must also be taken into account. The involvement of nonemployees in the work process means that a three-way struggle for control, with sometimes shifting alliances, replaces the familiar tug of war between workers and management. To understand the responses of workers and customers to managerial control strategies, we must therefore examine their effects on relations between workers and customers.

McDonald's: Routinizing Interactive Service Work

McDonald's has tried to control almost every aspect of its business by using the classic principles of routinization—make as many decisions as possible in advance and make sure that the work is carried out according to managerial dicta. In doing so, however, the company has had to go beyond the practices used to routinize manufacturing work by subjecting more aspects of people to control. by making nonemployees targets of control, and by using additional techniques of control.

Routinization is only one managerial approach to controlling work, and one that seems, on the face of it, to be ill-suited to interactive service work. In fact, many discussions of service companies stress that adding value through customization is increasingly central to competitiveness (e.g., Noyelle 1987). Moreover, it seems self-evident that the possibilities for routinizing service work are limited by the intrinsic fluidity and negotiability of human interactions. Whereas routinization is intended in part to insure that outputs of uniform quality are produced, the goal of uniformity is itself problematic in interactive work. Since good service is often equated with "personal service," standardization may necessarily undercut quality in human interactions.

Aside from the desirability of routinizing service interactions, the distinctive features of interactive service work would seem to make the process extremely difficult. First, the involvement of nonemployees in the work process complicates routinization considerably, since routines are only useful if the conditions and specifications of work are relatively predictable (Stinchcombe 1990). Service recipients' presence introduces an element of unpredictability (Mills 1986), so their behavior must somehow be standardized if the routines are to be workable. Second, the indivisibility of workers' selves from the work process and work product motivates some employers to extend their control efforts to aspects of workers' lives usually considered matters of individual personality or choice. Such intervention might well be resented and resisted.

McDonald's amply illustrates, however, that customization is only one route to success in a service business. Not only is routinization of service interactions quite possible, it can also be extremely profitable. With over 11,800 outlets worldwide, McDonald's is by far the world's largest fast-food company (*McDonald's Annual Report for 1990:* 1). It is also a major employer: in the United States alone, McDonald's restaurants employ about half a million people (Bertagnoli 1989: 33), including one out of fifteen first-time job seekers (Wildavsky 1989: 30). Ray Kroc, McDonald's founder, aimed to achieve the kind of tight control over work routines and product quality that centralized production in factories makes possible, in a business that is necessarily highly decentralized. He succeeded on a massive scale. Kroc instituted strict standardization of every element of the business. Although there are some matters that the company is legally obliged to leave to the discretion of its franchise owners, McDonald's has created centrally promulgated standards for how to perform every task associated with running its restaurants, as well as programs to teach these practices, equipment designed to implement the standards, and systems for monitoring the compliance of workers in both company-owned and franchise outlets.

Some service organizations grant front-line workers discretion to vary their work in response to the uncertainties and irregularities introduced into the work process by service recipients, but McDonald's has found ways to overcome the obstacles to routinization noted above. To deal with the tension between quality service and customization, it has minimized customers' expectations of individualized treatment while also trying to provide some semblance of personal service through the routinization of emotion work. It has greatly curtailed the unpredictability customers might bring to the work process by making sure they know how to fit into McDonald's routines. It has tried to make the standardization of personal characteristics palatable to workers and has also curtailed their ability to resist organizational dictates.

McDonald's has carried routinization so far that workers' decision-making power is almost eliminated. As one window worker told me, "They've tried to break it down so that it's almost idiot-proof." Most of the workers agreed that there was little call for them to use their own judgment on the job, since there were rules about virtually everything. If unusual problems arose, the workers were supposed to turn them over to a manager.

The interactive part of the job was standardized as the "Six Steps of Window Service," an unvarying routine for taking orders, assembling meals, and accepting payment. Greeting and thanking customers and asking for their return business were required, but workers were allowed some leeway to vary their phrases to avoid sounding like robots. Smiles, eye contact, and friendliness were monitored by managers (although workers who were speedy but minimally civil were tolerated).[3]

Many of the noninteractive parts of the window workers' job (as well as the grill workers') had been made idiot-proof through automation. At the franchise I studied, not only did the computerized cash registers make it unnecessary for the window workers to remember prices, calculate taxes, or make change, they also helped regulate some of the crew's interactive work by reminding them to try to increase the size of each sale through "suggestive selling." For example, when a customer ordered a Big Mac, large fries, and a regular Coke, the cash register buttons for cookies, hot apple pies, ice cream cones, and ice cream sundaes would light up, prompting the worker to suggest dessert.

To ensure that the detailed routines were carried out as intended, McDonald's management had to face two problems of control characteristic of interactive service work: how to standardize the self-presentation of workers and how to standardize the behavior of service recipients. Workers' self-presentation was subject to managerial control because McDonald's was selling customers a particular kind of experience as well as a meal. To create that experience, workers were asked not only to carry out physical tasks as specified but also to assume the cheerful, wholesome, agreeable persona McDonald's advertises. That is, they were asked to cede considerable control of their self-presentation to management.

The crew workers' appearance was standardized with uniforms and with rules detailing acceptable haircuts, jewelry, make-up, and fingernail length and color.[4] Window workers' words and manners were closely regulated, too. Their scripts, while not completely rigid, allowed quite limited variation in the service interaction. On some occasions workers were required to use specific sentences, such as, "Would you like to try our Bacon Double Cheeseburger?," in every encounter. There were also rules about what workers could *not* say. No matter how rude or insulting a customer was, crew members could not talk back, but were expected to remain polite and accommodating. To ensure that they conveyed cheerfulness and eagerness to serve, window workers' demeanor and body language were subject to regulation. Managers reprimanded those who did not follow through on their instructions to smile and make eye contact.

So that workers would be more likely to follow through on these requirements of their own accord, McDonald's taught "emotion rules" (Hochschild 1983) and ways of thinking that justified them. Managers acknowledged that some customers could be obnoxious, but guided workers to swallow their pride and suppress any annoyance they might feel. Several kinds of practices conveyed that message with varying degrees of subtlety. The "Ten Commandments of Service" studied by window workers preached, "The customer is not someone to argue with or match wits with," and "The customer does us an honor when he calls; we are not doing him a favor by serving him." Customers were usually called "guests," a term that made it somewhat easier for workers to accept the requirement that they remain politely deferential by invoking a familiar situation in which such behavior does not imply subservience. In encouraging workers not to take ill-treatment personally, McDonald's managers asked that they distance themselves from their jobs. However, the managers did want workers to identify with their jobs at least strongly enough to regard job performance as reflective of their discipline and capability. One low-level manager invoked the ideal of "professionalism," out of place as it might seem, to urge workers to take pride in doing their work well. "Don't let me catch you balling up the top of the bags," she cautioned the window workers. "You should fold it neatly twice so you look like a professional."

Through uniforms, rules about self-presentation, scripts, and emotion rules, McDonald's tried to control many aspects of its workers' selves. They required window workers to suppress some emotional reactions and simulate others, allowing them relatively little scope for self-expression. McDonald's window workers did not experience an extreme version of managerial manipulation, however. Although the inseparability of the worker, the work process, and the product meant that more aspects of the window workers' selves were subject to managerial control than is true in most manufacturing jobs, for example, for the most part the demands on them were limited to "surface acting" (see Hochschild 1983).

Many interactive service workers are subject to considerably more intensive manipulation of their thoughts and attitudes that McDonald's exerts. McDonald's did not find it necessary to attempt a thoroughgoing transformation of workers' personalities because it relied so little on workers' discretion. Organizations that depend on the decision-making of employees are likely to pay more attention to their hearts and minds. For example, insurance agents and direct sales distributors, who work without direct supervision and who must try to overcome the resistance of unwilling prospects, are subjected to quite sweeping attempts to change their characters (see Chapter 7; Biggart 1989; Butterfield 1985; Leidner 1993). In such cases, the effects of standardization are intended to extend beyond working hours, creating people who are, depending on the job, more optimistic, determined, assertive, materialistic, ruthless, or understanding.

Some elements of this more transformative approach to routinization were apparent in McDonald's management training. The company could not have removed decision-making authority from its crew workers' jobs so thoroughly were it not for the constant presence of managers whose capacity for decision-making it could trust. McDonald's went as far as it could in guiding that decision-making, issuing reams of directives and creating computer programs that standardized managerial techniques (see Garson 1988). But since it had to rely on managers to act in the company's interests in resolving unpredictable or difficult problems, it also worked on their selves in a variety of ways.

McDonald's encouraged management trainees to take Ray Kroc as a model, requiring Hamburger University students to read his autobiography (Kroc with Anderson 1977) and frequently quoting him in lectures and printed materials.[5] Since the managers worked within an organization that minimized flexibility, it was Kroc's determination and commitment to excellence that they were asked to emulate, not his entrepreneurial creativity. The training continually emphasized the tremendous success of the company, both to encourage managers to identify with that success and to drive home the message that managers and owners could rely on corporate directives. Managers' personal identities and styles of interaction were addressed most directly at Hamburger University through training in transactional analysis, as popularized in *I'm OK, You're OK* (Harris 1969). This training was intended to alter managers' style in dealing with workers, customers, and fellow managers, dissuading them from using tyrannical or belittling "parent-child" approaches and urging them to deal with others on an "adult-adult" level.

For both window workers and managers, then, McDonald's found ways to bring the selves of employees—whether merely self-presentations or personal identities—into line with organizational requirements. Persuading employees to accommodate themselves to the desired persona was an important element of the control of this interactive service work because of the difficulty of distinguishing between workers and their work processes. Employees were thus likely to experience at least some sense of disjuncture between their McDonald's persona and their self-identity, a disjuncture to which they could respond in a variety of ways: they might judge the McDonald's model of the self positively and embrace it (more common for managers than workers); try to maintain role distance (Goffman 1961b); focus on agreeable aspects of the role and resist others; or try to personalize the standardized role.

Extending the range of controls over employees' selves is one challenge for interactive service organizations, but employers must also concern themselves with the behavior of nonemployees. Service recipients partly determine the content of the work as the interactions are in progress, often by direct orders, and almost always by their attitudes and by their willingness and ability to cooperate in the service routine. Sometimes, as at McDonald's, they also perform part of the work that might otherwise be done by paid employees.[6] Concerted efforts to shape the personal identities of service recipients are not usually necessary, but organizational routines can proceed as planned only if service recipients' behavior can be made relatively predictable. An analysis of the control of interactive service work is thus incomplete without attention to the means by which customers' cooperation is marshaled.

It was obvious that the great majority of the customers at the McDonald's franchise I studied knew what they were supposed to do and were willing and able to play their parts in the service routines. They stood in line to order their food rather than waiting to be served at a table; they delivered their meal orders in the conventional sequence (hamburgers or other entrees, fries, drinks, desserts); they cleaned up after themselves. The customers had been trained in several ways. First, McDonald's advertising familiarized people with the service system and products. Second, the design of the restaurants provided cues to customers, guiding them toward the service line, for example, and making clear that they were supposed to use the well-marked trash cans (see Wener 1985). Moreover, most customers had been socialized through long experience with McDonald's and similar fast-food restaurants, and newcomers could take their cues from more experienced customers.

Not only were McDonald's customers able to play their roles properly, but they were generally willing to cooperate, since, of course, they had already made the decision to do business with McDonald's. It was the relative predictability of customer behavior that made it possible for McDonald's to create such inflexible routines for the window crew. When service recipients are less compliant or well informed, workers are likely to need more discretion to respond to contingencies.

The example of McDonald's demonstrates that basic assumptions about managerial strategies of workplace control need to be revised to make sense of interactive service work. Compared with manufacturing, *what* managers of service workers try to control is different. Not only are workers' physical tasks brought under managerial authority, but many more aspects of workers' selves are manipulated. Another major difference is in *whom* managers are trying to control: service recipients as well as workers are targeted. Meanwhile, the selves of managers may themselves be subject to standardization. In solving the problem of *how* to routinize interactive service work, McDonald's and other service organizations have employed control techniques uncommon in other kinds of work.

We should not assume, however, that the particular strategies McDonald's used to control the work process are available to all interactive service work organizations. Factors such as the complexity of the service transactions, the degree of supervision possible, and the stakes of service recipients and workers in the outcomes of interactions determine what strategies are appropriate for various organizations. The features of McDonald's window crew's routine—the extreme constriction of decision-making authority and the relative superficiality of standardization of workers' identities—reflect the brevity and simplicity of the service interaction, the presence of managers on the scene to handle difficulties, and the motivation of customers to cooperate. In service organizations where the service provided is complex and context-dependent or where only customized service will do, employers will be more dependent on workers' discretion, and workers' power relative to management will be accordingly enhanced. In cases where service recipients are not motivated to cooperate or where they are not sure how to do so, the service workers' routines may themselves be designed to channel the nonemployees' behavior, enhancing workers' control in a different way.

At McDonald's, however, workers' capacity to exercise control over their work was sharply limited. Richard Edwards (1979) has described three main types of control used by employers to direct, evaluate, and reward or punish workers: direct (or simple) control, technical control, and bureaucratic control. McDonald's crew workers were subject to all three of these forms. The ratio of supervisors to workers was quite high, so direct control was exercised by ever-present managers and trainers. Technical control was built into the computerized cash registers, which both dictated how window workers did their jobs and monitored their performance. Bureaucratic control of both the crew workers and the managerial staff was embodied in the detailed sets of regulations that described McDonald's standards for each task and prescribed criteria for evaluation. In addition, McDonald's window workers were further constrained by the direct supervision of customers, who could observe their work, make demands, and register complaints. The combination of these control methods left workers exceptionally little autonomy.

The Three-Way Dynamic of Control in Interactive Service Work

McDonald's efforts to manipulate the selves of workers and channel the behavior of customers illustrate that interactive service work organizations differ from other employers in what and whom they try to control. To understand the outcomes of these efforts, we must also reopen the questions of who tries to exercise control and how they define their interests.

A basic criticism of Harry Braverman's (1974) formulation of labor process theory was that it overstated management's success in achieving control (Edwards 1979; Littler and Salaman 1982). Numerous sociologists and labor historians have demonstrated that, although managers might try to achieve total control over the work process, their efforts are often met by workers' resistance (see Benson 1986; Edwards 1979; Halle 1984; Montgomery 1979). Even when workers do not fully succeed in withstanding these efforts, they may hold on to control over some matters, and their resistance can affect workplace outcomes in others.[7] We should not assume, therefore, that just because managers of interactive service workers have found ways to deal with the novel problems of regulating the behavior of nonemployees and of standardizing the self-presentations, ideas, and attitudes of workers, the outcomes of their control efforts are obvious. Workers and service recipients have their own preferences about how the interactions are to be carried out and their own resources for trying to act on those preferences.

To make sense of service work, we need to revise the model of workers and employers inevitably working to resist the other's control efforts. While the dynamic of conflict between workers and managers certainly does not disappear, the presence of service recipients greatly complicates the picture. Not only can workers resist employers' efforts to control the work, so too can service recipients. Moreover, customers can themselves try to exert control over workers, management, or both. Still, it is not enough to expand the resistance model of control by simply including service recipients as actors. The participation of three parties means that we can no longer take for granted that the interests of each are in conflict—that is, we cannot assume that workers or customers will resist managerial control efforts. In fact, the alignment of interests of these three parties varies in different kinds of work and even for different features of the same job (see Benson 1986; Wouters 1989).

Service recipients play varied roles in service encounters. They may give orders (restaurant customers) or follow them (doctors' patients) or both (airline passengers); they may have no choice but to participate (citizens dealing with government bureaucracies), or they may try to evade the interaction (fund-raising targets) or seek it out (prostitutes' customers); they may serve simultaneously as raw material and judge of the service (hair salon customers); they may contribute labor, willingly or not (fast-food customers). This variability means that how the interests of service recipients, workers, and management are balanced must be an empirical question. In some circumstances, workers' routines are designed to further their control over customers, in which case their motive to resist them is undermined but customers may try to resist. In others, routines can constrain workers, aligning the interests of managers and customers in controlling the workers. When customers and managers have different interests, workers are often put in the middle. Consequently, not only is the ability of workers and customers to evade managerial controls variable, so too is the interest of each group in doing so.

In interactive service work, we find not a stable pattern of workers and managers acting on interests that are directly opposed to each other, but a complex dynamic in which each of three groups of participants has interests that bring them sometimes into alliance, sometimes into opposition with each of the other two. The three-way play of interests can result in workers having less room to maneuver than they would if customers were not present, but it can also motivate managers to give workers leverage to control the interactions. Workers therefore might have reason either to resent routinization or to appreciate it. In some cases, customers and workers share an interest in avoiding the constraints of the employer-designed routine, but in others one party tries to enforce it on the other. The pattern at McDonald's is thus not generalizable to all interactive service work, but gives some sense of the complexity of the struggle over control in this type of work.

The routines of McDonald's window workers were designed primarily to give customers what they wanted, so long as they limited their wishes to the speedy delivery of a limited range of foods. For the most part, then, customers and managers shared an interest in having workers comply with their prescribed routines. Peter Mills (1986: 121) sees customers as subordinates of service providers, but at McDonald's they functioned more as supervisors. Since customers were generally quite familiar with the routine and since window work was done in full view of customers, service recipients joined management in pressuring workers to perform speedily, politely, and accurately. In other circumstances, such as commission sales jobs, managers and workers share an interest in persuading prospective customers to participate in service interactions they might wish to avoid. In such cases, workers' routines can be designed to enhance workers' control over service recipients, making customers rather than workers more likely to resist organizational control efforts (see Leidner 1993 on insurance sales).

Although particular service organizations generally have a dominant pattern of alliance, the interests of any two parties are unlikely to coincide precisely, creating cross-pressures and incentives for resistance. For example, while most elements of the McDonald's window workers' routine encouraged workers to behave deferentially to customers and to comply with their wishes rather than to manipulate them, there was one element of the routine that was intended to increase sales rather than to please customers: suggestive selling. In every interaction, window workers were required to suggest that the customer buy either another item ("Would you like a hot apple pie with that?") or a more expensive version of an item already ordered ("Will that be a large fries?"). Suggestive selling tended to irritate customers, bringing to the surface the organization's interest in manipulating customers and making the scripted nature of the interaction completely transparent. Most customers simply declined the proffered item, but some snapped, "If I'd wanted it, I'd have ordered it." When customers' and management's preferences differed, as in this matter, workers were put in the difficult position of having to please one party at the expense of the other. Since workers did not benefit directly from higher sales but did feel the effects of customers' annoyance, they usually resolved this dilemma in the customers' favor, omitting suggestive selling whenever they could get away with it.

To the extent that customers shared management's criteria for good work, they could reinforce management's control efforts, reprimanding workers for dawdling or behaving rudely, responding with gratitude and thanks to good work, complaining to workers' superiors when service did not meet their expectations (see Fuller and Smith, Chapter 4). When customers' preferences differed from those of management, workers were put in a still more difficult position.

Elsewhere, service recipients do not necessarily feel free to express their preferences and opinions so directly. If the service is understood to require special expertise, if the worker holds a higher status than the service recipient, or if the service recipient cannot easily take his or her business elsewhere, customer complaints are less commonly voiced than they are at McDonald's (see Goffman 1961a). McDonald's customers had clear expectations and were thus easily dissatisfied, but the window workers had no "status shield" (Hochschild 1983) to protect them from customers' expressions of dissatisfaction.

The workers were quite conscious that they bore the brunt of customers' irritation even when they were not directly to blame for a problem. Some McDonald's customers seemed to be angry for no particular reason and felt free to unleash their bad moods on workers. But others were irritated by the mistakes of backstage McDonald's workers who did not keep up a steady supply of food or who got an order wrong, and customer dissatisfaction often resulted directly from managerial choices. Rigid rules about which items could be served at which hours of the day disappointed some people, for example, and skimping on labor costs resulted in slower service. Since window workers were the most readily available targets, they were frequently blamed for things that were beyond their control. Evelyn Nakano Glenn and Roslyn L. Feldberg (1979) point out that interactive service workers, who often do not have the authority to change routines to meet customer requests, can serve as useful buffers who protect management from customer dissatisfaction.

In contrast, workers had relatively few resources for exercising control over customers or even for defending their dignity in the face of insult. Workers did try to guide customer behavior in some minor ways. For example, they sometimes conveyed by their manner that the customer should make decisions quickly, prompted customers with questions, or tried to preempt a display of impatience or anger by being especially cordial. But the workers' routines were not designed to empower them to control customers, except in the matter of suggestive selling, since most customers came to McDonald's willing and able to fit into the company's routine. Moreover, the rules about proper treatment of customers expressly ruled out most countermeasures by which workers might respond to obnoxious service recipients. Forbidden to talk back and unable to withdraw from unpleasant encounters by leaving their posts, workers could do little to counter rude or hostile customers or display their resentment other than scowl, for which they might be reprimanded, or project an icy distance. As one worker summed up the relation between crew and customers, "We're sort of at their mercy."

The balance of power between customers and workers varies considerably in different kinds of interactive service work. Some workers, who have the means to subject unpleasant service recipients to inconvenience or other trouble, may even feel that service recipients are at *their* mercy. Employers may contribute to workers' power over service recipients through the design of the service routines. The insurance agents I studied memorized scripts and practiced body language that made it as difficult as possible for prospective customers to interrupt them or turn down their sales pitch (Leidner 1993). In such cases, the interests of workers and employers are more closely aligned than those of service recipients and employers.

Whatever the dominant pattern of alliance in a given service organization, there are likely to be elements of the work process that set up different incentives, just as suggestive selling runs counter to the alliance of interest between McDonald's management and customers. For example, although the insurance agents and the company generally shared an interest in getting prospects to buy as much life insurance as possible, there were times when the prospect and the agent shared an interest that was contrary to the company's: an agent might be eager to get the commission on a sale to a willing customer who did not quite meet the guidelines for acceptable underwriting risk. Sometimes, of course, the worker's interests might be contrary to those of both the service recipient and the company, as when a greedy agent cheats customers and threatens the reputation of the company.

Furthermore, there can also be considerable individual variation in how much workers and customers value autonomy, custom service, and emotional investment, so members of these groups vary in the extent to which they try to evade organizational controls. At McDonald's, some window workers who resented the requirement that they be smiling and personable withheld an expression of involvement in interactions with customers (until rebuked for not smiling), protecting their own interests at the expense of management and customers. Some workers, in contrast, enjoyed chatting with customers or took pride in being able to provide a pleasant moment in someone's day. By following the scripted routine with enthusiasm or going a bit beyond it, they usually served both management's and customers' interests as well as their own. Still others focused their efforts on performing speedily rather than courteously, since that allowed them to challenge themselves without accepting a subservient stance. Their strategy satisfied certain customers and furthered some of management's interests, but their no-nonsense attitude and undisguised impatience with indecisive people made other customers feel rushed and pressured.

Customers as well as workers varied in their preferences, with some trying to engage the worker in conversation while others refused even to meet the worker's eye or otherwise acknowledge that they were dealing with a human being. Treatment that offended some workers was appreciated by others, who were grateful for undemanding and efficient interactions. Unlike salespeople's or fundraisers' prospects, McDonald's customers rarely made significant efforts to evade the routine imposed by management. Customer dissatisfaction was more often a response to what they felt was improper functioning of the routine, such as a long wait or a nondeferential worker.

Managerial success in instituting controls therefore depends in part on the balance of interests among the three parties. Do service recipients benefit when workers follow their prescribed procedures closely? Do workers' routines circumscribe customer behavior in ways that workers appreciate? Are employers' preferences about the conduct of service interactions closest to workers' or to service recipients'? How can workers and service recipients exercise control over each other in the course of the service interaction (see, e.g., Prottas 1979; Whyte 1946)? Because the answers to these questions vary, workers and customers may or may not try to resist the control efforts of management.

An appreciation of the triangular pattern of relations in interactive service work makes clear the limitations of the resistance model that has characterized studies of workplace control. Virtually all sociological and historical writing on this topic has taken for granted that managerial efforts to extend their control over the work process, especially through routinization, are contrary to the interests of workers. The literature therefore suggests a limited range of possible worker responses. They can try, individually or collectively, to resist managerial control; they can be dissatisfied with work they experience as alienating, unchallenging, and unconnected to themselves; or, suffering from false consciousness, they can fail to grasp that they should be unhappy or resistant. Attention to the three-way play of control reveals a wider range of worker responses and provides a framework for understanding them.

At McDonald's, some workers did dislike the stringent controls of routinization, and they expressed their resentment either directly or through behavior that demonstrated their determination to maintain an autonomous stance. Some seemed to be neutral rather than hostile toward their routinized work, however, and still others enthusiastically embraced either routinization in general or the content of their own work routines. The involvement of service recipients in the work process means that employers' control efforts can serve some of the interests of interactive service workers, so there is no reason for analysts to dismiss positive and neutral responses.

In the case of insurance sales, it was easy to understand why the agents showed little resistance to an extreme version of routinization. Because both they and management benefited when agents maintained the upper hand in inter-actions with potential customers, the agents' routines had been designed to max-imize their control over prospects. While routinization might have lessened the workers' autonomy vis-à-vis management, it gave them more control over their work. At McDonald's, even without the compensation of greater leverage over customers, workers did not consistently object to management's tight control over the work.[8]

There were several factors that muted McDonald's workers' resistance to routinization. First, the routine provided workers with some benefits. It gave them a clear sense of what was required of them, thus limiting the demands that could be placed on them and making them feel confident that they could do their jobs. Furthermore, while the literature on work tends to assume that workers prefer jobs that engage and challenge them, some McDonald's workers appreci-ated the way the routine allowed them to disengage from the work. Quite a few of the workers preferred interactions that did not require that they give their full attention to or make personal contact with a service recipient. When the work role is a subordinate one, role distance can be valuable, and a repetitive routine makes such distance easier to maintain. For that reason, the routine also pro-vided psychic protection from the rudeness or inconsiderateness of customers, since workers could avoid interpreting such behavior as an assault on the self. If the strict routines, by exasperating some customers, made poor treatment of workers more likely, it also made it easier for workers not to take it personally. Another factor that dampened workers' resentment of managerial control was the tendency of interactive service routines to refocus conflict between workers and service recipients. Not only did customers tend to direct their irritation at work-ers, but workers tended to focus on the unreasonableness of customers' behavior and demands, not of management's. For example, rather than deploring manage-rial pressure to hurry, they resented indecisive customers who held things up.

The literature does not provide a clear prediction of how service recipients will react to organizational controls. In most writing on work, nonemployees are simply absent. Among writers on service work there is little agreement, with some assuming that routinization makes it more difficult for customers to have their wishes met and others that customers would be better served if workers fol-lowed their routines more faithfully (Garson 1988; Koepp 1987; Roman 1979). In fact, whether service recipients' interests are furthered by routinization varies by organizational context and by individual circumstances and preferences. Standardization may benefit service recipients by defining their prerogatives clearly, mandating equal treatment, and providing a floor of competent service. However, some service routines are explicitly designed to constrain service recipients' behavior, and most limit the possibilities for delivering customized service to meet individual preferences or needs.

Thus the dynamics of control in interactive service work are not as easily predictable as the standard model of resistance would suggest. Both workers and service recipients can derive some benefits from employers' control strategies. How closely the interests of workers and service recipients are aligned with those of management varies, so the degree of acquiescence and resistance of both workers and customers varies as well. Furthermore, since participants have an assortment of interests and there is individual variation in how much workers and customers value autonomy, custom service, and emotional investment, members of these groups vary in the extent to which they choose to evade organizational controls. It is a mistake to believe, then, that the only reason that workers (or service recipients) would embrace routinization is that they misperceive their own interests.

Conclusion

This examination of workplace control at McDonald's calls into question some basic premises of theories of the labor process. The scope of employers' control efforts, the responses of workers to those efforts, the centrality of skill as a determinant of control, and the societal effects of regimes of workplace control each need to be reconsidered in light of the distinctive attributes of interactive service work.

The involvement of nonemployees in service interactions fundamentally alters the dynamics of the contest over control of the work process. Instead of a struggle between two parties whose interests are assumed to be directly contradictory, interactive service work presents a more variable three-way pattern. Employers must find ways to control service recipients if their operations are to run smoothly, and in some circumstances these service recipients try to resist that control. If customers share many interests with management and have the means to reinforce managerial control, workers will find that the presence of service recipients further weakens their position. However, in other circumstances, management's interests are served by enhancing workers' control over service recipients, in which case customers rather than workers look for ways to elude organizational control. The alignment of interests of the three parties to service interactions thus varies across types of services, depending largely on the degree to which workers are empowered to manage the behavior of service recipients. The assumptions of the "resistance model" of workplace control do not predict the behavior of interactive service workers well, because such workers have a stake in complying with those employer controls that enhance their capacity to control service recipients or to protect themselves psychologically from treatment they consider demeaning.

The inseparability of the worker, the work process, and the product of interactive service work means that employers extend their control efforts to workers' internal lives. To be sure, interactive service organizations are not the only employers to take an interest in their workers' thoughts and feelings. Managers of all sorts concern themselves with workers' motivation, willingness to cede authority to management, dedication, and loyalty to the organization. But interactive service organizations have reason to attempt more open and systematic control of workers' selves than other employers. Edwards (1979: 148–51) argues explicitly that employers take an interest in workers' attitudes to ensure the proper functioning of the control and reward system, not to direct the work process itself. In interactive service work, however, workers' attitudes, emotions, and ideas are clearly closely related to the accomplishment of their jobs. Employers may therefore make unusually invasive interventions without the legitimacy of those efforts being challenged.

Sociologists often make a distinction between workers' skill and their attitudes (see, e.g., Finlay and Martin 1991). Here, however, that distinction is hard to sustain, since the willingness and capacity of workers to manipulate and project their attitudes in the organization's interest are central to their competence on the job. The accounts of routinization provided by Braverman (1974) and subsequent analyses have treated deskilling as the crux of employer control, but skill is a misleading label for the attitudes, personal attributes, character traits, and interactional styles that interactive service employers try to standardize. Workers' subjectivity is at the heart of service employer efforts to control the labor process, and our theories must be reconsidered to give subjectivity a more central place. The self of the worker is the ground of workplace struggles for control in interactive service work, not just the worker's capacity and right to exercise skill.

Finally, the study of control in interactive service work provides a bridge between the sociology of work and broader studies of culture and society. Most studies of work assume that the struggle for control affects the society at large through its effects on workers' consciousness and on their degree of economic power. If, however, the Marxist argument that consciousness is determined at the point of production is valid, then the control efforts of interactive service organizations have a more direct impact on the culture at large. As service recipients, people find themselves at numerous points of production on their own time, forced to respond to organizational efforts to shape their interactions with other people. Understanding the effects of such manipulations on the cultural milieu and on social relations in general challenges sociologists of work to broaden their vision.

Notes

Acknowledgments: Thanks to Sam Kaplan and Annette Lareau for their help with this chapter.

1. Simpson (1985) does note the relevance of relations with clients to determining the extent of worker control.

2. The recent boom in business literature on managing services supports the contention that controlling such work presents novel challenges. Some early work argued that service productivity could be maximized by applying the principles of the assembly line, and simply extending industrial methods of production and assessment to new settings (e.g., Levitt 1972). The trend in advice to managers, however, has been to focus on the distinctive challenges of service provision: How can the quality of services be measured? How can managers inspire their front-line workers? Can the expectations and behavior of customers be managed? (See, e.g., Albrecht 1988; Albrecht and Zemke 1985; Cziepel, Solomon, and Surprenant 1985; Heskett, Sasser, and Hart 1990; Lovelock 1988; Mills 1986; Normann 1984; Zemke with Schaaf 1989.) The intangibility of the product and the real-time involvement of customers in service work complicate the control issues that are the heart of management.

3. Hochschild's (1983) work on flight attendants and bill collectors provides a detailed account of methods of standardizing the emotion work demanded of interactive service workers.

4. These rules sometimes impinged on workers' dignity as well as their self-expression. Many found their polyester tunic outfits degrading and were pleased when those uniforms were replaced by ones that more closely resembled street clothes. Some felt aggrieved at having to wear large Styrofoam Chinese peasant hats during a special promotion of "Shanghai McNuggets," which they believed made them ridiculous.

5. Biggart (1989) shows that direct sales workers are also frequently encouraged to model themselves on a charismatic leader.

6. Glazer (1984) has analyzed this trend, and many business writers (e.g., Lovelock and Young 1979; Normann 1984) strongly support it.

7. Furthermore, others have pointed out that it can be in employers' interests to allow workers some degree of autonomy to build their commitment or to add flexibility (see Burawoy 1979; Friedman 1977; Fuller and Smith, Chapter 4).

8. Given McDonald's high rates of employee turnover, however, it is reasonable to assume that my sample of current workers understated the level of dissatisfaction with these jobs.

References

Albrecht, Karl. 1988. *At America's Service: How Corporations Can Revolutionize the Way They Treat Their Customers.* Homewood, IL: Dow Jones–Irwin.

Albrecht, Karl, and Ron Zemke. 1985. *Service America! Doing Business in the New Economy.* Homewood, IL: Dow Jones-Irwin.

Benson, Susan Porter. 1986. *Counter Cultures: Saleswomen, Managers, and Customers in American Department Stores, 1890–1940.* Urbana: University of Illinois Press.

Bertagnoli, Lisa. 1989. "McDonald's: Company of the Quarter Century." *Restaurants & Institutions,* July 10, pp. 32–60.

Biggart, Nicole Woolsey. 1989. *Charismatic Capitalism: Direct Selling Organizations in America*. Chicago: University of Chicago Press.

Braverman, Harry. 1974. *Labor and Monopoly Capital: The Degradation of Work in the Twentieth Century*. New York: Monthly Review Press.

Burawoy, Michael. 1979. *Manufacturing Consent: Changes in the Labor Process under Monopoly Capitalism*. Chicago: University of Chicago Press.

Butterfield, Steve. 1985. *Amway: The Cult of Free Enterprise*. Boston: South End Press.

Cziepel, John A., Michael R. Solomon, and Carol F. Surprenant. 1985. *The Service Encounter: Managing Employee/Customer Interaction in Service Businesses*. Lexington, MA: Lexington Books.

Edwards, Richard. 1979. *Contested Terrain: The Transformation of the Workplace in the Twentieth Century*. New York: Basic Books.

Finlay, William, and Jack K. Martin. 1991. "Attitudes vs. Skill: Technology and Hiring Decisions in Electrical and Textile Plants." Paper presented at the annual meeting of the American Sociological Association, Cincinnati.

Friedman, Andrew. 1977. *Industry and Labour*. London: Macmillan.

Garson, Barbara. 1988. *The Electronic Sweatshop: How Computers Are Transforming the Office of the Future into the Factory of the* Past. New York: Simon and Schuster.

———. 1975. *All the Livelong Day: The Meaning and Demeaning of Routine Work*. New York: Doubleday.

Glazer, Nona Y. 1984. "Servants to Capital: Unpaid Domestic Labor and Paid Work." *Review of Radical Political Economics* 16: 61–87.

Glenn, Evelyn Nakano, and Roslyn L. Feldberg. 1979. "Women as Mediators in the Labor Process." Paper presented at the annual meeting of the American Sociological Association, Boston.

Goffman, Erving. 1961a. "The Medical Model and Mental Hospitalization: Some Notes on the Vicissitudes of the Tinkering Trades." In *Asylums: Essays on the Social Situation of Mental Patients and Other Inmates* (pp. 321–86). Garden City, NY: Anchor Books.

———1961b. "Role Distance." In *Encounters: Two Studies in the Sociology of Interaction* (pp. 83–152). Indianapolis, IN: Bobbs-Merrill.

Halle, David. 1984. *America's Working Man: Work, Home, and Politics among Blue Collar Property Owners*. Chicago: University of Chicago Press.

Harris, Thomas A. 1969. *I'm OK, You're OK: A Practical Introduction to Transactional Analysis*. New York: Harper & Row.

Heskett, James L., W. Earl Sasser, Jr., and Christopher W. L. Hart. 1990. *Service Breakthroughs: Changing the Rules of the Game*. New York: Free Press.

Hochschild, Arlie Russell. 1983. *The Managed Heart: Commercialization of Human Feeling*. Berkeley: University of California Press.

Kirkland, Richard I. 1985. "Are Service Jobs Good Jobs?" *Fortune*, June 10, pp. 38–43.

Knights, David, and Hugh Wilmott. 1990. *Labour Process Theory*. London: Macmillan.

Koepp, Stephen. 1987. "Pul-eeze! Will Somebody Help Me?" *Time*, February 2, pp. 48–55.

Kroc, Ray, with Robert Anderson. 1977. *Grinding It Out: The Making of McDonald's*. Chicago: Contemporary Books.

Leidner, Robin. 1993. *Fast Food, Fast Talk: Service Work and the Routinization of Everyday Life*. Berkeley: University of California Press.

Levitt, Theodore. 1972. "Production-Line Approach to Service." *Harvard Business Review* 50: 41–52.

Littler, Craig, and Graham Salaman. 1982. "Bravermania and Beyond: Recent Theories of the Labour Process." *Sociology* 16: 251–69.

Lovelock, Christopher H., ed. 1988. *Managing Services: Marketing, Operations, and Human Resources.* Englewood Cliffs, NJ: Prentice Hall.

Lovelock, Christopher H., and Robert F. Young. 1979. "Look to Consumers to Increase Productivity." *Harvard Business Review* 57 (May–June): 168–78.

McDonald's Annual Report. 1990. Oak Brook, IL.

Mills, Peter K. 1986. *Managing Service Industries: Organizational Practices in a Postindustrial Economy.* Cambridge, MA: Ballinger Publishing Co.

Montgomery, David. *1979. Workers' Control in America: Studies in the History of Work, Technology, and Labor Struggles.* Cambridge: Cambridge University Press.

Normann, Richard. 1984. *Service Management: Strategy and Leadership in Service Businesses.* Chichester: John Wiley and Sons, Ltd.

Noyelle, Thierry J. 1987. *Beyond Industrial Dualism: Market and Job Segmentation in the New Economy.* Boulder, CO: Westview Press.

Prottas, Jeffrey. *1979.* People Processing. *Lexington, MA: Lexington Books.*

Roman, Murray. 1979. *Telephone Marketing Techniques.* New York: AMACOM (American Management Association).

Silvestri, George T., and John M. Lukasiewic. 1987. "A Look at Occupational Employment Trends to the Year 2000." *Monthly Labor Review* 10 (September): 46–63.

Simpson, Richard L. 1985. "Social Control of Occupations and Work." *Annual Review of Sociology* 11: 415–36.

Smith, Joan. 1984. "The Paradox of Women's Poverty: Wage-Earning Women and Economic Transformation." *Signs* 10: 291–310.

Stinchcombe, Arthur L. 1990. *Information and Organizations.* Berkeley: University of California Press.

Thompson, Paul. 1989. *The Nature of Work: An Introduction to Debates on the Labour Process.* 2nd ed. London: Macmillan.

Wener, Richard E. 1985. "The Environmental Psychology of Service Encounters." In John A. Czepiel, Michael R. Solomon, and Carol F. Suprenant, eds. *The Service Encounter: Managing Employee/Customer Interaction in Service Businesses* (pp. 101–12). Lexington, MA: Lexington Books.

Whyte, William F. 1946. "When Workers and Customers Meet." In William F. Whyte, ed., *Industry and Society* (pp. 123–47). New York: McGraw-Hill.

Wildavsky, Ben. 1989. "McJobs: Inside America's Largest Youth Training Program." *Policy Review* 49: 30–37.

Wouters, Cas. 1989. "The Sociology of Emotions and Flight Attendants: Hochschild's *Managed Heart.*" *Theory, Culture, & Society* 6: 95–123.

Zemke, Ron, with Dick Schaaf. 1989. *The Service Edge: 101 Companies That Profit from Customer Care.* New York: NAL Books.

Reading 22

CASTING THE SELF: FRAMES FOR IDENTITY AND DILEMMAS FOR POLICY

Milbrey W. McLaughlin and Shirley Brice Heath

The few who do break through the hell-crust of prevalent conditions to
high ground should be crowned, extolled and emulated. This is the work
of the artist. [Paint, write,] let the submerged man and the world see those
who have proven stronger than the iron grip of circumstance.

Georgia Douglas Johnson
The New Negro Renaissance

Possible Selves: Different Perspectives

MRS. KNOWLTON (CIVIC ACTIVIST): There are a lot of crime problems and gangs,
but I think the bottom line of youth is that they're not motivated, which can
feed crime, can feed gangs. Citizens . . . and schools need to find a way to
motivate these kids. [However,] there are some children you will not be able
to touch regardless of what you do. It doesn't matter what you do, those children are untouchable. The parents are unmotivated, they don't care.

MRS. COBB (LEADER OF A VOLUNTEER ORGANIZATION): They [youngsters from
impoverished African American neighborhoods] have to learn to grow up and
improve themselves a little bit. And then let their children improve themselves. I mean, they gotta come up the ladder slowly . . . and when they see
people who have more, they want more, but they don't know how to get
more. You know, it's a vicious circle. They're unhappy and then they think,

McLaughlin, Milbrey W. and Shirley Brice Heath. "Casting the Self: Frames for Identity and
Dilemmas for Policy," in *Identity and Inner-City Youth : Beyond Ethnicity and Gender,* eds. Shirley
Brice Heath and Milbrey W. McLaughlin. New York : Teachers College Press, 1993. 210–239.

"I'll never get there; it'll never happen." This mind-set makes it hard to compete with the running of drugs for $500 a day rather than staying in school and working to get a degree and maybe make a little some day.

MR. MALLEN (CIVIC LEADER): Most of the youth have no motivation. It's learned at home from parents who don't work hard or work only when it is convenient for them. They come home at night and drink beer. Or maybe they don't even come home, a lot of them just carouse at bars. The kids do poorly in school. We need help to redirect the parent. Their main problem is that the parents have no respect for education.

RICKY (A GANG LEADER): The reason why a lot of kids drop out, it's a matter of a positive reception; you know, you gotta do better and if you don't do better, then you're a waste. And so, kids . . . ah, you know, it's not only pressure, it is a negative. And kids don't respond to that very well. And so, they want to go somewhere where they're accepted no matter what they do. When kids can't meet those expectations, they just get down on themselves. The only people who don't have expectations are gangbangers; they say just be yourself, do this for us, that's it.

MARCELLO (A GANGBANGER): A big reason why kids join gangs is that they are lonely . . . you're not getting enough attention in your house . . . your family's working too much or they got too many problems to pay much attention, and they forget all about you, you start feeling lonely so the only ones to hang around with is the guys on the corner. So, you start robbing your brothers and all that. Since [no one] is helping you out, you gotta help yourself out . . . you're gonna hang with someone who is gonna listen to you.

RICKY: I finally just lost it [in terms of academics]. I gave up. I just lost it because, uh, you couldn't please the teachers. You know, I tried hard to please the teachers, and you know, most of them are just beatin' you down. You know, the wear and tear of high school students, you know, you forget sometimes that some kids are really trying. . . . Kids' frustration comes from life, from the way they live. It's a buildup of negative energy. Kids are losing out. They get that frustration from school, from parents who aren't around, that's just more negative. And, just on the streets, it's just—you can feel "negative" everywhere.

ANGELA (A LEADER OF A NEIGHBORHOOD-BASED YOUTH ORGANIZATION): There is nothing there for these kids . . . they just go until they get killed or end up on the streets. These kids—the gangbangers, the dropouts, the criminals— they're the products of a community environment inundated with drug trafficking, unemployment, a school system which—I've seen kids graduate from [the local school] with a second-grade reading level and then they are expected to function. Talk about having self-confidence, talk about positive self-esteem, they don't know the meaning of that. No career goals, no support from home because parents don't understand what's going on, then you've got a school system that is so crazy. So, the kids get involved with gangs because that gives them the support structure they need, that gives them that "Wow! You are really something."

Frames for Identity

Ricky, Marcello, Angela, Mrs. Knowlton, Mrs. Cobb, and Mr. Mallen refer to the same reality: the barren contexts of inner-city youth, the dysfunctional activities and attitudes young people exhibit, and the bleak futures that face them. But their perspectives on the nature of the problem and, consequently, their thoughts about appropriate responses differ dramatically.

These youth and adults are among those we met in the course of 5 years of study of youth-based organizations in the inner cities of three major metropolitan areas.[1] Mrs. Knowlton and Mrs. Cobb, wealthy civic leaders and political activists, diagnose rising school dropout rates, increasing teen pregnancies, gang-related crime, and other destructive youth behaviors in terms of perceived deficiencies in the families of poor, urban youngsters and in the attitudes of youth. These women believe that insufficient motivation and willingness to work hard, compounded by parental indifference, derail low-income minority youth from productive, socially sanctioned lives. More incentives to achieve, such as promises of support for college attendance, can activate youngsters to take school and their achievements seriously. Mrs. Knowlton and Mrs. Cobb, well meaning though they are, "blame the victim" and seek solutions that fix deficiencies or control deviant behavior. Mr. Mallen, a community leader, echoes their indictment of the motivations and energies of the families and communities from which the youth come.

From Angela's, Marcello's, and Ricky's perspectives, these adults misunderstand thoroughly the sources of their alienation from so-called mainstream society, the signals and events that reinforce their low self-esteem and pessimistic sense of the future, and the reasons why they may choose to join a gang, to rob, to have a baby, or to drop out of school. They know well how they are characterized in the public media: Note their repetitions of key phrases abundant in the media's presentations of inner-city life. But Marcello, Angela, and Ricky maintain that outsiders also misunderstand the kinds of activities, programs, and institutions that could meet their needs and enable them to build a positive sense of personhood and future. Whereas Mrs. Knowlton, Mrs. Cobb, and Mr. Mallen locate the problems they see in the individuals concerned, these teens and workers in organizations that young people judge as effective see the roots of negative behavior in the failures of institutions that compose their social contexts.

[Our main aim has been] to distinguish between *objective* or outsider perspectives on youth and youth policy and *subjective* or insider views of the young people themselves, the view from the street, and the views of leaders of effective youth organizations that help young people to shape their sense of themselves. Our intent has been to examine the relationships between these two frames for identity—one, an objective target for policy defined by such variables as socioeconomic status, ethnicity, gender and race, and the other, a subjective sense of personhood constructed from collaborative involvement in group endeavors and engagement with long-running tasks and teams. The disjuncture between these frames forces reconsideration of identities and experiences salient to inner-city youth and a reconceptualization of the policies and practices that can enable these youngsters to find a firm footing on the path to maturity.

A youth's sense of personhood, self, and future results from the interplay of the multiple contexts in which he or she moves: community, neighborhood, family, peer group, social institutions, and labels of ethnic membership defined by larger society. These give multiple dimensions—son, Latino, student, Baptist, younger sister, gangbanger, athlete, immigrant, mother—and situate meaning and circumstance.

Productive Environments
for Inner-City Youth

Mrs. Knowlton, Mr. Mallen, and others—citizens, policymakers, and analysts—who share their assessment of the "youth problem" often wonder why young people who grow up in the desolate and hostile environments of urban, inner-city neighborhoods fail to take advantage of the many programs, interventions, and opportunities that public and private sources make available to them: tutoring programs, drug prevention efforts, skills training, remedial education, and so on. Inner-city youth behave "irrationally" when they avoid such efforts or refuse to cooperate when assigned to them.

However, from the perspective of the young people intended to benefit from these efforts, such youth policies and programs operate from a choice model that misunderstands their particular world views and circumstances. They, like their more advantaged peers, make choices based on what seems best for them at the time. Alternatives for inner-city youth are few, vision is limited, and the self-confidence necessary to "make it" is often lacking. Teens from inner-city neighborhoods, especially African American and Latino males, point to stereotypic conceptions of them as "delinquents" and "bad" as invidious forms of racism that obstruct their access to even the most menial of jobs.

Young men and women join gangs out of fear of the "nowhere jobs" and resulting social death they see in their parents or in neighborhood adults; young people join gangs to acquire the sense of legitimacy, productivity, and status denied them in an environment of high unemployment or limited opportunity as they understand it.[2] Individuals who are in gangs are not the "lowest of the low" or "just out to screw society" or interested only in easy gain, as some commentators suggest. They act out of their perceived best interest *within their context.* Young girls have babies because "that's all there is" and "to show I'm a woman" and "to have someone to love me." Teens drop out of school in search of a bonding supportive environment that will give some sort of recognition. Teens feel "all the negatives" from school and resent the almost exclusive focus on academic achievement geared toward college. They wonder at the lack of attention to "real work" in schools and point out that tracks in school are usually "college bound" and "non-college bound." The financial exigencies of their everyday lives tell teens that they must work—either before, during, or instead of, college—and yet they point out readily that high schools give no positive acknowledgement of the idea of work. Some teens also face logistical problems of getting to school: "I can't cross gang boundaries. It's easier to drop out." "I can't take my baby to day care until he is 8 months old."

Social science and social policy generally have failed to understand the perspectives of individuals growing up in inner cities of the 1990s, especially the several key ways in which these perspectives differ from those of the 1960s and 1970s. As relatively few social science studies have described the inner cities since those tumultuous decades, policymakers often formulate decisions on their view of inner cities as troubled, agitated, ethnically coherent, and impoverished neighborhoods. The extent of ethnic mixing (especially in public housing projects), exploitation by outsiders (ranging from drug dealers to insurance scam artists), and poor health (particularly among children) have reshaped inner cities since the early 1970s. Yet policymakers rarely have access to close-up descriptions of these situations; they learn of them only in disembodied statistical reports and sensationalist headlines that report the failures of local institutions, such as hospitals and schools.

Policymakers have not heard young people in their contexts and have not recognized the many signs, frustrations, and fears that young people believe signal society's disregard for them and their families, that foster and support low self-esteem, and that erode personal dignity. To a great extent, social scientists have since the 1960s prized the objective view from the outside, leaving aside what they have sometimes dismissed as the biased or narrow view of insiders. By the early 1990s, however, the coming together of humanistic interests with social science began to bring some recognition of the value of the indigenous sense of history.[3]

We have tried [in our research] to offer something of the rhythms of life in youth organizations to allow readers to hear young people and the youth organization leaders who work with them tell their own stories and give characterizations of themselves. For many of these youngsters, there is a "never for me" determination: "I'm not gonna end up like my brother, in jail with a kid he's never seen. Or like friends, blown away by gangs." This drive to survive—to construct a future—pushes them to get out of the only place they've known: the streets of the inner city. We have tried to convey the numerous ways in which both youth policymakers and those in inner-city youth organizations appropriate and misappropriate each other, which makes any kind of structural change extremely slow and highly dependent on new channels and messages of communication.

Those who find the objective perspective comforting and necessary as a means to stability will charge that the subjective view is too relativistic and that it asserts the equal validity of all norms and values, making moral judgments and cultural progress impossible. In the praises of youth and their leaders for local autonomy and contextualized responses, objectivists will hear a call for an end to all generalized, top-down schemes for the reform of inner-city youth.

Those who urge a more subjective view would respond that the essence of relativism lies in its plea for a fundamental respect for cultural differences among groups and for a recognition of the far-reaching and often unexpected results of top-down bureaucratic and political attempts to "shape up" inner-city families. Subjectivists would ask for ways of learning that center on communication within and between cultures and that challenge the need for youth policies to affirm universal values, usually from the mainstream, middle-class, nuclear family vantage point. Essential in this request is the need to recognize that the public ideal of leisured and paced mainstream middle-class childhood, adolescence, young adulthood, and adulthood, often portrayed in the media, lies outside the realm of possibility for those who grow up in inner cities anywhere in the world at the end of the 20th century.

Thus, policies framed on this ideal view of stage development with accompanying varying levels and types of support will not work for urban youth—or, quite possibly, for other segments of American youth. Closely linked to the need to see that adult responsibilities and realities push themselves on youngsters at an early age in inner cities is the recognition that academic achievement and advanced education must not be set out as the single measure of success for young people: jobs as bus drivers, warehouse managers, plumbers, electricians, and postal workers should stand as worthy of aspiration as either short-term, along-the-way, or long-term occupations. These jobs require decision making, technical skills, an ability to deal with the public, and commitment to accuracy and attention on the job.

The public's perceptions, like those of Mrs. Knowlton and Mr. Mallen, that inner-city youth "resist" social reform programs must be revised in light of the need for eminently pragmatic solutions that involve young people in their contexts. The public's perception that it is "too late" to intervene positively in the lives of youngsters once they are beyond the early elementary years must take into account the amount of responsibility and survival knowledge these young people must have by the age of eight or nine. If enrolled as part of the process and the planning, many of these young people can and will use opportunities to reshape their self-expectations and sense of the future. These same young people will indeed resist programs that try to control their behavior, that label them as deviant or deficient, that ignore their culture and context, that offer them little in the way of personal accomplishment and skill, or that hold them to low levels of expectation and accomplishment. They will resist youth organizations that attempt to herd them into ethnic membership as the single or primary key to self-identification. They will resent naive messages regarding safe sex and appropriate norms of gender behavior that disregard the actions of their local and media heroes and heroines. They will say quickly that when they assume adult responsibilities, take on decision-making, and handle financial and child-care tasks, they receive no recognition or support; ironically, especially for young women, their only hope for some support and recognition often comes only when they become mothers.[4]

An organization must add up to something for youth, must have significance for its members, and must allow them to reach out to other aspects of society than those they have known in the inner city. Travel, consistent sponsorship, and extended exposure to work situations of a wide variety enable young people to compare, critique, and contemplate choices available beyond their own streets. Such institutions are hard to franchise and hard to specify from outside the local setting in which they operate. The environments that support and engage inner-city youth—the organizations with which they choose to affiliate—are palpably local and are responsive to needs as defined by youth and to their context. Environments that succor and support youth are familylike organizations with productive, goal-directed activities. They differ in crucial elements of design and orientation from organizations that set out to serve youth. We distinguish between *youth-serving* and *youth-based* organizations—the latter being groups ever responsive to changing local needs and insistent on the importance of youngsters' input to the organizations.

Youth-based organizations share a conception of youth as a resource to be developed rather than a problem to be managed. Their conception of youth generates program activities that respect the views and abilities youngsters bring with them, that remain attuned to developmental needs and cultural differences, and that strive to provide the supports that mesh with their unmet needs. These organizations admit that the youngster who is one day responsible for getting a sick baby sister to the doctor and caring for her through the night may the next day fly into a temper tantrum to match that of a 2-year-old. Leaders of these groups talk of the need to expect rapid fluctuations among the young who carry many responsibilities and worries that would wear down their elders.

Activities in youth-based organizations embrace the whole person, not just a single issue or component such as ethnicity, pregnancy, substance abuse, or school success. Thus, although a single focus such as basketball, tutoring, or tumbling defines the organization, these activities are instrumental in helping attend to the fuller emotional, social, educational, and economic needs of participants. The basketball team holds regular study halls and homework sessions; the director of the tumbling team serves as employment counselor, emergency banker, and even emergency babysitter. The tutoring project takes field trips, finds money-making activities for youth, and often assists youths' families with crisis management in terms of social services or city bureaucracies. The community center becomes not only a place for basketball practice, homework tutoring, and puppet shows, but also a center where adults can come to prepare for taking the test for their General Education Diploma (GED), learn about jobs, and meet with attorneys who specialize in poverty law.

Youth-based organizations walk a thin line between heavy personalization of all who join their group and strict adherence to rules that apply to everyone. The janitor of the Girls Club may greet each group of girls as they enter between 6:30 and 7:00 each morning to get their breakfast, finish homework, and wait for a bus to take them to school, but he also insists each child sign in and turn in permission slips for the afternoon field trip. Those who fail to do so receive stern warnings and no club privileges until they adhere to the rules. The tumbling team member who is told to meet the van on a certain corner at a particular time but fails to show up on time is left behind; the basketball team member told to be in front of his apartment complex at 4:30 A.M. for a ride to the airport for a 6 A.M. flight knows if he is not there at the appointed minute, he will miss the team trip to the West Coast for tournament play. At the same time, leaders also allow older youth leeway in some of the organization's rules as a sign of respect and acknowledgement of tenure with the group. For example, a Boys and Girls Club that strictly enforces a requirement that youth carry their membership card at all times in the club excuse older members from doing so. But the rules that bind and advance youth and their activities are upheld with "tough love."

Activities driven by a conception of youth as a resource to be developed thus invest a significant measure of responsibility for maturation in the youth. All leaders believe that the rules of their organizations match those of the world of work and bureaucracy: If you don't do things on time, do them right, and fill out the paperwork, you'll lose out in the end. Entrusting plays a critical role in the group norms of social control; any latecomer knows not to expect sympathy from teammates as much as he or she knows nothing will be gained by pleading the case with the leader. The unflinching sense of responsibility and strict adherence to rules of youth-based organizations come wrapped in fairness, equity, consistent concern, and high expectations (as echoed by Ianni's [1989] formula for effective schools as firm, fair, and consistent). Again and again, those who complain about the rules describe their leaders as "fair," "sure," "certain," "making us work hard," and "making us believe we can do it." The discipline lies centrally in the expectations.

Their activities in these organizations suggest the sense of ownership these young people gain is a shared one—a sense of "being in this together" with the team, the center, or the troupe. Although each individual must be able to hold up his or her responsibilities, each does so with a view of connection and linkage. Letting down on the part of one person weakens the entire enterprise; thus, the youngsters work hard to keep each other up and to bring recalcitrants in line. A program attractive to teenagers is a program that is "theirs." A program attractive to adolescent youth empowers them, underscores their competence, and bolsters their sense of social worth.

Diversity within the group ensures access to a wide variety of types of expertise. Newcomers find themselves tested for what they know and can do within their first few visits to the Boys Club or the girls' softball team. The fact that becoming a member of a drama or dance group may call upon not only one's singing talents but also know-how with stereo equipment, access to a church auditorium, and ability to illustrate posters never leaves the mind of some of the old-timers in the group. Newcomers with diverse talents can help relieve others of some of the onerous tasks they have had to carry out. During the summer at a community center, new young people enrolled in day programs know that their leaders will be eyeing them with a view to whether they might be hired for some of the many jobs in the center that come up through the year. Adherence to daily sign-ins, cleanup rules, and safety regulations, as well as showing responsibility in helping younger participants to find their way through the maze of rooms, are the unspoken achievements that can win one notice as a possible junior employee at the center.

Important, too, is neighborhood investment, because it links the adults in a young person's life to the organization. For example, the director of a neighborhood Boys and Girls Club tells of the debilitating falloff of community volunteers and board members when the Club's financial authority was centralized "downtown." Youth-serving organizations that are vital and effective from the community's perspective have their roots deep in the community and so can draw on the local environment for political, financial, and instrumental support. Local investment can take the form of staff from the neighborhood, not just dollars. This local knowledge also enables program staff to understand the young people with whom they work in terms of family and neighborhood contexts and lets them interact with these young people as individuals. Local youth leaders face a dilemma of accessing the resources downtown without alienating or excising the resources of the neighborhood.

Knowing communities and families often adds up to not asking questions and not making ingenuous assumptions that each youngster has parents or guardians who are reliable, safe, and trustworthy. Youth leaders know that many of the youngsters in their groups have parents who rarely show up and are abusive and cruel when they do. Moreover, they know that young people every day see adults walk right back into situations that have previously harmed them; they hear too often from abused mothers that "there's nowhere else to go. I don't want to be alone." Some youngsters take their resentments out on parents, schools, and any form of authority, resisting any fencing in that might make them vulnerable to unfair and unpredictable treatment like that which they have known at home or in school.

Yet another important feature of successful programs for inner-city youth is responsiveness to "local ecology," or the resources and unmet needs of the community. Generic program models or standardized service menus, especially those created at some remove, risk redundancy or irrelevance. Not all neighborhoods have the same configuration of resources in terms of schools, recreational activities, social services, family coherence, political clout, economic outlets, or cultural opportunities. Not all youth programs need the same offerings of sports, education, social supports, or training. Efforts that have effectively engaged and sustained the participation of youth are efforts that have defined their emphases and offerings in terms of local topography and "fit" with the neighborhood, its resources, and its culture.[5]

Youth-based organizations attract young people by the safe, supportive, and personal environment they provide. Even within these organizations, however, teenagers present special emotional and social needs, difficult to meet in the context of general-purpose institutions intended to provide a broad range of activities and program to youth of all ages and interests. Even the most effective of these organizations often experiences a membership dropoff as youngsters enter their late teens; the organizations that met their needs in earlier years apparently do not continue to do so as they enter adolescence. Teens cite the absence of a space just for them, of programs or activities relevant to their interests, or of signs or symbols to mark their "elder" status as reasons why they believe the organizations they enjoyed earlier are now "just for kids."

One key to retaining adolescents' interest and involvement is the ability to employ these older youngsters within the youth-based organizations. In the relatively few situations in which this is possible, these young people serve as assistant coaches, apprentice electricians or custodians, assistant education directors for tutoring programs, and so on. Their continued role in the youth-based organizations offers these young members a sense of continuity and builds a financial base and sense of stability that often help them to translate future goals into attendance in vocational programs or a return to school.

Organizations in the inner cities that engender the commitment and engagement of young people beyond the age of 14 offer not only financial opportunities but also environments of small cohesive groups engaged in intense, demanding, goal-focused, and rewarding work. Long waiting lists of youth exist for activities that provide teenagers with involvement in a socially cohesive, distinctive group—evidence that youth will choose a positive identity or affiliation if such a choice is available. In even the most desperate inner-city neighborhoods, vibrant youth groups absorbed with such activities as theater, dance, basketball, or tumbling came by the early 1990s to have long waiting lists—sometimes of as many as 3,000 youngsters who wanted a chance to prove themselves and become part of a particular team or troupe. The similarity of these groups to the gangs that involve most of the neighborhood's adolescents are apparent: strong social identity, interdependence of members, and clear and stable relationships and roles.

These productive youth groups possess something difficult to create within the context of larger organizations: the group cohesiveness necessary to frame and sustain social identity in terms of group norms, values, and goals. In Lakeside, membership in the Liberty Theatre group [. . .] provides definite and positive social identity, membership by itself sufficient to escape pressures from gangs ("Who do you fly with?" "What do you be?") and to furnish a positive connection with status in mainstream society. So, too, is involvement with a winning, tournament-trekking basketball team a source of station, acknowledged identity, and positive comment on contribution and competence.

Involvement in such tightly structured, goal-focused, cohesive groups enables inner-city adolescents to reclassify the group to which they belong from "deviant" and "destructive" to "positive" and "productive" (Turner, 1987). Involvement in such groups shifts the ground for casting self and constructing social identity: It provides buffers from the fierce communion of the streets and the attractions of gangs and offers evidence of competence and worth. Cohesive, predictable groups license trusting relationships and mutual dependence, dimensions of human relations generally missing for most inner-city youth. One teen told us, "I don't have trust or faith in no one, nobody. We can't depend on someone to help us, protect us. You've got to protect yourself, help yourself. You are the only one you can trust." Learning to trust and to depend on others counts among the most important learning that occurs in inner-city youth-based organizations of the sort we describe here.

Ethnicity and gender figure in this construction in highly varying ways. Social self-concept, part of an individual's mental structural field, draws from the social groups with which an individual affiliates *together with* other emotional or personal associations—for example, male, Lakesider, sister, Latino, Hungarian, project-dweller, Catholic. Activities, products, performances, and even winning seasons form the core context from which youngsters build a sense of accomplishment and pride in their future and into which they can fit a sense of racial or ethnic pride.

Some groups focus on ethnicity and culture for some explicitly instrumental purpose: to provide the pride of heritage necessary to participate confidently in the broader culture. "When children's (or communities') identities become shrouded in shame, they lose the power to control their own lives in situations in which they interact with members of the dominant group."[6] But more often in the 1990s, youth organizations try to center pride in the actual spatial territory of community and the people there. When a youth organization originally founded in the 1960s to instill pride in being Puerto Rican tried to maintain that focus in a neighborhood of young people from mixed-ethnic families, as well as families from Mexico, South America, and Puerto Rico, young people balked. They admitted their irritation that one of the youth leaders was "always talkin' about Puerto Rican, Puerto Rican, Puerto Rican. . . ." This outburst provoked a discussion of the need to acknowledge other origins:

ALICIA: We don't like this, you know, 'cause she's always talkin' about Puerto Ricans. We're not even Puerto Ricans. We're Mexican and Peruvian.

RAOUL: I'm half Puerto Rican.

These young people and many of their peers see notions of "ethnic purity" or "cultural identity" as anachronistic symbols of another generation and political agenda.[7] In the hybrid demographics of urban institutions, ethnicity is reinterpreted and reinvented within the multicultural contexts of schools, housing projects, community organizations, and social life. Advocates of exclusionary, militant ethnic organizations generally represent *their* perspectives on ethnic identification, products of earlier eras of ethnic enclaves, not young people's conception of self.[8] For today's youth, ethnicity comprises not the primary identity but an additional "layer" of identity that youth—especially youth from minority cultures—can adopt as a matter of pride. Effective youth organizations assume this view of ethnicity as an aspect of multidimensional identity and thus celebrate ethnicities and accept differences.

Most of the successful groups and organizations we encountered viewed individual characteristics of ethnicity or race as instrumental to building a positive social identity and as part of the new ethnicity that equips individuals to have multiple perspectives on an issue or experience (Novak, 1980, elaborates the concept of "new ethnicity." [. . .]). Ethnic identity became most important when an individual had built a sense of immediate and primary team membership through sustained involvement in group activities. Beyond this foundation, a sense of ethnic membership helped enable these individuals to move confidently into larger society with a sense of linkage to a larger group with an identifiable proud history. Community-based organizations are in a unique position to provide links to the mainstream *and* to celebrate ethnic identities (Cahill, 1991). Key to ethnic identities within the contemporary urban context is recognition that youth inhabit multiple realities and that expressions of self represent multiple repertoires. In this embedded context, ethnicity signals only one part of a broader social identity, an aspect of self in which youth must take pride but which in and of itself is an insufficient social brief or inadequate guide for organization. In contemporary America, youth's ethnicity obtains meaning in the larger culture and is reinterpreted in each locale and by each generation.

Pride in gender identity further challenges the imagination and structure of many youth organizations. Even though Congress passed an amendment in 1974 that exempted voluntary youth organizations from the effects of Title IX of the Education Act Amendments of 1972, such groups have still felt pressure for increasing sex equity. In 1990, the Boys Clubs of America changed its name to Boys and Girls Clubs of America, largely as a result of the club's loss of a California court case concerning gender equity. With this change, the Girls Clubs of America, whose leaders felt that many particular needs and interests of girls would not be well served by a coeducational facility and program, reaffirmed their commitment to young women and changed the name of the Girls Clubs of America to Girls Incorporated. There, they could provide programs, schedules, personnel, and projects that catered to what they viewed as the needs of young women: birth control and child-care classes and cooking and tutoring programs. In recent years, Girls Clubs/Girls Incorporated have also developed major program components for girls on leadership skills, career development, basic sports skills, and math and science (Nicholson, 1987; Wahl, 1988) in recognition of the changing role of women in society and the uneven support that girls receive in developing confidence or expertise in these areas.[9] Little League and other sports teams occasionally felt public pressure to open membership to girls and boys, but most of these demands came in middle- and upper-class neighborhoods and not in inner cities.

Community centers, church youth groups, and artistic groups that foster dance, music, and theater consistently have included both boys and girls, although many such groups provide separate activities, places of meeting, and competitions for each. Rationales for such separations center around matters of identity and the need to have a safe, intimate place to talk about issues in which both adults and young believe the other gender has either no competence or interest. For young women, particularly, such occasions are most important for the opportunity they offer to talk about matters of sexuality and their confusion about the mixed signals they often receive from gangs and from adult women about relations with men. When adults fail them, girls cling together and often become appendages to gangs of young men. The desire for sexual favors from one male often fosters a competitive spirit among girls in gangs, which keeps them from talking among their gang peers. Yet our experience with such young women in community organizations indicates that they worry about how to meet the demands of a man while realizing that, by their own estimate, about 80% of males leave pregnant girls stranded and never help out with the baby.[10] In a supportive group in a community organization, girl gang members can confess that most of the girls "don't like to have babies. Like these chicks that I hang around with, if they're pregnant or anything and they see us cruising and everything . . . they go 'man, I can't wait till I get this thing out of my stomach.'" Some inner-city parents—male and female—have been gang members in their youth, and their children thus have to reconcile any admonitions their parents may give to them with what they know and see of their parents' behavior and with public and school admonitions against gang membership.

Having women within community organizations to direct activities, listen to girls, and understand the contradictions and dilemmas of their backgrounds is critically important. Yet finding women to direct such groups is difficult, and on the whole, most youth organizations that include boys and girls have male leaders. Short-term female volunteers who find the realities of the lives of inner-city youngsters too harsh and overwhelming do not last long in inner-city youth organizations. The few women who stay on in these groups tend to be those who share similar backgrounds with the youngsters or those whose personal or religious ideologies enable them to listen without judging and to accept without condition. These women play specialized roles for particular small groups within the organization. In our research, only a handful of organizations for teens were headed by women, and men far outnumbered women in youth organizations of all types—ranging from athletic to artistic.

However, contrary perhaps to public expectations, males within coeducational organizations tended to be highly sensitive to the needs of young women for support. For example, when a 13-year-old girl who had been a regular and exemplary member of a community center was hired to work as a junior leader for the next summer and became pregnant in the interim year, the male director accepted her dual roles of child and expectant mother. She participated in all the recreational opportunities of other junior leaders, but the center also arranged for her to have prenatal counseling. Plenty of time for small-group talk sessions, viewing of films, planning of puppet shows, and cross-age tutoring allowed males and females to talk about problems they had in common of resisting the dangers of both street and home life. Yet ample opportunity for private "girl talks" also ensured that young women's gender-specific concerns received attention. Cross-age groupings for females tended to center on personal and social concerns far more than did such occasions for males. Such conversations, especially in mixed-ethnic groupings, offered opportunities for young women to consider how parental expectations differed across cultures and how only certain norms and institutions could reinforce strong self-identities, counter to the generalized media image of young man or woman, young minority or majority ethnic member, and rich or poor.

Dilemmas for Policy

The matter of where norms and institutions might come from and what role youth policy should play in upholding these highlights the first of many dilemmas for youth policy. Often, youth leaders heard youngsters offering testimonies to their peers of how their church or their very traditional, old-fashioned grandmother kept them out of trouble. In many cases, youngsters able to stay in school and out of trouble also attended strict religious institutions. Community youth organizations funded either partially or fully by public sources or foundations could not endorse in public ways these institutions or their teachings, although they might wholeheartedly endorse the effects of the church on the lives of young people. These and other dilemmas highlight the fact that sensitive youth leaders often see both the inside and outside perspectives of the lives of youngsters and find themselves caught in the middle.

Policymakers and social scientists frequently give quiet nods to the importance of understanding and basing youth policy on the perspectives and actualities of young people—the subjective view that captures the multiple pressures, competing demands, and special rationality of young people's inner-city, urban context. But mere head nods usually do not lead to a serious grappling with contradictions and dilemmas. Economic demands for "efficiency," bureaucratic mandates for organizational control and accountability, and political calls for "equity" and neutrality with respect to religion deflect serious attention from the messy, noisy, undisciplined, and particular realities of urban youth.

Placed side by side, these two perspectives—that of the outsider and that of the insider—generate essential and uncompromising dilemmas for policymakers. The policy responses to these tough questions—the extent to which policy reflects Mrs. Knowlton's diagnosis of the "problem" and framework for "solution," or Ricky's and Angela's perspectives—has everything to do with whether urban youth will react as policymakers hope or whether youth policy initiatives aimed at benefiting both youth and society will again disappoint.

The dilemmas for youth policy run deep in our country's traditions of pluralism and democracy and of age-appropriate sexual behaviors and preparation for child rearing. These values underlie the procedures developed to assure taxpayers and foundation boards that their dollars are spent responsibly and fairly. The insiders' perspectives lead to a policy model and policy approaches that differ in critical, elemental ways from those in place today. We lay out here several examples of the tough interrelated choices we found among the 60 youth organization sites involving 24,000 youngsters in three major metropolitan areas.

"Value Neutral" Programs Versus Programs with Specific Religious or Moral Orientation

Few if any youth organizations could be called value free.[11] Most seek and hold a strong value base that they strive to inculcate in the young people who take part in their activities. For example, both the YWCA and Girls Incorporated have serious commitments to gender equality. The "One Imperative" of the YWCA—to eliminate racism by whatever means necessary—and the strong, proactive affirmative action position of the Girl Scouts signal strong organizational value positions about race and equity. The values on which the Boys Scouts organization builds—achievement, patriotism, community service, and religiosity—are everywhere evident in their program and protocols.

The policy dilemma involves not support for organizations that pursue these general philosophical positions but public backing of institutions that advocate specific religious or ideological positions (such as a specific religious denomination or a moral position on an aspect of private life). Tradition and constitutional law separate church from state in America; public norms resist the use of public dollars to support activities characterized by particular ideological perspectives. Yet organizations of such a "missionary" stripe are often among the more important resources for inner-city youth. Young people growing up in the oppressive contexts of depressed urban neighborhoods desperately need a clear, coherent value system—a secure, positive belief system in which to cast self and imagine futures. The significance of a cohesive, explicit value orientation (most often Christian) and its importance for young people were apparent in many of the effective youth organizations we observed. A number of youth told us personal stories similar to Jerrold's:

> When I got saved [as part of the church youth program], my whole attitude started to change. You know, that's when I started learning about God and started seeking for my own life. So, I finally gave in to all of that anger that I had built up from gangs and from my home life and, uh, just vented it on sports [that were part of the Christian youth group].

The insiders' perspective on such groups is that they offer to youngsters—often in the most difficult of circumstances—reliable, supportive, and firm environments for learning that do not exist in either families or schools. Moreover, certain types of youngsters can be reached by these groups when nothing else can offer them a way to achieve a sense of control over their destiny. Thus, the sweep of youth organizations available within inner-city communities should include churches or religious groups that are youth centered, strictly disciplined, and strongly demanding of loyalty and obedience. Yet the specific religious or moral teaching of such organizations raises fundamental questions as to their eligibility for public support.

Standardized Programs Versus Locally Constructed Practices

Ease of management and notions of equity promote standardized, "uniform" program approaches.[12] Policymakers, as well as leaders of national organizations, worry that decentralized programming could result in organizational chaos, defy management and control, and possibly support unequal programs and opportunities across sites. The insiders' perspective, however, suggests that whatever disorganization or inefficiency that may result would be far less costly in the long term than the expense of program dollars spent ineffectively. Programs that are irrelevant to local needs, incongruent with the local ecology, and insensitive to neighborhood cultures are bound to fall short. For example, one national organization's guidelines for facilities resulted in a well-equipped downtown athletic facility that is empty of youth, while glass-strewn parks in their neighborhoods are filled to capacity with young African American males unable or unwilling to travel downtown.

The dilemma for policy is to strike an effective balance between control or direction from the top and autonomy at the bottom, or the community level. Most national youth organizations recognize that rigid specification of standardized practices and insistence on uniformity or "program replication" are only apparent efficiencies and likely portend wasted dollars and energy at the level of youth. For example, a nationally sponsored educational program that proceeded on a centrally determined formula for collaboration among youth-based organizations succeeded in River City because the school partners that it collaborated with were strong and able to work with community agencies; however, it accomplished little in Lakeside, where the schools are notoriously weak and where deep animosity exists between schools and target neighborhoods. Neighborhood leaders could have designed and carried out a program to the same end, using other community resources, but were unable to do so because of national guidelines.

"What works" for inner-city youth conforms to the contexts in which an activity is embedded and to the subjective realities of the youth it intends to advance, not to distant bureaucratic directives. There are significant differences among national youth organizations on this dimension: Boy Scouts, Girl Scouts, and Camp Fire adhere to a top-down model of program development but permit and reward local innovation. Other organizations, such as Boys and Girls Clubs, Girls Incorporated, the YWCA, and the YMCA, follow a different model that stresses local autonomy in program development, within national guidelines. However, the trend within these organizations is more centralized development of program models as a strategy for reducing costly program development and incorporating proven notions of effective program strategies. These nationally developed models are not required of local affiliates and offer considerable flexibility. The challenge for national organizations is to find ways to integrate local knowledge, commitment, and realities with national models. As resources for youth programs shrink, the temptation to achieve economies of scale and efficiency by moving responsibility for program definition away from the local level becomes great, with the apparent benefit of being able to redirect dollars from program development to the maintenance of services and activities.

"Ethnic Blind" or Nondiscriminatory Policies Versus Policies That Acknowledge Ethnicity, Gender, and Race

Democratic values of fair play and nondiscrimination are the American way. Nonetheless, when important differences in design and implementation related to culture or gender are overlooked, programs often fall short of expectations.

For example, ignorance of culture caused a well-intended effort backed by the business community to fail in Big Valley. A fund to dispense up to $10,000 to any teenage mother willing to return to school went largely unspent. Sponsors overlooked the cultural norms of this largely Latino target group, which require Latinas to stay home and raise their children. The "benefit" attached to the program ran counter to cultural values and expectations.

Failure on the part of Boy Scouts to modify sufficiently their programming, based on European American, middle-class norms and values, continues to frustrate urban scouting efforts aimed at African American, Latino, and Asian American inner-city youth. The assimilation/accommodation debate that fired discussions of youth policy 100 years ago rages today. . . . A Boys and Girls Club facility that offered exactly the same locker room and shower facilities to boys and girls ignored girls' different needs of privacy and stirred resentment that the leaders were not "really" willing to have girls in their facility.

Policies that disregard cultural differences exhibit other public attitudes toward diversity—mind-sets that have little to do with fairness and much to do with comfort. The public's fear of digging down past the fluff of "cultural awareness"—past food and festivals—to confront the meaning of cultural differences in terms of such everyday factors as speech, conceptions of time, and views about child-rearing keeps policy intended to accommodate diversity at a superficial level. Furthermore, the unwillingness of the general public to address the implications of deeply seated cultural differences finds support in the cries of middle-class African Americans or Latinos of "stereotypes." Policymakers and the public often wrap themselves in the banner of "nondiscriminatory practices" to slide over the set of extremely sensitive, highly charged issues of ethnicity, race, or gender that are constantly subject to local demographics, youth perceptions, and economic possibilities.

Responsiveness to Constituents Versus Responsiveness to the Powerless

A tour of any urban center's park facilities, public schools, recreational buildings, hospitals, or other public services reveals profound disparities between what is available in wealthy parts of town and what is available in inner-city neighborhoods.[13] For the most part, city officials acknowledge these inequalities but defend them in terms of relative political voice and influence. Asked to explain the incongruities between the country club parks maintained in Lakeside's affluent neighborhoods and the barren, dangerous park facilities allocated to housing project neighborhoods, an official shrugged and said "the voters wouldn't stand for it" were it otherwise. The well-known political calculus that provides more and better resources to the affluent than to poverty-stricken neighborhoods not only denies equal treatment to poor neighborhoods but also deprives them of the very resources they need to construct a positive environment for youth: good schools; clean, well-equipped, and supervised recreation; responsive medical care; and other social services (Littell & Wynn, 1989, p. 66). City politics being what they are, the old adage holds: Those who have, get; those who don't, don't.

These wealth-based inequities are only one way in which urban youth are disadvantaged by local political processes. Only a small portion of voters in urban areas have a direct interest in the services available to youth; for example, in the cities we studied, only between 12% and 17% of voters had children in the public schools. The common responses across sites—that "there is really not much here for youth" and that there "is nothing to do," for teens especially—are not surprising. The remarks of the president of a neighborhood association in Big Valley are typical:

> We have a multipurpose center in our area, but beside that, there really is nothing. When the neighborhood association set priorities, youth probably ranked around third or fourth. And with the little funding we have to work with, that is a low priority. We focus more on public services such as road and drainage problems, then on senior services, and then youth. But there is never much left when we get to that.

Communities are concerned about the "youth problem," but demands from more powerful constituencies shove programs and resources for youth far down the priority list.

Professionalism Versus Local Knowledge

Issues of public safety, as well as assurances of program quality, drive demands for certification and the professionalization of youth programs. But a clear message from the effective youth organizations we observed is that the knowledge that matters most is local knowledge and sensitivity to neighborhood, families, and school contexts for young people. Many of the leaders of the organizations we studied had formerly been schoolteachers, and they had found their way to youth organizations to escape what they saw as schools' insensitive responses to urban youth needs. Others were committed locals or trained professionals with a strong commitment to place. The expertise gained through formal education had little to do with forging ties to the local context, which is so necessary for effective programs.

Local youth leaders resented the fact that city youth policy boards and administrators often included youth professionals whose career interests and mobility worked against these critical neighborhood connections. These professionals' commitment often was to the profession or to advancement within the national organization rather than to the neighborhood or a particular group of young people.

Beyond perpetual problems of funding, sustaining a healthy organization in an environment that thwarts its purpose and saps vitality from all institutions requires local knowledge, local ties, and local commitment to the community and its young people. Honor for local knowledge also signals respect for the community and its people. A Lakeside youth worker put it this way: "Residents of low-income communities are rarely heard—their voices are drowned out by 'those in the know,' those who really have no idea what it is like to live in the community."

Accountability Versus Adaptability

The demand from public and private funders for "accountability" tops youth workers' list as an impediment to the flexible, responsive programming associated with effective youth programs. Complaints are not about evaluation per se, but rather about the types of evidence demanded. Requirements to specify "treatments" and outcomes in advance lock in program and constrain program staff to identity "outputs" that can be easily measured, counted, and demonstrated. The "softer" outcomes, such as an improved self-concept, an expanded sense of possible futures, a connection with a coherent system of values and beliefs, and a sense of personal and emotional safety, elude typical evaluation instruments and so do not "count." Yet these are the outcomes that matter most to youth and to their productive futures. In addition, evaluations often call for a show of outcomes over very short periods of time. Insiders know that bringing about substantive change in young people whose lives have been and will in all likelihood continue to be buffeted by violence, poverty, abuse, and unpredictability takes time.

Furthermore, youth workers complain that their "success" is too often evaluated against bureaucratic criteria rather than in terms of what they accomplish for young people. In this view, rule-based accountability schemes reward the wrong things and lead to a "body count" or "audit" mentality that diverts organizational attention from youngsters' needs, that drives program decision making to focus on numbers and balance sheets, and that constrains adaptability.[14]

Enlightened Futures Versus Feasible Goals

Policies and programs aimed at the horizon and futures of inner-city youth through education and support for achievement—for example, programs that award scholarships to college-bound youngsters, that award honor roll status, or that bring professionals to inner-city schools as part of a career fair—may indeed motivate a small portion of inner-city youngsters. But for many young people, these programs further erode their sense of value and dignity because the expectations established are beyond them and the "options" given distinction are largely professional, white-collar positions. Absent is honor for the unexceptional, for the "average Joe"; absent is support and encouragement for simply finding balance in a productive social role. Ironically, many well-intended educational programs serve only to further disadvantage vulnerable inner-city youth.

Relaxation and Recreation Versus Remediation and "Work"

Youth workers and program planners confront choices of focus, message, and environment as activities are developed and programs designed for inner-city youth. It seems there is too much to attend to at once. Young people need to be able simply to relax in a supportive environment at safe remove from the endless succession of dangers, stresses, and challenges that characterize daily life in many inner-city neighborhoods. But they must also be able to find assistance, structure, and opportunity to acquire the basic skills and information essential for success in school and for the development of healthy, personally positive responses to invitations for involvement in drugs, unsafe sexual activity, crime, or other destructive behaviors.

Finding a balance between these objectives stretches slim resources and often countermands the directions of funders or public officials. Inner-city adolescents generally spurn programs that are purely recreational without concrete purpose or product. Such activities, in their view, are a waste of time because they do not add up to anything practical. Further, inner-city youth often see "fun" programs as demeaning because they fail to recognize the adult roles and responsibilities that many of these young people have carried since their early years. Programs based on organizations that have traditionally served European American, middle-class youth often err in this direction in program design and in their assumptions about the preferences and perspectives of the inner-city youth they hope to involve.

But adolescents, who can no longer be commanded by a parent or youth worker to show up for a tutoring session or counseling activity, also reject programs whose sole focus is on remediating, "fixing," or otherwise managing their behavior. Programs that focus on single issues, such as academic performance, substance abuse, sexual behavior, and parenting skills, frequently disappoint funders and planners, because young people fail to attend or to respond consistently.

The dilemma for policy, then, is to strike the appropriate balance between relaxation and serious work, between "time off" or recreational activities and a focused effort on developing the skills and attitudes necessary to negotiate successfully through inner-city environments to positive adulthood.[15] Many youth organizations have been unsuccessful in striking this balance and have defined themselves in terms of one or the other focus, as required by their institutional identity or policy mandate. And consequently, most youth organizations report a falloff in young people's participation once they reach teen years and can "vote with their feet." Yet conclusions that adolescents "won't participate in organized activities [outside gangs]" or are "uninterested in youth organizations" are unjustified. The exceptions to this general pattern are found in the organizations described here, whose activities derive from a conception of youth as a resource to be developed. These organizations link recreation and improvement together in a programmatic frame that expressly values and empowers young people. Moreover, these organizations do not define themselves as "after" or "out of" with respect to schools; they existed for young people and for the projects, performances, and participation they could create. The dilemma for policy involves moving from a programmatic stance that revolves around society's goals (e.g., reduction in crime, lowered rates of teen pregnancy and substance abuse, and lowered rates of school dropouts) or around particular institutional (often national) identities to organizations and activities that derive from the needs and perspectives expressed by youth. Unfortunately, this youth-centered position is not popular in state legislatures, foundation board rooms, or national organizations, whose conception of the problem, of solutions, and of ways to allocate scarce resources drive programs.

Professional or Bureaucratic Boundaries Versus Comprehensive Needs

Anyone who has lived, worked, or spent time in high-poverty, depressed inner-city neighborhoods knows that the problems of families and youths who live there come not in neat packages labeled "medical," "educational," "economic welfare," and so on, but in disorderly, complex bundles that mirror an individual's context and personal condition. Successful programs and their staff recognize the impossibility of meeting the needs of inner-city youth without crossing the boundaries of profession and agency. Successful programs take their substance, shape, and rhythm from the needs and nature of those they serve rather than from the precepts, strictures, or boundaries erected by professions or bureaucracies.

The fundamental disjunction between the traditional requirements of government agencies, bureaucracies, and professionalism and the needs of inner-city youth helps to explain the paucity of effective programs and the prevalence of disappointing initiatives. At root is perspective; how the problem is understood, where it is located, and the conception of promising responses compose the frame that drives policy.

The very small number of effective programs for inner-city adolescents also reflects a constraining myth: It is "too late" to do much with adolescents; they are a lost cause and thus an inefficient target for policy investment, Our extended fieldwork in youth-based organizations of inner-city neighborhoods provides abundant evidence to the contrary. Teens connected with groups or organizations such as those described in this book have recast their identity and purpose in ways that enable them not only to "duck the bullet" of early pregnancy, school failure, gangbanging, or death, but to move on to legitimate and productive futures as workers, parents, and citizens.

They may not do as policymakers would ideally wish them to do. They may become pregnant in their early teens, drop out of school, and go on welfare, but many sustain their connections with youth organizations, find their way to night school, and end up working for youth groups or serving as aides in their children's school. They may father several children, have scrapes with the law, and leave school, but if they emerge from these experiences through the athletic program of a youth organization and find their way to a vocational education program, they have some hope of supporting themselves and their families and of participating in larger society.

For such struggles to be seen as victories, institutions must give the clear message that such paths—unconventional from a purely academic or professional career orientation—warrant respect and support. Youth organizations often include leaders and workers whose lives have followed such directions, and they therefore offer clear and realistic models of hope and dignity for young people. Beyond the personnel of these youth organizations, their frame and ethos must fit the youth population in which their existence is based. Mrs. Knowlton and others who attempt to diagnose and prescribe from the outside, who derive policy goals primarily from society's needs rather than those of youth, and who place the burden of change on youth and their families rather than on the institutions that serve them must reframe policy responses to reflect the insiders' view and the rationality of inner-city neighborhoods.

The culture of the programs that "work" with inner-city youth supports the trust, social cohesion, and respectful relationships that enable young people to leave behind the cynicism, defeatism, disregard, and low self-esteem that generate the problems that concern society. Their work is artistry—helping young people to release themselves from the "iron grip of circumstance." Their programs must support and go beyond simplistic, single-identity labels of ethnicity, race, and gender to impart a positive social identity, broadly conceived; they seek not to control or remediate youth but to develop and nurture their spirit and their strength to negotiate successfully the cumulative entrapment—"the hell crust"—of the inner city. Establishment-defined, top-down policies that retain control of program design and implementation are bound to disappoint in the absence of knowledgeable, independent, and innovative local leadership because they usually reflect scant understanding of the socioeconomic milieu in which youth construct their sense of self and because they permit little ownership or social investment of the neighborhood or its youth in the program.

Frames for Identity and Principles for Policy

Frames for identity that enable inner-city youth to move to healthy, productive adulthood and that provide connections to society and the future derive from programs that are youth based. And from the youth's perspective, the principles fundamental to programs that "work"—activities and institutions that can support them along positive paths to maturity—are simple and few.

Most important are the motivations and goals that drive programs or policies for youth. Youth avoid programs defined in terms of society's goals of "social control"—for example, reduction of teen pregnancies, dropout rates, involvement in dangerous or illegal activities. Youth do not elect to participate in programs that label them as deviant, "at risk," or in some way deficient or negative. Inner-city youth, like youth in more advantaged circumstances, want to be involved with activities that take a positive view of them and their development. They choose activities that convey respect rather than condemnation for who they are and hope rather than fear for what they can become.

Positive programs and policies for inner-city teens avoid labels that sort youngsters into categories of more or less socially desirable behaviors or problems. Organizations in which inner-city adolescents get involved expressly challenge the many myths held by the general public about the value and potential of youth growing up in inner-city neighborhoods. These myths claim that youth:

- have little to offer the community
- cannot be trusted with responsibility
- have no interest in organizations
- are beyond redemption
- are lazy—just want to hang out or have fun
- have neither the interests nor abilities necessary to accomplish much

These myths constrain positive strategies for youth while they convey disrespect and preclude the empowering strategies essential to youth's productive development.

Inner-city youth and the adults who work with them point to the irony and waste of policy decisions that retain and reinforce social control objectives while abandoning developmental efforts. Recreation efforts scaled back to support beefed-up park security, jobs programs axed while drug prevention programs multiply, peer gang intervention programs dropped while "Green Beret" enforcement squads expand—policy choices such as these opt for fixing and controlling rather than developing and supporting. Dollars spent on development, the insiders agree, yield a higher return than those allocated to problem management and social control, and efforts to "fix" have a greater chance of success when located in a nurturing, positive context than in a punitive framework.

Youth quickly decide whether a program or an organization is attractive to them on other grounds as well. Their assessments of program appropriateness are conveyed in comments such as "it's just for kids," "there's nothing happening there," "the folks there just don't get it," or "it's too much like school."

Adolescents are unusually sensitive to whether activities or organizations are "developmentally appropriate." Programs that attract teens and sustain their interest and commitment are programs that exploit adolescents' needs in positive ways. Such programs provide a safe place in which peers can achieve a sense of belonging and of valued membership; here, youth both have mentors and can mentor others. Effective youth programs ensure that every member can come to feel he or she is an "expert" in something that others who are novices need to know. Such programs empower and entrust youth as young adults and give them meaningful roles within the organization. Programs that are developmentally appropriate for teens develop concrete competencies that are valued within the group and by the larger society. And appropriate programs for youth develop those competencies in a gratifying, not a punitive, way. "Good for you" activities are also fun and meet adolescents' social and psychological needs at the same time. The most powerful "treatments" craft coherent communities of youth and adults joined in enjoyable, productive purposes.

Young people also have clear but diverse preferences for the kinds of activities they enjoy and want to pursue. [E]ffective organizations [. . .] run the gamut from basketball teams, to dance groups, to baseball teams, to scout troops, to social organizations, to academic support groups. Each has its own clientele and its own niche within the community. Youth well served by one would likely be uninterested in another. Effective policies for youth attend to what the young people both want to do and see as needed for them and their community.

Inner-city youth, who live in the shadows of the so-called "helping institutions" as problems to be managed, want most of all for the public and policymakers to understand who they are and the resources they need. They want chances to communicate their views about what works for them. Both youth and the adults who work with them compare successful youth organizations to two seemingly disparate institutions: families and gangs. In the words of one youth leader:

> What teenagers need most is structured attention. And if you have something, it may not be the most sophisticated and it may not be in the most glamorous setting, but if you got some caring folks that want to give some time and attention, you're going to be able to help some kids. . . . gangs are those kinds of organizations, they provide the kinds of things we should be providing. They provide a family, they provide career opportunity. If you work hard, you can advance. They give you a sense of family. You don't have to be anything to join; you can

come as you are. You can find a niche and some funk that's gonna be your homies. I mean, you got a group, you've got support.

Inner-city youth have too much time on their hands, too little to do, and too few places to go. They flock to activities that protect them, nurture them, and respond positively to their needs and interests. Programs and policies based on the perspectives of youth acknowledge youth as fearful, vulnerable, cynical, and lonely but also frame them as capable, worthy young people eager to grow up to a healthy and productive future.

Acknowledgments

The close reading and comments of Arnetha Ball, Juliet Langman, and Jane Quinn enhanced and clarified this chapter; we thank them. The work reported here was supported by a grant from the Spencer Foundation to Shirley Brice Heath and Milbrey W. McLaughlin for a 5-year research project entitled "Language, Socialization, and Neighborhood-Based Organizations."

Notes

1. River City, Lakeside, and Big Valley are pseudonyms, as are all names of the organizations, neighborhoods, and individuals mentioned in this chapter. Except where otherwise noted, all quoted comments were made by respondents in the course of our fieldwork. To preserve the confidentiality of sites and individuals, we identify respondents only in terms of their community role.
2. See Jankowski, 1991, for elaboration of the isolation and diminished hopes of inner city youngsters.
3. Such works include Anderson (1990), Ianni (1989), Kotlowitz (1991), and Lefkowitz (1987). These works include not only extensive descriptive materials, but also some portrayal of the lives of the inner city by insiders—young and old.
4. Compare, for example, the cases in Lefkowitz (1987) that recount in youngsters' own words their reasons for running away from home and taking to the streets.
5. Based on an extensive literature review, researchers at the Chapin Hall Center for Children at the University of Chicago concluded that youngsters' affective, cognitive, and moral-social development is enhanced and enabled when they are linked explicitly to dimensions of their everyday life. Community-based organizations, with their strong ties to the neighborhood and normative congruity with the local setting, are in the best position to promote young people's positive growth (Wynn et al., cited in Cahill, 1991, p. 2).
6. Jim Cummins, 1989, *Empowering Minority Students,* as quoted in Cahill (1991, p. 4).
7. See Gomez-Pena (1988) for elaboration of the generational aspects of ethnicity and the distortions of ethnicity introduced by the "folkloric prism of Hollywood" (p. 132) and the ideological distortions of the media. Other scholars with this perspective include Nelson and Tienda (1989) and Sollors (1989).

8. Young people, as well as adults, resent the ignorant homogenizing wrought by labels like *Hispanic,* which obscure important differences. See Gomez-Pena (1988) for an example.

9. See, for example, descriptions of Operation SMART (Science, math and relevant technology), a Girls Clubs of America project, in Nicholson (1987) and Wahl (1988).

10. Researchers who studied girl gangs note that the women's movement has had the effect of moving girl gang members out of a totally passive role into some kind of independence and has caused a change in girls' roles in gang life (Campbell, 1991).

11. Jane Quinn's critique substantively improved this section by clarifying the important distinction between an organization's general philosophical or ideological position as seen in the Boy Scouts or the YMCA and its advocacy of specific religious or moral positions.

12. Jane Quinn provided important correction and detail to this section, most particularly in noting that many national youth organizations have worked diligently to avoid an autocratic, top-down approach to programs and activities at the local level.

13. Julia Littell and Joan Wynn detail these intra and inter-city discrepancies in their 1989 study of the availability and use of community resources in a major metropolitan area.

14. See chapter 6 [of *Identity and Inner-City Youth*] for elaboration of the conflicts that youth workers in various organizations experience as demands for "body counts" collide with assessments of programmatic responses appropriate for participating youth. The tension between bureaucratic requirements and the needs of youth derailed efforts at collaboration and eroded trust among organizations in all of the communities we studied.

15. Robert Halpern (1992) develops this point in his analysis of "after-school" programs for inner-city children aged 6 to 12 and concludes that programs that seem "too much like school" create inhospitable environments for urban youth.

References

Anderson, E. (1990). *Streetwise: Race, class, and change in an urban community.* Chicago: University of Chicago Press.

Cahill, M. (1991). *Community youth programs—bridging gaps in personal, cultural, and public identity: Ethnicity, race and gender in youth organizations.* Stanford University, Stanford, CA.

Campbell, A. (1991). *The girls in the gang* (2nd ed.). Cambridge, MA: Basil Blackwell.

Gómez-Peña, G. (1988). Documented/undocumented. In R. Simonson & S. Walker (Eds.), *The graywolf annual five: Multi-cultural literacy* (pp. 127–134). Saint Paul, MN: Graywolf Press.

Halpern, R. (1992). The role of after-school programs in the lives of inner-city children: A study of the "Urban Youth Network." *Child Welfare, 7*(3), 215–230.

Ianni, F. A. J. (1989). *The search for structure.* New York: Free Press.

Jankowski, M. (1991). *Islands in the street.* Berkeley, CA: University of California Press.

Kleinfeld, J., & Shinkwin, A. (1982). *Youth organizations as a third educational environment particularly for minority group youth: Final report to the National Institute of Education* (ERIC no. ED240194). Washington, D.C.: National Institute of Education.

Kotlowitz, A. (1991). *There are no children here.* New York: Doubleday.

Lefkowitz, B. (1987). *Tough change.* New York: Doubleday.

Littell, J., & Wynn, J. (1989). The availability and use of community resources for young adolescents in an inner-city and suburban community. Chicago: The Chapin Hall Center for Children at the University of Chicago.

Nelson, C., & Tienda, M. (1989). The structuring of Hispanic ethnicity: Historical and contemporary perspectives. In R. D. Alba (Ed.), *Ethnicity and race in the U.S.A.* (pp. 49–74). New York: Routledge.

Nicholson, H. J. (1987, July). *Operation SMART: From research to program—and back* (ERIC no. ED302403). Presented at the International Conference of Girls and Technology.

Novak, M. (1980). Pluralism in humanistic perspective. *Concepts of ethnicity* (pp. 27–56). Cambridge, MA: Belknap Press of Harvard University Press.

Sollors, W. (1989). Introduction: The invention of ethnicity. In W. Sollors (Ed.), *The invention of ethnicity.* (pp. ix–xx). New York: Oxford University Press.

Turner, J. C. (1987). *Rediscovering the social group: A self-categorization theory.* New York: Basil Blackwell.

Wahl, E. (1988, April). *Girls and technology: Stories of tools and power* (ERIC no. ED302402). Presented at the annual meeting of the American Educational Research Association, New Orleans, LA.

Reading 23

BRIDGES AND POLITICS

Henry Petroski

Large engineering projects usually have a long history, which in some cases stretches decades beyond any single engineer's career. There can be innumerable competing proposals and false starts, as well as long periods of inactivity and distraction caused by the need to work on other projects or by economic or political conditions seemingly beyond anyone's control. Elements of luck and timing enter in as well, as they do in any human endeavor. The story of the origins, design, financing, and construction of just about any major bridge can serve as a model for demonstrating this long and tortuous history and the many interrelated complexities that go along with all large engineering projects.

From ancient times to the Industrial Revolution, there prevailed a long and solid tradition of building bridges of stone and timber. Timber bridges were not only common in their own right, but a timber bridge of sorts (known as centering or falsework) had to be erected as a supporting form before a stone bridge could be put in place. Thus, in the late eighteenth century, when a new bridge was needed in the Severn Valley in England, there was a natural caution against the idea of using iron, despite the fact that the Darby family had made the valley well known for its iron production. The Darbys used the locally abundant coal residue known as coke in place of scarce timber in the smelting process, and the lack of timber made iron for bridge construction even more sensible. Yet the sketches that survive of early proposals for an iron bridge across the Severn River emphasize the strong bias toward traditional materials that had to be overcome.

Petroski, Henry. "Bridges and Politics." *Invention By Design: How Engineers Get From Thought to Thing*. Cambridge: Harvard U P, 1996. 160–187.

One of the sketches shows the iron cast into stonelike voussoirs, and the other shows iron mimicking timber. The bridge as built has the familiar overall appearance of a semicircular Roman stone arch bridge, while the assembly details are reminiscent of contemporary timber bridge construction. Such extra-technological deference to traditional materials and methods of construction overcame the resistance to technological change promoted by such vested interests as stonemasons, carpenters, and ferry boat operators. In the final analysis, however, clear and effective communication, ameliorating the sense of threat and uncertainty that the new material prompted, was a crucial factor in getting Iron Bridge built.

Once the bridge was successfully erected, its real advantages could speak for themselves. Because the cast-iron sections were so large and self-supporting, the bridge was put up in such a short time that there was a minimum disruption of river traffic. The promise of iron as an effective bridge material was further emphasized when Iron Bridge was the only bridge across the Severn to survive the flood of 1795. Stone bridges, because of their relatively small opening relative to their massive abutments and silhouettes, tended to clog up and act like dams under flood conditions. Timber bridges, although more open, tended to wash away because of their lack of strength against the force of water and trapped debris. Iron Bridge, on the other hand, being both open and strong, allowed the raging flood waters to pass through its lacy structure, which was seen eventually to possess an aesthetic of its own.

With the triumph of Iron Bridge, bridge designers increasingly began to think of iron as an innovative new material with which to work. But, whereas the design of Iron Bridge, based on the long-tested arch principle, required little sophisticated analysis of the forces acting on it, the bolder designs for iron bridges that were proposed in the early nineteenth century had little precedent upon which to argue for their safety. Suspension bridges, for example, used wrought iron in tension instead of cast iron in compression, and the structural action involved had no counterpart in stone or timber construction. Engineers proposing suspension bridges had to rely in public on their drawing, writing, and speaking talents as much as they did in private on their analytical and political abilities. Whereas they may have addressed to their satisfaction any strictly technical questions at the drawingboard or through experiments, the questions of strength, safety, economics, aesthetics, and the like that were raised by citizens, investors, politicians, and other lay persons required a talent for persuasive speaking and writing.

Proposals for a variety of different bridge types, and reports of progress on their construction, were models of nineteenth-century engineering. They were made possible by steady progress throughout the century in understanding beam action and in analyzing structures, and this new understanding was often conveyed to the lay public. However, in the 1840s in Britain, suspension bridges were not considered viable options for railroad structures, despite the great demand for crossings as rail routes were expanded. This poor stature of suspension bridges was attributable in part to the bridges' lack of stiffness and susceptibility to collapse in high winds, which were known to engineers and laypersons alike. As a result many alternative bridge designs were developed in Britain, including the iron tubular span exemplified in the Britannia Bridge. The extreme weight and cost of the Britannia, however, led to the evolution of open truss girder designs, which were to be taken to extremes of lightness in the Tay Bridge, as we shall see.

Doing the Doable Thing

As a young engineer, Othmar Ammann worked for Gustav Lindenthal, whose design for a massive suspension bridge between New York and New Jersey across the Hudson River was so ambitious and expensive that in over thirty years it had not gotten sufficient backing to progress very far. After trying unsuccessfully to get Lindenthal to redesign his bridge to less monumental proportions, in the early 1920s Ammann began to work independently on a more modest proposal for a Hudson River bridge.

Without informing Lindenthal, Ammann communicated his ideas to the future governor of New Jersey, who then promoted it as part of his administration. When Lindenthal found this out through newspaper accounts, he accused the younger engineer of unethical behavior. Did Othmar Ammann act in an unethical way?

Railroad bridge building in America followed a different evolutionary route, in part because the persuasive qualities of John Roebling's personality and writing complemented his engineering talents and acumen. Roebling's Niagara Gorge Suspension Bridge, completed in 1854, provided an incontrovertible counterexample to the British hypothesis that a suspension bridge could not carry railroad traffic. He went on to conceive and propose the landmark Brooklyn Bridge, and the story of the many long years that Roebling spent trying to convince others of his plan, after he had first persuaded himself, is one of the great dramas in the history of engineering. It often serves as a paradigm for all engineering projects precisely because the vicissitudes of that great project are far from unique.

But we might just as easily take as paradigmatic the story of Othmar Ammann and the George Washington Bridge, which was prefigured for almost a century by numerous plans for crossing the Hudson River at New York City. Ammann's pragmatic flexibility enabled him to achieve what his mentor, Gustav Lindenthal, could not, in large part because he could not adapt his railroad-age design for a behemoth of a bridge to the changing needs of a society that was developing a growing love for the automobile. In the early 1920s Ammann and Lindenthal parted ways, and the younger engineer was able to persuade political and business groups on both sides of the Hudson that his light and graceful $30 million bridge between Fort Lee in New Jersey and 179th Street in Manhattan was the route to go, even though technically it represented effectively a doubling of the longest suspension bridge span then in existence. Both Lindenthal and Ammann have left a voluminous legacy of written documents arguing the case for bridges, both built and unbuilt.

San Francisco Bridges

Among the major bridges of the world whose story is not as well known as it should be is the crossing of the bay between San Francisco and Oakland, California. Officially called the San Francisco–Oakland Bay Bridge, this enormous structure of over eight miles in total length has been overshadowed almost from the beginning of its operation by its neighbor, the Golden Gate Bridge, just a few miles to the northwest. Ideas for bridges at each of these locations go back to the nineteenth century, including a curious proposal issued in the form of a proclamation in 1869 by a fellow who declared himself Norton the First, Emperor of the United States and Protector of Mexico. Joshua A. Norton is believed to have been a fortuneseeker who went to California during the Gold Rush of 1849, struck it rich, but then lost everything, including his mind. He disappeared for a while but then reappeared as the self-declared emperor whose seat of power was in Oakland, where local people humored him and honored the paper money he issued. The fact that he proclaimed that a bridge be built from Oakland to Sausalito via San Francisco suggests that the idea was current in his time. However, it was not until the early decades of the twentieth century, when major bridges were being constructed all across the country, that proposals for various bridges in the San Francisco Bay area began to receive more serious attention.

Engineers who found themselves in California on other business became familiar with the need for bridges across the bay and its outlet to the sea—the strait known as the Golden Gate. One of these engineers was Joseph Strauss, who was president of his own Chicago-based Strauss Bascule Bridge Company. A bascule bridge is one whose roadway rotates on a hinge so that the span can be lifted out of the way of ships that need to pass. In this way the bridge can be built with a low clearance across a river, and thereby not require a lot of land on either side for long and high approaches. Strauss had become successful by designing and building such movable bridges in built-up and crowded cities like Chicago, where land for bridge approaches was very expensive, if available at all. With his experience in patenting and building moveable bridges, Strauss was also able to design an amusement ride known as the Aeroscope, in which passengers were carried up in a car as large as a two-story house and revolved at the end of a 265-foot cranelike boom over the grounds of the Panama-Pacific International Exposition, which was held in San Francisco in 1915 to commemorate the opening of the Panama Canal.

In that same year, the Strauss Bascule Bridge Company was awarded a contract to replace an old swing bridge across a San Francisco creek with a new bascule bridge. The Fourth Street Bridge, as it is known, is generally considered an ugly and purely functional design, as were many such bridges, with a heavy concrete counterweight suspended overhead. In any event, business travels relating to the Aeroscope and the Fourth Street Bridge caused Strauss to cross paths with the San Francisco City Engineer, Michael O'Shaughnessy, who dreamed of having a bridge across the Golden Gate.

Within a few years, Strauss had produced an uninspired design for a Golden Gate bridge. However, no matter how unattractive it was, Strauss's cost estimate of $17 million and his projection that toll revenues would in time more than cover that entire cost made the proposal very attractive to proponents of a bridge. Furthermore, Strauss's political savvy and entrepreneurial spirit, which drove him to talk up his proposal before any local civic or political group that would listen, eventually led to the dream becoming reality. The human story of Strauss and the Golden Gate Bridge is a long and acrimonious one, in which Strauss and O'Shaughnessy eventually became adversaries and in which Strauss dismissed and denied credit to his assistant engineer for design, Charles Ellis. However, in spite of the bridge's unglamorous beginnings and the difficult interpersonal relationships that ensued during its design and construction, the Golden Gate Bridge stands today as one of the most admired bridges in the world, at least in part because of its dramatic setting and the strikingly simple and beautiful design that eventually evolved.

The San Francisco–Oakland Bay Bridge, on the other hand, has a less unified appearance and occupies a site that does not lend itself to dramatic sunsets or to views that encompass the entire bridge. In contrast to the Golden Gate Bridge, whose single dominant 4200-foot main span was at one time the world's longest, the Bay Bridge is really made up of two distinctly different kinds of spans, each of which constituted a major bridge project in its own right, plus a significant tunnel through an island that rises high out of the water in the middle of the bay, a couple of miles from either shore. Although the construction of the Bay Bridge across deep water that was heavily traveled by ships presented enormous technical challenges to its engineers, it is not as widely recognized for the achievement it is because of the social and aesthetic accidents of its construction and appearance, and because of its being overshadowed by the contemporary project of the Golden Gate Bridge.

Early Proposals for a Bay Bridge

With most large bridge projects, a variety of proposals are put forth before a final design is settled upon. Just as Strauss's early and ungainly design for the Golden Gate Bridge was fortunately modified over the course of its design time to become an object of beauty as well as a technical achievement, so the Bay Bridge evolved slowly from early proposals to its final form. Among the more serious early proposals was one put forth by the civil engineer Charles Evan Fowler. Fowler was a Seattle-based consulting engineer who, like many of his contemporaries, dreamed of building the largest bridge in the world. Just as Strauss had become acquainted with the problem of bridging the Golden Gate while doing other business in San Francisco, so Fowler became interested in the problem of a bay bridge when he was engaged in designing the steelwork for one of the city's earliest steel-frame buildings. Like many a consulting engineer, Fowler was always looking for opportunities to secure new and prominent commissions. He prepared and printed at his own expense a booklet that laid out the problem of bridging the bay and presented his design for a solution.

Fowler published his booklet, entitled *The San Francisco–Oakland Cantilever Bridge,* in 1914. At that time, tunnel schemes for crossing the bay had been estimated to cost at least $25 million, and it was necessary to explain why any bridge costing a considerable amount more was a better choice. In fact, because of technical surprises that seemed invariably to accompany tunnel projects and because of the limited traffic capacity their necessarily small diameter tubes provided, comparative studies of tunnels and bridges were a matter of some heated debate not only in San Francisco but around the world. Thus, although Fowler's bridge proposal carried a price tag of $75 million, he argued that it was in the final analysis cost-effective and proceeded to describe it in the context of known bridge projects of the time.

Among the big decisions that faced bridge engineers in the early part of the twentieth century was the basic structural form that they would employ for long spans. Such a span would be required to bridge the deep-water distance between the city of San Francisco and the large island two miles out in the bay known variously as Yerba Buena Island or Goat Island or, more recently, as Treasure Island. This last name, strictly speaking, refers only to an artificial island formed adjacent to the large rock outcrop that comprises the natural island. Indeed, Treasure Island was created as the site of the 1939 West Coast World's Fair held to commemorate the engineering achievements of both the Golden Gate Bridge and the San Francisco–Oakland Bay Bridge.

Because the water was approximately 200 feet deep, the construction of foundations and piers to serve as bridge supports for a crossing would be costly and dangerous. It was thus desirable to have as few supports in the water as possible, and this meant that the superstructure should have spans as long as possible. In 1914, when Fowler was writing, the suspension bridge with the longest span was the 1600-foot Williamsburg Bridge in New York City. Although as early as the late 1880s engineers like Lindenthal had proposed bridges with suspended spans of the order of 3000 feet, such extra-long-span designs did carry very large cost estimates. Furthermore, they were so far beyond the experience of bridge building projects up to that time that the wisdom of making such large leaps in the state of the art was seriously questioned.

Cantilever Bridges

Fowler wrote in his report that the problem of bridging the bay between San Francisco and Oakland had been "uppermost" in his mind for a quarter of a century. That would have put his first thoughts on the matter in the late 1880s, when cantilever bridges were attracting a lot of attention among engineers. A cantilever bridge is a self-supporting structure that can be built out as large individual cantilever beams from piers or towers, thereby requiring no scaffolding underneath. This is an attractive design and construction technique because it eliminates the need to erect scaffolding that might obstruct shipping during bridge construction and that would certainly add to the bridge's cost.

The idea of a self-balancing cantilever was novel in the late 1880s, however, and a very large one was being built in Scotland only because other types of bridges had fallen into disrepute after a famous bridge collapse. The need for long bridges on the east coast of Scotland had developed when the North British Railway wished to eliminate the ferrying of railroad cars across the wide estuaries known as the Firth of Forth and the Firth of Tay. The bridge across the Tay was completed first, in 1878. It was a long, sinuous structure with many piers in the relatively shallow water. The most striking feature of the bridge was the high girders that rose, in almost 250-foot spans, above the main shipping channel. One night late in 1879, these fell or were blown into the water during a violent storm. About 75 people were killed in the horrendous accident, and there was a major inquiry into why it had occurred.

A Court of Inquiry found that the bridge's engineer, Sir Thomas Bouch (he had been knighted for the project), had been negligent in his design and in his supervision of construction. The force of the wind on the light bridge had been grossly underestimated by Bouch, and one theory of the failure was that the high girders and the train crossing them were simply toppled off their supports, to which the girders had not been sufficiently anchored. Another finding was that the iron columns on which the bridge stood were made of inferior castings, full of holes that weakened the structure. As with many early structural failures that left a mass of twisted metal, the exact cause remained somewhat debatable, but Bouch's reputation was irreparably damaged. A replacement bridge was designed and built across the Tay, but the task was to be given to other engineers.

At the time of the Tay Bridge failure, Bouch had also been overseeing the construction of a more ambitious bridge across the Firth of Forth, about 50 miles to the south. His design for that crossing had been a long-span suspension bridge, because the water was deep and he wanted to put as few piers in the water as possible, in order to work within allowable depths and to keep costs down. Not surprisingly, when the Tay Bridge fell, construction on Bouch's Forth bridge was halted. After he was found responsible by the Tay inquiry, Bouch's design was abandoned altogether. The task of designing a new bridge for the Firth of Forth was eventually given to the well-known and experienced British engineer Sir John Fowler. Since a major concern of the railroad company was to win back among passengers some degree of confidence in its bridges, a suspension bridge design, which was not generally favored in Britain anyway, became even more undesirable because it had been favored by Bouch. Sir John and his young assistant engineer, Benjamin Baker, thus came up with a relatively new idea for a British bridge—a cantilever.

The errors made in the design and construction of the Tay Bridge were described in considerable detail in the report of the Court of Inquiry, and the Tay accident led to the development of the massive cantilever bridge across the Firth of Forth. This bridge was the subject of many public lectures by Baker, and of numerous written reports reproduced around the world. Because the Forth Bridge was so ambitious a design, especially, in the wake of the collapse of the Tay, which was on the same railway line, it was necessary for Baker to communicate to the public the principles of cantilever construction.

Like most ideas, the cantilever bridge was not entirely new. Such bridges had been built in the Far East for some time, and some had of late been constructed in Germany and America. Thomas Bouch himself had even constructed a lesser-known one in Newcastle. However, the cantilever that Fowler and Baker proposed for the Firth of Forth was to be enormous, spanning about twice the distance of any then in existence. Because they were doing something so daring, Baker took great pains to explain the principle of the cantilever in the numerous public lectures he gave while the bridge was under construction. To illustrate the structural ideas behind the design, Baker employed a human model that consisted of two people on chairs and supporting a third person on a seat suspended between them. The arms of the people on the chairs and the struts that they held represented the cantilevers, with the counterweights of bricks providing balance. The swing represented a suspended portion of the bridge, but it looked nothing like the kind of suspension bridge Bouch had proposed, nor did it behave in principle like it. The distance from chair to chair thus came to be referred to, incorrectly, as the span of the cantilever itself.

The Firth of Forth Bridge was immensely successful. It became famous throughout the world and had many imitators, and by the end of the nineteenth century a cantilever was the bridge of choice for many designers, builders, and purchasers of bridges. When it became desirable to bridge the St. Lawrence River at Quebec, a cantilever with spans even longer than the record 1710 feet of the Firth of Forth was designed. Construction of the south arm of the Quebec Bridge had reached a distance of about 600 feet over the river in August 1907 when the bridge suddenly collapsed, killing about 80 workmen. Though the Quebec bridge was found to be grossly underdesigned, the failure called cantilevers of all kinds into question. The Quebec Bridge was eventually redesigned as a stronger structure and was finally completed in 1917. At the end of the twentieth century its span of 1800 feet remains the record for a cantilever bridge.

Such troubles with cantilever bridges were not thought to be likely when Charles Evan Fowler first began to think about bridging San Francisco Bay, for the Firth of Forth Bridge was thought to be a model for design. Perhaps because of its association with Sir John Fowler, whose surname he shared, or perhaps because later on Charles Evan Fowler knew that the Quebec incident was a case of bad design that need not condemn the whole genre of cantilever bridges, for decades he clung to the design he had come up with in his youth for a bridge between San Francisco and Oakland. Fowler proposed a Forth-like cantilever bridge with three main spans of 2000 feet each (two 650-foot cantilever arms supporting a suspended span of 700 feet between them), thus proposing a bridge longer than any in the world. Fowler dismissed still longer cantilevers of 2300-foot span and a suspension bridge alternative because of cost and "seismic conditions" in the bay area.

His report included a diagram showing the relative proportions of his 2000-foot cantilever span and a suitably proportioned outline of the 1710-foot spans of the Firth of Forth Bridge, which itself had once been compared to more familiar structures, such as the Eiffel Tower. Fowler also pointed out that the profile of his spans was chosen "not only for economical reasons, but to provide a structure of pleasing design." Such aesthetic considerations are often very high in the consciousness of engineers designing large, monumental structures.

Although Fowler did not mention the Quebec Bridge in his report, he knew that his readers would recall its relevance. It was well known that the Quebec Bridge failed because its lower chord members, corresponding to the struts held by the seated figures in Baker's model, were simply not strong enough to resist the great compressive forces being imposed upon them. The situation was analogous to those people holding not thick objects like baseball bats but slender ones like yardsticks. Pushing down too hard on such slender sticks, as we can readily verify by a chair-seat or desk-top experiment with a plastic yardstick or ruler, causes a phenomenon known as buckling, in which the stick suddenly springs out from under the pressure. Since such a situation had effectively occurred at the Quebec Bridge construction site in 1907, Fowler wanted to assure his readers that the same thing could not happen in his design. He did this by comparing the area of the lower chords of several well-known contemporary bridges. The Queensboro cantilever bridge, with a maximum span of almost 1200 feet, had recently been completed in New York City with a lower chord area of 1120 square inches. Also in New York at the time, a massive steel arch railroad bridge was under construction across a treacherous stretch of water known as Hell Gate, and its lower chords had an area of 1437 square inches.

Fowler's bay bridge was to have chords of octagonal cross section with an area of at least 3600 square inches, and he assured his readers that areas as great as 6000 square inches could be fabricated.

The great cantilevers proposed by Fowler were necessary to cross the bay between San Francisco's Telegraph Hill and Goat Island, the part of the waterway that required the widest and highest clearance for shipping. Fowler's plan for crossing the island was to excavate to the degree needed to provide a level path for four railroad tracks and two roadways. The considerable amount of excavated earth was to be used to fill in low areas and extend the island into some shallow water to the west, thus reducing somewhat the total length of bridge there. Over the East Bay between Goat Island and Oakland, Fowler proposed using earth fill to extend the land about two miles out into the bay. The remaining two miles of bridge needed to cross the water would consist of about a mile and a half of viaduct, which would essentially be a bridge of many modest spans on piers in relatively shallow water, plus another major cantilever bridge, but with a comparatively modest maximum span.

Proposing a bridge of the kind Fowler did would be only an exercise in structural design if he could not show it to be practical and economically feasible. Matters of practicality included getting railroad trains, vehicular traffic, and people on and off the bridge where it touched land. This was relatively easy on the Oakland side, where there could be a long bridge approach over filled land, thus providing a gradual grade. On the San Francisco side, however, it was another matter to bring traffic down from a bridge that had to be 165 feet above the water to allow ships to pass beneath it. Since the land that might be used for approaches in the city was developed and expensive to purchase and clear, it was desirable to minimize the length of approaches. To reduce the approach distance of railroad tracks while maintaining a reasonable grade, Fowler proposed that the railroad terminals be elevated. He also proposed that large elevators be installed capable of raising and lowering great numbers of pedestrians at a time from a bridge terminal on Telegraph Hill.

The economic justification for the elaborate bridge scheme Fowler proposed lay in the great increase in ferry traffic across the bay that had developed over the decades. During 1873, according to Fowler, there were about 2.5 million ferry passengers. By 1877 the number had doubled to over 5 million. By 1912 the number had reached 40 million annually and was projected to increase at the rate of about 2 million per year for the next ten years, the time estimated to build a bridge. Thus, by the time the bridge could be completed, in the mid-1920s, it would have to have a potential for carrying 60 million people annually.

Of Fowler's estimate that $75 million would be needed to build a bridge and terminals and pay interest on the money borrowed for the construction, two-thirds of the total, or almost $50 million, would be required for the massive cantilevers alone. Still, in Fowler's judgment, the "probable earnings" at the time of the bridge's completion would make it a paying proposition. Not everyone agreed, however, and in his massive two-volume 1916 treatise, *Bridge Engineering,* the prestigious and influential engineer J. A. L. Waddell doubted whether wagon and automobile traffic would pay for the upkeep of the roadway, let alone pay for the interest on the additional cost of construction for it.

To establish his own credentials for such a bold proposal, Fowler had appended to his report a list of his published works and photographs of some bridges for which he had served as chief engineer of design or as a consulting engineer. These included a steel arched cantilever in Knoxville, Tennessee, the towers of the Williamsburg Bridge in New York City, and a triangular railway arch bridge at White Pass, Alaska. Though several aspects of his main bridge design were remarkably similar in type and location to many others that would be presented over the next decade or so, Fowler was not to be involved in the bridge that was eventually built. In part, his timing was unfortunate, in that a second accident during the final stages of construction of the Quebec Bridge occurred in 1916, when the suspended span fell into the water as it was being hoisted into place. This incident cast further doubts on Fowler's judgment in proposing a cantilever bridge whose main spans would be even longer than those of the Quebec Bridge and thus even more difficult to erect. Furthermore, developments in international affairs turned people's minds and society's resources to other matters.

Further Proposals

World War I caused virtually all large bridge projects to be put aside, but in the 1920s schemes for crossing San Francisco Bay were revived. Especially popular were plans capable of relieving the growing traffic problems created by automobiles and trucks while at the same time turning a profit for investors who would build and operate toll bridges. Of course, ferries still carried vehicles across the bay from San Francisco to Oakland and Berkeley to the east and to Marin County to the north, but this mode of transportation was slow and frustrating, and during rush hours or over weekends the lines of cars waiting for a ferry could seem to be interminable. The ferry operators understandably opposed the building of bridges, but bridges were becoming increasing attractive alternatives.

In cities like New York, where colder winters could cause the Hudson River to ice over, thus interrupting ferry service altogether, cries for bridges and tunnels were loud and clear. Thus, the first vehicular tunnel under the river was begun in the early 1920s, amid considerable controversy regarding the nature of its design and construction and questions as to whether poisonous exhaust fumes could be effectively vented. The tunnel came to be named after its chief engineer, Clifford Holland, who died shortly before the tubes connecting New York and New Jersey were dug through, and the tunnel was an immediate success when it was opened to traffic in 1927. It was also loaded to capacity, for by that time the number of automobiles and trucks had grown to such numbers that new tunnels and bridges across the Hudson were already being designed, including the Lincoln Tunnel and the record-setting 3500-foot suspension bridge to be known as the George Washington Bridge, which would be completed in 1931. The successful financing of the Hudson River crossings by the Port of New York Authority, as well as that of other contemporary projects, by means of bonds that would be entirely repaid by the tolls charged to users of a tunnel or bridge, eventually helped gain final approval for projects like those in San Francisco.

Unlike Charles Evan Fowler's report, which proposed an expensive bridge but did not make a sufficiently convincing argument that it would pay for itself, Michael O'Shaughnessy and Joseph Strauss's 1921 proposal for a Golden Gate Bridge was a model of salesmanship. Not only was it better written than Fowler's bay bridge proposal, but it spelled out concisely and explicitly the costs and benefits in terms readily understood by anyone. Though O'Shaughnessy could elicit few formal proposals other than Strauss's for a crossing of the Golden Gate into the relatively unpopulated northern counties, proposals for crossing the bay to the east, where most commuters to the city lived, were numerous. In 1921, for example, thirteen applications were on record seeking franchises from the city of San Francisco to build a bridge to Oakland or other East Bay communities.

However, since San Francisco Bay was such a strategic waterway, the War Department, whose approval would eventually have to be won, held hearings on the matter of a bridge and placed strict limitations on what kind of structure could be built. Among these restrictions were that no bridge of any kind would be approved north of a location known as Hunter's Point, which was south of San Francisco; that no low bridge would be approved north of San Mateo, which was ten miles further south still; and that a 3000-foot-wide open channel had to be left on the San Francisco side of the bay.

The constraints imposed by the War Department, as well as the fact that the cost of a bridge across San Francisco Bay was expected to exceed that of any bridge built to that date in America, kept an easy decision from being made. By 1926, in addition to the cantilever design submitted by Fowler, seventeen proposals were before the San Francisco Board of Supervisors, who were being petitioned for a franchise to build a bridge with private funds. The designs ranged from combination tunnel and bridge schemes to major suspension bridges, and many of the proposals had associated with them the names of some of the most famous engineers of the time. These included J. Vipond Davies, who had been responsible for tunnels under the Hudson River; Ralph Modjeski, who was chief engineer for the suspension bridge then being completed across the Delaware River at Philadelphia, as well as many other bridges; George Washington Goethals, who had become famous as the engineer who finally completed the Panama Canal and who was advocating a tunnel scheme in New York; J. A. L. Waddell, the author of *Bridge Engineering,* who had built, among many others, a famous lift bridge in Chicago; and Gustav Lindenthal, who for almost 40 years had promoted a gigantic suspension bridge to carry rail and road traffic across the Hudson River and who had designed important bridges in Pittsburgh and New York City. Even Joseph Strauss, who at the time was promoting his Golden Gate project, had designed a Sunshine Transbay Boulevard Bridge that was to consist of cantilever spans and a bascule crossing between Hunter's Point and Alemeda. Furthermore, the longer a bay bridge remained unbuilt, the more designs were offered, and in 1928 the number of proposals put forth had reached 38.

Selecting a Site

While there was some question as to the legality of San Francisco unilaterally selecting a site and having plans prepared for a toll bridge to be built by a private company, the city's Board of Supervisors proceeded to ask the presidents of four local universities to provide a list of qualified and disinterested bridge engineers to serve in an advisory capacity. Three engineers were to be selected from the list to make "a study and investigation of the proper location of termini, foundations, clearance above the waters of the bay, space between piers, the loads which said bridge should carry, the facilities for traffic at both termini of said bridge, and the probable conditions of traffic incident to said bridge, and the financial problems involved." After so many years of indecision on the part of the city, the presidents of Berkeley, Stanford, the University of Santa Clara, and St. Mary's College were asked to produce a list of names within ten days. Since so many of the most famous bridge engineers in the country were already involved with the proposals that had been put forth, the list submitted contained names that might not have been immediately recognized. However, a distinguished board was appointed, made up of Robert Ridgeway from New York, Arthur N. Talbot from the University of Illinois, and John D. Galloway from San Francisco.

The board of engineers was given only 30 days to deliberate, and they came to the following conclusions in a report filed on May 5, 1927:

1. The most suitable location is from Rincon Hill to Alameda Mole [that is, breakwater], with a second choice from Potrero Hill to Alameda Mole, and a third from Telegraph Hill to Yerba Buena Island, thence to the Key Route Mole.
2. The longer spans should be two 1,250-ft. cantilevers.
3. Maximum grades should be 6 per cent for vehicles and 4 per cent for inter-urban [railway cars].
4. A double-deck bridge with a 42-ft. roadway on the upper deck and three inter-urban tracks on the lower deck will provide the desired capacity.

The board of engineers recognized a reliable cost estimate could not be made before information was available about the nature of potential foundation conditions beneath the bay. For all of the applications for franchises and preliminary design proposals that had been submitted, there had been remarkably little exploration of where exactly, and how deep, the bridge piers would be located. This should not be surprising, for the proposals were prepared on speculation, and few engineers or financial backers would have wanted to risk the time and money to explore the bed of the bay in any degree of detail before they had some kind of commitment that their efforts would have a reasonable chance of being rewarded. Thus, the board of engineers recommended that the city desiring the bridge explore the preferred site to determine exactly what kind of foundations could be supported and prepare a more detailed design on which to base cost estimates.

In the meantime, the War Department continued to be an obstacle. City officials attempted to deal with it by going to Washington to try to persuade army and navy authorities to relax their restrictions, and when this was not effective, the city got its elected representatives in Washington to introduce legislation to circumvent the War Department. This was not successful either, and further political efforts led to the idea of proposing the bridge as a publicly owned facility, which would enable it to be financed by revenue bonds in a manner not unlike the way the interstate Port of New York Authority was financing the George Washington Bridge. The idea of public ownership led to the notion of a governmental commission to oversee the project, and in 1929 a representative of Governor C. C. Young enlisted the support of President Herbert Hoover, a graduate of Stanford and a successful mining engineer before he became involved in public service and politics. He soon announced the appointment of a San Francisco Bay Bridge Commission, which came to be known as the Hoover-Young Commission. Legislation also created the California Toll Bridge Authority and designated the Department of Public Works as its agent to design, construct, and operate toll bridges. It further provided for their financing through revenue bonds and appropriated money for preliminary investigations.

The commission put California's state highway engineer, Charles H. Purcell, in charge of the project. Purcell, who was born in 1883 and who attended Stanford and the University of Nebraska, began his engineering career as a bridge designer for the Oregon Highway Department and worked for the U.S. Bureau of Public Roads before coming to California. State Bridge Engineer Charles E. Andrew was given immediate charge of the study. A systematic investigation of possible bridge locations was begun, and borings were made to determine foundation conditions. Detailed traffic studies were also initiated, including compilations of ferry records, in order to have accurate and up-to-date data on which to base projected bridge use and toll revenues. These studies led to the clear conclusion that the best route for the bridge was from San Francisco's Rincon Hill to Goat Island, along the route of an underwater rock ridge that provided a base for the least deep foundations, and thence on to Oakland, even though that community had been somewhat reluctant to have a bridge interjected into its harbor.

The Hoover-Young Commission received a report of the study, and by the middle of 1930 was able to conclude that bay bottom conditions made it clear that the route over Goat Island was the only technically and economically feasible one and that there should be no more than four main spans over the West Bay and that the two center spans should be high enough to provide a clearance of 214 feet over mean high water. This part of the bridge was as technically ambitious a construction project as any then under way or contemplated, and yet the final design was to be "such that it will conform with the scenic beauty of San Francisco Bay." The responsibility for designing and constructing such a bridge lay with the California Toll Bridge Authority.

The Final Design

With $650,000 appropriated in 1931, serious design work could begin, which meant that an engineering organization had to be established to look at the various options and details and come up with final plans so that War Department approval could be obtained and construction could begin. Such work necessarily involves a great number of engineers, with different ones focusing on different aspects of the project, which in this case included the West and East Bay crossings, the Goat Island crossing, and approaches in San Francisco and Oakland. Purcell was made chief engineer of the entire project, Andrew was appointed bridge engineer and as such headed the design team, and Glenn B. Woodruff was made engineer of design. As with all good engineering work, an independent group of engineers was established to advise on and check all engineering assumptions and calculations. This board of consulting engineers included Ralph Modjeski, whose Delaware River Bridge had been the longest when completed in 1926; the firm of Moran & Proctor, whose principals Daniel Moran and Carlton S. Proctor had been responsible for the foundations and piers of some of the country's most significant bridges; Leon Moisseiff, who would also work on the Golden Gate and Tacoma Narrows bridges; Charles Derleth, Jr., who was dean of engineering at the University of California in Berkeley; and Henry J. Brunnier, an established San Francisco consulting engineer who had been involved with many important West Coast structures. Consulting architects were also appointed to give advice on the physical appearance of the bridge and its approaches.

The final design of a great bridge is never a simple matter, for there are many different factors to be considered and many conflicting objectives to be met. The result is many possible designs, and it is engineering experience and judgment that play a key role in narrowing down the possibilities. The first design that was focused upon for the purposes of gaining War Department approval was a four-span symmetrical cantilever arrangement, in spite of the form's history. Because the 1700-foot spans were comparable to those of the well-considered Firth of Forth Bridge, the feasibility of the design and the clearances for shipping that it could provide were virtually unquestionable, and thus the critical approval was finally obtained. Any subsequent design changes that would be found desirable for technical or economic reasons would then be less likely to have approval withheld.

In fact, even before approval had been obtained for the cantilever design, it became clear to the engineers that a suspension bridge would be more economical, safer to erect, and more aesthetically pleasing. But exactly which suspension bridge design to adopt was still a matter of some thought and judgment, and required further calculations and tests.

It is always tempting for engineers to build a bridge with as long a span as possible, not only to have a sense of grandeur but also to reduce the number of obstacles in the water. Thus, a design with a single suspended span of 4100 feet between two towers would have been in keeping with the growth of suspension bridges while at the same time providing a structure of monumental proportions. In the end it was rejected, however, since it was found to be more expensive and less suited to the location than multiple span bridges. However, since the design of a multiple-span suspension bridge was indeed a departure from experience, special model tests were conducted by engineering professors R. E. Davis at the University of California and G. E. Beggs at Princeton University, in order to guide and check theoretical calculations about the dynamic behavior of such structures. In the end, these tests helped settle on a design comprising two complete suspension bridges in tandem, sharing a common central anchorage. The main spans of 2310 feet still made each of these individual bridges larger than all but the George Washington Bridge recently completed between New York and New Jersey and the Golden Gate Bridge under construction across the bay, but the spans were generally considered otherwise to be relatively conventional in design.

The crossing of Goat Island, on which there were military facilities, was to be through a tunnel of larger bore than any then in existence, making the overall project still more remarkable. As for the East Bay crossing, the wishes of Oakland had to be accommodated so that future development of its port facilities were not jeopardized by a low bridge. The original design calling for a main section comprising a 700-foot cantilever with a 161-foot clearance was modified to provide a 1400-foot cantilever section with a vertical clearance of 185 feet. Thus the project was to include a major cantilever span that would be the third largest in the world, ranking only behind the Firth of Forth and Quebec bridges.

The total cost of $75 million for the entire San Francisco–Oakland Bay Bridge was just what Fowler had estimated for his design, and the overall project was to include "the greatest bridge yet erected by the human race," according to ex-President Hoover, who spoke at ceremonies marking the beginning of construction in mid-1933. Chief engineer Purcell said he hoped to see traffic using the bridge by the beginning of 1937. In fact, construction would proceed ahead of schedule, and the bridge would be opened in 1936, well before the Golden Gate Bridge. In 1955, when it was almost 20 years old, the San Francisco–Oakland Bay Bridge was named by the American Society of Civil Engineers as one of the seven great modern civil engineering wonders of the United States.

Bridges and Traffic

The construction of the Bay Bridge was well documented in photographs, and though the bridge is their clear focus, it is difficult to overlook the large number of ferries that are in the background of so many of the shots of construction workers and the partially completed structure. By the 1930s commuter traffic across the bay had grown to such a volume that criss-crossing ferry boats making as many as 500 trips per day presented more of a hazard to navigation than did a limited number of bridge piers in the water. With the completion of the Bay Bridge, the Golden Gate, and other area bridges, ferry service naturally declined, and automobile traffic in and out of San Francisco became a much more convenient experience—until traffic volume grew to such a magnitude that the bridges themselves became choked with rush hour traffic. Building additional bridges today is considered financially prohibitive, not to mention environmentally threatening, and so ferry service has been reintroduced to relieve bridge traffic.

The Golden Gate Bridge, Highway and Transportation District, which developed as an independent entity as a direct result of engineer Strauss's political savvy and promotional skill, has developed alternative and innovative ways to alleviate congestion. For example, in 1968 the Golden Gate became the first bridge to collect tolls in one direction only. Under the assumption that the great bulk of users cross a bridge both ways, doubling the toll and collecting it only one way makes incontrovertible sense, and many toll bridges, including the Bay Bridge, have since adopted this practice. In 1970 the Golden Gate Bridge, Highway and Transportation District introduced a new ferry service between San Francisco and Sausalito, to further reduce traffic and congestion on the bridge.

When the required traffic capacity of the Bay Bridge was considered prior to design, it became clear that a single-deck bridge would have had to be about 100 feet wide, requiring a very strong and stiff floor structure. A double-deck roadway, approximately one third less wide, was found to result in considerable savings, and so it was adopted.

Other factors also affected the final design of the double-deck roadway. For example, as originally conceived, two interurban railway tracks would have been carried over or under the single vehicular roadway, but the double-deck concept made it possible to carry both sets of rapid transit rails more efficiently on the same level as truck traffic. Furthermore, the tracks were laid out side by side on the bridge's lower deck, even though this created the complication of a somewhat asymmetrical load on the structure. This kind of engineering decision was made to take into account more than just structural response to the loads, however. Locating the two rail lines symmetrically on opposite sides of the bridge would have meant that the vehicle traffic between them would have been interrupted and made more dangerous whenever trains had to cross over from one rail line to the other, which would be necessitated by repairs, accidents, and other circumstances. Commuter trains operated on the lower deck of the bridge until the late 1950s, when they were removed because ridership had dropped. The upper and lower roadways were then each dedicated to one-way traffic.

Bridges and Earthquakes

In the San Francisco Bay area a design consideration more critical than the arrangement of traffic lanes and commuter railroad tracks is the possibility of an earthquake moving the ground beneath the foundations of any structure, including a great bridge. If its traffic-carrying capacity is to be maintained under such abnormal circumstances, the bridge must be designed to withstand a certain amount of shaking. But how much extra strength a structure must have to withstand an earthquake is a matter of engineering judgment that must be tempered with economic reality. This means that reasonable assumptions about the size and characteristics of the kind of earthquake that is likely to strike during the lifetime of the bridge must be made. In the case of the Bay Bridge, Chief Engineer Purcell, in an article in *Civil Engineering* in 1934 describing the project when it was under way, revealed how earthquake resistance was built into the design:

> All elements of the bridge are designed for an acceleration of the supporting material of 10 per cent that of gravity. It was readily recognized that the usual criteria for earthquake design would not be satisfactory in dealing with this structure. In view of this, an exhaustive study was made and design methods were evolved which took into consideration the various peculiarities of the problem.
>
> In the case of the channel piers, the horizontal force created by the acceleration of the mass will be augmented by forces due to the movement of the pier through the water and the soft mud immediately below. In fact it is conceivable that the soft mud may have an acceleration of its own in a direction opposite to

that of the pier. These forces were incorporated in the analysis. In dealing with the superstructure, and particularly the suspension spans, the elastic and mechanical flexibility of the elements were fully considered. For earthquake design a 40 per cent increase in basic unit stress was permitted.

The same differences in character between the San Francisco–Goat Island crossing and the Goat Island–Oakland crossing that had necessitated two completely different kinds of structural design also turned out to complicate the attempt to design the Bay Bridge to withstand earthquakes. The West Bay section of the bridge would rest on bedrock, while the East Bay section would sit on mud that is vulnerable to seismic movement. It is this mud to which Purcell was referring in his description of the design problem.

In engineering-science courses like strength of materials and dynamics, engineering students learn to calculate the effects of loads and motion on structural elements. Working problems and exercises in these areas prepares engineers for the kinds of calculations alluded to by Purcell. However, unlike in textbook problems, where all the loads and conditions are clearly specified to give the student a well-defined example for analysis, in real design problems like those that faced the engineers of the Bay Bridge, the clearly essential and critical assumptions regarding what the basic accelerations moving the bridge will be and what additional strength it should have to resist them must be made as part of the calculations and design itself.

Because knowledge of the nature of earthquakes is largely empirical and historical, it becomes a matter of judgment as to what conditions will be designed for. As the earthquake of 1989 subsequently demonstrated, the design of the Bay Bridge was in fact not without its limitations, as a section of the upper roadway fell onto the lower, causing death and injury to motorists on the span at the time and closing the bridge to all traffic. The resulting inconvenience to commuters in the 260,000 vehicles that used the bridge each day demonstrated very forcefully not only the key role that the bridge played in bay area traffic patterns but also the vulnerability of all structures to key design decisions made decades earlier. Because the bridge was so important a traffic link across the bay, the repairs were completed with great speed and deliberation. The California Department of Transportation (known as Caltrans), which is responsible for all of California's toll bridges except the Golden Gate Bridge, reopened the Bay Bridge only 30 days after the earthquake. Subsequent analyses of the bridge suggested that the East Bay portion might have to be replaced entirely, and the total cost of all work needed may be as high as $1.3 billion.

By understanding the long history of a project like the San Francisco–Oakland Bay Bridge, not only do we better understand why its behavior in an earthquake is what it is but also we realize that the engineering and other decisions that went into its design and construction are really only fully meaningful in the context of engineering projects that preceded and were contemporary with it.

Engineering cannot take place in a social or technical vacuum, and thus the forces that shape any given engineering project are the same forces that shape the other news and world events that are taking place simultaneously. While engineers should never be ignorant of or ignore the technical aspects of engineering that are fundamental to a project and that give it its unique character, these technical aspects make up only part of any engineering problem, which is an invariably complex human endeavor. Every engineering effort is shaped by, and in turn shapes, the culture, politics, and times in which it is embedded.

Reading 24

PLAYING GOD IN THE GARDEN

Michael Pollan

Planting

Today I planted something new in my vegetable garden—something very new, as a matter of fact. It's a potato called the New Leaf Superior, which has been genetically engineered—by Monsanto, the chemical giant recently turned "life sciences" giant—to produce its own insecticide. This it can do in every cell of every leaf, stem, flower, root and (here's the creepy part) spud. The scourge of potatoes has always been the Colorado potato beetle, a handsome and voracious insect that can pick a plant clean of its leaves virtually overnight. Any Colorado potato beetle that takes so much as a nibble of my New Leafs will supposedly keel over and die, its digestive tract pulped, in effect, by the bacterial toxin manufactured in the leaves of these otherwise ordinary Superiors. (Superiors are the thin-skinned white spuds sold fresh in the supermarket.) You're probably wondering if I plan to eat these potatoes, or serve them to my family. That's still up in the air; it's only the first week of May, and harvest is a few months off.

Certainly my New Leafs are aptly named. They're part of a new class of crop plants that is rapidly changing the American food chain. This year, the fourth year that genetically altered seed has been on the market, some 45 million acres of American farmland have been planted with biotech crops, most of it corn, soybeans, cotton and potatoes that have been engineered to either produce their own pesticides or withstand herbicides. Though Americans have already

Pollan, Michael. "Playing God in the Garden," *The New York Times Magazine*. October 25, 1998, 6ff.

begun to eat genetically engineered potatoes, corn and soybeans, industry research confirms what my own informal surveys suggest: hardly any of us knows it. The reason is not hard to find. The biotech industry, with the concurrence of the Food and Drug Administration, has decided we don't need to know it, so biotech foods carry no identifying labels. In a dazzling feat of positioning, the industry has succeeded in depicting these plants simultaneously as the linchpins of a biological revolution—part of a "new agricultural paradigm" that will make farming more sustainable, feed the world and improve health and nutrition—and, oddly enough, as the same old stuff, at least so far as those of us at the eating end of the food chain should be concerned.

This convenient version of reality has been roundly rejected by both consumers and farmers across the Atlantic. Last summer, biotech food emerged as the most explosive environmental issue in Europe. Protesters have destroyed dozens of field trials of the very same "frankenplants" (as they are sometimes called) that we Americans are already serving for dinner, and throughout Europe the public has demanded that biotech food be labeled in the market.

By growing my own transgenic crop—and talking with scientists and farmers involved with biotech—I hoped to discover which of us was crazy. Are the Europeans overreacting, or is it possible that we've been underreacting to genetically engineered food?

After digging two shallow trenches in my garden and lining them with compost, I untied the purple mesh bag of seed potatoes that Monsanto had sent and opened up the Grower Guide tied around its neck. (Potatoes, you may recall from kindergarten experiments, are grown not from seed but from the eyes of other potatoes.) The guide put me in mind not so much of planting potatoes as booting up a new software release. By "opening and using this product," the card stated, I was now "licensed" to grow these potatoes, but only for a single generation; the crop I would water and tend and harvest was mine, yet also not mine. That is, the potatoes I will harvest come August are mine to eat or sell, but their genes remain the intellectual property of Monsanto, protected under numerous United States patents, including Nos. 5,196,525, 5,164,316, 5,322,938 and 5,352,605. Were I to save even one of them to plant next year—something I've routinely done with potatoes in the past—I would be breaking Federal law. The small print in the Grower Guide also brought the news that my potato plants were themselves a pesticide, registered with the Environmental Protection Agency.

If proof were needed that the intricate industrial food chain that begins with seeds and ends on our dinner plates is in the throes of profound change, the small print that accompanied my New Leaf will do. That food chain has been unrivaled for its productivity—on average, a single American farmer today grows enough food each year to feed 100 people. But this accomplishment has come at a price. The modern industrial farmer cannot achieve such yields without enormous amounts of chemical fertilizer, pesticide, machinery and fuel, a set of capital-intensive inputs, as they're called, that saddle the farmer with debt, threaten his health, erode his soil and destroy its fertility, pollute the ground water and compromise the safety of the food we eat.

We've heard all this before, of course, but usually from environmentalists and organic farmers; what is new is to hear the same critique from conventional farmers, government officials and even many agribusiness corporations, all of whom now acknowledge that our food chain stands in need of reform. Sounding more like Wendell Berry than the agribusiness giant it is, Monsanto declared in its most recent annual report that "current agricultural technology is not sustainable."

What is supposed to rescue the American food chain is biotechnology—the replacement of expensive and toxic chemical inputs with expensive but apparently benign genetic information: crops that, like my New Leafs, can protect themselves from insects and disease without being sprayed with pesticides. With the advent of biotechnology, agriculture is entering the information age, and more than any other company, Monsanto is positioning itself to become its Microsoft, supplying the proprietary "operating systems"—the metaphor is theirs—to run this new generation of plants.

There is, of course, a second food chain in America: organic agriculture. And while it is still only a fraction of the size of the conventional food chain, it has been growing in leaps and bounds—in large part because of concerns over the safety of conventional agriculture. Organic farmers have been among biotechnology's fiercest critics, regarding crops like my New Leafs as inimical to their principles and, potentially, a threat to their survival. That's because Bt, the bacterial toxin produced in my New Leafs (and in many other biotech plants) happens to be the same insecticide organic growers have relied on for decades. Instead of being flattered by the imitation, however, organic farmers are up in arms: the widespread use of Bt in biotech crops is likely to lead to insect resistance, thus robbing organic growers of one of their most critical tools; that is, Monsanto's version of sustainable agriculture may threaten precisely those farmers who pioneered sustainable farming.

Sprouting

After several days of drenching rain, the sun appeared on May 15, and so did my New Leafs. A dozen deep-green shoots pushed up out of the soil and commenced to grow—faster and more robustly than any of the other potatoes in my garden. Apart from their vigor, though, my New Leafs looked perfectly normal. And yet as I watched them multiply their lustrous dark-green leaves those first few days, eagerly awaiting the arrival of the first doomed beetle, I couldn't help thinking of them as existentially different from the rest of my plants.

All domesticated plants are in some sense artificial—living archives of both cultural and natural information that we in some sense "design." A given type of potato reflects the values we've bred into it—one that has been selected to yield long, handsome french fries or unblemished round potato chips is the expression of a national food chain that likes its potatoes highly processed. At the same time, some of the more delicate European fingerlings I'm growing alongside my New Leafs imply an economy of small market growers and a taste for eating potatoes fresh. Yet all these qualities already existed in the potato, somewhere within the range of genetic possibilities presented by *Solanum tuberosum*. Since distant species in nature cannot be crossed, the breeder's art has always run up against a natural limit of what a potato is willing, or able, to do. Nature, in effect, has exercised a kind of veto on what culture can do with a potato.

My New Leafs are different. Although Monsanto likes to depict biotechnology as just another in an ancient line of human modifications of nature going back to fermentation, in fact genetic engineering overthrows the old rules governing the relationship of nature and culture in a plant. For the first time, breeders can bring qualities from anywhere in nature into the genome of a plant—from flounders (frost tolerance), from viruses (disease resistance) and, in the case of my potatoes, from *Bacillus thuringiensis,* the soil bacterium that produces the organic insecticide known as Bt. The introduction into a plant of genes transported not only across species but whole phyla means that the wall of that plant's essential identity—its irreducible wildness, you might say—has been breached.

But what is perhaps most astonishing about the New Leafs coming up in my garden is the human intelligence that the inclusion of the Bt gene represents. In the past, that intelligence resided outside the plant, in the mind of the organic farmers who deployed Bt (in the form of a spray) to manipulate the ecological relationship of certain insects and a certain bacterium as a way to foil those insects. The irony about the New Leafs is that the cultural information they encode happens to be knowledge that resides in the heads of the very sort of people—that is, organic growers—who most distrust high technology.

One way to look at biotechnology is that it allows a larger portion of human intelligence to be incorporated into the plant itself. In this sense, my New Leafs are just plain smarter than the rest of my potatoes. The others will depend on my knowledge and experience when the Colorado potato beetles strike; the New Leafs, knowing what I know about bugs and Bt, will take care of themselves. So while my biotech plants might seem like alien beings, that's not quite right. They're more like us than like other plants because there's more of us in them.

Growing

To find out how my potatoes got that way, I traveled to suburban St. Louis in early June. My New Leafs are clones of clones of plants that were first engineered seven years ago in Monsanto's $150 million research facility, a long, low-slung brick building on the banks of the Missouri that would look like any other corporate complex were it not for the 26 greenhouses that crown its roof like shimmering crenellations of glass.

Dave Stark, a molecular biologist and co-director of Naturemark, Monsanto's potato subsidiary, escorted me through the clean rooms where potatoes are genetically engineered. Technicians sat at lab benches before petri dishes in which fingernail-size sections of potato stem had been placed in a nutrient mixture. To this the technicians added a solution of agrobacterium, a disease bacterium whose modus operandi is to break into a plant cell's nucleus and insert some of its own DNA. Essentially, scientists smuggle the Bt gene into the agrobacterium's payload, and then the bacterium splices it into the potato's DNA. The technicians also add a "marker" gene, a kind of universal product code that allows Monsanto to identify its plants after they leave the lab.

A few days later, once the slips of potato stem have put down roots, they're moved to the potato greenhouse up on the roof. Here, Glenda DeBrecht, a horticulturist, invited me to don latex gloves and help her transplant pinky-size plantlets from their petri dish to small pots. The whole operation is performed thousands of times, largely because there is so much uncertainty about the outcome. There's no way of telling where in the genome the new DNA will land, and if it winds up in the wrong place, the new gene won't be expressed (or it will be poorly expressed) or the plant may be a freak. I was struck by how the technology could at once be astoundingly sophisticated and yet also a shot in the genetic dark.

"There's still a lot we don't understand about gene expression," Stark acknowledged. A great many factors influence whether, or to what extent, a new gene will do what it's supposed to, including the environment. In one early German experiment, scientists succeeded in splicing the gene for redness into petunias. All went as planned until the weather turned hot and an entire field of red petunias suddenly and inexplicably lost their pigment. The process didn't seem nearly as simple as Monsanto's cherished software metaphor would suggest.

When I got home from St. Louis, I phoned Richard Lewontin, the Harvard geneticist, to ask him what he thought of the software metaphor. "From an intellectual-property standpoint, it's exactly right," he said. "But it's a bad one in terms of biology. It implies you feed a program into a machine and get predictable results. But the genome is very noisy. If my computer made as many mistakes as an organism does"—in interpreting its DNA, he meant—"I'd throw it out."

I asked him for a better metaphor. "An ecosystem," he offered. "You can always intervene and change something in it, but there's no way of knowing what all the downstream effects will be or how it might affect the environment. We have such a miserably poor understanding of how the organism develops from its DNA that I would be surprised if we don't get one rude shock after another."

Flowering

My own crop was thriving when I got home from St. Louis; the New Leafs were as big as bushes, crowned with slender flower stalks. Potato flowers are actually quite pretty, at least by vegetable standards—five-petaled pink stars with yellow centers that give off a faint rose perfume. One sultry afternoon I watched the bumblebees making their lazy rounds of my potato blossoms, thoughtlessly powdering their thighs with yellow pollen grains before lumbering off to appointments with other blossoms, others species.

Uncertainty is the theme that unifies much of the criticism leveled against biotech agriculture by scientists and environmentalists. By planting millions of acres of genetically altered plants, we have introduced something novel into the environment and the food chain, the consequences of which are not—and at this point, cannot be—completely understood. One of the uncertainties has to do with those grains of pollen bumblebees are carting off from my potatoes. That pollen contains Bt genes that may wind up in some other, related plant, possibly conferring a new evolutionary advantage on that species. "Gene flow," the scientific term for this phenomenon, occurs only between closely related species, and since the potato evolved in South America, the chances are slim that my Bt potato genes will escape into the wilds of Connecticut. (It's interesting to note that while biotechnology depends for its power on the ability to move genes freely among species and even phyla, its environmental safety depends on the very opposite phenomenon: on the integrity of species in nature and their rejection of foreign genetic material.)

Yet what happens if and when Peruvian farmers plant Bt potatoes? Or when I plant a biotech crop that does have local relatives? A study reported in *Nature* last month found that plant traits introduced by genetic engineering were more likely to escape into the wild than the same traits introduced conventionally.

Andrew Kimbrell, director of the Center for Technology Assessment in Washington, told me he believes such escapes are inevitable. "Biological pollution will be the environmental nightmare of the 21st century," he said when I reached him by phone. "This is not like chemical pollution—an oil spill—that eventually disperses. Biological pollution is an entirely different model, more like a disease. Is Monsanto going to be held legally responsible when one of its transgenes creates a superweed or resistant insect?"

Kimbrell maintains that because our pollution laws were written before the advent of biotechnology, the new industry is being regulated under an ill-fitting regime designed for the chemical age. Congress has so far passed no environmental law dealing specifically with biotech. Monsanto, for its part, claims that it has thoroughly examined all the potential environmental and health risks of its biotech plants, and points out that three regulatory agencies—the U.S.D.A., the E.P.A. and the F.D.A.—have signed off on its products. Speaking of the

New Leaf, Dave Stark told me, "This is the most intensively studied potato in history."

Significant uncertainties remain, however. Take the case of insect resistance to Bt, a potential form of "biological pollution" that could end the effectiveness of one of the safest insecticides we have—and cripple the organic farmers who depend on it. The theory, which is now accepted by most entomologists, is that Bt crops will add so much of the toxin to the environment that insects will develop resistance to it. Until now, resistance hasn't been a worry because the Bt sprays break down quickly in sunlight and organic farmers use them only sparingly. Resistance is essentially a form of co-evolution that seems to occur only when a given pest population is threatened with extinction; under that pressure, natural selection favors whatever chance mutations will allow the species to change and survive.

Working with the E.P.A., Monsanto has developed a "resistance-management plan" to postpone that eventuality. Under the plan, farmers who plant Bt crops must leave a certain portion of their land in non-Bt crops to create "refuges" for the targeted insects. The goal is to prevent the first Bt-resistant Colorado potato beetle from mating with a second resistant bug, unleashing a new race of super-beetles. The theory is that when a Bt-resistant bug does show up, it can be induced to mate with a susceptible bug from the refuge, thus diluting the new gene for resistance.

But a lot has to go right for Mr. Wrong to meet Miss Right. No one is sure how big the refuges need to be, where they should be situated or whether the farmers will cooperate (creating havens for a detested pest is counter-intuitive, after all), not to mention the bugs. In the case of potatoes, the E.P.A. has made the plan voluntary and lets the companies themselves implement it; there are no E.P.A. enforcement mechanisms. Which is why most of the organic farmers I spoke to dismissed the regulatory scheme as window dressing.

Monsanto executives offer two basic responses to criticism of their Bt crops. The first is that their voluntary resistance-management plans will work, though the company's definition of success will come as small consolation to an organic farmer: Monsanto scientists told me that if all goes well, resistance can be postponed for 30 years. (Some scientists believe it will come in three to five years.) The second response is more troubling. In St. Louis, I met with Jerry Hjelle, Monsanto's vice president for regulatory affairs. Hjelle told me that resistance should not unduly concern us since "there are a thousand other Bts out there"— other insecticidal proteins. "We can handle this problem with new products," he said. "The critics don't know what we have in the pipeline."

And then Hjelle uttered two words that I thought had been expunged from the corporate vocabulary a long time ago: "Trust us."

"Trust" is a key to the success of biotechnology in the marketplace, and while I was in St. Louis, I asked Hjelle and several of his colleagues why they thought the Europeans were resisting biotech food. Austria, Luxembourg and Norway, risking trade war with the United States, have refused to accept imports of genetically altered crops. Activists in England have been staging sit-ins and "decontaminations" in biotech test fields. A group of French farmers broke into a warehouse and ruined a shipment of biotech corn seed by urinating on it. The Prince of Wales, who is an ardent organic gardener, waded into the biotech debate last June, vowing in a column in *The Daily Telegraph* that he would never eat, or serve to his guests, the fruits of a technology that "takes mankind into realms that belong to God and to God alone."

Monsanto executives are quick to point out that mad cow disease has made Europeans extremely sensitive about the safety of their food chain and has undermined confidence in their regulators. "They don't have a trusted agency like the F.D.A. looking after the safety of their food supply," said Phil Angell, Monsanto's director of corporate communications. Over the summer, Angell was dispatched repeatedly to Europe to put out the P.R. fires; some at Monsanto worry these could spread to the United States.

I checked with the F.D.A. to find out exactly what had been done to insure the safety of this potato. I was mystified by the fact that the Bt toxin was not being treated as a "food additive" subject to labeling, even though the new protein is expressed in the potato itself. The label on a bag of biotech potatoes in the supermarket will tell a consumer all about the nutrients they contain, even the trace amounts of copper. Yet it is silent not only about the fact that those potatoes are the product of genetic engineering but also about their containing an insecticide.

At the F.D.A., I was referred to James Maryanski, who oversees biotech food at the agency. I began by asking him why the F.D.A. didn't consider Bt a food additive. Under F.D.A. law, any novel substance added to a food must— unless it is "generally regarded as safe" ("GRAS," in F.D.A. parlance)—be thoroughly tested and if it changes the product in any way, must be labeled.

"That's easy," Maryanski said. "Bt is a pesticide, so it's exempt" from F.D.A. regulation. That is, even though a Bt potato is plainly a food, for the purposes of Federal regulation it is not a food but a pesticide and therefore falls under the jurisdiction of the E.P.A.

Yet even in the case of those biotech crops over which the F.D.A. does have jurisdiction, I learned that F.D.A. regulation of biotech food has been largely voluntary since 1992, when Vice President Dan Quayle issued regulatory guidelines for the industry as part of the Bush Administration's campaign for "regulatory relief." Under the guidelines, new proteins engineered into foods are regarded as additives (unless they're pesticides), but as Maryanski explained, "the determination whether a new protein is GRAS can be made by the company." Companies with a new biotech food decide for themselves whether they need to consult with the F.D.A. by following a series of "decision trees" that pose yes or no questions like this one: "Does . . . the introduced protein raise any safety concern?"

Since my Bt potatoes were being regulated as a pesticide by the E.P.A. rather than as a food by the F.D.A., I wondered if the safety standards are the same. "Not exactly," Maryanski explained. The F.D.A. requires "a reasonable certainty of no harm" in a food additive, a standard most pesticides could not meet. After all, "pesticides are toxic to something," Maryanski pointed out, so the E.P.A. instead establishes human "tolerances" for each chemical and then subjects it to a risk-benefit analysis.

When I called the E.P.A. and asked if the agency had tested my Bt potatoes for safety as a human food, the answer was . . . not exactly. It seems the E.P.A. works from the assumption that if the original potato is safe and the Bt protein added to it is safe, then the whole New Leaf package is presumed to be safe. Some geneticists believe this reasoning is flawed, contending that the process of genetic engineering itself may cause subtle, as yet unrecognized changes in a food.

The original Superior potato is safe, obviously enough, so that left the Bt toxin, which was fed to mice, and they "did fine, had no side effects," I was told. I always feel better knowing that my food has been poison-tested by mice, though in this case there was a small catch: the mice weren't actually eating the potatoes, not even an extract from the potatoes, but rather straight Bt produced in a bacterial culture.

So are my New Leafs safe to eat? Probably, assuming that a New Leaf is nothing more than the sum of a safe potato and a safe pesticide, and further assuming that the E.P.A.'s idea of a safe pesticide is tantamount to a safe food. Yet I still had a question. Let us assume that my potatoes are a pesticide—a very safe pesticide. Every pesticide in my garden shed—including the Bt sprays— carries a lengthy warning label. The label on my bottle of Bt says, among other things, that I should avoid inhaling the spray or getting it in an open wound. So if my New Leaf potatoes contain an E.P.A.-registered pesticide, why don't they carry some such label?

Maryanski had the answer. At least for the purposes of labeling, my New Leafs have morphed yet again, back into a food: the Food, Drug and Cosmetic Act gives the F.D.A. sole jurisdiction over the labeling of plant foods, and the F.D.A. has ruled that biotech foods need be labeled only if they contain known allergens or have otherwise been "materially" changed.

But isn't turning a potato into a pesticide a material change?

It doesn't matter. The Food, Drug and Cosmetic Act specifically bars the F.D.A. from including any information about pesticides on its food labels.

I thought about Maryanski's candid and wondrous explanations the next time I met Phil Angell, who again cited the critical role of the F.D.A. in assuring Americans that biotech food is safe. But this time he went even further.

"Monsanto should not have to vouchsafe the safety of biotech food," he said. "Our interest is in selling as much of it as possible. Assuring its safety is the F.D.A.'s job."

Meeting the Beetles

My Colorado potato beetle vigil came to an end the first week of July, shortly before I went to Idaho to visit potato growers. I spied a single mature beetle sitting on a New Leaf leaf; when I reached to pick it up, the beetle fell drunkenly to the ground. It had been sickened by the plant and would soon be dead. My New Leafs were working.

From where a typical American potato grower stands, the New Leaf looks very much like a godsend. That's because where the typical potato grower stands is in the middle of a bright green field that has been doused with so much pesticide that the leaves of his plants wear a dull white chemical bloom that troubles him as much as it does the rest of us. Out there, at least, the calculation is not complex: a product that promises to eliminate the need for even a single spraying of pesticide is, very simply, an economic and environmental boon.

No one can make a better case for a biotech crop than a potato farmer, which is why Monsanto was eager to introduce me to several large growers. Like many farmers today, the ones I met feel trapped by the chemical inputs required to extract the high yields they must achieve in order to pay for the chemical inputs they need. The economics are daunting: a potato farmer in south-central Idaho will spend roughly $1,965 an acre (mainly on chemicals, electricity, water and seed) to grow a crop that, in a good year, will earn him maybe $1,980. That's how much a french-fry processor will pay for the 20 tons of potatoes a single Idaho acre can yield. (The real money in agriculture—90 percent of the value added to the food we eat—is in selling inputs to farmers and then processing their crops.)

Danny Forsyth laid out the dismal economics of potato farming for me one sweltering morning at the coffee shop in downtown Jerome, Idaho. Forsyth, 60, is a slight blue-eyed man with a small gray ponytail; he farms 3,000 acres of potatoes, corn and wheat, and he spoke about agricultural chemicals like a man desperate to kick a bad habit. "None of us would use them if we had any choice," he said glumly.

I asked him to walk me through a season's regimen. It typically begins early in the spring with a soil fumigant; to control nematodes, many potato farmers douse their fields with a chemical toxic enough to kill every trace of microbial life in the soil. Then, at planting, a systemic insecticide (like Thimet) is applied to the soil; this will be absorbed by the young seedlings and, for several weeks, will kill any insect that eats their leaves. After planting, Forsyth puts down an herbicide—Sencor or Eptam—to "clean" his field of all weeds. When the potato seedlings are six inches tall, an herbicide may be sprayed a second time to control weeds.

Idaho farmers like Forsyth farm in vast circles defined by the rotation of a pivot irrigation system, typically 135 acres to a circle; I'd seen them from 30,000 feet flying in, a grid of verdant green coins pressed into a desert of scrubby brown. Pesticides and fertilizers are simply added to the irrigation system, which on Forsyth's farm draws most of its water from the nearby Snake River. Along with their water, Forsyth's potatoes may receive 10 applications of chemical fertilizer during the growing season. Just before the rows close—when the leaves of one row of plants meet those of the next—he begins spraying Bravo, a fungicide, to control late blight, one of the biggest threats to the potato crop. (Late blight, which caused the Irish potato famine, is an airborne fungus that turns stored potatoes into rotting mush.) Blight is such a serious problem that the E.P.A. currently allows farmers to spray powerful fungicides that haven't passed the usual approval process. Forsyth's potatoes will receive eight applications of fungicide.

Twice each summer, Forsyth hires a crop duster to spray for aphids. Aphids are harmless in themselves, but they transmit the leafroll virus, which in Russet Burbank potatoes causes net necrosis, a brown spotting that will cause a processor to reject a whole crop. It happened to Forsyth last year. "I lost 80,000 bags"—they're a hundred pounds each—"to net necrosis," he said. "Instead of getting $4.95 a bag, I had to take $2 a bag from the dehydrator, and I was lucky to get that." Net necrosis is a purely cosmetic defect; yet because big buyers like McDonald's believe (with good reason) that we don't like to see brown spots in our fries, farmers like Danny Forsyth must spray their fields with some of the most toxic chemicals in use, including an organophosphate called Monitor.

"Monitor is a deadly chemical," Forsyth said. I won't go into a field for four or five days after it's been sprayed—even to fix a broken pivot." That is, he would sooner lose a whole circle to drought than expose himself or an employee to Monitor, which has been found to cause neurological damage.

It's not hard to see why a farmer like Forsyth, struggling against tight margins and heartsick over chemicals, would leap at a New Leaf—or, in his case, a New Leaf Plus, which is protected from leafroll virus as well as beetles. "The New Leaf means I can skip a couple of sprayings, including the Monitor," he said." I save money, and I sleep better. It also happens to be a nice-looking spud." The New Leafs don't come cheaply, however. They cost between $20 and $30 extra per acre in "technology fees" to Monsanto.

Forsyth and I discussed organic agriculture, about which he had the usual things to say ("That's all fine on a small scale, but they don't have to feed the world"), as well as a few things I'd never heard from a conventional farmer: "I like to eat organic food, and in fact I raise a lot of it at the house. The vegetables we buy at the market we just wash and wash and wash. I'm not sure I should be saying this, but I always plant a small area of potatoes without any chemicals.

By the end of the season, my field potatoes are fine to eat, but any potatoes I pulled today are probably still full of systemics. I don't eat them."

Forsyth's words came back to me a few hours later, during lunch at the home of another potato farmer. Steve Young is a progressive and prosperous potato farmer—he calls himself an agribusinessman. In addition to his 10,000 acres—the picture window in his family room gazes out on 85 circles, all computer-controlled—Young owns a share in a successful fertilizer distributorship. His wife prepared a lavish feast for us, and after Dave, their 18-year-old, said grace, adding a special prayer for me (the Youngs are devout Mormons), she passed around a big bowl of homemade potato salad. As I helped myself, my Monsanto escort asked what was in the salad, flashing me a smile that suggested she might already know. "It's a combination of New Leafs and some of our regular Russets," our hostess said proudly. "Dug this very morning."

After talking to farmers like Steve Young and Danny Forsyth, and walking fields made virtually sterile by a drenching season-long rain of chemicals, you could understand how Monsanto's New Leaf potato does indeed look like an environmental boon. Set against current practices, growing New Leafs represents a more sustainable way of potato farming. This advance must be weighed, of course, against everything we don't yet know about New Leafs—and a few things we do: like the problem of Bt resistance I had heard so much about back East. While I was in Idaho and Washington State, I asked potato farmers to show me their refuges. This proved to be a joke.

"I guess that's a refuge over there," one Washington farmer told me, pointing to a cornfield.

Monsanto's grower contract never mentions the word "refuge" and only requires that farmers grow no more than 80 percent of their fields in New Leaf. Basically, any field not planted in New Leaf is considered a refuge, even if that field has been sprayed to kill every bug in it. Farmers call such acreage a clean field; calling it a refuge is a stretch at best.

It probably shouldn't come as a big surprise that conventional farmers would have trouble embracing the notion of an insect refuge. To insist on real and substantial refuges is to ask them to start thinking of their fields in an entirely new way, less as a factory than as an ecosystem. In the factory, Bt is another in a long line of "silver bullets" that work for a while and then get replaced; in the ecosystem, all bugs are not necessarily bad, and the relationships between various species can be manipulated to achieve desired ends—like the long-term sustainability of Bt.

This is, of course, precisely the approach organic farmers have always taken to their fields, and after my lunch with the Youngs that afternoon, I paid a brief visit to an organic potato grower. Mike Heath is a rugged, laconic man in his mid-50's; like most of the organic farmers I've met, he looks as though he spends a lot more time out of doors than a conventional farmer, and he probably does: chemicals are, among other things, labor-saving devices. While we drove around his 500 acres in a battered old pickup, I asked him about biotechnology. He voiced many reservations—it was synthetic, there were too many unknowns—but his main objection to planting a biotech potato was simply that "it's not what my customers want."

That point was driven home last December when the Department of Agriculture proposed a new "organic standards" rule that, among other things, would have allowed biotech crops to carry an organic label. After receiving a flood of outraged cards and letters, the agency backed off. (As did Monsanto, which asked the U.S.D.A. to shelve the issue for three years.) Heath suggested that biotech may actually help organic farmers by driving worried consumers to the organic label.

I asked Heath about the New Leaf. He had no doubt resistance would come—"the bugs are always going to be smarter than we are"—and said it was unjust that Monsanto was profiting from the ruin of Bt, something he regarded as a "public good."

None of this particularly surprised me; what did was that Heath himself resorted to Bt sprays only once or twice in the last 10 years. I had assumed that organic farmers used Bt or other approved pesticides in much the same way conventional farmers use theirs, but as Heath showed me around his farm, I began to understand that organic farming was a lot more complicated than substituting good inputs for bad. Instead of buying many inputs at all, Heath relied on long and complex crop rotations to prevent a buildup of crop-specific pests—he has found, for example, that planting wheat after spuds "confuses" the potato beetles.

He also plants strips of flowering crops on the margins of his potato fields—peas or alfalfa, usually—to attract the beneficial insects that eat beetle larvae and aphids. If there aren't enough beneficials to do the job, he'll introduce ladybugs. Heath also grows eight varieties of potatoes, on the theory that biodiversity in a field, as in the wild, is the best defense against any imbalances in the system. A bad year with one variety will probably be offset by a good year with the others.

"I can eat any potato in this field right now," he said, digging Yukon Golds for me to take home. "Most farmers can't eat their spuds out of the field. But you don't want to start talking about safe food in Idaho."

Heath's were the antithesis of "clean" fields, and, frankly, their weedy margins and overall patchiness made them much less pretty to look at. Yet it was the very complexity of these fields—the sheer diversity of species, both in space and time—that made them productive year after year without many inputs. The system provided for most of its needs.

All told, Heath's annual inputs consisted of natural fertilizers (compost and fish powder), ladybugs and a copper spray (for blight)—a few hundred dollars an acre. Of course, before you can compare Heath's operation with a conventional farm, you've got to add in the extra labor (lots of smaller crops means more work; organic fields must also be cultivated for weeds) and time—the typical organic rotation calls for potatoes every fifth year, in contrast to every third on a conventional farm. I asked Heath about his yields. To my astonishment, he was digging between 300 and 400 bags per acre—just as many as Danny Forsyth and only slightly fewer than Steve Young. Heath was also getting almost twice the price for his spuds: $8 a bag from an organic processor who was shipping frozen french fries to Japan.

On the drive back to Boise, I thought about why Heath's farm remained the exception, both in Idaho and elsewhere. Here was a genuinely new paradigm that seemed to work. But while it's true that organic agriculture is gaining ground (I met a big grower in Washington who had just added several organic circles), few of the mainstream farmers I met considered organic a "realistic" alternative. For one thing, it's expensive to convert: organic certifiers require a field to go without chemicals for three years before it can be called organic. For another, the U.S.D.A., which sets the course of American agriculture, has long been hostile to organic methods.

But I suspect the real reasons run deeper, and have more to do with the fact that in a dozen ways a farm like Heath's simply doesn't conform to the requirements of a corporate food chain. Heath's type of agriculture doesn't leave much room for the Monsantos of this world: organic farmers buy remarkably little— some seed, a few tons of compost, maybe a few gallons of ladybugs. That's because the organic farmer's focus is on a process, rather than on products. Nor is that process readily systematized, reduced to, say, a prescribed regime of sprayings like the one Forsyth outlined for me—regimes that are often designed by companies selling chemicals.

Most of the intelligence and local knowledge needed to run Mike Heath's farm resides in the head of Mike Heath. Growing potatoes conventionally requires intelligence, too, but a large portion of it resides in laboratories in distant places like St. Louis, where it is employed in developing sophisticated chemical inputs. That sort of centralization of agriculture is unlikely to be reversed, if only because there's so much money in it; besides, it's much easier for the farmer to buy prepackaged solutions from big companies. "Whose Head Is the Farmer Using? Whose Head Is Using the Farmer?" goes the title of a Wendell Berry essay.

Organic farmers like Heath have also rejected what is perhaps the cornerstone of industrial agriculture: the economies of scale that only a monoculture can achieve. Monoculture—growing vast fields of the same crop year after year—is probably the single most powerful simplification of modern agriculture. But monoculture is poorly fitted to the way nature seems to work. Very simply, a field of identical plants will be exquisitely vulnerable to insects, weeds and disease. Monoculture is at the root of virtually every problem that bedevils the modern farmer, and that virtually every input has been designed to solve.

To put the matter baldly, a farmer like Heath is working very hard to adjust his fields and his crops to the nature of nature, while farmers like Forsyth are working equally hard to adjust nature in their fields to the requirement of monoculture and, beyond that, to the needs of the industrial food chain. I remember asking Heath what he did about net necrosis, the bane of Forsyth's existence. "That's only really a problem with Russet Burbanks," he said. "So I plant other kinds." Forsyth can't do that. He's part of a food chain—at the far end of which stands a long, perfectly golden McDonald's fry—that demands he grow Russet Burbanks and little else.

This is where biotechnology comes in, to the rescue of Forsyth's Russet Burbanks and, if Monsanto is right, to the whole food chain of which they form a part. Monoculture is in trouble—the pesticides that make it possible are rapidly being lost, either to resistance or to heightened concerns about their danger. Biotechnology is the new silver bullet that will save monoculture. But a new silver bullet is not a new paradigm—rather, it's something that will allow the old paradigm to survive. That paradigm will always construe the problem in Forsyth's fields as a Colorado potato beetle problem, rather than as a problem of potato monoculture.

Like the silver bullets that preceded them—the modern hybrids, the pesticides and the chemical fertilizers—the new biotech crops will probably, as advertised, increase yields. But equally important, they will also speed the process by which agriculture is being concentrated in a shrinking number of corporate hands. If that process has advanced more slowly in farming than in other sectors of the economy, it is only because nature herself—her complexity, diversity and sheer intractibility in the face of our best efforts at control—has acted as a check on it. But biotechnology promises to remedy this "problem," too.

Consider, for example, the seed, perhaps the ultimate "means of production" in any agriculture. It is only in the last few decades that farmers have begun buying their seed from big companies, and even today many farmers still save some seed every fall to replant in the spring. Brown-bagging, as it is called, allows farmers to select strains particularly well adapted to their needs; since these seeds are often traded, the practice advances the state of the genetic art—indeed, has given us most of our crop plants. Seeds by their very nature don't lend themselves to commodification: they produce more of themselves ad infinitum (with the exception of certain modern hybrids), and for that reason the genetics of most major crop plants have traditionally been regarded as a common heritage. In the case of the potato, the genetics of most important varieties—the Burbanks, the Superiors, the Atlantics—have always been in the public domain. Before Monsanto released the New Leaf, there had never been a multinational seed corporation in the potato-seed business—there was no money in it.

Biotechnology changes all that. By adding a new gene or two to a Russet Burbank or Superior, Monsanto can now patent the improved variety. Legally, it has been possible to patent a plant for many years, but biologically, these patents have been almost impossible to enforce. Biotechnology partly solves that problem. A Monsanto agent can perform a simple test in my garden and prove that my plants are the company's intellectual property. The contract farmers sign with Monsanto allows company representatives to perform such tests in their fields at will. According to *Progressive Farmer,* a trade journal, Monsanto is using informants and hiring Pinkertons to enforce its patent rights; it has already brought legal action against hundreds of farmers for patent infringement.

Soon the company may not have to go to the trouble. It is expected to acquire the patent to a powerful new biotechnology called the Terminator, which will, in effect, allow the company to enforce its patents biologically. Developed by the U.S.D.A. in partnership with Delta and Pine Land, a seed company in the process of being purchased by Monsanto, the Terminator is a complex of genes that, theoretically, can be spliced into any crop plant, where it will cause every seed produced by that plant to be sterile. Once the Terminator becomes the industry standard, control over the genetics of crop plants will complete its move from the farmer's field to the seed company—to which the farmer will have no choice but to return year after year. The Terminator will allow companies like Monsanto to privatize one of the last great commons in nature—the genetics of the crop plants that civilization has developed over the past 10,000 years.

At lunch on his farm in Idaho, I had asked Steve Young what he thought about all this, especially about the contract Monsanto made him sign. I wondered how the American farmer, the putative heir to a long tradition of agrarian independence, was adjusting to the idea of field men snooping around his farm, and patented seed he couldn't replant. Young said he had made his peace with corporate agriculture, and with biotechnology in particular: "It's here to stay. It's necessary if we're going to feed the world, and it's going to take us forward."

Then I asked him if he saw any downside to biotechnology, and he paused for what seemed a very long time. What he then said silenced the table. "There is a cost," he said. "It gives corporate America one more noose around my neck."

Harvest

A few weeks after I returned home from Idaho, I dug my New Leafs, harvesting a gorgeous-looking pile of white spuds, including some real lunkers. The plants had performed brilliantly, though so had all my other potatoes. The beetle problem never got serious, probably because the diversity of species in my (otherwise organic) garden had attracted enough beneficial insects to keep the beetles in check. By the time I harvested my crop, the question of eating the New Leafs was moot. Whatever I thought about the soundness of the process that had declared these potatoes safe didn't matter. Not just because I'd already had a few bites of New Leaf potato salad at the Youngs but also because Monsanto and the F.D.A. and the E.P.A. had long ago taken the decision of whether or not to eat a biotech potato out of my—out of all of our—hands. Chances are, I've eaten New

Leafs already, at McDonalds or in a bag of Frito-Lay chips, though without a label there can be no way of knowing for sure.

So if I've probably eaten New Leafs already, why was it that I kept putting off eating mine? Maybe because it was August, and there were so many more-interesting fresh potatoes around—fingerlings with dense, luscious flesh, Yukon Golds that tasted as though they had been pre-buttered—that the idea of cooking with a bland commercial variety like the Superior seemed beside the point.

There was this, too: I had called Margaret Mellon at the Union of Concerned Scientists to ask her advice. Mellon is a molecular biologist and lawyer and a leading critic of biotech agriculture. She couldn't offer any hard scientific evidence that my New Leafs were unsafe, though she emphasized how little we know about the effects of Bt in the human diet. "That research simply hasn't been done," she said.

I pressed. Is there any reason I shouldn't eat these spuds?

"Let me turn that around. Why would you want to?"

It was a good question. So for a while I kept my New Leafs in a bag on the porch. Then I took the bag with me on vacation, thinking maybe I'd sample them there, but the bag came home untouched.

The bag sat on my porch till the other day, when I was invited to an end-of-summer potluck supper at the town beach. Perfect. I signed up to make a potato salad. I brought the bag into the kitchen and set a pot of water on the stove. But before it boiled I was stricken by this thought: I'd have to tell people at the picnic what they were eating. I'm sure (well, almost sure) the potatoes are safe, but if the idea of eating biotech food without knowing it bothered me, how could I possibly ask my neighbors to? So I'd tell them about the New Leafs—and then, no doubt, lug home a big bowl of untouched potato salad. For surely there would be other potato salads at the potluck and who, given the choice, was ever going to opt for the bowl with the biotech spuds?

So there they sit, a bag of biotech spuds on my porch. I'm sure they're absolutely fine. I pass the bag every day, thinking I really should try one, but I'm beginning to think that what I like best about these particular biotech potatoes—what makes them different—is that I have this choice. And until I know more, I choose not.

Reading 25

SELECTIONS FROM:

DOMINATION AND THE ARTS OF RESISTANCE

James C. Scott

Behind the Official Story

I tremble to speak the words of freedom before the tyrant.
> —CORYPHAEUS, in Euripides, *The Bacchae*

The Labourer and Artisan, notwithstanding they are Servants to their Masters, are quit by doing what they are bid. But the Tyrant sees those that are about him, begging and suing for his Favour; and they must not only do what he commands, but they must think as he would have them [think] and most often, to satisfy him, even anticipate his thoughts. It is not sufficient to obey him, they must also please him, they must harass, torment, nay kill themselves in his Service; and . . . they must leave their own Taste for his, Force their Inclination, and throw off their natural Dispositions. They must carefully observe his Words, his Voice, his Eyes, and even his Nod. They must have neither Eyes, Feet, nor Hands, but what must be ALL upon the watch, to spy out his Will, and discover his Thoughts. Is this to live happily? Does it indeed deserve the Name of Life?
> —ESTIENNE DE LA BOETIE, *A Discourse on Voluntary Servitude*

And the intensest hatred is that rooted in fear, which compels to silence and drives vehemence into constructive vindictiveness, an imaginary annihilation of the detested object, something like the hidden rites of vengeance with which the persecuted have a dark vent for their rage.
> —GEORGE ELIOT, *Daniel Deronda*

Scott, James C. "Behind the Official Story" and "Domination, Acting and Fantasy." *Domination in the Arts of Resistance: Hidden Transcripts.* New Haven: Yale UP, 1990. 1–44.

If the expression "Speak truth to power" still has a utopian ring to it, even in modern democracies, this is surely because it is so rarely practiced. The dissembling of the weak in the face of power is hardly an occasion for surprise. It is ubiquitous. So ubiquitous, in fact, that it makes an appearance in many situations in which the sort of power being exercised stretches the ordinary meaning of *power* almost beyond recognition. Much of what passes as normal social intercourse requires that we routinely exchange pleasantries and smile at others about whom we may harbor an estimate not in keeping with our public performance. Here we may perhaps say that the power of social forms embodying etiquette and politeness requires us often to sacrifice candor for smooth relations with our acquaintances. Our circumspect behavior may also have a strategic dimension: this person to whom we misrepresent ourselves may be able to harm or help us in some way. George Eliot may not have exaggerated in claiming that "there is no action possible without a little acting."

The acting that comes of civility will be of less interest to us in what follows than the acting that has been imposed throughout history on the vast majority of people. I mean the public performance required of those subject to elaborate and systematic forms of social subordination: the worker to the boss, the tenant or sharecropper to the landlord, the serf to the lord, the slave to the master, the untouchable to the Brahmin, a member of a subject race to one of the dominant race. With rare, but significant, exceptions the public performance of the subordinate will, out of prudence, fear, and the desire to curry favor, be shaped to appeal to the expectations of the powerful. I shall use the term *public transcript* as a shorthand way of describing the open interaction between subordinates and those who dominate.[1] The public transcript, where it is not positively misleading, is unlikely to tell the whole story about power relations. It is frequently in the interest of both parties to tacitly conspire in misrepresentation. The oral history of a French tenant farmer, Old Tiennon, covering much of the nineteenth century is filled with accounts of a prudent and misleading deference: "When he [the landlord who had dismissed his father] crossed from Le Craux, going to Meillers, he would stop and speak to me and I forced myself to appear amiable, in spite of the contempt I felt for him."[2]

Old Tiennon prides himself on having learned, unlike his tactless and unlucky father, "the art of dissimulation so necessary in life."[3] The slave narratives that have come to us from the U.S. South also refer again and again to the need to deceive:

> I had endeavored so to conduct myself as not to become obnoxious to the white inhabitants, knowing as I did their power, and their hostility to the colored people. . . . First, I had made no display of the little property or money I possessed, but in every way I wore as much as possible the aspect of slavery. Second, I had never appeared to be even so intelligent as I really was. This all colored at the south, free and slaves, find it particularly necessary for their own comfort and safety to observe.[4]

As one of the key survival skills of subordinate groups has been impression management in power-laden situations, the performance aspect of their conduct has not escaped the more observant members of the dominant group. Noting that her slaves fell uncharacteristically silent whenever the latest news from the front in the Civil War became a topic of white conversation, Mary Chesnut took their silence as one that hid something: "They go about in their black masks, not a ripple of emotion showing; and yet on all other subjects except the war they are the most excitable of all races. Now Dick might be a very respectable Egyptian Sphynx, so inscrutably silent he is."[5]

Here I will venture a crude and global generalization I will later want to qualify severely: the greater the disparity in power between dominant and subordinate and the more arbitrarily it is exercised, the more the public transcript of subordinates will take on a stereotyped, ritualistic cast. In other words, the more menacing the power, the thicker the mask. We might imagine, in this context, situations ranging all the way from a dialogue among friends of equal status and power on the one hand to the concentration camp on the other, in which the public transcript of the victim bears the mark of mortal fear. Between these extremes are the vast majority of the historical cases of systematic subordination that will concern us.

Cursory though this opening discussion of the public transcript has been, it alerts us to several issues in power relations, each of which hinges on the fact that the public transcript is not the whole story. First, the public transcript is an indifferent guide to the opinion of subordinates. Old Tiennon's tactical smile and greeting mask an attitude of anger and revenge. At the very least, an assessment of power relations read directly off the public transcript between the powerful and the weak may portray a deference and consent that are possibly only a tactic. Second, to the degree that the dominant suspect that the public transcript may be "only" a performance, they will discount its authenticity. It is but a short step from such skepticism to the view, common among many dominant groups, that those beneath them are deceitful, shamming, and lying by nature. Finally, the questionable meaning of the public transcript suggests the key roles played by disguise and surveillance in power relations. Subordinates offer a performance of deference and consent while attempting to discern, to read, the real intentions and mood of the potentially threatening powerholder. As the favorite proverb of Jamaican slaves captures it, "Play fool, to catch wise."[6] The power figure, in turn, produces a performance of mastery and command while attempting to peer behind the mask of subordinates to read their real intentions. The dialectic of disguise and surveillance that pervades relations between the weak and the strong will help us, I think, to understand the cultural patterns of domination and subordination.

The theatrical imperatives that normally prevail in situations of domination produce a public transcript in close conformity with how the dominant group would wish to have things appear. The dominant never control the stage absolutely, but their wishes normally prevail. In the short run, it is in the interest of the subordinate to produce a more or less credible performance, speaking the lines and making the gestures he knows are expected of him. The result is that the public transcript is—barring a crisis—systematically skewed in the direction of the libretto, the discourse, represented by the dominant. In ideological terms the public transcript will typically, by its accommodationist tone, provide convincing evidence for the hegemony of dominant values, for the hegemony of dominant discourse. It is in precisely this public domain where the effects of power relations are most manifest, and any analysis based exclusively on the public transcript is likely to conclude that subordinate groups endorse the terms of their subordination and are willing, even enthusiastic, partners in that subordination.

A skeptic might well ask at this point how we can presume to know, on the basis of the public transcript alone, whether this performance is genuine or not. What warrant have we to call it a performance at all, thereby impugning its authenticity? The answer is, surely, that we cannot know how contrived or imposed the performance is unless we can speak, as it were, to the performer offstage, out of this particular power-laden context, or unless the performer suddenly declares openly, on stage, that the performances we have previously observed were just a pose.[7] Without a privileged peek backstage or a rupture in the performance we have no way of calling into question the status of what might be a convincing but feigned performance.

If subordinate discourse in the presence of the dominant is a public transcript, I shall use the term *hidden transcript* to characterize discourse that takes place "offstage," beyond direct observation by powerholders. The hidden transcript is thus derivative in the sense that it consists of those offstage speeches, gestures, and practices that confirm, contradict, or inflect what appears in the public transcript.[8] We do not wish to prejudge, by definition, the relation between what is said in the face of power and what is said behind its back. Power relations are not, alas, so straightforward that we can call what is said in power-laden contexts false and what is said offstage true. Nor can we simplistically describe the former as a realm of necessity and the latter as a realm of freedom. What is certainly the case, however, is that the hidden transcript is produced for a different audience and under different constraints of power than the public transcript. By assessing the discrepancy *between* the hidden transcript and the public transcript we may begin to judge the impact of domination on public discourse.

The abstract and general tone of the discussion thus far is best relieved by concrete illustrations of the possibly dramatic disparity between the public and the hidden transcripts. The first is drawn from slavery in the antebellum U.S. South. Mary Livermore, a white governess from New England, recounted the reaction of Aggy, a normally taciturn and deferential black cook, to the beating the master had given her daughter. The daughter had been accused, apparently unjustly, of some minor theft and then beaten while Aggy looked on, powerless to intervene. After the master had finally left the kitchen, Aggy turned to Mary, whom she considered her friend and said,

> Thar's a day a-comin'! Thar's a day a-comin'! . . . I hear the rumblin ob de chariots! I see de flashin ob de guns! White folks blood is a runnin on the ground like a ribber, an de dead's heaped up dat high! . . . Oh Lor! Hasten de day when de blows, an de bruises, and de aches an de pains, shall come to de white folks, an de buzzards shall eat dem as dey's dead in de streets. Oh Lor! roll on de chariots, an gib the black people rest and peace. Oh Lor! Gib me de pleasure ob livin' till dat day, when I shall see white folks shot down like de wolves when dey come hungry out o'de woods.[9]

One can imagine what might have happened to Aggy if she had delivered this speech directly to the master. Apparently her trust in Mary Livermore's friendship and sympathy was such that a statement of her rage could be ventured with comparative safety. Alternatively, perhaps she could no longer choke back her anger. Aggy's hidden transcript is at complete odds with her public transcript of quiet obedience. What is particularly striking is that this is anything but an inchoate scream of rage; it is a finely drawn and highly visual image of an apocalypse, a day of revenge and triumph, a world turned upside down using the cultural raw materials of the white man's religion. Can we conceive of such an elaborate vision rising spontaneously to her lips without the beliefs and practice of slave Christianity having prepared the way carefully? In this respect our glimpse of Aggy's hidden transcript, if pursued further, would lead us directly to the offstage culture of the slave quarters and slave religion. Whatever such an investigation would tell us, this glimpse itself is sufficient to make any naive interpretation of Aggy's previous and subsequent public acts of deference impossible both for us, and most decidedly for Aggy's master, should he have been eavesdropping behind the kitchen door.

The hidden transcript Aggy revealed in the comparative safety of friendship is occasionally openly declared in the face of power. When, suddenly, subservience evaporates and is replaced by open defiance we encounter one of those rare and dangerous moments in power relations. Mrs. Poyser, a character in George Eliot's *Adam Bede* who finally spoke her mind, provides an illustration of the hidden transcript storming the stage. As tenants of the elderly Squire Donnithorne, Mrs. Poyser and her husband had always resented his rare visits, when he would impose some new, onerous obligation on them and treat them with disdain. He had "a mode of looking at her which, Mrs. Poyser observed, 'allays aggravated her; it was as if you was an insect, and he was going to dab his fingernail on you.' However, she said, 'your servant, sir' and curtsied with an air of perfect deference as she advanced towards him: she was not the woman to misbehave toward her betters, and fly in the face of the catechism, without severe provocation."[10]

This time the squire came to propose an exchange of pasture and grain land between Mr. Poyser and a new tenant that would almost certainly be to the Poysers' disadvantage. When assent was slow in coming, the squire held out the prospect of a longer term farm lease and ended with the observation—a thinly veiled threat of eviction—that the other tenant was well-off and would be happy to lease the Poysers' farm in addition to his own. Mrs. Poyser, "exasperated" at the squire's determination to ignore her earlier objections "as if she had left the room" and at the final threat, exploded. She "burst in with the desperate determination to have her say out this once, though it were to rain notices to quit, and the only shelter were the workhouse."[11] Beginning with a comparison between the condition of the house—frogs on the steps of the flooded basement, rats and mice coming in through the rotten floorboards to eat the cheeses and menace the children—and the struggle to pay the high rent, Mrs. Poyser let fly her personal accusations as she realized that the squire was fleeing out the door toward his pony and safety:

> You may run away from my words, sir, and you may go spinning underhand ways o' doing us a mischief, for you've got old Harry to your friend, though nobody else is, but I tell you for once as we're not dumb creatures to be abused and made money on by them as ha' got the lash i' their hands, for want o' knowing how t' undo the tackle. An if I'm th' only one as speaks my mind, there's plenty o' the same way o' thinking i' this parish and the next to 't, for your name's no better than a brimstone match in everybody's nose.[12]

Such were Eliot's powers of observation and insight into her rural society that many of the key issues of domination and resistance can be teased from her story of Mrs. Poyser's encounter with the squire. At the height of her peroration, for example, Mrs. Poyser insists that they will not be treated as animals despite his power over them. This, together with her remark about the squire looking on her as an insect and her declaration that he has no friends and is hated by the whole parish, focuses on the issue of self-esteem. While the confrontation may originate in the exploitation of an onerous tenancy, the discourse is one of dignity and reputation. The practices of domination and exploitation typically generate the insults and slights to human dignity that in turn foster a hidden transcript of indignation. Perhaps one vital distinction to draw between forms of domination lies in the kinds of indignities the exercise of power routinely produces.

Notice also how Mrs. Poyser presumes to speak not just for herself but for the whole parish. She represents what she says as the first public declaration of what everyone has been saying behind the squire's back. Judging from how rapidly the story traveled and the unalloyed joy with which it was received and retold, the rest of the community also felt Mrs. Poyser had spoken for them as well. "It was known throughout the two parishes," Eliot writes, "that the Squire's plan had been frustrated because the Poysers had refused to be 'put upon,' and Mrs. Poyser's outbreak was discussed in all the farmhouses with a zest that was only heightened by frequent repetition."[13] The vicarious pleasure of the neighbors had nothing to do with the actual sentiments expressed by Mrs. Poyser—hadn't everyone been saying the same thing about the squire among themselves for years? The content, though Mrs. Poyser may have put it with considerable folk elegance, was stale; it was saying it openly (with witnesses) to the squire's face that was remarkable and that made Mrs. Poyser into something of a local hero. The first open statement of a hidden transcript, a declaration that breaches the etiquette of power relations, that breaks an apparently calm surface of silence and consent, carries the force of a symbolic declaration of war. Mrs. Poyser had spoken (a social) truth to power.

Delivered in a moment of anger, Mrs. Poyser's speech was, one might say, spontaneous—but the spontaneity lay in the timing and vehemence of the delivery, not in the content. The content had, in fact, been rehearsed again and again, as we are told: "and though Mrs. Poyser had during the last twelve-month recited many imaginary speeches, meaning even more than met the ear, which she was quite determined to make to him the next time he appeared within the gates of the Hall Farm, the speeches had always remained imaginary."[14] Who among us has not had a similar experience? Who, having been insulted or suffered an indignity—especially in public—at the hand of someone in power or authority over us, has not rehearsed an imaginary speech he wishes he had given or intends to give at the next opportunity?[15] Such speeches may often remain a personal hidden transcript that may never find expression, even among close friends and peers. But in this case we are dealing with a shared situation of subordination. The tenants of Squire Donnithorne and, in fact, much of the nongentry in two parishes had ample personal reasons to take pleasure in his being publicly humbled and to share vicariously in Mrs. Poyser's courage. Their common class position and their social links thus provided a powerful resolving lens bringing their collective hidden transcript into focus. One might say, without much exaggeration, that they had together, in the course of their social interchange, written Mrs. Poyser's speech for her. Not word for word, of course, but in the sense that Mrs. Poyser's "say" would be her own reworking of the stories, the ridicule, and the complaints that those beneath the Squire all shared. And to "write" that speech for her, the squire's subjects had to have some secure social space, however sequestered, where they could exchange and elaborate their criticism. Her speech was her personal rendition of the hidden transcript of a subordinate group, and, as in the case of Aggy, that speech directs our attention back to the offstage culture of the class within which it originated.

An individual who is affronted may develop a personal fantasy of revenge and confrontation, but when the insult is but a variant of affronts suffered systematically by a whole race, class, or strata, then the fantasy can become a collective cultural product. Whatever form it assumes—offstage parody, dreams of violent revenge, millennial visions of a world turned upside down—this collective hidden transcript is essential to any dynamic view of power relations.

Mrs. Poyser's explosion was potentially very costly, and it was her daring—some would have said foolhardiness—that won her such notoriety. The word *explosion* is used deliberately here because that is how Mrs. Poyser experienced it:

> "Thee'st done it now," said Mr. Poyser, a little alarmed and uneasy, but not without some triumphant amusement at his wife's outbreak. "Yis, I know I've done it," said Mrs. Poyser, "but I've had my say out, and I shall be the'easier for 't all my life. There's no pleasure in living, if you're to be corked up for iver, and only dribble your mind out by the sly, like a leaky barrel. I shan't repent saying what I think, if I live to be as old as the Squire."[16]

The hydraulic metaphor George Eliot puts in Mrs. Poyser's mouth is the most common way in which the sense of pressure behind the hidden transcript is expressed. Mrs. Poyser suggests that her habits of prudence and deception can no longer contain the anger she has rehearsed for the last year. That the anger will find a passage out is not in doubt; the choice is rather between a safer but less psychologically satisfying process of "dribbl[ing] your mind out by the sly" and the dangerous but gratifying full blast that Mrs. Poyser has ventured. George Eliot has, in effect, taken one position here on the consequences for consciousness of domination. Her claim is that the necessity of "acting a mask" in the presence of power produces, almost by the strain engendered by its inauthenticity, a countervailing pressure that cannot be contained indefinitely. As an epistemological matter, we have no warrant for elevating the truth status of Mrs. Poyser's outburst over that of her prior deference. Both are arguably part of Mrs. Poyser's self. Notice, however, that as Eliot constructs it, Mrs. Poyser feels she has finally spoken her mind. Inasmuch as she and others in comparable situations feel they have finally spoken truthfully to those in power, the concept truth may have a sociological reality in the thought and practice of people whose actions interest us. It may have a phenomenological force in the real world despite its untenable epistemological status.

An alternative claim, nearly a logical mirror image of the first, is that those obliged by domination to act a mask will eventually find that their faces have grown to fit that mask. The practice of subordination in this case produces, in time, its own legitimacy, rather like Pascal's injunction to those who were without religious faith but who desired it to get down on their knees five times a day to pray, and the acting would eventually engender its own justification in faith. In the analysis that follows I hope to clarify this debate considerably, inasmuch as it bears so heavily on the issues of domination, resistance, ideology, and hegemony that are at the center of my concern.

If the weak have obvious and compelling reasons to seek refuge behind a mask when in the presence of power, the powerful have their own compelling reasons for adopting a mask in the presence of subordinates. Thus, for the powerful as well there is typically a disparity between the public transcript deployed in the open exercise of power and the hidden transcript expressed safely only offstage. The offstage transcript of elites is, like its counterpart among subordinates, derivative: it consists in those gestures and words that inflect, contradict, or confirm what appears in the public transcript.

Nowhere has the "act of power" been more successfully examined than in George Orwell's essay "Shooting an Elephant," from his days as a subinspector of police in the 1920s in colonial Burma. Orwell had been summoned to deal with an elephant in heat that had broken its tether and was ravaging the bazaar. When Orwell, elephant gun in hand, finally locates the elephant, which has indeed killed a man, it is peacefully grazing in the paddy fields, no longer a threat to anyone. The logical thing would be to observe the elephant for a while to ensure that its heat had passed. What frustrates logic for Orwell is that there are now more than two thousand colonial subjects who have followed and are watching him:

> And suddenly I realized that I should have to shoot the elephant after all. The people expected it of me and I had got to do it; I could feel their two thousand wills pressing me forward, irresistibly. And it was at this moment, as I stood there with the rifle in my hands, that I first grasped the hollowness, the futility of the white man's dominion in the East. Here was I, the white man with his gun, standing in front of the unarmed native crowd—seemingly the leading actor of the piece; but in reality I was only an absurd puppet pushed to and fro by the will of those yellow faces behind. I perceived in this moment that when the white man turns tyrant it is his own freedom that he destroys. He becomes a sort of hollow posing dummy, the conventionalized figure of a sahib. For it is the condition of his rule that he shall spend his life in trying to impress the "natives," and so in every crisis he has to do what the "natives" expect of him. He wears a mask and his face grows to fit it. . . . A sahib has got to act like a sahib; he has got to appear resolute, to know his own mind and do definite things. To come all that way, rifle in hand, with two thousand people marching at my heels, and then to trail feebly away, having done nothing—no, that was impossible. The crowd would laugh at me. And my whole life, every white man's life in the East, was one long struggle not to be laughed at.[17]

Orwell's use of the theatrical metaphor is pervasive: he speaks of himself as "leading actor of the piece," of hollow dummys, puppets, masks, appearances, and an audience poised to jeer if he doesn't follow the established script. As he experiences it, Orwell is no more free to be himself, to break convention, than a slave would be in the presence of a tyrannical master. If subordination requires a credible performance of humility and deference, so domination seems to require a credible performance of haughtiness and mastery. There are, however, two differences. If a slave transgresses the script he risks a beating, while Orwell risks only ridicule. Another important distinction is that the necessary posing of the dominant derives not from weaknesses but from the ideas behind their rule, the kinds of claims they make to legitimacy. A divine king must act like a god, a warrior king like a brave general; an elected head of a republic must appear to respect the citizenry and their opinions; a judge must seem to venerate the law. Actions by elites that *publicly* contradict the basis of a claim to power are threatening. The cynicism of the taped Oval Office conversations in the Nixon White House was a devastating blow to the public transcript claim to legality and high-mindedness. Similarly, the poorly concealed existence of special shops and hospitals for the party elites in the socialist bloc profoundly undercut the ruling party's public claim to rule on behalf of the working class.[18]

One might usefully compare forms of domination in terms of the kinds of display and public theater they seem to require. Another, perhaps even more revealing way of addressing the same question would be to ask what activities are most sedulously hidden from public view by different forms of domination. Each form of rule will have not only its characteristic stage setting but also its characteristic dirty linen.[19]

Those forms of domination based on a premise or claim to inherent superiority by ruling elites would seem to depend heavily on lavish display, sumptuary laws, regalia, and public acts of deference or tribute by subordinates. The desire to inculcate habits of obedience and hierarchy, as in military organizations, can produce similar patterns. In extreme cases display and performance dominate, as in the case of the Chinese emperor Long Qing, whose public appearances were so minutely choreographed that he became virtually a living icon deployed in rituals that risked nothing to improvisation. Offstage, in the Forbidden City, he might carouse as he wished with princes and aristocrats.[20] This may be something of a limiting case, but the attempt by dominant elites to sequester an offstage social site where they are no longer on display and can let their hair down is ubiquitous, as is the attempt to ritualize contact with subordinates so that the masks remain firmly in place and the risk that something untoward might happen is minimized. Milovan Djilas's early critique of Yugoslavia's new party elite contrasted a meaningful but secret backstage with the empty ritual of public bodies: "At intimate suppers, on hunts, in conversations between two or three men, matters of state of the most vital importance are decided. Meetings of party forums, conferences of the government and assemblies, serve no purpose but to make declarations and put in an appearance."[21] Strictly speaking, of course, the public ritual Djilas denigrates does indeed serve a purpose inasmuch as the theater of unanimity, loyalty, and resolve is intended to impress an audience. Public ritual of this kind is both real and meaningful; Djilas's complaint is rather that it is also a performance designed to conceal an offstage arena of politics that would contradict it. Dominant groups often have much to conceal, and typically they also have the wherewithal to conceal what they wish. The British colonial officials with whom Orwell served in Moulmein had the inevitable club to repair to in the evenings. There, except for the invisible Burmese staff, they were among their own, as they might have put it, and no longer strutting before the audience of colonial subjects. Activities, gestures, remarks, and dress that were unseemly to the public role of sahib were safe in this retreat.[22] The seclusion available to elites not only affords them a place to relax from the formal requirements of their role but also minimizes the chance that familiarity will breed contempt or, at least, diminish the impression their ritually managed appearances create. Balzac captures the fear of overexposure, as it now might be termed, among the Parisian magistrates of the mid-nineteenth century,

> Ah what an unfortunate man your true magistrate is! You know, they ought to live outside the community, as pontiffs once did. The world should only see them when they emerged from their cells at fixed times, solemn, ancient, venerable, pronouncing judgment like the high priests of antiquity, combining in themselves the judicial and the sacerdotal powers! We should only be visible on the bench. . . . Nowadays we may be seen amusing ourselves or in difficulties like anybody else. . . . We may be seen in drawing rooms, at home, creatures of passion, and instead of being terrible we are grotesque.[23]

Perhaps the danger that unregulated contact with the public may profane the sacred aura of judges helps explain why, even in secular republics, they retain more of the trappings of traditional authority than any other branch of government.

Now that the basic idea of public and hidden transcripts has been introduced, I will venture a few observations by way of orienting the subsequent discussion. For the study of power relations, this perspective alerts us to the fact that virtually all ordinarily observed relations between dominant and subordinate represent the encounter of the *public* transcript of the dominant with the *public* transcript of the subordinate. It is to observe Squire Donnithorne imposing on Mr. and Mrs. Poyser on all those occasions on which, prior to the explosion, she managed to keep up the pretense of being deferential and agreeable. Social science is, in general then, focused resolutely on the official or formal relations between the powerful and weak. This is the case even for much of the study of conflict, as we shall see, when that conflict has become highly institutionalized. I do not mean to imply that the study of this domain of power relations is necessarily false or trivial, only that it hardly exhausts what we might wish to know about power.

Eventually we will want to know how the *hidden* transcripts of various actors are formed, the conditions under which they do or do not find public expression, and what relation they bear to the public transcript.[24] Three characteristics of the hidden transcript, however, merit clarification beforehand. First, the hidden transcript is specific to a given social site and to a particular set of actors. Aggy's oath was almost certainly rehearsed in various forms among the slaves in their quarters or at the clandestine religious services that we know were common. Orwell's peers, like most dominant groups, would risk less from a public indiscretion, but they would have the safety of the Moulmein Club in which to vent their spleen. Each hidden transcript, then, is actually elaborated among a restricted "public" that excludes—that is hidden from—certain specified others. A second and vital aspect of the hidden transcript that has not been sufficiently emphasized is that it does not contain only speech acts but a whole range of practices. Thus, for many peasants, activities such as poaching, pilfering, clandestine tax evasion, and intentionally shabby work for landlords are part and parcel of the hidden transcript. For dominant elites, hidden-transcript practices might include clandestine luxury and privilege, surreptitious use of hired thugs, bribery, and tampering with land titles. These practices, in each case, contravene the public transcript of the party in question and are, if at all possible, kept offstage and unavowed.

Finally, it is clear that the frontier between the public and the hidden transcripts is a zone of constant struggle between dominant and subordinate—not a solid wall. The capacity of dominant groups to prevail—though never totally—in defining and constituting what counts as the public transcript and what as offstage is, as we shall see, no small measure of their power. The unremitting struggle over such boundaries is perhaps the most vital arena for ordinary conflict, for everyday forms of class struggle. Orwell noticed how the Burmese managed to insinuate almost routinely a contempt for the British, while being careful never to venture a more dangerous open defiance:

> Anti-European feeling was very bitter. No one had the guts to raise a riot, but if a European woman went through the bazaars alone somebody would probably spit betel juice over her dress. . . . When a nimble Burman tripped me up on the football field and the referee (another Burman) looked the other way, the crowd yelled with hideous laughter. . . . In the end the sneering yellow faces of the young men that met me everywhere, the insults hooted after me when I was at a safe distance, got badly on my nerves. The young Buddhist priests were the worst of all.[25]

Tactical prudence ensures that subordinate groups rarely blurt out their hidden transcript directly. But, taking advantage of the anonymity of a crowd or of an ambiguous accident, they manage in a thousand artful ways to imply that they are grudging conscripts to the performance.

The analysis of the hidden transcripts of the powerful and of the subordinate offers us, I believe, one path to a social science that uncovers contradictions and possibilities, that looks well beneath the placid surface that the public accommodation to the existing distribution of power, wealth, and status often presents. Behind the "anti-European" acts Orwell noted was undoubtedly a far more elaborate hidden transcript, an entire discourse, linked to Burman culture, religion, and the experience of colonial rule. This discourse was not available—except through spies—to the British. It could be recovered only offstage in the native quarter in Moulmein and only by someone intimately familiar with Burman culture. Nor, of course, did the Burmans know—except through the tales that servants might tell—what lay behind the more or less official behavior of the British toward them. That hidden transcript could be recovered only in the clubs, homes, and small gatherings of the colonists. The analyst in any situation like this has a strategic advantage over even the most sensitive participants precisely because the hidden transcripts of dominant and subordinate are, in most circumstances, *never in direct contact.* Each participant will be familiar with the public transcript and the hidden transcript of his or her circle, but not with the hidden transcript of the other. For this reason, political analysis can be advanced by research that can compare the hidden transcript of subordinate groups with the hidden transcript of the powerful and both hidden transcripts with the public transcript they share. This last facet of the comparison will reveal the effect of domination on political communication.

Just a few years after Orwell's stint in Moulmein a huge anticolonial rebellion took the English by surprise. It was led by a Buddhist monk claiming the throne and promising a utopia that consisted largely of getting rid of the British and taxes. The rebellion was crushed with a good deal of gratuitous brutality and the surviving "conspirators" sent to the gallows. A portion, at least, of the hidden transcript of the Burmans had suddenly, as it were, leapt onto the stage to declare itself openly. Millennial dreams of revenge and visions of just kingship, of Buddhist saviors, of a racial settling of scores of which the British had little inkling were being acted on. In the brutality of the repression that followed one could detect an acting out of the admission that Orwell struggled against and that undoubtedly found open expression in the white's only club that "the greatest joy in the world would be to drive a bayonet into a Buddhist priest's guts." Many, perhaps most, hidden transcripts remain just that: hidden from public view and never "enacted." And we are not able to tell easily under what precise circumstances the hidden transcript will storm the stage. But if we wish to move beyond apparent consent and to grasp potential acts, intentions as yet blocked, and possible futures that a shift in the balance of power or a crisis might bring to view, we have little choice but to explore the realm of the hidden transcript.

Domination, Acting, and Fantasy

Jocasta: What is its nature? What so hard on exiles?
Polyneices: One thing is worst, a man cannot speak out.
Jocasta: But this is slavery, not to speak one's thought.
Polyneices: One must endure the unwisdom of one's masters.
—EURIPEDES, *The Phoenician Women*

Destinations

My broad purpose is to suggest how we might more successfully read, interpret, and understand the often fugitive political conduct of subordinate groups. The immodesty of this goal all but ensures that it will not be achieved except in a fragmentary and schematic form. This ambition grew from a prolonged effort to understand the politics of resistance by poor Malay peasants to changes in rice production that systematically worked to their disadvantage.[1] Given the power of landowning elites and officials, the struggle waged by the poor was necessarily circumspect. Rather than openly rebel or publicly protest, they adopted the safer course of anonymous attacks on property, poaching, character assassination, and shunning. They prudently avoided, with few exceptions, any irrevocable acts of public defiance. Anyone who regarded the calm surface of political life in "Sedaka" as evidence of harmony between classes would simply have been looking in the wrong place for political conflict.

For subordinate groups that find themselves in roughly the same boat as the poor of Sedaka, I reasoned, political life might assume analogous forms. That is, their politics too might make use of disguise, deception, and indirection while maintaining an outward impression, in power-laden situations, of willing, even enthusiastic consent.

An argument along these lines requires that we first understand how the public transcript is constructed, how it is maintained, and the purposes it serves. Why are public performances of deference and loyalty so important in power relations? Who is the audience for this symbolic display? What happens when angry or cheeky subordinates such as Mrs. Poyser spoil the performance?

The public transcript is, to put it crudely, the *self*-portrait of dominant elites as they would have themselves seen. Given the usual power of dominant elites to compel performances from others, the discourse of the public transcript is a decidedly lopsided discussion. While it is unlikely to be merely a skein of lies and misrepresentations, it is, on the other hand, a highly partisan and partial narrative. It is designed to be impressive, to affirm and naturalize the power of dominant elites, and to conceal or euphemize the dirty linen of their rule.

If, however, this flattering self-portrait is to have any rhetorical force among subordinates, it necessarily involves some concessions to their presumed interests. That is, rulers who aspire to hegemony in the Gramscian sense of that term must make out an ideological case that they rule, to some degree, on behalf of their subjects. This claim, in turn, is always highly tendentious but seldom completely without resonance among subordinates.

The distinction between the hidden and the public transcripts, together with the hegemonic aspirations of the public transcript allows us to distinguish at least four varieties of political discourse among subordinate groups. They vary according to how closely they conform to the official discourse and according to who comprises their audience.

The safest and most public form of political discourse is that which takes as its basis the flattering self-image of elites. Owing to the rhetorical concessions that this self-image contains, it offers a surprisingly large arena for political conflict that appeals to these concessions and makes use of the room for interpretation within any ideology. For example, even the ideology of white slave owners in the antebellum U.S. South incorporated certain paternalist flourishes about the care, feeding, housing, and clothing of slaves and their religious instruction. Practices, of course, were something else. Slaves were, however, able to make political use of this small rhetorical space to appeal for garden plots, better food, humane treatment, freedom to travel to religious services, and so forth. Thus, some slave interests could find representation in the prevailing ideology without appearing in the least seditious.

A second and sharply contrasting form of political discourse is that of the hidden transcript itself. Here, offstage, where subordinates may gather outside the intimidating gaze of power, a sharply dissonant political culture is possible. Slaves in the relative safety of their quarters can speak the words of anger, revenge, self-assertion that they must normally choke back when in the presence of the masters and mistresses.

A central argument of this book is that there is a third realm of subordinate group politics that lies strategically between the first two. This is a politics of disguise and anonymity that takes place in public view but is designed to have a double meaning or to shield the identity of the actors. Rumor, gossip, folktales, jokes, songs, rituals, codes, and euphemisms—a good part of the folk culture of subordinate groups—fit this description. As a case in point, consider the Brer Rabbit stories of slaves, and trickster tales more generally. At one level these are nothing but innocent stories about animals; at another level they appear to celebrate the cunning wiles and vengeful spirit of the weak as they triumph over the strong. I argue that a partly sanitized, ambiguous, and coded version of the hidden transcript is always present in the public discourse of subordinate groups. Interpreting these texts which, after all, are designed to be evasive is not a straightforward matter. Ignoring them, however, reduces us to an understanding of historical subordination that rests either on those rare moments of open rebellion or on the hidden transcript itself, which is not just evasive but often altogether inaccessible. The recovery of the nonhegemonic voices and practices of subject peoples requires, I believe, a fundamentally different form of analysis than the analysis of elites, owing to the constraints under which they are produced.

Finally, the most explosive realm of politics is the rupture of the political *cordon sanitaire* between the hidden and the public transcript. When Mrs. Poyser has her "say" she obliterates the distinction by making the hitherto hidden transcript public. In her case, the squire fled, but such moments of challenge and open defiance typically provoke either a swift stroke of repression or, if unanswered, often lead to further words and acts of daring. We will examine such moments for the insights they offer into certain forms of charisma and the dynamic of political breakthroughs.

Much of our attention will be devoted to what I have chosen to call the infrapolitics of subordinate groups. By this I mean to designate a wide variety of low-profile forms of resistance that dare not speak in their own name. A grasp of the substance of this infrapolitics, its disguises, its development, and its relationship to the public transcript, can help us clarify several vexed problems in political analysis.

The analysis of infrapolitics offers us a way of addressing the issue of hegemonic incorporation. It would be hard to find a subject on which more ink has been recently spilled—whether in the debates about community power or in the more subtle neo-Marxist formulations of Gramsci and his successors. Exactly what hegemonic incorporation might mean is subject to interpretation but, however one chooses to define it, a crude, one-dimensional answer to the query of whether slaves believe in the justice or inevitability of slavery is out of the question. If we seek instead to assess the ways in which subordinate groups may be socialized into accepting a view of their interests as propagated from above, then we may be able to provide a more complex answer. Evidence from the hidden transcript and from infrapolitics in general allows us, in principle at least, a way of approaching this problem empirically. We are not, in any case, reduced to waiting for open social protest to lift a veil of consent and quiescence. A view of politics focused either on what may be command performances of consent or open rebellion represents a far too narrow concept of political life—especially under conditions of tyranny or near-tyranny in which much of the world lives.

In a similar way, paying close attention to political acts that are disguised or offstage helps us to map a realm of possible dissent. Here, I believe, we will typically find the social and normative basis for practical forms of resistance (for example, what masters called shirking, theft, and flight by slaves) as well as the values that might, if conditions permitted, sustain more dramatic forms of rebellion. The point is that neither everyday forms of resistance nor the occasional insurrection can be understood without reference to the sequestered social sites at which such resistance can be nurtured and given meaning. Done in more detail than can be attempted here, such an analysis would outline a technology and practice of resistance analogous to Michel Foucault's analysis of the technology of domination.[2]

The hidden transcript and disguised forms of public dissent may also help to enlarge our understanding of charismatic acts. Charisma is not a quality—like, say, brown eyes—that someone possesses in any simple way; it is, as we know, a relationship in which engaged observers recognize (and may, in fact, help inspire) a quality they admire. Mrs. Poyser was not a charismatic character in the colloquial use of that term, but she undertook a charismatic act. Understanding that charismatic act, and many others like it, I would argue, depends upon appreciating how her gesture represented a shared hidden transcript that no one had yet had the courage to declare in the teeth of power.

My analysis emphasizes precisely those forms of subordination in which I anticipated finding the greatest divergence between the public transcript and the hidden transcript. Thus much of the evidence I use comes from various forms of tyranny chosen with an eye to how they might vindicate this perspective. Wherever possible, I have drawn material from studies of slavery, serfdom, untouchability, racial domination—including colonialism, and highly stratified peasant societies, which are my particular bailiwick. To a contemporary observer, these forms of domination might seem almost limiting cases; slavery and serfdom might even be considered antiquarian interests. Stressing such cases, however, has its advantages. As a historical matter, they surely represent a very large share of mankind's melancholy experience. Thanks to a growing attention to social history from below and to the recovery of otherwise mute voices—especially in the case of North American slavery—I have also been able to take advantage of much recently published work.

My strategy amounts to choosing forms of domination that bear a family resemblance to one another so as to lend some cohesion to comparisons across an already dangerously sprawling range of cases. These forms of domination are institutionalized means of extracting labor, goods, and services from a subject population. They embody formal assumptions about superiority and inferiority, often in elaborate ideological form, and a fair degree of ritual and "etiquette" regulates public conduct within them. In principle at least, status in these systems of domination is ascribed by birth, mobility is virtually nil, and subordinate groups are granted few if any political or civil rights. Although they are highly institutionalized, these forms of domination typically contain a strong element of personal rule.[3] Here I have in mind the great latitude for arbitrary and capricious conduct by the master toward his slave, the lord to his serf, the Brahmin to his untouchable. Thus these forms of domination are infused by an element of personal terror that may take the form of arbitrary beatings, sexual violations, and other insults and humiliations. Whether or not they occur to any particular subordinate, the ever-present knowledge that they might seems to color the relationship as a whole. Finally, like most large-scale structures of domination, the subordinate group has a fairly extensive offstage social existence which, in principle, affords it the opportunity to develop a shared critique of power.

This structural family resemblance is an essential analytical underpinning to my argument. I do not intend, in other words, to make "essentialist" assertions about the immutable characteristics of slaves, serfs, untouchables, the colonized, or subjugated races. What I do want to claim, however, is that similar structures of domination, other things equal, tend to provoke responses and forms of resistance that also bear a family resemblance to one another.[4] My analysis, therefore, is one that runs roughshod over differences and specific conditions that others would consider essential, in order to sketch the outlines of broad approach. Not only do I ignore the vast differences between each form of subordination, but I also overlook the great particularity of each instance of a given form—for example, between North American and Caribbean slavery, between French and Russian serfdom. If this approach has any merit, that merit would have to be demonstrated in case studies grounding these broad assertions in contexts that were both culturally specific and historically deep.

More than occasionally, I make reference to other forms of subordination that are at some remove from the core of structures mentioned above, but that have some similarities which I think will help advance and illustrate the argument. Evidence from "total institutions" such as prisons, reeducation camps, prisoner-of-war camps—especially where some effort is made at persuasion, even it if takes the form of brainwashing—has seemed helpful for comparative purposes. Similarly, public life in communist states in which the chasm between official ritual and the offstage political culture is often so large can tell us something about how a hidden transcript is elaborated.

The literature on gender-based domination and on working-class culture and ideology has proven insightful at many points. They share enough similarities to the cases I rely most heavily on to be suggestive. At the same time the differences limit the analogies that can be drawn. In the case of women, relations of subordination have typically been both more personal and intimate; joint procreation and family life have meant that imagining an entirely separate existence for the subordinate group requires a more radical step than it has for serfs or slaves. Analogies become more strained in contemporary settings where choice of marriage partner is possible and where women have civil and political rights. For the contemporary working classes in the West who can take or leave a particular job (though they typically *must* work) and who also have some mobility and have gained citizenship rights, many of the same difficulties arise. Both cases illustrate how essential the existence of some choice is in raising the possibility of hegemonic incorporation, and the case of gender highlights the importance of specifying exactly how separate separate spheres are.[5]

Given the choice of structures explored here, it is apparent that I privilege the issues of dignity and autonomy, which have typically been seen as secondary to material exploitation. Slavery, serfdom, and the caste system routinely generate practices and rituals of denigration, insult, and assaults on the body that seem to occupy a large space in the hidden transcripts of their victims. Such forms of oppression, as we shall see, deny subordinates the ordinary luxury of negative reciprocity: trading a slap for a slap, an insult for an insult. Even in the case of the contemporary working class, it appears that slights to one's dignity and close surveillance and control of one's work loom at least as large in accounts of oppression as do narrower concerns of work and compensation.

Preliminaries

[. . .] Before embarking on [the] enterprise [of analyzing the public transcript], however, a few working assumptions must be clarified. The first concerns the epistemological status of the hidden transcript and the nature of the *relative* freedom of the discourse found there. Second, I want to indicate how the distinctions between a public and a hidden transcript accord well with what we know from linguistic practice and from the phenomenology of distinctions between what's said in the face of power and what's said behind its back. Finally, I want to indicate how the hidden transcript receives its normative and emotional resonance from the impulses and assertions that are censored in the presence of power.

Deference and Back(stage) Talk

> The younger had always worn a Yoke, but is there any yoked creature without private opinion?
>
> —GEORGE ELIOT, *Middlemarch*

Any pattern of stratification provides a fairly reliable guide to who gives orders and who receives orders in that society. At the top are those who give orders to virtually all and take none; at the bottom are those who take orders from virtually anyone and give orders to none. Those at each position *defer* to those placed higher. Looked at in this fashion, deference is one of the consequences of a stratification system rather than its creator. We are in danger of making a serious mistake, therefore, whenever we infer anything at all about the beliefs or attitudes of anyone solely on the basis that he or she has engaged in an apparently deferential act. Strictly speaking, we have no basis for any such inference, and the term *deference* is best thought of as "the form of social interaction which occurs in situations involving the exercise of traditional authority."[6] There is little doubt that acts of deference—for example, a bow of greeting or the use of a superior's honorific in addressing him—are intended in some sense to convey the outward impression of conformity with standards sustained by superiors. Beyond this we may not safely go. The act may be performed almost automatically as a ritual or habitual act; it may be the result of calculating its advantages; it may be successful dissembling; it may spring from a conscious desire to honor a respected superior. In addition, since most acts of deference are routinized actions toward the holder of a particular status one might often wish to distinguish the attitude toward the individual from the attitude toward the status in general. One might defer to a particular priest, for example, out of a generalized respect for priests and for the faith they represent, while holding this particular priest in private contempt.

Each and every inference about the attitude behind an act of deference must therefore be based on evidence external to the act itself.[7] And when the acts of deference in question are those of a group that is systematically subject to domination, that evidence is all the more vital inasmuch as public rituals of deference may be highly routinized and shallow. In his comparative study of slavery, Orlando Patterson is at pains to insist that the servile acts of slaves in the presence of their masters are "the outward product of their interaction" and nothing more; we can say next to nothing about group psychology or beliefs on this basis.[8] In any established structure of domination, it is plausible to imagine that subordinate groups are socialized by their parents in the rituals of homage that will keep them from harm. A cruel paradox of slavery, for example, is that it is in the interest of slave mothers, whose overriding wish is to keep their children safe and by their side, to train them in the routines of conformity. Out of love, they undertake to socialize their children to please, or at least not anger, their masters and mistresses. How deep this conformity goes and how much of the backstage resentment and cynicism that may color it underlies the performance is impossible to say on surface evidence alone. Something along similar lines appears to occur in English working-class families. Compared to middle-class families, which emphasize feeling, guilt, and attitude, working-class parents, it is claimed, stress outward conformity and compliance with far less concern for the motives that lie behind it.[9] The pattern reflects to a great extent the kind of compliance to work life and to the class system that has been expected, and extracted, from their parents. It is as if working-class youngsters are being trained for a life in which there is no necessary connection—perhaps even a contradiction—between their public conformity to the realities of power and their confidential attitudes.

The problem we face in examining a public transcript of deference amounts to this: how can we estimate the impact of power relations on action when the exercise of power is nearly constant? We can only begin to measure the influence of a teacher's presence on a classroom of students once he or she leaves the room—or when they leave the room at recess. Aside from what they say, the typical explosion of chatter and physical exuberance released when school is out, compared with their previous behavior in the classroom, does tell us something retrospectively about the effect of the school and teacher on behavior. The motives behind acts of deference will remain opaque to us until and unless the power that prompts it weakens or else we can speak confidentially, backstage to those whose motives we wish to understand.

It is particularly in this latter realm of relative discursive freedom, outside the earshot of powerholders, where the hidden transcript is to be sought. The disparity between what we find here and what is said in the presence of power is a rough measure of what has been suppressed from power-laden political communication. The hidden transcript is, for this reason, the privileged site for non-hegemonic, contrapuntal, dissident, subversive discourse.

Hypothetical Discursive Sites, Arranged by Audience, under Slavery

Harsh master/ overseer	Indulgent master or overseer	Whites having no direct authority	Slaves and free blacks	Slaves of same master	Closest slave friends	Immediate family

|--| |--|

Public transcripts   Hidden transcripts

To this point I have used the terms *hidden* and *public transcript* in the singular when, in fact, the plural would be more accurate and would convey the great variety of sites where such transcripts are generated. The accompanying illustration—the crudity and linearity of which we shall later modify—provides an initial sense of this plurality of transcripts in the case of slavery.[10]

As a hypothetical slave finds himself among audiences progressively toward the more secluded (right) side of the continuum, his discourse is relatively freer of intimidation from above. Put in slightly different terms, power over discourse is typically, but not always, less lopsided the more the slave is cloistered within his most intimate circle. This is decidedly not, however, to assert that the slave's actions before a harsh master are necessarily sham and pretense while his conduct with his family and close friends is necessarily genuine and true. The reason we may not leap to this simplifying conclusion is that power relations are ubiquitous. They are surely different at opposite ends of the continuum, but they are never absent.[11]

The difference in power relations toward the hidden transcript segment of the continuum is that they are generated among those who are mutually subject, often as peers, to a larger system of domination. Although the slave may be freer vis-à-vis the master in this setting, it does not follow that relations of domination do not prevail among the slaves. Power relations among subordinates are not necessarily conducted along democratic lines at all. Among the inmates of prisons, who are all subject to a common domination from the institution and its officers, there frequently develops a tyranny as brutal and exploitive as anything the guards can devise. In this domination within domination the subordinate prisoner must measure his words and conduct perhaps more carefully before dominant prisoners than he does before prison officials.

Even if relations among subordinates may be characterized by symmetry and mutuality, the hidden transcript that develops in this case may be experienced as no less tyrannical despite the fact that all have had a hand in shaping it.

Consider, for example, the ethos that often prevails among workers which penalizes any laborer who would go out of his way to curry the favor of the bosses. The words used from below to describe such behavior (toady, ass-kisser, rate-buster, bootlicker) are designed to prevent it. These may be supplemented by glares, shunning, and perhaps even beatings.

The power relations generated among subordinate groups are often the only countervailing power to the determination of behavior from above. Tenant farmers in the Malaysian village I studied had developed a strong norm among themselves condemning anyone who might try to secure or enlarge his acreage by offering the landlord a higher seasonal rent than the current local tenant paid. Fifteen years ago someone apparently defied the norm; since then the family is poorly regarded and has not been spoken to or invited to feasts by any kin or friends of the offended family. In a comparable case no Andalusian farmworkers were said to dare work for less than the minimum wage. If they did, they would be given the cold shoulder, ostracized, or branded "low" or a "creeper."[12] The strength of the sanctions deployed to enforce conformity depends essentially on the cohesiveness of the subordinate group and on how threatening they view the defection. In nineteenth-century rural Ireland when a tenant broke a rent boycott by paying the land agent, he was likely to find his cow "houghed" in the morning: its Achilles tendon severed so that the tenant would have to destroy it himself. All such cases are instances of the more or less coercive pressure that can be generated to monitor and control deviance among a subordinate group.[13] This pressure serves not only to suppress dissent among subordinates but may also place limits on the temptation to compete headlong with one another—at the expense of all—for the favor of the dominant.

As shown in the figure, the dialectical relationship between the public and hidden transcripts is obvious. By definition, the hidden transcript represents discourse—gesture, speech, practices—that is ordinarily excluded from the public transcript of subordinates by the exercise of power. The practice of domination, then, *creates* the hidden transcript. If the domination is particularly severe, it is likely to produce a hidden transcript of corresponding richness. The hidden transcript of subordinate groups, in turn, reacts back on the public transcript by engendering a subculture and by opposing its own variant form of social domination against that of the dominant elite. Both are realms of power and interests.

The hidden transcript of the dominant is similarly an artifact of the exercise of power. It contains that discourse—gestures, speech, practices—which is excluded from the public transcript by the ideological limits within which domination is cast. It too is a realm of power and interests. Imagining a figure similar to the figure [cited earlier] in which we instead took the perspective of the slave master and ranging from audiences of his family and closest friends all the way to his interaction on ceremonial occasions with the slaves assembled, would yield a spectrum of discursive realms of the dominant. Here too, as with a diplomat whose discourse varies enormously depending on whether he is talking informally with his own negotiating team or formally with the chief negotiator of a threatening enemy power, is a realm of masks. The masks may get thicker or thinner, they may be crude or subtle, depending on the nature of the audience and the interests involved, but they are nevertheless performances, as are all social actions.

Power and Acting

> Your presence frightens any common man
> From saying things you would not care to hear
> But in dark corners I have heard them say
> how the whole town is grieving for this girl
> Unjustly doomed if ever woman was
> to die in shame for glorious action done . . .
>
> This is the undercover speech in town.
> —HAEMON TO CREON, *Antigone*

On a daily basis, the impact of power is most readily observed in acts of deference, subordination, and ingratiation. The script and stage directions for subordinate groups are generally far more confining than for the dominant. Putting it in terms of "paying respect" to status, Hochschild observes,

> to have higher status is to have a stronger claim to rewards, including emotional rewards. It is also to have greater access to the means of enforcing claims. The deferential behavior of servants and women—the encouraging smiles, the attentive listening, the appreciative laughter, the comments of affirmation, admiration, or concern—comes to seem normal, even built into personality rather than inherent in the kinds of exchange that low-status people commonly enter into.[14]

A convincing performance may require both the suppression or control of feelings that would spoil the performance and the simulation of emotions that are necessary to the performance. Practical mastery through repetition may make the performance virtually automatic and apparently effortless. In other cases, it is a conscious strain, as when Old Tiennon said that when he met his father's ex-landlord, "I forced myself to be amiable." We often talk in this schizophrenic way as if our tactical self exercises control over our emotional self, which threatens to spoil the performance.[15] The performance, as I shall continually emphasize, comprises not only speech acts but conformity in facial expression and gesture as well as practical obedience to commands that may be distasteful or humiliating.

More of the public life of subordinates than of the dominant is devoted to "command" performances. The change in the posture, demeanor, and apparent activity of an office work force when the supervisor suddenly appears is an obvious case. The supervisor, though she too is constrained, can typically be more relaxed about her manner, less on guard, for it is the supervisor, after all, who sets the tone of the encounter.[16] Power means not *having* to act or, more accurately, the capacity to be more negligent and casual about any single performance. So close was this association between power and acting in the French royal court that the slightest trace of an increase in servility could be taken as evidence of declining status and power: "Let a favorite pay close heed to himself for if he does not keep me waiting as long in his antechamber; if his face is more open, if he frowns less, if he listens to me a little further while showing me out, I shall think he is beginning to fall, and I shall be right."[17] The haughtiness associated with the bearing of power may, in a physical sense, contain more of the unguarded self, while servility virtually by definition requires an attentive watchfulness and attuning of response to the mood and requirements of the powerholder. Less of the unguarded self is ventured because the possible penalties for a failure or misstep are severe; one must be constantly on one's "best behavior."

The influence that the powerful exercise on public discourse is apparent in the findings of sociolinguists about language use and power. These findings indicate how hierarchies of gender, race, caste, and class are encoded in the domination of talk.

In her study of contemporary language-use differences between women and men, Robin Lakoff emphasizes that the history of male dominance has meant that women increasingly use men's language—imitating the higher status dialect—while the reverse is rarely the case.[18] In a face-to-face encounter the tone, grammar, and dialect of the dominant male is likely to prevail, not to mention that, as in other asymmetrical power relations, the dominant is typically the one who initiates the conversation, controls its direction, and terminates it. The fact of subordination can be read in the use of linguistic forms shaped so as to reflect and anticipate the response of the dominant. Thus Lakoff notes the far more widespread use by women of what linguists call the "tag question formation"—an "isn't it so?" or a rising tone at the end of what would otherwise be a declarative sentence, which indicates a request for reassurance and approval before continuing. Other linguistic marks of subordination include the greater use of hyperpolite forms ("Would you be so kind as to please . . ." in place of a command), of hyper-correct grammar, linguistic hedges ("sort of," "kind of") that weaken a declarative phrase, and a disinclination to tell jokes in public. When the subordination is extreme, as in slavery and racism, it is often observed that stammering is common, a stammering that reflects not a speech defect, since the stammerers can speak fluently in other contexts, but a fear-induced hesitation over producing the correct formula. One can, I think, read in these patterns a consistent risk-averse use of language by the powerless—an attempt to venture as little as possible, to use stock formulas when available, and to avoid taking liberties with language that might give offense. As a high-caste anthropologist conducting interviews among untouchable Chamars in Lucknow discovered, "The triter the inquiry the 'better' the Chamar's response. In less trodden areas, evasive devices—deflection, postponement, containment, cliché, rhetorical questions, and feigned ignorance were deftly employed."[19] Such performances require practice, mastery, and their own kind of improvisation if they are to be exercised successfully, but they are nevertheless all damage-control maneuvers in the face of power. As Lakoff concludes in the case of women's speech and dress conformity, "Her overattention to appearance and appearances (including perhaps overcorrectness and overgentility of speech and etiquette) is merely the result of being forced to exist only as a reflection in the eyes of others."[20]

Societies with long-established court cultures develop elaborate codes for speech-levels which in extreme cases can nearly constitute a separate language. Here the hyper-correctness of subordinates is institutionalized linguistically. Strong traces of such codes persist in the differences between Saxon and Norman English: the Saxon commoners ate while the Norman conquerors dined. In Malaysia a host of special verbs distinguish quite ordinary actions when the sultan is undertaking them: commoners bathe, the sultan sprinkles himself; commoners walk, the sultan progresses (implying a smooth, gliding motion); commoners sleep, the sultan reclines. Pronouns also change, as they do in most highly stratified societies, depending on the relative status of the speakers. When a commoner is addressing the sultan, he uses the term *hamba,* which translates roughly as "your slave," and he traditionally approached the throne in a posture of abject humility. Every encounter that brings together people of different statuses in such societies is designed to underline and reinforce those differences by rules about language, gesture, tone, and dress.

Terms of address, perhaps because they lend themselves to historical analysis, have been the object of considerable research by sociolinguists. In the past, the polite and the familiar forms of the second person pronoun (*vous* and *tu* in French, respectively) were used asymmetrically in a semantic of power.[21] The dominant class used tu when addressing commoners, servants, peasants and received back the more polite, dignified vous. No one who prudently used the formula could avoid thereby seeming to endorse the distinctions of worth and status inscribed in its use. Inasmuch as there was a determined effort by the revolutionaries in France immediately after 1789 to ban the use of vous, we can take it for granted that this semantic of power was not a matter of popular indifference. To this day, at socialist and communist gatherings, Europeans who are strangers will use the familiar form with one another to express equality and comradeship. In ordinary usage vous is now used *reciprocally* to express not status, but lack of close acquaintance.

A function equivalent to this nonreciprocity of address is the use of *boy* or first names by ruling groups when speaking with inferiors, and the latters' use of *Mister* to address their superiors. Common in systems of stratification by class and by race, this usage has not by any means disappeared in the West, though it is decidedly less universal today than fifty years ago. (It also survives as a kind of curiosity in the French *garçon,* for waiter, although *monsieur* is now increasingly favored.) Afrikaans, significantly, retains today both the asymmetrical use of the second person pronoun and the boy-Mister pattern.

We are in danger of missing much of their significance if we see linguistic deference and gestures of subordination merely as performances extracted by power. The fact is they serve also as a barrier and a veil that the dominant find difficult or impossible to penetrate. A striking example is the usually futile effort by sociolinguists to record "pure," "authentic" versions of lower-class dialect. Since the recorder is almost inevitably someone of higher status and education, a kind of linguistic Heisenberg effect takes place which drives out the more stigmatized forms of the dialect. The only way the semantics of power can be breached is by a highly unethical, surreptitious taping of conversations without the subject's knowledge or permission.[22] From one perspective this fact is merely an example of how power distorts communication. But from another perspective, it also preserves a sequestered site where a more autonomous discourse may develop. How are we to interpret the fact, for example, that lower-caste men in the pluralistic culture of the Punjab are likely to use any of several names, depending upon whom they were speaking to? Confronted with a Hindu, they called themselves Ram Chand, with a Sikh they called themselves Ram Singh, and with a Christian, John Samuel. The frustrated British census takers wrote of the "fickleness" of the lower castes with respect to religion, but it is not hard to recognize the evasive adoption of protective cover.[23] We also learn that black miners in Southern Rhodesia had several names which arose not simply from the confusion of languages but because the confusion could plausibly excuse a delay in responding to a summons or an otherwise unexplained absence.[24] The appearances that power requires are, to be sure, imposed forcefully on subordinate groups. But this does not preclude their active use as a means of resistance and evasion. The evasion, it must be noted, however, is purchased at the considerable cost of contributing to the production of a public transcript that *apparently* ratifies the social ideology of the dominant. Subordinates appear deferential, they bow and scrape, they seem amiable, they appear to know their place and to stay in it, thereby indicating that they also know and recognize the place of their superiors.

When the script is rigid and the consequences of a mistake large, subordinate groups may experience their conformity as a species of manipulation. Insofar as the conformity is tactical it is surely manipulative. This attitude again requires a division of the self in which one self observes, perhaps cynically and approvingly, the performance of the other self. Many of the accounts given by untouchables (notice how the term *untouchable* assumes a high-caste perspective) are frank in this respect. Noting that vital goods and services—sugar, kerosene, work, grain, loans—can be procured only by being on the good side of a member of the dominant castes, one observes, "We actually have to encounter, appease, and cajole the caste Hindus in a hundred different ways to secure our share."[25] Thus, conformity is far too lame a word for the active manipulation of rituals of subordination to turn them to good personal advantage; it is an art form in which one can take some pride at having successfully misrepresented oneself. Another untouchable emphasizes the tactical side of concealment: "We must also tactfully disguise and hide, as necessary, our true aims and intentions from our social adversaries. To recommend it is not to encourage falsehood but only to be tactical in order to survive."[26]

Blacks in the South, both before and after emancipation, had to thread their way among dangerous whites in much the same fashion. Thus it was possible for a black man speaking to a white abolitionist audience before the Civil War to explain, "Persons live and die in the midst of Negroes and know comparatively little of their real character. They are one thing before the whites and another before their own color. Deception towards the former is characteristic of them, whether bond or free, throughout the whole U.S."[27] The sense of achievement in a successful performance *and* the massive realities of power that make it necessary are each evident in this account of a black sharecropper between the wars:

> I've joked with white people, in a nice way. I've had to play dumb sometimes— I knowed not to go too far and let them know what I knowed, because they taken exception of it too quick. I had to humble down and play shut-mouthed in many cases to get along, I've done it all—they didn't know what it was all about, it's just a plain fact. . . . And I could go to 'em a heap of times for a favor and get it. . . . They'd give you a good name if you was obedient to 'em, acted nice when you met 'em an didn't question 'em 'bout what they said they had against you. You begin to cry about your rights and the mistreatin' of you and they'd murder you.[28]

Nate Shaw reminds us eloquently that the theater of power can, by artful practice, become an actual political resource of subordinates. Thus we get the wrong impression, I think, if we visualize actors perpetually wearing fake smiles and moving with the reluctance of a chain gang. To do so is to see the performance as totally determined from above and to miss the agency of the actor in appropriating the performance for his own ends. What may look from above like the extraction of a required performance can easily look from below like the artful manipulation of deference and flattery to achieve its own ends. The slaves who artfully reinforced their master's stereotyped view of them as shiftless and unproductive may well have thereby lowered the work norms expected of them. By their artful praise at celebrations and holidays, they may have won better food rations and clothing allowances. The performance is often collective, as subordinates collude to create a piece of theater that serves their superior's view of the situation but that is maintained in their own interests.[29] In fact, the stereotypes of the dominant are, from this perspective, a resource as well as an oppression to the subordinate, as Richard Hoggart's observation of the British working-class's use of deference makes plain: "the kind of obvious 'fiddling' of someone from another class which accompanies an overreadiness to say 'Sir,' but assumes . . . that it is all a contemptuous game, that one can depend on the middle class distaste for a scene to allow one to cheat easily."[30] Rituals of subordination, then, may be deployed both for purposes of manipulation and concealment. What was often called Uncle Tom behavior, from this angle, may be no more than a label for someone who has mastered the theater arts of subordination. Deference and a smile may be what a poacher habitually deploys before the gentry to avoid suspicion; rather like the normal walk of the fleeing suspect when he encounters a cop on the beat. This achievement is considerable, but we should not forget that it is won on a stage on which the roles have been largely scripted from above and on which the usual performances, no matter how artful, must reinforce the appearances approved by the dominant.

Such performances are seldom, of course, entirely successful. Dominant elites may well not know what lies behind the facade, but it is rare that they merely take what they see and hear at face value. An ancient text from Buddhist India seeks to instruct the master on what the facade conceals:

> O Bhante, our slaves . . . do another thing with their bodies, say another with their speech, and have a third in their mind.
>
> On seeing the master, they rise up, take things from his hands, discarding this and talking that; others show a seat, fan him with a hand fan, wash his feet, thus doing all that needs to be done. But in his absence, they do not even look if oil is being spilled, they do not turn to look even if there were a loss of hundreds or thousands to the master. (This is how they behave differently with the body). . . . Those who in the masters' presence praise him by saying, "our master, our Lord," say all that is unutterable, all that they feel like saying once he is away. (This is how they behave differently in speech.)[31]

The white slave master is always wary of being put on by his slaves; an eighteenth-century Japanese landlord can wonder, "Does anyone lie as much as a peasant?"[32] What is notable here, I believe, is not that the dominant should assume that wily subordinates will try to get around them. To believe this is not to be paranoid; it is merely to perceive reality. They attribute such behavior, however, not to the effect of arbitrary power but rather to the inborn characteristics of the subordinate group itself. In the ersatz science of race at the turn of the century the characteristics of subordination became traits of culture, gender, or ethnicity. Accounting for what he termed the negative and superficial quality of women's speech, Schopenhauer explained, "It arises immediately from the want of reason and reflection above alluded to, and is *assisted* by the fact that they, as the weaker, are driven by nature to have recourse not to force but to cunning: hence their instinctive treachery, and their irremediable tendency to lying."[33] Otto Weininger, who wrote a widely read study called *Sex and Character* not long after, made much the same point: "The impulse to lie is much stronger in women, because, unlike that of a man, her memory is not continuous, whilst her life is discrete, unconnected, discontinuous, swayed by the sensations and perceptions of the moment instead of dominating them."[34] Each author gives some evidence here of understanding the structural position of women that might account for the character of their observed speech; but each ultimately explains the difference by gender. In Weininger's case, the argument is extended to cover the "speech-character" of another subordinate group: the Jews. Both groups stood accused of the misuse of language and were "to be identified by the false, manipulative tone of their discourse."[35] The logic of the argument is marvelously perverse. Patterns of speech that are adaptations to inequalities in power are depicted as natural characteristics of the subordinate group, a move that has, in turn, the great advantage of underlining the innate inferiority of its members when it comes to logic, truth, honesty, and reason and thereby justifying their continued domination by their betters.

Control and Fantasy—The Basis of the Hidden Transcript

> When vengeance is tabled, it turns into an illusion, a personal religion, a myth which recedes day by day from its cast of characters, who remain the same in the myth of vengeance.
> —MILAN KUNDERA, *The Joke*

It is plain enough thus far that the prudent subordinate will ordinarily conform by speech and gesture to what he knows is expected of him—even if that conformity masks a quite different offstage opinion. What is not perhaps plain enough is that, in any established system of domination, it is not just a question of masking one's feelings and producing the correct speech acts and gestures in their place. Rather it is often a question of controlling what would be a natural impulse to rage, insult, anger, and the violence that such feelings prompt. There is no system of domination that does not produce its own routine harvest of insults and injury to human dignity—the appropriation of labor, public humiliations, whippings, rapes, slaps, leers, contempt, ritual denigration, and so on. Perhaps the worst of these, many slave narratives agree, was not personal suffering but rather the abuse of one's child or spouse while one had little choice but to look on helplessly. This inability to defend oneself or members of one's family (that is, to act as mother, father, husband, or wife) against the abuses of domination is simultaneously an assault on one's physical body and one's personhood or dignity. The cruelest result of human bondage is that it transforms the assertion of personal dignity into a mortal risk. Conformity in the face of domination is thus occasionally—and unforgettably—a question of suppressing a violent rage in the interest of oneself and loved ones.

We may capture the existential dilemma at work here by contrasting it briefly with Hegel's analysis of the duelist. A person challenges another to a duel because he judges that his honor and standing (including often that of his family) have been mortally insulted. He demands an apology or retraction, failing which his honor can be satisfied only by a duel to the death. What the challenge to a duel says, symbolically, is that to accept this insult is to lose standing, without which life is not worth living (the ideal code, seldom rigorously followed, of the warrior aristocrat). Who wins the duel is symbolically irrelevant; it is the challenge that restores honor. If the challenger loses, he paradoxically wins his point by demonstrating that he was willing to wager his physical life in order to preserve his honor, his name. The very logic of the duel makes its status as an ideal apparent; any code that preaches the assertion of standing and honor at the expense of life itself is likely to have many lukewarm adherents in a pinch.

For most bondsmen through history, whether untouchables, slaves, serfs, captives, or minorities held in contempt, the trick to survival, not always mastered by any means, has been to swallow one's bile, choke back one's rage, and conquer the impulse to physical violence. It is this systematic *frustration of reciprocal action* in relations of domination which, I believe, helps us understand much of the content of the hidden transcript. At its most elementary level the hidden transcript represents an acting out in fantasy—and occasionally in secretive practice—of the anger and reciprocal aggression denied by the presence of domination.[36] Without the sanctions imposed by power relations, subordinates would be tempted to return a blow with a blow, an insult with an insult, a whipping with a whipping, a humiliation with a humiliation. It is as if the "voice," to use Albert Hirschman's term, they are refused in the public transcript finds its full-throated expression backstage. The frustration, tension, and control necessary in public give way to unbridled retaliation in a safer setting, where the accounts of reciprocity are, symbolically at least, finally balanced.[37]

Later in this analysis I will want to move beyond the elementary, individual, and psychologistic view of the hidden transcript to its cultural determinants, its elaboration, and the forms in which it is expressed. For the moment, however, it is crucial to recognize that there is an important wish-fulfillment component to the hidden transcript.[38]

The greater part of Richard Wright's account, in *Black Boy,* of his youth in Mississippi is infused with his attempt to control his anger when in the presence of whites and, in turn, to give vent to that anger in the safety of black company.[39] His effort at stifling his anger is a daily, conscious effort—one that does not always succeed:

> Each day in the store I watched the brutality with growing hate, yet trying to keep my feelings from registering in my face. When the boss looked at me I would avoid his eyes.[40]

> I feared that if I clashed with whites I would lose control of my emotions and spill out the words that would be my sentence of death.[41]

Among his friends during work breaks, the talk frequently turned to fantasies of retaliation and revenge. The fantasies are explicit and often take the form of rumors about what has happened elsewhere. For example,

> "Yeah, if they hava race riot round here, I'm gonna kill all the white folks with my poison."

> "My momma says, that old white woman where she works talked 'bout slapping her and ma said, 'Miz Green, if you slaps me, I'll kill you and go to hell to pay for it!'"

> "They say a white man hit a colored man up north and that colored man hit that white man, knocked him cold, and nobody did a damned thing!"[42]

Wright explains that a "latent sense of violence" surrounded all the offstage talk about whites and that such talk was the "touchstone of fraternity" among the black boys who gathered at the crossroads.

Further evidence for the link between the practical need to control anger and its reflection in fantasy may be illustrated by the findings of a remarkable, if deeply flawed, study of the psychological consequences of racial domination on blacks written in the 1940s: Abram Kardiner and Lionel Ovesey's *The Mark of Oppression*.[43] As they understand it, any response to an all-powerful other will be some combination of idealization and hatred. The behavioral expression— whether with manipulative intent or not—of idealization would be ingratiation. Idealization might also take the form of emulation—the use of skin-lightening creams, hair straighteners, and other attempts to distance oneself from the oppressors' stereotype of blacks. This last strategy, for all but a very few, is bound to be futile. What is relevant for our purposes, however, is that both ingratiation and emulation (up to a point) readily find an outlet in the public transcript, precisely because they reaffirm the superiority of the dominant group. The equivalent manifestations of hatred—we may call them insolence and rejection— cannot, by definition, however, be expressed openly in the public transcript. They must either be insinuated cleverly into the public transcript to avoid retaliation or else be expressed offstage. The hidden transcript comes, in this way, to be the repository of the assertions whose open expression would be dangerous.

In their summaries of individual profiles, Kardiner and Ovesey emphasize that the major psychological problem for blacks was the control of aggression and its consequences. The aggression they find is not unconsciously repressed so much as consciously suppressed. One of their subjects, G. R., is described as being aware of his anger and capable of expressing it, but only when it is safe to do so. "This means that he is engaged in a constant process of control. He must be ever vigilant and he dare not act or speak on impulse."[44] Putting the issue in terms appropriate to virtually any subordinate group, they conclude,

> The conspicuous feature of rage lies in the fact that it is an emotion that primes the organism for motor expression. Hate is an attenuated form of rage, and is the emotion toward those who inspire fear and rage. The difficult problem for those who are constantly subject to frustration is how to contain this emotion and prevent its motor expression. The chief motive for the latter is to avoid setting into motion retaliatory aggression.[45]

The effort to control open aggression, in the knowledge that it leads almost inevitably to harsh retaliation, was not always successful. Those who did assert themselves defiantly won themselves a place in black folklore—that of the "baaaad Nigger"—that is one of both admiration and fearful awe. Admiration, for having acted out the hidden transcript and fearful awe, for having often paid for it with their lives. As we shall see later, the more common folk hero of subordinate groups—blacks included—has historically been the trickster figure, who manages to outwit his adversary and escape unscathed.

Some indirect evidence for the effort required to control anger comes from studies of slavery that indicate the circumstances under which the control might momentarily lapse. Gerald Mullin, in his study of slavery in eighteenth-century Virginia, finds repeated evidence that on those occasions when the masters declared a holiday and provided liquor, intoxicated slaves were said to become "aggressive and hostile, insolent, impudent, bold, stubborn."[46] It was as if alcohol loosened slightly the normal inhibitions against aggressive talk, thereby allowing a portion of the hidden transcript to find its way onto the stage.

Whenever a rare event legitimately allowed the black community to vicariously and publicly savor the physical victory of a black man over a white man, that event became an epoch-making one in folk memory. The fight between Jack Johnson and Jim Jeffries (the "White hope") in 1910 and Joe Louis's subsequent career, which was aided by instant radio transmission of the fights, were indelible moments of reversal and revenge for the black community. "When Johnson battered a white man (Jeffries) to his knees, he was the symbolic black man taking out his revenge on all whites for a lifetime of indignities."[47] Lest such moments be seen purely as a safety valve reconciling blacks to their quotidian world of white domination, there were racial fights in every state in the South and in much of the North immediately after the 1910 fight. The proximate causes varied, but it is clear that in the flush of their jubilation, blacks became momentarily bolder in gesture, speech, and carriage, and this was seen by much of the white community as a provocation, a breach of the public transcript. Intoxication comes in many forms.

Fantasy life among dominated groups is also likely to take the form of *schadenfreude:* joy at the misfortunes of others. This represents a wish for negative reciprocity, a settling of scores when the high shall be brought low and the last shall be first. As such, it is a vital element in any millennial religion. Natural events that seem to conform to this wish—as with the Johnson-Jeffries fight— will typically become the focus of symbolic attention. In the case of the black community in the twentieth century, the sinking of the *Titanic* was such an event. The drowning of large numbers of wealthy and powerful whites (the larger losses in steerage were ignored) in their finery aboard a ship that was said to be unsinkable seemed like a stroke of poetic justice to many blacks. It can be said to have "captured the imagination" of blacks in the nearly literal sense of being a prophetic enactment of their hidden transcript. "Official" songs about the loss of the *Titanic* were sung ironically ("It was *saaad* when the great ship went down . . ."). Other songs were composed and sung within the black community. A fragment of one serves to indicate the jubilation at the reversals:

> All the millionaires looked around at Shine [a black
> stoker] say, "Now Shine, oh, Shine, save poor me."
> Say, "We'll make you wealthier than one Shine can be."
> Shine say, "you hate my color and you hate my race."
> Say, "Jump overboard and give those sharks a chase."
> And everybody on board realized they had to die.
> But Shine could swim and Shine could float,
> And Shine could throw his ass like a motorboat.
> Say Shine hit the water with a hell of a splash,
> And everybody wondered if that Black sonovabitch could last.
> Say the Devil looked up from hell and grinned
> Say, "He's a black, *swimming motherfucker.* I think he's gon come
>   on in."[48]

At a more cosmic level we have the effort by subordinate groups to call down a curse on the heads of their aggressors. The elaborate curse, such as that cited earlier which Aggy invoked against her white master before emancipation, embodies a far more complex symbolic message than the individual dream of a specific revenge against a specific oppressor or the glee at the victory of a black prizefighter. The curse is an open prayer—even if confined to the backstage audience—embodying an intricate and lovingly ornate vision or revenge. From the perspective of magic, the curse, if properly prepared and recited, will bring about the wish it expresses. Long after emancipation, in the 1920s, Zora Neale Hurston, black novelist and anthropologist, collected such an elaborate curse from the Deep South. Its length precludes full quotation, but an excerpt will convey its controlled rage:

> O Man God, I beg that this I ask for my enemies shall
>   come to pass
> That the South wind shall scorch their bodies
>   and make them wither and shall not be tempered to
>   them
> That the North wind shall freeze their blood and numb
>   their muscles.
>   . . .

> I pray that death and disease shall be forever with them
> and that their crops shall not multiply and their
> cows, their sheep, their hogs and all their living
> possessions shall die of starvation and thirst.
> . . .
> I pray that their friends shall betray them and cause
> them loss of power, of gold and of silver, and that
> their enemies shall smite them until they beg for
> mercy, which shall not be given them.
> . . .
> O Man God, I ask you for all these things because they
> have dragged me in the dust and destroyed my good
> name; broken my heart and caused me to curse the
> day that I was born. So be it.[49]

Considering the curse in its entirety, it would be difficult to imagine a more comprehensive damnation with all the details visualized. The revenge is explicit in the curse itself, which begins and ends with the invocation of the oppressions for which the curse is just retribution.

To understand the more luxuriant fantasies of the hidden transcript, they must be seen not alone but as the reaction to domination in the public transcript. The inventiveness and originality of these fantasies lie in the artfulness with which they reverse and negate a particular domination.[50] No one recognized this more fully than W. E. B. Du Bois, who wrote of the double-consciousness of the American black arising from racial domination: "Such a double life with double thoughts, double duties, and double social classes, must give rise to double words and double ideals, and *tempt the mind to pretense or revolt, to hypocrisy or radicalism*."[51] Occasionally, Du Bois thought of individual blacks as representing one or the other consciousness. Those given to "revolt" or "radicalism" were those who "stood ready to curse God and die," while those given to "pretense" and "hypocrisy" had forgotten that "life is more than meat and the body more than raiment." We can, I think, more usefully think of the former as the hidden transcript and the latter as the public transcript embodied in the same individual; the former being the site of the rage and anger generated by the necessity of preserving a deferential or obsequious public demeanor despite humiliations. If Du Bois associated the radicalism more with the North and the hypocrisy with the South, this was probably because blacks were somewhat freer to speak their mind in the North.

At this point in the argument, a skeptic might wonder if the official, or public, transcript of power relations serves any purpose at all. Who takes it seriously? We have seen that subordinate groups are generally careful to comport themselves in ways that do not breach the etiquette of power relations determined largely from above. Even then, however, they are quite capable of tactically manipulating appearances for their own ends or using a show of servility to wall off a world beyond direct power relations where sharply divergent views may prevail. Dominant elites, for their part, are unlikely to be completely taken in by outward shows of deference. They expect that there is more here than meets the eye (and ear) and that part or all of the performance is in bad faith. They sense that they are being "jockeyed" even if the harness is of their own devising. If, then, this is all a gigantic shell game in which there is no real dupe, why bother with the pretence? The next chapter [in *Domination and the Arts of Resistance*] addresses this question.

Notes for "Behind the Official Story"

1. *Public* here refers to action that is openly avowed to the other party in the power relationship, and *transcript* is used almost in its juridical sense (*procès verbal*) of a complete record of what was said. This complete record, however, would also include nonspeech acts such as gestures and expressions.
2. Emile Gauillaumin, *The Life of a Simple Man,* ed. Eugen Weber, rev. trans. Margaret Crosland, 83. See also 38, 62, 64, 102, 140, and 153 for other instances.
3. Ibid., 82.
4. Lunsford Lane, *The Narrative of Lunsford Lane, Formerly of Raleigh, North Carolina* (Boston, 1848), quoted in Gilbert Osofsky, ed., *Puttin' on Ole Massa: The Slave Narratives of Henry Bibb, William Wells, and Solomon Northrup,* 9.
5. *A Diary from Dixie,* quoted in Orlando Patterson, *Slavery and Social Death: A Comparative Study,* 208.
6. Ibid., 338.
7. I bracket, for the moment, the possibility that the offstage retraction or the public rupture may itself be a ruse designed to mislead. It should be clear, however, that there is no satisfactory way to establish definitively some bedrock reality or truth behind any particular set of social acts. I also overlook the possibility that the performer may be able to insinuate an insincerity into the performance itself, thereby undercutting its authenticity for part or all of his audience.
8. This is not to assert that subordinates have nothing more to talk about among themselves than their relationship to the dominant. Rather it is merely to confine the term to that segment of interaction among subordinates that bears on relations with the powerful.
9. *My Story of the War,* quoted in Albert J. Raboteau, *Slave Religion: The "Invisible Institution" of the Antebellum South,* 313.
10. *Adam Bede,* 388–89.
11. Ibid., 393.
12. Ibid., 394.
13. Ibid., 398.
14. Ibid., 388.
15. We are, I think, apt to have the same fantasy when we are bested in argument among equals or insulted by a peer. The difference is simply that asymmetrical power relations do not interfere with the declaration of the hidden transcript in this case.
16. Ibid., 395. For readers unfamiliar with *Adam Bede* who would like to know how things turned out, the squire died providentially some months later, lifting the threat.

17. *Inside the Whale and Other Essays*, 95–96.
18. Similar inequalities are not nearly so symbolically charged in Western capitalist democracies, which publicly are committed to defend property rights and make no claims to be run for the particular benefit of the working class.
19. We all recognize homely versions of this truth. It is, parents sense, unseemly to argue publicly in front of their children, especially over their discipline and conduct. To do so is to undercut the implicit claim that parents know best and are agreed about what is proper. It is also to offer their children a political opportunity to exploit the revealed difference of opinion. Generally, parents prefer to keep the bickering offstage and to present a more or less united front before the children.
20. Ray Huang, *1571: A Year of No Significance*.
21. *The New Class*, 82.
22. I suspect that it is for essentially the same reason that the subordinate staff in virtually any hierarchical organization tend to work in open view while the elite work behind closed doors, often with anterooms containing private secretaries.
23. *A Harlot High and Low [Splendeurs et misères des courtisanes]*, trans. Reyner Happenstall, 505. The twentieth-century literary figure who made the masks of domination and subordination the center of much of his work was Jean Genet. See, in particular, his plays *The Blacks* and *The Screens*.
24. I overlook, deliberately for the moment, the fact that there are for any actor several public and hidden transcripts, depending upon the audience being addressed.
25. *Inside the Whale*, 91. A shouted insult seems hardly a hidden transcript. What is crucial here is the "safe distance" that makes the insulter anonymous: the message is public but the messenger is hidden.

Notes for
"Domination, Acting and Fantasy"

1. James C. Scott, *Weapons of the Weak: Everyday Forms of Peasant Resistance*.
2. *Discipline and Punish: The Birth of the Prison*, trans. Alan Sheridan.
3. My analysis is thus less relevant to forms of *impersonal* domination by say, "scientific techniques," bureaucratic rules, or by market forces of supply and demand. Much of Michel Foucault's work bears on those, for him, quintessentially modern forms of social control. While I believe many apparently impersonal forms of control are mediated by a personal domination that is, and is experienced as, more arbitrary than Foucault would allow, I take his point that there is something qualitatively different about claims to authority based on impersonal, technical, scientific rules.
4. For a similar argument about the structuralist or positional basis of feminist theory, see Lind Alcoff, "Cultural Feminism versus Post-structuralism: The Identity Crisis in Feminist Theory."
5. For an example of separate spheres analyzed in remarkable depth among Bedouin women, see Lila Abu-Lughod, *Veiled Sentiments: Honor and Poetry in a Bedouin Society*.
6. Howard Newby, "The Deferential Dialectic," 142. I am much indebted in this brief discussion to Newby's illuminating analysis.
7. The exception, perhaps, is when one can plausibly read in the act of deference itself the insinuation of another attitude altogether—for example, a "Yes, Sir" in a tone of

voice or with a sneer that implies contempt. Even here, however, we would want to verify such an impression.

8. *Slavery and Social Death,* 11.
9. Basil Bernstein, *Class, Codes and Control,* vol. 1.
10. A great deal of important information is purposely omitted from this illustration. As depicted, it is entirely static and does not allow for the development and interaction of transcripts over time. It fails to specify the location and circumstances as well as the audience; a slave speaking with a white shopkeeper while making an ordinary transaction is not in the same situation as he would be encountering whites on horseback at night. Finally, it adopts the vantage point of a single individual rather than what might be called the community of discourse. It does, however, serve to orient a discussion of power and discourse—a discussion that might have any number of illustrative cases: serfdom, caste, wage labor, bureaucracy, school.
11. No real social site can be thought of as a realm of entirely "true" and "free" discourse unless, perhaps, it is the private imagination to which, by definition, we can have no access. Disclosure to anyone else immediately brings power relations into play, and psychoanalysis, which aims at the disclosure of repressed truth in a tolerant, encouraging atmosphere, is, at the same time, a highly asymmetrical power relationship.
12. See Juan Martinez-Alier, *Labourers and Landowners in Southern Spain,* 126.
13. Where such domination within domination is pronounced it becomes possible to speak of a hidden transcript within the hidden transcript. Subordinates may be too intimidated by the exercise of domination within the group to say or do anything at odds with what is required. Notice also that when such a situation develops, power-holders among subordinates may well come to have something of a vested interest in the overall pattern of domination that is a precondition of their own power.
14. Arlie Russell Hochschild, *The Managed Heart: The Commercialization of Human Feeling,* 90–91. This fine, perceptive study of airline flight attendants who are paid, in part, for what Hochschild calls "emotional work" has helped me think through several important issues.
15. The effort to stifle anger necessary for a successful performance and its failure to prevail against a growing rage is the leit-motif of Jean Rhys's fine early novels. Julia, the central character in *After Leaving Mr. McKenzie,* knows how she must please men to live as she prefers, but she can rarely sustain her bad faith performance for long. As Rhys puts it, "She had fits of melancholy when she would lose the self-control necessary to keep up appearances," 27.
16. Thibaut, in an inventory of social psychology findings, agrees: "From the point of view of the individual member of the dyad, the possession of superior power has a number of advantages." "It tends to relieve him of the necessity of paying close attention to his partner's action and being careful in his own actions." John W. Thibaut and Harold Kelley, *The Social Psychology of Groups,* 125.
17. La Bruyère, quoted in Norbert Elias, *Power and Civility,* vol. 2 of *The Civilizing Process,* trans. Edmund Jephcott (originally published in Basel in 1939), 271.
18. *Language and Women's Place,* 10.
19. R. S. Khare, *The Untouchable as Himself: Ideology, Identity, and Pragmatism among the Lucknow Chamars,* 13.
20. *Language and Women's Place,* 27.
21. My discussion here is drawn largely from R. Brown and A. Gilman, "The Pronouns of Powers and Solidarity," in *Language and Social Context,* ed. Pier Paolo Giglioli, 252–82, and chap. 5 of Peter Trudgill, *Sociolinguistics: An Introduction to Language and Society.*

22. John R. Rickford, "Carrying the New Wave into Syntax: The Case of Black English BIN," in *Variation in the Form and Use of Language*, ed. Robert W. Fasold, 98–119.

23. Mark Jürgensmeyer, *Religion as Social Vision: The Movement against Untouchability in 20th Century Punjab*, 92.

24. Robin Cohen, "Resistance and Hidden Forms of Consciousness among African Workers," 8–22.

25. Khare, *The Untouchable as Himself*, 97. Khare and others alert us to the fact that subordinates are, generally, closer observers of the powerful than vice-versa because such observation is a vital safety and survival skill. The slave's or untouchable's "day" depends on an accurate reading of the master's mood; the master's "day" is far more impervious to the mood of his subordinate. For further evidence along these lines, see Judith Rollins, *Between Women: Domestics and their Employers*, and Joan Cocks, *The Oppositional Imagination: Adventures in the Sexual Domain*.

26. Khare, *The Untouchable as Himself*, 130.

27. Quoted in Lawrence Levine, *Black Culture and Black Consciousness*, 101.

28. Theodore Rosengarten, *All God's Dangers: The Life of Nate Shaw*, 545. Nate Shaw did join the Alabama Sharecroppers Union during the depression and used his pistol to defend a neighbor—and union member—whose livestock was being seized by the sheriffs. He was sent to prison for more than a decade, where the mere desire to live out his sentence required constant conformity and self-control. In the violent world of prison, as well, a harmless demeanor may be the most effective means to a successful attack. As Jack Henry Abbot wrote, "You learn to 'smile' him into position. To disarm him with friendliness. So when you are raging inside at anyone you learn to conceal it, to smile or feign cowardice." *In the Belly of the Beast*, 89.

29. See, along these lines, Erving Goffman, *Relations in Public: Microstudies of the Public Order*, 339.

30. *The Uses of Literacy: Aspects of Working Class Life*, 65.

31. Dey Raj Chanana, *Slavery in Ancient India*, 57, cited in Patterson, *Slavery and Social Death*, 207–08.

32. Tetsuo Nanta and Irwin Scheiner, *Japanese Thought in the Tokugawa Period, 1600–1868: Methods and Metaphors*, 40.

33. *Selected Essays of Arthur Schopenhauer*, trans. Ernest Belfort Bax, 341. Quoted in Sander L. Gilman, *Jewish Self-Hatred: Anti-Semitism and the Hidden Language of the Jews*, 243, emphasis added.

34. *Sex and Character*, 146, cited in Gilman, *Jewish Self-Hatred*, 245.

35. Gilman, *Jewish Self-Hatred*, 243–44.

36. One might, speculatively, imagine a useful parallel analysis of the cultural products of hatred and anger that cannot find direct expression on the one hand, and the cultural products of love that cannot find direct expression on the other. At one extreme, apocalyptic visions of a world upside down and, at the other, a poetry of complete mystical union with the beloved. If we were to proceed in terms of Habermas's analysis of the "ideal speech situation," the hidden transcript would represent the whole reciprocal conversational reply of the subordinate, which, for reasons of domination, cannot be spoken openly. Habermas excludes, by definition, all "strategic" action and dominated discourse from the ideal speech situation and, hence, from the search for rational consensus. What domination achieves, in this context, is the fragmentation of discourse, so that much of what would be a cohesive, integrated discourse is sequestered into the hidden transcript of the subordinate and the hidden transcript of the dominant. See, for example, Thomas McCarthy, *The Critical Theory of Jürgen Habermas*, 273–352.

37. Something very like this equilibrium view of the hidden transcript is invoked by Hochschild in the relatively benign world of flight attendants: "But in the public world of work, it is often part of an individual's job to accept uneven exchanges, to be treated with disrespect or anger by a client, all the *while closeting into fantasy the anger one would like to respond with.* Where the customer is king, unequal exchanges are normal, and from the beginning customer and client assume different rights to feeling and display. The ledger is supposedly evened by a wage." The fantasy in this case involves mostly imagined acts of retaliation to insults of the "what I would like to do if I didn't have to be prudent" kind. Flight attendants thus "pictured" themselves trading insults with abusive passengers, spilling drinks on their laps, putting large doses of a laxative in their coffee, and so forth. Wish fulfillment this most definitely is. *The Managed Heart,* 85–86.

38. Understanding the hidden transcript in this fashion might seem the equivalent of calling it the site of "ressentiment," as Nietzsche used the term. "Ressentiment" arises from the repeated repression of feelings of hatred, envy, and revenge that cannot be acted out. In this respect, at least, the term fits. But for Nietzsche, the psychological dynamics of "ressentiment" depend on these emotions having *literally* no possible outlet—no externalization—so that they come eventually to lie below the level of conscious thought. In our case, it is the social site of the hidden transcript that provides the opportunity for these emotions to take a collective, cultural form and be acted out. As Scheler notes, once an "ill-treated servant can vent his spleen in the ante-chamber, he will remain free from the inner venom of ressentiment" Max Scheler, *Ressentiment,* trans. William W. Holdheim, ed. Lewis A. Coser. See Friedrich Nietzsche, *On The Geneaology of Morals,* trans. Waiter Kaufman and F. J. Hollingsdale, particularly First Essay, sections 8, 10, 11, 13; Second Essay, sections 14–16. I was made aware of the relevance of Nietzsche's concept by the fine sociological study of contemporary domestic servants by Judith Rollins, *Between Women.*

39. *Black Boy: A Record of Childhood and Youth.*

40. Ibid., 159.

41. Ibid., 175.

42. Ibid., 67–69.

43. Subtitled *Explorations in the Personality of the American Negro.* This book is in the tradition of the "modal personality" school of cultural studies that Kardiner pioneered.

44. Ibid., 104.

45. Ibid., 304. Kardiner and Ovesey went to some lengths to secure an unbiased picture of the fantasy life of their subjects. Results of Rorschach Tests and Thematic Apperception Tests (TATS), both standard projective tests, were submitted to a panel for blind evaluation. Here, in an imaginative realm with few constraints, the assessment was that "the bulk of their emotional strivings are organized along the lines of aggression. Their inner existences are turbulent with the urge to hit out, hurt, and destroy." The protocols were frequently the mirror image of the control and measured words required in the public transcript of domination. Here one found much of the released violence and revenge that was otherwise suppressed. Ibid., 322.

46. *Flight and Rebellion: Slave Resistance in 18th Century Virginia,* 100. Wright, *Black Boy,* 162, quotes a drunken black man saying the following couplet: "All these white folks dressed so fine / Their ass-holes smell just like mine." For drink and self-assertion among women, see, for example, Mary Field Belenky et al., *Womens' Ways of Knowing: The Development of Self, Voice, and Mind,* esp. 25.

47. Al-Tony Gilmore, *Bad Nigger!: The National Impact of Jack Johnson,* 5. Knowing the likely impact of showing the film, local and state authorities passed ordinances against its being shown in local theaters. Ibid., 76–82.

48. D. C. Dance, ed., *Shuckin' and Jivin': Folklore from Contemporary Black Americans,* 215–16. The reversals here and elsewhere in the song are multiple. Shine, the black stoker from the hot engine room below decks, swims home to new sexual triumphs while the white passengers on the upper decks plunge with the ship to the cold bottom of the sea.

49. Quoted by Alice Walker, "Nuclear Exorcism," 20. Alice Walker began a speech at a nuclear disarmament rally with this curse in an effort to explain why many blacks were not much interested in signing nuclear freeze petitions. Their "hope for revenge" made them look on nuclear destruction brought about by a white-ruled world with equanimity if not malevolent pleasure. One has, she implies, no right expecting civic spiritedness from those whose experience of community has mostly been that of victims.

50. A standard and much commented on traditional woman's fantasy involves an inversion of dependency in which the dominant male, in this case the object of affection, would be imagined as becoming blind or crippled and thus helpless. The woman entertaining such a fantasy imagines both the harm and the devoted care that would demonstrate both power and affection.

51. "On the Faith of the Fathers," in his *The Souls of Black Folk,* 221–22.

Reading 26

THE GANGES' NEXT LIFE

Alexander Stille

Shortly after dawn, Veer Bhadra Mishra, a silver-haired Brahman in a traditional Indian dhoti, or loincloth, walks slowly and stiffly down a long, steep stairway from his temple in the city of Varanasi to the banks of the Ganges, as he has done almost every day of his fifty-eight years. All around him, along a seven-kilometre stretch of the river dominated by majestic, crumbling temples, palaces, and ashrams, the pageant of Indian life passes by. Tens of thousands of bathers, at eighty different ghats, or landing areas, plunge into India's holiest body of water. White-bearded ascetics raise their emaciated arms to salute the sun god; housewives in bright-colored saris toss garlands of marigolds to Mother Ganges, the river goddess; adolescent boys in G-stings do pushups, flex their muscles, and wash their bodies; naked children splash in the water; and families carry their dead to the "burning ghats" to cremate them and scatter their ashes on the river.

The tug of these traditions, some of which go back three thousand years, to the founding of Varanasi (also known as Banaras), the holiest city in India, pulls Mishra to the river, despite having suffered a broken thigh, which makes walking painful. But on this particular day, in early March, he remains on the bank, because of a nagging cold and also because of the poor quality of the water: it is filled with raw sewage, human and industrial waste, the charred remains of bodies, and animal carcasses. Normally, Mishra tries to perform five full immersions—five is an auspicious number, he explains. But even when he is feeling well he holds his nose as he puts his head in, and he no longer drinks the river water.

"There is a struggle and turmoil inside my heart," Mishra says. "I want to take a holy dip. I need it to live. The day does not begin for me without the holy

Stille, Alexander. "the Ganges' Next Life." *The New Yorker*. Jan. 19, 1998. 58–67.

dip. But, at the same time, I know what is B.O.D."—biochemical oxygen demand—"and I know what is fecal coliform." He is referring to some of the scientific indices of water pollution.

For Mishra, this struggle of the heart is particularly acute because he has a complex double identity: he is the mahant—the head—of Sankat Mochan Temple, one of the principal temples of Varanasi, and he is also a professor of hydraulic engineering at Banaras Hindu University.

As a devout Hindu, Mishra views the Ganges as a goddess, a river that, because of its divine origin, is pure and purifies all those faithful who immerse themselves in her. Just as Muslims vow to visit Mecca, it is the dream of all good Hindus to visit Varanasi and bathe in the Ganges at least once in their lives. It is said that one drop of Ganges water carried by a breeze that lands on your cheek hundreds of miles away is enough to cleanse a lifetime of sins. All Hindus seek to have their ashes scattered along the Ganges at their deaths, and it is considered particularly lucky to die in Varanasi, because from there your soul will travel straight to Heaven.

But, as a scientist, Mishra cannot forget what he knows about the condition of the river water. Up in the temple complex behind him stands a state-of-the-art laboratory where bacteria cultures are being grown in special incubators in order to measure the level of pathogens at various points along the river. In some places at Varanasi, the fecal-coliform count has been known to reach a hundred and seventy million bacteria per hundred millilitres of water—a terrifying three hundred and forty thousand times the acceptable level of five hundred per hundred millilitres.

Some five hundred million people—one out of every twelve people in the world—now live in the basin of the Ganges and its tributaries. A hundred and fourteen cities dump their raw sewage directly into the river, which starts at Nepal, in the Himalayas, flows fifteen hundred miles through India and Bangladesh, and empties into the Bay of Bengal at Calcutta. Not surprisingly, waterborne illnesses—hepatitis, amebic dysentery, typhoid, and cholera—are common killers, helping to account for the deaths of more than two million Indian children each year.

What is particularly disturbing about these numbers is that they come at the end of a ten-year government cleanup project called the Ganga Action Plan—a project that most people, even in government, concede has failed. Now the government is preparing for the second phase of the Ganga Action Plan, and Mishra is trying to keep the government from repeating its mistakes: he is pushing a new plan to save the river.

The battle to clean the Ganges is about much more than the environmental future of a river. Just as the river is a symbol of India, its cleanup is a test of India's condition fifty years after independence, and its outcome may answer some of the fundamental questions about the country's future. Will India (and other parts of the Third World) master its problems, or will it descend into a nightmarish Malthusian struggle over diminishing natural resources? Will India find creative ways to preserve its rich cultural traditions, or will it become homogenized into the new global economy? Will its ancient rituals, such as bathing in the Ganges, survive beyond the next century?

Varanasi is one of the oldest continuously occupied cities in the world, contemporary with the dynasties of ancient Egypt or Mesopotamia. But while no one sacrifices to the Egyptian sun god Ra or to Baal anymore, some sixty thousand devotees take the holy dip each day in Varanasi, lighting fires along the shores of the Ganges to Lord Shiva, the god who is believed to have caught the river in the tangled locks of his hair as it descended to earth from Heaven.

"Please consider them an endangered species, these people who still have this faith, this living relationship with the river," Mishra says with passion. "If birds can be saved, if plants can be saved, let this species of people be saved by granting them holy water."

Mishra, as the mahant of Sankat Mochan Temple, is himself the living link to one of Varanasi's most cherished legacies. He is spiritual heir to a greatly revered Hindu saint, Tulsi Das, who in the sixteenth century wrote a famous Hindi version of the Ramayana, one of the most important texts of Hinduism, originally written in Sanskrit. Mahantji, as Mishra is almost universally known in Varanasi (Indians add the suffix "ji" to a name to denote affection and respect), lives, with his family, in the house that Tulsi Das built, overlooking the Ganges and above the landing Tulsi Ghat. The house contains an original manuscript of Tulsi Das's Ramayana and a pair of the saint's wooden sandals. Mishra's position as mahant, which has been passed from father to son in his family for many generations, accords him a semidivine status among the disciples of Tulsi Das. As Mishra is speaking about things like biomass and biogas, a steady stream of worshippers stop by to touch his feet—a traditional sign of respect in India.

Mishra wears his status lightly. He is a person of exquisite courtesy and genuine warmth, without a hint of arrogance or self-regard. He has a handsome tan face, dark-brown eyes, an elegant head of white hair with a shock of black in the center, and a gray mustache. If his lower body is slow and awkward, from his broken thigh, his face is highly mobile and expressive, as if to underscore the Hindu belief that the body is but an imperfect vessel for the noble spirit. He smiles easily and laughs a lot, frequently at himself. He jokes about his "throne room"—the name his Western friends have teasingly given a room where he receives guests. It is in fact a modestly decorated room on the ground floor of his house, in which a large wooden platform covered with mattresses provides the mahant a place to sit cross-legged or lean back on a cushion. He dresses almost invariably in nothing but a light-blue dhoti—a single swath of cotton that wraps around his waist and covers his shoulders like a toga—and generally goes barefoot. The one exception is when he lectures at the university: then he puts on a pair of loafers and a brown Western-style suit, in which he looks somewhat ill at ease.

In 1982, after years of speaking out about the deteriorating condition of the river, Mishra founded, with two other engineers from Banaras Hindu University, the Sankat Mochan Foundation, a private secular organization dedicated to cleaning the Ganges. This has taken Mishra far from the traditional, religious role of mahant and brought him into contact with politicians in New Delhi, American State Department officials, and environmentalists and scientists around the world. Overcoming a certain amount of criticism and ridicule among some Hindus in Varanasi, he has travelled to places like Sydney, New York, and San Francisco in order to attend water-resource conferences and explore alternative waste technologies. Like India itself on the eve of the millennium, Mishra is trying to incorporate what is best from the West in order to preserve the Hindu traditions that he loves.

In his attempt to clean the Ganges, the mahant finds himself teamed with a seeming unlikely partner—William Oswald, an emeritus professor of engineering at Berkeley, who is a gray-haired seventy-eight-year-old with elephantlike ears, two hearing aids, an impish smile, and an earthy sense of humor. On being told that the Hindus believed that they would go straight to Heaven if they died in Varanasi, Oswald replied, "They'll get there a lot faster if they go in that water."

Mishra and Oswald were brought together by Friends of the Ganges, a San Francisco–based group of environmentalists who have been working closely with the Sankat Mochan Foundation to help find a solution to Varanasi's water-pollution problems.

Oswald is the pioneer of a kind of "back to the future" approach to modern urban waste, called Advanced Integrated Wastewater Pond Systems, in which sewage is treated in a carefully engineered series of natural algae ponds. Waste decomposes naturally in water through a combination of microbial fermentation and photosynthesis. It works like this: In a pond, bacteria grow on sewage and, in the process, decompose it into its elements—carbon, nitrogen, hydrogen, oxygen, etc. Algae in the pond assimilate these nutrients and, as their green biomass grows, produce oxygen through photosynthesis. Algae are the most efficient producers of oxygen on the planet: they supply more than one and a half times their weight in oxygen, and are the largest single source of atmospheric oxygen in the air we breathe. The oxygen that algae produce sustains the aquatic life of a pond or a river; fish both feed on algae and breathe the oxygen that algae produce; bacteria also use the oxygen to keep the process of decomposition going in a self-sustaining cycle of creation and decay.

Oswald is to algae what Michael Jordan is to basketball. When he and I first met, in Delhi, he excused himself in advance for not remembering my name: "For every new person's name I learn, I forget the name of an alga." Back in the late sixties, at the request of the United States Air Force's space program, Oswald invented something called the Algatron—a system for growing algae in space to provide oxygen for astronauts. Although it has been tried out only on mice in a California laboratory, Oswald proved, in principle, that you could create a self-sustaining ecosystem in a weightless environment. In his view, algae are among the great unacknowledged heroes of the planet. Algae and bacteria have a symbiotic relationship that performs miracles in converting toxic or disease-carrying waste into oxygen, new plant life, and valuable protein for other forms of life to feed on.

Oswald's system is not a utopian environmentalist's fantasy. Before the age of mechanical treatment plants, ponds were one of the primary means of taking care of sewage. They are cheaper than mechanical treatment plants and clean wastewater more thoroughly, but they generally require more land. As a result, most major United States cities have switched to mechanized plants in recent decades, relegating pond systems to smaller cities and towns—some seventy-five hundred of them throughout the United States.

Oswald has devoted his life to devising pond systems that improve on nature's by handling waste in an accelerated fashion while using less space. He has created a system that moves water, by means of gravity and paddle wheels, through a linked sequence of ponds, each with its own special environment, meant to encourage a particular kind of waste treatment. The first group of ponds are dug very deep, in order to create a dark, sunless environment without oxygen, where anaerobic bacteria decompose the heavier solid wastes. The second group are shallow, so that all the water is exposed to sunlight in order to encourage algae to grow through photosynthesis and kill off harmful bacteria. The third ponds are deep, still ponds, in which the algae settle and can be easily "harvested," to be fed to pigs or chickens, or else left in the water for fish farming. In the final phase, the water passes into large, reservoirlike ponds from which it will be reused in irrigation.

This technology appears ideally suited to India, one of whose most abundant resources is sunlight. And it seems fitting that the scientific key to the modern problems of Varanasi, one of India's most ancient cities, could be one of the most ancient and also one of the simplest life-forms: algae.

In 1994, Mishra travelled to Northern California and visited three pond systems built by Oswald. Last summer, Earl Kessler, a member of the State Department's Agency for International Development, or AID, sent a delegation as well. Kessler was sufficiently impressed to commission both Oswald and Mishra's Sankat Mochan Foundation to prepare a feasbility study for a waste-pond system at Varanasi. Last spring, Oswald and his partner, Bailey Green, an acquaintance of mine, were scheduled to fly to India in order to complete the study and try to win Indian government support for the plan, and I decided to accompany them.

When we arrived, Mishra and two of his close colleagues at the foundation presented the American engineers with a surveyor's map they had prepared of the area where the ponds would be constructed, with carefully traced markings for ground elevation and soil composition. Oswald and Green have proposed a system of thirty-two ponds in a dried-up river channel near the island of Dhab, downstream from Varanasi. They spread the map on a table in a guesthouse overlooking a grassy lawn where a colored tent and a marigold-festooned stage were decked out for the foundation's annual festival of *dhrupad*—the most ancient form of Indian classical music—which was to begin later that evening.

As they pored over the map, Oswald worried about possible hitches in the successful completion of the pond project, which, if it should be carried out, would be the largest of his career. "Are you sure that a dike that is seventy-five metres above sea level will be high enough for the monsoon?" he asked. During the last thirty years, Oswald had seen many ambitious pond projects in the Third World evaporate for a host of technical, political, and financial reasons. But, after fifteen years of work, the mahant was anxious that the project's momentum not be slowed by nettlesome details. "We will show that Dr. Oswald's pond system can work even in India," he said grandly.

"I don't want to be a hero," responded Oswald the pragmatist. "I just want to be right."

The musicians outside began to tune up their instruments, and the conversation about the soil composition of the proposed pond site continued to the drone of sitars. The musicians played until six-thirty in the morning, and as we lay under our mosquito nets later that night ancient ragas ran through our waking and sleeping thoughts.

The following afternoon, we set off by boat down the Ganges to examine the site where the ponds would be constructed. There were about twenty of us on a long, flat, beat-up wooden boat with a put-put motor and a canvas sheet stretched over us for protection against the midday sun. Besides us visitors and the mahant, the passengers were mostly volunteers from the Varanasi area, devotees of the temple who also donated their time to the Clean the Ganges campaign. (The foundation can afford only two full-time staff members. Its laboratory was provided through the efforts of the Swedish chapter of Friends of the Ganges, and one of Mishra's household servants doubles as a laboratory assistant.)

Because Tulsi Ghat is at the far south end of Varanasi, the trip took us in slow motion past the entire city. The ghats rise up dramatically out of the water, at the top of tall stairways, and so serve as a kind of two-way theatre: people on the ghats observe the activity on the river below, while those passing by in boats observe the doings of people up above.

Although Varanasi is the chief center of Hindu learning and culture, almost every religious practice and every region of India are represented along the river. There is a ghat for the Dandi Panth ascetics and a ghat leading to a temple surrounded by erotic Nepalese sculptures. There are pagodalike ghats reminiscent of southern India, and fortresslike ghats, which recall the Mogul conquerors of the north. Some ghats are old and are built of sombre, earth-colored stone; others are made of modern concrete and are painted white, yellow, pink, red, or green.

Along with all the different religious practices, all the different forms of pollution along the Ganges were similarly evident. There were ghats where herds of water buffalo cooled off in the water. At others, washerwomen rinsed out their laundry on the shore while a rainbow of colored saris lay drying on the steps. Hinduism contains many rituals of purification and hygiene, including a prohibition against using soap in the Ganges, which is widely ignored.

After a few minutes, we slowly passed the first of the burning ghats. At all hours of the day and night, the funeral pyres burn on the shore, with family members circling the fire and saying prayers. When the firewood has been consumed, the remains of the dead are consigned to the river to begin their journey from this world to the next, but in some cases the bodies may not have been fully consumed. On the average, about forty thousand traditional funerals are performed on the banks of the Ganges at Varanasi each year. In addition, about three thousand other dead bodies—those of people too poor to afford a funeral—and about nine thousand dead cattle are tossed into the river annually. As part of the government's Ganga Action Plan, close to twenty-nine thousand turtles were released at Varanasi a few years ago, in the hope that they would consume any decomposing body parts. But the turtle farm is now empty, and there are no turtles in the river. Many people suspect that they were poached for food.

The government cleanup, however, did include the building of an electric crematorium at one of the two main burning ghats, in order to cut back on the traditional funerals. The program seems to be working, for the lines in front of the brick crematorium are much longer than the ones in front of the firewood sellers. This, in Mishra's view, is an instance of India's adaptability: "The reasons are economic," he explained. "A traditional funeral today will cost between fifteen hundred and two thousand rupees, and the charge for the electric crematorium is seventy rupees."

The traditional forms of Indian life visible along the shores of the Ganges—the funeral pyres, the water buffalo, the washerwomen—are not the principal source of pollution at Varanasi. Looking closely, even along the bathing ghats you can see large sewage pipes draining directly into the river. The city's trunk sewer, which was built by the British in 1917, is strained beyond capacity. As recently as fifty years ago, the population of Varanasi was just over a quarter million; how it is a million four hundred thousand, and growing.

Upon leaving Varanasi, we reached the point where the Varuna River meets the Ganges, and there the surface of the water was bubbling like soup on a low flame—raw sewage turning into methane gas. Just a mile or so up the Varuna is a huge new pumping station, which is supposed to transport Varanasi's sewage to a large treatment plant a few miles downstream. Able to handle but a fraction of the city's two hundred million litres of sewage per day, the plant pumps the sewage of Varanasi up several hundred yards, only to dump the bulk of it into the Varuna, where it then travels back to the Ganges.

A few miles farther downstream, there was a sudden explosion of algae blooms, in such unnatural quantities that for several hundred yards the Ganges took on the unhealthy appearance of a swamp. It is here that the Indian government has placed its treatment plant, but the plant only performs what in the waste business is called "primary treatment"—the equivalent of going through just the first of Oswald's four ponds. Because the plant's "cleaned" effluent is still full of sewage and harmful bacteria, it, together with the hot Indian sun, stimulates the growth of far more algae than the natural resources of the river can absorb. As they decompose they consume, rather than create, oxygen, putting a strain on the marine life of the river. This condition shows up when the oxygen level of the water is tested in a laboratory: biological oxygen demand, or B.O.D., is one of the principal measures of water pollution. Where pollution places a high demand on oxygen, less is available for fish and other organisms.

The central government, in New Delhi, has recently spent about a hundred and fifty million dollars building Western-style high-technology wastewater plants along the Ganges, like the one we just passed, which are particularly ill-suited to Indian conditions. The treatment facilities run on electricity, and when the power goes out—as happens several times a day in many Indian cities—they stop operating. Similarly, the plants become overwhelmed during the monsoon season and simply shut down. Even when they are working, the facilities are so expensive and so difficult to operate that many of the cities say they cannot afford to maintain them.

In Varanasi, sewage is backing up into people's toilets or forming fetid puddles in their yards and in the streets. Local residents became so enraged about a year ago that they forced a city water engineer to stand for several hours in a pool of sewage in order to better acquaint him with the problem.

After decades of supporting this type of expensive, high-technology project, the United States State Department is now a proponent of "sustainable technology"—projects like Oswald's ponds, which cost less, use little electricity, and can be maintained with relatively little training by local people. (The pond system designed for Varanasi is estimated to cost between ten and sixteen million dollars, as opposed to twenty-five million for the city's mechanized treatment plant, which handles only a quarter to a third as much waste.)

In 1985, the government in New Delhi also adopted Western waste-treatment technology without considering the radically different ways that people use the rivers in India. It is still common in Europe for sewage-treatment plants to discharge partly cleaned effluent into rivers, but the inhabitants of London and Paris would not dream of bathing in or drinking out of the Thames or the Seine. "They have made such blunders," the mahant said. "It is like a theme park of failed technology."

Although our trip downriver to the island of Dhab was only about ten miles long, it took us nearly five hours, because the boat kept running aground. With each successive stop, more members of our party were out in the river pushing the boat and fewer of us were in it. The small Western contingent was calculating the probability of catching some dread tropical disease if it was forced to take an unanticipated holy dip to reach shore.

The Ganges is generally a mile wide throughout its course, but it becomes shallow in the dry months leading up to the summer monsoon. The problem has grown worse in recent years as more and more river water has been diverted for irrigation. Throughout our journey, we saw large pipes sucking water out of the Ganges toward distant fields. While India has twenty per cent of the world's people, it has only four per cent of the world's fresh water. With its population approaching a billion, the country is scheduled to overtake China as the world's most populous nation, and its future growth could mean mass starvation. Some three hundred million Indians are already classified as "Food Insecure"—a bad monsoon away from starvation.

Under these circumstances, wars over water—a prospect that haunts the twenty-first century—have already become a reality in India. India and Bangladesh have come close to breaking off diplomatic relations over the use of Ganges water. And in 1994 the Indian state of Haryana simply diverted a sizable portion of New Delhi's water supply, claiming it needed the water for irrigation. The struggle for water can only get worse as India's growing urban population demands Western standards of plumbing. The seventeen five-star hotels of New Delhi consume eight hundred thousand litres of water daily—enough to fulfill the requirements of a million three hundred thousand slum dwellers, who have no plumbing whatever. And as the number of flush toilets increases so will the amount of sewage.

As I was contemplating the prospect of ecological Armageddon during our on-again, off-again voyage in the shallow waters of the Ganges, we heard the distant sound of a brass band. A large crowd was massed on the banks of the island of Dhab, and, even though it was nearly sunset and they had been waiting all afternoon, they greeted the arrival of the Sankat Mochan Foundation and its Western guests with triumphal music and wild jubilation.

Dhab is one of the pockets of rural India that have been largely left out of the past fifty years of development: it has no electricity and no year-round bridge to the mainland. About ten miles long, Dhab, with a population of forty thousand, has a curious geographical configuration: it is an island during the rainy season and a tenuous part of the mainland the rest of the year. As the course of the Ganges gradually shifted over centuries toward the southeast, it exposed a former channel to the north of the island, which can be crossed during the drier months of the year but still floods during the summer. This wide former river channel is sandy and infertile, and has no proper road. It is here that the Sankat Mochan Foundation would like to put its system of wastewater ponds. The plan also involves building three main roads across the dikes of the ponds to connect Dhab to the mainland—roads that cable could be laid in, providing the electric spark that would connect the people of Dhab to the rest of the world.

Amid cries of "Hail to the gods!" we climbed up the banks of a shore thick with eagerly waiting crowds, who were waving painted banners and were ready to hand us armfuls of carefully stitched flower wreaths. So we proceeded slowly, in cars sent ahead by the foundation, stopping at every village cluster for a new celebration. Again and again, there were bands and painted banners, and entire canopies of marigolds. At each stop, mothers sent their children forward to touch our feet, lay on wreaths, and say prayers.

It was dark before we reached our final stop and the main ceremony, in which we were invited to eat a sticky orange sweet and drink some lemon tea. The mahant and the elected chiefs of the villages read a declaration. The people of Dhab stated their support for the Oswald pond project. The declaration ended with the fervent hope that this good deed would bring them *mukti* and *bhukti*— liberation in the next life and happiness in this one.

The wild sense of expectation and hope on the island—the sense that the pond project would instantly transform people's lives for the better—was both moving and sobering. While there is a legitimate worry about the levelling effect of every remote outpost's plugging into the world grid, Dhab's desire to be part of the wider world is palpable and overpowering. On a clear night, villagers on certain parts of the island can see the lights of a distant railroad yard. They stand and watch this bright symbol of the world they yearn to be a part of—a world of lights, power tools, modern appliances, and, of course, television.

"Our moral responsibility is now very great," the mahant said as we set off for Varanasi amid final cheers.

The next ten days back at Tulsi Ghat were filled with activity on various fronts. The foundation members were trying to set up a series of high-level seminars in which to present the American engineers and their plan to local officials, including the mayor of Varanasi; to technocrats at the Water Commission in Lucknow, the capital of the state of Uttar Pradesh, the region in which Varanasi lies; and to national ministers, politicians, and environmental activists at a major conference in New Delhi. Oswald and Green were working day and night with their pencils and calculators, as they drew up a new set of site-specific engineering plans and came up with precise figures on the money and the land that would be needed to build the pond system. Staff members and volunteers of the foundation were trying to track down things like the cost of moving a ton of earth in Varanasi.

Also during those ten days a stream of special visitors passed through the mahant's "throne room": engineers, village chiefs, politicians, local bureaucrats, university professors—anyone thought to have access to some important decision-making body. In between meetings, the mahant was on his cordless phone,

lining up support and making sure that people who had promised to attend a particular meeting would actually show up.

The day after we returned from the island, Mishra received a phone call
from a member of the Indian parliament representing Varanasi, who was eager
to hear about the trip. The people of Dhab had evidently become so disappointed
with the traditional politicians that they would no longer receive them. It seemed
that the mahant had inadvertently uncovered a small political gold mine—a unified group of approximately twenty-five thousand highly motivated voters. As a
result, the mahant found himself in the role of power broker—a role in which he
felt some discomfort. "We are not political people, and it is still not clear to me
what we should do with this consensus," he explained to me, as we sat in the
throne room overlooking the Ganges.

And yet perhaps the only way to realize the pond project is through judiciously applied political pressure. "We have to have a more effective way to
influence the politicians and harness the support we have built," Mishra said. So
far, the political work appears to be paying off. The foundation has succeeded in
winning the support of both the central government in New Delhi and the
municipal government of Varanasi. The final obstacle to building the ponds
remains the state government of Uttar Pradesh.

In the midst of all this engineering, organizing, and politicking, life at Tulsi
Ghat continued as if it were a medieval village within the city: Devotees trooped
through at all hours to worship at one of several pagodalike shrines in the courtyard. Sanskrit students passed through on their way to a school that the temple
runs. Behind Mishra's house is an arena with a round corrugated-tin roof, in
which each morning young men practiced a traditional form of Hindu wrestling.
Sacred cows also wandered through, while goats walked into the shrines to eat
the flowers that worshippers had left for the gods.

While this ritual-filled life moved at the stately pace of the Ganges, the
activity of the Sankat Mochan Foundation marched to the high-pitched squeal of
the fax machine. Mishra himself shuttled between these two worlds, finding
time, despite long meetings and conferences, to keep up his religious duties,
from his holy dip at dawn to the closing ceremonies at the temple, which sometimes did not end until midnight. Somewhere in between, he and I managed to
have a series of conversations about his own double role as holy man and environmental activist, and about his own curious blend of science and Hinduism.
"Even in my wildest dreams, I would not have thought that something like this
would happen in my life," the mahant said, with a burst of laughter. Nothing in
Mishra's early life prepared him for a life of science and political activism. "My
father and my grandfather had the traditional education, which means Sanskrit
and wrestling and music," he said. "There was no reason to deviate." In 1952,
Mishra's father died, and Mishra, only fourteen, had the role of mahant thrust
upon him. His destiny seemed even more fixed. "From that time onward, there

would be a distance between me and the other people," he said, rather ruefully. "Because of traditional respect, even old people would come and touch my feet to pay respect, so there was no intimate interaction. My life was very protected."

When Mishra reached the age of seventeen, however, he made a radical and unprecedented move: he enrolled at Banaras Hindu University: "I don't know why this happened," he said, his voice rising with genuine perplexity. "In my family, I am the first person to go to the university." When he got there, his path became even more unusual: he started taking science courses. "Why I studied physics, chemistry, and mathematics, I don't know. Why I became a civil engineer with a specialty in hydraulics, I don't know. I can now see this as a scheme of the god."

Although there are no other known cases of someone's combining the vocation of mahant and that of civil engineer, it seems typical of India's uncanny ability to preserve its culture while surviving countless foreign occupations and absorbing new influences, from the Persians and the Islamic Mogul conquerors to the departure of the British, in 1947. The Indian writer Gita Mehta, in her latest book "Snakes and Ladders," tells a story that sums up this quality of Indian culture very well:

There were two men who were considered the holiest in India, one called the Diamond-Hard Ascetic and the other called the Field of Experience. The Diamond-Hard Ascetic challenged his rival to a duel to prove that he was the holiest of all. I have become so hard through countless austerities, he said, that you can strike me with a sword of steel. And indeed the sword bounced off him. When he took the sword to the Field of Experience, it simply went through him, at which point the Ascetic conceded that the other man was holier.

The Field of Experience is India: seeming to offer no resistance, it is nevertheless impregnable. Other traditional societies—like China, Burma, and nations governed under strict Islamic law—preserve themselves by steeling themselves against the outside world, but they may become much more vulnerable as they begin to open up. India is a wide-open society, through which numerous armies have marched, and yet it remains remarkably itself.

India's economy, which has been frequently written off, came to life as a result of a policy of liberalization started in 1991. Growing at the rate of six per cent a year ever since, India has been enjoying a boom similar to China's, but it has done so while remaining the world's largest democracy. Though its problems, in their scale, are almost unimaginable, so are its assets. It has more poor people than any other country in the world, but it also has a huge well-educated middle class. More than a hundred million Indians speak English, the lingua franca of the computer world, which is more than the number of speakers of English in Great Britain, Australia, and New Zealand combined. It is not an accident that software developers have turned to India for highly skilled software engineers. Half a world away, computer companies in Silicon Valley send their work problems to technicians in Bangalore, and those technicians work on them all day while the people in California sleep. Bill Gates arrived in Delhi while I was there, and his arrival was accorded the pomp of Queen Victoria's Diamond Jubilee during the days of Raj.

"These things—satellite television, this Internet surfing—are with us whether we like it or not," Mishra says. "They are means. They can be used in a beautiful way. It is as if you were riding a lion—you should be strong enough to tame the lion, or it will eat you." In keeping with that spirit, the Sankat Mochan Foundation is believed to be the first group in Varanasi to sign up for an E-mail and Internet connection.

This extremely open attitude toward the outside, however, has—so far, at least—in no way lessened the country's intense religiosity. To a remarkable degree, Indians have adapted new technology to their own traditional purposes. When Indian television broadcast a movie version of the Ramayana, many Indian families moved their sets up onto their household altars and worshipped before them. Some observers might be scandalized by this, but these people were not worshipping the television; they were worshipping their gods. In Varanasi, on the night celebrating the wedding anniversary of the gods Shiva and Parvati, I saw numerous shrines to Shiva elaborately decorated with flashing electric lights, pulsing to the beat of Indi-pop disco music. To Western eyes, these shrines, built around an ancient phallic symbol and decked out like entrances to Las Vegas night clubs, seemed sacrilegious and surreal, but ordinary Indians were clustered around them in devout worship, just as they would have been a generation or a millennium ago.

"I think in India this lion will be tamed!" Mishra said, with a delighted laugh, when I mentioned the disco shrine.

The mahant is also convinced that science and religion have to mesh if the Ganges is to be saved. The Western approach, based on fear of a possible ecological disaster, will not work, he said. "If you go to people who have a living relationship with Ganga and you say, 'Ganga is polluted, the water is dirty,' they will say, 'Stop saying that. Ganga is not polluted. You are abusing the river.' But if you say 'Ganga is our mother. Come and see what is being thrown on the body of your mother—sewage and filth. Should we tolerate sewage being smeared on the body of our mother?' you will get a very different reaction, and you can harness that energy."

One attraction of the Oswald pond system is that it seems to combine modern science with traditional Hindu ideas, relying mainly on the self-cleansing properties of nature. Indeed, there is a curious parallel between Oswald's descriptions of the self-sustaining ecology of a pond system and certain traditional Hindu beliefs about the fundamental nature of the universe. "All living organisms fit into one of three categories," Oswald explained to me. "Either they are producers, like algae and other plants that create oxygen, or they are consumers, like cows, which eat plants, or human beings, who eat plants and cows, or they are decomposers, like fungi, which dispose of things when they're dead." Hinduism, in its mythopoetic description of the universe, may have intuited something similar. Mishra told me, "There are three gods: Brahma, the creator, Vishnu, the sustainer, and Shiva, the god who provides us happiness in this world, which is decaying every day."

When I pointed out the analogy to Mishra, he seemed fascinated. "What did Professor Oswald say when you mentioned this?" he asked. I told him that Oswald had replied, with humor, "I'll leave that to your literary imagination. If I go back to California talking about Lord Shiva, they'll put me in a straitjacket."

Mishra, however, sees no necessary contradiction between the mythological and the scientific. Indeed, the practice of harnessing the metaphors of Hindu mythology to create a new environmental ethos is common in India. Even secular magazines, like *India Today,* invoke Lord Krishna's love of the forest in writing about the need for protection against the denuding of the Indian landscape. "With the Clean the Ganges campaign," Mishra says, "a meaning has been given to my religious background and to my scientific background. If both these backgrounds were not there, probably I would not have done this." He concludes by saying, "Life is like a stream. One bank is the Vedas"—the earliest Hindu Sanskrit texts—"and the other bank is the contemporary world, which includes science and technology. If both banks are not firm, the water will scatter. If both banks are firm, the river will run its course."

Reading 27

THE ROOTS OF DEBATE IN EDUCATION AND THE HOPE OF DIALOGUE

Deborah Tannen

The teacher sits at the head of the classroom, feeling pleased with herself and her class. The students are engaged in a heated debate. The very noise level reassures the teacher that the students are participating, taking responsibility for their own learning. Education is going on. The class is a success.

But look again, cautions Patricia Rosof, a high school history teacher who admits to having experienced that wave of satisfaction with herself and the job she is doing. On closer inspection, you notice that only a few students are participating in the debate; the majority of the class is sitting silently, maybe attentive but perhaps either indifferent or actively turned off. And the students who are arguing are not addressing the subtleties, nuances, or complexities of the points they are making or disputing. They do not have that luxury because they want to win the argument—so they must go for the most gross and dramatic statements they can muster. They will not concede an opponent's point, even if they can see its validity, because that would weaken their position. Anyone tempted to synthesize the varying views would not dare to do so because it would look like a "cop-out," an inability to take a stand.

One reason so many teachers use the debate format to promote student involvement is that it is relatively easy to set up and the rewards are quick and obvious: the decibel level of noise, the excitement of those who are taking part. Showing students how to integrate ideas and explore subtleties and complexities is much harder. And the rewards are quieter—but more lasting.

Tannen, Deborah. "The Roots of Debate in Education and the Hope of Dialogue." *The Argument Culture: Moving from Debate to Dialogue.* New York: Random House, 1998. 256–290.

Our schools and universities, our ways of doing science and approaching knowledge, are deeply agonistic. We all pass through our country's educational system, and it is there that the seeds our adversarial culture are planted. Seeing how these seeds develop, and where they came from, is a key to understanding the argument culture and a necessary foundation for determining what changes we would like to make.

Roots of the Adversarial Approach to Knowledge

The argument culture, with its tendency to approach issues as a polarized debate, and the culture of critique, with its inclination to regard criticism and attack as the best if not the only type of rigorous thinking, are deeply rooted in Western tradition, going back to the ancient Greeks.[1] This point is made by Walter Ong, a Jesuit professor at Saint Louis University, in his book *Fighting for Life.* Ong credits the ancient Greeks[2] with a fascination with adversativeness in language and thought. He also connects the adversarial tradition of educational institutions to their all-male character. To attend the earliest universities, in the Middle Ages, young men were torn from their families and deposited in cloistered environments where corporal, even brutal, punishment was rampant. Their suffering drove them to bond with each other in opposition to their keepers—the teachers who were their symbolic enemies. Similar in many ways to puberty rites in traditional cultures, this secret society to which young men were confined also had a private language, Latin, in which students read about military exploits. Knowledge was gleaned through public oral disputation and tested by combative oral performance, which carried with it the risk of public humiliation. Students at these institutions were trained not to discover the truth but to argue either side of an argument—in other words, to debate. Ong points out that the Latin term for school, *ludus,* also referred to play or games, but it derived from the military sense of the word—training exercises for war.

If debate seems self-evidently the appropriate or even the only path to insight and knowledge, says Ong, consider the Chinese approach. Disputation was rejected in ancient China as "incompatible with the decorum and harmony cultivated by the true sage."[3] During the Classical periods in both China and India, according to Robert T. Oliver, the preferred mode of rhetoric was exposition rather than argument. The aim was to "enlighten an inquirer," not to "overwhelm an opponent." And the preferred style reflected "the earnestness of investigation" rather than "the fervor of conviction." In contrast to Aristotle's trust of logic and mistrust of emotion, in ancient Asia intuitive insight was considered the superior means of perceiving truth. Asian rhetoric was devoted not to devising logical arguments but to explicating widely accepted propositions. Furthermore, the search for abstract truth that we assume is the goal of philosophy, while taken for granted in the West, was not found in the East, where philosophy was concerned with observation and experience.

If Aristotelian philosophy, with its emphasis on formal logic, was based on the assumption that truth is gained by opposition, Chinese philosophy offers an alternative view. With its emphasis on harmony, says anthropologist Linda Young, Chinese philosophy sees a diverse universe in precarious balance that is maintained by talk. This translates into methods of investigation that focus more on integrating ideas and exploring relations among them than on opposing ideas and fighting over them.

Onward, Christian Soldiers

The military-like culture of early universities is also described by historian David Noble, who describes how young men attending medieval universities were like marauding soldiers: The students—all seminarians—roamed the streets bearing arms, assaulting women, and generally creating mayhem. Noble traces the history of Western science and of universities to joint origins in the Christian Church. The scientific revolution, he shows, was created by religious devotees setting up monastery-like institutions devoted to learning. Early universities were seminaries, and early scientists were either clergy or devoutly religious individuals who led monklike lives. (Until as recently as 1888, fellows at Oxford were expected to be unmarried.)

That Western science is rooted in the Christian Church helps explain why our approach to knowledge tends to be conceived as a metaphorical battle: The Christian Church, Noble shows, has origins and early forms rooted in the military. Many early monks[4] had actually been soldiers before becoming monks. Not only were obedience and strict military-like discipline required, but monks saw themselves as serving "in God's knighthood," warriors in a battle against evil. In later centuries, the Crusades brought actual warrior-monks.

The history of science in the Church holds the key to understanding our tradition of regarding the search for truth as an enterprise of oral disputation in which positions are propounded, defended, and attacked without regard to the debater's personal conviction. It is a notion of truth as objective, best captured by formal logic, that Ong traces to Aristotle. Aristotle regarded logic as the only trustworthy means for human judgment; emotions get in the way: "The man who is to judge would not have his judgment warped by speakers arousing him to anger, jealousy, or compassion. One might as well make a carpenter's tool crooked before using it as a measure."[5]

This assumption explains why Plato wanted to ban poets from education in his ideal community. As a lover of poetry, I can still recall my surprise and distress on reading this in *The Republic* when I was in high school. Not until much later did I understand what it was all about.[6] Poets in ancient Greece were wandering bards who traveled from place to place performing oral poetry that persuaded audiences by moving them emotionally. They were like what we think of as demagogues: people with a dangerous power to persuade others by getting them all worked up. Ong likens this to our discomfort with advertising in schools, which we see as places where children should learn to think logically, not be influenced by "teachers" with ulterior motives who use unfair persuasive tactics.

Sharing Time: Early Training in School

A commitment to formal logic as the truest form of intellectual pursuit remains with us today. Our glorification of opposition as the path to truth is related to the development of formal logic, which encourages thinkers to regard truth seeking as a step-by-step alternation of claims and counterclaims.[7] Truth, in this schema, is an abstract notion that tends to be taken of context. This formal approach to learning is taught in our schools, often indirectly.

Educational researcher James Wertsch shows that schools place great emphasis on formal representation of knowledge. The common elementary school practice of "sharing time" (or, as it used to be called, "show-and-tell") is a prime arena for such training. Wertsch gives the example of a kindergarten pupil named Danny who took a piece of lava to class.[8] Danny told his classmates, "My mom went to the volcano and got it." When the teacher asked what he wanted to tell about it, he said, "I've always been taking care of it." This placed the rock at the center of his feelings and his family: the rock's connection to his mother, who gave it to him, and the attention and care he has lavished on it. The teacher reframed the children's interest in the rock as informational: "Is it rough or smooth?" "Is it heavy or light?" She also suggested they look up "volcano" and "lava" in the dictionary. This is not to imply that the teacher harmed the child; she built on his personal attachment to the rock to teach him a new way of thinking about it. But the example shows the focus of education on formal rather than relational knowledge—information about the rock that has meaning out of context, rather than information tied to the context: Who got the rock for him? How did she get it? What is his relation to it?

Here's another example of how a teacher uses sharing time to train children to speak and think formally. Sarah Michaels spent time watching and tape-recording in a first-grade classroom. During sharing time, a little girl named Mindy held up two candles and told her classmates, "When I was in day camp we made these candles. And I tried it with different colors with both of them but one just came out, this one just came out blue and I don't know what this color is.' The teacher responded, "That's neat-o. Tell the kids how you do it from the very start. Pretend we don't know a thing about candles. OK, what did you do first? What did you use?" She continued to prompt: "What makes it have a shape?" and "Who knows what the string is for?" By encouraging Mindy to give information in a sequential manner, even if it might not seem the most important to her and if the children might already know some of it, the teacher was training her to talk in a focused, explicit way.

The tendency to value formal, objective knowledge over relational, intuitive knowledge grows out of our notion of education as training for debate. It is a legacy of the agonistic heritage. There are many other traces as well. Many Ph.D. programs still require public "defenses" of dissertations or dissertation proposals, and oral performance of knowledge in comprehensive exams. Throughout our educational system, the most pervasive inheritance is the conviction that issues have two sides, that knowledge is best gained through debate, that ideas should be presented orally to an audience that does its best to poke holes and find weaknesses, and that to get recognition, one has to "stake out a position" in opposition to another.

Integrating Women in the Classroom Army

If Ong is right, the adversarial character of our educational institutions is inseparable from their all-male heritage. I wondered whether teaching techniques still tend to be adversarial today and whether, if they are, this may hold a clue to a dilemma that has received much recent attention: that girls often receive less attention and speak up less in class.[9] One term I taught a large lecture class of 140 students and decided to take advantage of this army (as it were) of researchers to answer these questions. Becoming observers in their own classrooms, my students found plenty of support for Ong's ideas.

I asked the students to note how relatively adversarial the teaching methods were in their other classes and how the students responded. Gabrielle DeRouen-Hawkins's description of a theology class was typical:

> The class is in the format of lecture with class discussion and participation. There are thirteen boys and eleven girls in the class. In a fifty-minute class:
> Number of times a male student spoke: 8
> Number of times a female student spoke: 3
> . . . In our readings, theologians present their theories surrounding G-D, life, spirituality and sacredness. As the professor (a male) outlined the main ideas about the readings, he posed questions like "And what is the fault with

/Smith's/ basis that the sacred is individualistic?" The only hands that went up were male. Not one female <u>dared</u> challenge or refute an author's writings. The only questions that the females asked (and all female comments were questions) involved a problem they had with the content of the reading. The males, on the other hand, openly questioned, criticized, and refuted the readings on five separate occasions. The three other times that males spoke involved them saying something like: "/Smith/ is very vague in her theory of XX. Can you explain it further?" They were openly argumentative.[10]

This description raises a number of fascinating issues. First, it gives concrete evidence that at least college classrooms proceed on the assumption that the educational process should be adversarial: The teacher invited students to criticize the reading. (Theology, a required course at Georgetown, was a subject where my students most often found adversarial methods—interestingly, given the background I laid out earlier.) Again, there is nothing inherently wrong with using such methods. Clearly, they are very effective in many ways. However, among the potential liabilities is the risk that women students may be less likely to take part in classroom discussions that are framed as arguments between opposing sides—that is, debate—or as attacks on the authors—that is, critique. (The vast majority of students' observations revealed that men tended to speak more than women in their classes—which is not to say that individual women did not speak more than individual men.)

Gabrielle commented that since class participation counted for 10 percent of students' grades, it might not be fair to women students that the agonistic style is more congenial to men. Not only might women's grades suffer because they speak up less, but they might be evaluated as less intelligent or prepared because when they did speak, they asked questions rather than challenging the readings.

I was intrigued by the student's comment "/Smith/ is very vague in her theory of XX. Can you explain it further?" It could have been phrased "I didn't understand the author's theory. Can you explain it to me?" By beginning "The author is vague in her theory," the questioner blamed the author for his failure to understand. A student who asks a question in class risks appearing ignorant. Prefacing the question this way was an excellent way to minimize that risk.

In her description of this class, Gabrielle wrote that not a single woman "<u>dared</u> challenge or refute" an author. She herself underlined the word "dared." But in reading this I wondered whether "dared" was necessarily the right word. It implies that the women in the class wished to challenge the author but did not have the courage. It is possible that not a single woman *cared* to challenge the author. Criticizing or challenging might not be something that appealed to them or seemed worth their efforts. Going back to the childhoods of boys and girls, it seems possible that the boys had had more experiences, from the time they were small, that encouraged them to challenge and argue with authority figures than the girls had.

This is not to say that classrooms are more congenial to boys than girls in every way. Especially in the lowest grades, the requirement that children sit quietly in their seats seems clearly to be easier for girls to fulfill than boys, since many girls frequently sit fairly quietly for long periods of time when they play, while most boys' idea of play involves at least running around, if not also jumping and roughhousing. And researchers have pointed out that some of the extra attention boys receive is aimed at controlling such physical exuberance. The adversarial aspect of educational traditions is just one small piece of the pie, but it seems to reflect boys' experiences and predilections more than girls'.

A colleague commented that he had always taken for granted that the best way to deal with students' comments is to challenge them; he took it to be self-evident that this technique sharpens their minds and helps them develop debating skills. But he noticed that women were relatively silent in his classes. He decided to try beginning discussion with relatively open questions and letting comments go unchallenged. He found, to his amazement and satisfaction, that more women began to speak up in class.

Clearly, women can learn to perform in adversarial ways. Anyone who doubts this need only attend an academic conference in the field of women's studies or feminist studies—or read Duke University professor Jane Tompkins's essay showing how a conference in these fields can be like a Western shoot-out. My point is rather about the roots of the tradition and the tendency of the style to appeal initially to more men than women in the Western cultural context. Ong and Noble show that the adversarial culture of Western science and its exclusion of women were part and parcel of the same historical roots—not that individual women may not learn to practice and enjoy agonistic debate or that individual men may not recoil from it. There are many people, women as well as men, who assume a discussion must be contentious to be interesting. Author Mary Catherine Bateson recalls that when her mother, the anthropologist Margaret Mead, said, "I had an argument with" someone, it was a positive comment. "An argument," to her, meant a spirited intellectual interchange, not a rancorous conflict. The same assumption emerged in an obituary for Diana Trilling, called "one of the very last of the great midcentury New York intellectuals."[11] She and her friends had tried to live what they called "a life of significant contention"—the contention apparently enhancing rather than undercutting the significance.

Learning by Fighting

Although there are patterns that tend to typify women and men in a given culture, there is an even greater range among members of widely divergent cultural backgrounds. In addition to observing adversarial encounters in their current classrooms, many students recalled having spent a Junior year in Germany or

France and commented that American classrooms seemed very placid compared to what they had experienced abroad. One student, Zach Tyler, described his impressions this way:

> I have very vivid memories of my junior year of high school, which I spent in Germany as an exchange student. The classroom was very debate-oriented and agonistic. One particular instance I remember well was in physics class, when a very confrontational friend of mine had a heated debate with the teacher about solving a problem. My friend ran to the board and scribbled out how he would have solved the problem, completely different from the teacher's, which also gave my friend the right answer and made the teacher wrong.

> STUDENT: "You see! This is how it should be, and you are wrong!"
> TEACHER: "No! No! No! You are absolutely wrong in every respect! just look at how you did this!" (He goes over my friend's solution and shows that it does not work.) "Your solution has no base, as I just showed you!"
> STUDENT: "You can't prove that. Mine works just as well!"
> TEACHER: "My God, if the world were full of technical idiots like yourself! Look again!" (And he clearly shows how my friend's approach was wrong, after which my friend shut up.)

In Zach's opinion, the teacher encouraged this type of argument. The student learned he was wrong, but he got practice in arguing his point of view.

This incident occurred in high school. But European classrooms can be adversarial even at the elementary school level, according to another student, Megan Smyth, who reported on a videotape she saw in her French class:

> Today in French class we watched an excerpt of a classroom scene of fifth-graders. One at a time, each student was asked to stand up and recite a poem that they were supposed to have memorized. The teacher screamed at the students if they forgot a line or if they didn't speak with enough emotion. They were reprimanded and asked to repeat the task until they did it perfectly and passed the "oral test."

There is probably little question about how Americans would view this way of teaching, but the students put it into words:

> After watching this scene, my French teacher asked the class what our opinion was. The various responses included: French schools are very strict, the professor was "mean" and didn't have respect for the students, and there's too much emphasis on memorization, which is pointless.

If teaching methods can be more openly adversarial in European than American elementary and high schools, academic debate can be more openly adversarial there as well. For example, Alice Kaplan, a professor of French at Duke University, describes a colloquium on the French writer Céline that she attended in Paris:

> After the first speech, people started yelling at each other. "Are you suggesting that Céline was fascist!" "You call that evidence!" "I will not accept ignorance in the place of argument!" I was scared.[12]

These examples dramatize that many individuals can thrive in an adversarial atmosphere. And those who learn to participate effectively in any verbal game eventually enjoy it, if nothing else than for the pleasure of exercising that learned skill. It is important to keep these examples in mind in order to avoid the impression that adversarial tactics are always destructive. Clearly, such tactics sometimes admirably serve the purpose of intellectual inquiry. In addition to individual predilection, cultural learning plays a role in whether or not someone enjoys the game played this way.

Graduate School as Boot Camp

Although the invective Kaplan heard at a scholarly meeting in Paris is more extreme than what is typical at American conferences, the assumption that challenge and attack are the best modes of scholarly inquiry is pervasive in American scholarly communities as well. Graduate education is a training ground not only for teaching but also for scientific research. Many graduate programs are geared to training young scholars in rigorous thinking, defined as the ability to launch and field verbal attacks.

Communications researchers Karen Tracy and Sheryl Baratz tapped into some of the ethics that lead to this atmosphere in a study of weekly symposia attended by faculty and graduate students at a major research university. When they asked participants about the purpose of the symposia, they were told it was to "trade ideas" and "learn things." But it didn't take too much discussion to uncover the participants' deeper concern: to be seen as intellectually competent. And here's the rub: To be seen as competent, a student had to ask "tough and challenging questions."

One faculty member commented, when asked about who participated actively in a symposium,

> Among the graduate students, the people I think about are Jess, Tim, uh let's see, Felicia will ask a question but it'll be a nice little supportive question.[13]

"A nice little supportive question" diminished the value of Felicia's participation and her intelligence—the sort of judgment a student would wish to avoid. Just as with White House correspondents, there is value placed on asking "tough questions." Those who want to impress their peers and superiors (as most, if not all, do) are motivated to ask the sorts of questions that gain approval.

Valuing attack as a sign of respect is part of the argument culture of academia—our conception of intellectual interchange as a metaphorical battle. As one colleague put it, "In order to play with the big boys, you have to be willing to get into the ring and wrestle with them." Yet many graduate students (and quite a few established scholars) remain ambivalent about this ethic, especially when they are on the receiving rather than the distribution end. Sociolinguist Winnie Or tape-recorded a symposium at which a graduate student presented her fledgling research to other students and graduate faculty. The student later told Or that she left the symposium feeling that a truck had rolled over her. She did not say she regretted having taken part. she felt she had received valuable feedback. But she also mentioned that she had not looked at her research project once since the symposium several weeks before. This is telling. Shouldn't an opportunity to discuss your research with peers and experts fire you up and send you back to the isolation of research renewed and reinspired? Isn't something awry if it leaves you not wanting to face your research project at all?

This young scholar persevered, but others drop out of graduate school, in some cases because they are turned off by the atmosphere of critique. One woman who wrote to me said she had been encouraged to enroll in graduate school by her college professors, but she lasted only one year in a major midwest university's doctoral program in art history. This is how she described her experience and her decision not to continue:

> Grad school was the nightmare I never knew existed. . . . Into the den of wolves I go, like a lamb to slaughter. . . . When, at the end of my first year (masters) I was offered a job as a curator for a private collection, I jumped at the chance. I wasn't cut out for academia—better try the "real world."

Reading this I thought, is it that she was not cut out for academia, or is it that academia as it was practiced in that university is not cut out for people like her. It is cut out for those who enjoy, or can tolerate, a contentious environment.

(These examples remind us again of the gender dynamic. The graduate student who left academia for museum work was a woman. The student who asked a "nice little supportive question" instead of a "tough, challenging one" was a woman. More than one commentator has wondered aloud if part of the reason women drop out of science courses and degree programs is their discomfort with the agonistic culture of Western science. And Lani Guinier has recently shown that discomfort with the agonistic procedures of law school is partly responsible for women's lower grade point averages in law school, since the women arrive at law school with records as strong as the men's.)

The Culture of Critique:
Attack in the Academy

The standard way of writing an academic paper is to position your work in opposition to someone else's, which you prove wrong. This creates a *need* to make others wrong, which is quite a different matter from reading something with an open mind and discovering that you disagree with it. Students are taught that they must disprove others' arguments in order to be original, make a contribution, and demonstrate their intellectual ability. When there is a *need* to make others wrong, the temptation is great to oversimplify at best, and at worst to distort or even misrepresent others' positions, the better to refute them—to search for the most foolish statement in a generally reasonable treatise, seize upon the weakest examples, ignore facts that support your opponent's views, and focus only on those that support yours. Straw men spring up like scarecrows in a cornfield.

Sometimes it seems as if there is a maxim driving academic discourse that counsels, "If you can't find something bad to say, don't say anything." As a result, any work that gets a lot of attention is immediately opposed. There is an advantage to this approach: Weaknesses are exposed, and that is surely good. But another result is that it is difficult for those outside the field (or even inside) to know what is "true." Like two expert witnesses hired by opposing attorneys, academics can seem to be canceling each other out. In the words of policy analysts David Greenberg and Philip Robins:

> The process of scientific inquiry almost ensures that competing sets of results will be obtained. . . . Once the first set of findings are published, other researchers eager to make a name for themselves must come up with different approaches and results to get their studies published.[14]

How are outsiders (or insiders, for that matter) to know which "side" to believe? As a result, it is extremely difficult for research to influence public policy.

A leading researcher in psychology commented that he knew of two young colleagues who had achieved tenure by writing articles attacking him. One of them told him, in confidence, that he actually agreed with him, but of course he could not get tenure by writing articles simply supporting someone else's work; he had to stake out a position in opposition. Attacking an established scholar has particular appeal because it demonstrates originality and independence of thought without requiring true innovation. After all, the domain of inquiry and the terms of debate have already been established. The critic has only to say, like the child who wants to pick a fight, "Is not!" Younger or less prominent scholars can achieve a level of attention otherwise denied or eluding them by stepping into the ring with someone who has already attracted the spotlight.

The young psychologist who confessed his motives to the established one was unusual, I suspect, only in his self-awareness and willingness to articulate it. More commonly, younger scholars, or less prominent ones, convince themselves that they are fighting for truth, that they are among the few who see that the emperor has no clothes. In the essay mentioned earlier, Jane Tompkins describes how a young scholar-critic can work herself into a passionate conviction that she is morally obligated to attack, because she is fighting on the side of good against the side of evil. Like the reluctant hero in the film *High Noon,* she feels she has no choice but to strap on her holster and shoot. Tompkins recalls that her own career was launched by an essay that

> began with a frontal assault on another woman scholar. When I wrote it I felt the way the hero does in a Western. Not only had this critic argued *a, b,* and *c,* she had held *x, y,* and *z!* It was a clear case of outrageous provocation.[15]

Because her attack was aimed at someone with an established career ("She was famous and I was not. She was teaching at a prestigious university and I was not. She had published a major book and I had not."), it was a "David and Goliath situation" that made her feel she was "justified in hitting her with everything I had." (This is analogous to what William Safire describes as his philosophy in the sphere of political journalism: "Kick 'em when they're up.")[16]

The claim of objectivity is belied by Tompkins's account of the spirit in which attack is often launched: the many motivations, other than the search for truth, that drive a critic to pick a fight with another scholar. Objectivity would entail a disinterested evaluation of all claims. But there is nothing disinterested about it when scholars set out with the need to make others wrong and transform them not only into opponents but into villains.

In academia, as in other walks of life, anonymity breeds contempt. Some of the nastiest rhetoric shows up in "blind" reviews—of articles submitted to journals or book proposals submitted to publishers. "Peer review" is the cornerstone of academic life. When someone submits an article to a journal, a book to a publisher, or a proposal to a funding institution, the work is sent to established scholars for evaluation. To enable reviewers to be honest, they remain anonymous. But anonymous reviewers often take a tone of derision such as people tend to use only when talking about someone who is not there—after all, the evaluation is not addressed to the author. But authors typically receive copies of the evaluations, especially if their work is rejected. This can be particularly destructive to young scholars just starting out. For example, one sociolinguist wrote her dissertation in a firmly established tradition: She tape-recorded conversations at the company where she worked part-time. Experts in our field believe it is best to examine conversations in which the researcher is a natural participant, because when strangers appear asking to tape-record, people get nervous and may change their behavior. The publisher sent the manuscript to a reviewer who was used to different research methods. In rejecting the proposal, she referred to the young scholar "using the audiotaped detritus from an old job." Ouch. What could justify the sneering term "detritus"? What is added by appending "old" to "job," other than hurting the author? Like Heathcliff, the target hears only the negative and—like Heathcliff—may respond by fleeing the field altogether.

One reason the argument culture is so widespread is that arguing is so easy to do. Lynne Hewitt, Judith Duchan, and Erwin Segal came up with a fascinating finding: Speakers with language disabilities who had trouble taking part in other types of verbal interaction were able to participate in arguments. Observing adults with mental retardation who lived in a group home, the researchers found that the residents often engaged in verbal conflicts as a means of prolonging interaction. It was a form of sociability. Most surprising, this was equally true of two residents who had severe language and comprehension disorders yet were able to take part in the verbal disputes, because arguments have a predictable structure.

Academics, too, know that it is easy to ask challenging questions without listening, reading, or thinking very carefully. Critics can always complain about research methods, sample size, and what has been left out. To study anything, a researcher must isolate a piece of the subject and narrow the scope of vision in order to focus. An entire tree cannot be placed under a microscope; a tiny bit has to be separated to be examined closely. This gives critics the handle of a weapon with which to strike an easy blow: They can point out all the bits that were not studied. Like family members or partners in a close relationship, anyone looking for things to pick on will have no trouble finding them.

All of this is not to imply that scholars should not criticize each other or disagree. In the words of poet William Blake, "Without contraries is no progression."[17] The point is to distinguish constructive ways of doing so from nonconstructive ones. Criticizing a colleague on empirical grounds is the beginning of a discussion; if researchers come up with different findings, they can engage in a dialogue: What is it about their methods, data, or means of analysis that explains the different results? In some cases, those who set out to disprove another's claims end up proving them instead—something that is highly unlikely to happen in fields that deal in argumentation alone.

A stunning example in which opponents attempting to disprove a heretical claim ended up proving it involves the cause and treatment of ulcers. It is now widely known and accepted that ulcers are caused by bacteria in the stomach and can be cured by massive doses of antibiotics. For years, however, the cure and treatment of ulcers remained elusive, as all the experts agreed that ulcers were the classic psychogenic illness caused by stress. The stomach, experts further agreed, was a sterile environment: No bacteria could live there. So pathologists did not look for bacteria in the stomachs of ailing or deceased patients, and those who came across them simply ignored them, in effect not seeing what was before their eyes because they did not believe it could be there. When Dr. Barry Marshall, an Australian resident in internal medicine, presented evidence that ulcers are caused by bacteria, no one believed him. His findings were ultimately confirmed by researchers intent on proving him wrong.[18]

The case of ulcers shows that setting out to prove others wrong can be constructive—when it is driven by genuine differences and when it motivates others to undertake new research. But if seeking to prove others wrong becomes a habit, an end in itself, the sole line of inquiry, the results can be far less rewarding.

Believing as Thinking

"The doubting game" is the name English professor Peter Elbow gives to what educators are trained to do. In playing the doubting game, you approach others' work by looking for what's wrong, much as the press corps follows the president hoping to catch him stumble or an attorney pores over an opposing witness's deposition looking for inconsistencies that can be challenged on the stand. It is an attorney's job to discredit opposing witnesses, but is it a scholar's job to approach colleagues like an opposing attorney?

Elbow recommends learning to approach new ideas, and ideas different from your own, in a different spirit—what he calls a "believing game." This does not mean accepting everything anyone says or writes in an unthinking way. That would be just as superficial as rejecting everything without thinking deeply about it. The believing game is still a game. It simply asks you to give it a whirl: Read *as if* you believed, and see where it takes you. Then you can go back and ask whether you want to accept or reject elements in the argument or the whole argument or idea. Elbow is not recommending that we stop doubting altogether. He is telling us to stop doubting exclusively. We need a systematic and respected way to detect and expose strengths, just as we have a systematic and respected way of detecting faults.

Americans need little encouragement to play the doubting game because we regard it as synonymous with intellectual inquiry, a sign of intelligence. In Elbow's words, "We tend to assume that the ability to criticize a claim we disagree with counts as more serious intellectual work than the ability to enter into it and temporarily assent."[19] It is the believing game that needs to be encouraged and recognized as an equally serious intellectual pursuit.

Although criticizing is surely part of critical thinking, it is not synonymous with it. Again, limiting critical response to critique means not doing the other kinds of critical thinking that could be helpful: looking for new insights, new perspectives, new ways of thinking, new knowledge. Critiquing relieves you of the responsibility of doing integrative thinking. It also has the advantage of making the critics feel smart, smarter than the ill-fated author whose work is being picked apart like carrion. But it has the disadvantage of making them less likely to learn from the author's work.

The Socratic Method—Or Is It?

Another scholar who questions the usefulness of opposition as the sole path to truth is philosopher Janice Moulton. Philosophy, she shows, equates logical reasoning with the Adversary Paradigm, a matter of making claims and then trying to find, and argue against, counterexamples to that claim. The result is a debate between adversaries trying to defend their ideas against counterexamples and to come up with counterexamples that refute the opponent's ideas. In this paradigm, the best way to evaluate someone's work is to "subject it to the strongest or most extreme opposition."[20]

But if you parry individual points—a negative and defensive enterprise— you never step back and actively imagine a world in which a different system of ideas could be true—a positive act. And you never ask how larger systems of thought relate to each other. According to Moulton, our devotion to the Adversary Paradigm has led us to misinterpret the type of argumentation that Socrates favored: We think of the Socratic method as systematically leading an opponent into admitting error. This is primarily a way of showing up an adversary as wrong. Moulton shows that the original Socratic method—the *elenchus*—was designed to convince others, to shake them out of their habitual mode of thought and lead them to new insight. Our version of the Socratic method—an adversarial public debate—is unlikely to result in opponents changing their minds. Someone who loses a debate usually attributes that loss to poor performance or to an adversary's unfair tactics.

Knowledge as Warring Camps

Anne Carolyn Klein, an American woman who spent many years studying Tibetan Buddhism, joined a university program devoted to women's studies in religion. It was her first encounter with contemporary feminist theory, which she quickly learned was divided into two warring camps. In one camp are those who focus on the ways that women are different from men. Among these, some emphasize that women's ways are equally valid and should be respected, while others believe that women's ways are superior and should be more widely adopted. Both these views—called "difference feminism"—contrast with those in the other camp, who claim that women are no different from men by nature, so any noticeable differences result from how society treats women. Those who take this view are called "social constructionists."[21]

Klein saw that separating feminist theory into these two camps reflects the Western tendency to rigid dichotomies. Recalling how Buddhist philosophy tries to integrate disparate forces, she shows that there is much to be gained from both feminist views—and, in any case, both perspectives tend to coexist within individuals. For example, even though the constructionist view of gender has won ascendancy in academic theory (that's why we have the epithet "essentialist" to describe those who hold the view that is in disfavor but no commonly used epithet to sneer at the constructionist view), "feminists still struggle to recognize and name the commonalities among women that justify concern for women's lives around the world and produce political and social alliances." Klein asks, "Why protest current conditions unless the category 'women' is in some way a meaningful one?"[22] She shows, too, that the very inclination to polarize varied views of women and feminism into two opposing camps is in itself essentialist because it reduces complex and varied perspectives to simplified, monolithic representations. This also makes it easy to dismiss—and fight about—others' work rather than think about it.

Reflecting this warring-camps view, journalist Cynthia Gorney asked Gloria Steinem, "Where do you stand in the current debate that the feminist world has divided into 'equity' feminism versus 'difference' feminism—about whether women are to be treated like men or as different from men?" This question bears all the earmarks of the adversarial framework: the term "debate" and the separation of a complex domain of inquiry into two opposed sides. Steinem responded:

> [*Sighs.*] Of course, you understand that I've turned up in every category. So it makes it harder for me to take the divisions with great seriousness, since I don't feel attached to any of them—and also since I don't hear about the division from women who are not academics or in the media. The idea that there are two "camps" has not been my experience. The mark to me of a constructive argument is one that looks at a specific problem and says, "What shall we do about this?" And a nonconstructive one is one that tries to label people. "Difference" feminist, "gender" feminist—it has no meaning in specific situations.[23]

In this short comment, Steinem puts her finger on several aspects of the argument culture. First, she identifies academics and journalists as two groups that have a habit of—and a stake in—manufacturing polarization and the appearance of conflict. Second, she points out that this view of the world does not describe reality as most people live it. Third, she shows that polarizing issues into "a debate" often goes along with "labeling" the two sides: Lumping others together and sticking a label on them makes it easy to ignore the nuances and subtleties of their opinions and beliefs. Individuals are reduced to an oversimplification of their ideas, transformed into the enemy, and demonized.

False dichotomies are often at the heart of discord.

Question the Basic Assumption

My aim is not to put a stop to the adversarial paradigm, the doubting game, debate—but to diversify: Like a well-balanced stock portfolio, we need more than one path to the goal we seek. What makes it hard to question whether debate is truly the only or even the most fruitful approach to learning is that we're dealing with assumptions that we and everyone around us take to be self-evident. A prominent dean at a major research university commented to me, "The Chinese cannot make great scientists because they will not debate publicly." Many people would find this remark offensive. They would object because it generalizes about all Chinese scientists, especially since it makes a negative evaluation. But I would also question the assumption that makes the generalization a criticism: the conviction that the only way to test and develop ideas is to debate them publicly. It may well be true that most Chinese scientists are reluctant to engage in public, rancorous debate. I see nothing insulting about such a claim; it derives from the Chinese cultural norms that many Chinese and Western observers have documented. But we also know that many Chinese have indeed been great scientists.[24] The falsity of the dean's statement should lead us to question whether debate is the only path to insight.

Consensus Through Dissension?

The culture of critique driving our search for knowledge in the scientific world of research is akin to what I have described in the domains of politics, journalism, and law. In those three institutions, an increasingly warlike atmosphere has led many people already in those professions to leave, and many who would have considered entering these professions in the past are now choosing other paths. Those who remain are finding it less fun; they don't look forward to getting up and going to work in the same way that they and others used to. And in all these areas, raised voices and tempers are creating a din that is drowning out the perhaps more numerous voices of dialogue and reason. In law, critics of the principle of zealous advocacy object on the grounds of what it does to the souls of those who practice within the system, requiring them to put aside their consciences and natural inclinations toward human compassion—just what some among the press say about what aggression journalism is doing to journalists.

Forces affecting these institutions are intertwined with each other and with others I have not mentioned. For example, the rise of malpractice litigation, while prodding doctors to be more careful and providing deserved recompense to victims, has also made the doctor-patient relationship potentially more adversarial. At the same time, physicians are finding themselves in increasingly adversarial relationships with HMOs and insurance companies—as are the patients themselves, who now need the kind of advice that was offered under the headline "When Your HMO Says No: How to Fight for the Treatment You Need—and Win."[25]

People in business, too, report an increasingly adversarial atmosphere. There are, of course, the hostile takeovers that have become common, along with lawsuits between companies and former employees. But there is also more opposition in the day-to-day doing of business. A man who works at a large computer company in Silicon Valley told me that he sees this daily. Disagreement and verbal attack are encouraged at meetings, under the guise of challenging assumptions and fostering creativity. But in reality, he observes, what is fostered is dissension. In the end, the company's ability to do business can be threatened. He has seen at least one company virtually paralyzed by trying to seek consensus after assiduously stirring up dissension.

Who Will Be Left to Lead?

If this seems to describe an isolated phenomenon in a particular industry, take note: A comparable situation exists in our political life. The culture of critique is threatening our system of governance. Norman Ornstein, a political analyst at the American Enterprise Institute, articulates how.[26]

Ornstein offers some astonishing statistics: Between 1975 and 1989, the number of federal officials indicted on charges of public corruption went up by a staggering 1,211 percent. During the same period, the number of nonfederal officials indicted doubled. What are we to make of this? he asks. Does it mean that officials during that decade were far more corrupt than before? Not likely. Every systematic study, as well as all anecdotal evidence, suggests just the opposite: Public officials are far less corrupt now; fewer take bribes, get drunk in the middle of their duties, engage in immoral conduct, and so on.

What we have is the culture of critique. The press is poised to pounce on allegations of scandal, giving them primacy over every other kind of news. And the standards by which scandals are judged have declined. Allegations make the news, no matter where they come from, often without proof or even verification. (Remember the ruckus that accompanied reports that planes were forced to circle and travelers were delayed while President Clinton got a haircut on Air Force One in the Los Angeles airport?[27] And that George Bush did not know what a supermarket scanner was? Both turned out to be false.) Political opponents seize on these allegations and use them to punish or bring down opponents. The sad result is that laws designed to improve ethics have not improved ethics at all. Instead, they have made government almost impossible. Allegations trigger long investigations that themselves damage reputations and suggest to the public that terrible things are going on even when they aren't.

Prosecutors, too, are part of the web, Ornstein continues. In the past, an ambitious prosecutor might set out to snare a criminal on the FBI's ten most wanted list. Now the temptation is to go after a senator or cabinet member—or a vice president. That's where attention is paid; that's where the rewards lie.

The threat is not only to those at the highest levels of government but to public servants at every level. I spoke to someone prominent in the arts who was invited to join a federal commission. But first there was a questionnaire to fill out—pages and pages of details requested about the prospective nominee's personal, professional, and financial life. Special request was made for anything that might be embarrassing if it became public. The person in question simply declined the invitation.

The artist I spoke to typified a situation Ornstein described: It is becoming almost impossible to get qualified people to serve in public positions, from the highest executive nominations to part-time or even honorary appointments. Leaving private life for public service has always required personal sacrifice: Your family life is disrupted; you take a pay cut. But now those contemplating such a move must be willing to make an even greater sacrifice: putting their personal reputation at risk. Instead of enhancing reputations, going into public services now threatens them, whether or not the officials have done anything to be ashamed of.

Disruption of family life is intensified, too, by the inordinate delay, Ornstein explained. While a nominee waits to be confirmed, life goes on hold: A spouse's job is in limbo; children await a change in schools; houses must—but can't—be found or rented or bought or sold. What is causing the delays to become so much more protracted than they were before? Every step in the process: Presidents (and their staffs) must take much more time in choosing potential nominees, to make absolutely sure there is nothing in their lives or backgrounds that could embarrass not just the nominee but the president. Once people are selected, the FBI takes weeks or months longer than it used to for background checks, because it too wants to make sure it is not embarrassed later. Finally, the nomination goes to the Senate, where political opponents of the president or the nominee try to go for the jugular on ethics charges.

The result of all these forces is a much smaller pool of qualified people willing to consider public service, long periods when important posts are left vacant, a climate of suspicion that reinforces public doubts about the ethics of people in government, and real disruption in the running of our country.

We have become obsessed with the appearance of impropriety, as Peter Morgan and Glenn Reynolds show in a book with that title. Meanwhile, real impropriety goes unnoticed. We have to ask, as Ornstein does, whether the price we're paying to have pristine individuals fill every public post is worth what we're getting—and he (like Morgan and Reynolds) doubts that what we're getting is less impropriety.

The Cost in Human Spirit

Whatever the causes of the argument culture—and the many causes I have mentioned are surely not the only ones—the most grievous cost is the price paid in human spirit: Contentious public discourse becomes a model for behavior and sets the tone for how individuals experience their relationships to other people and to the society we live in.

Recall the way young boys on Tory Island learned to emulate their elders:

> All around milled little boys imitating their elders, cursing, fluffing, swaggering, threatening. It was particularly fascinating to see how the children learned the whole sequence of behavior. Anything that the men did, they would imitate, shouting the same things, strutting and swaggering.[28]

Tory Island may be an especially ritualized example, but it is not a totally aberrant one. When young men come together in groups, they often engage in symbolic ritual displays of aggression that involve posturing and mock battles. Without pressing the parallel in too literal a way, I couldn't help thinking that this sounds a bit like what journalists and lawyers have observed about their own tribes: that the display of aggression for the benefit of peers is often more important than concrete results.

Consider again law professor Charles Yablon's observation that young litigators learn to value an aggressive stance by listening to their elders' war stories about "the smashing victories they obtained during pretrial discovery in cases which ultimately were settled." Litigators

> derive job satisfaction by recasting minor discovery disputes as titanic struggles. Younger lawyers, convinced that their future careers may hinge on how tough they *seem* while conducting discovery, may conclude that it is more important to look and sound ferocious than act cooperatively, even if all that huffing and puffing does not help (and sometimes harms) their cases.[29]

Against this background, recall too the observations made by journalists that their colleagues feel pressured to ask tough questions to get peer approval. Kenneth Walsh, for example, commented that "it helps your stature in journalism" if you ask challenging questions because that way "you show you're tough and you're independent." Just as litigators trade war stories about how tough they appeared (whether or not that appearance helped their client), Walsh points out that a journalist who dares to challenge the president takes on a heroic aura among his peers. He recalled a specific incident to illustrate this point:

> Remember Brit Hume asking the question . . . about the zigzag decision-making process of President Clinton? And of course President Clinton cut off the questions after that one question because he felt it was not appropriate.

That's what we all remember about the Ruth Bader Ginsburg period, is that Brit asked that question.[30]

Let's look at the actual exchange that earned Brit Hume the admiration of his peers. President Clinton called the press conference to announce his nomination of judge Ruth Bader Ginsburg to the Supreme Court. After the president introduced her, Judge Ginsburg spoke movingly about her life, ending with tributes to her family: her children, granddaughter, husband, and, finally, her mother, "the bravest and strongest person I have known, who was taken from me much too soon." Following these remarks, which moved listeners to tears, journalists were invited to ask questions. The first (and, as it turned out, also the last) asked by correspondent Hume was this:

> The withdrawal of the Guinier nomination, sir, and your apparent focus on Judge Breyer and your turn, late, it seems, to Judge Ginsburg, may have created an impression, perhaps unfair, of a certain zigzag quality in the decision-making process here. I wonder, sir, if you could kind of walk us through it and perhaps disabuse us of any notion we might have along those lines. Thank you.

This question reminded everyone—at the very moment of Judge Ginsburg's triumph and honor—that she was not the president's first choice. It broke the spell of her moving remarks by shifting attention from the ceremonial occasion to the political maneuvers that had led up to the nomination—in particular, implying criticism of the president not from the perspective of substance (whether Judge Ginsburg would make a good Supreme Court Justice) but strategy (the decision-making process by which she was chosen). Remarking, "How you could ask a question like that after the statement she just made is beyond me," the president closed the event.

The answer to how Brit Hume could have asked a question like that lies in Walsh's observation that journalists value a display of toughness. In this view, to worry about Judge Ginsburg's feelings—or those of the viewing audience—would be like an attorney worrying about the feelings of a witness about to be cross-examined. But public ceremonies play a role in the emotional lives not only of participants but also of observers, an enormous group in the era of television. Viewers who were moved by Judge Ginsburg's personal statement shared in the ceremony and felt connected to the judge and, by implication, to our judicial system. Such feelings of connection to public figures whose actions affect our lives is a crucial element in individuals' sense of community and their feeling of well-being. Breaking that spell was harmful to this sense of connection, contributing a little bit to what is often called cynicism but which really goes much deeper than that: alienation from the public figures who deeply affect our lives and consequently from the society in which we live.

In this sense, the valuing of the appearance of toughness is related to another theme running through all the domains I discussed: the breakdown in human connections and the rise of anonymity. Lieutenant Colonel Grossman points out that this, too, was one of many ways that the experience of serving in Vietnam was different for American soldiers than was the experience of serving in previous wars. Remember my Uncle Norman, who at the age of eighty-seven was still attending annual reunions of the "boys" he had served with in World War II? This was possible because, as Grossman describes, soldiers in that war trained together, then went to war and served together. Those who were not killed or wounded stayed with the group until they all went home together at the end of the war. No wonder the bonds they forged could last a lifetime. Vietnam, in contrast, was a "lonely war" of individuals assigned to constantly shifting units for year-long tours of duty (thirteen months for Marines). Grossman's description is graphic and sad:

> In Vietnam most soldiers arrived on the battlefield alone, afraid, and without friends. A soldier joined a unit where he was an FNG, a "f——ing new guy," whose inexperience and incompetence represented a threat to the continued survival of those in the unit. In a few months, for a brief period, he became an old hand who was bonded to a few friends and able to function well in combat. But then, all too soon, his friends left him via death, injury, or the end of their tours. . . . All but the best of units became just a collection of men experiencing endless leavings and arrivals, and that sacred process of bonding, which makes it possible for men to do what they must do in combat, became a tattered and torn remnant of the support structure experienced by veterans of past American wars.[31]

Though this pattern is most painful in this context, it parallels what we have seen in all the other domains of public dialogue. Recall attorney Susan Popik's observation "You don't come up against the same people all the time. That encouraged you to get along with them because you knew that in six months, you would be across the table from them again."[32] Recall journalists' lamenting that the present White House press corps is a large group, often unknown to aides and leaders, kept at a distance from the leaders they are assigned to cover: confined in a small room, in the back of the president's plane, behind ropes at public events. Contrast this with the recollections of those old enough to remember a small White House press corps that had free run of official buildings and lots of private off-the-record meetings with public officials, including the president and first lady, so that they actually got to know them—as people. And recall departing Senator Heflin's regret about the decline of opportunities for legislators of opposing parties to socialize, which led to friendships developed "across party and ideological lines" that "led to more openness and willingness to discuss issues on a cordial basis" and to finding "common ground." We could add the demise of the family doctor who came to your home, replaced by an overworked internist or family practitioner—if not an anonymous emergency room—and, if you're unlucky enough to need them but lucky enough to get to see them, a cadre of specialists who may not talk to each other or even much to you, or surgeons who may spend hours saving your life or limb but hardly ever see or speak to you afterward.

In all these domains, wonderful progress has been accompanied by more and more anonymity and disconnection, which are damaging to the human spirit and fertile ground for animosity.

Getting Beyond Dualism

At the heart of the argument culture is our habit of seeing issues and ideas as absolute and irreconcilable principles continually at war. To move beyond this static and limiting view, we can remember the Chinese approach to yin and yang. They are two principles, yes, but they are conceived not as irreconcilable polar opposites but as elements that coexist and should be brought into balance as much as possible. As sociolinguist Suzanne Wong Scollon notes, "Yin is always present in and changing into yang and vice versa."[33] How can we translate this abstract idea into daily practice?

To overcome our bias toward dualism, we can make special efforts not to think in twos. Mary Catherine Bateson, an author and anthropologist who teaches at George Mason University, makes a point of having her class compare *three* cultures, not two.[34] If students compare two cultures, she finds, they are inclined to polarize them, to think of the two as opposite to each other. But if they compare three cultures, they are more likely to think about each on its own terms.

As a goal, we could all try to catch ourselves when we talk about "both sides" of an issue—and talk instead about "all sides." And people in any field can try to resist the temptation to pick on details when they see a chance to score a point. If the detail really does not speak to the main issue, bite your tongue. Draw back and consider the whole picture. After asking, "Where is this wrong?" make an effort to ask "What is right about this?"—not necessarily *instead,* but *in addition.*

In the public arena, producers can try to avoid, whenever possible, structuring public discussions as debates. This means avoiding the format of having two guests discuss an issue, pro and con. In some cases three guests—or one—will be more enlightening than two.

An example of the advantage of adding a third guest was an episode of *The Diane Rehm Show* on National Public Radio following the withdrawal of Anthony Lake from nomination as director of central intelligence. White House Communications Director Ann Lewis claimed that the process of confirming presidential appointments has become more partisan and personal.[35] Tony Blankley, former communications director for Newt Gingrich, claimed that the process has always been rancorous. Fortunately for the audience, there was a third guest: historian Michael Beschloss, who provided historical perspective.

He explained that during the immediately preceding period of 1940 to 1990, confirmation hearings were indeed more benign than they have been since, but in the 1920s and the latter half of the nineteenth century, he said, they were also "pretty bloody." In this way, a third guest, especially a guest who is not committed to one side, can dispel the audience's frustration when two guests make opposite claims.

Japanese television talk shows provide a window on other possibilities. Sociolinguist Atsuko Honda compared three different current affairs talk shows televised in Japan. Each one presents striking contrasts to what Americans take for granted in that genre. (The very fact that Honda chose to compare three—not two—is instructive.) The Japanese shows were structured in ways that made them less likely to be adversarial. Within each structure, participants vigorously opposed each other's ideas, yet they did so without excessively polarizing the issues.

Consider the formats of the three shows: *Nichiyoo Tooron (Sunday Discussion)* featured a moderator and four guests who discussed the recession for an hour. Only the moderator was a professional news commentator; two guests were associated with research institutes. The two other shows Honda examined concerned Japanese involvement in a peacekeeping mission in Cambodia. *Sunday Project* featured three guests: one magazine editor and two political scientists; the third show was a three-and-a-half-hour discussion involving fourteen panelists sitting around an oval table with a participating studio audience composed of fifty Japanese and Cambodian students. Viewers were also invited to participate by calling or faxing. Among the panelists were a history professor, a military analyst, a movie director, a scholar, a newscaster, and a legislator.

It is standard for American shows to provide balance by featuring two experts who represent contrasting political views: two senators or political consultants (one Republican, one Democrat), two journalist commentators (one on the left, one on the right), or two experts (one pro and one con). These Japanese shows had more than two guests, and the guests were identified by their expertise rather than their political perspectives. Another popular Japanese show that is often compared to ABC's *Nightline* or PBS's *Jim Lehrer News Hour* is called *Close-up Gendai.*[36] Providing thirty minutes of nightly news analysis, the Japanese show uses a format similar to these American TV shows. But it typically features a single guest. Japanese shows, in other words, have a wide range of formats featuring one guest or three or more—anything but two, the number most likely to polarize.

The political talk shows that Honda analyzed included many disagreements and conflicts. But whereas moderators of American and British talk shows often provoke and stoke conflict to make their shows more interesting, the Japanese moderators—and also the other guests—expended effort to modulate conflicts and defuse the spirit of opposition, but not the substance of disagreement. One last example, taken from Honda's study, illustrates how this worked.

In the long discussion among fourteen panelists, a dispute arose between two: Shikata, a former executive of the Japanese Self-Defense Forces, supported sending these forces to Cambodia. He was opposed by Irokawa, a historian who believed that the involvement of these forces violated the Japanese constitution. This exchange comes across as quite rancorous:

SHIKATA: Why is it OK to send troops to the protecting side but not OK to the protected side?
IROKAWA: Because we have the Japanese Constitution.
SHIKATA: Why is it so, if we have the Constitution?
IROKAWA: Well, we have to abide by the Constitution. If you don't want to follow the Constitution, you should get rid of your Japanese nationality and go somewhere else.

These are pretty strong words. And they were accompanied by strong gestures: According to Honda, as Shikata posed his question, he was beating the table with his palms; as Irokawa responded, he was jabbing the air toward Shikata with a pen.

Yet the confrontation did not take on a rancorous tone. The television cameras offered close-ups of both men's faces—smiling. In Japanese and other Asian cultures, smiling has different connotations than it does for Americans and Europeans: It tends to express not amusement but embarrassment. And while Shikata and Irokawa smiled, other panelists rushed to add their voices— and everyone burst out laughing. The laughter served to defuse the confrontation. So did the loud cacophony of voices that erupted as several panelists tried to speak at once. When individual voices finally were distinguished, they did not take one side or the other but tried to mediate the conflict by supporting and criticizing both sides equally. For example, Ohshima, a movie director, said:

OHSHIMA: I think that both parties overestimate or underestimate the realities for the sake of making a point.

Atsuko Honda found this to be typical of the televised discussions she analyzed: When a conspicuous conflict arose between two parties, other participants frequently moved in with attempts to mediate. In this way, they supported the Japanese ideal of avoiding winners and losers and helped everyone preserve some measure of "face." This mediation did not prevent varying views from being expressed; it resulted in different kinds of views being expressed. If two sides set the terms of debate and subsequent comments support one side or the other, the range of insights offered is circumscribed by the original two sides. If the goal instead is to mediate and defuse polarization, then other panelists are more likely to express a range of perspectives that shed nuanced light on the original two sides or suggest other ways of approaching the issue entirely.

Moving from Debate to Dialogue

Many of the issues I have discussed are also of concern to Amitai Etzioni and other communitarians. In *The New Golden Rule,* Etzioni proposes rules of engagement to make dialogue more constructive between people with differing views. His rules of engagement are designed to reflect—and reinforce—the tenet that people whose ideas conflict are still members of the same community.[37] Among these rules are:

- Don't demonize those with whom you disagree.
- Don't affront their deepest moral commitments.
- Talk less of rights, which are nonnegotiable, and more of needs, wants, and interests.
- Leave some issues out.
- Engage in a dialogue of convictions: Don't be so reasonable and conciliatory that you lose touch with a core of belief you feel passionately about.

As I stressed [. . .] earlier [. . .], producers putting together television or radio shows and journalists covering stories might consider—in at least some cases—preferring rather than rejecting potential commentators who say they cannot take one side or the other unequivocally. Information shows might do better with only one guest who is given a chance to explore an idea in depth rather than two who will prevent each other from developing either perspective. A producer who feels that two guests with radically opposed views seem truly the most appropriate might begin by asking whether the issue is being framed in the most constructive way. If it is, a third or fourth participant could be invited as well, to temper the "two sides" perspective.

Perhaps it is time to reexamine the assumption that audiences always prefer a fight. In reviewing a book about the history of *National Geographic,* Marina Warner scoffs at the magazine's policy of avoiding attack. She quotes the editor who wrote in 1915, "Only what is of a kindly nature is printed about any country or people, everything unpleasant or unduly critical being avoided."[38] Warner describes this editorial approach condescendingly as a "happy-talk, feel-good philosophy" and concludes that "its deep wish not to offend has often made it dull." But the facts belie this judgment. *National Geographic* is one of the most successful magazines of all time—as reported in the same review, its circulation "stands over 10 million, and the readership, according to surveys, is four times that number."

Perhaps, too, it is time to question our glorification of debate as the best, if not the only, means of inquiry. The debate format leads us to regard those doing different kinds of research as belonging to warring camps. There is something very appealing about conceptualizing differing approaches in this way, because the dichotomies appeal to our sense of how knowledge should be organized.

Well, what's wrong with that?

What's wrong is that it obscures aspects of disparate work that overlap and can enlighten each other.

What's wrong is that it obscures the complexity of research. Fitting ideas into a particular camp requires you to oversimplify them. Again, disinformation and distortion can result. Less knowledge is gained, not more. And time spent attacking an opponent or defending against attacks is not spent doing something else—like original research.

What's wrong is that it implies that only one framework can apply, when in most cases many can. As a colleague put it, "Most theories are wrong not in what they assert but in what they deny."[39] Clinging to the elephant's leg, they loudly proclaim that the person describing the elephant's tall is wrong. This is not going to help them—or their readers—understand an elephant. Again, there are parallels in personal relationships. I recall a man who had just returned from a weekend human development seminar. Full of enthusiasm, he explained the main lesson he had learned: "I don't have to make others wrong to prove that I'm right." He experienced this revelation as a liberation; it relieved him of the burden of trying to prove others wrong.

If you limit your view of a problem to choosing between two sides, you inevitably reject much that is true, and you narrow your field of vision to the limits of those two sides, making it unlikely you'll pull back, widen your field of vision, and discover the paradigm shift that will permit truly new understanding.

In moving away from a narrow view of debate, we need not give up conflict and criticism altogether. Quite the contrary, we can develop more varied—and more constructive—ways of expressing opposition and negotiating disagreement.

We need to use our imaginations and ingenuity to find different ways to seek truth and gain knowledge, and add them to our arsenal—or, should I say, to the ingredients for our stew. It will take creativity to find ways to blunt the most dangerous blades of the argument culture. It's a challenge we must undertake, because our public and private lives are at stake.

Notes

1. This does not mean it goes back in an unbroken chain. David Noble, in *A World Without Women*, claims that Aristotle was all but lost to the West during the early Christian era and was rediscovered in the medieval era, when universities were first established. This is significant for his observation that many early Christian monasteries welcomed both women and men who could equally aspire to an androgynous ideal, in contrast to the Middle Ages, when the female was stigmatized, unmarried women were consigned to convents, priests were required to be celibate, and women were excluded from spiritual authority.

2. There is a fascinating parallel in the evolution of the early Christian Church and the Southern Baptist Church: Noble shows that the early Christian Church regarded women as equally beloved of Jesus and equally capable of devoting their lives to religious study, so women comprised a majority of early converts to Christianity, some of them leaving their husbands—or bringing their husbands along—to join monastic communities. It was later, leading up to the medieval period, that the clerical movement gained ascendancy in part by systematically separating women, confining them in either marriage or convents, stigmatizing them, and barring them from positions of power within the church. Christine Leigh Heyrman, in *Southern Cross: The Beginnings of the Bible Belt,* shows that a similar trajectory characterized the Southern Baptist movement. At first, young Baptist and Methodist preachers (in the 1740s to 1830s) preached that both women and blacks were equally God's children, deserving of spiritual authority—with the result that the majority of converts were women and slaves. To counteract this distressing demography, the message was changed: Antislavery rhetoric faded, and women's roles were narrowed to domesticity and subservience. With these shifts, the evangelical movement swept the South. At the same time, Heyrman shows, military imagery took over: The ideal man of God was transformed from a "willing martyr" to a "formidable fighter" led by "warrior preachers."

3. Ong, *Fighting for Life*, p. 122. Ong's source, on which I also rely, is Oliver, *Communication and Culture in Ancient India and China.* My own quotations from Oliver are from pp. 259.

4. Pachomius, for example, "the father of communal monasticism . . . and organizer of the first monastic community, had been a soldier under Constantine" and modeled his community on the military, emphasizing order, efficiency, and military obedience. Cassian, a fourth-century proselytizer, " 'likened the monk's discipline to that of the soldier,' and Chrysostom, another great champion of the movement, 'sternly reminded the monks that Christ had armed them to be soldiers in a noble fight" (Noble, *A World Without Women*, p. 54).

5. Aristotle, quoted in Oliver, *Communication and Culture in Ancient India and China*, p. 259.

6. I came to understand the different meaning of "poet" in Classical Greece from reading Ong and also *Preface to Plato* by Eric Havelock. These insights informed many articles I wrote about oral and literate tradition in Western culture, including "Oral and Literate Strategies in Spoken and Written Narratives" and "The Oral/Literate Continuum in Discourse."

7. Moulton, "A Paradigm of Philosophy"; Ong, *Fighting for Life.*

8. The example of Danny and the lava: Wertsch, *Voices of the Mind,* pp. 113–14.

9. See David and Myra Sadker, *Failing at Fairness.*

10. Although my colleagues and I make efforts to refer to our students—all over the age of eighteen—as "women" and "men" and some students in my classes do the same, the majority refer to each other and themselves as "girls" and "boys" or "girls" and "guys."

11. Jonathan Alter, *"The End of the Journey,"* Newsweek, Nov. 4, 1996, p. 61. Trilling died at the age of ninety-one.

12. Kaplan, *French Lessons,* p. 119.

13. Tracy and Baratz, "Intellectual Discussion in the Academy as Situated Discourse," p. 309.

14. Greenberg and Robins, "The Changing Role of Social Experiments in Policy Analysis," p. 350.

15. These and other quotes from Tompkins appear in her essay "Fighting Words," pp. 588–89.

16. Safire is quoted in Howard Kurtz, "Safire Made No Secret of Dislike for Inman," *The Washington Post,* Jan. 19, 1994, p. A6.

17. I've borrowed the William Blake quote from Peter Elbow, who used it to open his book *Embracing Contraries.*

18. Terence Monmaney, "Marshall's Hunch," *The New Yorker,* Sept. 20, 1993, pp. 64–72.

19. Elbow, *Embracing Contraries,* p. 258.

20. Moulton, "A Paradigm of Philosophy," p. 153.

21. Social constructionists often deride the ideas of those who focus on differences as "essentialist"—a bit of academic name-calling; it is used only as a way of criticizing someone else's work: "Smith's claims are repugnant because they are essentialist." I have never heard anyone claim, "I am an essentialist," though I have frequently heard elaborate self-defenses: "I am not an essentialist!" Capturing the tendency to use this term as an epithet, *Lingua Franca,* a magazine for academics, describes "essentialist" as "that generic gender studies *j'accuse!*" See Emily Nussbaum, "Inside Publishing," *Lingua Franca,* Dec.–Jan. 1977, pp. 22–24; the quote is from p. 24.

22. Klein, *Meeting the Great Bliss Queen,* pp. 8–9.

23. Cynthia Gorney, "Gloria," *Mother Jones,* Nov.–Dec. 1995, pp. 22–27; the quote is from p. 22.

24. See, for example, Needham, *Science and Civilization in China.*

25. Ellyn E. Spragins, *Newsweek,* July 28, 1997, p. 73.

26. This section is based on an interview with Ornstein. See also Ornstein's article, "Less Seems More."

27. The story behind the haircut story is told by Gina Lubrano, "Now for the Real Haircut Story . . . ," *The San Diego Union-Tribune,* July 12, 1993, p. B7. That the supermarket scanner story was not true was mentioned by George Stephanopoulos at a panel held at Brown University, as reported by Elliot Krieger, "Providence Journal/Brown University Public Affairs Conference," *The Providence Journal-Bulletin,* Mar. 5, 1995, p. 12A.

28. Fox, "The Inherent Rules of Violence," p. 141.

29. Yablon, "Stupid Lawyer Tricks," p. 1639.

30. Kenneth Walsh made this comment on *The Diane Rehm Show,* May 28, 1996.

31. Grossman, *On Killing,* p. 270.

32. Susan Popik made this comment on the *U.S. Business Litigation* panel.

33. Suzanne Wong Scollon: Personal communication.

34. Mary Catherine Bateson: Personal communication.

35. At the time of this show, Ms. Lewis was deputy communications director.

36. Yoshiko Nakano helped me with observations of *Close-up Gendai.*

37. Etzioni, *The New Golden Rule,* pp. 104–106. He attributes the rule "Talk less of rights . . . and more of needs, wants, and interests" to Mary Ann Glendon.

38. Marina Warner, "High-Minded Pursuit of the Exotic," review of *Reading National Geographic* by Catherine A. Lutz and Jane L. Collins in *The New York Times Book Review,* Sept. 19, 1993, p. 13.

39. I got this from A. L. Becker, who got it from Kenneth Pike, who got it from . . .

Reading 28

TOWARD AN EXPERIENCE-NEAR ANTHROPOLOGY

Unni Wikan

One day in Bali I was sitting with a couple trying to make out—once again—how notions of "balance" and "harmony" translate into personal experience. From the literature it seemed clear that such notions were crucial in Bali-Hindu cosmology and person constitution. But how, I wondered, did they compel action? What did they actually mean for people whose lives they presumably governed?

With my friends I explored linkages I thought I could detect between bodily imbalance, emotional imbalance and moral and ritual transgressions; logically all cohered, yet my friends seemed bewildered by my questions. In the end the man cut me short and gracefully said, "You know it's right what you say, but it is not the way we think."

And he went on to expound how Balinese think, substituting the notion of "balance" I had used with more experience-near[1] concepts of pragmatic consequence in everyday life, and relegating my kind of usage to the discourse of literary and textual specialists.

To me his warning came timely. As I saw it, he did not merely juxtapose two kinds of discourse, two ways of knowing, one expert, one folk, or even two different cultural models.[2] More was at stake.

And now I have to admit to you that I have been misleading you all along, making it seem as if he told me "It is not the way we think," when actually what he said was something different—for he said "feel-think," *mekench.* In rendering his words into English I am misconstruing him. I have to say either "think"

Wikan, Unni. "Toward an Experience-Near Anthropology." *Cultural Anthropology.* V. 6., No. 3. Aug , 1991. 285–305.

or "feel," or I have to coin a new concept, "feel-think," which seems slightly cumbersome in English.

Yet in going for the easier solution I am dissecting a process of knowing, splitting it off from its ontological base, as if lived experience could be reduced to a way of thinking or even the latter reigned supreme.

This might seem much ado about little. "Think" or "feel-think": what difference does it make? Well, from a Balinese point of view it makes all the difference, for whoever separates feeling from thought will be bereft of moral guidance and—which might concern social scientists more—unable to reach genuine insight. Balinese have a proverb that says:

> If you have a short string,
> you should not try
> to reach for the sky

They use it to refer to precisely the sort of people who split feeling off from thought, letting the latter be their driving ambition, when to climb high in any venture—also the pursuit of knowledge—one has to exercise feeling-thought.

There are no third-world people among keynote speakers here, and I am using my privileged position to interject a word of warning from people who figure large in anthropological discourse, yet have to little extent been given their say. In thinking about the concept of culture, I suggest we stand to gain by taking up challenges posed by ways of knowing alien from ours. Holland and Quinn, in their fine book on *Cultural Models in Language and Thought,* note that culture is "what one sees *with,* but seldom what one *sees*" (1987:14). I interject a Balinese model here to help us see more clearly some premises that are grounded in our way of thought, and that also inform our approaches to knowledge about other cultures.

In a perceptive conclusion to their essay on "The cognitive model of anger inherent in American English," Lakoff and Kovecses pose a number of important questions: How much of the model they have uncovered do people actually use? Do they have awareness of the model? How much of it do they believe? And finally, and in their own words "most intriguingly, does the model have any effect on what people *feel?*" (1987:221).

The Balinese vision of knowledge I espouse here would render superfluous the latter question, for it postulates feeling-thinking to be *the* way to understanding, integral to valid knowledge. If so, a cognitive model would be flawed in its very conception for segregating one part of a more encompassing process that shapes everyday thought. The only way we can comprehend (appreciate— *menghati* is their word) what others experience, is by recognizing its feeling-thinking character.

Anger in their cultural model is felt-thought, so are black magic, social inequality and power, or the jurisdiction of the gods. Indeed, the man who brushed aside my use of "balance" as misperecived, if right and true, proceeded to set out precisely those "basic-level concepts" (Lakoff and Kovecses 1987:218) that were sensible, felt thought. They were used, they were conscious, they were believed, and they were embodied.

Much writing on culture and thought presumes cultural models to be largely out-of-awareness: "Tacit and unexamined, [they] embed a view of 'what it means' that seems wholly natural" and goes unquestioned (Holland and Quinn 1987:11). In my own dealings with Balinese the opposite has struck me: how explicit, how aware, how able people are to ponder even those models that grant "a seeming necessity to how [they] . . . live their lives" (1987:11).

Perhaps, if feeling-thinking is *the* crucial process of gaining knowledge about oneself and the world, then awareness is increased because it is embodied. Perhaps it is our Western thought-splitting tendency to shut feeling off as all too irrational, subjective, no partner for thought, that accounts, in part, for the degree to which we lead shallow lives, unaware of basic presuppositions?

Obeyesekere (1981) has remarked how South Asian conceptions of reality leave open pathways between the unconscious and the conscious as valued or privileged sources of insight. Balinese, while not recognizing an unconscious component of the soul,[3] emphasize the body as a medium of most relevant existential insight. And never is knowledge a product of mere thought. "Can anyone think but with their heart?" they ask, incredulous.

Western epistemology is premised on the belief that yes, one can indeed, that the sky can only be reached with what Balinese term a short string. And so I suggest that our models of cultural models are fundamentally culture-bound and may need refeel-thinking to allow for *different* constructions of reality.

I pose this problem as part of my challenge to the concept of culture. But I want to go further and ask some more general questions: What if Balinese are right that feeling-thinking is one integral process that should be implicated in any successful venture, what then would be the implications for a theory of culture? What if Balinese are right, that we amputate our endeavor if we dismiss the feeling part of thought—how then should we proceed methodologically to enhance the string of our knowledge?

What concerns me then, is more than the distributive or situated character of knowledge in recognition that we are all feeling-thinking subjects with different vantage points. The more fundamental problem implicated in the vision of things I illustrate here concerns the ontological status of experience contra interpretation and the production of knowledge. It was first brought home to me with the man's gentle warning: "But it is not the way we feel-think."

Essentially the challenge he posed (as I saw it) concerned epistemology and ways of knowing: How do we come to know what we think that we know? What is to count as truth, and for what purpose? It was a problem that was to confront me time and again in fieldwork; for instance, when after a year an expert told me that the knowledge I had gained that Balinese lose their vital spirit *(bayu)* when they are frightened or suddenly surprised was a misconception. In believing this, the expert said, both the people and I were confused, for whoever loses his *bayu,* his vital spirit, even only for a moment, will be dead. Yet here were all those Balinese I knew who had lost their *bayu,*[4] and were most undeniably alive. Where then was truth? What was I to believe?

I carried my confusion to a friend and shared with her my sense of the problem. She thought for a moment, for she too was perplexed, then she shrugged her shoulders and said: "Well, I suppose it's right what the balian[5] says, but it is not the way we feel think." And she went on to describe so graphically the sensations of emptiness. trembling, confusion and fear that ensue when one loses one's bayu that anyone who thought otherwise was made to seem slightly bewildered.

I don't suppose my friend thought any more about this. It was I as the anthropologist who was left with the problem of how to reconcile these different views or even account for the fact that people could be so confused. To be frank, what came to trouble me more was the realization that *I* could be so gullible. Clearly, I had not done my homework, nor read the literature well, or I would not have been misled in the first place. To think that people lost their souls!

With time what has come to trouble me more is the insight that might have been lost had I *not* been so naive. Had I gone to the experts first, or been more familiar with Bali-Hindu philosophy, would I have been able to take in earnest the notion that people lose their vital spirit? Instead of trying hard to feel-think what they meant, would I not have shrugged their claim off as some lesser version of the truth—a misconception—as the experts said?

Now instead I fought back, as I fell committed to those who had first taught me. Much in the spirit of Festinger's *When Prophecy Fails* (1956) I clung the more firmly to our shared convictions when they were contradicted, and it came to matter to me to defend their good sense.

Yet the feeling of unease has not left me. My husband suggested that in extension of this experience I write an essay "On the Virtues of Ignorance." Instead I take the occasion here to engage you with me in reflection on some issues this experience raised for me. The import is epistemological and methodological. And some questions I would ask are these:

How valid is knowledge that is not anchored in experience? Why take in earnest what experts say? Or if we must, why credit them with privileged insight or even join forces with them to let contesting visions appear invalid or less than true? To follow this line of logic to its bitter end: Why not just follow the example of my Balinese friend and shrug our shoulders and say, "Well, I suppose it's right what they say, but. . . ."

We cannot, for we are sky-climbers—with short strings—bent on building conceptual castles in our pursuit of abstract, generalized knowledge. We join forces with some experts in privileging logic and coherence above messy inchoate experience, dismissing things as insignificant when they do not fit, rather than taking my friend's more humble, but also more self-assured stance, and credit contesting versions with a grain of truth. Where she can be generous, relaxedly unconcerned, we tend toward the defensive, all too concerned with the truth of what we call culture, a hegemonic structure that acts with the self-importance of a divine mission in driving heretics off.

The question of folk versus expert models cannot be resolved in the Balinese context (or any other, I think) by redefining them as alternative cultural models and granting them equal status. They are *not* equal, and framing the issue thus sidesteps the problem of how to identify valid knowledge, relevant knowledge from different existential viewpoints. Nor does a view of culture as distributive and situated resolve what is at stake—for it is not a question of fitting pieces into a jigsaw puzzle but of grasping lived-in worlds of compelling significance.

That the vital life force cannot be lost, or that "balance" is the key cosmic principle may be good for some to ponder, but singularly inept to live by and thus rather irrelevant *compared* to models that "work" (Obeyesekere 1985), that guide and compel experience and have, as D'Andrade puts it, "directive force" (1984). In Bali what works with directing force are models anchored in bodily experience that draw on feeling-thoughts like "calm," "confused," "happy," and "angry" as "key concepts" (Quinn 1987).

This has implications for how experts are considered: While we tend to assume that "cultural understandings . . . gain force from their identification with expert knowledge" (Holland and Quinn 1987:15), in societies where the body is the medium (source) of authoritative experience experts lose out—because they stand too removed—unless they, too, can compel experience, as healers, ancestors, possessing spirits, bodily felt-thought.

Our split-mind vision of culture, then, impedes understanding of alternative epistemologies like those based in feeling-thinking as the vital premise and the *key of relevance* to lived experience. And now we are in a position to understand why "balance" would function poorly as a waysign in daily life. A contingent variable that depends on how you feel, it compels only indirectly, via experience-near feeling-thoughts of "calm" or "confusion." Nor is "imbalance" much invoked to account for disasters in the world. It is anger that is salient/operative, anger of the gods, of the ancestors, of fellow beings, even anger within oneself.

"I say to myself he is a mad man so I will not be angry and sick," said a woman of a man who was always chiding her publicly. Another observed: "Have you noticed how I always act immature what that man? I do it on purpose, so he will think I am childish, and not be angry with me." A healer said of his client: "The man is sick because the gods are angry with him—he has two priests reincarnated in him, and yet he eats cow's meat and drinks milk."

Such embodied and supremely relevant models have to a great extent been overlooked by us in our preoccupation with "culture," a hegemonic concept that until recently and even today holds us in a straitjacket. Renato Rosaldo (1989) has set out the salient aspects of this essentialist structure: It was a monolithic formation of logically coherent parts with the observer as the authoritative adjudicator of what does and does not belong. What we term emotions, or Balinese feeling-thoughts, played a most subsidiary role when culture was prefigured as cognitive, a matter of categories, symbols and signs. The string was short, but we did not see it.

Order reigned, at the expense of uncertainties, ambiguities, contesting visions, not to speak of the disorder and unpredictability of much of everyday life. Norms, rules and regularities carried the day to coalesce into a harmonious whole of pattern, consistency—in short, a culture.

It was a fiction, as Geertz has said (1973a:15) in the sense of written, inscribed, constructed. What many of us did not see equally well was that it was also a figment of the mind, our minds, that ignored pragmatic meanings, embodied truths.

Eyes set on cosmic balance, it is not easy to keep track of messy, murky, mundane realities, as I can vouch for myself. The same goes when other elevated concepts like "honor" or "hierarchy," or today's guest of honor—"culture"—are in focus. Let an example illustrate:

Sitting in Cairo, as I recently did, with poor people, friends whom I had known for years,[6] and listening to their complaints I was myself overcome with the sense of their misery, and it was some ten days before I suddenly thought: "Culture! My God, culture! I'll be speaking of it soon, but where is it?"

And I looked above, as if expecting to find it dangling in the air. But all I saw were cracks in the ceiling and the paint coming off and so my mind set again on poverty while "culture" exited after its brief entrance—too stylish, overdressed, unfit for the occasion.

The experience left a mark on me for I was all too well aware that when in Bali, with poor people, "culture" is none the less there, a seemingly fitting partner to "poverty." What's going on?

I think the answer is multifaceted and has in some way to do with exoticism, in some way with beauty (it is easier to see "culture" among people who carry themselves well). Appadurai's notion of "gate-keeping concepts" (1986) may also apply. Bali has been an arena for studying "the cultural dimension" of persons—par excellence.[7] And so Balinese appear "cultural", to us, however materially destitute or despairing.

The fundamental lesson I draw from the experience is this: that "culture" must be refelt-thought to become as transparent in sheer poverty as in the most glamorous of ceremonies. It must, as Renato Rosaldo (1989) suggests, be made part and parcel of pragmatic meanings, humdrum visions or else, I'd say, discarded altogether as discriminatory, arbitrary, laden with value judgments.

Acting on this suggestion might prove more painful to us anthropologists than we are ready to acknowledge, for it entails modifying die-hard habits of work and moving down on the social ladder away from association with "culture's" spokesmen and evocateurs to more ordinary people of humdrum, inostensible concerns. The essentialist construct of culture, as Rosaldo makes clear, has been built on a complicity between people in power and us. They were the vocal ones, the eloquent, the experts we sought out while the poor, the infirm, women and youths were disregarded as uninformed about "truth."

And so it is that the concept of culture as a seamless whole and of society as a bounded group manifesting inherently valued order and normatively regulated response, effectively masked human misery and quenched dissenting voices. There was little room for a man's soft-spoken protest, "But it is not the way we feel-think."

The last ten years have seen the gradual dismantling of this culture concept. As Marilyn Strathern has observed: "What is of interest [now] is why a once-convincing analytical strategy no longer convinces. . . . The present mood, which . . . regards culture as dangerous reification is bound to be expressed in images of disintegration. The interpretive quest is imagined not so much as decoding signs on a map as capturing the elusive" (1987:173).

Several anthropologists have played significant roles in this: cutting the culture concept down to size.[8] Personally, I am particularly impressed with the challenge posed by Keesing in his "Anthropology as Interpretive Quest" (1987a) where he effectively exposes the ideological vogue of the old-time culture concept and renders "deeply problematic premises about culture as a system of shared meanings" (1987a:16). Keesing cites Scholte to the effect that "few do the actual spinning while the . . . majority is simply caught" in the webs of significance we posit as comprising "a culture" (Scholte 1984:140, quoted in Keesing 1987a:162). Cultures thus are as much webs of mystification as of signification with meanings differently situated, distributed and controlled and "differently read, differently construed, by men and women, young and old, experts and nonexperts, even in the last complex of societies" (Keesing 1987a:161).

The main theoretical challenge Keesing poses is to suggest that meanings might better be seen as *evoked* by cultural symbols, rather than inherent in them. And thus, if we may speak of "a culture" at all, it lives "in the emergent creations and evanescent structures of ongoing social life" and is constructed by us as anthropologists "from situational shreds and patches" (1987a:164–165).

Over the past decade a number of anthropologists have shown how social life evokes meanings not only of cognitive but "intensely meaningful" emotional experience. The concept of emotion, in Lutz's words, draws our attention to "things that matter rather than things that merely make sense" (1988:5). Michele Rosaldo spoke of emotions as giving the sense that "I am involved"; of being like "embodied thoughts" (1984:143)—a kind of judgment, in Robert Solomon's term (1984) that is "*preeminently* cultural" (Lutz 1988:5) and bridges personal and social worlds.

The lesson for anthropology was clear: No longer a mere cognitive structure, culture must be made to encompass emotion and to account for the elusive but intensely meaningful experiences that cultural symbols also evoke.

I stand on the shoulders of all of these when I proceed in my challenge to the concept of culture. Drawing on field materials from Bali I would stress the need to redesign our ways of observing and conceptualizing if we are to proceed further to grasp what I choose to call "lived experience," which is something different than "emotional experience" and combines both the "dreary" *and* "the intensely meaningful." Balinese are concerned that people "carry their hearts always with them," and that there is "so much to care about" in social life. I want to elevate such experiential statements to key analytical status, that is, I am not using them metaphorically but as technical, analytical constructs in the belief that an anthropology of experience requires a revitalization and redesign of concepts.[9]

I want to present to you some such concepts and show how they may be used to help us better grasp *connecting* links in people's lives. Lives are inevitably lived as wholes, of some kind. Rather than compartmentalizing with our dissecting categories I want to try to recapture some of that continuity, which makes, as Kleinman says, "of each life a seamless whole" (1988:79). Or to remain with the Balinese conceptualization: "hearts carried across."

Methodologically, I argue that we have to attend to people's multiple, simultaneous, compelling concerns and to follow them, *as* they move, bridging scenes and encounters, if we are to grasp what is at stake and how they, people in various positions, feel-think and act. I stress the need for a discovery procedure that seeks out knowledge *they* deem relevant to their lived experience as the basis on which to frame cultural understandings. But before I proceed to ethnography, a couple of observations regarding my vantage points.

Perhaps I part ways with some emotion analysts when I say that I don't think continued emphasis on the study of "emotion" will help us best, at this stage, to grasp what I choose to call "lived experience." Immense achievements have been made by elevating "emotion" to analytical status, and demonstrating its crucial role in culture and society.[10] But I think the time has come now when continued emphasis on this, as a phenomenon in its own right, might prove counterproductive.

Two issues concern me here. First, I question whether "emotion" as a concept connotes the "intensely meaningful" any more than thought does. Second, I think that elevating "emotion" to analytical status reifies a dichotomy ingrained in Western culture despite our best efforts to define emotion as also cognitive (e.g., Scheper-Hughes and Lock 1987).

To revert to the first point again: Does indeed emotion generally refer to intensely meaningful experience, or is not most of our emotion, most of the time, rather dour and dull? Is the feeling that "I am involved" any more telling of everyday, ordinary emotion than of everyday ordinary thought? Does perhaps the distinction take as its prototype certain more deepfelt emotions as the sign of authenticity, and generalize those—beyond validity? I think so, and also that an emphasis on emotion is bound to reify a notion we entertain of separate mental processes in which flow different types of experience—when it is only by taking the full consequences of a view that the Western emotion/thought split might be a myth that theory building will proceed fruitfully.

At issue is indeed the culturally constructed character of emotion as subverting its natural link with thought in one process on which culture operates. I suggest we grant Balinese that no one can think but with their feelings, indeed, that feeling and thought are the same, for "when you use one, you use the two," and that, in consequence, feeling-thought be made our analytical label in order better to grasp experience, predicaments and what is at stake.[11]

Another observation regarding my vantage point: I stand outside of American anthropology, a member of a minority culture, and look with much awe and admiration—and some distress—at what goes on. Magnificent achievements have been made by interpretive anthropology alerting us all to the need for reflexivity and consciousness about our representational tools and genes. Yet something seems amiss, and what I miss most in interpretive anthropology is greater concern with methodology, *and,* paradoxically, with the voice of "the other."

There is a proverb that says: "If the tool you have is a hammer, it's tempting to treat everything as if it were a nail." From my vantage point it seems as if there is an awful lot of hammering going on with texts being constructed and deconstructed, again and again, and much of anthropology's subject matter lost in the process.

In his epoch-setting *The Interpretation of Cultures* Geertz predicted that what would get better, as one analysis "better informed and better conceptualized" would run alongside another, would be "the precision with which we vex each other" (1973b). Has this been borne out? Was this ever a goal? Or why, when the writings of fellow anthropologists are critiqued would the vexed ones so often be those who can be counted on *not* to answer back, souls eternally silenced like Evans-Pritchard, Malinowski, Benedict and Griaule—beside an occasional high brow European like Lévi-Strauss who won't answer anyway (Clifford 1988; Geertz 1988).

Reading the texts, from a distance, I wonder if anthropologists are too dedicated to their roles as *besserwissener,*[12] ever speaking *for* mute others.

When now I embark on a short analysis of aspects of Balinese ethnography it is not to lay claim to privileged truth but to exercise some methodological and theoretical issues that became salient for me in my own fieldwork and which I judge relevant to challenge the concept of culture. Bali serves well as a showcase, it being truly one of "anthropology's most favoured of favourite cases." So you can all be counted on to have some familiarity with the place, and take an interest in "what manner of men are these."

Balinese indeed have become like anthropologists' next-door neighbors, closely present, though we do not know them well. They are inscribed in anthropology in a manner that makes it impossible to know them well for they are said never to "meet"—even one another (Geertz, 1973a:365).

Enigmatic, they are frozen on the scene, a people of masks, not faces, engaged in theatrical display, their selves comprised by the spectacles and masks, ever shunning emotionality and individuality.[13] With this as the anthropological representation, you will be rather ill-prepared when a Balinese attempts to meet you as a person with compelling concerns. Let me tell you of my first encounter and proceed to draw some lessons from that. I use a story that has already been recounted in *Ethos* (Wikan 1987), but permit me to use it again.

It was the second day of fieldwork and I was sitting on a bus with a young woman, aged 22, when she mentioned to me in passing that a friend of hers had died suddenly, two days before. She proceeded to tell the fragments of a story with such a glittering smile, I could not know if it was an event, something to talk about, or more deeply, personally significant.

Two days later she brought up the story again asking to borrow a great deal of money so that she could go to a memorial service for him. When I asked, she confided that he had been very special to her—the boy she had planned to marry. But as she spoke, she exuded such cheerfulness, her face was so bright *(cedang)* as to leave me wholly confused. Could bereavement parade as seeming happiness? Was the story to be believed?

Many elements made me slightly incredulous. Not only her posture, gestures and tone of voice, but also the sense of her words: She said she had never met the boy's parents but now would travel to a very distant place to see them— alone, and yes, with her parents' permission, her brother would come along. Her conduct, as I interpreted it, incorporated elements that seemed not only incongruous but wholly incompatible. And so I said, I was sorry, our money had not yet arrived. And Suriati smiled and left, not a sign of distress.

In the evening I told the story to my husband. He was impressed with the sense of Suriati's words for he did not need to struggle like me with the glaring discongruity between word and gesture. "Just think, if . . ." said he. And so Suriati was given the benefit of the doubt, and with it the money, and off she went, cheerful *(girang)* and bright as ever.

Information continued to come in over the next few days indicating that things were not quite as Suriati had said. There was a letter from her, telling how her parents had absolutely refused to let her go, but she had cried for two days until they gave in. But now she was stuck in the capital. She did not have the money for a plane ticket, only an uncle working at the airport who might help her get a cheap seat, but the planes were full, et cetera.

When I went to her parents to ask about her a few days later, they were all smiles and cheerfulness, nothing to indicate a personal disaster. What was going on?

And as in the meantime I learned that most marriages in Bali are conducted by elopement, my suspicion grew that this was perhaps the essence of the matter.

A week later Suriati came back. I'll never forget the impression she made on me as she walked the long path toward our house. She carried herself with such composure, her face was so cheerful and bright, I was in little doubt; she must come from a happy encounter.

Would I like to see the photos of her friend? And she laid them out, two thick folders in all, showing a handsome and vivacious young man, in many situations. Then there was a photo of him reclining on his bed, playing the tape recorder, and in the next photo he was lying on that same bed, all draped in white. I had a split moment's thought, "well the Balinese have many rituals. . . . But in the next he was lowered into the coffin and borne to the grave. The last photo showed herself kneeling on his grave.

I was numb, not knowing what to say. Friends assembled to hear her story and see the pictures. Their reaction was the same: they laughed. Nothing to be sad about in this. The world is full of men! No use grieving over one. Where one stick is broken, another will grow. Go on, be happy—let bygones be bygones! The world is bigger than a *kelor* leaf.[14]

What are we to make of all this? That Balinese shrink from emotionality and individuality as Geertz has claimed (1973b, 1984). Or that they lack the qualities of empathy or thoughtfulness, as Mead has claimed (1942:11)? How are we to get at the meanings that were evoked by this encounter, seen as an emergent creation in ongoing social lives, of my friend, her companions, and others who were not present, but vicariously involved, her parents for instance? What is at stake?

I suggest that we have first to grant that the persons involved are feeling-thinking subjects who, to maintain the Balinese perspective, carry their hearts always with them. It means that concerns often cannot be shed, but carry across encounters, and thus the above incident cannot be disconnected from its experiential context in persons (feeling-thinking subjects) with multiple, simultaneous compelling concerns.

Suriati is not merely grappling with death, her friends not merely with a bereaved companion. Life must go on, here as whenever, and I suggest it is fruitful to keep this in mind also when we deal with what to us might appear more mundane and insignificant events. Energies are limited, resources scarce, concerns multiple, and it takes an effort, in much of our lives to carry through and manage.

This then is my second admonition, feeling-thinking was the first. The second, in keeping with a Balinese notion of "so many cares" *(liu anu kenchange)*, to think of concerns as shed only with difficulty. And then proceed to ask, methodologically, how are we to capture the meanings that are invoked (by symbols and acts) when there are these multiple compelling concerns that people carry always with them?

I suggest, and this is my third point, that we have to follow people, *as* they move, bridging scenes and encounters. I stress the aspect of bridging because much social analysis proceeds by compartmentalizing life into distinct domains (for example, a "public" and a "private"), not seeing that a life-line is cut in the process, and with it compelling concerns.

Two amputated halves do not necessarily make a whole. Adding "public" onto the "private," each as a commentary on the other, might make good reading but is beside the point in the way that we are also bound to misunderstand Suriati if we take her cheerful "public" face and add it onto her "privately" expressed sorrow.[15] The stereotypes are there, ready to be applied. But what are her concerns? What is the heart, the feeling-thought which carries across? And how does this heart, this feeling-thought,[16] *experience* the predicament of never-ceasing criss-crossing that is entailed in a life of "so many cares."

I argue that it matters to bridge thresholds along with people, and to note how women and men often keep on, in the Balinese term, "a bright face" *(mue cedang)*, when they cross the thresholds to their homes. There is something at stake, and we have to discover it. It matters also to discover what intangible thresholds and bridges people construct: points of demarcation at which the priorities of these concerns may be reordered or shed.

Said a 13-year-old to her mother who was trapped, as the daughter knew, in a terrible family tragedy: "Do you hate us, Mama, when with the guests you are always cheerful and laughing but with us children moody and grim?" She alerted the mother that she had overstepped boundaries, crossed an inoperative threshold. But we should be cautious in thinking we know what this means. The fiction of masked, stereotyped Balinese precludes discovery of their existential concerns.

I proceed soon to Suriati and the enigma she presents, but first a word on "public/private." In my opinion application of this dichotomy to Bali has proved disastrous, for it perpetuates a divide *we* draw, and applies deeply connotative labels to another world, thereby begging crucial questions regarding how *they* construe and experience social space and social relations.

I suspect that if Balinese were confronted with our gloss on their world as composed variously of a warm and intimate private sphere contrasted with one which is public, formal, and restraining, they might remark, "Well, I suppose it's right what they say, but . . ." And the big *but* in this case would refer to an overpowering existential awareness of black magic and sorcery ever threatening in *domestic* encounters; of casualties and misfortunes wrought, not by "contemporaries," but by close "consociates"[17] who are held responsible for approximately 50% of all deaths by North Balinese,[18] according to my evidence.

In view of this, places that we term public (streets, markets, et cetera), emerge as relatively safe and nonthreatening, for the fear of shame is so much less than that of black magic. But we need not go into that here except as a perspective on Suriati's compelling concerns: Bereaved people are living in the world, and black magic does not take a vacation. It offers no respite, no hiding place, even for the bereaved, but may penetrate to the deepest corners and at all times of night and day. I ask you to keep this in mind as we revert to Suriati.

Over the next few months Suriati appeared to act precisely as her friends had advised. She was cheerful and bright, indeed so exquisite *(anggun)*, by Balinese standards, that I heard people who did not know her tease her saying she was secretly in love. And I derived a secret sense of triumph from this. It was not only I as an outsider who was fooled by her appearance. The enigma was real, and Balinese were also taken in.

But did I not have access to the "private"? Did not that offer privileged entry to her personal universe? I did, and it only aggravated my sense of confusion. For she shone, most of the time, and particularly with her mother whom she engaged in constant laughing and joking. What was going on? Did she not *feel* her sorrow?

Suriati, as I shall show, not only felt her sorrow but she felt-thought it, and it was therefore that she acted as she did. Hers was a deliberate, self-conscious response that was also in keeping with how a Balinese young woman should be, but no less deliberate for that.

She had many concerns, not one. And they were not handled one at a time. They were continuous, overflowing and included compassion for a mother with despairs of her own. This is what she told me after a few months.

"I am afraid to think of my sorrow, that I might go mad and also that if I show it, people might mock me. They will laugh and say "Oh, you're a widow!" or "brokenhearted." But *I* don't want to be called a widow or broken-hearted. . . ." Her testimony ended thus: "It is very bad if you are sad and people laugh. That's why we keep our sorrow."

It was one of those enlightened moments in fieldwork, of which I have written elsewhere, when patches waiting for their interpretive context suddenly fall into place (Wikan 1983). Suriati at long last made sense. It is *rational* to laugh if otherwise people will mock you. Her testimony touches strings that appear universal, and perhaps you could share some of my feeling of relief?

Yet I must tell you that you have again been misled as I was on that day, and not because her words were not true, they were, but because they were expressed in a state of confusion. And here we are with the crux of Balinese lived experience. Feeling shapes thought, for they are linked and every interpretation bears testimony to that.[19] Thus when Suriati a year later was in a state of bliss from new-found love, she denied her previous interpretation: "Oh, no, they laughed for my own good! Perhaps they were afraid that I might kill myself because I was so confused due to my sadness. They all laughed to make my heart happy from sadness" (Wikan 1989b).

How laughter can make hearts happy from sadness is a theme to which I shall return. But first a consideration regarding cultural symbols: They do not have meaning in and of themselves, as Suriati's diverse interpretations make clear. Balinese laughter or the ever "bright face" *(mue cedang)* do express politeness, friendliness and concern, yet always the question arises: Concern with what and from whose point of view? Said a man who was gripped with despair because the brother-in-law whom he had carefully chosen himself had committed double murder.[20] "It was in all the papers, so everyone knows, yet no one speaks a word to me about it. I don't understand," said he, questioning me mutely.

He was alluding to the bright faces and the said within the unsaid. Grace and demeanor were all that he encountered. Did he rest content with that—find relief in the still life of masks? Far from it, for masks was not what he saw, but faces, imbued with hearts *(keneh)*, with feeling-thoughts *(keneh)*, and variously responding to his own predicament.

When he could take his doubts no longer, he threw a grandiose party, to which everyone "had" to come (for he was very powerful). And he said to me afterwards, "I cried for I was so overcome with all the attention showered on me."

Is this how Balinese are supposed to act? No, you have to imbue people with a heart to enable them to cry, and hearts are what Balinese attribute to each other. No masks and faces, but faces with hearts—it makes a world of difference. Think of a Pagliacci, Leon Cavallo's tragic clown, stripped of his heart; what would he be but a comic figure? Balinese, as inscribed in anthropology remind me of this pitiful image: Slightly clownish in their single-minded aesthetic pursuit when in fact they have hearts that cry and laugh and imprint themselves on reality, as did this man (or his murderous brother-in-law!), or Suriati determined not to be branded brokenhearted *(patah hati)* because she, like every Balinese, has an identity to defend.

This heart, a metaphor of will, desire, motivation, feeling-thought and character, asserts itself full force when a challenge is made, as when Suriati was chided by another, far superior in rank, with being inferior in math, and replied in her most gracious tone: "And does the rat beget lions for children?" Lions and rats—evocative images for social privilege and handicap that bespeak a world of compelling concerns, throbbing behind that smooth and bright face that Balinese should present always to the world. This face shows ripples at times, at times flashes into tempestuous clouds. Always it comes across with composite meanings depending on actors, context, and circumstance. It does because hearts carry across, they cannot be shed, and this in turn explains the ultimate value of keeping a bright face. In a world of untold covert violence, wrought by angry hearts, one has to tread carefully to please as virtue pleases. The bright face protects in three important ways: It is an expression of friendliness and good relations that makes a *moral* claim on another to be friendly in turn; it cushions against the offense and revenge one might provoke should others see one's true heart; and it is a therapeutic device that molds feeling by good expression and thus strengthens the vital spirit that protects against illness and black magic.[21]

So bright faces do not only communicate, they work *to* effects and *from* compelling concerns. The 13-year-old's rebuke of her mother belongs within this frame: Gloom and bad mood endanger not only the person herself but a collectivity of people, for feelings are perceived to spread, when expressed. And laughter is used as a shock therapy to shake people out of a despair that threatens the wellbeing of many (much the same way contagious diseases do).

Crisscrossing scenes and encounters, Balinese carry with them many concerns, with health, survival, power, a mother's love, and into all weave interpretive problems. Life's episodes evoke, they do not "have" meaning, and the following case exemplifies a common predicament: I once witnessed a grisly marital scene between a couple. *He* abused her ferociously; *she* broke down and cried: *I* feared for her sanity; she was sole provider for eight. Afterwards the man told me he did it all on purpose: His wife was a victim of black magic, and he needed to make her cry to drive the black magic out. I thought to myself he was mad, indeed it was so rumored. But when I told the wife of his "misconception" (to help her cope), her eyes widened and she whispered, "It's true what he says. I was. . . . But I am conscious now, only he does not believe it, yet. . . ."[22]

A year later the man believed, and excused himself. He himself had been victim of black magic, hence controlled by another's mind (actually, soul *atma* or *roh*). Here then are layers upon layers of interpretation and its "mis," with feeling-thought the critical point of reference. But power also enters—the man had power to humiliate his wife. Others had power over him. He had been fired from his job after he tried to teach pupils the value of self-reliance by making them see for themselves that ghosts of the dead *(jerangkong)* are a superstition. He made them camp by the graveyard one night. The whole scheme failed because all except him "saw" the ghosts, and parents panicked with fright on their children's behalf.

So a question of truth was decided by experiential knowledge, the superior evidence of feeling-thinking. But the stark consequences that ensued from this nightly meeting with ghosts was decided by sheer power, he was fired. The unbeliever was widely esteemed as the kindest and most brilliant of men, and yet when people in power, looking for a pretext to sack him, reacted to his unfortunate rendez-vouz "everyone" was outraged, yet no one spoke in his defense. In Bali too much is at stake. The fear of black magic quenches political protests, and mollifies feelings of oppression into so many huddled voices, flowing softly from bright and cheerful faces, often masking—the evidence is unequivocal—hearts of fury.[23]

So wars are waged, battles are fought, but in massive indirect violence, with black magic a weapon of weak and powerful alike.[24] It is against this existential background that we should see Suriati's endeavor to keep smiling and bright, or a 13-year-old's rebuke of her gloomy mother.

Balinese cannot retreat to the "private" and feel safe. There is no place into which black magic cannot penetrate. The closest to a sanctuary a person can come is her own self. By cultivating and nourishing her "life force" or "heart" (the two are used as idioms for one another) one develops that measure of calm and equanimity that offers the only protection against black magic. Bright faces work to such ends, molding feeling onto expression. But the existential dilemma of how to persevere with and balance a life of so many cares is inescapable. Both the problem and its attempted solution focus on one experiential fact, that people carry their hearts always with them.

With this fragmentary glimpse into a Balinese world I have tried to field a challenge to our current concept of culture by marshalling an ethnography that hews more closely to the concepts people actually employ when coping with their many concerns. I urge that we must not move so swiftly from the patterns we have discerned in sets of data we ourselves have selected and extracted, and then construct further abstractions arising from our own culture-bound notions.

The essence of methodology is centered on the existential concerns of particular Balinese. I have argued for the need to bridge domains and cross thresholds along with people, if we are to grasp those connecting links that they forge in their lives, and to attend closely to the analytical concepts *they* use to shape their action on the world and their moral sensibilities in it.

Central among them is the Balinese conception of feeling-thinking, transcending our own deep distinction between cognition and emotion. Putting it to use, I have sought to articulate what their acts and concerns evoked on *my* feeling-mind. Balinese say there will be no "resonance" *(ngelah keneh)* except if we use our feelings—we will be captives of illusions. Feelings are essential so that we may appreciate facts of knowledge.

Also in Bali, people try at times to deafen themselves to the feeling part of thought, for feeling may be bothersome since it compels compassion and empathy *(kelangen)*. Such people have short strings and they can neither live morally nor attain high knowledge. Indeed, say Balinese, feeling is more essential for intellectual comprehension for it spawns intuition, evaluation and moral judgment. From this perspective a Western epistemology based on intellectual reasoning and objective thought alone appears an act of hubris. I submit that it cannot prove adequate to an anthropology that aspires to know the women and the men of this world.

This may have been the insight Kroeber was groping toward as early as 1949, when he made his unheeded plea for a unified conception of affect-idea system (I could have used the term to translate the Balinese feeling-thinking), wishing to make it the very core of our analysis of culture (Kroeber 1949:136). But we should not need to appeal to an anthropological authority to legitimate the concept. Let us show humility for other traditions of knowledge and that we are open to the insights they teach.

There has been much emphasis lately on "letting their voice be heard" in our writings—but in a patronizing way this has almost always been limited to their accounts of themselves and their particular worlds. We should also be willing to learn general lessons from their insights and analyses of the human condition.[25] It is in this spirit that I propose to employ a Bali-inspired model of "feeling-thinking" or "thinking-feeling" (written with a dash and not a slash) to replace the previously so successful, but Western culture-bound notion of "emotion."

In Bali a couple of months ago I sat with a group of people discussing this paper and testing my exposition on them. They listened intently and laughed heartily when I explained that "emotion" had gained acceptance in anthropology recently after years of neglect when it was deemed irrational and subjective. "Do Westerners also regard thinking as irrational?" they asked. "Well, then, how can feeling be—when they are one and the same?"

The expert among them[26] then took the word and spoke: "Westerners do not understand about feeling because they don't understand about the soul. They don't see that thinking-feeling emanates from the soul as one process and so they think that they think with their thoughts when actually they use their feelings—for they are one. If we do not use our feelings, there will be no resonance with life, we will be captured by the illusion only." He paused a moment, then went on like this:

"I have one piece of advice for you: When you go to Washington, tell Suriati's story and when you finish ask the audience 'What did you think when you heard this?'" Made's face brightened into a wide smile and he went on: "Then tell them: 'That which you thought, it was not your thinking, it was your feeling.' Then they will understand."

Notes

Acknowledgments. This paper was delivered to the Society for Cultural Anthropology meetings in Washington, D.C. May 1989 under the theme "Challenges to the Concept of Culture." I am indebted to Naomi Quinn for extending the invitation, and to I Made Bidja Arya Wang Bang Pynatih, Dr. Soegianto Sastrodiwiryo, Professor Arthur Kleinman, and my husband Fredrik Barth, for a wealth of useful suggestions. Fieldwork in Bali was conducted over 20 months in 1984–1989. The paper is printed as originally given.
1. During the discussion following my presentation and superbly led by Bradd Shore, the issue was raised that "experience-near" might be a problematic concept. There seems to be a tacit notion that somehow experience-near is more authentic than experience-distant, because it invokes praxis (rather than structure), events (rather than generalization), and feeling rather than thinking. I, of course, took the concept from Clifford Geertz who again took it from Heinz Kohut (Geertz 1984:124). I see the problem, but choose to keep the term precisely because it evokes lived experience, and *is* in that sense, more authentic.
2. For a discussion of the fruitfulness of glossing "folk" and "expert" models as of one kind, namely, "cultural models," see Quinn and Holland 1987 and Keesing 1987b.
3. The soul *(atma)* is the source of feeling, thinking, will, desire and instinct. Consciousness *(kesadaran)* is its essence. Balinese do not accept the notion of an unconscious in which feelings, memories, thoughts may be stored. Persons may, however,

lose their consciousness as when the soul is captured or vanquished by an evil spirit, or lost through fright (cf. Wikan 1989a).

4. *Bayu* is life force, vital energy, power, (cf. Winan 1989b and 1990, chapter 9). It is generally joined to, but distinct from, the soul *(atma* or *roh)* as the representation of God in the person. But people often confound the two and use *bayu* to refer to either. *Bayu* has clear bodily referents and is thus experience-near whereas the *atma* is etheral and abstract. *Bayu* may also be called *jiwa* or *tenaga.*

5. Balians are traditional healers (see Connor 1986 and Wikan 1990, chapters 12 and 13). The one in question was a *balian usada,* a category of literate medical specialists whose practice is founded on the possession of classical texts about healing *(usada)* and who acquire their skills by a formalized learning process. However, not all *balian usada* know how to read these texts, which are believed to be efficacious in themselves because of their mystical power *(sakti).* The Balian in question was, however, widely respected for his knowledge and ability to decipher the old texts. On *balian usada* see Connor 1986.

6. I conducted fieldwork in Cairo over two and a half years in the early 1970s, with yearly revisits thereafter for 16 years (Wikan 1980, 1983).

7. On the proclivity of studies of "the cultural construction of person and self" to tend toward an overrepresentation of exotic features, see Keesing 1989.

8. The need for this in Balinese studies has been incisively argued by Mark Hobart in a series of essays, especially 1985, 1986a, and 1986b. His compelling analyses have applicability and power far beyond the particular field of Bali.

9. I am indebted to Arthur Kleinman for this insight and formulation.

10. The works of M. Rosaldo and Lutz are, of course, crucial here.

11. Both Catherine Lutz and Fitz John Porter Poole make use of labels that join feeling and thought in their analyses of Ifaluk and Bimin-Kuskusmin, namely: "thought/ emotion" (Lutz 1988:92) and "thinking/feeling" (Poole 1987:4). Lutz emphasizes how "it is not simply that thought evokes, or is accompanied by an emotion; the two are inextricably linked" (1988:93). Poole notes how "Bimin-Kuskusmin claim that the 'forces of the heart' . . . that is, the vital processes of 'thinking/feeling' . . . are bound up in the very constitution of person and self" (1987:4). I would go further than these two, however, in suggesting that "feeling-thought" or "feeling-thinking" *substitutes* for the anthropological key concept "emotion." I regard the latter as fundamentally culture-bound, an Anglo-Saxon gloss on the world that does not even translate into some other Western languages, such as my own Norwegian (except in the loan-word "emosjon," a rather experience-distant and recent usage). The Balinese "feeling-thought" *(keneh)* or Ifaluk "thought/emotion" *(nunuwa),* or Bimin-Kushusmin "thinking/feeling" *(iboorop araar-taan)* are also, naturally, culture-bound, yet we stand to lose nothing by elevating one of those to analytical status, and trying out the implications. I suggest the notion "feeling-thought" as the better of these three in that the slash, to my mind, emphasizes the divide. I prefer to put "feeling" first, in accordance with Balinese popular notions; but this could be debated. I am quite willing to reverse the order.

   On the peculiar culture-boundedness of the Anglo Saxon term "mind," its intranslatability into languages like German or French, and the mistranslation involved in glossing German and French concepts that also connote spiritual aspects of the person into an English despiritualized "mind," see the brilliant essay by A. Wierzbicka (1989).

12. A *besserwissener* is someone who tends always to know things better than others— even than the person herself/himself—and makes no secret of it.

13. Cf. C. Geertz (1984:128–29): "Physically men come and go, mere incidents in a happenstance history, of no genuine importance, even to themselves. But the masks they wear, the stage they occupy, the parts they play, and, most important, the spectacle they mount remain and comprise not the facade but the substance of things, not least the self."

14. The *kelor* leaf is the size of a little fingernail.

15. This argument is set out in detail in my book (1990), especially chapters 3 and 4.

16. Balinese use the same word, *keneh,* for heart, feeling and thought.

17. Cf. Mary Zurbuchen: "Fears of the bad results of a relative's jealousy or disaffection play a powerful role in the management of kin-group and hamlet relations; the Balinese fear that supernatural force will be enacted by even the closest associates— hence the saying, *musuh tekén gigi* 'the enemy is as close as your teeth'" (1989:263–264).

18. Evidence is obtained by Hindus from the souls of the dead themselves when they are contacted, through a medium, 42 days after death. Muslims (roughly 8% of the population in the North) do not "believe" (though some do) that one can converse with the dead. Their evidence for death by black magic is sudden, unexplicable death, strange symptoms preceding death and other "unnatural" indications.

19. On this point, see also Hobart (1985:123): "The agent's thoughts or feelings are seen as an active part of knowledge, speculation and speech."

20. He had hanged his lover who was pregnant with a child.

21. How this works is set out in detail in Wikan 1990, especially chapters 3, 6, 8, and 9.

22. The story is told in detail in Wikan 1990, chapter 11.

23. I am struck with the stark contrast to Cairo's poor who, however destitute and "oppressed," *always* have people who will speak in their defense and fight a battle for them, *even* against persons in power. Everyone will always have *some* allies and co-contenders. In Bali, by contrast, people may be left utterly alone, with no allies except for closest family who would not dare to confront the enemy. Others will express sympathy and compassion privately, but they dare not risk their own well-being (or even lives) and that of their kin (see Wikan 1990, chapter 11). In Cairo, there *is* no such risk.

24. But the powerful, while also threatened, stand a better chance of hiring a good magician. Thus we could say black magic is more a weapon of the powerful than of the weak.

25. Again I choose to draw attention to the work of Mark Hobart, who urges compellingly that the "voice of the other" be listened to, also for its analytical input to the corpus of anthropological knowledge and epistemology.

26. He was a balian *usada.*

References Cited

Appadurai, Arjun. 1986. Theory in Anthropology: Center and Periphery. Comparative Studies in Society and History. 28 (2):356–374.

Clifford, James. 1988. The Predicament of Culture. Cambridge: Harvard University Press.

Connor, Linda. 1986. Balinese Healing. *In* Jero-Tapakan: Balinese Healer. L. Connor, P. Asch and T. Asch, eds. pp. 21–36. Cambridge: Cambridge University Press.

D'Andrade, Roy. 1984. Cultural Meaning Systems. *In* For Culture Theory: Essays on Mind, Self and Emotion. R. A. Shweder and R. A. deVine, eds. pp. 88–119. Cambridge: Cambridge University Press.

Festinger, Leon. 1956. When Prophecy Fails. Minneapolis: University of Minnesota Press.

Geertz, Clifford. 1973a [1996]. Person, Time, and Conduct in Bali. *In* The Interpretation of Cultures. pp. 360–411. New York: Basic Books.

1973b. Thick Description: Toward an Interpretive Theory of Culture. *In* The Interpretation of Cultures. pp. 3–30. New York: Basic Books.

1984 [1974] "From the Native's Point of View": On the Nature of Anthropological Understanding. *In* Culture Theory: Essays on Mind, Self, and Emotion. R. A. Shweder and R. A. LeVine, eds. pp. 123–136. Cambridge: Cambridge University Press.

1988. Works and Lives: The Anthropologists as Author. Stanford: Stanford University Press.

Hobart, Mark. 1985. Anthropos through the Looking-Glass: Or How to Teach the Balinese to Bark. *In* Reason and Morality. Joanne Overung, ed. pp. 104–134. London: Tavistock.

1986a. Summer's Days and Salad Days: The Coming of Age of Anthropology. London: Department of Anthropology. School of Oriental and African Studies (ms.).

1986b. Thinker, Thespian, Soldier, Slave: Assumptions about Human Nature in the Study of Balinese Society. *In* Context, Meaning and Power in Southeast Asia. Mark Hobart and Robert H. Taylor, eds. pp. 131–156. Ithaca: Cornell Southeast Asia Program.

Holland, D., and N. Quinn, eds. 1987. Cultural Models in Language and Thought. Cambridge: Cambridge University Press.

Keesing, Roger. 1987a. Anthropology as Interpretive Quest. Current Anthropology. 28(2):161–169.

1987b. Models "Folk" and "Cultural": Paradigms Regained? *In* Cultural Models in Language and Thought. D. Holland and N. Quinn, eds. pp. 363–393. Cambridge: Cambridge University Press.

1989. Theories of Culture Revisited. Paper presented at the American Anthropological Association Meetings, Washington, D.C.

Kleinman, Arthur. 1988. The Illness Narratives: Suffering, Healing and the Human Condition. New York: Basic Books.

Kroeber, A. L. 1949. The Nature of Culture. Chicago: University of Chicago Press.

Lakoff, G., and Z. Kovecses. 1987. The Cognitive Mind of Anger Inherent in American English. *In* Cultural Models in Language and Thought. D. Holland and N. Quinn, eds. pp. 195–221. Cambridge: Cambridge University Press.

Lutz, Catherine. 1988. Unnatural Emotions. Chicago: University of Chicago Press.

Mead, Margaret. 1942. Introduction. *In* Balinese Character. Gregory Bateson and Margaret Mead, eds. New York: Academy of Sciences.

Obeyesekere, Gananath. 1981. Medusa's Hair: An Essay on Personal Symbols and Religious Experience. Chicago: University of Chicago Press.

1985. Depression, Buddhism, and the Work of Culture in Sri Lanka. *In* Culture and Depression. A. Kleinman and B. Good, eds. pp. 134–152. Berkeley: University of California Press.

Poole, Fitz John Porter. 1987. The Voice of "Thinking/Feeling" and the Power of Speech: Ethnopsychological Discourse among Bimin-Kuskusmin. Paper presented at the American Anthropological Association meetings. La Jolla: University of California, San Diego (unpublished manuscript).

Quinn, Naomi. 1987. Convergent Evidence for a Cultural Model of American Marriage. *In* Cultural Models in Language and Thought D. Holland and N. Quinn, eds. pp. 173–192. Cambridge: Cambridge University Press.

Quinn, Naomi, and D. Holland. 1987. Culture and Cognition. *In* Cultural Models in Language and Thought. D. Holland and N. Quinn, eds. pp. 3–40. Cambridge: Cambridge University Press.

Rosaldo, Michelle Z. 1984. Toward an Anthropology of Self and Feeling. *In* Culture Theory: Essays on Mind, Self and Feeling. R. A. Shweder and R. A. LeVine, eds. pp. 137–157. Cambridge: Cambridge University Press.

Rosaldo, Renato. 1989. Culture and Truth: The Remaking of Social Analysis. Boston: Beacon Press.

Scheper-Hughes, N., and M. Lock. 1987. The Mindful Body: A Prolegomenon to Future Work in Medical Anthropology. Medical Anthropology Quarterly 1(1):6–41.

Solomon, Robert C. 1984. Getting Angry: The Jamesian Theory of Emotion in Anthropology. *In* Culture Theory, Essays on Mind, Self, and Emotion. R. A. Shweder and r. A. LeVine, eds. pp. 238–257. Cambridge: Cambridge University Press.

Strathern, Marilyn. 1987. Comment on Keesing's "Anthropology as Interpretive Quest." Current Anthropology 28(2):173–174.

Wierzbicka, Anna. 1989. Soul and Mind: Linguistic Evidence for Ethnopsychology and Cultural History. American Anthropologist 91(1):41–58.

Wikan, Unni. 1989 [1976]. Life Among the Poor in Cairo. London: Tavistock.

1983. Tomorrow, God Willing: Lives in the Back Streets of Cairo. Oslo: The University Press (in Norwegian).

1987. Public Grace and Private Fears: Gaiety, Offense and Sorcery in North Bali. Ethos 15:337–365.

1989a. Illness from Fright or Soulless: A North Balinese Culture-Bound Syndrome. Culture, Medicine and Psychiatry 13:25–50.

1989b. Managing the Heart to Brighten Face and Soul: Emotions in Balinese Morality and Health Care. American Ethnologist 17:294–310.

1990. Managing Turbulent Hearts: A Balinese Formula for Living. Chicago: University of Chicago Press.

Zurbuchen, Mary Sabina. 1989. Internal Translation in Balinese Poetry. *In* Writing on the Tongue. A. L. Becke, ed. pp. 215–279. Michigan Papers on South and Southeast Asia, No. 33. The University of Michigan.

Reading 29

BEGINNINGS AND ENDINGS

Annie Tremmel Wilcox

A *Circumstantial Narrative of the Campaign in Russia.* This book has come downstairs to my workbench in Conservation from Special Collections because it needs treatment. It's not old—it was printed in 1817—and will be a good book for me to practice conservation techniques with. I pull out a treatment survey and report sheet and begin to fill it out.

This book's major problem is that it doesn't have any covers. All that remains attached to the text block is the original leather spine of the binding with its label. The leather appears to be calf and has red rot, a condition of older leather that causes it to turn red and crumble at the slightest touch. As I examine it, the spine leaves leather smudges all over my hands. Since this is a tight-back book where the leather cover is glued directly to the back of the text block, I will probably not be able to save the spine piece. With luck, however, I will be able to remove and reuse the label.

Next I begin to examine the text block. As I open it, I notice the faint musty smell older books often have. I can see that the pages are foxed (spotted with rust from bits of iron in the paper there as a result of the way the paper was made or sized). I will probably be able to lighten the stains as I treat the paper but not remove them. Foxing this bad usually doesn't come out in the wash.

I page through the text block carefully. Facing the title page is a frontispiece—the stereotypical picture of Napoleon, lock of hair over his forehead, hand in his coat front. The foxing is worse on these two pages, and as a result Napoleon has a very ruddy complexion. The rust stains continue throughout the rest of the book. The edges of the pages are ragged in places, and the frontispiece has a tear that extends from the fore edge of the page down through Napoleon's portrait and goes just past his left ear and into his shoulder.

Wilcox, Annie Tremmel. "Beginnings and Endings." *A Degree of Mastery: A Journey through Book Arts Apprenticeship.* Minneapolis: New Rivers Press, 1999. 3–43.

The other major problem with *Campaign* is that the paper of the text block is very soft. The edges of the pages are slightly ruffled and torn in places. Whatever internal or external sizing this paper may have will wash away, leaving these pages even softer and more vulnerable. This will be a problem. I will probably have to resize the paper to strengthen it before I reassemble the text block. One of the primary things my job as a book and paper conservator entails is leaving an item in better condition than it was when I received it.

I complete the survey sheet, noting everything I can about *Campaign* and its condition. Not only will this serve as my record of the treatment, but a copy will stay here in the Conservation Department to answer any questions someone may have later about the condition of this book before treatment. Then I take a set of documentation slides that show the book's lack of covers, its spine, the title page and frontispiece of Napoleon, and sample interior pages. Once I have finished treating the book, I will take another set of slides to show how it's been improved. I take a pencil and letter the pages that aren't numbered, mostly front matter, so that I can get the pages back in the correct order later. The graphite won't hurt the book or come off during treatment.

Now I am ready to begin "pulling" the text block—the process of taking it apart for treatment. I open a tool drawer and take out my lifting knife.

It was a sunny day in October 1983 the first time I met Bill Anthony. I was busy setting type at Windhover Press, the University of Iowa's letterpress, where I was a student of Kim Merker's. I had been working there for three years, slowly learning all that goes into the letterpress printing of fine books. I liked the rhythm of setting type by hand and pulling freshly printed sheets of text. Eventually I hoped to become Kim's assistant at the press. I was the only person working in the shop that afternoon when he asked if I would like to go over to the health sciences library with him. A bookbinder and conservator from Chicago named Bill Anthony was bringing back some of the books he had worked on for the library's John Martin Rare Book Room. Anthony was going to show slides of the treatments he'd performed, and Kim wanted to see them.

I had been in the health sciences library before, but never in the rare book room. It's stuck in an out-of-the-way corner on the second floor. When we arrived, a few other people were milling about looking at the books in the display cases. Kim knew who they were and went to talk to them. As I looked at the books, I noticed I was the only woman in the room. A slide projector was set up on one of the long tables. After a few minutes people began taking seats. I sat down next to Kim just as the lights were dimmed.

The first slide was a before-treatment picture of a Vesalius, a mid-seventeenth-century medical book, that appeared to be in bad shape. The pages looked dirty and broken in places—not a book that could be handled easily. My attention was drawn, however, away from the slide to the man narrating. He appeared to be in his midfifties, a gentle man with a serious face and a soft voice. it was the voice that caught me with its strong hint of Ireland. This was Bill Anthony.

I was fascinated as he continued through the slides. He had taken this book completely apart to treat it. I was only familiar with putting together new books. How did he get the pages apart? How was it possible to wash and dry a book? How did he ever get all the pages together again, in the right order, and bound? I was enthralled. One man off to the side kept asking questions. When the slide show was over and Kim introduced me to people, I was to discover that this was Dr. John Martin, the man who had donated a large number of valuable and rare historical medical books to the university and the man for whom this room was named. He had come all the way from Clarinda, Iowa, to see how Bill Anthony had treated his books. The Vesalius had been one of the jewels of his collection.

The last slide showed the book, now rebound and covered in alum-tawed pigskin, a rich white leather, with tooled lines that crisscrossed in a diamond pattern on the cover. When the lights came up, the book was on a table in the front of the room. It seemed like magic that this book was now restored to a condition where people could pick it up and easily turn the pages without harming it. Dr. Martin and the others examined the Vesalius while Kim introduced me to Mr. Anthony, who warmly shook my hand. He had red hair, now going to gray, and wore khaki pants and a blue oxford shirt with the sleeves rolled up to the elbows. He smiled and patted Kim on the back as he shook his hand.

I had just managed to tell him how much I enjoyed seeing his slides when Dr. Martin came up with the Vesalius to ask some more questions. Kim and I left, and on the way back to the press, he told me Bill Anthony was thinking of closing his business in Chicago. Kim was trying to convince the university that Bill should come to Iowa and begin a conservation department in the Main Library. Maybe Bill would even teach bookbinding classes.

Kim knew I was interested in bookbinding as a sideline to printing because I was working a couple of afternoons a week for the local binder of the Windhover Press books. In the afternoons when I worked at the press setting type, Kim would often tell me about the Center for the Book he was scheming to create at Iowa. Having a bookbinder-conservator around sounded like a good plan. He had an idea about a young papermaker who might like to come and teach at the university too. I had liked Mr. Anthony and was amazed that he could successfully take books apart and put them back together again in better condition. I had no idea that there were people who did this sort of thing.

As I suspected, the spine leather is so rotted it comes easily away from where it is glued to the back of the text block. I slide the edge of the lifting knife under one side of the leather and slice the spine off in crumbling strips. Carefully, I remove the leather label in one piece. I'll clean the back of the rotted leather later. For now I place it in a labeled envelope so that it won't get mislaid.

Once I slice and scrape the rest of the leather off the back of the book, I must remove the animal-hide glue that holds the spine lining material on and the backs of the sections together. It has dried hard, resembling the mucilage glue I had used as a child in school. When this glue is removed the book will come apart more easily.

The book is already in the job backer, a large iron standing press that clamps the text block firmly so that the spine is facing up and can be worked on. I prepare a dry paste about the consistency of Cream of Wheat that has sat too long and heap it in mounds all along the spine's surface. The paste allows moisture to slowly soften the lining and glue so that they can be scraped off. The book must sit for half an hour, so I drape a piece of Saran Wrap over the paste to keep it from drying out too quickly.

Later I remove the Saran Wrap and scrape the paste off the back of the book carefully with my bone folder—a long, slender, polished piece of bone reminiscent of a tongue depressor. The mull, an open-mesh, starched fabric that was glued onto *Campaign* as a spine lining, is soft now and peels up from the backs of the sections. Next I take the pointed end of my bone folder and scrape the brown animal-hide glue off the backs of the sections of paper that make up this book. It comes off in most places, but another application of wheat paste is needed before it comes off completely. Moisture has softened the back of the sections, and I have to be careful not to scrape away any of the paper.

Quickly I take the book out of the job backer and put it on my workbench. I have to pull the text before the backs of the sections dry out again. I reach into one of my tool drawers and take out a pair of curved dissecting scissors and a pair of hemostats, the delicate gripping tools used by surgeons. I open the text block to the very center of the first section where the threads of sewing show. Lifting them up just a bit with the hemostats, I clip the threads with the scissors. Then I close the section again and, grabbing it gently by the fore edge of the pages, pull it away from the rest of the text block. If there is any glue left along the spine of the section, the sections will still come away because it is damp and soft. I continue to do this for the rest of the text block. If I tried to pull the book dry, I would tear off the backs of the sections, making more repair work for myself later. Since *Campaign* is so thick, I have to continually redampen the spine of the sections with a large, wet cotton swab.

Now that the sections have been pulled, it's time to wash the book. I get out several white photographic trays that are large enough to hold the sections of *Campaign* when they are opened flat into folios—sheets folded once in the middle. I also get out a stack of wet-strength paper that is cut to fit these trays. This paper is used to support pages during washing and deacidification. It is almost impossible to handle wet sheets of paper without tearing them. Ordinary paper loses eighty percent of its strength when it's wet. Wet-strength paper holds up because it's impregnated with a resin that coats the fibers and keeps it strong in water.

Since there is so much foxing and staining on the pages of *Campaign*, I half fill one of the trays with heated deionized water out of a sterling silver tap resistant to the water's corrosive powers on metal. Warm water floats more impurities out of the paper than cold. I submerge one piece of wetstrength paper and follow by submerging two folios of *Campaign* on top, watching to make sure the paper wets out completely. The old book smell suddenly becomes much more pungent. I continue alternating wet-strength paper with folios of the text, adding more water to the tray as necessary. The whole book takes up two trays.

By the time I have finished with the second tray, the water in the first is bright yellow with the impurities that have washed out of the paper. I drain off this water and add fresh, repeating this process over the course of several hours until the water ceases to turn yellow, changing the water in the trays every half hour. Now it is time to deacidify the paper.

Kim's dream for the Center for the Book began to materialize, and in the spring of 1985, I was among the students in the first bookbinding class Bill Anthony taught after setting up the Conservation Department in the university's Main Library. My work with Kim at Windhover Press had led me to a job at a local edition bindery, and I was thrilled to have a chance to move beyond the simple types of bindings I did there to study with Bill. He had seemed very nice when I had gone to get his signature on my registration sheet. He asked polite questions about the job I'd had at the bindery.

The class met on Wednesday nights for two and a half hours in a makeshift book arts room in the Art Building. We had book presses and workbenches, but no paper cutter. Bill had to bring materials to class precut. He had planned several bindings for us to do, and each class began with a demonstration of the steps we would do that evening. Then, as we worked, Bill moved among us answering questions and helping with any problems we had. it was a tight squeeze, and my first impression was that he was genial and easy to work with, although the lack of a paper cutter obviously bothered him.

The class was an odd mix of students. There were two schoolteachers with fancy manicures and clean work aprons. There was Tom, the only male in the class, who soon became one of Bill's racquetball partners. And there was Nadine. She was a graduate student in the Math Department who was good with numbers, but not with her hands. She also took everything Bill said literally.

For example, the first night of class Bill showed slides of a conservation treatment. The slide projected on the wall depicted pages of a book washing in a tray of water. Nadine asked if the spin cycle of the washer didn't damage the pages of the book. And what about the dryer? I knew from having been at various book arts lectures with her that Nadine had a habit of asking serious questions that seemed to show a complete lack of common sense. It was a while before Bill learned to ignore her and just go on with his explanations. Never before had he taught a class where he hadn't handpicked the students from a pool of interested binders.

And there was Greta. She worked with me at Windhover, filling book orders and keeping track of who owed what. Expecting her first child, she grew in size as the semester progressed. One night as she was putting a book in the nipping press, Greta turned the handle the wrong way so that the platen of the press flew up instead of clamping down on her book. Bill was standing next to her, watching.

"That's the problem with women," he said to Greta, watching the platen go down toward the book as she spun the handle the other way. "They can never screw right."

Greta looked down at her expanding waistline and back up at him and replied, "Oh, I don't know. I think I've proved that I'm pretty good at screwing." Fair-skinned Bill turned a deep crimson and laughed.

I had no idea at the time that this gentle man with his sly sense of humor was one of the most famous book conservators and binders in the country. He and his apprentices in his shop in Chicago had bound editions for the foremost printers in the United States. His fine, one-of-a-kind leather bindings sold for thousands of dollars. He conserved rare and valuable books for libraries throughout the Chicago area and beyond. Books like the giant folio editions of Audubon's *Birds of America*. I knew none of this. At this point he was just another teacher, although he was one I liked and respected very much.

One evening we were learning the Coptic, a four-needle stitch that has been used to bind Egyptian books since the second century. Bill had explained the sewing pattern to the class and was facing me over the workbench, trying to guide me through it. Nadine was sitting next to me trying to thread one of her needles.

Bill, finally frustrated at my botched sewing of the sections of the book, came over and made me get up so that he could show me how to do it. He took up the slightly curved needles and began sewing the next section of paper to the text block. But he got mixed up at the point where the needles passed each other, changing sewing directions, and had to take the stitches out and start over again. At this point I leaned over and asked, "Are you sure you've done this before?"

Again he turned crimson. Then he laughed and replied, "I think so." He got the sewing started again, showed me how to attach the section correctly, and I took my place at the workbench to finish sewing the text block. Nadine was still threading her needles.

I stand the photographic trays up in the big sink to drain off the deionized wash water from the folios of *Campaign*. After half an hour, I lay the trays back down and pour a solution of magnesium bicarbonate into them. We prepare this buffer ourselves by bubbling carbon dioxide through two large glass containers of magnesium carbonate powder mixed with deionized water, siphoning out the resulting solution into plastic jugs. Once in the trays, the buffer is adjusted with the addition of more deionized water until the pH is around 8, indicating that the solution is alkaline. The folios soak in the magnesium bicarbonate between the sheets of wet-strength tissue for about half an hour.

This is one of the standard procedures for buffering paper. Through washing, I have removed as many soluble acids as possible, and this next bath will deposit a buffer in the paper that I hope will neutralize any acids that remain in the sheets. Although it is possible to age paper artificially and see how well it lasts after being treated this way, conservation science is still too new to know how well such treatments will endure over the years.

After half an hour, I stand the trays up again and drain off the magnesium bicarbonate solution. I carefully place the sets of wet-strength, each with two folios of the text trapped between them, on the drying racks to air-dry overnight. The next morning, I remove the papers from the drying racks, peel apart the sets, and separate the folios from the wet-strength paper. It amazes me to see how little the sheets have cockled in the drying process. Because this paper is so soft, the slight tear across Napoleon's portrait has lengthened during handling. Other edge tears will also need repair. But the pages are noticeably cleaner and less stained and spotted after treatment.

I can feel how much softer the pages have become as a result of being washed and buffered. The sizing in the paper, put in originally to protect and strengthen it like spray starch on shirts, contributed greatly to the yellow color of the wash water and is almost completely gone. I could go ahead and mend the sheets and rebind the book, but the pages would be more susceptible to dirt and tears if left this way. It will be better if I resize them first.

I make the solution for resizing by mixing a third of a cup of Methocel 4AC into hot water. The fine white methyl cellulose powder disperses in hot water but does not dissolve. I then add a cup of room-temperature deionized water and the mixture begins to thicken. Adding another cup of cold deionized water from the refrigerator causes the Methocel to thicken more into a smooth solution not unlike runny Jell–O. This is the magic powder that is sold by the ton to McDonald's to keep their shakes thick. I thin mine out a little more until it's runny, but still a bit slimy to the touch, and pour it into one of the trays.

I place each folio of *Campaign* between two sheets of Hollytex, a thin sheet of spun polyester, and submerge it into the Methocel. The Hollytex has an open texture, and the liquid passes through it easily. Yet it is strong enough to support the weight of the wet, resized sheet as I lift it out of the solution and lay it to drain on a slanted sheet of Plexiglas in the sink. I blot each folio to remove excess moisture, carefully transfer it to dry sheets of Hollytex, and place it back on the drying rack. To do this for more than two hundred pages of text takes a very long time. Several days, in fact, because I can only lay out a dozen sets of folios on the drying racks at once.

As the sheets are finished, I carefully refold them into sections following the pagination and my own penciled notations. I layer the sections between pieces of binder's board and weight them gently over several days, gradually pressing out what slight cockling has occurred as a result of resizing, but not pressing out the impression made by the type when the pages were printed. Next the tears will be mended.

During that first semester I studied with Bill, I began to feel a companionship with him I had never known with any other teacher. He had a deep love for his work that I found contagious. He was always enthusiastic. He always listened to his students when we spoke to him. Even Nadine was a valued and important member of the class, no matter how far from common sense she strayed. For me, it was like being in a room with a chocolate cake: I always wanted more. Late that spring I also discovered the great talent of this craftsman.

In February, Bill had mounted an exhibit of bindings in the University of Iowa Museum of Art, *The Art and Craft of Bookbinding*. One class night in April just before the exhibit was to come down, he arranged for a museum guard to let us see the exhibit after hours. As we waited on the steps of the museum to be let in, I had no idea what to expect. Other than the work Bill had demonstrated in class, I had only seen the Vesalius he had treated for the health sciences library. I had no idea what other types of work he did. The binder I had I worked for took letterpress editions and put them into plain paper and cloth covers a lot like what you find under the dust jackets of hardcovers in the bookstore. I was about to be enlightened.

A guard wearing a gun met us at the door and let us in the museum, showing us where to hang up our coats and backpacks. Lighting was low except in a small gallery up the stairs to the right as we went in. Bill handed each of us a glossy exhibit brochure containing a brief history of bookbinding and told us to look around and let him know if we had any questions. Freestanding cases throughout the room were filled with books of designs and styles that I could never have imagined. I walked from one Plexiglas-covered case to another in a state of openmouthed amazement.

There were conservation treatments Bill had done for the library. A fourteenth-century manuscript written on vellum had been rebound in a warm honey-brown leather with windowpane lines tooled into the covers. I wanted to pick it up and open the small brass clasps holding it shut to see the pages inside. Another one of Bill's bindings was a German book from 1687 bound in vellum with intricate lettering on its wide spine. It was held closed by tiny pegs resembling small bone folders slipped through alum-tawed pigskin thongs. A big book, it looked quite light in its vellum cover. I wanted to open it and see how the vellum cover moved in my hands.

There were cases and cases of French and English "fine bindings." Bill explained to us that these were books decorated more artistically than the conservation bindings—usually in colored leathers with designs of leather inlaid and edged with gold tooling. Many were on loan from Dr. Samuel Rosenthal, a friend of Bill's from Chicago. A number of the fine bindings had been done by Bill.

I was transfixed in front of a case containing a large book by Bill covered in bright green leather. On its cover were onlaid strips of bright red leather that formed a rectangle with a diamond interwoven with it. These were framed by two larger red leather-strip rectangles. Everywhere the red and the green met was a perfectly straight line of gold tooling. The colors were more vivid than any I had ever seen before on a book cover. I looked up to see Bill standing on the other side of the case, looking at me with amusement.

"How did you do this?" I asked him. "How did you keep the gold line so straight?" As he proceeded with an explanation involving gold foil and things called "rolls" and "pieces of line," I knew that whatever the process, I wanted to learn how to do it. I wanted to be this man's student until I knew how to make books as beautiful as these. I wanted the whole chocolate cake.

So I continued to take Bill's class. In the fall of 1985, he moved us from the Art Building to the Conservation Department in the Main Library so that we could have access to the equipment we needed. There were some new students (we had lost the two tidy school teachers—but the rest of the class remained). Bill decided to have everyone do the same initial project, and then let us each choose what we wanted to do after that.

We started out by making three small quarter-cloth bindings with marbled paper on the front and back covers. None of us had ever done any case binding, which, unlike the nonadhesive bindings we had done the semester before, required using adhesives. We learned quickly that it was a bit tricky to keep the glue only where we wanted it. I enjoyed making these three books, all exactly the same except for the different marbled papers I used on their covers.

Bill had given us free rein over the materials in the department, and I was often paralyzed by the choices. I spent most of one evening just leafing through the two drawers of marbled papers, each sheet carefully decorated by hand. They were the most beautiful sheets of paper I had ever seen. Bill finally came over and teased me about taking so long to make up my mind, even though I was still ahead of almost everyone else in getting my books completed. I was to learn later he didn't much care for marbled papers and almost never used them on his own bindings. He generously bought these for his students to use. Some of them had been given to him by former students and friends who made marbled papers.

I responded to his teasing by picking out three of the brightest and wildest papers I could find. The first had fine veins of teal blue, brown, and two shades of bright orange. The second had a fine feathery pattern in glowing turquoise and green. And the third was scalloped in purple, sky blue. and white. But they were all made on base sheets of dark cream that almost matched perfectly the cloth I chose for the spines. My books turned out well and felt nice in my hands.

And the colors made Bill wince noticeably. Many years later, I discovered that these vivid papers were marbled by Norma Rubovits, one of America's foremost paper marblers and a former binding student of Bill's in Chicago.

By the time the semester was over I was hooked. The previous summer, I had quit working for the edition binder in town who did the Windhover books. I had definitely decided that doing one or two similar bindings was much more agreeable than doing two hundred and fifty exactly alike. I liked Bill's approach to his work. He was meticulous and didn't panic when things didn't go right with our books. He simply helped us correct them, calmly and carefully. He said that there was no mistake in binding that you couldn't correct or redo, and I found that comforting.

Paper mending can be a tedious and time-consuming process. I am lucky in this case. The tears in *Campaign* are along the edges of the pages and, with the exception of Napoleon's portrait, will go quickly. The principle is simple: a tear in paper is stabilized by gluing another piece of paper to it—just like adhesive tape, only better. I lay out the tools and supplies I will need on the top of my bench and prepare my adhesive.

Ever conservator I talk to has different opinions about adhesives. Some use pure starch paste—derived from flours with the proteins and glutens removed—for their work. Some use "mix"—pastes combined with other adhesives such as PVA (polyvinyl acetate—a kissing cousin of Elmer's glue) or methyl cellulose. Others use rabbit or fish glues. The choice of adhesive depends on a number of things, but, for most, the ideal is to use the purest adhesive in the weakest strength that will accomplish a specific task. Adhesives applied in conservation are supposed to be reversible, so that if for any reason they need to be removed later, they can be.

For mending *Campaign* I will use *zin shofu,* a Japanese wheat-starch paste. I measure a third of a cup of the thin off-white powder and mix it with three cups of deionized water to soak for twenty minutes before it is cooked. Conservators used to spend the cooking time stirring the paste in a saucepan over a hot plate. Now the mixture is put into the nonstick saucepan of a Cook'n'Stir, the type of kitchen appliance used to make hollandaise sauce. It has a heating element with temperature control and a rotating blade that stirs continuously. Once the *zin shofu* sits for twenty minutes, I simply turn on the machine, and it stirs and cooks the paste for me.

Twenty minutes later the opaque white mixture has thickened considerably and turned translucent. I remove it from the pan, sieve it while adding deionized water to thin it to the consistency of smooth gravy, and pour it into a plastic container that has been sprayed on the inside with Lysol to retard spoilage and the growth of mold. I spoon paste into a small clear glass bowl and thin it further with water until it is almost runny.

While the paste cooks, I lay out the tools I need for mending on my bench: a piece of clear, thin Mylar, several brushes, the bowl of paste, another bowl of deionized water, some tweezers, large cotton swabs, and an assortment of mending papers made from kozo, a long-fibered plant resembling bamboo that produces a tough yet thin paper. I also prepare a corner of my bench with strips of heavy blotter and Hollytex and weights.

I decide to begin with the frontispiece of Napoleon and do the difficult mend first. It is a jagged tear, but it has not warped during drying. The edges also meet all along their length, so there will be no gaps. If both sides of a tear don't meet evenly, the resulting gap must be filled in with kozo because pulling them together would cause warping elsewhere in the sheet. I turn the page over to do my primary mend from the back.

I wet-tear a strip of kozo three-eighths of an inch wide from a sheet similar in color to the text paper. This is done by running a thin lining brush full of water down the length of the kozo and pulling the narrow strip away. Because the kozo paper is made of long fibers, the tear is furry, resembling a thin paper centipede. I put the frontispiece under the sheet of Mylar and position the strip on top so that I can check how well it adheres to the contours of the tear. This tear is fairly straight; for crooked tears, the kozo can be wet-torn to match its configuration. I pull the page back out, and, leaving the mend strip on the Mylar. I paint it with the thin paste, making sure that my strokes pull the fibers out at right angles to the strip. I pull the kozo off the Mylar with the tweezers and lay it on the mend, carefully rolling it down with a large cotton swab that applies pressure and helps soak up extra moisture. Slowly, I make sure the two edges of the tear match. Long tears are usually mended in sections. I quickly sandwich the mend in between two pieces of Hollytex and two pieces of blotter, and weight till dry. Drying the mend under tension like this keeps it from cockling from the moisture I have introduced into a small area of the page. While this first tear dries, I do another, smaller edge tear in another page. Soon I have several mends drying on the corner of my bench.

I go back and check the frontispiece. The mend has dried flat and looks good from the back. I turn it over. The two portions of Napoleon are now rejoined. But just by handling the page I can tell that it has a tendency to bend along the tear line, so I need to reinforce it from the front as well. I attach another kozo strip across the front margin of the page and dry it. But I can't run a kozo mend across the portrait of Napoleon (the kozo mend will dry an opaque off-white and will obscure the fine black lines of the illustration). I tease another strip of kozo into a much smaller piece, spider shaped, that I can use to tack the tear at a point where I won't interfere with the illustration. I use the white space of Napoleon's epaulet. I have heard of conservators mending important texts with single kozo fibers so as not to obscure the printing, but fortunately Napoleon doesn't command such attention.

The page is stable when I have finished and will turn without buckling when the book is rebound. But the staining on the portrait side of the paper makes the kozo mends obvious. I touch them up lightly with colored pencils so that they blend in better. I don't want to hide the fact that the page has been mended, but I don't want my mends to distract from Napoleon either. The rest of the work goes quickly. I reassemble the folios into sections and order them into a text block. Finally, *Campaign* is ready to be resewn.

Bill and I had settled into a routine that fall semester. I was always the first one to class on Wednesday nights. I would wait in the hallway for Bill to come back to the library after having gone home for dinner. He would unlock the door, we would walk down the long corridor to Conservation, and talk about this and that. Books. Things I was working on at Windhover. What I was working on in class. He would show me what he was busy with at his bench. The rest of the students would drift in, and class would begin at seven.

At this point, after teaching the class for three semesters, Bill no longer assigned bindings that all the students were to do at the same time. Instead, each of us, after a chat with him, worked on whatever project we wanted to. Another schoolteacher had joined the class, driving to Iowa City each week from Anamosa. She spent her time repairing her own books or books of friends. I was doing a sketchbook that would have a spine of leather (the first time I had worked with this material). Greta was making a book for the baby due mid-semester.

Bill would usually make a trip around the room, going from bench to bench as class began. He would answer any questions we had, and once everyone was busy working, he would go to his own bench and work on whatever project he had to do. Sometimes it was private commission work. Sometimes it was work for Special Collections. We knew that we could always interrupt him with any questions we had. Bill never made anyone feel like an intruder, and he gave his full attention to his answer, often putting down what he was doing to help a student at his or her bench.

When I came up behind him—his workbench faced the wall—I would always stop to see what he was doing before I asked my question. Often Bill would describe to me what he was doing and why. I was fascinated by his job and its privileges. To be able to handle rare and valuable books on a regular basis. To examine them and understand their structures.

That fall, Bill was working on the Petrus Comestor. This was a large book that had previously been rebound during the nineteenth century in a cloth-and-paper case binding. An incunabulum printed in 1473 during the earliest days of movable type, the Petrus was quite valuable. Bill had taken it out of its most recent binding and was rebinding it more appropriately. For several weeks, we watched the progression as Bill dry-cleaned the pages, mended them, resewed the text block, and prepared to recover it.

For this new cover, Bill laced on huge oak boards, as the book measured roughly sixteen by eleven inches. From my studies of the history of printing and binding, I knew that books had once had wooden covers, but to actually see them placed on a book was impressive. Bill had sanded and stained the wood, fitting the boards to the shape and size of the text block. Watching him, I realized book conservation required knowledge of many things—including woodworking!

The next week during class, Bill was getting ready to put on a spine covering of leather that would extend over and cover a third of the front and back boards. He had ordered the leather from a woman in New York and showed it to us that night in class. It was goatskin, something Bill called "Super Chieftain." When he unrolled it, there was the unmistakable aroma of leather. He held up the supple skin and we could see from its shape that it had been an animal. In fact, it reminded me too vividly of some creature run over on the highway. But I liked the smell and feel of the skin, smooth and slightly knobby on one side and rough on the other, like the inside of one of my mother's leather handbags.

By the end of the semester, the binding was complete and Bill showed it to us one last time before it was boxed and returned to its home in Special Collections. The supple pages turned easily in their new binding. I could see that the first twenty pages still had some dirt and fingerprints on them that Bill hadn't been able to remove. The first pages of a book are almost always the dirtiest since they get handled the most. I could see that the rubrication—the highlighting by hand in red—of each of the woodcut capital letters ended two-thirds of the way through the book. Obviously, the scribe had gone blind by that point. I stood and paged through the book with the others for quite some time. It was much better off in its new binding.

I fold new endsheets for *Campaign* and tip linen hinges to them with a thin stripe of adhesive. These hinges are strips of unbleached linen about an inch and a half wide and the length of the endsheets. They are creased lengthwise with the material on one side of the fold only one-sixteenth of an inch wide. The narrow sides are glued out and the hinges are adhered to the first and last sections, with the larger, unglued flaps of linen left free on the sides that will face the covers. These flaps will be adhered later to the inside of the covers, reinforcing the weakest area of the cover where the book swings open.

Now that the text block is complete, I can punch the holes in the folds of the sections and resew the book. There are already holes where the book was sewn previously. I use those and have to punch only three new holes in each section. using a thin card strip with notches cut in one edge. Each section is opened and placed fold down in a punching through—a V-shaped jig made out of wood. The card is placed down into the center of the section, and using the notches as guides, I punch through the section with my awl. Even though there are many sections to this book, punching holes this way doesn't take more than five minutes. Now the text block is ready for sewing.

This book consists of a number of thin sections. To keep down the swelling that could occur in the spine area due to too many lengths of sewing running back and forth through the sections, I am going to sew *Campaign* "two-on." I have never done this before, and just diagramming the sewing and getting it straight in my mind takes most of one morning. Unlike standard sewing, in which the thread runs up the length of one section and down the length of the next, I will weave in and out, running the length of thread up through two sections and down through two more. This was a technique first used in the nineteenth century to speed up book production in a era when all books were still sewn by hand. Binders found it much quicker to sew text blocks together two sections at a time.

I am going to sew this book on half-inch linen tapes and attach three of them to a sewing frame. This holds them taut at spaced intervals perpendicular to the text block, allowing me to sew up and back through the sections and weave the thread around these tapes for more stability. Later the tapes will be glued to the covering boards to help attach the text block securely.

I thread a needle with a thin linen thread, wax it so that it is less likely to knot, and begin to sew the sections. I follow the two-on diagram, making several false starts. Weaving up and back through two sections at a time is slow and confusing, and, although I can do it more quickly after sewing a third of the book, it takes me more than three hours to get all the sections sewn and to cut the tapes loose from the frame.

Next I must "forward" the text block—the steps done before the covers are attached. I return the book to the job backer, with the folded creases of the spine of the text block facing up. The tapes running across the back of the text block are held securely by the thin expanses of thread that run over them. I tighten the backer gently—just enough to hold the text block securely and keep it from falling through onto the floor. Then I glue up the spine of the text block with some of the *zin shofu* I used for mending. After a few minutes when it has dried, I apply a second layer of paste and a lining strip of the Japanese mending tissue—a slightly thicker weight than used to mend tears—that is the length and width of the spine area. This will stabilize the backs of the sections and begin to hold the spine rigid.

While the spine linings dry, I make new endbands for the book. In the early days of bookbinding, the endbands consisted of a core of leather or cord that was sewn onto the top and bottom of the text block with a series of windings of thread to wrap it. They were tacked periodically through the section folds below, and helped protect the head and tail of the text block's spine. Fine bindings still use ornate endbands made this way using colored silks. Usually for conservation work, I sew new endbands of unbleached linen thread. But in the early nineteenth century, when *Campaign* was published, endbands consisted of pieces of striped cloth folded over a cord core, cut to the width of the text block, and glued onto the book at the head and tail. Like two-on sewing, this type of "stuck-on" endband significantly speeded up the binding process. Since I am putting a new cover on this book, I choose to put on a new endband that approximates what *Campaign* might have had originally.

I take a small piece of unbleached linen and dilute a little forest green acrylic paint in a glass bowl. Using the edge of a plastic drafting triangle, I paint thin, evenly spaced stripes on the linen. I have made endbands like this before and it goes quickly. When the piece of linen is dry, I glue it in half with a piece of cord inside the fold. When the new endband material is dry, I cut off two widths and glue them on the text block—still in the press—at the head and tail with PVA, a heavier adhesive. Then I line the spine with PVA and three more layers of handmade cotton paper running the length of the spine and the endbands. There are three slight bulges in the paper linings where they run over the sewing tapes. When the linings are dry, I sand these areas lightly until the entire spine is flush and smooth. Forwarding complete, the book is now ready for covering, and I take it out of the job backer.

Periodically, Bill brought items of special interest down from Special Collections for us to look at during class. It was a chance to examine styles of bindings that we would never get the chance to make in class. One night he showed us a jeweled binding (a copy of *King Florus and the Fair Jehane*). I knew such bindings existed, but had never seen one up close. It was covered in green leather with a fine gold filigree decorating the edges of the boards, set with tiny opals and rubies. But the ornate binding also kept the book from opening easily. This was obviously a case in which the binding mattered more than the content of the book inside.

Another night, I remember that we were all hard at work when Bill asked quietly if we would like to see a page from the Gutenberg Bible. Suddenly everyone was standing around the middle workbench as he opened a tall black leather-covered book—a slender volume containing an essay about the Gutenberg Bible in general and this single page in particular. I had never seen a leaf-book before and was amazed that we were looking at a page from the famous forty-two-line Bible, the first book printed in Europe.

It was a beautiful, creamy page with dark type in two heavy columns. Bill let us examine both sides and touch it. I had no idea that our own Special Collections held such an item.

"Why would just one page be bound up like this?" someone asked.

"It's a presentation binding," Bill answered. "Incomplete copies of famous and valuable books are cut up and sold as single sheets. Dealers can get more money for the pages individually than they can for the volume as an incomplete copy of something."

I was appalled. It seem barbaric to cut up a text—even if it wasn't complete.

Another time Bill showed us a magnificent illuminated book of hours that he was going to rebind—a fifteenth-century French manuscript that had been horribly mutilated. None of us had seen a book like this before. Bill paged through it carefully, his hands supporting the fragmented pages, to show us the one remaining illustration and the pages where the other illuminated capitals and decorative borders had been cut out. Slowly he turned pages that resembled Swiss cheese. So much material had been cut away that in places only stubs of text remained along the gutter. Apparently such treatment had once been common practice. Victorians kept "border books" of the illustrations and decorative borders they had cut from manuscripts. I was amazed that people would brutalize such obvious works of art. I could see that part of conservation was coming to terms with such injuries. But how do you compensate in a text for things that were missing or removed? Bill told us he planned to inlay new, blank pieces of vellum, restoring the integrity of the manuscript pages so that readers could more easily turn them to enjoy the beauty that remained.

I line two pieces of binder's cardboard with acid-free paper on each side to add stability, cutting them down to the size I want for the covers. I have to allow enough extra for the "square" of the boards—that strip that sticks out beyond the edges of the text block. A spacer strip of cord is glued down on what will become the inner edge of each board. This will be removed after the leather cover of the book has dried and will keep the hinge area from becoming too tight as the leather shrinks and dries on the book.

I fit the boards on the book and use PVA to glue the tapes to the inside of the boards. When they dry, I paste three layers of a thin, hard machine-made paper over them, ending the paper just past the edges of the tapes. When this too is dry, I sand the paper smooth so that there are no ridges from the tapes. I press the book—with the boards now attached—under weight for several days to help the book and board adjust to their new configuration.

While *Campaign* is under weight, I prepare the leather for covering it. I cut a piece of dark brown calf from a large skin and shave the edges thin with a French bookbinder's paring knife. When I had first learned to pare leather, my specimens resembled lasagna noodles—flat in the middle with waves along the edges from being stretched by the blade. Now I can pare well enough to take the thickness off the edge neatly. Keeping my knife extremely sharp helps.

In the areas where the leather needs to be slightly thinner—such as in the hinge areas or at the corners where the leather will fold back on top of itself—I use a spokeshave to pare the leather. Bookbinding and conservation make a practice of borrowing and adapting tools from other professions. This is a regular woodworker's spokeshave—a plane with handles on both sides—from Sears. I have reground and sharpened the blade, shaping it for leatherwork. Paring leather is a tricky process, and I have to proceed carefully or I will nick holes in the leather. I once went through five strips of leather while preparing a leather spine piece for a binding. This paring, however, goes quickly.

I stir up a bowl of cold-water paste that doesn't have to be cooked, mixing it with water until I get the consistency of oatmeal. I don't need a paste as pure (or as expensive) as *zin shofu* for this step. The paste will be trapped away from the text block. I also lay out the brushes, knives, and other materials I will need to put the leather on the book.

Lifting the book from under the weights, I wrap the text block with waste paper to protect it from the paste. With a wad of cotton, I dampen the leather from the right side with some water. This will put moisture into the skin and keep the first application of paste from drying out completely. With a large brush, I then paste out the leather. I fold the piece gently in half without creasing it and let it sit for a minute or two. Then I scrape off all the paste and apply a second layer. The previous application has charged the skin with water, allowing the new layer of paste to stay tacky and workable. I lay the book down onto the leather and begin to work the skin onto the book. I wish I had two more hands.

This step requires dexterity and patience. The leather must be turned over the edges and slipped down in a neat tuck behind the endbands. The corner areas must be pared again while wet and folded over into neat pleats that will protect the corners of the covers. All of this must be done carefully—wet leather marks easily—and it must he done before the leather and paste dry out. I always find it a nerve-racking procedure, rather like getting all the dishes for Thanksgiving prepared and on the table at the same time.

Once I have finished, a piece of card—a "fence"—is slipped inside each cover, extending beyond its edges to keep moisture from migrating from the wet leather into the text block. I wrap the book with a piece of felt to keep it from getting marked and weight it under a board to dry overnight.

As I continued to take Bill's class each semester, I tried to figure out where I could go to continue my bookbinding studies. Even though I had advanced to become Kim's printing assistant at Windhover, my experiences with Bill convinced me that my passion lay in binding rather than printing. I preferred restoring books one at a time to printing them in batches of two hundred and fifty. I asked Kim one day if he knew where I could go to study. Somewhere in Europe perhaps? I was certain I could convince my husband to continue his own graduate studies abroad for a year.

"You could go to Camberwell in England," he replied, "but why would you want to leave Iowa City when one of the best bookbinders and conservators in the business is across the parking lot in the library?"

I explained to him how taking a class that only met once a week was great, but that there was so much more I wanted to learn. It would take forever at such a snail's pace.

"Well, maybe Bill will ask you to be his next apprentice," Kim replied. "But your work will have to be exceptional, and you'll have to impress him with your attitude. He's never taken a woman as an apprentice before."

Yes, that was one thing that had been made clear to me by this time. Bill had always had only male apprentices. The tradition under which he had trained in Ireland was male dominated. Women only worked in the shops sewing books. Men trained as apprentices with a master and moved on in the profession, often serving as journeymen, until they were masters themselves. This was the course Bill had followed.

"Mark's apprenticeship with Bill will be up this fall," Kim continued. "He'll have to think of taking on someone new." Mark Esser was apprenticed to Bill when he had moved to Iowa City from Chicago. One of Bill's agreements with the university was that Mark would move too, receive a salary, and be able to finish his training. Now in the spring of 1986, Mark was beginning to look for a job. "You'll just have to show Bill you're interested," Kim finished.

I was indeed interested and thought for days about the possibility of becoming an apprentice. But how would I go about convincing Bill that I could be a good one? And would he even consider me? Early in the semester, one Wednesday night after class over a beer at a local microbrewery, he had told me of a woman who had asked to be his apprentice whom he had turned down. At the time he told me the story, I wasn't sure that he had refused her because she wasn't talented enough or because she was a woman. This was not encouraging.

Even now I am not sure *what* I did to convince Bill that I would be a good choice for an apprentice. The previous semester he had asked me in passing if I was interested in studying bookbinding—he knew from conversations that we had had about my work at Windhover that printing was not going to be my life's profession—but I was also working on a Ph.D. In English literature and was teaching rhetoric. I was in Iowa so that I could teach writing someday.

I only know that I worked very hard in class and was meticulous in my work. I made plans to continue learning as much as possible about book arts and signed up to take a class in the fall with Tim Barrett, the papermaker Kim had just brought to the university. I figured that if I were going to spend all this time making books out of paper, it would be to my advantage to know more about its properties and how it was made. Before I began working at Windhover, paper was just paper. Then it gradually became a vehicle for impressing type, distinct in color and surface texture. Now I knew that there were papers made and used just for conservation techniques. Tim Barrett was one of the foremost producers of those papers.

The next day I take *Campaign* out from under the weight and remove it from the felt. The leather looks smooth and dry across the cover. With a wet swab, I dampen the hinge area from the outside and open both the front and back covers, acquainting the leather with this movement. I remove the fences and strip the spacer cord with tweezers. Finally, I remove the waste-paper wrap from around the text block.

Now it is time to finish the covering. I take a scalpel and ruler and carefully trim the leather turn-ins on the inside of the covers so that they form a neat rectangle. The leather forms a slight ridge that would be noticeable under a pastedown, so I cut a thin piece of card to the exact size and glue it into the opening. Then I glue out the linen hinge that is wrapped around the end section of new paper that I had added to the text and work it across the hinge area and onto the inside of the cover, smoothing it flat with my bone folder. The book is dried open for a few minutes, then shut. I cut a piece of paper for the pastedown that matches the new endpapers and glue it down to the inside of the board, again slipping in the piece of card back to act as a moisture barrier, and weight the book for a few minutes more to allow the pastedown to adhere. I repeat the procedure for the other cover and place the book back under weight.

While the pastedowns dry, I set up the tooling stove on my bench. This affair is similar to an electric hotplate with a fixed ring like a halo that surrounds it and supports the finishing tools. These roughly resemble screwdrivers. Usually they are made up of rounded wood handles with a brass extension. The brass is shaped on the tip into numerous ornate flowers, lines, curves, and alphabets. I lay out a piece of line that will be used to make the decorative rules across the spine of the book, dividing it into the traditional five panels.

The endpapers dry just as the stove is hot. I place the book in the finishing press—a wooden press that holds the book clamped spine up for tooling—with felt wrapped around it to protect it from pressure marks. The spine is parallel to the edge of my bench. I test the heat of the tool by touching the brass to a wet sponge in a bowl, and it hisses briefly. I have marked out the spine of the book with evenly spaced needle pricks to show me where to make the lines. Single lines at top and bottom, double lines to divide the panels in the traditional style. I wrap a piece of thin card over the curve of the spine as a guide and place the edge of the tool against it. Quickly, I roll the polished surface of the line across the back of the spine in one smooth motion. I step back to see how it turned out. A nice even line blind embossed into the leather. I reheat the tool briefly, cool it down on the sponge, and tool the rest of the panel divisions. They go well and most are complete on the first pass.

Once I have tooled the lines, I dampen them one at a time with a small piece of cotton, retooling them with the heated piece of line. The moisture and leather react together to leave a blackened mark in the leather. This adds more definition to the impression.

Tooling leather like this is a another nerve-racking business. It is very easy to have the tool too hot or to emboss too deeply. It is also very easy to have the tool so hot it burns completely through the leather to the spine lining paper below. I did this once. Fortunately, it was in the second panel from the top where the lettering of the title of the book traditionally goes. I simply put a piece of colored leather in that panel and tooled the title into that. Such overlabeling is a common practice among binders and it looked nice when I was finished. I wonder how many books with labels onlaid onto leather spines had other crispy lettering underneath? Dampening and darkening these spine lines goes quickly.

When I have finished my tooling, I prepare the original label from the spine of *Campaign* that I had saved. It is a fairly thick but weakened leather. With my lifting knives I gently scrape away excess material from the back, thinning it down. Because of the condition of the leather this is done easily, although I must be careful not to chip off pieces at the edges. I paste a layer of the Japanese mending tissue to the back to strengthen it. When this is dry, I glue the label into the second panel from the top of the new binding. Since I had calculated the size of the panels according to the length of this label, it's a perfect fit.

The conservation of this book is now complete, and I will make it a protective box before it goes back to Special Collections. This work has taken several weeks to complete. I lean over my workbench, pull out the book's treatment survey sheet, and begin to complete the sections on what has been done to *Campaign*.

I will never forget that early March evening. I was working at one of the end benches putting the cover on a book for my father, when Bill suddenly faced me from the other side of the bench. Usually when he wanted to see what I was doing he came up next to me. He wasn't smiling, but looked very intent standing there in his usual khaki pants and pinstriped oxford shirt, sleeves rolled up just below the elbows.

"How would you like to become my next apprentice?"

Suddenly a large pit opened up in the bottom of my stomach. How did he know what I wanted more than anything? He was really asking *me*—a woman— to become his apprentice. I couldn't believe it. I took a deep breath and answered him.

I told him no.

Not no, I didn't want to be his apprentice. But no, I couldn't do it right away. I explained that I still had a year left of my agreement with Kim to be his printing assistant for two years. I explained to Bill that I didn't want to go back on my word even though his offer was tempting. I told him that I had signed up to take papermaking because I thought a knowledge of how paper was made would make me a better bookbinder. On and on I babbled, blowing my chances, letting myself and all of womanhood down. The pit in my stomach, born of excitement, was now hard and cold.

When I had finished, Bill stood there for a moment and said, "All right. I can understand your obligation to Kim. How would you like to start as soon as the next school year is over?"

Calmly, I told him that would be fine. He said that he would just find someone else who could start first. He turned and walked away. I went quietly back to work, putting the cover on my father's book upside down.

Reading 30

A BROADER VISION
Social Policy Options in
Cross-National Perspective

William Julius Wilson

Changes in the global economy are placing strains on the welfare state in both the United States and Europe and are contributing to growing social dislocations, including racial conflicts. The question that Secretary of Labor Robert Reich raised at a 1994 conference of finance and labor ministers from seven industrial democracies is central and timely: "Are we condemned to choose between more jobs but greater inequality and insecurity, as we have in this country, or better jobs but higher unemployment and a thicker social safety net, as in Europe?"[1] This question implicitly asks whether Europeans and Americans can learn from one another in the creation of programs that simultaneously address the problems of economic growth, joblessness, and wage inequality.

There is a growing recognition that proposed solutions to the problems of jobs and wages in any of the major industrial democracies cannot ignore developments in the highly integrated global marketplace. Indeed, because of concerns about the problem of creating good jobs in the global economy, the finance and labor ministers from the major industrial democracies (Britain, Canada, France, Germany, Italy, Japan, and the United States, or the Group of Seven, commonly called G7) held a jobs conference in Detroit in March 1994. In previous years, only heads of state and finance ministers met "to discuss high diplomacy and the high finance exchange rates and interest rate management."[2]

Wilson, William Julius. "A Broader Vision: Social Policy Options in Cross-National Perspective." *When Work Disappears: The World of the New Urban Poor.* New York: Vintage Books, 1997. 207–238.

However, that exalted approach was considered insufficient to address the concrete issue of jobs that now confronts all of these nations.

In addition to the more familiar themes, such as the importance of stimulating economic growth and of avoiding protectionist policies to safeguard shrinking job markets, the officials at the conference also agreed "that the only way to create more jobs in the face of rapid technological change was to upgrade education, particularly for those who are least skilled." It was the first time the G7 policymakers had addressed, as a global problem, the widening gap in wages between skilled and unskilled workers and the strong association between low levels of education, joblessness, and poorly paid work.[3]

Although the conference did more to highlight than to solve these problems, the main hope of the ministers was that the discussions could "teach them something about what each of them has done right, and wrong, in confronting the jobs question."[4] As I examine possible policy prescriptions in cross-national perspective, a framework for discussing the appropriateness of long-term solutions to the jobs problem in the United States (solutions that take several years before the desired ends are achieved or realized) and one for discussing more immediate solutions come to mind.

My framework for long-term solutions outlines two types of relationships in an effort to address the issues of generating good jobs and combating the growing wage inequality among workers—namely, the relationship between employment and education and family support systems and, in the metropolitan context, the relationship between the cities and the suburbs. My framework for immediate solutions delineates ways in which to either revise current programs or create new programs to decrease joblessness among disadvantaged adults. Each framework involves the integration of programs that involve both the public sector and the private sector.

I hasten to point out that the following presentation and discussion of policy frameworks is not constrained by an awareness of the current political climate in the United States. The dramatic retreat from using public policy as a means to fight social inequality has effectively discouraged calls for bold new social programs. Indeed, at the time of this writing, the trend is toward slicing or reducing social programs and the spending for such programs. The emphasis is on personal responsibility, not inequities in the larger society, and therefore the assumption is that people should help themselves and not turn to the government for handouts. It is said that the growth of joblessness and welfare receipt mainly reflects a declining commitment to the core values of society and therefore that the incentives for idleness or the factors that lead to a lack of personal and family responsibilities ought to be removed.

These arguments have been advanced with such force and consistency in public discussions since the 1994 congressional elections that even some of the most dedicated liberals feel intimidated and powerless. Accordingly, traditional programs benefiting the poor, such as AFDC, Medicaid, and the earned income tax credit, have either been eliminated or are being threatened with severe reductions.

This retreat from public policy as a way to alleviate problems of social inequality will have profound negative consequences for the future of disadvantaged groups such as the ghetto poor. High levels of joblessness, growing wage inequality, and the related social problems discussed in this book are complex and have their source in fundamental economic, social, and cultural changes. They therefore require bold, comprehensive, and thoughtful solutions, not simplistic and pious statements about the need for greater personal responsibility. Progressives who are concerned about the current social conditions of the have-nots and the future generation of have-nots not only have to fight against the current public policy strategies; they are morally obligated to offer alternative strategies designed to alleviate, not exacerbate, the plight of the poor, the jobless, and other disadvantaged citizens of America.

My aim, therefore, is to galvanize and rally concerned Americans to fight back with the same degree of force and dedication displayed by those who have moved us backward, rather than forward, in combating social inequality. I therefore do not advance proposals that seem acceptable or "realistic" given the current political climate. Rather, I have chosen to talk about what *ought to be done to address the problems of social inequality,* including record levels of joblessness in the inner-city ghetto, that threaten the very fabric of our society.

Some who acknowledge the need to confront the growing social inequality also feel that new social programs should be put on hold until the huge budget deficit has been significantly reduced. In the final analysis, however, we must recognize that spending is directly related to political priorities. Decisions about budget cuts for federal programs now indisputably favor the advantaged segments of the population at the expense of the disadvantaged.

I believe that steps must be taken to galvanize Americans from all walks of life who are concerned about human suffering and the public policy direction in which we are now moving. I therefore present policy frameworks that call for the integration and mobilization of resources from both the public and the private sectors. We need to generate a public/private partnership to fight social inequality. In the final analysis, I hope to stimulate thought about what ought to be done and how we should do it among those who support positive social reforms and see the need for action now. The following policy frameworks, therefore, are suggestive and provide a basis for further discussion and debate. Let me begin by first focusing on the part of my framework for long-term solutions that involves relationships between employment and education, and family support systems.

The United States can learn from industrial democracies like Japan and Germany. These countries have developed policies designed to increase the number of workers with "higher-order thinking skills," including policies that require young people to meet high performance standards before they can graduate from secondary schools and that hold each school responsible for meeting these national standards. As Ray Marshall points out, "Standards are important because they provide incentives for students, teachers and other school personnel; information to employers and postsecondary institutions; and a means for policymakers and the public to evaluate schools. Indeed, by strengthening linkages, standards have helped fashion systems out of disjointed activities."[5]

Students who meet high standards are not only prepared for work, they are ready for technical training and other kinds of postsecondary education. Currently, there are no national standards for secondary students or schools in the United States. Accordingly, students who are not in college preparatory courses have severely limited options with respect to pursuing work or secondary technical training after high school. A commitment to a system of national performance standards for every public school in the United States would be an important first step in addressing the huge gap in educational performance between the schools in advantaged and disadvantaged neighborhoods.

But because the quality of local public schools in the United States is in large measure related to the resources of local governments, national standards may not be attractive to taxpayers and local officials in some areas. Also, some schools will encounter greater difficulties in meeting a national performance standard because of fewer resources and a greater concentration of students from disadvantaged backgrounds and neighborhoods. The question raised by the Columbia University educator Linda Darling-Hammond is important in this connection: "Can the mere issuance of standards really propel improvements in schooling, or are there other structural issues to contend with—issues such as funding, teachers' knowledge and capacities, access to curriculum resources, and dysfunctional school structures?" She goes on to state:

> If the goal of standard setting is the improvement of education for all children, rather than merely a more efficient means of sorting students and schools into "worthy" and "unworthy" categories, attention must be paid to building the capacity for schools to teach in the manner envisioned by these learning goals. This requires carefully developed policy efforts in the areas of teacher development, school development, and equalization of resources.[6]

Accordingly, if standard-setting is to be a meaningful route to reform, it will have to address the current inequalities in the public school system in the United States. In contrast to the more central and equal supports for schools in European countries, funding for public education in the United States is dramatically uneven, "with wealthy schools commonly spending two to three times as much as poor ones."[7] The result is significant differences in educational experiences. Whereas public school students in advantaged neighborhoods enjoy airy facilities and well-equipped small classes, those in poor neighborhoods are more likely to enter dilapidated schools and attend classes that are large and poorly equipped. Even more important is the differential student access to a high-quality curriculum and well-trained teachers, all of which can be traced to the unequal allocation of funds. As Iris C. Rotberg and James J. Harvey put it:

> More often than not, the "best" teachers, including experienced teachers offered greater choice in school assignment because of their seniority, avoid high-poverty schools. As a result, low-income and minority students have less contact with the best-qualified and more experienced teachers, the teachers most likely to master the kinds of instructional strategies considered effective for all students.[8]

Recent research on the nationwide distribution of science and mathematics opportunities indicates that low-income, minority, and inner-city students are in school environments that are not as conducive to learning because of less qualified teachers, fewer material resources, less engaging activities for learning in the classroom, and considerably less exposure to good training and knowledge in mathematics and science.[9] The problem of finding qualified teachers is particularly acute. Teacher shortages in many central-city and poor rural schools have resulted in a disproportionate number of underprepared and inexperienced teachers, many of whom provide instruction in fields outside their areas of preparation, and a continuous flow of short-term and long-term substitutes.[10]

A system of national performance standards should include the kind of support that would enable schools in disadvantaged neighborhoods to meet the standards that are set. State government, with federal support, not only would have to create equity in local school funding and give birth to programs that would foster teacher development (through scholarships and forgivable loans for teacher education to attract more high-quality teachers, through increased supports for teacher training in schools of education, and through reforms in teacher certification and licensing) but would also have to ensure that highly qualified teachers are distributed in local school districts in ways that provide all students with access to excellent instruction. In some cases this would require greater flexibility in the public school system, not only to attract and hire qualified teachers, but also to displace those who perform poorly in the classroom and lack a dedication to teaching. Local education agencies and state education departments should be helped to identify schools that need support in curriculum development and assessment, teacher development, educational and material resources, and so on.

One important area that could be addressed in programs to equalize resources in the public schools is the availability of computer facilities. Since two-thirds of all new jobs will require the use of computers, all schools should require that students become competent in the use of computers.[11] According to the U.S. Bureau of the Census, only 35 percent of black youths ages 3 to 17 use a computer at school.[12] Half of their white counterparts have access to in-school computers. It is imperative that the public schools provide each student with a computer workstation in the elementary, secondary, and high schools and develop linkage to the information superhighways, including access to the Internet. Some public schools already have this capacity and will not need to be upgraded, but others, such as many inner-city schools, must be earmarked for more resources.

Targeting education would be part of a national effort to raise the performance standards of all public schools in the United States to a desirable level, including schools in the inner city. Every effort should be made to enlist the support and involvement of the private sector in this national effort. Corporations, local businesses, civic clubs, community centers, churches, and community-based organizations should be encouraged to work with the schools to enhance computer-competency training. Some examples of private-sector involvement in such endeavors should be touted to spur others on. For example, Frank C. Weaver, director of the Office of Commercial Space Transportation at the U.S. Department of Transportation, reported:

> Bell Atlantic and Tele-Communications, Inc. announced in 1994 that they would provide free linkage to the information superhighways for 26,000 elementary and secondary schools in areas served by the two companies. Under the plan, known as the Basic Education Connection (BEC), the school would receive free educational cable television programming and free access to certain data and online services, such as access to the Internet.
>
> Another project, the Hughes Galaxy Classroom, is enabling 51,000 elementary school children around the country to access more of the educational resources on television available via satellite. Under the auspices of the Galaxy Classroom Foundation, which provides antenna dishes and related equipment to schools, the project offers a science and English curriculum beamed into classrooms through satellite transmissions. Student feedback and questions are faxed to the producers of the program for inclusion in subsequent shows. Particular attention is paid to inner-city and minority schools. There are 480 schools participating this year, and the goal for next year is 1,500 schools with 150,000 to 200,000 students.[13]

Since the creation of national performance standards would provide a clear means for the public to evaluate the different schools, data on school performances could be widely disseminated. This would enable parents of all backgrounds, including those in disadvantaged neighborhoods, to compare nearby schools and make appropriate decisions about which ones their children should attend. However, families from disadvantaged neighborhoods would be in a much better position to make and act on such decisions if an effective public school choice program were in place. This would involve the availability not only of vouchers for the selection of public schools but also information about school performance that could be interpreted with ease. Although the empirical data on the effectiveness of existing school choice programs on student achievement is scant,[14] new evidence suggests that increased competition among public schools (as reflected by a larger number of school districts in a metropolitan area) improves average student performance and restrains levels of spending.[15]

A step toward the development of national performance standards was taken in the spring of 1994 when Congress passed the Goals 2000: Educate America Act. This act identified a number of goals to be achieved by the year 2000, ranging from student-demonstrated competence in challenging subjects (science, English, mathematics, geography, and history) to the professional development of teachers. The basic assumption underlying the act is that the role of the federal government is to "encourage experimentation within the framework of broad federal guidelines," not to mandate uniform changes in the educational system.[16]

Congress appropriated $125 million for Goals 2000 in 1994 and $700 million for 1995.[17] The act encourages states to apply for grants so that their schools can participate in educational improvements outlined in the legislation. Communities and local schools are encouraged to develop clear and high standards pertaining to instruction, curriculum, technology, professional development, and parental and community involvement. The Goals 2000: Educate America Act is a first step toward the development of national performance standards, but since it is not mandatory and only a small amount of money was appropriated, it is unlikely to produce major and widespread changes in the nation's educational system. Yet educational issues are critical and, as suggested in my discussion of the requirements for an adequate system of national performance standards, will require a much stronger commitment to change.

The learning system in other industrial democracies has also been strengthened by family policies to support children.[18] Among industrialized countries, the United States is alone in having no universal preschool, child-support, or parental leave programs. "The absence of such policies makes many of our families, particularly low-income families, very poor learning systems," states Ray Marshall. "Many of our children therefore start school far behind their more advantaged counterparts, and subsequently receive inadequate learning opportunities at home as well as in school."[19] The family structure has undergone fundamental changes in the last several decades. There has been a sharp increase in single-parent families, and many of them are trapped in persistent poverty. Also, in many "intact" families both the husband and wife must work outside the home to make ends meet. The absence of widely available high-quality preschool and child-support assurance programs places additional stress on these families and hampers their ability to provide a learning environment that prepares children for school and reinforces the learning process.

The French system of child welfare stands in sharp contrast to the American system. In France, children are supported by three interrelated government programs—child care, income support, and medical care. The child care program includes establishments for infant care, high-quality nursery schools *(écoles maternelles),* and paid leave for parents of newborns. The income support program includes child-support enforcement (so that the absent parent continues to contribute financially to his or her child's welfare), children allowances, and welfare payments for low-income single mothers.[20] Finally, medical care is provided through a universal system of national health care financed by social security, a preventive care system for children, and a group of public health nurses who specialize in child welfare.

The *école maternelle* is perhaps the most distinctive institution in the French system. Children who are no longer in diapers may enter the nursery school and attend until they are enrolled in the first grade. Because parents view participation in the *école maternelle* as highly beneficial to their children, even those mothers who are not working send their children.

As the economist Barbara Bergmann points out:

> The *école maternelle* serves the integration of all children, minority children included, to full participation in regular school and as future citizens. One of its most important functions, especially for the 4- and 5-year-olds, is getting the children ready for the regular school. Each year a child spends at an *école maternelle* reduces considerably the likelihood that the child will fail the rigorous first grade and have to repeat it. Of children from poorer backgrounds who have not attended an *école maternelle,* more than half fail the first grade. Four years of preschool attendance for such poorer children cuts their first grade failure rate in half. Children from more affluent backgrounds are also materially helped to pass.[21]

The combination of a system of national performance standards in public schools and family policies to reinforce the learning system would greatly facilitate the transition from school to work in the United States. "America has the worst school-to-work transition process of any industrialized nation," states Ray Marshall. "Put simply, we have no systematic processes to assist high school graduates to move smoothly from school into employment."[22] The focus of U.S. secondary schools and counseling programs is to encourage young people to enter college and obtain a degree. But high school graduates who are not college-bound represent nearly one-half of each graduating class. Thus, they "are left to sink or swim—without advice or career counseling and without any job placement assistance."

Unlike employers in Germany and Japan, employers in the United States who have jobs that offer good wages, career potential, and attractive benefits usually do not hire workers immediately out of high school. America's largest and best corporations virtually ignore youthful workers. As Marshall points out, "Only a handful of the Fortune 500 firms hire fresh high school graduates for entry jobs offering career opportunities."[23] The larger firms in America do eventually hire high school graduates, but normally not until they have reached their mid–20s, have accumulated some work experience, and have "matured and settled down." The practices of the larger firms are emulated by other employers. Even the "average starting apprentice in the United States is in his/her late twenties. This delay in hiring for career-track jobs results in many youths spending five or six years floundering in jobs that offer neither learning nor advancement opportunities."

The delay in hiring youths has a number of critical consequences for school-to-work transition in the United States. It gives young people in Germany and Japan a five-to-ten-year head start in obtaining access to crucial occupational skills training; it removes our best corporations and their important learning systems from involvement in the processes of molding young workers; it eliminates a natural communication network for feeding employer information to schools about the changing skills required in the workplace; and, most important, it disconnects achievements in school from rewards in the workplace, thereby undermining the incentive for academic success.

The problem of school-to-work transition confronts young people of all ethnic and racial backgrounds, but it is especially serious for black youths. According to a recent report by the U.S. Bureau of Labor Statistics, only 42 percent of black youths who had not enrolled in college had jobs in October after graduating from high school a few months earlier in June, compared with 69 percent of their white counterparts.[24] The figures for black youngsters in inner-city ghetto neighborhoods are obviously even lower. The inadequate system of school-to-work transition has also contributed significantly to the growing wage gap between those with high school diplomas and those with college training. In the 1950s and 1960s, when school-to-work transition was compatible with the mass production system, the average earnings of college graduates was only about 20 percent higher than those of high school graduates. By 1979, it had increased to 49 percent, and then rapidly grew to 83 percent by 1992.

Thus, the school-to-work transition is a major problem in the United States, and it has reached crisis proportions in the inner-city ghetto. In an initial step meant to address this problem, Congress passed the School-to-Work Opportunities Act (SWOA) in the spring of 1994. Providing the framework for the development of a national school-to-work program, the basic objective of the SWOA "is to build on the high standards encouraged by the Goals 2000 Act."[25] The SWOA assumes that the best way to develop a national system of school-to-work transition is to begin with voluntary demonstrations by state and local areas, including demonstrations whereby businesses work with educators in reforming school systems and integrating work and school. The act encourages federal, state, and local partnerships. It also, through an emphasis on business and education partnerships in local areas, follows the lead of Germany and Japan in stressing the critical importance of private-sector investment in education.

But once again, only a relatively small amount of money was allocated for this program. Total funding for SWOA for fiscal years 1994 and 1995 is less than $500 million. Also, there is no guarantee that the demonstration grants to states will ultimately lead to a more comprehensive national program of school-to-work transition. But such a program is critically needed not only to address the overall problem of growing wage inequality and economic marginality among high school graduates but also as one important weapon in the fight against acute joblessness in the inner-city ghetto.

If the other industrial democracies offer lessons for a long-term solution to the jobs problem involving relationships between employment, education, and family support systems, they also offer lessons on the importance of another solution from a metropolitan perspective—namely, city-suburban integration and cooperation. None of the other industrialized democracies has allowed its city centers to deteriorate as has the United States. In European countries, suburbanization has not been associated with the abandonment of cities as residential areas. "The central governments continued to treat cities as a national resource to be protected and nurtured."[26] Indeed, the city centers in Europe remain very desirable places to reside because of better public transportation, more effective urban renewal programs, and good public education that is more widely available to disadvantaged students. Moreover, unlike in the United States, cheap public transportation makes suburbanized employment sites more accessible.

It will be difficult to address growing racial tensions in U.S. cities unless we tackle the problems of shrinking revenue and inadequate social services and the gradual disappearance of work in certain neighborhoods. The city has become a less desirable place in which to live, and the economic and social gap between the cities and suburbs is growing. The groups left behind compete, often along racial lines, for declining resources, including the remaining decent schools, housing, and neighborhoods. The rise of the new urban poverty neighborhoods has exacerbated these problems. Their high rates of joblessness and social disorganization have created problems that often spill over into other parts of the city at large. All of these factors aggravate race relations and elevate racial tensions.

Ideally, we need to restore the federal contribution to the city budget that existed in 1980 and to sharply increase the employment base. Regardless of changes in federal urban policy, however, the fiscal crisis in the cities would be significantly eased if the employment base could be substantially increased. Indeed, the social dislocations caused by the steady disappearance of work have led to a wide range of urban social problems, including racial tensions. Increased employment would help stabilize the new poverty neighborhoods, halt the precipitous decline in density, and ultimately enhance the quality of race relations in urban areas.

Perhaps at no other time in the nation's history has it been more important to talk about the need to promote city and suburban cooperation, not separation.

The political fragmentation of many metropolitan areas in the United States has contributed to the problems of joblessness and related social dislocations of the inner-city poor. As David Rusk, the former mayor of Albuquerque, New Mexico, has pointed out, because the older cities of the East and the Midwest were unable to expand territorially through city-county consolidation or annexation, they failed to reap such benefits of suburban growth as the rise of shopping malls, offices, and industrial parks in new residential subdivisions. As areas in which poor minorities live in higher and higher concentration, these cities face an inevitable downward spiral because they are not benefiting from suburban growth. Rusk argues, therefore, that neighborhood revitalization programs, such as community development banks, nonprofit inner-city housing developments, and enterprise zones, will not be able "to reverse the downward slide of inner cities" if they are not carried out within "a framework of actions to bring down the walls between city and suburb."[27]

Efforts to promote city and suburban cooperation will not benefit cities alone. There is mounting evidence that cities and suburbs are economically interdependent. The more central cities are plagued by joblessness, dysfunctional schools, and crime, the more the surrounding suburbs undergo a decline in their own social and economic fortunes. Suburbs that experienced increases in income during the 1980s tended to be linked to a thriving urban center. In the global economy, metropolitan regions continue to compete for jobs.[28] Suburbs that will remain or become competitive are those with a well-trained workforce, good schools, a concentration of professional services, first-class hospitals, a major university and research center, and an efficient transportation network to link executives with other parts of the United States and with countries around the world. However, many of these elements cannot come solely from suburbs. They require a viable central city. It is important for Americans to realize that city-suburban *integration* is the key to the health of metropolitan regions and to the nation as a whole.

Reforms put forward to achieve the objective of city-suburban cooperation range from proposals to create metropolitan governments to proposals for metropolitan tax base sharing (currently in effect in Minneapolis/St. Paul), collaborative metropolitan planning, and the creation of regional authorities to develop solutions to common problems if communities fail to reach agreement.[29] Among the problems shared by many metropolises is a weak public transit system. A commitment to address this problem through a form of city-suburban collaboration would benefit residents of both the city and the suburbs. Theoretically, everyone would benefit from mobility within the metropolitan areas, and inner-city residents would have greater means to prevent high joblessness.

The problems of joblessness and social dislocation in the inner city are, in part, related to the processes in the global economy that have contributed to greater inequality and insecurity among American workers in general, and to the failure of U.S. social policies to adjust to these processes. It is therefore myopic to view the problems of jobless ghettos as if they were separate from those that plague the larger society.

In using this cross-cultural perspective I am not suggesting that we can or even should simply import the social policies of the Japanese, Germans, or other West Europeans. As Ray Marshall has appropriately pointed out, the approaches in these other countries are embedded in their own cultures and have their "own flaws and deficiencies, as well as strengths." We should instead "learn from the approaches used in other countries and adapt the best aspects into our own homegrown solutions."[30]

The strengths of some of the approaches in other countries are apparent. For example, in Japan and Germany most high school and college graduates leave school with skills in keeping with the demands of the highly technological marketplace in the global economy.[31] In the United States, by contrast, only college graduates and those few with extra-specialized post–high school training acquire such skills. Those with only high school diplomas or less do not.

The flaws and deficiencies of some of the approaches in the other countries are also apparent. Except for Germany, European countries have the same gap in worker skills.[32] Because of the generous unemployment benefits, however, the low-skilled European workers tend to be less willing to accept the lower-paying jobs that their counterparts in the United States are often forced to take. Therefore, the problems of unskilled European workers are not only restricted to low wages, they also include high levels of unemployment. [T]he growing problems of unemployment among low-skilled European workers is placing a strain on the welfare state. Immigrant minorities are disproportionately represented among the jobless population, and therefore tend to be publicly identified with the problem of maintaining welfare costs. These perceptions contribute to growing intergroup tensions. Accordingly, the problems of race, unemployment, and concentration of urban poverty that have traditionally plagued the United States are now surfacing in various countries in Europe.

Just as the United States can learn from some of the approaches in the other countries, the Europeans could learn from the United States how to make their workforces more flexible instead of paying them to stay unemployed indefinitely. In particular, they could learn how to get unskilled workers into low-wage jobs that would be buttressed by maintaining certain desirable aspects of the safety net, such as universal health insurance, that prevent workers from slipping into the depths of poverty, as so often happens to their American counterparts.

It is important to discuss immediate solutions to the jobs problem in the United States. Because of their level of training and education, the inner-city poor and other disadvantaged workers mainly have access only to jobs that pay the minimum wage or less and are not covered by health insurance. However, recent policies of the federal government could make such jobs more attractive. The

United States Congress enacted an expansion of the earned income tax credit (EITC) in 1993. By 1996, the expanded EITC will increase the earnings from a minimum-wage job to $7 an hour. Families with incomes from $8,400 to $11,000 will receive cash payments of up to $3,370.[33] This expansion, and the previous expansions of the EITC in 1986 and 1990 under the Reagan and Bush administrations, reflected a recognition that wages for low-paying work have eroded and that other policies to aid the working poor—for example, the minimum wage—have become weaker.[34]

However, even when the most recent expansion of the EITC is fully in effect in 1996 (as shown in Table 8.1), it will still fall notably short of compensating for the sharp drop in the value of the minimum wage and the marked reductions in AFDC benefits to low-income working families since the early 1970s. Nonetheless, "the 1993 law set the EITC for a family with two or more children at the level that would bring a family of four with a full-time minimum wage worker to the poverty line if the family also received food stamps and the minimum wage was modestly raised."[35]

If this benefit is paid on a monthly basis and is combined with universal health care, the condition of workers in the low-wage sector would improve significantly and would approach that of comparable workers in Europe. The passage of universal health care is crucial in removing from the welfare rolls single mothers who are trapped in a public-assistance nightmare by the health care needs of their children. It would also make low-paying jobs more attractive for all low-skilled workers and therefore improve the rate of employment.

TABLE 8.1

Average Disposable Income for a Mother and Two Children from Wages, Food Stamps, EITC, and Federal Taxes (in 1993 Dollars)

	Number of Hours Worked at Minimum Wage Throughout the Year		
Year	20 Hours	30 Hours	40 Hours
1972	$13,482	$14,602	$15,656
1980	11,479	12,870	13,792
1990	9,830	10,467	11,509
1993 (with EITC at fully phased-in 1996 levels)	10,612	11,956	13,653

	Percentage Change in Average Disposable Income for a Mother and Two Children		
1972–1993	-21%	-18%	-13%

Source: Department of Health and Human Services. Adapted from Center on Budget and Policy Priorities (1995).

However, at the time of this writing, not only has legislation for universal health care been shelved, but the traditional bipartisan support for the EITC is beginning to erode in the Republican-controlled Congress. In May 1995, the Senate passed a budget resolution that includes an assumption that the EITC would be cut by roughly $13 billion over five years and $21 billion over seven years. As pointed out by the Center on Budget and Policy Priorities, a nonprofit public policy organization that examines federal and state fiscal policies:

> More than two-thirds of these cuts would be achieved by repealing the final phase of the 1993 EITC expansion for families with two or more children scheduled for 1996 and reducing the EITC below current levels (tax year 1995 levels) for both families with two or more children and families with one child. Ten million families with children would receive smaller EITCs than they otherwise would. . . . The 1993 EITC expansion is being phased in over several years. The final stage of the phase-in for families with more than one child is scheduled to occur in tax year 1996. *If this last stage of the expansion is repealed and the 1995 expansion is scaled back, a family of four in which a parent works full-time, year-round at the minimum wage will be pushed about $445 deeper into poverty.*[36]

Instead of rolling back the modest expansion of the EITC, it could be argued that the earned income tax credit could be further expanded at reasonable cost to lift all poor working families who work full-time year-round out of poverty, not just those who are currently working at the minimum wage. Further expansion of the EITC and the creation of universal health care legislation ought to be issues at the top of any progressive public policy agenda today. I return to these issues in the next and final section of this chapter, but first I need to complete my discussion of proposed immediate solutions to the jobs problem.

The mismatch between residence and the location of jobs is a special problem for some workers in America because, unlike in Europe, the public transportation system is weak and expensive. This presents a special problem for inner-city blacks because they have less access to private automobiles and, unlike Mexicans, do not have a network system that supports organized car pools. Accordingly, they depend heavily on public transportation and therefore have difficulty getting to the suburbs, where jobs are more plentiful and employment growth is greater.[37] Until public transit systems are improved in metropolitan areas, the creation of privately subsidized car-pool and van-pool networks to carry inner-city residents to the areas of employment, particularly suburban areas, would be a relatively inexpensive way to increase work opportunities.[38]

In the inner-city ghettos, the problems of spatial mismatch have been aggravated by the breakdown in the informal job information network. In neighborhoods in which a substantial number of adults are working, people are more likely to learn about job openings or be recommended for jobs by working kin, relatives, friends, and acquaintances. Job referrals from current employees are important in the American labor market. Individuals in jobless ghettos are less likely to gain employment through this process. But the creation of for-profit or not-for-profit job information and placement centers in various parts of the inner city not only could significantly improve awareness of the availability of employment in the metropolitan area but could also serve to refer workers to employers.[39]

These centers would recruit or accept inner-city workers and try to place them in jobs. One of their main purposes would be to make persons who have been persistently unemployed or out of the labor force "job-ready" so that a prospective employer would be assured that a worker understands and appreciates employer expectations such as showing up for work on time and on a regular basis, accepting the orders of supervisors, and so on. When an information and placement center is satisfied that a worker is job-ready, then and only then would the worker be referred to an employer who has a job vacancy. Moreover, information and placement centers could coordinate efforts with the car-pool and van-pool networks to get those job applicants who lack private transportation to the employment sites.

As much of the foregoing economic analysis suggests, however, the central problem facing inner-city workers is not improving the flow of information about the availability of jobs, or getting to where the jobs are, or becoming job-ready. The central problem is that the demand for labor has shifted away from low-skilled workers because of structural changes in the economy.[40] During certain periods, this problem can be offset to some extent by appropriate macroeconomic levers that can act to enhance economic growth and reduce unemployment, including fiscal policies that regulate government spending and taxation and monetary policies that influence interest rates and control the money supply.[41] But given the fundamental structural decline in the demand for low-skilled workers, such policies will have their greatest impact in the higher-wage sectors of the economy. Many low-wage workers, especially those in high-jobless inner-city neighborhoods who are not in or have dropped out of the labor force and who also face the problem of negative employer attitudes, will not experience any improvement in their job prospects because of fiscal or monetary policies. Despite some claims that low-skilled workers fail to take advantage of labor-market opportunities,[42] available evidence strongly suggests not only that the jobs for such workers carry lower real wages and fewer benefits than did comparable jobs in the early 1970s, but that it is harder for certain low-skilled workers, especially low-skilled males who are not being absorbed into the expanding service sector, to find employment today.[43] As the economists Sheldon Danziger and Peter Gottschalk put it:

> In our view, the problem is not that more people have chosen not to work, but rather that demand by employers for less-skilled workers, even those who are willing to work at low wages, has declined. We find it paradoxical that so much

attention has been focused on changing the labor-supply behavior of welfare recipients and so little has been given to changing the demand side of a labor market that has been increasingly unable to employ less-skilled and less-experienced workers.[44]

If firms in the private sector cannot use or refuse to hire low-skilled adults who are willing to take minimum-wage or subminimum-wage jobs, then the jobs problem for inner-city workers cannot be adequately addressed without considering a policy of public-sector employment of last resort. Indeed, until current changes in the labor market are reversed or until the skills of the next generation can be upgraded before it enters the labor market, many workers, especially those who are not in the official labor force, will not be able to find jobs unless the government becomes an employer of last resort.[45] This argument applies especially to low-skilled inner-city black workers. It is bad enough that they face the problem of shifts in labor market demand shared by all low-skilled workers; it is even worse that they confront negative employer perceptions about their work-related skills and attitudes.

If jobs are plentiful even for less skilled workers during periods of economic expansion, then labor shortages reduce the likelihood that hiring decisions will be determined by subjective negative judgments concerning a group's job-related traits. Prior to the late 1970s, there was less need for the creation of public-sector jobs. Not only was economic growth fairly rapid during periods of expansion, but "the gains from growth were widely shared." Before the late 1970s, public jobs of last resort were thought of in terms of "a counter-cyclical policy to be put in place during recessions and retired during recoveries. It is only since the late 1970s that the disadvantaged have been left behind during recoveries. The labor market changes . . . seem to have been permanently reduced private sector demand for less-skilled workers."[46]

Given the current need for public jobs to enhance the employment opportunities of low-skilled workers, what should be the nature of these jobs and how should they be implemented? Three thoughtful recent proposals for the creation of public jobs deserve serious consideration. One calls for the creation of public-sector infrastructure maintenance jobs, the second for public service jobs for less-skilled workers, and the third, which combines aspects of the first two, for WPA-style jobs of the kind created during the Franklin D. Roosevelt administration.

Edward V. Regan has advanced a proposal for a public-investment infrastructure maintenance program. He points out that "infrastructure maintenance and upgrading can . . . benefit the economy by creating jobs, particularly for the relatively unskilled, and by raising productivity, thereby contributing to long-term economic growth."[47] According to one estimate, $1 billion spent on road maintenance will directly generate 25,000 jobs and indirectly put 15,000 people to work.[48] On the other hand, new construction creates fewer jobs at higher wages. Another study reports that new building projects or major construction employs 40 percent fewer workers than do maintenance projects.[49] Just as other low-skill jobs are made more attractive by programs of health care, child care, and earned income tax credits, so would low-skill jobs in infrastructure maintenance.

Aside from creating jobs, infrastructure maintenance could lead to higher productivity. On this point, Regan states:

> Intuitively, fixing roads and bridges means less axle damage to trucks, fewer road mishaps and congestion, lowered costs of goods, and increased transportation productivity. Congested and deteriorated highways, broken water mains, inadequate sewage treatment, reduced transit services—all of these infrastructure deficiencies reduce productivity, drive up costs of goods and services, and inhibit people's access to employment. Any state or local government official who has tried to attract business facilities to a particular area and has watched business decision makers turn up their noses at cracked concrete and rusting bridges knows the practical meaning of those statements.[50]

Regan also points out that there are many other benefits stemming from an improved infrastructure that are not accounted for in standard economic measures, including shortened commuting times and reduced traffic congestion. If well selected, public investment in infrastructure maintenance could contribute to economic growth. According to the Congressional Budget Office, the national real rate of return for investments to maintain the current quality of the highway system would be 30 to 40 percent, those involving selected expansion in congested urban areas would be 10 to 20 percent.[51]

Although the creation of infrastructure maintenance jobs will provide some employment opportunities for low-skilled workers, the condition of today's labor market makes it unlikely that many of these jobs will actually go to high school dropouts or even to high school graduates with little or no work experience. To address this problem, the economists Sheldon Danziger and Peter Gottschalk, in a recently published book, have advocated the creation of a labor-intensive, minimum-wage public service jobs program of last resort for today's low-skilled and jobless workers.[52] They have in mind jobs such as day-care aides and playground assistants who can supervise in school gyms and public parks during after-school hours. These would be jobs for poor workers who cannot find a place in the private sector, jobs providing services that the fiscally strapped cities can no longer afford to supply through local resources.

Their plan for public service jobs differs in two important respects from recent proposals aimed at increasing work requirements and work incentives for recipients of welfare. First, their proposal is directed not just at welfare recipients but at *all poor workers* adversely affected by current economic shifts, including those who have been ineligible for, or who have chosen not to participate in, welfare. Only a small proportion of those whose labor-market prospects have diminished since the early 1970s have been welfare recipients. Second, their proposal addresses changes in the demand side of the labor market by emphasizing work opportunities and earnings supplements rather than work requirements or incentives.

It is important to distinguish clearly the view of public service jobs embodied in the proposal outlined in the Clinton administration's welfare reform plan that was pushed aside after the Republicans gained control of Congress in 1994. Under the Clinton proposal, welfare would change from an entitlement to a transitional system through which cash assistance would last only two years. For those welfare recipients who reach the time limit but fail to find jobs in the private sector, transitional public-work slots would be made available. However, as Danziger and Gottschalk appropriately point out:

> A program offering jobs of last resort *only* to welfare recipients who exhaust two years of cash assistance would have the potential for perverse incentives and serious inequities. Families who either were not eligible for welfare or chose not to participate would not have access to these jobs. Even if the incentive to go on welfare in order to gain access to the PSE jobs were small, offering jobs to welfare recipients but not to equally needy families who were trying to make it in the labor market could cause resentment.[53]

Danziger and Gottschalk recognize the fact that if programs provided "good" public-sector jobs, local officials would be tempted to fill them with displaced but experienced workers from manufacturing and other goods-producing industries. Therefore, workers with limited experience, skills, and training from high-jobless inner-city neighborhoods would very likely be passed over. Moreover, their proposal is designed to create public service jobs that produce goods and provide services that are not available in the private sector and would not displace private-sector workers.

Their proposal offers a subminimum-wage public service job to any applicant. They would set compensation at 10 to 15 percent below the minimum wage to encourage movement into private-sector jobs as they become available. Graduated job ladders would provide rewards to workers who succeed on the job, "but wages would always be lower than [that which] an equally successful worker would receive in the private sector." These wages would be supplemented with the expanded earned income tax credit and other wage supplements (including a federal child care subsidy in the form of a refundable income tax credit for the working poor and refundable state tax credits for the working poor).

The Danziger and Gottschalk proposal obviously would not provide a comfortable standard of living for the workers forced to take public service jobs. Such jobs are minimal and are "offered as a safely net to poor persons who want to work but are left out of the private labor market." However, they maintain that their proposal is an improvement over the current system, "which offers a minimum wage if you find a job, but leaves millions of poor persons searching for work and many others poor even though they have jobs."

The final proposal under consideration here was advanced by the perceptive journalist Mickey Kaus of *The New Republic*. Kaus's proposal is modeled on the Works Progress Administration (WPA), a large public works program announced in 1935 by Franklin D. Roosevelt in his State of the Union address. The public works jobs that Roosevelt had in mind included highway construction, slum clearance, housing construction, rural electrification, and so on. As Kaus points out:

> In its eight-year existence, according to official records, the WPA built or improved 651,000 miles of roads, 953 airports, 124,000 bridges and viaducts, 1,178,000 culverts, 8,000 parks, 18,000 playgrounds and athletic fields, and 2,000 swimming pools. It constructed 40,000 buildings (including 8,000 schools) and repaired 85,000 more. Much of New York City—including LaGuardia Airport, FDR Drive, plus hundreds of parks and libraries—was built by the WPA. . . . Lester Thurow has suggested that New York's infrastructure is now decaying because no WPA has existed to replace these public works in the half-century since.[54]

Kaus advances what he calls a neo-WPA program of employment for every American citizen over 18 who wants it. The program would provide useful public jobs at wages slightly below the minimum wage. Kaus's proposed program would not only eliminate the need to provide public assistance or "workfare" for able-bodied workers but, unlike welfare, the WPA-style jobs would be

> available to everybody, men as well as women, single or married, mothers and fathers alike. No perverse "anti-family" incentives. It wouldn't even be necessary to limit the public jobs to the poor. If Donald Trump showed up, he could work too. But he wouldn't. Most Americans wouldn't. There'd be no need to "target" the program to the needy. The low wage itself would guarantee that those who took the jobs would be those who needed them, while preserving the incentive to look for better work in the private sector.

Kaus maintains that the work relief under his proposal, like the work relief under Roosevelt's WPA, would not carry the stigma of a cash dole. People would be earning their money. Although some workers in the WPA-style jobs "could be promoted to higher-paying public service positions," most of them would advance occupationally by moving to the private sector. "If you have to work anyway," asks Kaus, "why do it for $4 an hour?"

Kaus's proposal would also place a time limit on welfare for able-bodied recipients. After a certain date they would no longer be eligible for cash payments. However, unlike the welfare program proposed in 1995 by the Republican-controlled Congress, public jobs would be available to those who move off welfare. Kaus argues that to allow poor mothers to work, government-funded day care must be provided for their children if needed. But this service has to be integrated into the larger system of child care for other families in the United States to avoid creating a "day-care ghetto" for low-income children.

In Kaus's proposal the WPA-style jobs would be supplemented with the earned income tax credit, which could be expanded at reasonable cost to lift all poor working families who work full-time throughout the year out of poverty, Because this subsidy would augment the income of all low-wage workers, those in low-level private-sector jobs would not be treated unfairly and their wages on average would be slightly higher than those in the guaranteed subminimum-wage public jobs.

Kaus maintains that there will be enough worthwhile WPA-style jobs for anyone who wants one. The crumbling infrastructure in American cities has to be repaired. Services cut back by the government for financial reasons, such as picking up trash two times a week and opening libraries every evening and on Saturdays, could be reinstated. Jobs for men and women could range from filling potholes and painting bridges to serving as nurse's aides, clerks, and cooks. "With a neo-WPA maintaining highways, schools, playgrounds, and subways, with libraries open every evening and city streets cleaned twice a day, we would have a common life more people would find worth reclaiming."[55]

In reviewing these three proposals, the Kaus neo-WPA jobs plan is the most comprehensive because it would include not only the kind of infrastructure maintenance advocated by Regan but also the labor-intensive public service jobs proposed by Danziger and Gottschalk. And unlike the program proposed by Danziger and Gottschalk, neither Kaus's WPA-style jobs program nor Regan's infrastructure maintenance program would be targeted to poor workers. Whereas Kaus explicitly states that the pay scale for the neo-WPA jobs would be set below the minimum wage, Regan does not address the question of pay scale for his infrastructure maintenance jobs. It is reasonable to assume, however, that the pay scale for the infrastructure maintenance jobs would be lower than that for comparable levels of employment in the private sector. Nonetheless, both of these programs would very likely attract a substantial number of displaced experienced workers willing to take lower-paying public-sector jobs until they find higher-paying work in the private sector.

Given the broader scope of Kaus's neo-WPA jobs program, a higher proportion of workers with few skills and little or no work experience would be employed than would be possible under the Regan program of infrastructure maintenance. Accordingly, Kaus's program would provide many more job opportunities for workers in high-jobless inner-city ghetto neighborhoods.

The labor-intensive public service jobs program advanced by Danziger and Gottschalk is designed to generate immediate employment opportunities for workers with low skills and little or no work experience. However, since it is explicitly aimed at poor workers, it runs the risk of carrying a stigma. The WPA-style jobs advocated by Kaus avoid this problem. The program would be presented as offering jobs to any American who wants a job. Given the subminimum-wage scale, it is likely to attract only a handful of workers who could readily find higher-paying jobs in the private sector. And even if local authorities succumbed to the temptation to fill the "good" WPA jobs with displaced experienced workers, there would still be a sufficient number of labor-intensive jobs requiring little skill, training, or experience. Moreover, the experienced and higher-paid workers who accept WPA-style jobs because of layoffs in the private sector would be likely to remain in the program for only a short period of time.

Furthermore, the Kaus program of WPA-style jobs would lend itself to the kind of progressive public rhetoric that focuses on problems afflicting not only the poor but the working and middle classes as well. Thus, the program would promote social and economic improvements benefiting all groups in society, not just the truly disadvantaged segments of the population. This is consistent with my argument that the joblessness of the poor, including the inner-city poor, represents the more extreme form of economic marginality experienced by large segments of the population and stems in large measure from changes in the organization of the economy, including the global economy.

Because it is comprehensive, less likely to carry a stigma, and lends itself to a progressive public rhetoric of social reform, I include the Kaus neo-WPA jobs plan in my package of proposed immediate solutions to the jobs problem. However, there is the problem of administering a neo-WPA program, which is not discussed by Kaus. This program must be administered by the federal government (as was the earlier WPA program under the Roosevelt administration) in order to avoid the problem of "fiscal substitution"—that is, the shifting of spending on public employment projects from the local or state level to the federal government.[55] This problem accompanied the implementation of the Comprehensive Employment and Training Act (CETA). The creation of public service employment through CETA in the 1970s did very little to increase the *aggregate* number of jobs in the economy because states and localities over time used the program to substitute subsidized positions for previously nonsubsidized public service jobs.[56] This had the effect of shifting jobs from one funding source to another. Our goal here is to increase the number of jobs, and thus broad federal oversight is required.

As another way to avoid the problem of worker displacement, I would also recommend that the workers in the federal WPA-style program only produce goods and services that are not being produced in the private sector and are not presently provided by regular public-sector workers.[57] If this problem is not addressed, considerable opposition to such a program could arise from both private- and public-sector unions and from businesses in the private sector. Accordingly, following Klaus, I have in mind useful public work that is currently not being done for financial reasons.[58] This would include regular infrastructure maintenance; the cleaning of streets twice, not once, a day; the collection of trash twice a week instead of once a week; the opening of libraries on Saturday and in the evenings; the cleaning of municipal parks, playgrounds, and other public facilities at a level and with a frequency that would ensure their attractiveness and invite use; and the supervision of public playgrounds that would maximize safer, adult-sponsored recreation for all neighborhood children.

It is reasonable to anticipate that as WPA-style workers are used to replenish or revitalize, public service staffs, certain states and localities might be tempted to scale back their regular workforce during periods of severe fiscal constraints and rely more on subsidized public service workers. To discourage this type of displacement of regular government workers, I would recommend that one WPA worker be removed for every regular worker's slot that is eliminated or not filled within a certain time period.

A WPA-style jobs program will not be cheap.[59] In the short run, it is less expensive to give people cash welfare than it is to create public jobs. Including the costs of supervisors and materials, it is estimated that each subminimum-wage WPA-style job would cost at least $12,000. That would represent $12 billion for every 1 million jobs created. This figure does not include additional funds to augment the subminimum wage from the earned income tax credit, nor does it reflect any long-run national real rate of return for public investment in infrastructure maintenance that would contribute to economic growth.

None of the immediate solutions I am proposing involves retraining workers for higher-paying positions in the highly technological global economy. The need to retrain low-skilled workers is generally recognized by policymakers and informed observers in both Europe and the United States. However, the most serious discussions about training for the new economy have focused on young people and their transition from school to work or from school to postsecondary training. The cost of retraining adult workers is considerable, and none of the industrial democracies has advanced convincing proposals indicating how to implement such a program effectively.[60] Moreover, a heavy emphasis on skill development and job retraining is likely to end up mainly benefiting those who already have a good many skills that only need to be upgraded.

Also, none of my immediate solutions offers a remedy for the growing wage inequality in the United States. The long-term solutions I have presented, which include those that prepare the next generation to move into the new jobs created in the global economy, are designed to combat that problem. But my specific recommendations for immediate action would address the employment problems of many low-skilled workers, including those from the inner city. They would confront the current and serious problem of the disappearance of work in the inner-city ghetto. The jobs created would not be high-wage jobs but, with universal health insurance, a child care program, and earned income tax credits attached, they would enable workers and their families to live at least decently and avoid joblessness and the problems associated with it. The United States Congress has already expanded the earned income tax credit. Universal health insurance and some kind of flexible child care program would be costly, but these programs would support *all* Americans. Furthermore, the nation has recognized the need for such social benefits and there remains considerable public support in favor of moving forward on both programs—especially in the area of health insurance—despite Congress's retreat from public policy programs to combat social inequality following the 1994 congressional elections.

Ironically, at the same time there is growing pressure in Europe to reduce the social safety net, especially the entitlement of indefinite unemployment insurance. What might evolve in the future is a movement in both directions—toward a stronger social safety net in the United States and a weaker one in Europe—that would result in similar or more comparable social welfare programs sufficient to allow workers on both sides of the Atlantic to live free of economic deprivation or severe hardship. For this to occur, however, Americans concerned about combating social inequality will have to counter the current retreat in the U.S. Congress away from public policy issues that address joblessness and poverty.

Programs proposed to increase employment opportunities, such as the creation of WPA-style jobs, should be aimed at broad segments of the U.S. population, not just inner-city workers, in order to provide the needed solid political base of support. In the new, highly integrated global economy, an increasing number of Americans across racial, ethnic, and income groups are experiencing declining real incomes, increasing job displacement, and growing economic insecurity. The unprecedented level of inner-city joblessness represents one important aspect of the broader economic dislocations that cut across racial and ethnic groups in the United States. Accordingly, when promoting economic and social reforms, it hardly seems politically wise to focus mainly on the most disadvantaged groups while ignoring other segments of the population that have also been adversely affected by global economic changes.

Yet, just when bold new comprehensive initiatives are urgently needed to address these problems, the U.S. Congress has retreated from using public policy as an instrument with which to fight social inequality. Failure to deal with this growing social inequality, including the rise of joblessness in U.S. inner cities, could seriously worsen the economic life of urban families and neighborhoods.

Groups ranging from the inner-city poor to those working- and middle-class Americans who are struggling to make ends meet will have to be effectively mobilized in order to change the current course and direction taken by policymakers. Perhaps the best way to accomplish this is through coalition politics that promote race-neutral programs such as jobs creation, further expansion of the earned income tax credit, public school reform, child care programs, and universal health insurance. A broad-based political coalition is needed to successfully push such programs through the political process.

Because an effective political coalition in part depends upon how the issues to be addressed are defined, it is imperative that the political message underscore the need for economic and social reform that benefits all groups, not just America's minority poor.[61] The framers of this message should be cognizant of the fact that changes in the global economy are creating growing social inequality and situations which intensify antagonisms between different racial and ethnic groups, and that these groups, although often seen as adversaries, are potential allies in a reform coalition because they suffer from a common problem—economic distress caused by forces outside their own control.

In the absence of an effective political coalition, priorities will be established that do not represent the interests of disadvantaged groups. For example, in the House of Representatives, 67 percent of proposed spending cuts from the federal budget for the year 2000 would come from low-income programs, even though these programs represent only 21 percent of the current federal budget. Without an effective political coalition it is unlikely that Congress would be willing to finance the kinds of reforms that are needed to combat the new social inequality. At the time of this writing, the momentum is away from, not toward, social programs. Instead of recognizing and dealing with the complex and changing realities that have led to economic distress for many Americans, policymakers seek to assign blame and associate the economic problems of families and individuals with personal shortcomings such as lack of initiative, work ethic, or motivation. Consequently, there is very little support in favor of financing any social programs—even the creation of public service jobs for the limited number of welfare recipients who reach a time limit for receipt of welfare checks. Considering the deleterious consequences this shortsighted retreat from public policy will have for so many Americans, it is distressing that progressive groups, far from being energized to reverse the public policy direction in which the country is now moving, seem to be almost intimidated and paralyzed by the rhetoric of the Republican Contract with America.

Accordingly, the kinds of long-term and immediate-term solutions that I have proposed stand little chance of being adopted, not to mention seriously considered, in the absence of a new political coalition of groups pressing for economic and social reform. Political leaders concerned about the current shift in public policy will have to develop a unifying rhetoric, a progressive message that resonates with broad segments of the American population, a message that enables groups to recognize that it is in their interest to join a reform coalition dedicated to moving America forward.

The solutions I have outlined were developed with the idea of providing a policy framework that would be suitable for and could be easily adopted by a reform coalition. The long-term solutions, which include the development of a system of national performance standards in public schools, family policies to reinforce the learning system in the schools, a national system of school-to-work transition, and ways to promote city-suburban integration and cooperation, would be beneficial to and could draw the support of a broad range of groups in America. The short-term solutions, which range from the development of job information and placement centers and subsidized car pools in the ghetto to the creation of WPA-style jobs, are more relevant to low-income Americans, but they are the kinds of opportunity-enhancing programs that Americans of all racial and class backgrounds tend to support.

Although my policy framework is designed to appeal to broad segments of the population, I firmly believe that if adopted, it would alleviate a good deal of the economic and social distress currently plaguing the inner cities. The immediate problem of the disappearance of work in many inner-city neighborhoods would be confronted. The employment base in these neighborhoods would be increased immediately by the creation of WPA-style jobs, and income levels would rise because of the expansion of the earned income tax credit. Programs such as universal health care and day care would increase the attractiveness of low-wage jobs and "make work pay."

Increasing the employment base would have an enormous positive impact on the social organization of ghetto neighborhoods. As more people become employed, crime, including violent crime, and drug use will subside; families will be strengthened and welfare receipt will decline significantly; ghetto-related culture and behavior, no longer sustained and nourished by persistent joblessness, will gradually fade. As more people become employed and gain work experience, they will have a better chance of finding jobs in the private sector when they become available. The attitudes of employers toward inner-city workers will undergo change, in part because they would be dealing with job applicants who have steady work experience and would furnish references from their previous supervisors.

This is not to suggest that all the jobless individuals from the inner-city ghetto would take advantage of these employment opportunities. Some have responded to persistent joblessness by abusing alcohol and drugs, and these handicaps will affect their overall job performance, including showing up for work on time or on a consistent basis. But they represent only a small segment of the worker population in the inner city. Most workers in the inner city are ready, willing, able, and anxious to hold a steady job.

The long-term solutions that I have advanced would reduce the likelihood that a new generation of jobless workers would be produced from the youngsters now in school and preschool. We must break the cycle of joblessness and improve the youngsters' preparation for the new labor market in the global economy.

My framework for long-term and immediate solutions is based on the notion that the problems of jobless ghettos cannot be separated from those of the rest of the nation. Although these solutions have wide-ranging application and would alleviate the economic distress of many Americans, their impact on jobless ghettos would be profound. Their most important contribution would be their effect on the children of the ghetto, who would be able to anticipate a future of economic mobility and share the hopes and aspirations that so many of their fellow citizens experience as part of the American way of life.

Notes

1. Quoted in Friedman (1994a).
2. Friedman (1994a).
3. Friedman (1994b).
4. Friedman (1994b).
5. Marshall (1994).
6. Darling-Hammond (1994), p. 480.
7. Darling-Hammond (1994), p. 499. Also see Educational Testing Service (1991).
8. Rotberg and Harvey (1993).
9. Oakes (1990).
10. Darling-Hammond (1990 and 1994).
11. Hundt (1995).
12. Weaver (1995).
13. Weaver (1995), p. 7. Also see Krieg (forthcoming).
14. Katz (1995).
15. Hoxby (1994) and Katz (1995).
16. Marshall (1994), p. 21.
17. Marshall (1994).
18. Marshall (1994).
19. Marshall (1994), p. 7.
20. Bergmann (1993).
21. Bergmann (1993), pp. 343–44.
22. Marshall (1994), p. 3.
23. Marshall (1994), p. 9.
24. U.S. Bureau of Labor Statistics (1994).
25. Marshall (1994), p. 22.
26. Weir (1993a), p. 26.
27. Rusk (1993), p. 12 I.
28. Bok (1994).
29. Bok (1995), p. 13. Also see Weir (1993b).
30. Marshall (1994), p. 26.
31. Marshall (1994).
32. Friedman (1994b).
33. *New York Times* (1994).
34. Center on Budget and Policy Priorities (1995a and 1995b).
35. Center on Budget and Policy Priorities (1995b), p. 2.
36. Center on Budget and Policy Priorities (1995b), p. 2.
37. See Hughes (1993).
38. Based on several local transportation programs in Chicago (especially the "Job-Express" program created by the Suburban Job Link Corporation), Public/Private Ventures, a nonprofit research organization, "has designed a research demonstration

to test a transportation strategy that links inner-city residents to job opportunities outside city centers. The elements of Bridges to Work are transportation (public or private), a mechanism for connecting trained workers with available suburban jobs (a regional alliance of providers of employment services), and special support services (provided by a community agency). A four-year demonstration of the model is planned to begin in up to nine sites in Fall 1995." Public/Private Ventures (1994), p. 9.

39. For this short-term policy recommendation I am indebted to James S. Tobin.
40. See the discussion in Chapter 2 in [*When Work Disappears*]. Also see Danziger and Gottschalk (1995).
41. Bloch (1994).
42. See, for example, Mead (1992).
43. Danziger and Gottschalk (1995), p. 155, Holzer (1995), and Carlson and Theodore (1995).
44. Danziger and Gottschalk (1995), p. 156.
45. Danziger and Gottschalk (1995).
46. Danziger and Gottschalk (1995), p. 174.
47. Regan (1994), p. 43.
48. Montgomery and Wyes (1992).
49. Wieman (1993).
50. Regan (1994), p. 44.
51. Regan (1994).
52. Danziger and Gottschalk (1995).
53. Danziger and Gottschalk (1995), p. 173.
54. Kaus (1992), pp. 259, 125.
55. Danziger and Gottschalk (1995).
56. Danziger and Gottschalk (1995).
57. Danziger and Gottschalk (1995).
58. Kaus (1992).
59. For a discussion of the cost of public-sector employment, see Danziger and Gottschalk (1995) and Kaus (1992).
60. According to one estimate, it would take an investment in education and training of "$1.66 trillion (in 1989 dollars) to restore the 1979 earnings ratios of less-skilled workers to workers with some college education, while holding workers with some college education at their 1989 levels of earnings." See Heckman, Roselius, and Smith (1994), p. 84.
61. Wilson (1987).

Reading 31

MAKING CHOICES: FROM SHORT-TERM ADJUSTMENTS TO PRINCIPLED LIVES

Robert Wuthnow

With increasing levels of burnout, career dissatisfaction, substance abuse, alcoholism, and costly job-stress suits, a growing number of American corporations have started paying attention to the possibility that people are simply working too hard, taking on responsibilities that do not nurture themselves as human beings, and putting themselves under too much pressure. General Motors has more than 100 staff psychologists dealing with problems of drugs, alcohol, burnout, and depression on the assembly line. Motorola, Xerox, Levi Strauss, and a few other large firms have initiated task forces in recent years to study the relationship between work and family problems among their employees.[1] But thus far the response from business has been mainly to invoke stricter policing in hopes of curtailing substance abuse and to encourage workers to live healthier lives through fitness programs and health evaluation clinics. Stimulating productivity while protecting their firms from undue costs has been management's top priority.

Quick-Fix Solutions

Typifying this priority is the kind of advice found routinely in managerial columns for employers faced with stress and burnout among their employees. One such column advises readers to screen employees better for preexisting

Wuthnow, Robert. "Making Choices: From Short-Term Adjustments to Principled Lives." *Poor Richard's Principle: Recovering the American Dream Through the Moral Dimension of Work, Business, and Money.* Princeton: Princeton U P, 1996. 37–58.

"mental maladies" and to solicit information from other workers that might be useful in warding off lawsuits. Presuming that it is the worker's own responsibility to limit stress, the column makes no mention of firms themselves trying to reduce job pressures.[2] Other columns suggest that managers deal with work-related stress by making corporate myths more visible to middle-level employees.

More generally, analyses of the work and money pressures facing the American population usually take a sadly limited view, attributing them to bothersome but endemic features of corporate life, the managerial personality, and the business cycle. Most of the trouble, say the analysts, springs from crisis situations such as being laid off, landing under the thumb of a dictatorial boss, or simply having a sudden string of bad luck.[3] Others emphasize economic and demographic factors, both of which have simply made it more difficult for the present generation to realize the American Dream.

What to do? Find ways to cope. Here, for example, is the advice given by a leading news magazine:

> Maintain a sense of humor.
> Meditate.
> Get a massage.
> Exercise regularly.
> Eat more sensibly.
> Limit intake of alcohol and caffeine.
> Take refuge in family and friends.
> Delegate responsibility.
> Stand up to the boss.
> Quit.[4]

These tips are not dissimilar from ones found in countless advice columns, employee newsletters, and self-help books. They encourage people to take more minivacations, play softball, go fishing, collect stamps, see the doctor regularly, and take themselves less seriously. Meditation and physical exercise are increasingly among the most frequently cited recommendations. Other hints include visualizing a pastoral scene while sitting at one's desk, making lists of fun things to do after work, and cultivating friends who stroke one's ego. A few corporations have even begun trying to help their employees relieve stress in these ways. Ben & Jerry's Ice Cream Company, for example, has initiated a Joy Committee to help employees lighten up. The Fun Committee at Odetics, a robotics firm in California, has been sponsoring Hula-Hoop contests and bubble-gum-blowing competitions for the same reason.[5]

Such activities and advice may be helpful for getting through a particularly stressful day, but they will not do anything to solve the underlying problem. "Stress cannot be dealt with by psychological tricks," Sam Keen has written, "because for the most part it is a philosophical rather than a physiological problem, a matter of the wrong worldview."[6] Coming from a writer who himself has long been associated with the pop-psychology industry, this is a sobering warning indeed.

The reason quick-fix solutions can be of little enduring value is that stress and overwork are built into the American way of life. They are not just the nettlesome by-products of having an ill-tempered boss or seeing a prospective contract turn sour. They are rooted in endemic characteristics of the modern workplace and the international markets in which most corporations now compete. Certainly these economic realities play a significant role in the work and money pressures so many middle-class Americans are experiencing. But there is an even deeper source of many of these pressures. They are part of the values we have inherited and the way we think. They reflect both long-standing and changing conceptions of ourselves as individuals, of our responsibilities and what we most cherish in our lives.

Research evidence points clearly to the inadequacy of quick-fix solutions. If these ideas were really that useful, we would expect to find people faced with stress on a frequent basis using them more. If they actually worked, we might also observe that people who used them were less likely to register feelings of stress than people who didn't. But neither of these is the case. When faced with stress, large numbers of the American workforce resort to such tactics: 71 percent talk to close friends, 60 percent engage in physical exercise, 56 percent work on a hobby, 40 percent go shopping, and 30 percent take a few days off. But those faced with frequent stress are neither more nor less likely to engage in these activities than other people. Nor are those who engage in these activities any more satisfied with their work or any less likely to be worried than other people.[7]

The evidence also points clearly to one of the reasons why quick-fix solutions do not work. Job-related stress stems from factors other than just those associated with unpleasant situations at work, and it raises questions about a much broader and deeper range of issues. Of people in my survey who said they experienced job-related stress almost every day, for example, only a quarter complained of conflict with co-workers (26 percent), an unsupportive boss (25 percent), or an unpleasant work environment (22 percent). In comparison, nearly half complained of not having enough time for their family (49 percent), feeling burned out (49 percent), needing more time for themselves (48 percent), and wanting other things in life (42 percent).

To be sure, unpleasant situations at work can contribute significantly to job-related stress. For instance, among those who said they experience stress on a daily basis, 26 percent said they had had an argument with the boss in the past year, 21 percent felt they had experienced discrimination, 16 percent had been reprimanded, and 8 percent claimed to have been sexually harassed—all higher percentages than among those who registered little or no stress. And yet the percentages for whom stress had raised broader issues were much higher. Among the frequent-stress group, 53 percent had been wondering if they were in the right line of work, and 55 percent had been feeling seriously burned out within the past year.

The one thing that stress relates to more powerfully than anything else, in fact, is thinking about basic values in life and trying to juggle commitments to a wide range of values. In the labor force as a whole, for example, 29 percent said they think a lot about their values and priorities in life; but this proportion rose to 40 percent among persons experiencing stress almost every day in their jobs and was 56 percent among those who felt they were working themselves to death. Moreover, the more frequently respondents experienced stress, the more likely they were to say they attached value to other commitments such as family, morality, taking care of themselves, and relating to God.

Fun committees and advice columnists seldom pay any attention to these underlying values. They simply assume that people are going to work too hard, try to buy too many things, and eventually burn out. So the only thing to be done is provide a little humor along the way. They are part of the current mentality that tells us we must also work hard at keeping fit and keeping our stress down, our self-esteem up, and our outlook bright. It is little wonder that we find everything from getting a massage to quitting our jobs on the same list. The advice columnists can think up easy solutions to our problems, but they help little in thinking through the hard issues of what we really want in life.

Brad Diggins illustrates well how tough these issues can be. Owner of a travel agency in southern California, he finds he has to work twelve hours a day, six days a week, to keep the business afloat. For years he's been searching for a way to stop putting his work first. But every time he thinks he's figured out how to change things, he laments, "it doesn't change; it just gets to be more." Nearing his mid-forties, he knows he has to change things before it's too late. "Somehow I've got to create a life," he ponders. But much of the time he isn't even sure anymore what kind of life he wants.

The Disease Model

If quick-fix solutions are too shallow, the disease model that has been advanced in recent years to understand problems with work, money, and other economic commitments goes to an extreme in the other direction. Rather than linking stress and burnout to specific situations at work, it associates them with an underlying malady in the worker's personality. The problem, say proponents of this view, is "workaholism"—a malady taken to be exactly parallel with alcoholism. Suffering from some fundamental insecurity, the workaholic tries to discover true happiness by working too hard. Compulsiveness is often present, causing the individual to "binge" on day-and-night working sprees and then to feel utterly dissatisfied and unmotivated. Money problems may stem from the same problem:

an insatiable longing for happiness that is wrongly pursued by trying to accumulate riches or by spending money wildly on unneeded purchases.

The disease model is valid up to a point. It does recognize the importance of questions about personal identity, commitments, values, and the need to settle on priorities. The compulsive behavior it describes does characterize a segment of the population. But, like so many other contemporary applications of the literature on addictions, it carries the argument too far. Workaholism may be similar to alcoholism in some respects, but its chemical basis is fundamentally different. Just how widely applicable it may be is also debatable. That it may have limited applications is suggested by the fact that only one person in six actually feels like he or she is working to death, and only one in seven claims to experience stress on a daily basis. Moreover, of this frequent-stress group, only 4 percent say they are seeing a therapist to help them with stress, and only 6 percent try to find help in a support group.

Proponents of the disease model, of course, argue that the fact people are not seeking help is all the more reason to be concerned. But the model ultimately suffers thereby from being impossible to confirm or disconfirm empirically. Many of its assertions focus so broadly on such "problems" as rushing, busyness, making lists, and caring about one's work that virtually everyone falls into the category of the diseased. Other assertions make valuable connections and yet lead away from a valid understanding of these connections. For example, one widely publicized book on the subject asserts that "work addicts are dishonest, controlling, self-centered, perfectionistic, and abusive to themselves and others." It is little wonder, the author expostulates, that "their morality" is askew. "You cannot lead such a life without losing your moorings. Your grounding in basic values is lost in the relentless pursuit of the addiction."[8] Clearly the important point is that basic values must somehow be brought back into focus. It helps little to describe the underlying problem as an addiction, however.

The broader problem is not that people who work hard have abandoned other values. Indeed, it is clearly the opposite. People like Brad Diggins want it all. They are committed to their work and to the good life that money can buy; they also want more out of life. Indeed, when work and money are compared with other values in our society, they come out on top fairly infrequently. In my survey, for example, 29 percent of the labor force said their work was absolutely essential to their sense of personal worth, and only 15 percent said this about "making a lot of money." In comparison, 69 percent said their family was absolutely essential to their personal worth; 56 percent said this about their moral standards, 43 percent did so about taking care of themselves, and 39 percent did about their relationship to God. The study also shows that the minority who did say work and money were absolutely essential were actually *more* likely to value these other commitments, rather than less likely to value them.[9]

If something is wrong, it is that we want too much out of life, not too little. And yet to say that people want to spend time with their families, that they value their moral standards and their relationship to God, or that they want to serve the needy is surely not something to decry. The American Dream has always championed these other pursuits as part of what the good society should encourage its members to be doing. What has contributed to the difficulty of engaging in these pursuits in recent years is that social conditions and cultural understandings alike have been shifting rapidly. As a result, more and more people are having to think through their values in ways that were neither possible nor necessary in the past.

We shall want to consider the basis for claims such as this more carefully [at another time]. For now, however, it is worth observing that most of the pressures and uncertainties surrounding economic commitments [. . .] are in fact associated with the extent to which fundamental questions about values and priorities are being raised in our society. Feeling that one is working harder than before and wishing that one could work fewer hours, for example, are associated with a greater likelihood of thinking a lot about values and priorities in life. So are feeling burned out and feeling that one is not getting enough time for oneself. And so are feeling that one has a lot of financial obligations, worrying about how to fulfill these obligations, feeling that one is under a lot of pressure, and wanting more time for one's family. All these worries and concerns are associated with raising questions about one's values in general.

Fundamentally, then, the issue people like Brad Diggins are confronting is the need to make choices, of deciding when to say no, or even saying yes, but doing so in a way that keeps the material life in proper perspective. We are bombarded by the appeals of the leisure industry to spend more time relaxing and by the business world itself to do what we must to take care of our health. And yet the question remains whether there are principles other than self-interest, pleasure, and bodily preservation that should be factored into our thinking. The question is not simply how to rest up so we can be more productive at work the next day. The question is how to weigh the other priorities that have always characterized the human spirit against those to which the dollar sign can be affixed. Should we be willing to sacrifice an hour pursuing another business deal in order to visit a friend in the hospital? Or can we be content, as one writer discovered when he posed this question to a class of prospective MBAs at Harvard Business School, to regard such moral commitments as patently absurd?

Reforming the System

Historically, the most common way of placing limits around the economic system has been to invoke governmental restrictions. From early attempts to limit the workday, pass old-age- and disability-insurance measures, and promote greater safety in the workplace, to more recent efforts to outlaw discrimination and implement redistributive taxation schemes, legislation has been regarded as the principal means of combating the ill effects of the marketplace. One of the major axes around which modern political debate has revolved has thus been its position on how much or how little the state should intervene in economic matters.[10]

The reason why recourse to political means has so often been taken is that the state's powers seem the only measure strong enough to make a difference. Against the entrenchment of profit-motivated interests and the social influences of those in control of economic resources, only coercion can call a halt. Pragmatic arguments, indicating that political means have in fact accomplished much in terms of ameliorating the worst excesses of the marketplace, have often been advanced as well. Compared with schemes for overturning capitalism itself, these reformist measures have proven decidedly more attractive. Yet political solutions can go only so far in guiding and restraining economic life.

Government restrictions work best within a legitimating framework of fundamental human rights, including norms of justice and equal treatment before the law. They can help prevent the worst excesses of economic production and distribution, such as the exploitation of disadvantaged minorities, conditions injurious to health, or ones that pollute the environment. Government initiatives have sometimes been able to mitigate undesirable social conditions by encouraging long-range economic growth itself. Public expenditures on transportation systems, education, and basic research are often cited as examples. Where government restrictions cannot legitimately attempt to regulate economic life is in those realms deemed to lie within the domain of individual discretion.

Discretion to make fundamental decisions affecting the course and quality of individual life has come to be regarded as a culturally legitimate and constitutionally guaranteed manifestation of personal freedom. Government can pass legislation prohibiting an employer from dumping toxic waste on public land or from discriminating against racial minorities, but it cannot pass laws telling that employer to be at work by a certain hour in the morning, to spend Thursday evenings at home with the family, or to give $5,000 to charity rather than purchase a new wide-screen television set. All government can do in those areas is to provide gentle nudges in one direction or another. For example, it can encourage charitable contributions by making them tax deductible or it can discourage spending on luxury items by adding a surtax.

Anything further violates the individual freedoms so widely cherished in democratic societies. As efforts to legislate a thirty-hour work week, add new holidays to the national calendar, and mandate social service among the young all have demonstrated, it is extremely difficult for social reformers to legislate new conceptions of the American Dream, not only because of the costs of these programs, but because they can also be opposed on grounds of curbing fundamental human liberties.

The extent to which such opposition is present in the American population is clearly evident in opinion polls. Some questions, for example, suggest that the majority of Americans view government restrictions as an unwelcome intrusion in their lives, in much the same way that they dislike having to work in large bureaucracies or jostling through traffic jams on the way to their jobs. In one survey, two-thirds of the public expressed this dislike by saying government regulations were a serious or extremely serious problem in American society, while only 6 percent said they were not a problem.[11] Other questions indicate that part of the resistance to government intervention in the economy is that Americans simply do not feel such programs are effective. For example, in the same survey when people were asked whether spending more money on government welfare programs would help make America better, only 21 percent said it would help a lot, compared with 36 percent who thought it would help only a little, and 42 percent who said it would not help at all.

In contrast to these patterns, people are much more likely to think that economic solutions are the best way to deal with social problems. When asked how much it would help improve the society to keep our economy going at a steady rate, 71 percent said this would help a lot, compared with only 25 percent who said it would help a little, and 3 percent who said it would not help. Even when the issue is not so much income distribution or general well-being, but matters of social goals and priorities, the American public registers deep skepticism about government playing too large a role. One indication of this attitude is that 71 percent of the public thinks politicians have too much influence in shaping the nation's goals and values, whereas only 47 percent think this about business leaders.[12]

Social critics are correct in suggesting that much of the public's resistance to government intervention in the economy stems from raw self-interest instead of well-schooled conceptions of civic liberty. The critics also need to be taken seriously when they point out that civic responsibility requires people to press for government solutions to such problems as discrimination in the workplace, corporate greed, exploitation of the poor and the disadvantaged, fraud, and environmental destruction. But the same critics who voice these concerns have also come increasingly to recognize that government restrictions are unlikely to be instituted in the first place—or be effective—unless people are willing to subject themselves to some kind of moral restraint. In short, a society that places high responsibility on the individual must look not only to government to rein in its economic commitments, but to a better understanding of the ethics and values on which institutional and individual commitments are based.

The Growing Role of Discretion

In advanced industrial societies individual discretion has become increasingly significant. Not only has it been championed in various ways by conservative and liberal political theoreticians; it is also built increasingly into the fabric of economic life itself. With late-modern levels of economic development, fewer people have to work from sunrise to sunset to eke out a subsistence living, nor do people spend as large a percentage of their earnings on food, shelter, clothing, and other necessities, thus leaving a larger share of their time and money available for discretionary uses. In the workplace itself greater emphasis is likely to be placed on autonomous decision making, with fewer tasks being mandated specifically by someone in authority. The choice of careers themselves and decisions about particular places of employment have increasingly become matters of personal discretion. Indeed, the very meaning of discretion, once connoting caution and prudence, has been subtly redefined to mean the exercise of choice.

Discretion is part of the normative order of most institutions as well. The individual is expected to make ethical decisions and to choose how he or she will achieve desired work goals. Greater discretion is expected of individuals in their private lives, from choosing sexual and marriage partners to deciding how to school their children. With nonworking hours being defined as free time involving a wide variety of options, people are expected to exercise discretion in allocating time to various leisure activities or to community service. They are expected to exercise discretion in deciding how to allocate surplus financial resources among various consumer products and benevolent causes. All these decisions have enormous implications for the economy itself and for the quality of people's lives, but they are decisions over which most people feel government has very little rightful control.

For Davis Reskin, 35, a middle manager in New York's garment district, it is precisely this ability to exercise discretion that makes him glad he's alive. Like so many other people of his generation, he believes the future holds whatever he decides to choose for himself. He has a wife and one child but does not feel "encumbered" by his family the way his parents did. Living in Manhattan, he picks and chooses his friends, trying hard to be kind to them, but not getting himself bogged down in community organizations like his mother did. He revels in having enough cash to amuse himself in his spare time. At work, he compares himself with the women he sees bent over their sewing machines ten hours a day stitching garments. He thanks his lucky stars that he has the freedom to set his own pace. He likes the creativity and artistry that his work requires. At the same time, he finds himself restless and ready to move on whenever the opportunity arises. "I'm very open," he asserts. "I never close doors. Never say no. I'm interviewing tomorrow as a matter of fact. Headhunters call me all the time and I always go. I never say no. Only a fool would say that. I could do lots of different things." He certainly does not want government telling him what to do. In his view, that smacks of socialism, a system he believes is rapidly becoming a thing of the past.

In the absence of guiding legal or coercive norms, discretionary behavior for millions of people like Davis Reskin has increasingly become the domain in which economic influences are permitted to reign with virtually unlimited authority. Individuals define themselves as economic decision makers, allocating time and financial resources to various services, leisure activities, and consumer goods. Economic institutions can rightfully try to influence these individual decisions through marketing and advertising, or in the workplace, by offering financial incentives. The individual is assumed to be free to make economic choices, so no constitutional issues are at stake, and is regarded as being motivated to participate in the marketplace as a consumer. Economic institutions are even said to have special claim to the individual because they are, it is sometimes claimed, the source of this discretionary time and income in the first place.[13]

How Much Freedom Do We Have?

To those who have considered how much economic institutions shape our lives, the claim that people are increasingly free to do whatever they want is of course recognizably overstated. They know that even the relatively affluent professionals and managers who are said to enjoy the greatest freedoms often find themselves with little room to maneuver at all. Their corporations have a rigid set of expectations to which they must conform in order to survive and succeed. These may include everything from dress codes to formal objectives to unstated rules about how to greet the boss in the morning. Professionals who work in other settings may also be subjected to bureaucratic norms requiring them to perform efficiently, to meet fixed work schedules, and to participate in unrewarding gatherings of their peers.

Sociologist Robert Jackall, in an intensive study of the work lives of corporate managers, has provided a compelling account of how the bureaucracies in which most people now work shape their goals, their expectations, and their perceptions of themselves.[14] He argues that bureaucracy has fundamentally altered the rules by which people pursue the American Dream. From the outside, bureaucracies may appear as highly rational, hierarchically coordinated systems for getting the complex tasks of the modern economy done. From the inside, they appear more to be what Jackall appropriately terms "moral mazes." They encourage unwavering loyalty to bosses and patrons and divide people into floating alliances among coteries and cliques. Within these unstable networks, workers learn relativistic and often contradictory standards of trustworthiness.

They turn to each other for behavioral cues, but what they experience is often too ambiguous to codify. Ethics and values take a back seat to yea-saying, pragmatism, and glib talk.

The result is that work gets done, but sooner or later most people begin to experience conflict between their work and the standards of value they perceive in other spheres of their lives. Jackall points especially to the tension that may arise between struggles for dominance in the bureaucracy and wider norms of friendship, honesty, and compassion. He also perceives tension between the standards of excellence that many individuals aspire to and the inevitable mediocrity that he feels plagues most organizations. Like other critics, he believes bureaucracy is fundamentally at odds with finding overall meaning at work because what is good for the organization may not be good for the individuals who work in it or for the wider society.

This line of analysis suggests that very little can be done to rectify the current situation. People may think they can exercise discretion, but this perception is fundamentally an allusion. Economic institutions not only operate according to their own laws, governing our workday and our pocketbook; they also determine the way we think. Furthermore, bureaucracies are unlikely to disappear anytime soon. In the meantime, we can delude ourselves by talking about the freedom we have, but we must realize that this apparent sense of control over our lives really operates to perpetuate the institutions that dominate modern society.

The trouble with this kind of analysis is that it attributes too much casual influence to the blind forces of which bureaucracy presumably consists. It buys too strongly into the kind of social structural determinism that sociologists have so often assumed they must defend in order to advance their own profession. Yet a more nuanced reading of studies like Jackall's reveals that "bureaucracy" is often little more than a metaphor for the patterns of language and behavior that are observed in the workplace. These patterns are not determined by something else; they are the stuff of which organizations are constituted. It is the conventional languages and norms that must be understood, not some deep force that exercises irresistible control over our lives.

Viewed this way, the same ambiguities that lead some observers to be cynical about the modern workplace provide small beacons of hope. If bureaucracy presents people with uncertainty rather than rigid structures, then there is indeed room for discretion after all. If most people make up their moral norms to satisfy each other, then these norms are by no means fixed from on high. Moreover, the assumption that economic institutions tie people down to the point that they despair of finding any meaning in their work flies in the face of evidence we have already considered. Perhaps people are simply deluded by the organizations for which they work. They may, however, find their work sufficiently meaningful that they would like to integrate it more effectively with the other parts of their lives. Only if they assume their choices are entirely free or entirely determined by the economic realm itself will they find it impossible to pursue this integration.

The Need for Moral Discourse

The individual is thus left to make an increasing number of decisions about how to use his or her resources largely without any government restrictions interfering with these decisions, and yet within a normative context in which he or she is defined as an economic actor subject only to the guiding hand of economic institutions and an ethos of economic interest maximization. But how is the individual to make these decisions? On the basis of what value orientations, conceptions of the good, ethical considerations, or moral commitments does the individual decide to participate or withdraw from participating in the marketplace? Economic considerations may specify a range of options and attach various costs and benefits to these options, but they neither exhaust the range of conceivable options nor provide standards of individual or social good to be weighed in selecting among various options.

For this reason, all societies have in fact encouraged conceptions of the good that in one way or another limit their members' participation in the economic realm and provide autonomous moral standards for the governance of behavior within this realm. In traditional societies a minority of the population generally opted out of the so-called productive vocations to pursue careers in monastic and religious orders. In many cases people of sufficient means abandoned the pursuit of ever greater wealth in order to engage in public service, cultivate the intellectual life of the salons and universities, or participate in the leisure activities of the court. In still other instances people restricted their economic ambitions in order to raise families or to care for aging relatives. Although these activities were sometimes mandated by the state, they were more often done voluntarily. Economic interest maximization was seldom a primary consideration. A commitment to values that were deemed more basic than economic pursuits erected moral limits around the economic life.

In modern societies, for reasons that include the declining salience of an all-embracing conception of cosmic order and the extension of rational decision-making processes to most matters of personal life, the concept of moral limits has largely been restricted to behaviors that have little to do with the economic realm. Morality has come to focus on such issues as sexual fidelity, honesty, and propriety in personal relations, rather than referring to a deeper sense of what is fundamentally good. Indeed, we might venture to say that economic thinking has itself penetrated the moral domain to the extent that technical solutions to the perplexing questions of personal life often seem preferable to old-fashioned conceptions of duty and obligation. British sociologist Bryan Wilson observes:

"As for purely personal morality, that quaint concept, so vital to communities in the past, modern man might ask whether it has not become redundant. In modern language, to be moral is to be 'uptight'; to express moral attitudes is to inhibit people when they want—as modern men say that they have a right to want—'to do their own thing.'"[15]

But if morality connotes unwelcome strictures on personal behavior in general, it is likely to be all the more so conceived when these activities are defined simply as consumer preferences. When someone decides to purchase a new automobile instead of spending the money on an expensive vacation, it thus seems correct to speak of the decision as one of maximizing alternative utilities, but it would seem odd to say that certain that moral understandings have been expressed. That we do make decisions about economic commitments that have broader moral overtones may still be beyond dispute, but exactly how we do this is less clear. It is thus to the realm of moral discourse that we must look if we are to gain a better understanding of how the deeper commitments of the human spirit relate to the economic realm.

The Nature of Moral Discourse

Because it has so often been conceived narrowly, we need to consider just what moral discourse is and how in the best of all worlds it might be constructed in order to guide and curtail our economic pursuits in effective, satisfying, and meaningful ways. Moral discourse has been the subject of growing attention in recent years, especially among ethicists, but we must select judiciously from this literature.[16]

Ethical absolutes or moral truths of the kind "courage is a virtue" or "slavery is evil" will be of little concern. Ethicists worry a lot about such statements—and they think ordinary people should too—because they want to know how such claims can be defended and, if they cannot, fear there may be no basis for opposing fanatics and fools.

As one of these "ordinary people," I believe we often do not care much what ethicists have to say on these questions. The problem is not, as ethicists themselves will assert, that more compelling philosophical grounds need to be discovered for making these kinds of ethical claims. Most of us ordinary people, probably to ethicists' dismay, are quite willing to accept on faith that courage is good or slavery is evil and leave the fanatics and fools for others to dispute. The problem we sense with ethicists is that none of this has very much to do with the real questions we face in our ordinary lives.

Somewhere between the absolute good and the absolute evil with which ethics is concerned lie the questions we face routinely about what should be done, what is desirable or undesirable, and which of several options may be best for us to pursue. When a physician decides to take an afternoon to play golf, the issue is not one of absolute good or evil. Even though, by some larger calculation, there may be slightly more suffering—or even death—in the world than there might have been otherwise, we would not ordinarily consider this a question of virtue or vice. Nevertheless, there is a moral dimension to such a decision, and it is this broader moral dimension that should interest us here. How does a person decide when it is preferable to spend an afternoon playing golf instead of treating the sick?

Moral discourse in this sense is about preferences, but not strictly so, at least not in a way that suggests applying the various models of decision-making behavior that abound in the philosophical literature. In the present case, I am not really concerned with figuring out why one physician decides to quit working at 1 p.m. and another decides to continue working till 5:30. The moral dimension of importance is concerned with broader questions about the modes of reasoning and talking that define things as legitimate.

In his book *Theory of the Moral Life,* John Dewey framed a conception of moral reasoning that will be useful for us to incorporate into the present discussion.[17] First published in 1908, Dewey's arguments sometimes seem overly optimistic, placing too much faith in education, reason, and scientific progress to be credible in the more complex world of today. Yet there is still much to be learned from this book. Dewey's clear-headed, moderate style resonates far more deeply with the American experience than do many of the arguments that have been borrowed in recent decades from other traditions.

At the heart of Dewey's conception of morality is the distinction (to which we have already referred) between right and wrong, on the one hand, and value preferences, on the other hand. Citing the case of a man torn between his religiously inspired commitment to pacifism and his sense of civic responsibility, Dewey writes: "Now he has to make a choice between competing moral loyalties and convictions. The struggle is not between a good which is clear to him and something else which attracts him but which he knows to be wrong. It is between values each of which is an undoubted good in its place but which now get in each other's way. He is forced to reflect in order to come to a decision."[18]

This is precisely the kind of moral dilemma most people find themselves confronted with as they consider the relationship between their economic commitments and other values. The problem generally is not choosing between something good, like working hard, and something evil, like laying around the house all day in a drunken stupor. It is usually choosing between two activities of "undoubted good" that get in each other's way, such as working hard and taking one's children to the dentist, or serving people through one's profession and being a more responsible member of one's community. These, we recognize with Dewey, are often more difficult choices than making decisions between good and evil.

Dewey also draws a useful distinction between customary morality and reflective morality, The former depends on force of habit, on doing things the way they have always been done. It is the morality of the tribe, the ancestral home, the parental rules that have never been questioned. Reflective morality, in contrast, emerges from conscious deliberation. It "springs from the heart, from personal desires and affections, or from personal insight and rational choice."[19] It often requires criticizing existing customs and institutions from a new point of view.

Customary morality is of considerable importance because it often provides a reliable guide in matters of right and wrong. In principle at least, long-established norms about telling the truth, not stealing from one's neighbors, and the like still pertain appropriately to most people in most situations. Customary morality also serves a positive function in everyday life simply by permitting us to *avoid* thinking about some things. Dewey suggests there is something "sick" about a person who goes through life questioning the morality of everything. But customary morality becomes a negative force when people let institutionalized norms make their basic decisions for them. The economic realm can of course be a strong source of customary morality.

Reflective morality requires conscious effort on the part of the individual. It involves questioning one's behavior, knowing what options are available, thinking through the consequences of various choices, and recognizing one's responsibility to choose wisely. It comes into play most visibly when people are faced with choices about their basic values and how to realize these values in their daily lifes. Indeed, Dewey goes so far as to say that an immoral decision is one that has been made unreflectively, while a moral act takes the form of a well-considered judgment. Saying "I meant well" (when things turn out badly) is not a good excuse, Dewey asserts, because the person probably did not really pause to reflect on what he or she was about to do.

Unlike customary morality, which can often be articulated in simple moral dictums, *reflective morality* cannot be codified in terms of absolute rules. It is instead a matter of theory, process, and character. Theory—or, perhaps better, "outlook"—is a frame of reference, a set of beliefs and values that inform the individual's thinking. It includes a conception of individual freedom and responsibility, an understanding of the importance of reflection itself, and an awareness of the need to balance self-interest with the needs of others. Process is the ongoing act of reflection itself. It is not so much a matter of making air-tight, logical choices, but of bringing one's outlook into conscious engagement with one's experience and behavior. It requires individual soul searching, but is also a social activity, benefiting from formal education, reading, and interacting with others. "Character" signals the fact that reflective morality is integrally rooted in the self. This means moral worth is ascribed less to single, discrete activities than to longer-term patterns of behavior. It also means that morality and the self are fundamentally intertwined in a mutually reinforcing, and hopefully upward, spiral of development. In short, moral reflection is conducive to personal growth.[20]

In American society (probably in most societies), economic modes of moral argumentation command enormous respect. They do so because they are rooted in powerful institutions that compete to derive profits from the appropriation and deployment of scarce resources. These institutions provide the only places in which most people can find gainful employment, and these same institutions search constantly for new markets, attempting to define people as consumers and lure them into consumerist activities. The "lifeworld" in which people live is, as German sociologist Jürgen Habermas has put it, increasingly subject to the "colonizing" forces of these institutions.[21]

But economic demands stem as much from the ways in which people think as from the power of multinational corporations or commercial advertising agencies. The citizens of democratic societies may be ideologically opposed to Marxism, but they are nevertheless Marxists in practice, taking it for granted that economic considerations are fundamental. They talk about economic laws and principles as the determining features of human behavior, view the entire future more favorably when the economy is good than when it is bad, and simply assume that certain economic realities exist. They base their thinking on how much certain investments will earn, or how much certain items will cost, and throughout history they have been driven to war to protect the raw materials and transportation routes on which their way of life depends.

Economic thinking thus becomes a powerful form of legitimation. Even the most "scientific" arguments presented by economists generally go beyond mere descriptive statements to draw normative conclusions about what is right and good. "It is an extremely rare economist," writes sociologist Alan Wolfe, "who stops at the point of simply asserting the ethical benefits of self-interest; most continue on to make a point about obligations to others as well: because the pursuit of my self-interest contributes to some collective good . . . my obligation to you is to do what is best for me."[22] We have, in short, adopted a "market mentality," as Karl Polanyi termed it some years ago, that reifies the economic institutions we have created, turning them into forces we no longer believe we can control or even resist, but at the same time making of this necessity a moral virtue.[23]

Because of the enormous legitimating power of these economic assumptions, a reasonable place to begin in identifying the characteristics of an ideal moral discourse is to say that it must be capable of challenging economic norms and providing alternative ways of thinking. Moral discourse with this capacity may invoke a variety of substantive arguments, but these arguments should be based on something other than economic calculations or assumptions about economic laws alone. To carry authority, they are also likely to need institutional moorings. Thus, it would be more likely to find these moral languages in institutions such as families, neighborhoods, voluntary associations, public interest groups, universities, and religious communities than to imagine them existing simply in the abstract.[24] These are the institutions in which values are learned and reinforced voluntarily, as part of personal discretion, unlike political institutions that impose collective norms on individuals through coercion and principles of legality.

In saying that moral discourse should be capable of challenging economic assumptions, it should also be stated that moral restraint need not be inimical to hard work, material success, self-interest, or other canons of the economic life. It should only be understood, contrary to what economists have often argued, that moral conduct is not necessarily the same as, or always compatible with, these economic norms. For example, a value such as freedom is not necessarily contingent on economic growth, and hard work and material success do not necessarily indicate a life of moral virtue.

As long as moral discourse can be distinguished from economic norms, it can guide and constrain economic behavior in at least two ways. Internal to the economic realm itself, it can influence the norms governing economic behavior, causing these norms to be guided by ethical considerations as well as self-interest. Externally, it can establish the outer limits of the economic realm, showing where its assumptions and demands no longer apply. It can lead a parent, for instance, to spend time with a child, not as an "investment," but for the sake of the human relationship itself.

It is also worth remembering that morals and ethics have always (but perhaps especially so in modern societies) focused particular attention on the individual. This is because matters of right and wrong, and of what is more or less desirable, are understood to be matters of choice. For these choices to be legitimate, the individual must be able to make sense of them, giving reasons (if only in private) why something is an appropriate thing to do. Moral discourse is composed not so much of abstract principles but of personalized narratives, told to ourselves as much as to anyone else, to explain who we are, why we are good and decent human beings, and how we should respond to the choices we experience. Moreover, these choices have significant consequences for our lives, determining not only how time and energy are spent but also what values will be realized. Indeed, they play a significant role, as Dewey reminds us, in shaping the kind of self we will become. They involve the deepest longings and aspirations of the individual and are fundamentally concerned with how to live the good life. "Human spirit" is thus an appropriate reference for much of what moral discourse is about.

But moral discourse is also concerned with more than the individual, for implicit in it are assumptions about civil society. Individuals can make moral decisions only if civil society guarantees certain basic rights, such as respect for the individual and freedom of choice. Moreover, it is largely through the informal networks of association of which civil society is composed that the individual learns to practice reflective morality and finds ways to integrate these reflections with everyday behavior. At the same time, moral discourse generally assumes that the good life for the individual depends on sociality, friendship, and a sense of community. Hence, notions of responsibility to others and identification with the whole society in which one lives are also integral features of moral discourse.

For moral discourse to be effective, it must provide clear, unambiguous guidance about how to live individually and collectively. If it does not, people will be unable to make informed choices and in the face of uncertainty may well follow the dictates of unstated economic assumptions rather than consciously placing limits around these assumptions. But moral discourse should also provide room for a wide range of individual choices and lifestyles. Modern society is too diverse, too complex, too changeable for moral discourse to be codified as authoritative behavioral maxims. Communities of moral discourse function best when they provide opportunities for collective reflection and role models to emulate. Moral strictures may discourage greed and ambition as a general rule, yet provide arguments about individual talent or social service that legitimate exceptional endeavors for a few. Reasons for *not* following the rest of the herd, and stories of people who make a difference by leading alternative lives, may be one of the most beneficial functions moral discourse can provide.

In all this, it should also be evident that moral discourse, while terribly personal, must be a feature of the public life of any society. It must be codified in language, in the common stock of tradition and narrative, so that it can be communicated and provide a basis for shared understandings. Without this public dimension, moral discourse could not be transmitted intergenerationally or internalized to the point that it becomes taken for granted. This means that moral discourse, as discourse, matters in its own right and is distinguishable from ethical behavior. What people say about their lives—how they talk about greed and ambition—is at least as important as the implicit social norms that can be inferred from how they behave.

An ideal moral discourse, then, is one that can challenge, question, guide, and set limits around the economic sphere by giving voice to deeper considerations of what is good for the individual and the society. Rather than setting up an autonomous conception of morality that can be fulfilled entirely within the economic realm itself, it forces questions to be raised about the connections between this realm and broader conceptions of the human spirit. It provides a way of thinking and talking about what is legitimate that necessitates discussion of human values. In doing so, it makes room for diverse talents and interests but also defines broad categories in which thinking can take place and questions of good and bad—and, even more importantly, questions of better and best—can be deliberated.

Notes

1. Hugh A. Mulligan, "Companies Give Workers Piece of the Action," *Trenton Times* (May 19, 1991).
2. LaVan, Katz, and Hochwarter, "Employee Stress," 64.
3. For example, see those quoted in Annetta Miller, "Stress on the Job," *Newsweek* (April 28, 1988), 40–45.
4. *Ibid.*
5. David J. Abramis, "Finding the Fun at Work," *Psychology Today* (March 1989), 36–38.
6. Keen, *Fire in the Belly,* 61.
7. Economic Values Survey.
8. Diane Fassel, *Working Ourselves to Death: The High Cost of Workaholism and the Rewards of Recovery* (San Francisco: Harper San Francisco, 1990), 46.
9. Economic Values Survey.
10. Useful surveys of recent debates concerning the role of the state in regulating economic forces include Alan Wolfe, *Whose Keeper? Social Science and Moral Obligation* (Berkeley: University of California Press, 1989); Robert Dahl, *A Preface to Economic Democracy* (Berkeley: University of California Press, 1985); and Fred Block, *Post-Industrial Possibilities* (Berkeley: University of California Press, 1990).
11. This result and the other figures reported in the text are from the "Values Survey." See chapter 1, note 30, [in *Poor Richard's Principle*].
12. Government intervention in the economy is also favored less than the work of the voluntary sector. For example, in the "Values Survey," 72 percent agreed that "private charities are generally more effective than government programs."
13. The relationship between economic institutions and personal discretion is clearly described in Milton Friedman, *Capitalism and Freedom* (Chicago: Univesity of Chicago Press, 1962); for more recent statement, see Peter L. Berger, *The Capitalist Revolution: Fifty Propositions about Prosperity, Equality, and Liberty* (New York: Basic books, 1986), especially chapter 5.
14. Robert Jackall, *Moral Mazes: The World of Corporate Managers* (New York: Oxford University Press, 1988). I have benefited greatly from the insightful analysis presented in this book.
15. Bryan Wilson, *Religion in Sociological Perspective* (Oxford: Oxford University Press, 1982), 161. Wilson also discusses the ways in which moral questions have been moved into the sphere of political reform.
16. As a guide to this literature, I have found especially valuable the work of my colleague Jeffrey Stout, *Ethics after Babel: The Languages of Morals and Their Discontents* (Boston: Beacon, 1988). I have also borrowed quite selectively from Alasdair MacIntyre, *After Virtue: A Study in Moral Theory,* 2d ed. (Notre Dame: University of Notre Dame Press, 1984), and Stanley Hauerwas, *Truthfulness and Tragedy* (Notre Dame: University of Notre Dame Press, 1977).
17. John Dewey, *Theory of the Moral Life* (New York: Holt, Rinehart and Winston, 1960 [1908]).
18. *Ibid.,* 6–7.
19. *Ibid.,* 3.

20. "There is not simply a succession of disconnected acts but each thing done carries forward an underlying tendency and intent, *conducting,* leading up, to further acts and to a final fulfillment or consummation" (*Ibid.,* 11).
21. The thesis of "lifeworld colonization" is developed in Jürgen Habermas, *The Theory of Communicative Action,* 2 vols. (Boston: Beacon, 1984, 1987) especially 2:332–73.
22. Wolfe, *Whose Keeper?,* 7.
23. Karl Polanyi, *The Livelihood of Man* (New York: Academic Press, 1977).
24. On the importance of institutions for moral language, see Bellah et al., *The Good Society.*